W9-ATK-299

PRAISE

FOR

AMERICA'S NEW DEMOCRACY

BY FIORINA, PETERSON, AND VOSS

"The text provides a thematically driven, comprehensive review of American politics and government."

—Peter Watkins, Saint Joseph's College

"The best, most affordable textbook for freshmen level American national government. Nothing is left out . . . and the students will gain so much from it."

—Cheryl A. Brown, Marshall University

"It's an informative, engaging book that offers both breadth and depth on the standard topics in American politics. The theme—that elections are at the center of American politics, and have wide-ranging causes and consequences—is a natural one, both for teachers and students of American politics."

—Charles R. Shipan, University of Iowa

"This text covers the many aspects of American government. It is supported by excellent graphics and additional reading that would entice a class to discussion."

—Sarah Miller, Lourdes College

"This book links the study of American government and politics with political science. It emphasizes explanation and description, and students become familiar not only with the substance of American politics, but also how political scientists go about their work. This is how we ought to teach American government."

—Daniel E. Ponder, University of Colorado at Colorado Springs

ABOUT
THE AUTHORS

MORRIS P. FIORINA

Morris P. Fiorina is Professor of Political Science and Senior Fellow of the Hoover Institution at Stanford University. He received a B.A. from Allegheny College in Meadville, Pennsylvania, and a Ph.D. from the University of Rochester. Before moving to Stanford, he taught at the California Institute of Technology and Harvard University.

Fiorina has written widely on American government and politics, with special emphasis on representation and elections. He has published numerous articles, and five books: *Representatives, Roll Calls, and Constituencies; Congress— Keystone of the Washington Establishment; Retrospective Voting in American National Elections; The Personal Vote: Constituency Service and Electoral Independence* (coauthored with Bruce Cain and John Ferejohn); and *Divided Government*. He has served on the editorial boards of a dozen journals in the fields of political science, economics, law, and public policy, and from 1986 to 1990 he served as chairman of the Board of Overseers of the American National Election Studies. He is a member of the National Academy of Sciences.

In his leisure time, Fiorina favors physical activities, including hiking, fishing, and sports. Although his own athletic career never amounted to much, he has been a successful youth baseball coach for fifteen years. Among his most cherished honors is a plaque given by happy parents on the occasion of an undefeated Babe Ruth season.

PAUL E. PETERSON

Paul E. Peterson is the Henry Lee Shattuck Professor of
Government and Director of the Center for American
Political Studies at Harvard University. He received his B.A.
from Concordia College in Moorhead, Minnesota, and his
Ph.D. from the University of Chicago.

Peterson is the author of numerous books and articles
on federalism, urban politics, race relations, and public policy, including studies of education, welfare, and fiscal and
foreign policy. He received the Woodrow Wilson Award
from the American Political Science Association for his book
City Limits (Chicago, 1981). In 1996 his book *The Price of Federalism* (Brookings, 1995) was
given the Aaron Wildavsky Award for the best book on public policy. He is a member of
the American Academy of Arts and Sciences.

It is not only when writing a textbook that Peterson makes every effort to be as
accurate as possible. On the tennis courts, he always makes correct line calls and has seldom been heard to hit a wrong note when tickling the ivories.

D. STEPHEN VOSS

D. Stephen Voss is Assistant Professor of Political Science at
the University of Kentucky. He received his Ph.D. from
Harvard University, studying with Gary King, and special-
izes in voting and elections with a particular focus on racial
politics in the U.S. South. A New Orleans native, Voss also
has two bachelor's degrees from Louisiana State
University—one in history and one in print journalism.

Voss has authored or coauthored articles in various
political science journals, including the *American Journal of
Political Science, Journal of Politics, Public Opinion Quarterly, State
Politics and Policy Quarterly,* and *American Politics Research.* He also coauthored
CliffsQuickReview American Government and is working on the Federal Elections Project
with David Lublin of American University. Prior to entering academia, Voss was a political reporter for Gannett News Service and edited a top-selling travel guide, *Let's Go: USA.*

Voss spends his leisure time shooting pool, playing poker or blackjack, enjoying
warlike computer games, watching David Lynch videos, and listening to hard-edged
music of all sorts. He used up his 15 seconds of fame while in graduate school, thanks to
an unscripted cameo appearance as the blue spaceman in Phish's "Down with Disease"
music video.

Penguin Academics

AMERICA'S NEW DEMOCRACY

Penguin Academics

AMERICA'S NEW DEMOCRACY

SECOND EDITION

MORRIS P. FIORINA
Stanford University

PAUL E. PETERSON
Harvard University

D. STEPHEN VOSS
University of Kentucky

PEARSON
Longman

New York   San Francisco   Boston
London   Toronto   Sydney   Tokyo   Singapore   Madrid
Mexico City   Munich   Paris   Cape Town   Hong Kong   Montreal

Vice President and Publisher:	Priscilla McGeehon
Executive Editor:	Eric Stano
Senior Marketing Manager:	Megan Galvin Fak
Development Director:	Lisa Pinto
Media Editor:	Patrick McCarthy
Supplements Editor:	Kristi Olson
Managing Editor:	Bob Ginsberg
Production Manager:	Joseph Vella
Project Coordination, Text Design, and Electronic Page Makeup:	Thompson Steele, Inc.
Senior Cover Designer/Manager:	Nancy Danahy
Cover Photo:	Democratic National Convention © Franklin McMahon/CORBIS, Inc.
Photo Research:	Photosearch, Inc.
Manufacturing Manager:	Dennis J. Para
Manufacturing Buyer:	Lucy Hebard
Printer and Binder:	Quebecor World—Taunton
Cover Printer:	Phoenix Color Corp.

For permission to use copyrighted material, grateful acknowledgment is made to the copyright holders on pp. C-1–C-2, which are hereby made part of this copyright page.

Library of Congress Cataloging-in-Publication Data

Fiorina, Morris P.

America's new democracy / Morris P. Fiorina, Paul E. Peterson, D. Stephen, Voss.

    p. cm. -- (Penguin academics)

Includes bibliographical references and index.

ISBN 0-321-12963-6

    2. Democracy--United States. 2. United States--Politics and government. I. Peterson, Paul E. II. Voss, D. Stephen (Dennis Stephen), 1968- III. Title. IV. Series.

JK1726.F56 2004

320.473--dc21   2003052282

Copyright © 2004 by Pearson Education, Inc.

All rights reserved. No part of this publication may be reproduced, stored in a retrieval system, or transmitted, in any form or by any means, electronic, mechanical, photocopying, recording, or otherwise, without the prior written permission of the publisher. Printed in the United States.

Visit us at http://www.ablongman.com

For more information about the Penguin Academic Series, please contact us by mail at Longman Publishers, attn. Marketing Department, 1185 Avenue of the Americas, 25th Floor, New York, NY 10036, or via the Internet at http://www.ablongman/feedback

ISBN 0-321-12963-6

2 3 4 5 6 7 8 9 10—QWT—06 05 04

To Michael and Joseph,
citizens of the new
American democracy
—M. P. F.

To David, Sarah, and John
—P. E. P.

To Sir Gareth, the humble knight,
and Princess Corrine, our fairy maiden
—D. S. V.

CONTENTS

PART TWO
CHANNELS OF INFLUENCE IN AMERICA'S NEW DEMOCRACY
87

PART THREE
THE INSTITUTIONS OF
AMERICA'S NEW DEMOCRACY
277

PART FOUR
OUTPUTS FROM
AMERICA'S NEW DEMOCRACY
429

CHAPTER 15 | PUBLIC POLICY 501

APPENDIX A-1

PREFACE

College-age people are instinctively pessimistic when they approach the study of American government. Students do not struggle with the concept that institutions or practices may malfunction. Hidden motives, corrupt bargains, social injustice, rampant incompetence—these are precisely what many (if not most) undergraduates today expect to encounter. Of course, not all students react to bad news in the same way. Some smirk knowingly. Some thump their chests and demand radical reform. Most shrug or yawn. Precious few, however, gasp in surprise.

Many popular political science works reinforce the pessimism of the age, especially with regard to democratic politics. They downplay the importance of mass political behavior—and teach that elites actually run the U.S. government, with limited regard for the voting public.[1] This book, by contrast, offers a guardedly upbeat message, one that stresses the system's responsiveness. Our purpose is not to suppress healthy skepticism. Rather, it is to cultivate a mirror image of analytical techniques already in place—to get readers in the habit of looking beyond the surface when appearances are *negative,* not only when they are rosy. We encourage readers to approach sky-is-falling-down political rhetoric with the same critical eye that they automatically reserve for sunny optimism.

Admittedly, institutions or practices that seem to function effectively in fact sometimes do not. Yet sometimes institutions or practices that appear dysfunctional—those that draw on base motives, express questionable values, or seem to lack an underlying logic—actually perform surprisingly well. This is an even-handed orientation, one that seeks the virtues as well as the vices of American government. Our cautious optimism may sound alien to modern readers, especially those who have learned about politics primarily from journalistic sources. But it dates back to the Enlightenment "political science" of the nation's founders (in particular, James Madison) and is a dominant mode of thinking among several contemporary schools in the political science discipline.

The intellectual perspective described here motivates the book's central theme: Elections (or at least the anticipation of them) matter more in America's political system now than they have in the past, than they do in other industrialized democracies, or than other political writers usually recognize. Votes are the main currency in the political market, so influencing them motivates political behavior even when the connection is not obvious. Fiorina and Peterson first articulated this claim while writing a textbook in 1993, and at the time they expected the argument to meet with substantial resistance. Most of the developments they described were fairly recent. But a decade under the Clinton and Bush administrations has lessened the novelty of the the argument—and, if anything, turned it into conventional wisdom.[2] This new book lies squarely in the mainstream of scholarly thinking about American politics.

A UNIFIED APPROACH TO AMERICAN GOVERNMENT

Regardless of whether one accepts this book's central argument, it serves as a valuable organizing framework for learning about American government. The book's theme and its intellectual perspective link every chapter. An introductory chapter announces the emphasis on popular influence, especially as transmitted through democratic elections. The remaining 14 chapters then each deal with a subject conventionally covered by American government texts. Rather than consign culture, opinion, and electioneering to single chapters, however, we continue to trace their effects through American political institutions all the way to the shape of public policies.

Every chapter begins with a vignette that either illustrates the voting public's power or seems to contradict it. We then use the stories to draw larger lessons about popular influence on each component of the American political system. We emphasize the electoral incentives that political actors face, how those incentives shape institutions, and how the institutions translate competing pressures into public policy. Thus, the result is more a unified book than a textbook, albeit one written for newcomers to the topic.

CHALLENGING TODAY'S STUDENT

This volume differs from an introductory textbook in one other sense as well. Instructors often operate on the implicit view that their students are not adequately motivated to undertake college work. They presume that undergraduates will not endeavor to learn new words or to think through complex ideas. This viewpoint has led some instructors to oversimplify their courses and some textbook authors to avoid sophisticated arguments. Having each taught American government for many years, we are not unsympathetic with the pressures these educators face.

Nevertheless, we suspect that the main problem for typical students is neither stupidity nor laziness but simple boredom. Our experiences as educators at both private and public universities suggest that most students who are engaged by a subject are perfectly willing to do the work necessary to learn, even if it means checking a dictionary occasionally or reading a paragraph a second time. Rather than blame students for their boredom, therefore, we hypothesize that political science textbooks need to do a better job of conveying why political science is both interesting and relevant to students who lack an inherent love of the subject.

Given our premise, this book intentionally challenges college undergraduates. We treat readers as mature and thoughtful people, curious about their world but impatient with authors who waste their time. To meet the requirements of this demanding audience, we have done everything possible to streamline the book's presentation and spice up the book's language without sacrificing substance. Each chapter is an extended essay told in a uniform authorial voice, not a series of disembodied topics. We tell stories. We emphasize meaning and significance, the "bottom line." We use the active voice, straightforward sentences, and nontechnical language whenever possible. We do not just define or describe; we interpret and sometimes provoke. Our hope is that readers will find this approach as satisfying an antidote for their boredom as our own undergraduate students have.

FEATURES
OF THE SECOND EDITION

The first edition of this book grew out of a textbook by Fiorina and Peterson called *The New American Democracy*.[3] It is not just an "essentials edition" of the parent text, however. As part of the *Penguin Academics* series from Longman Publishers, *America's New Democracy* is an alternative for instructors and readers who want to move away from standard textbooks—those who prefer a learning tool unified by a strong framework upon which to attach facts picked up along the way. Voss has adapted the book so that it differs substantially from the source, taking on its own distinct personality. The key changes are as follows:

- Greater focus on the book's underlying theme, including transition sections (a) linking each introduction to the book's central argument and (b) explaining how the body of the chapter illustrates popular influence in the political system. Chapters are organized to work readers through the logic connecting each topic to electoral influences.

- Large sections of new or substantially revised material, including new introductions for almost every chapter, up-to-date Election Connection boxes showing how elections have influenced each chapter topic, and new Aftershock sections at the end of half the chapters discussing the role of public opinion in policy changes carried out after 9/11.

- A reorganized table of contents, with the material broken up to facilitate use in a 15-week course. This is accomplished by offering larger, merged chapters on public opinion and the media, on elections (including presidential and congressional elections), on political factions (including parties and interest groups), and on public policy (including domestic, economic, and foreign policy).

- Contemporary information on current events, including *elections* (updated through the 2002 congressional contests), *judicial decisions* (updated through the 2003 Supreme Court term's decisions on affirmative action, sodomy, and state sovereign immunity), *foreign and defense policy* (updated through the wars against Afghanistan and Iraq), *economic affairs* (updated through the 2002 financial scandals), and *budgetary politics* (updated through the state budget crisis of 2002–2003).

Note that this new edition also differs substantially from the first edition. Eight of the introductions, eight of the Election Connection boxes, and almost all of the Aftershock discussions are new. Numerous other sections have been improved as well, based on feedback from a dozen reviewers, various helpful fellow professors, and hundreds of our own students. Instructors familiar with the first edition or its election update are encouraged to request a copy of the instructor's manual (see the next section). It provides clear chapter-by-chapter detail on the changes in the new edition, thereby minimizing the amount of new course preparation necessary to make the transition to the updated book.

SUPPLEMENTS

INSTRUCTOR'S MANUAL / TEST BANK
Prepared by D. Stephen Voss and Candice Y. Wallace of the University of Kentucky, this resource manual contains an overview of what each chapter tries to accomplish and how the material fits into an undergraduate classroom. For each chapter, it provides instructors with a list of learning objectives, suggests possible pedagogical strategies to assist with classroom use of the book, outlines in detail the arguments and evidence contained in the body of the book, and lists numerous test questions drawn directly from the readings.

TESTGEN-EQ COMPUTERIZED TESTING SYSTEM
This easy-to-master electronic supplement on CD-ROM includes all the test items in the printed test bank. The software allows you to edit existing questions and add your own items. Tests can be printed in several different fonts and formats.

ACKNOWLEDGMENTS

We want to thank the many people who helped out during the preparation of this book. Candice Y. Wallace, Gareth J. Voss, and Kathleen J. Elliott performed superbly as research assistants. University of Kentucky Professors Brad Canon, Don Gross, Stuart Kaufman, and Mark Peffley all provided advice on chapters relating to their areas of expertise (judicial politics, congressional elections, ethnic conflict, and media politics, respectively). Our editor, Eric Stano, and project manager, Karla Maki, patiently guided the second edition to publication despite numerous authorial delays. Also, Voss is grateful for the encouragement he has received as a faculty member in the University of Kentucky's College of Arts and Sciences, not only from the college's administration but also from the many University of Kentucky undergraduates who have toiled to make his experience teaching American Government so stimulating. He dedicates the book to his two children, Gareth James Voss and Corrine Faye Elliott, whose knight-and-princess fantasies suggest rather royalist leanings but who nevertheless tolerate their father's interest in mass political behavior.

We also wish to express the deepest gratitude to those who have assisted with editions of the text from which this book draws. Bruce Nichols first argued the need for a new-century approach in introductory texts on American government. The Center for Advanced Study in the Behavioral and Social Sciences provided generous support for Peterson's work on the first edition during his academic year there. Harding Noblitt of Concordia College read the entire first-edition manuscript in search of errors of fact and interpretation, which saved the authors much embarrassment. In addition, portions were read by Danny Adkison, Sue Davis, Richard Fenno, Gary Jacobson, Barry Rabe, and Chris Stamm, whose comments helped with fact checking. Larry Carlton supplied important factual material. Rebecca Contreras, Alison Kommer, Shelley Weiner, and Sarah Peterson provided staff assistance. Research assistants included Ted Brader, Jay Girotto, William Howell, Donald Lee, Jerome Maddox, Kenneth Scheve, Sean Theriault, and Robert Van Houweling. Martin West of Harvard University and Sam Abrams of Stanford University performed a multitude of tasks to develop the second edition of *The New American Democracy,* from which the first edition of this book borrowed heavily. Finally, and perhaps most importantly, we extend our special thanks to Bert Johnson of Carleton College. Bert performed invaluable research to develop the second edition and helped author the third edition of the textbook from which *America's New Democracy* draws some of its material. Hence, although Bert is not credited as a full-fledged author of this particular book, some of his words undoubtedly found their way onto its pages. We are indebted to him for any and all inadvertent borrowings that appear inside.

Finally, we would like to thank the reviewers who provided comments on the first edition to help us prepare the second:

Cheryl A. Brown, Marshall University
Debbie Daniels, University of Minnesota
Jim Enelow, University of Texas at Austin
Sarah Miller, Lourdes College
Daniel E. Ponder, University of Colorado at Colorado Springs
Charles R. Shipan, University of Iowa
James Toole, Indiana University
Peter Watkins, Saint Joseph's College

We regret that this edition could not reflect all of their useful suggestions. Nonetheless, any improvements in the second edition of *America's New Democracy* owe much to their extraordinarily helpful advice.

M. P. F.
P. E. P.
D. S. V.

FOUNDATIONS
OF
AMERICA'S NEW DEMOCRACY

1

DEMOCRACY IN THE UNITED STATES

Election night 2000 was not a proud moment in the annals of American journalism. The problems began at 8:00 P.M. EST, just after polls had closed in the first handful of states. Americans were still casting votes across the heartland and up and down the West Coast when news anchors announced a major development in the presidential race. One after another the networks declared, on the basis of election-night polls, that Democratic Vice President Al Gore had taken Florida—even though some of the state's voting booths had not yet even closed.[1]

Losing Florida, the state governed by his brother, would have dealt a crushing blow to the presidential ambitions of Republican nominee George W. Bush. Most observers thought—rightly, as it turned out—that the Texas governor could not take the White House without solid support from southern states.[2] But when Bush appeared on television soon afterward, seated in his shirtsleeves with tie askew, he was joking with companions on screen. He turned to the cameras and announced that no one should write him off yet. "The networks called this thing awfully early, but the people who are actually counting the votes are coming up with a little different perspective," he warned. Bush did not appear particularly worried. "I'm pretty darn upbeat about things," he claimed.[3]

Bush staffers were much less jocular. They jumped quickly to chastise the networks for making declarations so early in the night, when they could still influence many voters across the country. "This is an unfortunate rush to judgment by the media," Mark McKinnon, Bush's senior media consultant, told ABC. No doubt reporters initially assumed that Bush's smiles were false bravado, hiding his campaign advisers' knowledge that the election was lost. The election, though, was not lost.

As the numbers poured in from Florida, it became clear that Gore was not receiving the levels of support estimated by the day's polls. The networks finally threw out their predictions after half of Florida's precincts had reported results. "We realized we were in trouble, and we pulled it back," explained one ABC spokeswoman, describing the situation faced by all the networks. They declared Florida once again "too close to call" and stuck to that judgment throughout the night, even as the Florida tally mounted—no doubt wishing to avoid a second embarrassment.

Finally, in the wee hours of the morning, the networks could no longer resist and set themselves up for humiliation again. They declared Florida for Bush this time and announced his election as the nation's 43rd president. The few TV screens still shining across the United States showed smiling pictures of Governor Bush, with the American flag rippling behind him. Only later did watchers learn that Florida law would require a recount, leaving the state still much too close to call.

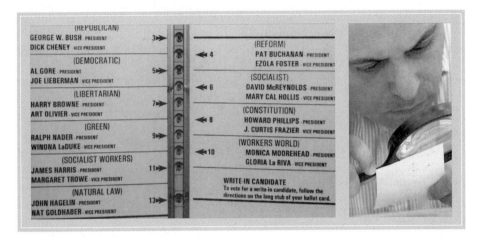

A butterfly doomed to extinction
Palm Beach County, Florida, used a "butterfly ballot" in the 2000 presidential election that caused many voters to choose Reform party candidate Pat Buchanan accidentally. Many specialists argue that Gore lost the bulk of these miscast votes. Other Florida ballots had to be counted by hand because voters did not punch out their "chads" properly. Florida followed the debacle with a major overhaul of its election law. Why might Gore supporters have been more likely than Bush supporters to make mistakes with these ballots?

If election night 2000 marked the low point in political news coverage, many observers considered the days that followed the low point of twentieth-century American politics. The presidential vote was so close nationally that the candidate who won Florida also would win the election—and it quickly became clear that Florida's election laws and voting technologies were not precise enough to resolve such a close contest in a manner satisfactory to everyone. The unofficial vote totals gave Bush a tiny lead, but technical issues resolved during the recount process could make him lose that edge (see Chapter 6).

Someone had to figure out a way to determine who had won the presidency. Thousands of ballots had gone uncounted. Many thousands more had been miscast by voters who did not understand what they were supposed to do with the ballot. In one Florida county, Palm Beach, a poorly designed ballot resulted in perhaps 3000 votes being miscast for Reform party candidate Pat Buchanan. It is hard to say who deserved those votes, because Buchanan's spot on the ballot placed him between the two major-party candidates, but the quantity involved was more than enough to make up any difference between votes for Bush and those for Gore.[4] Media reports turned up examples of dead people and felons voting, of people being turned away at the polls because precincts could not handle the traffic, and of absentee military ballots being disqualified on technicalities.[5]

Florida began the slow process of recounting votes to make sure that Bush had beaten Gore. But the two sides disputed where ballots should be counted, which votes should be eligible, and how much time the procedure could take.

With so many of the rules in doubt, it seemed inevitable that ultimate resolution of the contest would have to come from the courts. Legal teams for both candidates began filing suits and countersuits, throwing around provisions in Florida law and constitutional doctrine to swing the state over to their cause.

The legal battle took five weeks. It did little to increase national confidence in the election. Florida's Republican secretary of state made a series of judgments about the timing of recounts—judgments that would benefit the Republicans. The Democratic state attorney general responded with contrary legal interpretations that would benefit the Democrats. The Florida Supreme Court, dominated by Democratic judges, favored an interpretation of state law that favored Gore. But the U.S. Supreme Court, dominated by Republican appointees, overruled the lower court's judgment as unconstitutional—only then guaranteeing a Bush victory. The debate operated under a veneer of legal reasoning, but if anything, it only added to the sense that Americans might never know who really won the 2000 election.

One election result did appear certain: This "debacle" could only fuel feelings of impotence and political cynicism already rampant in the country. Many Democrats charged that the GOP had stolen the election, but concern over the electoral process ran deeper than mere partisan disappointment. If campaigns in the United States could be resolved by such a haphazard (and seemingly partisan) procedure, many asked, why should anyone bother to vote? Who would accept that the attitudes, opinions, and values of regular citizens can influence elected leaders? Who would believe that elections really matter anymore?

NEVERTHELESS, THE CENTRAL THEME OF THIS BOOK is that elections are the key to understanding contemporary American democracy. Elections not only matter, they are more important in the United States than in other democracies and more important today than they were in most earlier periods of U.S. history.

Those who focus on the messy process that put President Bush in the White House ignore the many steps that preceded it. Bush and Gore planned their presidential bids far in advance of the contest. They compiled proposals and worked hard to frame successful political messages. They cultivated the leaders of interest groups that voters join. They campaigned aggressively to win over unaffiliated voters, visiting cities and towns across the country. It was their joint sensitivity to public demands—their electioneering—that produced such a close contest. And even if the battle's chaotic final resolution seemed no more democratic than a coin toss, haphazard forces gained so much influence only because the election results did not communicate a clear favorite. Voters mattered from start to finish.

Elections drive the political system because Americans have developed *a unique conception of democracy* that requires frequent citizen participation, with the result that *elections are plentiful* and *politicians are permanently campaigning*. The need to please a fickle and demanding electorate shapes the nation's institutions, both the formal ones set up by law and the informal ones—such as political parties, interest groups, and the mass media—that express public demands to elected leaders.

A UNIQUE CONCEPTION OF DEMOCRACY

Americans were cynical long before the 2000 Florida debacle. Citizens generally do not trust government as much as they did a generation ago (see Figure 1.1). They believe that government costs too much and delivers too little. They think politics is needlessly contentious and often corrupt. They do not respect public servants, whether elected or appointed. They are unenthusiastic about major-party presidential candidates and yearn for a new style of leader.[6]

FIGURE 1.1

Americans have grown increasingly skeptical of the national government

Are Americans today too cynical, or were those in the past too trusting?

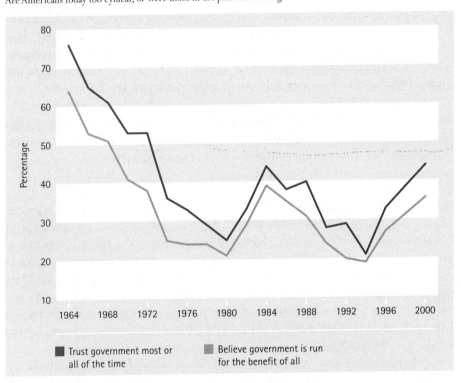

- ■ Trust government most or all of the time
- ■ Believe government is run for the benefit of all

NOTE: Data on the 1986 responses to the second question do not exist.

SOURCE: The American National Election Studies.

[handwritten margin notes: "views of government — laissez faire or" and "functions of government school/mail"]

To some extent, suspicion of government is healthy. Governments threaten human liberty by their very nature. The great German sociologist Max Weber wrote that government is the only institution in society with a "monopoly of the legitimate use of physical force."[7] Government is the only institution that *legally* can take people's property (by taxing them), restrict their movements (by imprisoning them), and even kill them (by executing them). As George Washington put it a century before Weber, "Government is not reason, it is not eloquence—it is force."[8]

Why have governments at all, then? Different thinkers have provided different answers to that question. Thomas Hobbes, a great English political philosopher, made the most basic case. A world without government would be nothing less than "a war of all against all," he claimed. Life would be "nasty, brutish and short."[9] Because he saw the consequences of anarchy as so dire, Hobbes determined that government must possess absolute power to protect itself. Few Americans accept this drastic conclusion. At the same time, almost everyone accepts that some form of government is necessary, and for much the same pessimistic reason Hobbes offered: to protect people from each other, if nothing else. In former president James Madison's words, "If men were angels, no government would be necessary."[10]

Those who participate in politics today usually want more than just basic protections, though. Most want to use government's great power to realize their visions of a better society. Obviously there are other ways to improve a community, a nation, or the world—such as through charities and service organizations—but these associations rely on voluntary cooperation. Government is a convenient means to force everyone else to work toward the same vision, and to do so speedily. In other words, government is designed to be a legitimate means for resolving disagreements, one that can back up society's decisions with violence if necessary. For that reason, citizens *should* be wary of its power.

REPRESENTATION

British author Samuel Johnson once commented, "I would not give half a guinea to live under one form of government rather than another. It is of no moment to the happiness of an individual."[11] Johnson's comment is silly, at best. Lives can be saved or destroyed, depending on the type of government under which people live. The scope and structure of government are among the most critical decisions that a society must make. Aristotle recognized this fact 23 centuries ago, prompting him to work out a classification scheme for political institutions. He divided governments into three general categories: government by one person, by the few, and by the many.

Few Americans today support government dominated by a small number of people. When a single ruler, such as an emperor or a tsar, controls the state, that individual may put the people's welfare first, last, or anywhere in between. An

Hail to the Chief

Elected leaders have no monopoly on popular support. Dictators like Saddam Hussein may enjoy at least some celebrity in their home countries too. What sets apart government by a small number of people is how they treat citizens who do not support them.

absolute ruler answers to no one. Government by the few may appear slightly better, because members of a ruling class can compete with each other. They may try to improve social conditions as a means of attracting public support during internal disputes. But without periodic elections, a small ruling group generally can remain unified enough to exploit its position. Americans, therefore, overwhelmingly favor **democracy** (from the Greek word *demos,* meaning "people"), a form of government in which citizens share power.

Knowing that most Americans support rule by the many does not settle all questions regarding the form of government. Different systems of representation give voters varying amounts of influence, depending on the extent to which citizens exercise power directly. Pure, **direct democracy** still exists in a few New England villages, where citizens determine policies together at town meetings, but otherwise, elected representatives make most of a government's decisions. Just about every democracy more complicated than a small town is a representative democracy, or **republic,** in which citizens elect officials to govern them rather than selecting most policies themselves.

A republic's institutions require some means to ensure that representatives do not undermine the democratic system after taking office. James Madison, architect of the Constitution, believed that written rules—which he called "parchment barriers"—would not protect freedoms effectively. Nor could citizens rely on the virtue of their leaders. In this sense, Madison anticipated modern distrust of government. As a solution, he endorsed a system of institutions that would divide power among different representatives chosen in different elections at different times. Give them authority to resist each other, Madison explained, and elected officials desiring to protect their own authority naturally would keep an eye on rivals who tried to gather excessive power. Self-interest would encourage leaders to check (that is, block) each other's abuses, resulting in a safe, balanced system. "Ambition must be made to counteract ambition," he wrote.[12]

Madison did not view majority rule as a foolproof solution to the dangers of strong government, though. On the contrary, the system of **checks and balances** promised one other benefit: It was a form of representation that placed clear limits on popular whims. It may prevent a minority from abusing governmental powers, but it also can frustrate a majority trying to abuse those powers. Electing representatives is a fairly blunt instrument for manipulating public policy. Unless voters are fairly unified and fairly patient, the government responds sluggishly to public demands.

POPULAR INFLUENCE

Political theorists disagree over how much popular control is desirable. Some prefer that citizens take a more active role in government. Democracy is more than just a decision-making procedure for them; it is also an educational forum. A citizenry improves itself while deciding the community's future. By being inclusive, by transforming "conflict into cooperation," the process combines everyone's perspectives to produce better policy.[13] Elections play a critical role in this *popular model of democracy* because they are the mechanism for instructing officials about public wishes. Obviously, this idea requires informed citizens who are capable of voting prospectively—that is, by looking to the future.

Other theorists question whether the average citizen should take more than a passive role in government. Too much participation produces lots of talk but little action and also makes compromises more difficult. Citizens may be capable of judging a candidate retrospectively—that is, by looking at past performance when they vote, keeping good leaders and removing bad ones. But they are neither equipped for, nor interested in, selecting among competing policy proposals.[14] These critics favor instead a *responsible model of democracy,* in which elected officials choose policies but must answer to the people afterward for the outcomes of their decisions.

In the real world, of course, pure types do not exist; all democracies combine popular and responsible features. Yet the United States has always been a more popular democracy than its European counterparts. Indeed, from the earliest days of the republic, the principles of popular democracy have been an important part of American thought. "Where annual elections end, there slavery begins," said the second president, John Adams, arguing that citizens must have frequent opportunities to instruct and judge their representatives.[15] When the French scholar Alexis de Tocqueville visited the United States during the 1830s, he was astounded by the extent of popular participation. "It must be seen to be believed. No sooner do you set foot on American ground than you are stunned by a kind of tumult," he exclaimed to his fellow French citizens. "Almost the only pleasure an

American knows is to take part in the government and discuss its measures."[16] The system's responsiveness has only increased since then.

For this reason, one brand of American cynicism strikes us as particularly unhealthy. Many citizens believe they have little influence over government. Unlike the other forms of distrust, which are prudent given government's vast powers, we find this brand of pessimism discouraging because it is so misguided. Whatever the flaws of American government, inadequate opportunity for citizen input is certainly not one of them. The American political system allows frequent opportunities to give leaders feedback. We turn to that topic now.

ELECTIONS ARE PLENTIFUL

American politics has evolved over the course of two centuries to allow greater popular participation. The connection between representatives and the public has become increasingly direct. National institutions are less insulated from popular influence than they once were. And the number and frequency of elections, coupled with the more extensive campaigning that accompanies them, have increased. These trends have accelerated dramatically in recent decades—to the extent that calling the system America's "new democracy" is no exaggeration.

HALF A MILLION ELECTED OFFICIALS, AND THEN SOME

The United States has more elections, selecting more officials for public office, than any other country on Earth. This simple fact is one important key to understanding why elections are so influential. Unbelievable as it may seem, more than half a million people in the United States are elected officials, about one official for every 500 Americans. If all elected officials lived in one place, the population would exceed that of Cleveland.[17]

National elections, which determine the officials of the federal government, occur every two years. Voters must pick 435 voting members of the House of Representatives and a third of the Senate's 100 members. Every four years, voters also choose the president and vice president. But these elections, which receive the bulk of news coverage, are just the tip of the iceberg.

State elections allow the citizens of each of the 50 states to choose their public officials. In every state, voters elect the governor and the state legislature, and in nearly all states they also elect the lieutenant governor, the treasurer, the state's attorney, the auditor, and perhaps state public utility commissioners.

The number of elections explodes at the local level. In *local elections,* voters in cities elect mayors and city councils. Voters in the more than 3000 counties elect sheriffs, county treasurers, and county boards, among other officials. Voters elect the members of 90 percent of the nation's 16,000 school boards, as well as numer-

judicial

ous officials responsible for the governance of towns, villages, and special districts.

Even the judicial system—often viewed as insulated from political pressure—is permeated by elections. In 37 states, voters elect at least some judges.
Altogether, Americans select more than 1000 state judges and about 15,000
county, municipal, and other local officers of the court.[18] Moreover, in recent
years judges have been increasingly subject to **recall elections,** in which dissatisfied citizens try to remove sitting officials during their terms. The result? Americans must vote constantly to stay involved. To take just one example, professors
at the University of Houston estimate that a resident of Houston is represented by
126 elected officials, judges included.[19]

Although half a million elected officials sound like a lot, there are far more
elections than there are elected officials. First, many officials must win two or
more elections before they can take office. In the **primary election,** each party
chooses a nominee, who then squares off against the other parties' nominees in
the **general election**—which selects the officeholder. *Nonpartisan elections,*
where candidates do not run with party labels, also sometimes use primaries to
narrow the field of candidates.

Some elections do not choose officials at all. In 27 states and the District of
Columbia, voters may influence public issues directly by making law at the ballot
box.[20] Some states allow **initiatives,** proposed laws or constitutional amendments placed on the ballot by citizen petition. Some decide policy through **referenda,** laws or state constitutional amendments proposed by a legislative body
that require voter approval before going into effect. These forms of direct democracy show little sign of losing their popularity. A few states, such as California,
frequently have more initiatives and referenda on the ballot than elected offices to
be filled.

Other countries do not have nearly so many elections. Consider Great Britain,
which elected Tony Blair prime minister in 1997 and reelected him in 2001. In each
of these elections, Britons voted for only one person—a candidate for parliament.
Between these two elections, Britons voted on only two other occasions, for only
two offices—local councillor and representative to the European Community.

In the time between Bill Clinton's two election victories, the French voted
four times: for Parliament in 1993, for president in April and May of 1994
(France has a two-round system), and for local mayors in 1995. Similarly,
between 1992 and 1996 the Japanese voted five times, twice each for the upper
and lower houses of the Diet (their parliament) and once for local officials.

U.S. citizens even vote a lot more often than other North Americans. A
Mexican citizen votes at most four times in a four-year period: in presidential,
congressional, state, and municipal elections. A Canadian votes at most three
times (national, provincial, and municipal) in a four-year period, except for an
occasional referendum, such as Québec's 1995 vote on sovereignty.[21]

Observers from other countries are struck by the seemingly constant presence of Americans at the polling booths. British analyst Anthony King observes,

> Americans take the existence of their elections industry for granted. Some like it; some dislike it; most are simply bored by it. But they are all conscious of it, in the same way that they are conscious of Mobil, McDonald's, Larry King Live, Oprah Winfrey, the Dallas Cowboys, the Ford Motor Company, and all the other symbols and institutions that go to make up the rich tapestry of American life. In a meaningful sense, America is about the holding of elections. [22]

THE LIMITS OF VOTING

Stressing the importance of elections may paint a rather rosy picture. To avoid any misunderstanding, therefore, we must emphasize three qualifications: (1) Elections involve more than what takes place in the voting booth. (2) Elections do not always express the popular will. (3) Elections are not the only important force in American politics.

First, our notion of electoral influence is very broad. We are referring not just to what happens in the voting booth, nor even just to what goes on during campaigns. Rather, when we write about the importance of elections, we include the anticipation of, and the preparation for, future elections. Political actors would be foolish indeed if they waited until election day to worry about what the public wants. Looking ahead affects what presidents propose, what they sign, and what they veto; what Congress passes and what it kills; whom groups support and whom they oppose; and what the media cover or ignore. Voters wield much of their power passively.

A second important clarification is that when we stress the importance of elections, we are *not* making a naïve claim that "the people" rule. Just as the winner of an Olympic event may have been determined on the training fields years earlier, so the outcomes of elections may be determined by the actions of candidates, groups, contributors, the media, and other political actors far in advance of the actual campaigns. Most fund raising is done by groups who wish to promote special political interests. Liberal and conservative groups, economic and environmental groups, women's groups, minority groups, or whatever—all have a perfectly legitimate right to participate in politics. But all have a point of view, usually one that is narrower than that of the typical voter. These groups furnish money, campaign volunteers, and endorsements, so their leaders carry extra weight with most elected officials.

Once elections are under way, many potential voters choose not to participate. Even in the 2000 presidential election, only 51 percent of the adult population voted (see Chapter 6). Turnout rates in other elections are much lower—in the single digits(!) in some local races. Groups of people who vote at higher rates, such as the elderly, therefore enjoy disproportionate political influence. [23] Pri-

The permanent campaign
Candidates begin campaigning far in advance of the actual presidential election and often find the whole experience terribly draining. Texas Governor George W. Bush's exhaustion shows in this election-night photo, in which he tries to nap on wife Laura's shoulder. Is it feasible, or even a good idea, to limit the time candidates may campaign?

mary elections have especially low turnout. The primary electorate is much better educated, and much more interested in politics, than the average American citizen. Republican primary voters tend to be more conservative than the typical American, and Democratic primary voters tend to be more liberal. To win primary elections, candidates may appeal to the more extreme elements of their parties. By the time typical voters get involved in the general election, their choice may be between two unappetizing candidates.

Sometimes elections allow powerful special interests to block actions desired by a majority. Sometimes leaders elected by different majorities at different times or in different regions fight each other to a standstill. It is possible for inattentive voters to be manipulated by biased information or confused by complex political issues. These various forces prevent any simple assumption that the people rule. Elections are not always free, accurate, and effective expressions of national sentiment.

Finally, to say that elections are a key ingredient in American democracy—even *the* key ingredient—is not to deny that other elements are important as well. Elections are part of a complex political system. Comprehending how they operate in America's new democracy sometimes requires understanding the historical evolution of American government, the political behavior of individual Americans, the workings of the country's basic institutions, and the policies that the government produces. All of these topics, which are closely bound up with elections, thus receive thorough treatment in the chapters that follow. First, though, we consider one important drawback to a system driven by elections: the cost of the stressful contests themselves.

THE PERMANENT CAMPAIGN

The new American democracy is marked by a **permanent campaign**.[24] The term literally means that campaigning never ends; the next election campaign begins as soon as the last one has finished, if not before. Commentators began speculating on President Bush's likely 2004 opposition before he even took office.* Behind-the-scenes planning for the 2004 contest began in 2001. Nine Democratic candidates had already entered the race by early 2003, only halfway into Bush's term.

The deeper meaning of the term *permanent campaign* is that the line between campaigning and governing has disappeared. How an elected official governs is, in effect, just another strategic campaign decision. This change could be good or bad. On the good side, it might enhance democracy by encouraging leaders to consider public desires throughout their time in office. On the bad side, injecting campaign tactics into government may result in short-term thinking, a more combative governing style, and more emphasis on image than on substance.[25] Either way, though, the permanent campaign has transformed the political system.

CAUSES OF THE PERMANENT CAMPAIGN
At least seven developments have moved American democracy in a popular direction by contributing to the permanent campaign. Some of these receive more in-depth treatment in later chapters, but let's review them briefly here.

SEPARATION OF ELECTIONS   A century ago, public officials were all elected on the same day. Citizens in most states could cast votes simultaneously for president, senator, representative, governor, mayor, state representative, state senator, city councillor, and so forth. A graduate student named Woodrow Wilson claimed, in 1885, that "This is preeminently a country of frequent elections, and few states care to increase the frequency by separating elections of state from elections of national functionaries."[26] But over time, Americans did separate those elections

---

*One favorite topic of discussion: a presidential bid by First Lady Hillary Clinton, who had not even been sworn in as New York's junior U.S. senator.

and increased the frequency of elections in other ways as well.[27] Most Americans now turn out to vote for president at one general election, for governor at another, and for mayor at yet another. Primary elections, as well as those for local offices, occur earlier in the election year. Initiatives and referenda may take place on still other occasions. As a result, Americans repeatedly receive their summons to the polls. For example, a conscientious Californian generally has to vote on eight separate occasions every two years. There is very little "quiet time."

DECAY OF PARTY ORGANIZATIONS   The two major parties in the United States are the Democrats and the Republicans (or GOP, for "Grand Old Party"). Those two have dominated the political system for a long time. The GOP started just before the Civil War and, ironically, the Democrats are even older, tracing their lineage back to supporters of Thomas Jefferson's 1800 presidential bid. These parties give voters a choice by advocating different ideologies (see Chapter 4). Republicans tend to be conservative politically, which means they are "the right" or "right wing." Democrats tend to be liberal and are called "the left" or "left wing."* A party's issue positions shift only gradually, providing continuity and familiarity to political life. For this reason, parties simplify the choices voters must make.

A century ago many of the state and local party organizations were called machines, because they were strong, disciplined organizations that could mobilize large numbers of voters. Candidates relied on their parties when elections rolled around. But various reforms and social changes killed the machines (see Chapter 8). Today's politicians cannot depend on party workers; they must build their own organizations almost from scratch.[28] Such personalized support requires extensive time and resources to maintain.[29]

SPREAD OF PRIMARIES   In most countries, party leaders select candidates for office. This was the standard procedure in the United States a century ago as well. According to reformers, candidates were picked in "smoke-filled rooms" by party "bosses." To eliminate the corruption that often accompanied such deal making, reformers passed laws giving voters the right to select party nominees in primary elections (see Chapter 7). Each public office then required twice as many visits to the voting booth, shortening the gap of time between elections. Some members of the House of Representatives face primaries more than six months before their two-year terms end. On April 9, 1996, for example, a Texas Republican was defeated in a primary scarcely 15 months after he had taken the oath of office.

---

*The origins of this terminology lie in the French Assembly that sat after the French Revolution (1789–1795). In the Assembly, conservatives sat on the right side of the chamber and liberals on the left (as you face the podium). The U.S. Congress and some other world legislatures follow a similar practice today.

FIGURE 1.2

The number of presidential primaries has increased greatly in the past three decades.
Would party leaders select better standard bearers than the voters do?

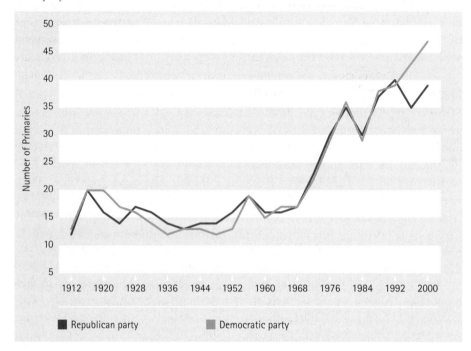

■ Republican party   ■ Democratic party

SOURCE: Harold Stanley and Richard Niemi, Vital Statistics on American Politics. (Washington, DC: CQ Press, 2000), p. 62, and data compiled by Sam Abrams.

Although they came into use about a century ago, primaries did not become the dominant mechanism for nominating presidential candidates until after World War II (see Figure 1.2). The first presidential candidate who owed his nomination in any significant degree to winning primaries was Dwight D. Eisenhower, elected in 1952. As late as 1968, the Democratic nominee, Hubert Humphrey, did not enter a single primary. Now participation is necessary.

MASS COMMUNICATIONS   Today's candidates must exploit the mass media or their opponents will gain an advantage. They work to get their names in the papers and their pictures on television. Dozens of cable television channels enable candidates to communicate with small, well-defined audiences. C-SPAN provides continuous coverage of congressional debates, giving people outside Washington a chance to observe public officials directly. Radio talk shows have increased in popularity. Candidate and interest-group Web sites on the Internet have proliferated, and conversation on the Internet (although often erroneous and conspiratorial) is perhaps the fastest-growing mode of political communication.

The effects of technological development have been intensified by changing journalistic norms. Media outlets demand content, and they do not shy away from criticizing political figures (see Chapter 5). Any move a politician makes might end up on television, and virtually every move a prominent politician makes is now evaluated for its political motives and implications. Partly as a consequence of the media's insatiable appetite for news, the distinction between public and private life has eroded. The financial and medical histories of elected officials are treated as public business, and reporters ask candidates almost any question imaginable, no matter how tasteless or unrelated to government. Campaigning never ends because the public never stops watching.

PROFUSION OF INTEREST GROUPS   The campaign organizations that today's candidates assemble are built in large part from the numerous interest groups created during the past generation (see Chapter 8). When political scientists wrote about interest groups at mid-century, they referred mostly to a few large business, labor, and agricultural organizations. Now there are thousands of generally smaller, more narrowly focused organizations. Many are outgrowths of the social movements of the 1960s (such as the antiwar, civil rights, women's, and environmental movements). These groups monitor elected officials and report to voters about what the politicians are doing. They may post information on Web sites, send blanket e-mail to their members, or even buy television advertisements. In the spring of 2001, groups aired ads attacking California Governor Gray Davis for his handling of the state's energy crisis, even though he did not yet have an opponent for the 2002 election. Such tactics force politicians to consider the electoral implications of whatever they do.

PROLIFERATION OF POLLS   The permanent campaign owes much to the profusion of polling (see Chapter 5). Leaders always have been concerned about public opinion, of course. The framers of the U.S. Constitution were particularly concerned with how others would perceive their handiwork, because they wanted the document ratified and respected. Abraham Lincoln waited for a military victory before issuing the Emancipation Proclamation, which abolished slavery in the Confederate states, so that a happy northern public would be more inclined to support it. Politicians traditionally are portrayed as having their "ears to the ground" and their "fingers to the wind." But until the introduction of modern polling, beliefs about the state of public opinion were only guesses. Modern polling techniques are much more precise tools when elected officials are hungry for information about the state of the public mind.

Polling contributes to the permanent campaign by making opinions immediately available. When a new issue arises, politicians no longer wonder about the savvy position to take; they find out within days or sometimes hours. Even if elected officials wanted to make decisions free from political calculation, it would

FIGURE 1.3

Poll coverage exploded between the mid-1960s and mid-1970s

Do opinion polls serve a useful social or political function?

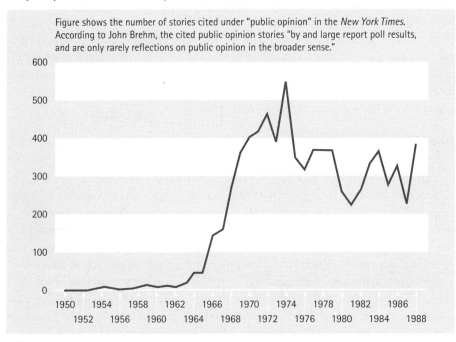

Figure shows the number of stories cited under "public opinion" in the *New York Times*. According to John Brehm, the cited public opinion stories "by and large report poll results, and are only rarely reflections on public opinion in the broader sense."

SOURCE: John Brehm, The Phantom Respondents (Ann Arbor, MI: University of Michigan Press, 1993), p. 4.

be difficult to do so. They are bombarded with such information at every turn because the media have become increasingly focused on polling (see Figure 1.3). Some critics charge that the media find it easier to "manufacture" news by taking a poll than to identify and write about real events.

MONEY Campaigning is expensive. Polls, political consultants, and TV ads cost a great deal of money (see Chapter 7). And because candidates now have personal organizations, they do not share many resources with each other. The total cost of election campaigns thus has increased dramatically in the past three decades (see Figure 1.4). Campaigns for the House of Representatives, for example, were more than five times more expensive in 1996 than in 1976.[30]

Elections may occur every few years, but the quest for money is continuous. U.S. senators serve six-year terms. The framers thought that such long terms would help insulate senators from popular pressures and allow them to act more deliberately than members of the House. But most contemporary observers believe that the Senate today is just as electorally sensitive. One reason is that sen-

FIGURE 1.4

The total costs of American elections have increased dramatically in the last five decades.
Should Congress try to limit spending in election campaigns?

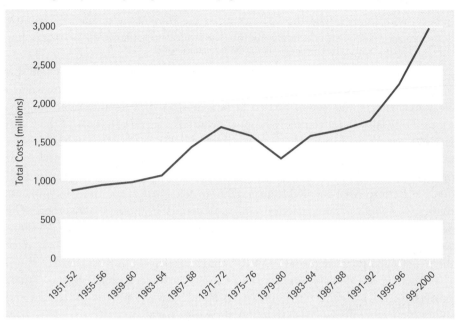

NOTE: All figures have been adjusted for inflation in terms of 2001 CPI constant dollars.

SOURCES: Common Cause, the Center for Responsive Politics, and respective volumes of Herbert E. Alexander, *Financing the 1951–1952* [and 1995–2000 vols.] *Election* (Washington, DC: CQ Press).

ators must raise more than $15,000 every week of their six-year terms to run for reelection.[31] Of the 28 gubernatorial incumbents who won reelection from 1998 to 2000, the average candidate spent more than $4.5 million. This would equate to more than $22,000 raised every week of a four-year term.[32]

In recent years the scramble for money has led to a series of fund-raising scandals, some involving public officials with long-standing reputations for honesty and integrity. In consequence, public interest groups have placed the issue of campaign finance on the public agenda (see Chapter 8). Another, more basic cost of this need for cash is that public officials must be concerned with the next election even when it is years away.

MORE DEMOCRACY?

The United States pays a price for the pervasiveness of its elections. Continuous electioneering creates a governmental system that is unattractive in many respects. Scandals—real and trumped up—are common; inefficiency and stalemate are widespread; important social problems fester; delays and compromises undermine the effectiveness of public policies.[33] Reformers often call for further movement toward popular democracy—more elections, more opportunities to exert popular pressure, or less power for appointed officials. Americans apparently believe, with John Dewey, that "The cure for the ailments of democracy is more democracy."[34] Such reforms overlook the tremendous popular pressure that political leaders already face.

Single-issue voters and other kinds of special interests at times do wield disproportionate influence. However, such groups lose much of their clout when a clear majority of the voters takes a strong interest in a highly visible subject. Elected officials cannot routinely support positions contrary to those of their voters and expect to escape the wrath of the electorate indefinitely. Moreover, majorities remain potentially powerful even when the public is uninformed about or unaware of an issue. Elected officials realize that the media spotlight may suddenly shine into what seemed to be a dark corner. Most of the time, incumbents think twice before taking actions in back rooms if those actions cannot be defended once the doors are opened.[35] Leaders are never sure which decisions will explode into campaign issues, so they tend to be cautious in handling all of them—which limits the power of well-connected special interests.

America is a diverse country, and those who elect public officials—their **constituencies**—reflect that diversity. People have conflicting interests and values. If elected officials wish to follow their **electoral incentives,** and remain in office, they must attend to the demands generated by these diverse constituencies. Reconciling so many demands requires compromise. Unlike chief executives in the business world, presidents cannot fire members of Congress, governors cannot remove members of their state legislatures, and mayors cannot dismiss members of their city councils. Political leaders either must persuade their opponents or bargain for their support, a process that becomes harder when the public is more attentive and involved. In short, popular influence on government is often a cause of the very problems reformers wish to address.[36] This being the case, reforms that shift American politics in a still more popular direction may worsen problems of stalemate and delay rather than eliminate them.

EVALUATING AMERICA'S
NEW DEMOCRACY

Too often, critics apply unrealistic standards of evaluation to government performance. Any policy or institution will fall short when judged against abstract standards of perfection. Perfection does not exist in the real world, but the wish for it may make people unhappy with their government and their leaders. The search for perfection can cause harm because people often abandon the "pretty good" for something worse. As Winston Churchill once remarked, "Democracy is th form of government except all those other forms that have been tried."[37]

We began this chapter by noting an irony of America's new democracy: Americans have been growing increasingly unhappy with a government over which they have more influence than ever before. Now that we have explained how thoroughly American majorities exercise their influence, it should be clear that the sour national mood is difficult to justify. Serious problems and unresolved conflicts certainly exist, but most are the natural result of an active and diverse voting public, not the result of an arrogant and inattentive government.

More than ever before, and more than in other democracies, electoral influences drive politics in the United States. Elections have always played a central role in American political thought because the framers relied on a system of checks and balances to protect freedom. But the power of elections has grown because there are so many elected offices in the United States, because terms of office generally are short, and because Americans select candidates in primaries and vote directly on propositions. Public officials must permanently campaign as a result of numerous technological, institutional, and social changes; electoral considerations can never be far from their minds. The result is a responsive political system that, although imperfect, is still the envy of much of the world.

Across the entire sweep of human history, most governments have been controlled by one or a few. Many were tyrannical; a government that did not murder and rob its subjects was about as good a government as people could expect. Tragically, tyrannical governments are not just a matter of ancient history. Only a bare majority of the world's population today lives under governments that can reasonably be considered democratic, and in the twentieth century governments caused the deaths of 170 million people, a number that *does not include those who died in wars*.[38] The death toll has not ended: China's government executed somewhere between 5000 and 10,000 of its subjects in 2001 alone.[39] To quote the great American judge Learned Hand, "Even though counting heads is not an ideal way to govern, it is at least better than breaking them."[40]

To be sure, Americans should not set too low a standard for their political life. No one would seriously argue that Americans should be satisfied just because their country has avoided dissolving into chaos. But Americans must apply realistic standards when evaluating their political system. Critics selectively cite statistics showing that the United States is worse than Canada in one respect, worse than Japan in another respect, worse than Sweden in some other respect, and so on. But can one conclude with confidence that any comparable national government works better on the whole? We think the answer is no.

Only when comparing the United States with other countries do we see that American democracy, for all its faults, has an unmatched record of maintaining order, encouraging prosperity, protecting freedom, and redressing injustices. Citizens in the United States enjoy rights and privileges that citizens in other lands die to achieve. Not only can American citizens vote more often, but Americans also can speak their minds more freely, find out more easily what their government is doing, and deal with a government less likely to discriminate against them. On average, citizens of the United States are wealthier than citizens of any other comparably large country. They are better housed, better fed, and better clothed. Their physical environment is better protected against degradation. Their nation owes less money than most other industrialized countries.

Of course, the United States is not best at everything. Poverty rates are higher in the United States than in countries with comparable living standards. The distribution of income is less even than in other developed democracies, and more people lack access to adequate medical care. More people are murdered and more are imprisoned than in almost any other industrialized country. Just why the United States does poorly at some things and well at others is considered in the pages that follow. But for all its problems, the United States has as good a government as exists anywhere, and a better one than most.

Shock to the system

Less than a year after the 2000 presidential election provoked a constitutional crisis, another tragedy struck the United States—one that made the election controversy seem trivial by comparison. This tragic event did more than simply upset the American public. The shock waves it sent throughout the nation's political system rapidly altered public attitudes and sharply rearranged the policy environment. We will refer to the topic repeatedly in later chapters because of its widespread impact. Rather than summarizing the main details of the event every time it comes up, therefore, we present the detailed story here.[41]

> *A pleasant morning greeted New Englanders who awoke early on September 11, 2001. The sky was sunny, the temperature just chilly enough to hint at autumn's approach. Egyptian engineer Mohammed Atta had spent the night in Portland, Maine—but he pulled himself out of bed in the wee hours, before any sunshine could warm the crisp air. He had to catch a 6 A.M. commuter flight to Boston.*
>
> *The serious-minded young Muslim had written out his plans for the morning. "Be happy, optimistic, calm," he told himself. It was a big day for Atta, a day that would force the world to remember him long after he was gone—much of it to despise him. But he reassured himself in the note, "You are heading for a deed God loves and will accept." Atta had titled the document "The Last Night" because he did not expect or intend to return alive from his mission to Boston. Instead, Atta anticipated spending the evening with more heavenly company. He wrote of his hopes: "It will be the day, God willing, you spend with the women of paradise."*
>
> *Atta boarded American Airlines Flight 11, a jumbo jet bound for Los Angeles, with four colleagues. They were armed with knives and box cutters. The plane departed from*

The two towers

Terrorists destroyed the World Trade Center's twin towers on September 11, 2001. The 9/11 tragedy changed more than just New York City's skyline, though. It fundamentally changed American politics.

Boston's Logan International Airport before 8 A.M. Around 15 minutes later, another Los Angeles–bound jet left Boston. Five more conspirators sat on United Airlines Flight 65, similarly armed. Neither airliner reached cruising altitude. The terrorists commandeered both flights and turned them toward New York City at a speed of more than 500 miles per hour. Atta probably piloted his plane, which hurtled into the one of the World Trade Center towers just before 9 A.M. Around 15 minutes later, the second flight crashed into the 90th floor of the other tower.

The Big Apple's public-service workers responded quickly to the disaster. Police attempted to restore order and get people to safety. Health workers treated cuts, burns, and other injuries in the vicinity of the crashes. Firefighters rushed up the stairwells of the Twin Towers laden with hoses and fire gear, urging survivors to leave the building in an orderly fashion but as rapidly as they could. It was advice that the brave firefighters, sadly, did not follow themselves. Above them, and down the elevator shafts around them, *thousands of gallons of jet fuel were burning at temperatures almost three times hotter than the point at which steel beams lose their strength. The 1362-foot South Tower collapsed before 10 A.M., taking many of the would-be rescuers with it. The North Tower followed within the hour, adding to the carnage.*

But the day's horrible events had not ended. Cell-phone calls began to emanate from American Airlines Flight 77 out of Washington, DC. The callers reported that five foreign terrorists had hijacked their plane, herding passengers and crew to the rear. Television commentator Barbara Olson phoned her husband, U.S. Solicitor General Theodore K. Olson, at least twice from the plane. At the end of her second call, she reportedly asked what the pilot should do. No one knows what the crew actually did or tried. But at 9:45 A.M. the airliner crashed into the Pentagon Building, heart of the Department of Defense and symbol of America's military might. Terror had spread to the nation's capital.

Another flying weapon of mass destruction hurtled toward Washington, DC. The four hijackers on American Airlines Flight 93 apparently intended to take out the president's home (the White House) or the Capitol building where Congress meets. But they failed because passengers already knew about the attacks on the World Trade Center. If Mohammed Atta now personifies the cowardice that allows a man to terrorize and murder civilians, a young California businessman has come to symbolize the heroism that can rise up to resist the cowards. Thomas E. Burnett, Jr., managed to call his wife four times from Flight 93—the last time informing her that he was joining an effort by a few passengers to overcome the terrorists. They succeeded. The airliner crashed into the sparsely populated Pennsylvania countryside, harmless to everyone except the 45 people on board.

The total 9/11 death count was astronomical, perhaps 3000 people. Mostly Americans, but also foreign nationals from dozens of countries, lost their lives in the worst act of terrorism ever committed on American soil. The news could have been much worse. An estimated 50,000 potential victims worked in the Twin Towers and 22,000 in the Pentagon, but enough individuals resisted the urge to panic, and adapted to the chaos around them, that they were able to limit the death toll. Nevertheless, people across the world expressed their horror, their grief, and their sympathies. Foreign leaders, even some with strained U.S. relations, communicated their dismay and offered to help track down those responsible. Americans vowed that they would concentrate on the most important things in life, such as spending time with their families. They turned out in droves to donate blood, in case survivors needed it. The culture also shifted perceptibly, at least for a time. Things once thought funny had suddenly lost their humor. Cynicism faded, and in its place rose a desire to celebrate heroes such as Mr. Burnett and New York City's firefighters.

Of course, wounds heal. Vows lapse. Tastes evolve. Leaving aside those directly hurt by the tragedy, the vivid feelings associated with 9/11 seem to be abating. Younger Americans may have little more than fuzzy memories of the crisis itself, especially if their youth prompted adults to protect them from the details. In short, we realize that the immediate events of 9/11 may already feel like "old news," like an historical event rather than a personal one. Then why spend so much space telling the story here, and why include sections in later chapters—the Aftershock sections—that discuss how the event relates to American government? We have two, equally important reasons.

Government institutions usually change incrementally. They lock into place the mood dominant at the time they were created or at the last time they were changed significantly. The government's response to 9/11 has fundamentally altered the American political system in numerous ways: the money available to fund public policies (see Chapter 3), the legacy of a president elected under controversial circumstances (see Chapter 10), the organization of law enforcement agencies (see Chapter 11), and the philosophy underlying American foreign and defense policy (see Chapter 15). Many of these changes will long outlast any memory of what prompted them.

A second reason is that 9/11 serves as an invaluable way to illustrate the argument offered in this book. Our thesis, after all, is that elections and public opinion drive American institutions. The best way to evaluate this claim is to see what happens when public attitudes shift suddenly, as they did in the wake of the crisis. Responsive institutions will reflect the rapid change in preferences—and indeed, we find that policy did respond quickly to new ways of thinking in areas such as immigration (see Chapter 4), the rights of suspects (see Chapter 13), and racial profiling (see Chapter 14). In short, feelings about 9/11 may be fading, but in terms of understanding America's new democracy, aftershocks from the tragedy will not be old news for a long time to come.

KEY TERMS

checks and balances, p. 9

constituencies, p. 20

democracy, p. 8

direct democracy, p. 8

electoral incentives, p. 20

general election, p. 11

initiatives, p. 11

permanent campaign, p. 14

primary election, p. 11

recall elections, p. 11

referenda, p. 11

republic, p. 8

SUGGESTED READINGS

Cronin, Thomas. *Direct Democracy: The Politics of Initiative, Referendum, and Recall.* Cambridge, MA: Harvard University Press, 1989. A comprehensive study of direct democracy in the United States that takes a

balanced view of the costs and benefits of citizen policy making.

Downs, Anthony. *An Economic Theory of Democracy.* New York: Harper, 1957. Seminal theoretical discussion of how elections shape the activities of voters, candidates, parties, and interest groups.

King, Anthony. *Running Scared: Why Politicians Spend More Time Campaigning Than Governing.* New York: Free Press, 1996. Provocative study by a British political scientist who shows how elections shape contemporary American politics.

Morone, James A. *The Democratic Wish.* New York: Basic Books, 1990. Brilliant historical analysis that shows how Americans have long tried to cure the ills of democracy by extending citizen participation.

Schattschneider, E. E. *The Semi-Sovereign People.* New York: Holt, 1960. Classic analysis that explains why elections do not ensure equal political influence.

Tocqueville, Alexis de. *Democracy in America,* Vols. I and II, Philips Bradley, ed. New York: Knopf, 1945. Nineteenth-century French observer's insightful interpretation of the democratic experiment in the United States.

ON THE WEB

DemocracyNet
www.dnet.org
This online voter guide with state-specific information is a project of the Center for Governmental Studies and the League of Women Voters.

The Federal Election Commission (FEC)
www.fec.gov
This online portal of the FEC provides easy-to-use information regarding all aspects of elections—from electoral histories to campaign finance contributions.

Project Vote Smart
www.vote-smart.org
This richly informative site is supported by a nonpartisan group. It contains biographical histories, voting records, campaign finances and promises, and performance evaluations of elected officials and candidates.

THE U.S. CONSTITUTION

The soldiers who straggled home after America's Revolutionary War often encountered desperate conditions upon their return. Many had abandoned their sources of livelihood for months or even years so that they could fight for independence, leaving businesses to dry up and farms to fall into disrepair. Some had contracted crippling diseases or suffered irreparable wounds on the battlefield. Others had lost their homes and families to the violence of war.

The new country's financial turmoil only added to whatever difficulties Americans faced trying to rebuild their lives.[1] The national government entered peacetime deeply in debt, but initially it could not repay war bonds. It also could not pay veterans the pensions they had been promised. Many soldiers did not even receive full wages for their service. Private finances were not much better. The states contained few mature industries. Restrictive European trade laws blocked access to the most desirable export markets. And the English did not show much interest in extending loans to their recent enemies. Little money circulated through the economy.

Four out of five New Englanders lived on family farms, a **yeoman** population that grew what it required to live and not much more. The postwar economy hit them hardest of all. They relied on costly trade with Europe and the West Indies to provide essential household items like gunpowder, glassware, basic medicines, and metal goods such as nails. Many needed to clear land, purchase seed, buy livestock, and build new homesteads after the war—but the limited availability of credit meant that, to receive loans, they had to accept exorbitant interest rates.

Not all of them could afford the interest payments. So much produce flooded the postwar market, and economic competition with European colonies grew so fierce, that agricultural prices dropped sharply. By the late 1780s, rural America was suffering. Hundreds of farmers landed in debtor's court for failing to meet their financial obligations. Some saw their property auctioned off, at a fraction of its true value, to distant owners with no intention of farming the land themselves. Others, including Revolutionary War veterans, went to prison for days, weeks, even months.

Conditions were worst in Massachusetts. In some western counties as much as a third of the population faced legal action because they owed money. Coastal merchants and bankers seized, through lawsuits, the same land that British troops could not overrun with guns. One farmer lamented, "Those who gloriously supported our independence now find their moveables vanishing like empty shades, their lands sinking under their feet."[2] Small farmers soon filled the prisons, often for failing to repay tiny sums.

Legislators in some states tried to help farmers survive. New Hampshire, for example, eventually agreed to accept tax payments in paper money. Sympathy ran so high in Rhode Island that a new political party won control of the state legislature. The Country party lived up to its motto, "To Relieve the Distressed," taking such aggressive steps to assist debtors that merchants and money lenders called the state "Rogue Island" and proposed that it be broken up. However, leaders in other states turned a deaf ear to calls for aid.

The top political figures in Massachusetts all hailed from the eastern seaboard, where lawyers, bankers, and big merchants tended to live. They not only supported aggressive debt collection in the courts, they also drew most of the state's revenue from taxes on land—taxes that farmers had to pay in coin. Nor did those sympathetic to the debtors have much chance of taking over the legislature. Almost half of the western townships lacked representation, mostly because they could not afford to house someone in Boston. Strict property requirements excluded many yeomen from public office altogether.

New England's farmers gradually turned to violence as a way to protect their homes. They harassed tax collectors and disrupted court hearings. When those who spoke out against commercial interests faced arrest, locals armed to protect the speakers or to spring them from jail. Two hundred militants shut down the New Hampshire statehouse for five hours, holding the governor and state assembly as hostages.

But, not surprisingly, the confrontation reached its peak in western Massachusetts, where it took on the name **Shays's Rebellion**.* Rebels may have numbered as much as half the population in some counties, a third of them veterans. After the state started imprisoning people without trial, they grew militant, raiding wealthy homes and even trying to seize a government armory. State leaders wanted to crush the rebellion, but members of the militia deserted rather than attack their fellow citizens. Other states refused to send troops. Eventually a privately funded army, led by members of a secret society of former revolutionary officers, took up arms for the government.† They found a cluster of rebels outside Sheffield and fired upon them at close range for six minutes, slaughtering 30 and effectively ending the resistance.

WHEN AMERICANS SPEAK OF THEIR "FOUNDING FATHERS," they typically do not mean the defeated participants in this 1786 uprising, most of whom remain nameless or forgotten. Nor do they have in mind the many independent farmers who opposed ratification of the U.S. Constitution in 1789 or helped vote the party of George Washington, John Adams, and Alexander Hamilton out of office

---

*Daniel Shays, a Pelham native and former Continental Army captain, helped lead part of the Massachusetts rebellion. But naming the confrontation after him exaggerates the extent of his influence over a wave of resistance that swept the region.

†George Washington was the titular head of the group, which was known by various names (for example, the Order of the Cincinnati). Membership was hereditary.

in 1800. Quite the contrary. Whether one takes the founders to include those who signed the Declaration of Independence, those who led the revolution against Britain, or those who wrote the U.S. Constitution, most of them lined up on the other side.

Consider the role a few famous politicians played in Shays' Rebellion itself. Massachusetts Governor John Hancock, whose sweeping signature adorns the Declaration of Independence, ordered his troops to kill the Shaysites "if necessary, and conquer [them] by all fitting ways." Sam Adams, the great rabble-rouser who once dressed as a Mohawk and tossed British tea into Boston Harbor, engineered a Riot Act to outlaw public gatherings. Violators faced 39 lashes and months of imprisonment. Nathaniel Gorham, who presided over the Congress, wrote a Prussian prince to ask whether the nobleman would be willing to assume kingly powers in America.[3] Gorham later chaired the Constitutional Convention's Committee of the Whole.

The unrest in New England frightened national leaders, convincing them of the need for a strong federal government that could prevent future debtor uprisings.* The Constitution they proposed a year later was, in part, an act of self-defense, an attempt to keep the yeomen in their place. Although the document contained rules to protect popular majorities from the government, including the scheduling of frequent elections (see Chapter 1), it also contained provisions to limit the political system's responsiveness and therefore to protect unpopular minorities—especially property owners.

At the same time, America's independent farmers shaped the political system because they were a large portion of the founders' audience and of their potential opposition. Part of the influence was indirect. To ensure the Constitution's legitimacy across the countryside, its authors proposed a strategic document, one that drew heavily on *inherited political traditions*, on *revolutionary experiences*, and on lessons learned during the *early years of independence*. They did not just force it on the nation. They were clever politicians who developed a proposal that voting majorities could accept.

Some of the yeoman influence was more direct. Many leaders from rural regions demanded that the U.S. Constitution contain a Bill of Rights to restrict governmental power. Those provisions have gained importance over time. Rural Americans jealously guarded the rights of state governments, electing leaders such as Thomas Jefferson who would exercise federal powers modestly (see Chapter 3). Voters often favored "men of the people" such as Andrew Jackson (see Chapter 8), men who embodied rural America's social and political ideals. They counted on these "populist" leaders to emphasize liberty and equality when interpreting the founders' handiwork, values that eventually pushed the system toward

*Most states appointed their delegates to the Constitutional Convention only after Shays' Rebellion.

greater openness. In short, rural radicals who fought the growth of federal power are, in some ways, as much the "fathers" of America's new democracy as the founders themselves.

INFLUENCES ON
THE U.S. CONSTITUTION

As we have noted, the U.S. Constitution proposed in 1787 drew heavily on inherited political traditions, on revolutionary experiences, and on lessons learned during the early years of independence. Before describing the document itself, we briefly review those influences here.

INHERITED POLITICAL TRADITIONS

A small group of religious dissenters, now remembered as the Pilgrims, set sail for England's Virginia colony in 1620. To cover costs for the voyage, they had loaded the ship *Mayflower* with passengers who did not share their religious beliefs and who simply wanted to seek their fortunes. The ship never reached its destination (either because it was blown off course, as claimed, or because the Pilgrim leaders never really intended to live in a colony led by Anglican tobacco planters). Instead, the *Mayflower* arrived in what is now Provincetown, Massachusetts. Imagine the dismay of the ship's ambitious immigrants when they looked out and, instead of seeing rich tobacco fields, encountered New England's bare and rocky shoreline!

The Pilgrim leaders knew that they would have to pacify the disappointed passengers if they were going to found a new colony.[4] They also wanted a framework for governing that, at least in principle, allowed individuals to decide religious and political matters for themselves. Before disembarking, therefore, the settlers signed the Mayflower Compact, the first document in colonial America in which the people gave their express consent to be governed. Democratic principles were established very early in New England's colonial settlement.[5]

Few English settlements began as radical social or religious experiments. Most formed as "proprietary" colonies under companies or prominent English nobles. The proprietors founded these settlements, such as the Jamestown colony, almost exclusively for economic gain. Later, most of the colonies ran into financial difficulty, at which point they reverted to royal control. Even the royal colonies indirectly promoted democratic ideals, though, mostly because English monarchs seldom paid attention to settlements so far from the throne. The king would appoint a representative, but elected assemblies made many important decisions in the colony, including the proper level of taxation.

The colonies were not fully democratic in the modern sense of the word. Women, slaves, and indentured servants could not vote (see Table 2.1). Even

TABLE 2.1

VOTING QUALIFICATIONS BY COLONY

Are elections democratic if part of the population may not vote? What makes a system democratic—the process through which it selects leaders, the proportion of the population that takes part in it, or something else?

COLONY	QUALIFICATIONS
Massachusetts	Male, 21 years old, property owner
New Hampshire	Male, 21, except paupers
Rhode Island	Male, 21, debt-free
Connecticut	Male, 21, property owner, civil in conversation
New York	Male, 21, property owner or renter, six months residence
New Jersey	Male, 21, one year residence
Pennsylvania	Male, 21, taxpayer, two years residence
Virginia	Male, 21, property owner
Maryland	Male, 21, property owner, one year residence
North Carolina	Male, 21, property owner, one year residence
South Carolina	Male, 21, white, taxpayer, property owner, two years residence
Georgia	Male, 21, taxpayer, six months residence

SOURCES: Robert J. Dinkin, *Voting in Revolutionary America: A Study of Elections in the Original Thirteen States, 1776–1789* (Westport, CT: Greenwood Press, 1982); Robert J. Dinkin, *Voting in Provincial America: A Study of Elections in the Thirteen Colonies, 1689–1776* (Westport, CT: Greenwood Press, 1977).

white, male citizens usually had to meet certain property qualifications: In Virginia they had to own 25 acres and a house. In Maryland and Pennsylvania, voters needed to be worth 50 acres or 40 pounds. By 1750 these qualifications disenfranchised more than a quarter of the male population.[6] But a habit of local control nonetheless developed in America's towns and villages. When Thomas Jefferson wished to clear the Rivanna River for navigation by trading boats, for example, he did not petition the king. He organized his community to carry out the enterprise—a leadership role that later won him election to the Virginia assembly.[7]

Regardless of whether settlements began with democratic ideals or only developed them out of habit, radical principles took root in the colonial soil. Americans in the Revolutionary period gravitated toward a political philosophy based on three core principles, ideals that the U.S. Constitution eventually embodied:

1. Government arises from the consent of the governed.
2. Government power should be separated across multiple institutions.
3. Citizens should participate in determining the direction of government.

CONSENT OF THE GOVERNED   Few eighteenth-century Britons believed that their leaders ruled by **divine right**, by the command and authority of God. They knew full well that the Parliament, their national legislature, had set a new family line on the English throne more than once—most recently in 1689, after Stuart King James II threw his royal seal into the Thames River and tried to flee the country on a fishing boat. But if royal lines might come and go, Europeans needed some other explanation for why governments could exercise legitimate authority.

To grapple with this puzzle, political thinkers such as Thomas Hobbes, John Locke, and Jean-Jacques Rousseau engaged in a thought experiment. They asked themselves, "What might life have looked like before government existed, and why would such institutions develop?" The three came up with varying answers, with Hobbes painting the most pessimistic picture of life's natural state and Rousseau imagining a savage existence of some nobility. But all three basically agreed that humans must have given up certain freedoms intentionally, as part of a contract with the rest of society, so that they could reap the benefits of communal life. These social-contract theorists concluded that for government to enjoy legitimacy, its right to rule must have been built on the consent of the governed.

SEPARATION OF POWERS   **Social-contract theory** could imply a wide range of institutions, depending on exactly what the governed agreed to give up and what the government agreed to do in exchange for the right to rule. John Locke, an English writer whose *Second Treatise on Government* (published in 1690) prefigured both the language and the ideas in America's Declaration of Independence, concluded that people must have entered communities as a means to protect preexisting rights to life, liberty, and property. They sacrificed some freedoms to ensure the continuation of more important ones.

Because Locke placed these **natural rights** at the center of government's reason for being, he required little effort to figure out the best type of government: one that could not enslave citizens or otherwise threaten their health, freedom, or possessions. The best way to prevent such tyranny, the Englishman decided, was to set up institutions similar to those in his home country (which had a relatively long history of citizen independence). In particular, he endorsed dividing up the legislative and executive functions of government so that they did not reside in the same institution.[8] Nearly 60 years later, the French philosopher Montesquieu added to this list a third governmental function—the judicial power—but the logic remained the same. A **separation of powers** would allow branches of government to check each other, just in case one got out of hand and tried to grab too much influence.

PARTICIPATORY DEMOCRACY   Merely stacking up multiple branches of government to compete with each other does not ensure liberty. The British system had that much: a king with executive power, a noble House of Lords that appointed judges, and an elected House of Commons that exercised legislative power. But not long after Locke wrote, the British system lost its balance. The crown began using royal privileges to concentrate power in a small circle of ministers drawn from Parliament but appointed by the king.[9]

A group of politicians, scattered around the English countryside, decided that government periodically should have to seek a renewal of popular consent. The **Whigs,** as they were known, argued against a system that allowed monarchs to buy influence through the distribution of money and public offices. They proposed that ordinary citizens should select virtuous leaders from among their own number, since locally elected representatives would be most likely to protect citizen freedoms.[10] Thomas Paine laid out the Whig theory of representation forcefully in an essay called *Common Sense*, which American colonials read avidly in the months before seeking their independence.[11]

THE REVOLUTIONARY EXPERIENCE

Whig criticism of the British government made sense to many American colonists, especially after Lord of the Treasury George Grenville imposed several taxes to help defray the empire's rising military costs. He experimented in 1765 with the Stamp Act, which imposed a tax on pamphlets, playing cards, dice, newspapers, marriage licenses, and other legal documents. Colonial taxes were lower than those the British paid, but Parliament imposed the stamp levy without consulting colonial representatives and so it seemed an unjust imposition.[12]

Violent protest spread throughout the colonies. A group in Boston called the Sons of Liberty hanged the city's proposed tax collector in effigy and then looted his home–and that of the lieutenant governor for good measure. Tax collectors resigned their positions, others refused to take their places, and colonial assemblies banned the importation of English goods. Colonists showed their opposition to the tax by wearing homespun clothes and drinking native beverages such as hard cider (rather than English ale).[13]

Parliament repealed the legislation within a year but still ignored American demands for representation.[14] Instead, the British government switched to a tax on colonial imports, including tea, which further ignited passions across the Atlantic. Antitax groups led by community leaders such as Samuel Adams and John Hancock stirred up rebellious sentiments until, finally, a group of colonists boarded British ships in a nighttime foray and dumped chests of tea in the harbor. The Boston Tea Party of 1773 represented an open act of law breaking that outraged members of Parliament, who withdrew the Massachusetts colony's charter, closed its elected assembly, banned town meetings, blockaded the harbor, and strengthened the armed garrison stationed in the city.

The colonists responded to British encroachments by organizing a Continental Congress in 1774. Attended by delegates from 12 of the colonies, the gathering issued a statement of rights and called for a boycott of British goods. Patriots assembled guns and trained volunteers for military exercises in Massachusetts.

To put down the rising insurrection, British soldiers marched out from Boston's harbor in search of weapons hidden in the nearby countryside. Paul Revere helped spread a warning that British redcoats were coming, though, so 600 patriots were able to arm themselves. Ralph Waldo Emerson later claimed that the first shots they fired were "heard 'round the world." Word of the shots at least spread southward to the Virginia assembly, where Patrick Henry cried, "Give me liberty, or give me death!"

Delegates from all 13 colonies soon journeyed to Philadelphia to participate in a **Second Continental Congress**. This Congress withdrew America's "united states" from the British Empire on July 4, 1776. Their formal announcement, a document written mainly by Thomas Jefferson and called the **Declaration of Independence**, clearly reflects the influence of John Locke on colonial thought (see Table 2.2). It denounces King George III for failing to protect rights of "life, liberty, and the pursuit of happiness" in his colonies.[15]

The Congress also prepared for war. One of its inspired decisions was to appoint George Washington, a Virginia plantation owner, as commander of the Continental Army; this helped create an aura of unity, because most soldiers initially came from northern colonies. Constitutional decisions took much longer than military decisions. The nation's first constitution, the **Articles of Confederation**, was not ratified until 1781.

Americans refined their political ideals during the war. The conflict generated intense discussion of philosophical concepts, the sort of debate that rarely takes place in a stable society. Americans rejected taxation without representation and instead embraced consent of the governed, separation of powers, and the importance of popular participation. Their new state governments implemented these ideals.

Eight of the 13 states eased property qualifications for voting, and 5 lowered them for candidates to the lower houses of state legislatures.[16] Over time, fewer state legislators possessed great wealth, especially in the North—giving new political opportunities to those from modest backgrounds. Six states limited the number of terms that governors could serve, and 10 required that they face annual elections.[17]

TABLE 2.2

Social-contract theory
and the Declaration of Independence

Although Thomas Jefferson denied that John Locke was a central reference for his draft of the Declaration of Independence, the ideas and even the phrasing are so similar in their writings that few dispute the influence of social-contract theory on America's revolutionaries. Do you think Jefferson plagiarized Locke, or could these similarities have resulted from indirect influences?

LIBERAL PRINCIPLE	DECLARATION OF INDEPENDENCE	LOCKE'S SECOND TREATISE ON GOVERNMENT
Natural Law	. . . the laws of nature and of nature's God . . .	The state of nature has a law to govern it, which obliges every one . . . (Ch. II.6)
Egalitarianism	. . . all men are created equal . . .	. . . all men are naturally in . . . a state . . . of equality . . . (Ch. II.4)
Natural Rights	. . . they are endowed by their Creator with certain unalienable rights . . .	. . . men being all the workmanship of one omnipotent, and infinitely wise maker, . . . all men may be restrained from invading others rights . . . (Ch. II.6–7)
Inventory of Rights	. . . among these are life, liberty, and the pursuit of happiness . . .	. . . no one ought to harm another in his life, health, liberty, or possessions . . . (Ch. II.6)
Purpose of Government	. . . to secure these rights, governments are instituted among men . . .	. . . The great and chief end . . . of men's . . . putting themselves under government, is . . . the mutual preservation of their lives, liberties, and estates . . . (Ch. IX.123–124)
Consent	. . . deriving their just powers from the consent of the governed . . .	. . . all peaceful beginnings of government have been laid in the consent of the people . . . (Ch. VIII.112)
Unlikelihood of Rebellion	. . . mankind are more disposed to suffer . . . than to right themselves by abolishing the forms to which they are accustomed . . .	People are not so easily got out of their old forms . . . [T]he people, who are more disposed to suffer than right themselves by resistance, are not apt to stir . . . (Ch. XIX.223, 230)
Right of Rebellion	. . . when a long train of abuses . . . evinces a design to reduce them under absolute despotism, it is their right, it is their duty, to throw off such government, and to provide new guards for their future security . . .	. . . if they see several experiments made of arbitrary power . . . if a long train of actions shows the councils all tending that way . . . whenever the legislators endeavour to . . . reduce them to slavery . . . it devolves to the people . . . to resume their original liberty, and, by the establishment of a new legislative . . . provide for their own safety and security . . . (Ch. XVIII.210 and Ch. XIX.222)

NOTE: The bulk of the Declaration (see this book's Appendix) lists specific injustices allegedly condoned by King George III. Many of these specific claims also echo Locke's language. Some mimic his specific examples of tyranny.

The patriots valiantly fought British soldiers for seven years. Numerous Europeans, excited by the radical ideals of freedom and equality behind the revolution, journeyed to the Americas to help with the war effort (see Chapter 4). Loyal colonists who opposed independence, meanwhile, lost their property and were imprisoned or chased off. Some 80,000 fled to London, Nova Scotia, or the West Indies. In 1783, the British recognized American independence in the Treaty of Paris.

GOVERNMENT AFTER INDEPENDENCE

The new country faced an uncertain future after achieving independence. Certainly it contained abundant resources: fertile lands for farming, rivers and lakes teeming with fish, lush forests stocked with game for hunting or trapping, mountains and hills that one day would furnish valuable minerals and fuels. The nation's citizens, although spread thinly across the 13 states, were relatively young and ambitious. Soon they would be joined by equally capable immigrants, many fleeing poverty or oppression back home, as well as able-bodied African slaves imported by force.* The long-term economic prospects looked hopeful.

A GROWING SENSE OF DREAD   Threats surrounded the Americans, though (see Figure 2.1). Resentful English colonies challenged them from the north, and their warships periodically dragooned U.S. sailors into British service. Ambitious Spanish colonies pushed upward from the south, creeping beyond the Florida border to claim large segments of what is today Alabama and Mississippi. Ruthless pirates ranged up and down their eastern shoreline, striking without warning and then retreating around jagged islands or up narrow rivers to avoid capture. Unpredictable Native American tribes roamed the lands to the west, and other tribal settlements dotted the interior of the United States itself. Even France, a revolutionary ally, blocked U.S. trade with its islands in the West Indies and demanded repayment of war loans.

Especially worrisome to many former revolutionaries was the rise of a "levelling spirit" among the common people.[18] Commoners took revolutionary ideals of liberty and equality to heart. They put on airs, wearing fancy clothing once restricted to the higher orders. They showed disrespect toward their social betters and an overriding desire to make money. Most of all, they applied the same disruptive tactics and radical ideas to their new governments that the revolutionaries had once applied to the British, such as gathering in informal conventions to void unpopular laws and electing leaders from among their own number.[19] The

---

*This is not to suggest that all slaves arrived after independence. The first Africans apparently arrived in 1619, before the landing of the *Mayflower,* and thousands of African descent took up arms during the revolutionary conflict, both for and against Britain. See George Brown Tindall, *America: A Narrative History* (New York: Norton, 1984).

FIGURE 2.1

Map of competing claims

This map shows only some of the competing claims being made in North America in 1787. Because the British had a superior navy and pirates sometimes ranged the coast, the United States was, in a sense, besieged on all sides. Should a nation shape its Constitution on the basis of emergency conditions such as these?

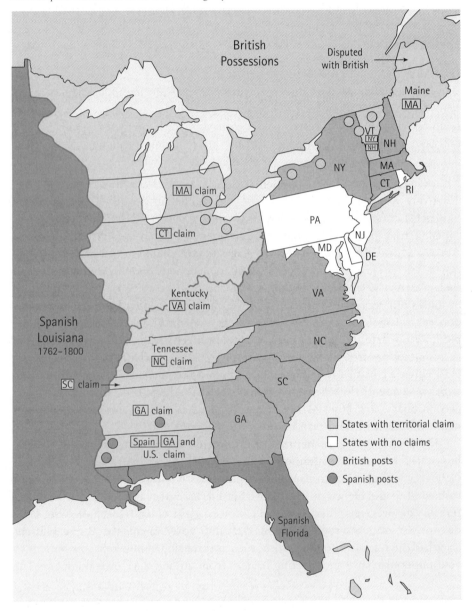

SOURCE: Edgar B. Wesley, *Our United States: Its History in Maps* (Chicago: Denoyer-Geppert Co., 1965), p. 37.

biggest problem came from former revolutionary soldiers, who were not being treated very well after the war.* Leaving aside their supporting role in Shays' Rebellion, as discussed in the chapter introduction, ex-soldiers also organized their own protests. A group of veterans descended on Congress in 1783, for example, and demanded their rightful back pay. Legislators fled to Princeton College to avoid the mob.

PROBLEMS WITH THE ARTICLES The Articles of Confederation, in their own words, amounted to little more than a "firm league of friendship" in which "each state retains its sovereignty, freedom and independence." The national government lacked authority for dealing with most threats or with most social problems. The Articles granted the Continental Congress limited power. Congress could declare war but could raise an army only by requesting states to muster their forces. Congress could not tax citizens; it had to rely on voluntary state contributions, so the government could not pay its debts.

Most significantly, the Continental Congress could not promote commerce effectively. States coined their own money, flooding the country with multiple currencies. Constant quarrels over the relative worth of different state coins impeded trade among the states. Congress could negotiate **tariffs** (taxes on imports and exports) with other nations, but so could each state. States also imposed trade barriers on one another. New York, for example, taxed New Jersey cabbage and Connecticut firewood.[20]

State legislatures elected members of the Continental Congress annually. Each state, no matter how large or small, received equal representation. On all important issues, a supermajority of 9 states (out of 13) had to agree before action could be taken, and changing the Articles required unanimity. Congress often lacked a **quorum**, the minimum number who must be present for official business to take place, which meant that much of the legislature's work fell upon an unwieldy Committee of the States. Nine of the 13 delegates had to agree before the committee could take any action.

The Articles of Confederation did not create a system of divided powers along the lines Locke had envisioned. Instead, the Continental Congress wielded all national powers, such as they were. There was no independent executive. Judicial functions were left to the states, except that disputes between states were settled by ad hoc committees of judges selected by the Continental Congress. Discontent with the Articles grew as the national government proved too weak to grapple with peacetime problems.

---

*Indeed, they had not been treated very well *during* the war. At one point the Continental Congress had to pass a law limiting soldier beatings to restrain George Washington's whip! See Merrill Jensen, *The New Nation: A History of the United States During the Confederation, 1781–1789* (New York: Vintage, 1965), p. 33.

THE CONSTITUTIONAL CONVENTION

A group of reformers met to discuss constitutional changes in 1786 at what became known as the Annapolis Convention, but only five state delegations attended. Hamilton persuaded the convention to propose another meeting in Philadelphia for the next year, a plan that Madison easily sold to the Congress after Shays' Rebellion. Every state legislature except Rhode Island's sent delegates to the Constitutional Convention with instructions to formulate amendments for the Articles of Confederation.

AN UNSEEMLY PROCESS

The 55 men who gathered in Philadelphia in 1787, to write the charter that has become the world's longest-living constitution, arrived there under false pretenses. State legislators had instructed them to repair the current government, not to start from scratch and write a new Constitution. Yet they tossed out the Articles on the fourth day and, instead, started working on a new document drafted in advance by Virginia delegate James Madison.

The Articles of Confederation were quite explicit about the proper legal procedure for changing them: Alterations had to be "confirmed by the legislatures of every state." The framers knew, however, that the new constitution they envisioned would never get past Rhode Island and might not clear North Carolina. They saw little justice in allowing one or two small states to prevent the rest of the nation from adopting a new political system. So they ignored the law and wrote in the Constitution that the proposed government would take effect if it had the approval of only nine states. They also did not trust the state legislatures who had appointed them to give up power voluntarily, so they ignored the law a second time. The Constitution specified that the states would decide whether to ratify it, making no mention of the currently elected legislatures.

If word of these plans had leaked out, the Constitutional Convention might have faced disruption from angry mobs. The nation's many poor farmers might have viewed the proceedings as a threat to individual liberties as well as to their home states. Therefore, to keep their discussions private, the framers imposed a gag rule, swearing members to secrecy. Today such a promise may sound silly, because it is hard to keep news bottled up among such a large number of people. But at the time a gentleman's word of honor was one of his most prized possessions.[21] The deliberations proceeded with very few leaks about what was taking place inside. Indeed, most of our knowledge of the convention comes from Madison's notes, which he kept from the public until after his death.[22]

Once the framers finished, the Confederation Congress did not delay their "legal revolution." Congress submitted the Constitution to the states for approval 11 days after the convention adjourned. Some of the most supportive states moved swiftly to build up momentum behind the document—and to do so before opponents could prepare themselves for a fight. The states held elections to select delegates for their individual constitutional conventions, elections in which many poor Americans could not vote. The process moved so quickly, and news spread so slowly, that participation was quite low even among eligible voters.

Those supporting the Constitution were much better prepared than opponents were. Their leaders knew the document intimately and possessed the resources to promote it. Some well-known figures did fight hard to stop ratification. Patrick Henry, the great American patriot, was one of these. "Before the meeting of the late Federal Convention at Philadelphia a general peace, and a universal tranquility prevailed in this country," Henry warned. But now, "I conceive the republic to be in extreme danger. Here is a revolution as radical as that which separated us from Great Britain. . . . All pretensions to human rights and privileges are rendered insecure, if not lost."[23] But neither talent nor time was on the opponents' side, and the Constitution eventually won ratification.

In sum, the whole process was rather unseemly. A group of young discontents appointed to do a specific job instead ignored both their instructions and the law. They worked in secrecy to redesign the political system and then exploited numerous strategic advantages to win official approval for their plans. It was not what most Americans envision when they think of "free and fair elections." Was the country from its beginning nothing more than a sham democracy?

In fact, elections played a minor role in constitutional ratification only because the framers were good politicians. They worked hard to anticipate problems that their Constitution might face with the voters. They made compromises from start to finish to minimize those difficulties. It was precisely the Constitution's success at meeting these requirements that allowed its rapid adoption and ensured its continuing legitimacy.

A SUCCESSFUL PRODUCT

The delegates to the Constitutional Convention did not constitute a cross section of the population. They were wealthy, young "demi-gods," as Thomas Jefferson called them, not typical citizens—bankers, merchants, plantation owners, and speculators in land west of the Appalachians.[24] These leaders were willing to spend a hot summer in a poorly ventilated hall without pay, debating the fine points of governance, only because they had ambitious plans for changing the political system. They believed the country needed a centralized government that could provide political stability, mediate conflicts among the states, defend the nation—and, incidentally, promote their own interests.[25]

Most of those content with the existing system stayed away. Patrick Henry refused to be a delegate, saying he "smelt a rat." Others simply were not interested. Of the few skeptics who did attend, ten abandoned the convention before the Constitution was completed. Only three more refused to sign the finished product; support was almost unanimous.

TABLE 2.3

COMPARING THE CHARTERS

The Articles of Confederation were a "league of friendship" and seldom allowed the national government to give orders to states. Did the Articles have any advantage over the U.S. Constitution?

WEAKNESSES OF THE ARTICLES OF CONFEDERATION	HOW ADDRESSED IN CONSTITUTION
Congress could not levy taxes.	Congress has power to levy taxes (Article I, Section 8).
States could restrict commerce among states.	States cannot regulate commerce without the consent of Congress (Article I, Section 10).
States could issue their own currency.	States are prohibited from coining money (Article I, Section 10).
Executive was not independent of Congress.	An independently elected president holds the executive power (Article II).
There was no national judicial system.	The Supreme Court was created, and Congress was granted the power to establish lower federal courts (Article III, Section 1).
Amendments to Articles had to have unanimous approval of states.	Large majorities are necessary to amend the Constitution, but there are several different ways to do so (Article V).

SOURCE: Articles of Confederation; U.S. Constitution, articles listed. See Appendix.

Yet the delegates did not agree on everything. Some disagreements were tactical; they disputed which sorts of changes voters would accept. However, delegates did represent varied regions with conflicting interests: large versus small states, southern versus northern states, and so on. Some disputes derived from genuine differences. The delegates therefore used numerous strategies to construct a plan on which they could agree and that voters might accept. The result was a Constitution quite different from the Articles (see Table 2.3).

On sharply drawn conflicts, the delegates *split the difference*, compromising between the two sides. When their ideal system was unlikely to win voter approval, they often used vague language that would allow flexibility of interpretation later. With other conflicts, they simply *delayed the decision*, either by giving someone else the authority to choose or by writing language whose implications would be unclear until some time had passed.

SPLITTING THE DIFFERENCES   The delegates' differences were submerged during the opening weeks of the convention, when a spirit of unity and reform filled the Philadelphia hall. But as the four-month convention progressed, delegates pulled back from some of the more far-reaching ideas and began fighting over issues that divided their states. The convention leaders searched for compromises that would keep most delegates happy.[26]

Large and small states disagreed over how to structure the legislative branch. Madison had prepared a constitutional draft, with Washington's active involvement, prior to the Philadelphia gathering. His **Virginia Plan** created a separation of powers along the lines that Locke recommended. Instead of a single congress like the one established under the Articles, Madison proposed two chambers, each with state representation determined by population.

Delegates from smaller states, especially New Jersey and Delaware, were not pleased. They offered an alternative plan, which gave each state a single vote in a one-chamber congress. But a convention majority rejected the proposal, prompting delegates from the small states to consider pulling out of Philadelphia. The large states flirted with the idea of forming their own union and then using economic pressure to force small states to join later.

Instead, this divisive issue was turned over to a committee controlled by moderates. They brought back a proposal, from the middle-sized state of Connecticut, that created a senate with equal state representation and a house with seats proportionate to population. The **Connecticut Compromise** allowed both small states and large states to block legislation they opposed: small states in the senate, large states in the house (see Figure 2.2).

The second major split divided the southern, slave states from the northern states, whose economies relied on free labor. The delegates never seriously contemplated using the Constitution to eliminate slavery (although one delegate said it was their moral duty to do so). Indeed, the Constitution avoided mentioning slavery by name, because southern states never would have ratified a constitution that threatened their economic system. The debate over slavery took other forms.

For example, the North and South split over taxes on imported goods. Southerners feared that tariffs would protect northern industries at the expense of slave plantations. Meanwhile, northerners wanted to end the international slave trade sooner than the South did. The two sides compromised, with southern delegates accepting tariffs in exchange for a guarantee that the slave trade could continue for 20 years. Congress could not interfere with the "importation of such persons as any of the states now existing shall think proper to admit" until 1808.

Northern delegates did not want to count slaves when figuring state representation in the House. Southerners thought they should be counted. On the other hand, southerners did not want slaves counted for purposes of taxation, which northerners endorsed. The two sides came up with the **three-fifths compromise,** in which a state's quantity of slaves would be multiplied by 3/5 when determining both taxes and House seats. Although this computational device obviously has no practical relevance today, it may be the constitutional

FIGURE 2.2

The Connecticut Compromise

Vital to the success of the Constitutional Convention, the Connecticut Compromise gave both large and small states a voice in Congress. These pie charts illustrate the proportions of seats in each congressional chamber that were controlled by the original 13 colonies. Are there still reasons today why states should receive equal representation as well as people?

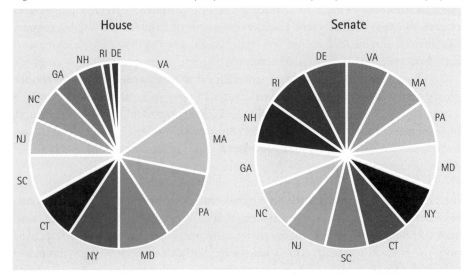

provision that most offends modern sensibilities, because it implies that the framers did not consider African Americans full people.

USING VAGUE LANGUAGE   Most of the framers desired a strong government but doubted that their ideal system would make it past voters. To help their cause, the framers often included vague language that later Americans could interpret broadly to give the federal government greater influence. For example, the Virginia Plan gave Congress vast powers, including the ability to negate "all laws passed by the several states," a power it could back with force.[27] Small-state representatives wanted to restrict the legislative branch to a specific list of powers, though. The final document provided a list, but also gave Congress the power to "make all laws which shall be necessary and proper for carrying into Execution" its duties. Eventually, views about the proper actions of government would change, and the **necessary and proper clause** would be elastic enough to allow congressional influence to grow.

Many convention delegates wanted a strong executive.[28] Alexander Hamilton even proposed granting powers comparable to those of a British monarch. But the delegates knew that voters would reject a constitution that threatened the return of another King George III. Hence they placed clear limits on presidential power, to please those who wanted an executive that was little more than a glorified clerk carrying out congressional orders, but left enough flexibility to allow the evolution of presidents who were strong political leaders. For example, the president is commander-in-chief of the armed forces, but only Congress can declare war. The president may veto congressional legislation, but Congress can override the veto with a two-thirds vote. The president appoints judges and executive-branch officers and also negotiates treaties, but these actions require the Senate's advice and consent.

Most convention delegates wanted a federal judiciary to settle conflicts among the states, but they apparently disagreed on whether federal courts should possess the controversial power of **judicial review**—that is, authority to strike down laws that violate the Constitution. So convention delegates simply inserted a clause binding judges to treat the Constitution as the "supreme Law of the Land." The **supremacy clause** allowed the Supreme Court, 20 years later, to claim powers of judicial review.

DELAYING THE DECISION Many disagreements in the Constitutional Convention did not require single, definitive answers. As long as the Constitution provided some way to determine the proper procedure for resolving later disputes, it did not have to declare what the resolution would be. For example, the delegates differed over whether the Supreme Court needed lower federal courts to assist it. They compromised by letting Congress decide whether to create lower federal courts. The first Congress established a system of lower courts whose essentials remain intact today.

The question of property qualifications for voting was a delicate one, because northern merchants preferred limitations based on wealth and southern planters preferred limitations based on land ownership. Rather than settle the dispute, the Constitution let states establish their own qualifications, aside from requiring that anyone eligible to vote for the lower chamber of a state legislature could vote in elections for the House of Representatives. The wording therefore allowed states to exclude poor citizens from voting however they liked and yet guaranteed the vote to everyone already eligible (that is, those who would decide whether to ratify the Constitution). This open-ended language later permitted the gradual, state-by-state extension of the right to vote to many who were excluded from the electorate in 1787.

The method for presidential selection once again divided big and small states. A president chosen by the House or by popular vote would owe allegiance to big states, whereas selection in the Senate would give small states extra clout. The delegates compromised by constructing a two-stage **Electoral College** system whose implications depended on how people would vote in the future. The first stage lets each state select the same number of electors as it holds seats in

Congress, a provision that favors large states.* For example, Texas now picks 34 electors because it has 2 Senate and 32 House seats; New Hampshire gets only 3. After their selection, the nation's electors all vote. If a candidate receives a majority of the Electoral College vote (50 percent plus 1 vote, or 270 votes today), that person wins. If no candidate receives a majority, the action moves to the House, where each state delegation votes as a unit. This stage favors small states but has not occurred since 1824.

The Constitution does not require that voters choose members of the Electoral College. Instead, the manner of selecting electors was left up to the states. Constitutional silence on this key matter was not accidental. Some delegates thought the president should be elected by the people; others believed this could lead to mob rule. Not until 1864 did the last state, South Carolina, give voters the power to select electors directly (although by the 1820s, electors were chosen by the voters in the great majority of states).[29]

AMENDING THE CONSTITUTION

The delegates to the Constitutional Convention, realizing that the document they were writing was imperfect, discussed methods for amending the Constitution. Small states wanted unanimous consent of state legislatures, which would sharply limit amendments. Southern states also feared an easy amendment process that might endanger slavery. Big states, on the other hand, believed that a unanimity rule would lead to stagnation and protracted conflict.

The resulting compromise allowed proposal and then ratification of amendments by any one of four different procedures (see Figure 2.3). The simplest, and the most frequently used, way to amend the Constitution requires a two-thirds vote in both houses of Congress and then ratification by three-quarters of the state legislatures. Of the 27 amendments to the Constitution, 26 followed this procedure. On one occasion, the amendment repealing Prohibition, state legislatures were bypassed in favor of state ratifying conventions attended by elected delegates (the same procedure used to ratify the Constitution itself).

Amending the Constitution requires such overwhelming majorities that, despite thousands of proposals, only 17 amendments have been enacted since the Bill of Rights. A proposed amendment must clear hurdles so high that even popular ideas falter. For example, in the 1970s many people thought that the Equal Rights Amendment would win approval because all it did was grant men and women "equality of rights under the law." The amendment received overwhelming support from both houses of Congress in 1971–1972 and was quickly ratified by 34 states. But when debate turned to consider what federal courts might do with those innocent-sounding words, opinion shifted and the ERA fell 3 states short (see Chapter 14).

---

*In addition, as a result of passage of the Twenty-Third Amendment, the District of Columbia casts 3 votes.

FIGURE 2.3

Amending the Constitution: A two-stage process

Why did the founders make the amendment process so difficult? Should amending the Constitution be easier so that judges would not have to reinterpret provisions to fit with changing times?

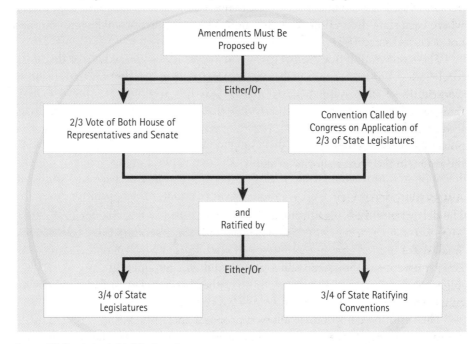

SOURCE: U.S. Constitution, Article V. See Appendix.

The one kind of amendment that seems capable of jumping the high hurdles it must clear to achieve adoption is one that extends democratic electoral practices. Amendments have tightened the electoral connection between government and governed well beyond what was originally envisioned by the Constitution—by broadening the electorate, by extending civil liberties, or by making more direct the linkages between leaders and voters. Five amendments specifically extended suffrage to citizens previously excluded from voting: African Americans, women, young people (aged 18 to 21), residents of the District of Columbia, and those unwilling or unable to pay a poll tax.

THE FIRST NATIONAL ELECTION

The Articles of Confederation were unpopular, but ratification of the Constitution was hardly inevitable. Many revolutionary war heroes, such as Patrick Henry and Sam Adams, feared a stronger government. Powerful state politicians, such as New York Governor George Clinton, did not want their powers reduced. And numerous provisions clashed with the sympathies and interests of America's inland farm population. These voters faced a difficult choice: either accept the new document, which seemed likely to favor the nation's commercial interests, or stick with a governmental framework that most considered inadequate.

Americans quickly polarized over the new proposal. The **Federalists**, who supported the Constitution, included many prominent national politicians and well-funded newspapers. Benjamin Franklin, a soft-spoken elder statesman, promoted the Constitution in Pennsylvania. Alexander Hamilton, a hero at the decisive battle of Yorktown, emerged as a rising star during the New York ratification campaign. Especially important was General George Washington, America's revolutionary leader, whom everyone expected to become the first U.S. president after ratification.

The Federalists faced one of their toughest battles in the state of New York. A series of newspaper essays, written under the pen name "Publius," appeared there defending the provisions of the Constitution in great detail. The essays drew on history, philosophy, logic, and occasionally wit to counter the opposition; they are generally regarded as the finest essays on American political theory ever written.[30] Three men wrote the *Federalist Papers*, as they are now called: Alexander Hamilton, James Madison, and diplomat John Jay. Hamilton wrote the greatest number, Madison the most influential (including No. 10 and No. 51, which appear in this book's appendix). Because the *Federalist Papers* were public statements, they are a valuable source for judges and elected officials trying to interpret what constitutional law meant to the people who ratified it.

The **Anti-Federalists,** those who opposed ratification of the Constitution, lacked a leader of national stature. Thomas Jefferson, the one man who could have galvanized the opposition, bowed out. He strongly sympathized with the inland farmers and worried that the Constitution did not protect civil liberties adequately, but he admitted to his friend Madison that the document still deserved ratification. At any rate, Jefferson was posted in Paris, serving as Minister to France. The burden of opposition fell mostly on local figures, including many country politicians who lacked the funding and skills of their opponents.

The Constitution's most famous critics tended to be men of an older generation, with ideas formed during the rebellion against England—such as Patrick Henry, who wanted the convention investigated as a conspiracy. The Anti-Federalists drew on Whig theories explicitly and attacked the Constitution as a blueprint for national tyranny. They said undercutting the states would take power from the people. The number of representatives in Congress would be too small to include a wide variety of citizens from all parts of the United States. Presidents would become virtual kings, because they could be reelected again and again for the rest of their lives. The reelection of senators and representatives would create a political aristocracy.[31]

With energy and organization on their side, the Federalists easily won the first rounds in the struggle. Conventions in four of the smaller states—Delaware, New Jersey, Georgia, and Connecticut—ratified the document by an overwhelming vote within four months of its signing (see Table 2.4).[32] Pennsylvania also approved it quickly, thanks to some strong-arm tactics. However, a vocal minority at the Pennsylvania convention opposed the Constitution. They distributed a stinging critique of both the document and the ratification process, a critique that the opposition elsewhere could use for ammunition.

Of all their criticisms, though, only one seemed powerful enough to derail ratification. The framers neglected to protect important civil liberties in the proposed Constitution. Their proposal did not mention freedom of religion, free expression, or even rights against abusive law enforcement (which the English took for granted). Silence on civil liberties was not a mere oversight. The framers explicitly rejected South Carolina delegate Charles Pinckney's proposal to guarantee a free press,[33] and they never addressed the topic of a Bill of Rights directly,

TABLE 2.4

VOTING OF DELEGATES AFTER THE FIRST NATIONAL ELECTION

Americans elected delegates in each state, who then voted on whether to ratify the Constitution. At what point did the founders have enough states on board to start a feasible government?

STATE	DATE	YES VOTES	NO VOTES	PERCENTAGE YES
Delaware	Dec. 7, 1787	30	0	100.0
Pennsylvania	Dec. 11, 1787	46	23	66.7
New Jersey	Dec. 18, 1787	38	0	100.0
Georgia	Jan. 2, 1788	26	0	100.0
Connecticut	Jan. 9, 1788	128	40	76.2
Massachusetts	Feb. 6, 1788	187	168	52.7
Maryland	Apr. 26, 1788	63	11	85.1
South Carolina	May 23, 1788	149	73	67.1
New Hampshire	June 21, 1788	57	47	54.8
Virginia	June 25, 1788	89	79	53.0
New York	July 26, 1788	30	27	52.6
North Carolina	Nov. 21, 1789	194	77	71.6
Rhode Island	May 29, 1790	34	32	51.5

SOURCE: Lauren Bahr and Bernard Johnson, ed., *Collier's Encyclopedia*, Vol. 7 (New York: P. F. Collier, 1992), p. 239.

ELECTION CONNECTION

James Madison's House Campaign and the Bill of Rights

Despite harboring doubts about the necessity of the Bill of Rights, James Madison emerged in the first Congress as the driving force behind its passage. Madison's willingness to defer to the desire of others can be explained by the same constituency pressures that shape the views of modern-day members of Congress. Although a Federalist, Madison came from Virginia, home state of the acclaimed Virginia Bill of Rights and of the country's most influential Anti-Federalists, George Mason and Patrick Henry. Henry had successfully fought to prevent Madison from being selected as one of Virginia's two senators, and Madison had won a seat in the House of Representatives only by promising to work for the passage of a Bill of Rights.

That Madison was influenced more by election pressures than by constitutional scruples is evident from the fact that, at the Constitutional Convention itself, he had seen little need for such a document. Even after the convention, Madison wrote, "I have never thought the omission [of a bill of rights] a material defect, nor been anxious to supply it even by subsequent amendment, for any other reason than that it is anxiously desired by others."

In Madison's hands, the meaning of the Bill of Rights underwent a significant transformation. Whereas the Anti-Federalists had wanted amendments to protect state governments, Madison's amendments focused on individual liberties. Only two amendments addressed state prerogatives. Madison thus was able to avoid the central issue of contention between Federalists and Anti-Federalists: the balance of power between levels of government. The ten amendments Congress eventually agreed upon were quickly and quietly ratified in 1791 by all but two states, apparently because few people thought the amendments would have much practical effect. Their protections include the following:

- Freedom of religion (Amendment I)
- Freedom of speech, press, and assembly (Amendment I)
- Right to bear arms (Amendment II)
- Security against unreasonable searches and seizures (Amendment IV)
- Protection from being be forced to testify against oneself (Amendment V)
- Guarantee of trial by jury (Amendments VI and VII)
- Protection against cruel or unusual punishment (Amendment VIII)

What do you think?

- If, as historians believe, Madison promoted the Bill of Rights under electoral pressure, should this change our understanding of these rights or how we interpret them?
- Should it change our opinion of Madison?

Sources: Robert A. Rutland, *The Birth of the Bill of Rights* (Chapel Hill: University of North Carolina Press, 1955); Stanley Elkins and Eric McKitrick, *The Age of Federalism* (New York: Oxford University Press, 1993); Thornton Anderson, *Creating the Constitution: The Convention of 1787 and the First Congress* (University Park: Pennsylvania State University Press, 1993), p. 176.

even though they knew that many other state constitutions explicitly defended fundamental freedoms. In fact, the author of Virginia's famous statement of rights, George Mason, sat in the hall as one of the delegates.*

---

*Mason was one of the three who, at the end, refused to endorse the proposal.

The absence of a Bill of Rights almost undermined all of their hard work, and the Constitution's ratification ultimately relied on a promise from Federalist politicians that they would add a Bill of Rights later. The Federalists first recognized their mistake during the fight over ratification in Massachusetts. They narrowly secured the state's support, and did so only after promising to amend the Constitution so that it would protect freedoms explicitly. Victories in Virginia and New York required similar guarantees. Two states, North Carolina and Rhode Island, remained unsatisfied. They withheld ratification until the Constitution's first ten amendments, the **Bill of Rights,** passed through the Federalist-controlled Congress.

It is surprising that the framers made such a serious miscalculation, given the sound political judgment they otherwise exhibited. This one temporary setback is instructive, though, because it clearly reveals to what extent the many Federalist successes depended on anticipation of popular sentiment. The one time they ran directly against public opinion, they were forced to back down. Specific politicians also flip-flopped on the Bill of Rights rather than resist a popular idea (see the accompanying Election Connection, "James Madison's House Campaign and the Bill of Rights").

EVALUATING THE CONSTITUTION

Debate over the Constitution did not end with its ratification. The influential historian Charles Beard wrote in 1913 that the Constitution primarily represented a victory for commercial interests over landowners.[34] Beard pointed out that wealthy people wrote the document and that only people with property were allowed to vote on ratification. The Constitution contained provisions to protect contracts, ensure the repayment of war bonds, prevent wealth-based taxes, and protect slavery—none of which was necessary to grapple with the foreign threats that the Confederation seemed incapable of handling. It is easy to exaggerate these criticisms, but they nonetheless contain a fair bit of truth.

On the other hand, evaluating the Constitution requires more than just an assessment of whether the founders had personal motivations for what they wrote or whether the procedures they followed would be acceptable today. What matters, ultimately, is whether the document they produced did its job and provided a sound, but flexible, framework of government. Modern-day historians Bernard Bailyn and Gordon Wood point out that the Constitution gave practical expression to important ideals such as citizen rights and fair representation, the same Whig beliefs that motivated revolutionary patriots.[35] It established three branches of government—president, courts, and the House and Senate—with fairly distinct powers. It ultimately grounded all three branches in the people, setting up frequent elections. This electoral connection grew after 1789, because the Constitution allowed a more popular democracy to evolve.

That the Constitution could win support from a uniformly white, male, property-owning population—and still leave open the possibility for greater democratization in the centuries to come—is to the honor, not the discredit, of those who met in Philadelphia.

Most flaws written into the Constitution were necessary to achieve ratification. The most obvious of these is the stain of slavery, which remains indelible. The Constitution validated the slave trade and counted each slave as three-fifths of a person. The Constitution required free states to return escaped slaves to the places from which they had fled. It also divided powers so well that, when a national majority turned against the tyranny of slavery, they could not end such an immoral institution peacefully. Other, less democratic nations abolished slavery more rapidly than the United States could, and with less bloodshed. It is not easy to think how delegates could have designed a constitution that would have both freed slaves and won ratification by the voters of 1788, but the fact remains that they did not try very hard.

By contrast, the delegates wrote a document that contributed to solutions for three of the most immediate and pressing problems facing the United States. First, the new Constitution facilitated economic development by outlawing the chaos created by state currencies and tariffs. As a result, trade among states flourished, and the United States grew into an economic powerhouse faster than any had expected. The states of Europe are only now experimenting with what the United States accomplished in 1789: establishing a single currency, dropping barriers to trade, and guaranteeing citizens the same "immunities and privileges" as they cross borders.

Second, the Constitution created a unified nation at a time when Britain, France, and Spain were all looking for a piece of the action in the New World. The compromise document incorporated the interests of big states and small states, northerners and southerners, commercial entrepreneurs and farmers, property owners and debtors—all woven into a constitutional fabric that was able to establish the government's legitimacy and ultimately to secure national loyalty. Instead of falling prey to European ambitions, the United States profited from European divisions by seizing the opportunity to make the Louisiana Purchase of 1803, which doubled the size of the country. The new lands were eventually incorporated into the Union as member states.

Finally, the Constitution created a strong executive branch that could adapt to an increasingly complex world, taking on additional duties (such as budgeting and regulation) as well as mastering the duties that became increasingly complicated (such as defending the nation and organizing the government bureaucracy). George Washington, the country's most beloved political leader, agreed to serve as the first president, lending his great prestige to a national government that needed the additional strength to overcome its growing pains (see the accompanying Election Connection, "George Washington Is Elected").

ELECTION CONNECTION

George Washington Is Elected

The first presidential election was extremely dull. No issues arose and no campaign allegations were made; the vote was unanimous. Yet the votes cast by the Electoral College on February 4, 1789, may have been as important as any ever cast. The election of George Washington as the nation's first president got the country off to a good start.

Unanimity was certainly an advantage, because the election process itself raised many questions. In only five states did the voters choose the electors. Electors in two states—Rhode Island and North Carolina—did not vote because their states had yet to ratify the Constitution. The New York legislature, still opposed to the Constitution, refused to pick any electors. In New Jersey the electors were designated by the governor and his council. In four other states the electors were chosen by the legislatures.

Yet virtually everyone was pleased with the new president. Though a great war hero, he had always deferred to the Continental Congress. As a former member of the Virginia colonial legislature, he did not disdain politics. Because he was both a speculator in western lands and a slave owner (known for his generous treatment of those who worked for him), he was acceptable to both northern and southern states.

What do you think?
- Are war heroes as politically popular today as Washington was?
- Should the powers of a public office be influenced by who is likely to hold it?

SOURCE: Stanley Elkins and Eric McKitrick, *The Age of Federalism* (New York: Oxford University Press, 1993); Thomas A. Lewis, *For King and Country: The Maturing of George Washington, 1748–1760* (New York: HarperCollins, 1993.)

In the two centuries that have followed, the main lines of conflict have changed. People no longer worry much about the political divisions that captivated the framers. But the Constitution still allows American government to reconcile the demands and opinions of many different groups and interests. Even the ambiguities embedded in the Constitution have provided benefits, because they have had the elasticity necessary to accommodate powerful social and political changes that the framers could not have anticipated. Subsequent chapters discuss ways in which the compromises of 1787 have been redefined in response to changing political circumstances, allowing the U.S. Constitution to become the longest-lasting Constitution in the world.

CHAPTER SUMMARY

The yeoman farmers who participated in Shays' Rebellion lost their uprising; some were killed and others fled to adjoining states. The Anti-Federalists, who were especially dense in America's inland agricultural regions, lost their battle against constitutional ratification. However, America's rural radicals strongly shaped both the Constitution and the government it created. Their opposition required the framers to draft laws that would be acceptable to voters—both at the time of ratification and afterward, when the nation would need their loyalty. Many powers that the founders wanted to claim for the government were left undeclared, couched in vague language that later Americans could interpret according to the needs and beliefs of their age. The Constitution left the state governments with their own authority and independence. The presidency did not receive royal prerogatives, and the Congress was restricted to a specific list of powers. Many compromises were necessary.

The convention delegates erred by excluding a Bill of Rights, but they ultimately agreed during the ratification debate to add one. Rights to free expression, to religion, and to legal due process have had a dramatic impact on government and society. The rights of free speech and free press, in particular, have been an important component of the permanent campaign because of the vibrant and aggressive political debates they protect. The opposition also helped force the framers to defend their handiwork in the *Federalist Papers* and to explain what different constitutional provisions meant.

Finally, the members of America's agricultural population continued to participate in the new government's political life. Their intensity and their large numbers inspired politicians such as Thomas Jefferson, James Madison, and (later) Andrew Jackson to shape policies that could attract rural votes. These elected officials were so successful that during much of the nineteenth century, the Constitution was a mixture of Federalist words and Anti-Federalist ideals. In particular, such leaders espoused an ideology of liberty, equality, limited government, and state autonomy. Their beliefs tamed some of the more expansive constitutional provisions. In sum, the openness and responsiveness characteristic of American government owes much to the battles fought by the nation's agrarian population. Both they and the Constitution's actual authors collaborated to produce America's new democracy, described in the chapters to follow.

KEY TERMS

Anti-Federalists, p. 48
Articles of Confederation, p. 35
Bill of Rights, p. 51
Connecticut Compromise, p. 43
Declaration of Independence, p. 35
divine right, p. 33
Electoral College, p. 45
Federalist Papers, p. 48

Federalists, p. 48
judicial review, p. 45
natural rights, p. 33
necessary and proper clause, p. 44
quorum, p. 39
Second Continental Congress, p. 35
separation of powers, p. 34
Shays's Rebellion, p. 29
social-contract theory, p. 33

supremacy clause, p. 45
tariffs, p. 39
three-fifths compromise, p. 43
Virginia Plan, p. 43
Whigs, p. 34
yeoman, p. 28

Suggested Readings

Adams, Willi Paul. *The First American Constitutions: Republican Ideology and the Making of the State Constitutions in the Revolutionary Era.* Chapel Hill: University of North Carolina Press, 1980. Reveals that much of what seems original in the Constitution was already in place in many states.

Bailyn, Bernard. *The Origins of American Politics.* New York: Knopf, 1968. Identifies the sources of the American Revolution in colonial thought and practice.

Beard, Charles A. *An Economic Interpretation of the Constitution of the United States.* New York: Free Press, 1913. Interprets the writing of the Constitution as an effort by the wealthy to protect their property rights.

Elkins, Stanley, and Eric McKitrick. *The Age of Federalism.* New York: Oxford University Press, 1993. Authoritative account of political life during the first decade after the adoption of the Constitution.

Morgan, Edmund S., and Helen M. Morgan. *The Stamp Act Crisis: Prologue to Revolution.* Chapel Hill: University of North Carolina Press, 1953. Readable account of key events leading to the Revolution.

Roche, John P. "The Founding Fathers: A Reform Caucus in Action." *American Political Science Review* 55 (December 1961): 799–816. Identifies the election connection at the Constitutional Convention.

Wood, Gordon S. *The Radicalism of the American Revolution.* New York: Knopf, 1992. Portrays the unleashing of a democratic ideology during the struggle for independence.

On the Web

National Archives and Records Administration
www.nara.gov/exhall/charters/ constitution/conmain.html
The National Archives and Records Administration provides the full text of the Constitution, biographies of each of its signers, and high-resolution images of the document itself.

PBS
www.pbs.org/ktca/liberty/
This site, the companion to a PBS series on the American Revolution, provides a comprehensive overview of the Revolutionary War, including timelines, accounts of battles, and biographies of key figures.

Avalon Project at Yale Law School
www.yale.edu/lawweb/avalon/ avalon.htm
The Avalon Project at Yale Law School is an excellent resource for major documents in law, history, and diplomacy. For the project's home page, see the Web site.

Amendments Passed and Rejected
www.usconstitution.net/constam. html#proposed
www.usconstitution.net/constam. html#failed
Offers a list of proposed amendments to the Constitution, including those that failed to make it through the approval process.

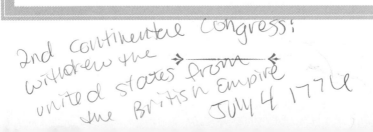

3

FEDERALISM

CHAPTER OUTLINE

I t took Clarence William Busch only two days out on bail from his hit-and-run drunken-driving charge before he killed a little girl. Thirteen-year-old Cari Lightner was in the middle of a Saturday afternoon stroll when Busch's car careened straight across a bicycle path, struck the slim teen from behind, and left her mangled body in its wake. She died within the hour.[1]

That Busch's personal struggles finally resulted in a death was not particularly surprising. As he climbed behind the wheel that fateful day, Busch already had two drunken-driving convictions under his belt, not counting the most recent charge. More surprising was that the repercussions from this all-too-common tragedy spread far beyond the devastation it brought to Cari's family. Her mother, a Sacramento real estate agent, quickly transformed her grief into a political crusade— one that would affect the lives of college students across the nation.

Candy Lightner formed the organization Mothers Against Drunk Driving (MADD) within a week of her daughter's death and, just four years later, commanded a national organization claiming 258 chapters and 300,000 members. MADD initially focused on strengthening penalties for those caught driving under the influence of alcohol. But Candy's thirst for "revenge" did not stop with individuals who had already done something wrong. Instead, her organization decided to target young adults (even though Busch himself was 47 years old on the day he took Cari's life). Teenagers account for a disproportionate share of drunk-driving accidents, so MADD demanded federal laws to take away the whole age group's right to drink.[2]

At first, President Ronald Reagan and other Republicans resisted tampering with the drinking age; modern conservatives generally prefer to let states set their own social regulations (see Chapter 4). But the political situation grew stickier as many states delayed changing their age limits. By the middle of 1984, only 23 states forbade drinking for those under 21, and 19 states had passed up the opportunity to do so.[3] The final blow came when New York's legislature failed to raise the state's age limit, despite a strong push by the governor. New York was a mecca for young drinkers from New Jersey and Pennsylvania, who created a "blood zone" on the state borders as they journeyed back home.

Congressional delegations from New York's two neighboring states placed MADD's agenda on the front burner. One New Jersey Democrat's legislative assistant explained, "The day of more rights for kids has passed." However, the Twenty-first Amendment gives the states authority over liquor laws, so Congress could not simply set a national drinking age itself. Representative James Howard of New Jersey suggested trying economic pressure, instead—the same strategy he used in 1973 to force states to lower their speed limits to 55 miles per hour. He proposed legislation yanking away millions of dollars in federal highway funds from any state whose drinking age remained below 21.*

---

*States that did not raise their drinking ages would lose 5 percent of their highway construction funds in 1986 and 10 percent starting in 1987.

Public opinion left national politicians little wiggle room: Polls supported raising the minimum, and those who wanted the age limit raised were a lot madder than the young people who faced a loss of privileges. The House passed the indirect federal drinking age by voice vote, with very little opposition—prompting the White House to switch positions. Transportation Secretary Elizabeth Dole announced during a MADD rally on the Capitol steps that President Reagan now supported their bill. It then passed the Senate 81 to 16, opposed primarily by conservatives unhappy with the strong-arm treatment that states would face.[4]

Reagan signed the National Minimum Drinking Age Act into law, but the battle did not end there. Eight states refused to cave in until the 1986 deadline arrived, and four actually passed on the "blackmail portion" of federal highway funds for a year by holding out until June 1987.[5] Others changed their laws only in protest. Florida, for example, specified that the age would drop again the minute any federal court struck down the Act.[6] South Dakota, supported by the other holdout states, took a challenge all the way to the U.S. Supreme Court.

South Dakota's attorneys explained that their state preferred lower drinking ages because, otherwise, teenagers would engage in dangerous "surreptitious drinking."[7] They charged that Congress was trying to do an end run around the state's constitutional right to make this judgment. But the Court wouldn't swallow it. Chief Justice Rehnquist wrote for a seven-justice majority in *South Dakota v. Dole* (1987) that Congress can use federal budgetary power to pressure states—regardless of whether the law Congress wants changed falls under its responsibilities. He called the potential million-dollar losses "relatively mild encouragement," prompting a spokesperson for the National Conference of State Legislatures to scoff, "I don't think many of them will hold out. They simply need the money."[8]

No state held out against the letter of the law; the blackmail worked. But Louisiana's state legislature did resist the *spirit* of the law. It was no accident that Louisiana would be the last to surrender. The state began as a French colony and later fell under Spanish control. Latin Catholicism still heavily influences her southern region,[9] so alcoholic beverages are more likely to be part of normal family life there. Often visitors to New Orleans are struck by the city's casual approach to drinking, perhaps best symbolized by the many drive-up daiquiri shops that patrons frequent on hot days. Louisiana also attracts a substantial (and young) tourism trade, hosting numerous music festivals as well as Mardi Gras—a carnival celebration called the "greatest free show on Earth." Raising the drinking age simply did not conform to the state's interests or to her culture.

Accordingly, the Louisiana legislature left a major loophole in its 1986 alcoholic beverage regulation. Legislators made it illegal to drink under age 21 but imposed no penalty for selling alcohol to someone 18 or older. This loophole made consistent enforcement impossible for a decade. And when the loophole finally collapsed in 1995, worn down by continued federal pressure, the Louisiana

Let the good times roll

States have varying cultures, and this diversity can lead to wide differences in law. The state of Louisiana's southern region features a spicy Latin culture, augmented by carnival celebrations and musical festivals—which leads to a more tolerant attitude toward alcohol than is found in states with an Anglo-Saxon heritage. Here we see the city's French Quarter inundated with revelers, many drinking beer on a public street. If a state's attitudes seem "unenlightened," when should the nation impose its cultural preferences?

Supreme Court responded by trying to roll the entire age limit back to 18, ruling that a higher limit represented age discrimination!

But one New Orleans columnist, at least, knew that the resistance could not last. James Gill predicted, somewhat tongue-in-cheek, that raw federal power would force a reversal of the decision: "So long as they got the bomb, and we [only] got the Tenth Amendment, the feds are going to win every time."[10] He was right. Louisiana's court reheard the case in the face of severe threats from the Clinton administration and then backpedaled, with one judge switching his vote and a new judge joining the majority. "Totally political," grumbled the state's top liquor lobbyist.[11] The drinking age went up again, loopholes gone.

At long last Louisiana conformed to national norms, and young adults were saved from demon liquor in every state, right? Wrong. Not even Louisiana's 1996 surrender was final. One poll showed that fewer than half of Louisiana men endorsed the higher drinking age and that respondents aged 18 to 20 overwhelmingly opposed it.[12] A strong majority of the legislators in the statehouse, unimpressed by the federal mandate, voted in favor of a 1999 constitutional amendment to restore the old limit—although they fell 18 votes short of the supermajority needed.[13]

And Louisiana still has loopholes. For example, both chambers of the legislature explicitly rejected an attempt to curtail teenage access to bars. Despite complaints from law enforcement officials, young adults are still free to enter entertainment establishments that serve liquor in order to "hear good music."[14] And there's always the question of how aggressively police enforce a law imposed by the national government that lacks local sympathy. Two teenage brothers interviewed in 1996 said they had little trouble finding booze in the New Orleans French Quarter. "Once in a while we'll get hassled trying to buy liquor in a supermarket," 17-year-old Patrick Grimmace explained. "But never on Bourbon Street."[15]

THE WINDING PATH FOLLOWED BY AMERICA'S NATIONAL DRINKING AGE illustrates why the structure of intergovernmental relations—seemingly so technical—has been an intense source of conflict since the nation's founding. It shows the important value preserved by letting states do their own thing: social regulations that better fit the culture and interests of people in each state and less danger of a national majority bullying regional minorities. It indicates how hard states will fight to retain their distinctiveness. At the same time, it reveals how a determined national majority can force deviant states to conform to its demands, especially when a few states seem bound to a policy that the rest of the nation considers backward or unwise. States often capitulate to national public opinion in a way that is "totally political."

The story also illustrates why the American political system has tilted over time toward the national government. It shows that federal courts ultimately bear the burden of deciding between competing claims of authority—a responsibility that, more often than not, they exercise to expand the power of the national government of which they are part. It exhibits another reason why the balance has tipped as well: the muscle provided by congressional grants. But the story also shows that, even in their weakened condition, state and local governments still have influence. As long as the nation relies on them to implement programs, local officials will enjoy some discretion.

THE FEDERALISM DEBATE

Deciding how much to centralize power has been a challenge since the country's founding. The Federalists favored a strong central government, whereas the Anti-Federalists wanted state governments to retain as much power as possible because they were closer to the voters (see Chapter 2). As a compromise, the framers developed a principle called **federalism**—the belief that multiple sources of government authority could coexist, each with its own sphere of responsibility.

TABLE 3.1

CONSTITUTIONAL DIVISION OF POWER
BETWEEN NATIONAL AND STATE GOVERNMENTS

[handwritten: "national" above first column header, "States" above second column header]

POWERS GRANTED TO THE ~~STATE GOVERNMENTS~~	POWERS GRANTED TO THE ~~NATIONAL GOVERNMENT~~
Conduct foreign affairs	
Raise armies and declare war	Maintain state militias (the National Guard)
Regulate imports and exports	
Regulate interstate commerce	Regulate commerce within the state
Regulate immigration and naturalization	
Establish and operate federal court system	Establish and operate state court systems
Levy taxes	Levy taxes
Borrow money	Borrow money
Coin money	
Provide for the general welfare	
Make laws "necessary and proper" to accomplish the above tasks	Exercise powers not granted to national government

The U.S. Constitution established a federal system, laying out the areas of law in which each level of government enjoyed unchecked (or "sovereign") authority (see Table 3.1). The result is a system of **dual sovereignty** with two formal units, the *national government* and the *state governments.**

Few nations follow the principle of federalism. Most have unitary political systems, in which all authority is held by national governments. Such a system may divide the country into local jurisdictions, but these are simply administrative outposts that lack sovereignty. Indeed, as a principle of government, federalism attracts a fair bit of skepticism. The great fighter for Venezuelan independence, Simón Bolívar, once observed, "Among the popular and representative systems of government, I do not approve of the federal system: It is too perfect; and it requires virtues and political talents much superior to our own."[16] Splitting up authority can prevent a nation from responding quickly during a crisis and may exacerbate problems during times of conflict.

*Local governments—such as cities, counties, towns, and school districts—are also important parts of government in the United States, but they are not fundamental units in the U.S. federal system in the same way that the national and state governments are. According to a long-standing legal doctrine known as *Dillon's rule* (after the Iowa state judge John Dillon), local governments are in legal terms mere "creatures of the state" that a state legislature may alter or abolish at any time.

Yet federalism seems ideally suited to a nation characterized by geographic, ethnic, and cultural diversity. By allowing subdivisions to "do their own thing," it provides a useful way to resolve conflicts that can tear other countries apart. Federalism also promotes economic development, because it gives states the authority and interest to focus on local needs. As early as the 1830s, the keen French observer Alexis de Tocqueville noted, "One can hardly imagine how much division of sovereignty contributes to the well-being of each of the states that compose the Union."[17]

Both elections and court decisions have defined and redefined the nature of American federalism. Leaving aside any indirect influence that elections have on the Supreme Court, they also mold what leaders try to accomplish by determining how elected officials envision their responsibilities. For much of early American history, the national government remained weak precisely because elected officials intentionally limited their exercise of power. Centralization increased only when voters selected new leaders who promised to do more.

FEDERALISM IN THE COURTS

The Constitution does not indicate who should settle disputes between the national government and the states. Before the Civil War, some opponents of centralized power argued that states could nullify, or invalidate, national laws that infringed on their authority (see the accompanying Election Connection, "The Nullification Doctrine"). The doctrine of **nullification** was seldom invoked, however. Instead, the Supreme Court granted itself the power to decide how the Constitution divided up sovereignty, in the sweeping 1819 decision *McCulloch v. Maryland*—among the most important the Court has ever made.[18] This assumption of responsibility became accepted over time.

Supreme Court decisions have had a fundamental impact in defining American federalism because national courts exercise the power of **judicial review**—that is, the authority to declare laws null and void on the grounds that they violate the Constitution (see Chapter 12). When the Supreme Court declares a national law unconstitutional, which it does rarely, it also expands the arena in which states are sovereign. When it declares state laws unconstitutional, which it does much more frequently, the result is a stronger national government.

A few constitutional amendments attempted to protect state governments from federal encroachment. The Tenth Amendment, added in part to satisfy revolutionary hero Sam Adams, emphasizes that states retain all powers not delegated specifically to the national government. The Supreme Court rarely invokes this provision, though. The Eleventh Amendment also protects states. It gives them **sovereign immunity** from suits filed under national law, a provision that conservative members of the Supreme Court began giving teeth in the mid-1990s.

The Nullification Doctrine

Many Americans considered the Constitution a limit on national government—an understandable impression, given the strong wording of the Tenth Amendment and the ambiguity of other clauses. Indeed, some thought state sovereignty so complete that they propounded the doctrine of nullification, which says that state legislatures can invalidate unconstitutional acts of Congress.

States first used this doctrine in 1798. In that year, Federalist members of Congress were upset by criticism of their party, especially criticism of President John Adams during a foreign policy crisis with France. They feared the growing power of Vice President Thomas Jefferson and the Democratic–Republican party he led. Congress passed the Sedition Act, a ban on criticizing national leaders (except Jefferson). Opposition newspaper editors were soon imprisoned, and even Congressman Matthew Lyon was sentenced to four months in jail for insulting Adams. Federalists no doubt hoped censorship could suppress Jefferson's presidential campaign against Adams.

Outraged Jeffersonians in Virginia and Kentucky initially invoked the nullification doctrine, passing state resolutions to void the laws. Jefferson and his protégé, James Madison, wrote the resolutions, arguing that the Sedition Act of 1798 was unconstitutional. The doctrine's legal status remained unresolved, however, because their attempt to shut off debate backfired on the Federalists.

Jefferson won the 1800 election, and his party trounced the Federalists in Congressional contests across the country. Jeffersonians took firm control of the national government, and a new Congress discontinued the Sedition Act.

The main application of the Nullification Doctrine took place when regional conflict between the North and South started heating up. During the Jackson administration the conflict focused on tariffs, or taxes on imports, which Southern planters generally opposed but Northern merchants generally supported. Former Vice President John Calhoun's supporters in South Carolina called a state convention, which declared the tariff null and void in their state. President Jackson prepared to use armed force to crush the dissidents, but cooler heads prevailed. Congress passed a new tariff, and South Carolina agreed to pay it.

Southern leaders continued to espouse the nullification doctrine—including their right to withdraw peacefully from the Union—because they were afraid that the national government would end slavery. Abraham Lincoln's election brought the issue to a head in 1860, because Lincoln represented the antislavery Republican party. The South seceded from the Union in response to his election. Only after half a million soldiers had died and the countryside had been laid to waste was the nullification doctrine finally repudiated.

What do you think?

- If the national government passed unconstitutional legislation today, should state governments refuse to cooperate?
- If so, what prevents states from ignoring any federal law they dislike?
- If not, how can states protect themselves?

SOURCE: Stanley Elkins and Eric McKitrick, *The Age of Federalism* (New York: Oxford University Press, 1993).

For example, in a 2001 opinion written by Chief Justice William Rehnquist, the Court ruled that a woman suffering from breast cancer could not sue the state of Alabama for discrimination under the federal Americans with Disabilities Act.[19] States cannot rely on this constitutional protection, however. Rehnquist wrote another opinion in 2003 that opened states to suits filed under the Family and Medical Leave Act, explaining that the federal government's interest in preventing sex discrimination trumped state sovereignty.[20]

Federal judges have found numerous phrases in the Constitution to permit expanded federal power. Four are especially important: the **supremacy clause** declaring national law superior to state law, the **commerce clause** giving Congress control over interstate trade, the **spending clause** giving Congress access to a very deep purse, and the **necessary and proper clause,** which gives Congress great flexibility in carrying out its enumerated powers. Combined, these ambiguous phrases laid the groundwork for a significant centralization of power in the national government, to which the Fourteenth Amendment added after the Civil War (see Chapters 13 and 14).

THE SUPREMACY CLAUSE   The Constitution states that national laws "shall be the supreme Law of the Land . . . Laws of any State to the Contrary notwithstanding." This statement comes close to saying (yet does not quite say) that only the national government is truly sovereign. It was used early in the nation's history, in *McCulloch* v. *Maryland* (1819). The case revolved around the Bank of the United States, an entity that commercial interests thought vital to economic prosperity but that many farmers and debtors resented. Responding to popular opinion, the state of Maryland levied a steep tax on the bank. James W. McCulloch, an officer of the bank's Maryland branch, refused to pay and took his case to the Supreme Court. The Court ruled in favor of McCulloch. Maryland could not tax a federal bank, Chief Justice John Marshall explained. The "power to tax involves the power to destroy."[21] If a state government could tax a federal agency, then states could undermine national sovereignty—which the supremacy clause would not allow.

THE NECESSARY AND PROPER CLAUSE   The Constitution gives Congress authority "to make all laws which shall be necessary and proper for carrying into Execution the . . . Powers vested by this Constitution in the government of the United States." The words *necessary and proper* were first analyzed by Justice Marshall in the same decision that fleshed out the supremacy clause, *McCulloch* v. *Maryland*.

Maryland argued that Congress had no authority to establish a national bank, because a bank was not *necessary* for Congress to carry out its delegated power to coin money. But Justice Marshall, an ardent Federalist, rejected such an interpretation. The language, he explained, does not mean *absolutely* necessary; it only means convenient. "Let the end be legitimate," he said. "Let it be within the scope of the Constitution, and all means which are appropriate, which are plainly adapted to that end, which are not prohibited, but consistent with the letter and spirit of the Constitution, are constitutional."[22]

Since the *McCulloch* v. *Maryland* decision, courts have generally found that almost any means selected by Congress is "necessary and proper." As a result, the necessary and proper clause has come to be known as the **elastic clause.** Over the centuries it has stretched to fit almost any circumstance.

THE COMMERCE CLAUSE   The Constitution gives Congress power "to regulate commerce . . . among the several states." The meaning of these words has been the subject of heated dispute. In the nineteenth century, the courts understood *interstate* (between-state) commerce to exclude exchanges that did not overtly cross state lines. Thus, for example, the Supreme Court's 1895 ruling in *United States* v. *E. C. Knight Co.* said that Congress could not break up a monopoly that had a nationwide impact on the price of sugar because the monopoly refined all its sugar within the state of Pennsylvania.[23]

The Great Depression eventually led to a change in how courts understood the commerce clause, because it ushered in a long period of Democratic dominance (see Chapter 8). In particular, voters sent Franklin Delano Roosevelt (FDR) to the White House because he promised to fight the Depression aggressively. FDR initiated what he called the **New Deal**—a wide array of proposals expanding the federal government's power to stimulate economic recovery. The Supreme Court resisted empowering the national government at first, but after Roosevelt's landslide reelection in 1936, the Court began reinterpreting the commerce clause to suit his proposals (see Chapter 12).

At first, doctrine changed slowly. For example, the Supreme Court permitted the Wagner Act, a New Deal law protecting union organizers, only because "industries organize themselves on a national scale."[24] But FDR's appointees increasingly expanded the definition of interstate commerce. In 1941, a farmer sowed 23 acres of winter wheat on his own land to feed his own family and his own livestock. This act violated crop limits imposed under New Deal legislation, but the farmer challenged the quotas as unconstitutional. What took place entirely on his farm, he argued, bore no relation to commerce "among the several states." Yet the Supreme Court ruled against the farmer in *Wickard* v. *Filburn* (1942), reasoning that, if he did not "resort to the market," he was depressing worldwide wheat prices.[25] In other words, the government could prevent a farmer from growing food to take care of his own needs! With such an expansive definition of interstate commerce, almost nothing falls outside the reach of Congress.

Waves of grain?
Before the New Deal, the Supreme Court ruled that the power of Congress to regulate commerce generally applied only to goods produced or processed in multiple states. But the New Deal court decided that Congress can prevent farmers from growing food even if their produce will never leave the farm. Do you think the framers envisioned a national government with such power?

This broad interpretation of the commerce clause went unquestioned until 1992, when Alphonso Lopez, a teenager with neither a criminal record nor a history of making trouble, foolishly carried a .38-caliber handgun to his San Antonio high school. Needless to say, this was a violation of Texas state law. Rather than leave the matter to the local justice system, though, a U.S. district attorney decided to prosecute Lopez using 1990's Gun-Free School Zone Act. This law made bringing a dangerous weapon near school grounds a federal offense. Lopez received a sentence of six months in the penitentiary, but he appealed the case, arguing that Congress had exceeded its enumerated powers by trying to control the state's public schools. *U.S. v. Lopez* (1995) resulted in a victory for Lopez, who avoided jail and instead joined the Marines.

The *Lopez* case also represented a victory for states trying to slow expansion of the federal government. Chief Justice Rehnquist dismissed arguments that

Congress could regulate the "business" of public schools because they influence interstate commerce. Since then, the Supreme Court has continued to place limits on Congress's ability to intervene in state and local affairs. In 2000, the Court expanded the thrust of the *Lopez* decision by invalidating another federal law that had been justified using the commerce clause. The Violence Against Women Act gave battered spouses and rape victims the power to sue their attackers, but the Court did not see much connection between this 1994 law and the power of Congress to regulate interstate commerce.

THE SPENDING CLAUSE   The Constitution gives Congress authority to collect revenues for the "general welfare." The New Deal Supreme Court considered the meaning of this clause when it ruled on the constitutionality of the social security program for senior citizens enacted in 1935. A taxpayer had challenged the program as oriented toward the specific welfare of the elderly and not the general welfare. But the Supreme Court, in tune with FDR's enlarged conception of federal power, said it was up to Congress to decide whether any particular program was for the general welfare "unless the choice is clearly wrong."[26] So far, the Court has never found Congress "clearly wrong."

Not only has the Supreme Court refused to restrict the purposes for which Congress can spend money, it has also granted Congress the right to attach almost any rule to the money it distributes. *South Dakota* v. *Dole* (1987), discussed in the introduction to this chapter, shows the thin connection permissible between the "strings attached" to federal money and the purpose for which the money would be spent. South Dakota argued that a state's drinking age bore no relation to how it used highway funds, but the Supreme Court decided that both involve "highway safety."[27] Only one justice expressed general concern with Congress buying "compliance with the few things that otherwise exceed its grasp."[28]

Authority to tax and spend has remained one of the broadest congressional powers because the federal government's scope expands every time it raises taxes. The more revenue that is extracted from state economies by federal taxation, the more that cash-strapped state governments need to get the funds back through federal grants—and therefore the more willing they must become to meet congressional stipulations. Some scholars consider the national government's spending authority "the greatest threat to state autonomy."[29] For this reason, it is important to understand how the national government distributes funds to state and local government. That is the subject of the next section.

FEDERALISM AND GOVERNMENT GRANTS

The classic understanding of federalism envisions levels of government as distinct and separate, each sticking to its own duties. As governmental interactions became more complicated after World War II, though, this conception seemed inadequate; different levels of government usually worked together in the same policy areas to solve problems. For example, law enforcement requires cooperation among such agencies as the Federal Bureau of Investigation, state highway traffic control, the county sheriff's office, and local police departments.

Political scientist Morton Grodzins helped focus attention on the gap between how people viewed federalism and how it actually operated by using the contrast between two sorts of dessert. He compared the classic model of federalism to a traditional layer cake: stacked levels, each one separate from and independent of the other, perhaps with a strip of icing buffering one level from the next.[30] Grodzins preferred an alternative, cooperative view of federalism in which agencies from different levels of government worked together, combining and intertwining their functions. As an image for this view of intergovernmental relations, Grodzins selected a dessert popular at the time he was writing: the marble cake, in which light and dark batters were swirled before baking to give the cake a mottled look like cut marble. This image has persisted among scholars who study federalism.

CATEGORICAL GRANTS   Grodzins made clear that he favored **cooperative (or marble-cake federalism)** because it would accommodate a growth in government power. The national government should raise taxes, he suggested, and distribute the resulting revenue to state governments as an inducement for them to become more active.[31] For this reason, cooperative federalism is particularly well suited to Democratic party philosophy (see Chapter 8). Many Democrats see federal grants as a way to address social needs that state and local governments otherwise would ignore. In particular, they favor **categorical grants**—grants with fairly specific regulations about how the money must be spent. Categorical grants often have social welfare purposes, such as job training, elimination of hunger through food stamps, and educational programs for the disabled.

The Democratic party's electoral successes in the early 1960s provided an opportunity to experiment with the sort of cooperation Grodzins proposed. Congress greatly enlarged the number, size, and complexity of programs funded in part by the federal government but administered more locally. Only $85.8 million was spent on grants to local governments in 1930, but these funds grew to $43.6 billion by 1962.[32] By 1982, they had more than tripled to $147.5 billion.* The **War on Poverty,** a wide-ranging set of programs designed to enhance economic opportunities for low-income citizens, became the most famous and controversial set of all categorical grant programs. Enacted in 1964, at the behest of President Lyndon Baines Johnson (LBJ), this series of poverty initiatives created

*Unless otherwise indicated, all amounts in this chapter are calculated in 1998 dollars.

such popular programs as Head Start, which helps preschoolers from impoverished families prepare for grade school, and the Job Corps, a residential education
and training program.

Other programs in the War on Poverty attracted more enemies. The liberal
social values expressed in LBJ's welfare policies caused some of the attacks. Riots
swept through American cities in 1964 and 1965, shortly after the War on Poverty
began, so some conservatives blamed the initiative for unsettling urban ghettoes.
Other detractors criticize how the War on Poverty effort was implemented—that
is, how it was administered on the local level. Critics note three specific reasons
why such intergovernmental grants failed to meet expectations:[33]

1. *National and local politicians block one another, making it impossible to get much
   done.* Local officials often feuded with the poverty warriors. The officials
   accused government workers of being insensitive to their community's
   needs, and the activists accused officials of trying to undermine the beneficial intent of the programs. For example, when LBJ tried to build "new
   towns" for the poor on vacant federal land, local officials balked because
   they thought the program would undermine property values.[34] Virtually
   no new towns were built.
2. *When many participants are involved, delays and confusion are almost inevitable.*
   It took more than four years to get a job creation program in Oakland
   under way. Political scientists Jeffrey Pressman and Aaron Wildavsky point
   out that the long delay was caused at least in part by the sheer number of
   agencies involved in the decision. The program required 70 separate
   clearances. Even if each took an average of only three weeks (not an
   unreasonable length of time), the total delay would be over four years.[35]
3. *Federal policy makers often raise unrealistic expectations* by using exaggerated
   rhetoric, thereby guaranteeing disappointment. It was a mistake to equate
   moderately funded programs with a war.

Although categorical grants no longer enjoy the widespread popularity they
once had, Congress shows little enthusiasm for reducing their size or number (see
Figure 3.1). The precise rules accompanying categorical grants give members of
Congress more control over what the money buys, which means that constituents
who need funds must go to the legislator for help rather than to a local official.

Categorical grants also make it easier for legislators to claim credit for whatever the grant accomplishes. Constituents rarely criticize their elected officials
for bringing money home from Washington. Sometimes programs that seem
wasteful to those outside a congressional district can be quite important to the
constituents of a member who secures the dollars. An embankment protecting
West Fargo from floods, erected at the behest of a North Dakota senator, apparently saved the town from disaster when the Red River flooded in 1997.[36]

FIGURE 3.1

Growth of federal grants to states and localities

Expenditures for intergovernmental grants continue to rise, and with decreasing flexibility for how states may spend the money. Why would categorical grants rise and block grants fall at a time when the Republicans controlled Congress?

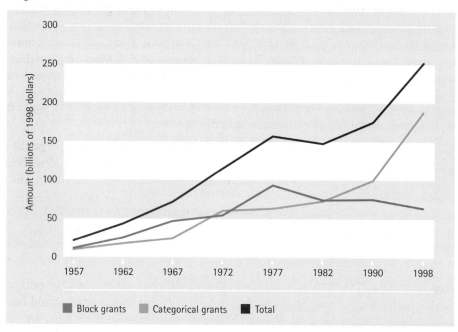

SOURCES: Paul E. Peterson, *The Price of Federalism* (Washington, DC: Brookings, 1995), Ch. 5; U.S. Bureau of the Census, *Federal Aid to the States for Fiscal Year 1998*. (*Note:* Totals exclude defense expenditures. Deriving precise estimates of block and categorical grants is a difficult undertaking. Here we have employed grants used mainly for developmental purposes as a proxy for block grants and grants used mainly for redistributive purposes as a proxy for categorical grants.)

BLOCK GRANTS   Republicans typically dislike categorical grants because of the influence they give the national government at the expense of the states. But they may not call for shrinking the federal budget. Sometimes they simply endorse giving states more flexibility in spending federal money. To simplify federal policy, therefore, Congress occasionally replaces categorical grants with **block grants**—intergovernmental grants with a broad set of objectives, a minimum of restrictions, and maximum discretion for local officials.

The move toward block grants occurred in three distinct waves, each influenced by the political circumstances prevailing at the time. The first wave of block grants began under President Nixon. They did not replace categorical grants so much as supplement them—a compromise that enabled Nixon to get block grants past Democrats in Congress. As a consequence, grant spending grew throughout the decade, eventually totaling more than $155 billion. One block grant program, general revenue sharing, took the idea of removing categorical rules to its logical extreme: It gave state and local governments a share of federal tax revenues to be used for any purpose whatsoever.

The second wave of block grants came at the beginning of Ronald Reagan's administration, which enjoyed a Republican majority in the Senate. Reagan succeeded in converting a broad range of categorical grants in education, social services, health services, and community development to block grants. During this second wave, the new block grants not only had fewer restrictions than those they replaced, their funding levels also fell.[37] The amount spent on block grants dropped from $93.5 billion in 1977 to $64.1 billion in 1998. Most of this reduction occurred in the early 1980s—general revenue sharing was eliminated in 1985, and a major grant program for cities across the country, the community development block grant, was cut from $7.7 billion in 1980 to $5 billion in 2001.[38]

The third wave of block grants took place after the congressional election of 1994, when Republicans captured control of Congress. Earlier grant reorganizations had not touched large social programs, such as Medicaid and Aid to Families with Dependent Children (AFDC, or "welfare"). But in 1996, Congress transformed the AFDC program into a block grant that gave states almost complete discretion over the way monies could be used (see Chapter 15). Congress also tried to transform the Medicaid program into a block grant, but this effort was forestalled by a presidential veto.

THE DEBATE OVER GRANTS   Federal grants carry such an awesome potential for increasing the power of national government that some critics would like to do away with just about all of them. Supporters, meanwhile, would like to see a wide variety of grants, as well as increased spending on the ones that already exist. This debate polarizes the two sides, but it is possible that both of them are partially correct.

One common argument for federal grants is that they equalize wealth across the country.[39] The numbers indicate, however, that the federal budget does not operate like Robin Hood, taking from the rich states and giving to the poor. In fact, the opposite is true: Rich states receive more funding per capita than anyone else (see Figure 3.2)! Critics are probably right to suggest that Congress distributes grants on the basis of political calculations rather than simple policy needs.

Centralizing welfare policies may help the poor in a different way, though— by overcoming state government's natural tendency to squeeze social programs. When states are not subject to federal regulation, they try to shift the burden of serving the needy to other states. More importantly, they want to keep benefits low enough that they will not attract "other people's poor." In Minnesota, a state with generous poverty programs, the proportion of new out-of-state welfare recipients increased from 19 to 28 percent between 1994 and 1995, a time when other states were placing limits on benefits. "We're really concerned," a county official said.[40] Fear of migration from other places creates a vicious cycle of cuts

FIGURE 3.2

Block grants for traditional governmental services

Richer states usually get more money than poorer states. Is this unfair, or do rich states deserve more because they pay more to the federal government in taxes?

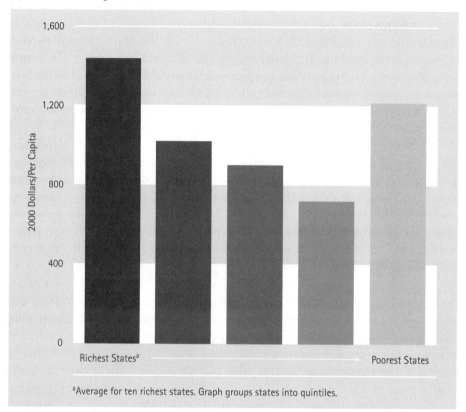

Richest States[a] ⟶ Poorest States

[a]Average for ten richest states. Graph groups states into quintiles.

SOURCE: U.S. Bureau of the Census, *Federal Aid to the States for Fiscal Year 1998*, April 1999, Table 1.

that President Clinton has called a "race to the bottom." This phenomenon lends some credibility to the argument that only federal grants will compel states to provide generous social welfare benefits.

It may be possible to reconcile the two sides in this polarized debate by keeping in mind that not all federal grants are created equal. States and localities customarily provide traditional services, such as transportation, sanitation, and education, regardless of whether they face federal pressure to do so. States are also likely to know their needs in these policy areas better than the federal government would. Congress, meanwhile, tends to spend money poorly in these areas, using political considerations to drive the policy choices. It may be appropriate to keep the federal role to a minimum. But in other areas, such as Medicaid and food stamps, it may be important to establish federal standards so that states do not "race to the bottom." Congress and President Clinton compromised on a position not unlike this one in 1996, making the biggest cuts in traditional programs while keeping the largest social programs as federally funded categorical grants.

THE FEDERALISM DEBATE TODAY

The debate over federalism continues. It divides the two major political parties. Republicans tend to prefer a decentralized government because state and local officials are closer to the people, more in touch with their needs, and less likely to waste taxpayer dollars. Conversely, Democrats tend to think that many serious social problems require a national solution; they do not trust local majorities to be fair.

In the early 1990s, debate focused on the issue of **unfunded mandates,** which occur when the national government imposes regulations on state and local governments without covering the costs. This strategy is tempting to members of Congress because it allows them to "solve" social problems without paying for the solutions. By 1993, countless mandates had reached the statute books. For example, state and local governments had to ensure equal access to public facilities by disabled persons but were given little money to cover the new construction costs. Medicaid required that expanded services be provided for low-income recipients, but for many states the law funded only half the cost of the program.[41]

Despite the long-standing popularity of unfunded mandates on Capitol Hill, the 1994 election at least temporarily slowed their growth. Republicans campaigned in favor of **devolution,** the return of governmental responsibilities to state and local governments. After taking over Congress, they passed a statute banning any new law that is not adequately funded. This stricture certainly did not eliminate unfunded mandates, though. At the spring 2003 National League of Cities meeting, mayors complained about the layoffs and tax increases that federal orders were forcing. "When we get federal mandates, where do we get the money?" one Kentucky major asked. "We would hope that the federal government would be more understanding."[42]

States also faced additional mandates after 1994. In 1998, for example, the federal Department of Health and Human Services required state Medicaid programs to buy Viagra for patients suffering from impotence, at an estimated cost to the states of $100 million a year. The *Chicago Tribune* acidly noted that the states had better use for their health insurance dollars than paying for "improved recreational sex." This mandate was one of the many federal regulations that caused Medicaid costs to surge in the 1990's.[43]

The Supreme Court has also worked to limit the elasticity of the necessary and proper clause through rulings that have attracted some criticism. For example, in *New York v. U.S.* (1992), the Supreme Court declared that Congress cannot give direct orders to states. This case dealt with the disposal of radioactive waste. Millions of cubic feet of such waste must be buried someplace where it cannot be disturbed for thousands of years. The dilemma has become an elected official's nightmare: Something needs to be done, and there is no way of doing it without making some people really angry.

Citizens organize protests whenever a town is mentioned as a potential radioactive dump. Everyone knows the stuff has to go somewhere, but everyone also says, "Not In My Back Yard." This response is generally known as the **NIMBY problem.** Congress opted for a politically painless solution to the buildup of radioactive wastes: It required each state either to find an adequate burial site for its waste or to become legally responsible for any damages the waste might cause. Rather than make tough decisions itself, Congress decided to impose an unfunded mandate on governors and state legislatures.

As a result, the debate over domestic radioactive waste shifted to the states. In no state was the issue more hotly debated than in New York.[44] Pressured by the federal law, New York officials decided to ignore public opposition and dump the waste in Cortland and Allegany counties. But the elected boards for the two counties filed suit claiming that the federal law was unconstitutional. Supreme Court Justice Sandra Day O'Connor, writing for the majority, said Congress could not force states or local governments to bury their nuclear waste; such direct orders violate state sovereignty.[45] The debate over dual sovereignty clearly has not died.

STATE AND LOCAL GOVERNMENT

American government may have become more centralized, but that does not mean the states and localities are withering away. Quite the contrary. The national government has increased its authority, but lower levels of government usually bear responsibility for implementing policy. These lower levels are often the ones actually spending the funds collected through federal taxation and distributed via competitive grants or according to specific formulas. State and local governments are the ones hiring new bureaucrats to implement federal mandates (see Chapter 11). For this reason, anyone who wants to understand America's new democracy needs to consider how these independent administrative units actually operate.

LOCAL GOVERNMENT

Local governments now play a more prominent role in the federal system than they have for decades. Even before the most recent devolution, nearly half of all domestic government expenditures operated at the state and local level. This pattern is in keeping with long-standing American traditions (see Figure 3.3). Local governments maintain roads; take care of the parks; provide police, fire, and sani-

FIGURE 3.3

Domestic government expenditures

State and local governments spend almost as much as the national government.

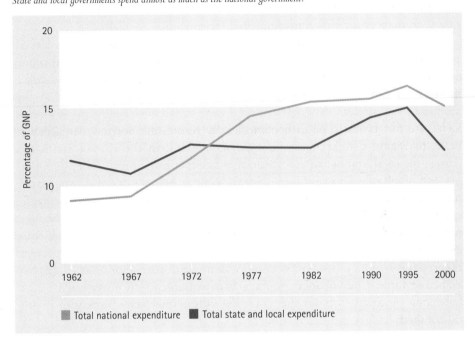

SOURCES: Paul E. Peterson, *The Price of Federalism* (Washington, DC: Brookings, 1995); U.S. Bureau of the Census, *Statistical Abstract of the United States, 1998*.

tation services; run the schools; and perform many other functions that affect the everyday lives of citizens.

THE NUMBER AND TYPES   Local governments constitute a growing presence, at least in sheer numbers. There were over 73,000 in 1997, up from about 46,000 in 1942. The basic unit in most states is the county, although not all counties are alike. In some states they manage school systems, welfare programs, local roads, sanitation systems, sheriff's offices, and an array of other governmental activities. In other states they have hardly any duties. Many counties are divided into townships—there are nearly 17,000 of them nationwide—which take care of local road maintenance and other small-scale activities. As the population has become concentrated in urban areas, the total number of municipalities—cities, suburbs, and towns—has increased to nearly 20,000. In most states, these municipal governments have assumed many of the responsibilities once performed by counties.

States, counties, and municipalities have also created an extraordinary array of special districts—nearly 35,000 in all. Each special district has responsibility for only one or a few specific governmental functions. Such governments are unique in that they overlap the boundaries of other local governments, sometimes spanning many different municipal jurisdictions. Special districts account for most of the increase in the number of local governments over the last 50 years. Some special districts run schools, others manage parks, and still others administer transportation systems or garbage collection. Even as specific a task as mosquito abatement can be the responsibility of a special district.

LOCAL ELECTIONS Elected officials run most local governments, although heads of special districts are sometimes appointed. In the United States as a whole, the total number of elected local officials approaches half a million people. But despite the large number of local elections, actual rates of citizen participation in them are surprisingly low. If a particularly colorful candidate runs for mayor, or if ethnic or racial issues arise, large numbers of voters can show up at the polls. But usually the local electorate is about half the size of the presidential electorate.[46] The sheer number of elected officeholders often makes local elections confusing. The near invisibility of local elections also helps reduce local participation rates.[47] Newspaper coverage is haphazard. Local governments often hold their elections at times that coincide with neither state nor national elections, which further reduces turnout.[48]

POPULARITY OF LOCAL GOVERNMENT This diverse, half-democratic system might seem irrational and doomed to fail. Yet local governments remain popular. According to survey results, 37 percent of the population trust their local governments more than other levels of government, compared to only 19 percent who trust the federal government the most (see Figure 3.4). Only 8 percent feel their local governments are most wasteful of their tax dollars, compared to 66 percent who feel this way about the federal government.

One explanation for the apparent popularity of local government, despite the low profile of its elections, is the ability of people to "vote with their feet"—that is, to move from one community to another—if they are unhappy. Americans are a mobile people: Each year, over 17 percent move.[49] Every local government official knows that if the government is inefficient or unresponsive, population and property values will drop. As a result, most local governments have good reason to be mindful of their constituents' needs and desires.

The ability to move is important, because it allows people to "shop" for the type of locality in which they wish to live. Some people favor sex education programs and condom distribution in schools; others do not. Some people think refuse collection should be publicly provided; others prefer to recycle their own garbage. Some people think police protection should be intensive; others think an intrusive

FIGURE 3.4

Evaluations of federal, state, and local governments

Why do you think more people trust local government than trust other governments?

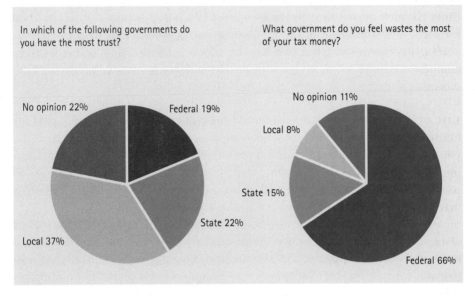

In which of the following governments do you have the most trust?

No opinion 22%
Federal 19%
State 22%
Local 37%

What government do you feel wastes the most of your tax money?

No opinion 11%
Local 8%
State 15%
Federal 66%

SOURCE: Thomas R. Dye, "Federalism: A Return to the Future," *Madison Review* 1 (Fall 1995): 3.

police presence violates civil liberties. People can choose where to live based upon the quality of a school system, the level of taxes, the types of recreation available, or a community's access to airports and highways. By giving people a choice, the diversity of local governments reduces conflict and enhances citizen satisfaction.

THE JOBS RACE   Local governments compete with each other to attract businesses that generate economic activity. Although such competition has benefits, in that it keeps localities sensitive to the needs of their wealth producers, sometimes the competition can get out of hand. With state help, one county in Kentucky outbid its neighbors for a Canadian steel mill employing 400 people. The deal ended up costing the state $350,000 for every job created. Such bidding wars have spread across the country. As one Michigan official put it, "Right now, all we are doing is eating each other's lunch. At some stage we have to start thinking about dinner."[50]

Localities pour substantial resources into attracting and retaining sports teams, a symbol of prestige and a source of citizen entertainment. In 1995, Cleveland Browns owner Art Modell abruptly decided to move his football franchise to Baltimore, which had promised a new stadium and other financial incentives. Baltimore's mayor and Maryland's governor participated in the negotiations for the team and helped announce the move. To honor author Edgar Allen Poe's ties to Baltimore, the team took on the name Ravens. Cleveland officials were incensed. Mayor Michael White likened the move to "a kick in the teeth."[51] Undaunted, the city worked with major financial backers to resurrect the Browns, this time as an expansion team. In 1999, a new incarnation of the team played its first season in a brand-new $283 million stadium. The drama surrounding the Browns is rare, but sports franchise owners commonly threaten to move their teams if they do not receive assistance from the cities where they are located.

EDUCATION POLICY Primary responsibility for education resides at the state and local level. Today, 95 percent of the cost of public education is paid for out of state and local budgets, each contributing approximately half the cost (the exact percentage paid varies widely from one state to another). This decentralization means that taxes for education often go straight to the local community and so are not as unpopular as many other taxes. Nevertheless, elderly voters often defeat bond issues intended to increase school funding.[52]

The public's commitment to local public schools is historically rooted. As early as 1785, Congress set aside the revenue from the sale of one-sixteenth of the land west of the Appalachian Mountains to help pay for "the maintenance of public schools."[53] Support for public schools intensified with the flood of immigrants that arrived in the nineteenth century, because these institutions helped build American democracy. Public schools fostered a common language among people from disparate parts of the world and reinforced a common American identity. They also educated the workforce to operate the new machines that eventually turned the country into an industrial power.

Nevertheless, public schools are not as popular as they once were. From 1973 to 1999, the percentage of Americans expressing "a good deal" or "quite a lot" of confidence in the public schools dropped from 58 percent to 34 percent (see Figure 3.5).[54] Critics argue that public institutions are local monopolies that perform badly, pointing to weak performance by American students in reading, science, math, and geography.[55] Schools serve the interests of the adults teaching in and administering them, they say, not those of the students. Modern educators are more interested in making all children equal than in helping children reach their full potential. They no longer unify American children, instead advancing a multicultural agenda that undermines the nation's individualism.

All of these criticisms have added up to a loss of faith. Public schools have not benefitted from the generous funding increases enjoyed by other government programs. The share of resources dedicated to elementary and secondary education has increased only slightly over the past 25 years.[56] Between 1985 and 1995, spending inched upward from 4.7 percent to 5 percent of the country's gross domestic product (a measure of economic productivity).[57] Teacher salaries, relative to salaries in other occupations, have hardly improved at all.[58]

FIGURE 3.5

Fewer Americans have confidence in public schools

Widespread criticism of public schools seems to have influenced public opinion. What accounts for the decreased confidence in public schools?

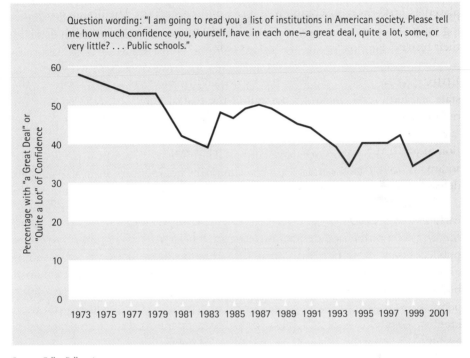

Question wording: "I am going to read you a list of institutions in American society. Please tell me how much confidence you, yourself, have in each one—a great deal, quite a lot, some, or very little? . . . Public schools."

SOURCE: Gallup Poll, various years.

STATE GOVERNMENT

The federal government's design was adapted from constitutions in many states. Thus it is not surprising that the basic organization of most state governments bears a strong resemblance to that found in the U.S. Constitution. Just as Congress has the Senate and the House, legislatures have an upper and a lower chamber in all states except Nebraska (which has only one chamber). All states have multi-tiered court systems roughly comparable to the federal system. And every state has an independently elected governor, the chief executive of the state, whose responsibilities roughly parallel those of the president.

State governments differ in many important ways, however. State legislatures vary greatly in size. Most lower houses have around 100 representatives, but New Hampshire's lower house contains 398 legislators whereas other states have 40. Some state governments hold their elections in even-numbered years, in conjunction with federal races; others do not. In some states, administrative officers such as the secretary of state and the attorney general are elected, whereas in other states the governors appoint these officials.

State policies vary as well. One reason is that different states have different cultures, with varying voter preferences and varying traditions of conducting government. Cultural differences may explain why states vary significantly in how they treat abortion, assisted suicide, or social welfare. Until the federal government clamped down on them, states varied widely in their minimum drinking ages as well. Another reason for policy variation is that states serve as "laboratories of democracy"—places where policy makers can experiment with solutions to social problems. If a solution works at the state level, other states may copy it or the federal government may try to imitate it at the national level.[59]

STATE ELECTIONS Despite differences among states, state elections bear a strong resemblance to national elections. The same two political parties—the Republicans and Democrats—are the dominant competitors in nearly all state elections. A new trend toward competitive politics and divided government has developed in most states (see Figure 3.6). The voters may like this split in power:

FIGURE 3.6

States with divided government

Increasingly, the governor of a state belongs to a party different from the party that controls one or both houses of the state legislature. Is this pattern an accident or the result of conscious decisions by voters?

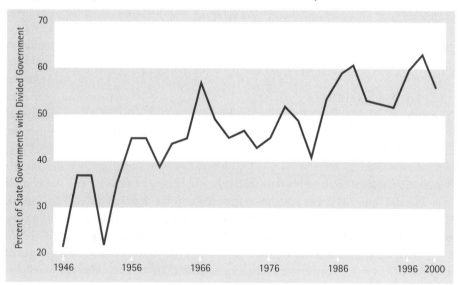

SOURCES: Morris Fiorina, *Divided Government* (Needham Heights, MA: Allyn and Bacon, 1996); *The Book of the States,* Vol. 32: 1998–1999 (Lexington, KY: The Council of State Governments, 1998).

Each party can act as a check on the other, and government does not drift to either political extreme.[60]

VARIATION IN RESPONSIBILITIES The size and range of state responsibilities have grown dramatically in recent decades. As a percentage of GNP, state expenditures increased by over 60 percent between 1962 and 1995. States bear heavy responsibilities for financing education at all levels. They maintain parks, highways, and prisons. They manage welfare and Medicaid programs that serve low-income populations. They give grants to local governments to help pay for police, fire, and other basic governmental services.

The amount spent on governmental services varies from state to state. For one thing, wealthier states spend much more on public services. In 1996, the state and local governments in the ten richest states spent an average of $7,791 per person on public services, whereas in the ten poorest states they spent, on average, less than $4,730 (although, of course, the purchasing power of a dollar may be greater in a poor state).[61] Federal grants have done little, if anything, to reduce fiscal inequalities. Expenditures are also affected by elections. Each party has its favorite type of public service. Democrats in the legislature tend to prefer high expenditures for social services. The more Republicans who win, the higher the expenditure for traditional government services.[62]

As state government has become more complicated, state legislatures have also become more professional. That is, they have lower turnover rates, higher salaries, more staff, and longer sessions. In 1995, California's legislature was among the most modern. Its members remained in session throughout the year, enjoying $72,000 in salary, retirement benefits, and handsome daily expense payments, as well as the services of a full-time staff. Turnover rates were only about 18 percent. By contrast, Wyoming paid its legislators $125 dollars a day and limited its legislative sessions to a maximum of 40 working days in odd-numbered years and 20 days in even-numbered years. It had a turnover rate twice that of California.[63] During the 1990s, voters reacted against the professionalization of state government, as many states limited the terms of legislators, cut their staffs, and reduced their salaries and benefits.

THE RESURGENT GOVERNORS Being governor of a medium- to large-sized state has become one of the best ways to prepare for a presidential run. Four of the last five U.S. presidents have been governors, and former governors have been major candidates in every presidential election campaign since 1976. George W. Bush's popularity as governor of Texas, coupled with the advantages of a well-known family name, quickly catapulted him into the presidential limelight.

Since 1950, many states have strengthened the office of governor by lengthening terms of office, reducing term limitations, and enhancing the governor's veto power over legislation. Most governors now have a **line item veto,** a power that allows them to reject specific parts of a bill. Ten governors have a particularly strong form of the line item veto that allows them to eliminate or cut particular spending items.[64] In part because of their newfound strength, governors became influential players in several national policy debates in the 1980s and 1990s, and they lobbied Congress to increase spending on homeland security in 2001.[65]

STATE ECONOMIC ACTION   In the nineteenth century, state governments played an active role in state economies, granting charters to private corporations and investing their resources to assist in the development of key industries. After the New Deal, the states faded in importance, but many became active again in the 1980s and 1990s—seeking to reinvigorate their business climate through tax incentives, worker-training programs, and active recruitment of out-of-state firms.

States with large economies and significant international exports, such as California and Texas, often arrange trade missions to foreign countries. Some of these missions meet with surprising success. In 1987, California governor George Deukmejian traveled to Japan to promote the sale of California rice. Most experts scoffed at his efforts, arguing that native Japanese rice was central to the country's national pride, culture, and self-sufficiency. "Negotiating for rice is like negotiating for Mt. Fuji," one trade consultant scoffed. Nevertheless, the governor's efforts did not go unrewarded: By the late 1990s, Japan imported $100 million worth of rice from California, accounting for 20 percent of the state's rice crop. The skeptics had to admit they were wrong.[66]

AFTERSHOCK:
THE STATE BUDGET CRUNCH

State budgets collapsed in 2002. Across the country their revenues fell short by a combined total of $40 billion. Governors and state legislatures needed to identify some combination of tax hikes and spending cuts that would balance their budgets—and, as they customarily do, the states dealt with their financial woes by scaling back programs for the young.[67] Indiana's Democratic governor cut a huge sum from the state's school for the blind and also closed campgrounds and pools. Tennessee scuttled a summer program for gifted and talented high school students. Oregon's legislators cut their school budget by $112 million in special session. Illinois planned to cut pre-kindergarten classes for low-income children.

The budget crunch especially hurt America's young adults, because more than half of the cash-strapped states sliced spending for higher education. Many colleges and universities immediately responded by raising tuition. Pennsylvania cut spending by 5 percent, so students at Penn State paid a tuition increase of

8 percent in 2001–2002 and faced another hike (as well as $600 more in fees) for the year that followed. Iowa retreated from paying 77 percent of the budget for its three biggest state universities to paying only 60 percent, with tuition increases making up most of the difference. The University of Washington's budget proposed an astronomical 16 percent tuition increase. Wisconsin, meanwhile, froze undergraduate admissions at its 26 campuses.

Presumably, Americans disliked all this slash-and-burn budgeting by their state governments. A poll by the Public Education Network, as reported in *Education Week,* found that respondents overwhelmingly picked education as their top policy priority when states dealt with budget cuts. So why did states have to slash educational funding? Why did state officials not protect education, as voters seemed to want?

The 9/11 terrorist attacks partly explain the sudden reversal in state finances. States and localities increased their spending on law enforcement, firefighting, disease control, and other policy areas related to terrorism, which squeezed other programs. Meanwhile consumers, jittery about being vulnerable in public places such as malls, turned heavily to Internet shopping, beginning with the 2001 Christmas season: Online sales climbed a third over the previous year's.[68] States cannot collect sales taxes on most online purchases, so the change in buying habits undermined an important source of revenue.

The attacks dampened state revenues indirectly, too, by perpetuating national economic problems. The attacks helped prolong a recession that began near the end of the Clinton presidency, which undercut corporate income taxes and increased worker's compensation payments. An accompanying stock market decline, which 9/11 reinforced and the buildup to war with Iraq exacerbated, reduced taxes from stock manipulations. In short, the terrorist attacks caused serious and sudden budget shortfalls, which struck much too quickly for states to adjust their tax codes.

The federal government did very little to help states. For example, the U.S. Senate rejected a proposal to tax Internet sales, which would have leveled the playing field between online and in-store purchases. National leaders also did very little to help dampen the explosion of health care costs, which allowed Medicaid spending to grow 13.4 percent in a single year! On the other hand, despite increased security needs and a growing deficit, the Bush administration's budget did not cut back in any significant way on domestic spending. It even proposed a 2.8 percent spending increase for education. Of the many culprits responsible for state budget shortfalls, therefore, national leaders seem to share little blame.

And yet, when states began to struggle economically, the governors quickly demanded more federal money, especially in health and transportation. Journalists, meanwhile, put the blame for state shortfalls squarely on the national government, sometimes in bitter terms. "The states are being hit from all sides—and

Washington is doing little to help them," wrote columnist David Broder.[69] "It looks as if Washington has turned its back on America." No one seemed to recognize the peculiarity of this reaction in a nation where voters strongly prefer authority to rest with states.

Attacks especially centered on President Bush, who had pushed tax cuts and signed a federal farm aid bill. This reaction was even more peculiar. For many years, the conventional wisdom for fighting recessions was that Congress should cut taxes and/or increase spending (see Chapter 15)—and this is exactly what Bush's policies enabled the national government to do. If states needed more money, why did they not take advantage of the additional funds that Bush's tax cut allowed to circulate through the economy? Why did they not exploit the additional funding that Congress distributed to agricultural areas with the farm bill? (See Chapter 9.)

Part of the answer is that various laws prevent states from solving their own problems in hard times. State laws give governors and legislators little flexibility in budgeting. Some state constitutions limit certain taxes or make taxes harder to approve. Most states require balanced budgets, whereas the federal government can spend far more money than it actually collects. States often operate under unfunded mandates imposed by the national government. Federal court decisions and federal agency rules constrain the choices that state and local governments can make—forcing them to update facilities for handicapped access or to refurbish prisons, for example. Numerous federal programs, such as Medicaid, require states to provide matching funds if they want to receive grant money. The overall impact of this maze of limitations and requirements is that state budgets cannot respond quickly to new priorities or rapid economic changes, and education is the one expensive policy area flexible enough to absorb the damage.

But that cannot be the whole story. All of those laws and restrictions ultimately do not prevent the states from funding education adequately if they really wish to do so. Not only could voters pressure the federal government to back off their states, they also could demand that their states overcome the difficulties of raising additional funding. But voters are doing just opposite. *Washington Post* staff writer Robert Pierre reports that states are using taxes to make up only a third of their shortfalls and are resorting to cuts to compensate for the rest.[70]

Whatever survey respondents say about their values, the reality is that public opinion in America's new democracy does not allow states to maintain their programs for the young. Two governors who did try to hike taxes significantly (Democrat Mike Easley in North Carolina and Republican Don Sundquist in Tennessee) faced picketing demonstrators pumped up by radio talk shows. It is this reality that forces governors to plead with the federal government for aid and allows journalists to assume that the states cannot tap into the money that tax cuts and federal spending inject directly into their local economies.

CHAPTER SUMMARY

Federalism divides sovereignty between the states and the national government. Its existence in the United States is the result of a compromise between Constitutional Convention delegates who believed that a strong national government was necessary to preserve stability and those who feared that centralized power would lead to tyranny. The compromise that resulted does not define governmental powers clearly. As a result, the nature of American federalism has changed in response to numerous events, including both elections and court decisions.

The election of strong Democratic majorities in the 1960s allowed the national government to put in practice a theory known as cooperative (marble-cake) federalism, which holds that all levels of government can and should work together. The national government used increasing tax revenue to establish extensive grants, which have helped state and local governments overcome their own difficulties raising revenue but have also made them more vulnerable to congressional power. Republicans occasionally try to limit the restrictions placed on states by federal grants, but with only modest success.

Despite the expansion of federal power, state and local governments remain vital components of the federal system. Nearly half of domestic spending by government comes out of state and local budgets, so these governments can play key roles in economic development. Governors are well-known political figures, often positioned to seek the presidency. Although few citizens participate in local elections, local governments are the most popular of all governmental levels, in part because people can "vote with their feet"—that is, they can choose local communities suited to their tastes.

The growing power of the national government in some ways represents a frustration of popular desires, because Americans generally trust their local officials more. They are annoyed by a federal bureaucracy that hands down orders, ignoring local needs. Yet support for the principle of federalism is not strong, and often the national government can find solutions for problems that voters do not allow state and local government to address. Frustration with centralized government should not conceal an important fact: The new balance in favor of national power has made it easier for popular majorities to change American social life rapidly, and voters often compel the national government to do exactly that.

KEY TERMS

block grant, p. 70
categorical grant, p. 68
commerce clause, p. 64
cooperative federalism, p. 68

devolution, p. 73
dual sovereignty, p. 61
elastic clause, p. 65
federalism, p. 60
judicial review, p. 62

line item veto, p. 82
marble-cake federalism, p. 68
McCulloch v. Maryland, p. 62

[handwritten: FDR proposals expanded government power]

necessary and proper clause, p. 64

New Deal, p. 65

NIMBY problem, p. 74 *[handwritten: not in my back yard]*

nullification, p. 62

sovereign immunity, p. 62

spending clause, p. 64 *[handwritten: right to collect revenues for general welfare]*

supremacy clause, p. 64

unfunded mandates, p. 73

War on Poverty, p. 68 *[handwritten: programs designed to help low-income citizens.]*

[handwritten: with ammendment protecting states]

SUGGESTED READINGS

Conlan, Timothy. *From New Federalism to Devolution: Twenty-Five Years of Intergovernmental Reform.* Washington, DC: Brookings, 1998. Excellent analysis of changing federal policy.

Elazar, Daniel. *American Federalism: A View from the States.* New York: Harper & Row, 1984. Discussion of various regional political cultures in the United States.

Elkins, Stanley, and Eric McKitrick. *The Age of Federalism.* New York: Oxford University Press, 1993. Account of the first decades of the federal system under the Constitution.

Fiorina, Morris. *Divided Government.* New York: Macmillan, 1992. Explains why control of many state governments is divided between the Democratic and Republican parties.

Peterson, Paul E. *The Price of Federalism.* Washington, DC: Brookings, 1995. Contrasts the responsibilities of national, state, and local governments.

Riker, William H. *Federalism: Origin, Operation, Significance.* Boston: Little, Brown, 1964. Theoretical treatise on federalism.

ON THE WEB

National League of Cities
National Conference of State Legislatures

National Governor's Association
www.nlc.org
www.ncsl.org
www.nga.org
Several interstate governmental organizations provide information and policy priorities for state and local governments.

Urban Institute
newfederalism.urban.org/
On this Web site, the Urban Institute's "Assessing the New Federalism" project presents information about the impact of programs devolving authority to state and local government.

Federalism
www.min.net/~kala/fed/
Created by a doctoral student at George Washington University, this Web site covers nearly every aspect of federalism, from philosophy to economics to history.

CHANNELS OF INFLUENCE
IN AMERICA'S
NEW DEMOCRACY

AMERICAN POLITICAL CULTURE

A merican schoolchildren who study the Revolutionary War typically learn
about numerous acts of heroism that helped free their nation from English
rule. Textbooks may emphasize the Minutemen's brave stand at Lexington
Green or Paul Revere's midnight ride, two days earlier, to warn Concord that
British troops were coming. Students might probe the details of Thomas
Jefferson's profound statement of freedom, the Declaration of Independence, or
discover that John Hancock boldly signed the final draft in large letters so that
primary responsibility would fall on his shoulders. They may be inspired by
Patrick Henry's boast that he would accept death if he could not have liberty, or
by schoolteacher and spy Nathan Hale's reported final words before execution:
that his main regret was having only one life to give for his new country.

Whatever their symbolic importance, though, small skirmishes, philosophical musings, and eloquent speeches from the gallows do not win a war on their
own. Notably absent from the schoolbook version of the Revolutionary War is
any credible explanation of how a few underpopulated North American colonies
managed to turn back the finest standing army in the world. About the only military advantage mentioned in the conventional story is that colonial forces mimic-
ked Native American warriors by wearing camouflage and hiding behind rocks or
trees during battle—a self-preservation tactic that would not have been enough
to prevent veteran British troops under experienced leadership from achieving
just about any military objective they sought. To lose the war, the "redcoats" had
to lose real battles with real armies. Yet, if one accepts the legends at face value,
all they confronted was ragtag militia of small farmers and their sons, men who
lacked both equipment and experience on the battlefield.[*]

How did colonial forces prevail? An important, and usually neglected, part of
the answer is that the colonists had a lot of help from the outside. The French
Marquis de Lafayette and the German Baron Johann de Kalb were among
Washington's top generals (although de Kalb died after suffering 11 wounds in
hand-to-hand combat).[1] When Washington's army was shivering at Valley Forge
and the American cause seemed lost, another German, Baron Friedrich Wilhelm
von Steuben, arrived on the scene. An expert in military drill, von Steuben transformed the untrained Americans into a disciplined force that could stand against
British regulars.

A young Spanish commander in New Orleans, Don Bernardo de Galvez, organized a force of 1200 men, including 80 free blacks and 160 Indians, and sailed
up the Mississippi, taking British forts as far north as Natchez. Then he captured
Mobile and Pensacola. In all, de Galvez's racially diverse unit took about 3000
British soldiers out of the fight.[2] A Polish general, Casimir Pulaski, known as the
father of the American cavalry, was mortally wounded leading an international

[*]They also occasionally faced women. George Washington recognized Molly Pitcher—the wife of a cannoneer who took
over her husband's post during the Battle of Monmouth after he was wounded—by giving her a warrant as a noncommis-
sioned officer.

unit (Americans, Poles, Irish, French, and Germans) against British fortifications at Savannah.[3] Another Pole, Thaddeus Kosciuszko, designed the defenses at Saratoga, where Americans stopped the British from separating New England from the other colonies. He also designed the fortifications at West Point that Benedict Arnold tried to betray to the enemy.

At the time, it was not unusual for soldiers to serve under a foreign flag. Generally, such troops were mercenaries—professional soldiers who fought for pay. For example, the Hessians whom Washington defeated on his famous midnight raid across the Delaware River were British employees. Soldiers on the American side, though, often were volunteers. High-ranking officers worked without pay until after the war. Kosciuszko donated his military compensation to the emancipation of slaves. These outsiders joined up, at least in part, because of their attraction to the kind of country Americans were creating. Without all of this "foreign aid," Americans might be singing "God Save the Queen" at the start of baseball and football games.

The international contribution to the "American" Revolution is insufficiently appreciated, but it foreshadowed the extent to which migrants would contribute to shaping the United States after the war. Millions of people have followed in the footsteps of those eighteenth-century soldiers, opting to become part of the democratic experiment. As a result, Americans are more diverse in ethnicity and religion than the citizens of other democracies, an unusual example of different peoples coexisting peacefully under the same democratic government.[4]

Carl Friedrich, a professor who immigrated to the United States from Germany, explained in 1935 why so many immigrants find it possible to adopt America as a new homeland: "To be an American is an ideal, while to be a Frenchman is a fact."[5] In other words, the meaning of American citizenship differs from that found in most of the world. Other nations define citizenship by race or ethnicity. Members of a dominant racial or ethnic group automatically enjoy a citizen's rights and privileges, whereas others may not be eligible at all. By contrast, an American may belong to any ethnic group. To be a "good American" refers not to a nationality but to a set of beliefs and values that people of any heritage may choose to embrace.

Yet Friedrich's comment hints at a strange contradiction. For all their diversity, Americans share a political "ideal"—a set of basic assumptions about the nature of a good society—more so than do citizens in other democracies. Certainly the United States has its share of controversy and disagreement, such as the political struggle between "liberals" and "conservatives" or between Democrats and Republicans. But it lacks strong parties on the extreme left or the extreme right, a surprising political uniformity for such a diverse nation.

THE MIXTURE OF *UNIFORMITY* AND *DIVERSITY* FOUND IN THE UNITED STATES may seem puzzling, but this chapter shows that the two traits actually fit together.

[handwritten margin notes: conservatism (cultural issues) e.g. abortion, gay marriage; liberalism]

[handwritten annotation above first paragraph: reciprocity: states must accept other states' licenses, and other contracts]

[handwritten left margin: Will Miller; traditional Southern democrats are much different from Northern democrats]

Historical experiences mold a citizenry's values, and they especially shape the fundamental beliefs about politics and government that some scholars call a nation's **political culture.** In the United States, immigration has been a dominant historical experience. The precise contents of America's political culture (the unity) developed out of the waves of people who have swept over the nation's shores (the variety). Early settlers brought distinct beliefs favoring individualism, freedom, and equality—values that later migrants helped reinforce and refine. The resulting world view forms the context for America's new democracy, the electoral environment that shapes its laws and its policies.

SOCIAL DIVERSITY

John Jay wrote in the second *Federalist Papers* essay that Americans were "one united people; a people descended from the same ancestors, speaking the same language, professing the same religion." Such statements remind us that the *Federalist Papers* were primarily campaign documents, for Americans were not nearly so similar as Jay alleged. His exaggeration of American unity was a political tactic, an appeal to rise above serious divisions that threatened ratification of the Constitution.

Contrary to Jay's claim, the New World was not settled by "one united people." The British were especially numerous, of course, but they were not all of a kind. Puritans settled New England, while Virginians professed loyalty to the Church of England. Lord Baltimore invited his fellow Catholics to Maryland, while Pennsylvania welcomed Quakers. Moreover, after 1700, British immigration came increasingly from Scotland, Wales, and Ireland rather than from England.

Other nationalities settled in the American colonies. The Dutch founded New York—although they called it New Amsterdam—and the Swedes established settlements in what are now Delaware and eastern Pennsylvania. The French were present on the northern and western borders, the Spanish in the south (although the latter never were very numerous). Indentured servants (who made up half the populations of Pennsylvania, New York, and New Jersey) included thousands of Germans, Scandinavians, Belgians, French, and Swiss. And these were only the voluntary immigrants; the involuntary immigrants—slaves— came from Africa.* Historians estimate that, in 1763, only 50 percent of the colonial population was English and nearly 20 percent was African American.[6]

You may react skeptically to this description of colonial variety. After all, a mixed group of Europeans and their slaves does not correspond to the modern-day notion of "diversity"—a term contemporary Americans might reserve for instances when people of color live peacefully among a white majority, when people who follow Christian traditions coexist with those who hold other religious beliefs, or when people with unconventional lifestyles enjoy the same rights

*Native Americans, whose numbers had been decimated by wars and disease, were viewed as separate nations altogether.

and privileges as those who are more traditionally oriented. But diversity is relative to time and place.

Take the case of religious differences. In the sixteenth and seventeenth centuries, Protestants looked upon Catholics with no more understanding (and possibly with less) than that with which a Christian looks upon a Muslim today. Northern European Christians (Catholics, Calvinists, and Lutherans) pillaged, raped, and murdered each other on a monumental scale during the Thirty Years' War (1618–1648); one-third of the population of what is now Germany died during the conflict. Near the end of that period, Puritan dissenters from the Church of England fought Royalist defenders of Church and Crown in the English Civil War (1642–1653). Ultimately, the king and the archbishop both lost their heads. For perhaps the most appalling contradiction of the notion that European Christians were all alike, consider the St. Bartholomew's Day Massacre. French Catholics wielding swords, axes, and crude firearms moved from door to door and farm to farm to kill 30,000 French Calvinists in 1572.

Nor has the United States been immune to bloodshed inspired by religion. The English Civil War echoed faintly in Maryland, where Catholics, Puritans, and Anglicans engaged in a "minor civil war."[7] Illinois Protestants murdered Mormon leader Joseph Smith in 1844 because, among other things, he taught that men could have multiple wives (see the accompanying Election Connection, "The Mormons in Illinois Elections"). Of course, like *Federalist Papers* author John Jay, Americans seeking peace in their communities often have tried to downplay the importance of internal differences. One myth holds that the nation is a Melting Pot, in which many peoples are melted down to form a new metal tougher than any of the ingredients.[8] The national motto, *E Pluribus Unum,* translates into a message of unity: "Out of many, one." But the simple truth is that, relative to the time and the place, the United States has always been especially diverse. And each wave of immigrants has faced uneasiness, fear, or even hatred from the citizens of their adopted country.

A NATION OF IMMIGRANTS THEN

The United States had an open-door immigration policy at the time of its founding, but not everyone was happy about it. One of the most cosmopolitan Americans of the time, Benjamin Franklin, expressed his resentment of Germans in various letters: "Why should *Pennsylvania,* founded by the English, become a colony of Aliens, who will shortly be so numerous as to Germanize us instead of our Anglifying them, and will never adopt our Language or Customs any more than they can acquire our Complexion?" [emphasis in original].[9]

Despite such misgivings, land was plentiful and labor scarce. The more rapidly the territory filled up, the more rapidly economic development would follow, so borders remained open. Immigration gradually increased, until by mid-century immigrants from England, Ireland, and Germany were arriving in numbers as

modern democrats tend to be socially liberal
and economically conservative.
libertarianism; protect individual rights
                    minimal governments
abortion rights, legalized drugs

ELECTION CONNECTION

The Mormons and Illinois Elections

In 1844 Nauvoo was the largest city in Illinois, with just over 20,000 residents (Chicago was second). Founded in the spring of 1839, this Mormon community flourished and grew quickly. But by the winter of 1846 it was almost utterly abandoned—the church leaders and virtually all of the members had left it to trek across Iowa and eventually to the Great Basin valleys of Utah. The story of Nauvoo's collapse illustrates only too clearly how cultural conflict can manifest itself in politics.

"Mormons" acquired their somewhat derisive nickname in New York, where Joseph Smith, the founder and prophet for the church, claimed to have seen God the Father and Jesus Christ. Smith went on to produce a book—*The Book of Mormon*—that he claimed was a record of God's work among some of the native inhabitants of the Americas. Smith called for church

members to gather in "communities of Saints," settlements governed by religious leaders. Perhaps most scandalously, he announced a revelation that some church members should take multiple wives. Smith's unconventional theological views earned him and the Mormons many enemies. Mormons accordingly were driven west to Illinois.

The cultural tensions between Mormons and their more conventional neighbors were exacerbated by politics. As soon as enough Mormons gathered in one place, elections—and therefore representatives and judges—quickly fell under their control. For example, in 1844 the Mormon-backed Democratic candidate for Congress from Illinois's sixth district (which contained Nauvoo) won 76 percent of the vote. Elections for local office were no less one-sided: The 1845 Hancock

A religious martyr
An Illinois mob murders Mormon prophet Joseph Smith in 1844. The diversity represented by his religion's polygamist practices was intolerable, especially in light of growing Mormon electoral influence. When does a community have a right to enforce its morality, to enforce conformity rather than diversity?

(continued)

(continued from previous page)

County sheriff's race saw the "Mormon" candidate receive 2334 votes to his opponent's 750. Some particularly angry anti-Mormons expressed their frustration in an open letter to the governor of Illinois: "When we approach the ballot box we find we are virtually disfranchised; for the Mormons greatly outnumber us."[a]

Smith, who was mayor of Nauvoo, and the Nauvoo city council closed a press that they labeled "libelous." Local citizens were outraged that this voice of dissent had been silenced. The governor of Illinois asked him to stand trial in Carthage (the Hancock County seat) in front of a non-Mormon jury, and against his better judgment Smith went. He never returned. A mob of men with blackened faces broke into the Hancock jail and shot Joseph and his brother Hyrum Smith to death (a third man was shot four times but somehow survived). Five men were eventually tried for inciting the murder, but a jury of non-Mormons found them not guilty.

If the murderers of Joseph Smith had expected to destroy Mormonism, they failed. Yet, they successfully ended Mormon political influence in Illinois, by driving the Mormons west once again. In 1847 the Mormon pioneers settled in the Rocky Mountains, believing that they would be safe once they were far from civilization. Their presence kept Utah from statehood until 1896 (after plural marriages officially ended). Local legend has it that to obtain statehood, the church asked specific members to become Democrats or Republicans (up until that point, Mormon and non-Mormon political parties had dominated state politics while the national parties played little role).

This religious/political conflict probably seems like something deep in America's past.

And it is certainly true that assassination is not an element of modern American politics. But the conflict between Mormons and their local neighbors has not completely disappeared. Nor is it true that Americans have become notably more tolerant of the beliefs that once caused Mormons to be despised. Radical Mormons who ignore their church's rules and take multiple wives today still face violence, as they had 150 years before—only now the show of force is more likely to come from the government than from a mob.

What do you think?

- Are there examples (less extreme, one would hope) of conflict over diversity in your community today? Are there limits to diversity? Are there things that society simply ought not to tolerate?
- Utah state politics tends to be dominated by one party (the Republicans), which is also often identified with the local dominant culture. How would persons unaffiliated with the Morman church react to such a political situation?
- Utah hosted the Winter Olympics in 2002. The secular mayor of Salt Lake City went through a protracted battle to alter liquor laws but was ultimately unsuccessful in altering anything other than advertising restrictions. What—if any—options are available to members of Utah's minority population with respect to changing such laws?
- What would happen if Mormon religious leaders endorsed plural marriage again?

[a]*Quincy Herald* Editorial, July 5, 1844, quoted in Dallin H. Oaks and Marvin S. Hill, *Carthage Conspiracy,* Urbana: University of Illinois Press, 1975) p. 31.

[handwritten annotations in top margin: "religious diversity — protestants — puritans — menonites, quakers / catholics / seculars / unitarians" and "linguistic diversity / English Dutch Spanish / German French / Swedish"]

high as 400,000 per year. Irish immigration became a major political controversy. Some Protestants feared that Catholics would put their allegiance to the Pope above their loyalty to the United States—and might even plot to overthrow the government on his behalf. Cartoonists of the period depicted the Irish as hairy, ape-like people. In the 1854 elections, an anti-Catholic party won 43 seats in the House of Representatives (comparable to 80 seats in today's House).

Immigration increased considerably after the Civil War. The first of an eventual half-million French Canadians crossed the northeastern U.S. border in the 1860s and 1870s, and several million Scandinavians joined a continuing stream of English, Irish, and Germans (see Figure 4.1). Again, by today's standards such groups may seem alike, but their "ethno-cultural" differences often produced severe social conflicts.[10] Indeed, the era's political parties usually squared off over cultural issues. Northern Republicans appealed to native Protestants by calling for the prohibition of alcohol, for "blue laws" to restrict commerce on Sundays, and for regulations that would promote public schools at the expense of parochial or bilingual education. All of these proposals inconvenienced the immigrant Catholic communities, where northern Democrats sank their roots.

The German Lutherans were an important swing group in some midwestern states. They generally voted Republican but swung to the Democrats when

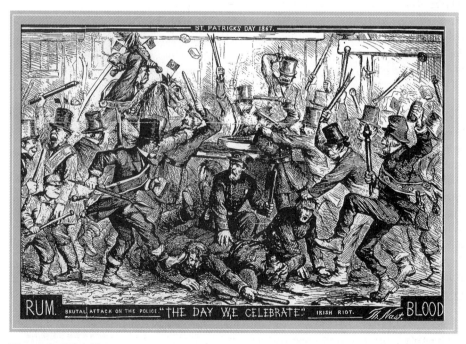

Riot on St. Patrick's Day

Thomas Nast's cartoon of a clash between police and Irish revelers clearly reveals his sympathies. He portrays the Irish as violent, ape-like brutes. Which groups receive unflattering portrayals in popular entertainment today?

FIGURE 4.1

Timeline: Immigration to the United States

The quantity and origin of immigration to the United States has changed sharply over time. Why might interest in emigrating to the United States rise and fall?

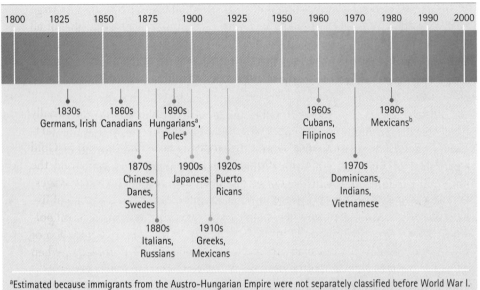

Old Immigration   New Immigration

| 1800 | 1825 | 1850 | 1875 | 1900 | 1925 | 1950 | 1960 | 1970 | 1980 | 1990 | 2000 |

1830s   1860s   1890s
Germans, Irish   Canadians   Hungarians[a],
Poles[a]

1870s   1900s   1920s
Chinese,   Japanese   Puerto
Danes,   Ricans
Swedes

1880s   1910s
Italians,   Greeks,
Russians   Mexicans

1960s   1980s
Cubans,   Mexicans[b]
Filipinos

1970s
Dominicans,
Indians,
Vietnamese

[a]Estimated because immigrants from the Austro-Hungarian Empire were not separately classified before World War I.
[b]Mexican immigration first reached 100,000 in the 1910s. However, in terms of new immigration, Mexican immigration peaked in the 1980s with over 1.65 million immigrants to the United States.

NOTE: During these decades, immigration by the indicated nationality group first reached 100,000.

SOURCES: Stephanie Bernado, *The Ethnic Almanac* (Garden City, NY: Doubleday, 1981), pp. 22–140; U.S. Immigration and Naturalization Service (www.ins.gov).

conservative Protestants within the Republican party attempted to legislate on cultural issues. In Wisconsin, for example, the Republicans lost only two statewide elections between 1858 and 1890. One came after the party raised liquor license fees, the second after it passed a measure requiring English-language instruction in the schools. According to Richard Wayman, "Throughout much of Eastern Wisconsin, German immigrants jealously guarded what they regarded as their right to preserve many of the customs they brought with them from Europe."[11]

IMMIGRATION AND RACIAL FEARS The United States attracted millions of people from southern and eastern Europe beginning in the 1880s, an influx that encouraged anti-immigrant sentiments. Some of the criticisms echoed those heard in the past: Immigrants differed from "real Americans" because they spoke

[handwritten margin notes: "Ethnic Diversity Swedes English Spanish Dutch French"; "founding fathers were primarily English but wanted America to be independent of these countries"]

foreign tongues and worshiped in alien churches. By this time, though, the rhetoric shifted focus to emphasize genetic characteristics. "Real Americans" perceived Italians, Greeks, and other immigrants of the period to be people of color who threatened their nation's racial purity.[12]

Such sentiments were by no means limited to a small fringe of the population. A best-selling book by Madison Grant of the American Museum of Natural History, published in 1916, warned that the United States was receiving "a large and increasing number of the weak, the broken, and the mentally crippled of all races drawn from the lowest stratum of the Mediterranean basin and the Balkans, together with hordes of the wretched, submerged populations of the Polish ghettoes."[13] Ethnic stereotypes even appeared within official government documents.[14]

The growing visibility of non-European peoples added urgency to racially charged political appeals. Asians began to immigrate on a significant scale—starting with the Chinese, thousands of whom participated in the California Gold Rush of 1849.[*] Later, more than 100,000 Chinese laborers helped build the transcontinental railroads. These "coolies" worked dangerous jobs for low wages, provoking complaints that they were undermining the American standard of living.[15] African Americans, meanwhile, began to play an active role in electoral politics after the Civil War, especially in the U.S. South, where a large population of former slaves could vote but many former rebels could not.[16] Employers, when challenged by their workers, often used black laborers to break strikes.

[handwritten margin note: "1418?"] World War I strengthened anti-immigrant sentiments, especially after revolutionaries installed a communist government in Russia. The world seemed a frightening and unstable place, leading many Americans to question the wisdom of admitting immigrants who might subscribe to the same dangerous ideas that were tearing Europe apart. An anti-communist hysteria, the first "Red Scare," swept the United States. Religious bigotry also surged: Anti-Catholic and anti-Jewish sentiments spawned a second Ku Klux Klan in the 1920s that counted 25 to 30 percent of the adult male Protestant population in its membership.[17]

OUTLAWING DIVERSITY   As public opinion turned against people of other races and ethnic groups, policy quickly followed. It initially focused on non-Europeans. To combat the "Yellow Peril," Congress passed the Chinese Exclusion Act of 1882, a ban on Asian immigration that was later expanded to include the Japanese and other nationalities. Around the same time, many state governments began depriving African Americans of fundamental social and political rights, a process completed by the turn of the century (see Chapter 14).

[handwritten margin note: "civil war 1860?"]

[*]Only two-thirds of the forty-niners were Americans, and only two-thirds of the Americans were white. Large numbers of Cherokee Indians and African Americans panned for gold. On the multicultural character of California after it was annexed to the United States, see Ronald Takaki, *A Different Mirror* (Boston, MA: Little, Brown, 1993), Ch. 8.

The backlash eventually spread. An immigration law adopted in 1917 required a literacy test that favored English speakers.[18] Law enforcement officials cracked down on immigrant communities during the Red Scare, perceiving them as incubators for radical politics. A series of laws passed in the 1920s restricted immigration and gave explicit preference to those from northern and western Europe.[19] By 1930, the era of the open door had ended.*

Before the United States closed its doors, more than 35 million people had left hearth and home to "look for America." These newcomers and their children formed a large component of population growth in the United States, transforming a country of 10 million inhabitants in 1820 into one of more than 100 million by 1920. The change did not come smoothly, however. Along the way, native-born citizens exhibited strong and tenacious doubts about tolerating so many immigrants from countries and cultures so different from theirs.

Contemporary Americans may be dismayed by the ignorance and hatred that, historically, often greeted outsiders. But anti-immigrant anxieties reflected a truth easy to forget today, which is that no one really knew whether a democratic government could manage the conflicts spawned by a rapid influx of foreigners. Most of the world's multiethnic governments have been either short-lived (like Yugoslavia) or authoritarian (like the Austro-Hungarian and Soviet empires). For much of its history, by contrast, the United States has coped successfully with the risk of maintaining open political institutions while absorbing a population of unprecedented variety. Diversity is a critical, but often overlooked, component of America's democratic experiment.

A NATION OF IMMIGRANTS NOW

The Great Depression distracted Americans from their concern with ethno-cultural politics. Several bigoted radio personalities commanded a large audience during that period of economic troubles, and discrimination against Catholics and Jews continued into the 1930s. But tensions were dying down. The cumulative effects of economic troubles, World War II, revulsion against the Holocaust, the Cold War, and generational change led to a reduction in discrimination.

As soon as public policy opened American borders again, however, anti-immigration sentiment revived, indicating that the quiet period was only a brief interlude between the cultural conflict of yesterday and that of today. The Immigration Act of 1965 permitted the largest surge of foreigners since the 1890s. The 1965 legislation abandoned the national-quotas system, which had favored northern Europeans. As a result, immigration from Latin America and

---

*Mexicans continued to enter the southwestern states to work in American agriculture (joining those who had been incorporated when the United States took the territory from Mexico), and after World War II, Puerto Ricans emigrated in significant numbers to New York City.

[handwritten margin notes: Fears crime / anti-catholicism / lack of assimilation / take jobs / over population / fear of color / Chinese exclusion Act / Jim Crow laws and segregation]

the West Indies increased rapidly. In addition, hundreds of thousands of new immigrants from Vietnam, Korea, Cambodia, India, Iran, the Philippines, and other countries became the first numerically significant Asian groups since the Japanese (see Figure 4.1).

In the 1980s the absolute number of immigrants—about 9 million—was higher than in any previous decade, though lower as a proportion of the population than it had been at the turn of the century. Three million came from Mexico, Central America, and the Caribbean, and nearly as many from Asia. Nearly half a million came from South America and almost 200,000 from Africa. These figures include only legal immigrants; millions of people now live in the United States illegally.[20]

As a result of this newest wave of immigration, by 1995 the proportion of the population of European origin had dropped to about three-quarters, and it is projected to fall to less than two-thirds in the next two decades. Whites of European origin have lost their majority status in California, as well as in many large cities. This dramatic shift in the U.S. population has fueled political conflicts over immigration that echo those from previous centuries.

EVALUATING THE NEW IMMIGRATION

Immigration is once again a political issue. In 1994, California voters overwhelmingly passed Proposition 187, an initiative that denied state services to illegal immigrants and their children. Support for the measure was high even in counties where very few immigrants lived.[21] And from 1995 to 1996, the question of eligibility for governmental services such as welfare was a matter of intense controversy at the national level. Much of this contemporary debate over immigration would sound familiar to Americans of the early 1900s. Does providing services to immigrants impose a burden on native citizens? Do immigrants take jobs from native workers and drive native shopkeepers out of business?

Such fears are not new, but that does not mean they are totally groundless. There are four tangible reasons why immigration today differs from that encountered in the past. First, in contrast to earlier periods in American history, immigrants are not entering an economy hungry for unskilled labor. There is no exploding railroad industry to absorb today's immigrants as it absorbed the Irish and the Chinese. There is no expanding steel industry sending representatives to Eastern Europe to recruit workers. The American economy is moving away from manufacturing to a globally integrated service and information economy. Many Americans, especially those who lack skills, face severe difficulties in the transition. Research indicates that competition from immigrants undercuts the wages of low-skilled Americans who are already struggling to make ends meet.[22]

Second, levels of government do not share the burdens and benefits of immigration equally.[23] Studies show that immigrants strengthen the national economy.

They pay nearly as much in taxes as they consume in government services. But most of the taxes paid by immigrants are federal income and social security taxes. This revenue does not go directly to the states and cities responsible for providing services to new migrants. Yet during the 1980s, more than 75 percent of new immigrants went to six states: California, New York, Texas, Florida, New Jersey, and Illinois. This disparity focuses the costs of immigration much more narrowly than the benefits. Heavy immigration forces local and state governments to cut services, raise taxes, and beg for money from higher levels of government—options that elected officials naturally view as unpleasant.

Third, both the United States and the world face a looming environmental crisis tied to an expanding population. The fertilizers and pesticides used to grow food eventually contaminate water used for drinking or for recreation. Chemicals needed to produce consumer goods, and fuels used to transport both people and products, all cause health problems. Trees are cut down and unpopulated areas devastated to make room for housing developments and roads. Isolated locales once treasured for vacations, for outdoor sports, or just for their natural beauty may not be so isolated any more. Providing utilities like energy and water sometimes strains communities, as does disposing of garbage and other wastes.

All of these concerns worsen as the population increases, and immigrants account for half of the country's current population growth. Obviously, many sorts of policies can address the declining quality of life associated with over-crowding, and shifts in population from one country to another may not worsen global problems. But concern with the environment does prompt many to question the wisdom of admitting even more people from other countries.[24]

Finally, whereas late-nineteenth-century law barred a person "likely to become a public charge," the immigration law adopted in 1965 gives preference to those with relatives already in the country. Two-thirds of all immigrants today are relatives of those already present. In consequence, a higher proportion of dependent persons—especially older people—have been admitted in recent years than in previous eras.[25] Current U.S. immigration policy admits fewer tax-payers and more people in need of services than the law that gave first preference to productive workers. Even if immigrants as a group pay as much in taxes as they consume in services, many American taxpayers ask why they should admit *anyone* likely to be a drain on resources.

These are all material explanations for opposition to immigration. Over and above economic costs, however, many opponents of immigration regard it as a threat to America's political culture. They believe that people who speak different languages, believe in different religions, and practice different customs could threaten American unity and possibly American safety. They fear a divided society, in which groups retain their own narrow identities and fight each other for power and influence. They urge the United States to close the door before too much *pluribus* destroys the *unum.*[26] To understand these fears, however, we need to know precisely what these Americans seek to defend.

PHILOSOPHICAL UNITY

From the French visitor Alexis de Tocqueville in the 1830s to the Swede Gunnar Myrdal in the 1940s, visitors have claimed that Americans agree on a common core of values defining what it is to be American. These beliefs usually are described as "individualist," and the political culture they produce is generally referred to as a "liberal" one.[27]

Classical liberalism emerged in Europe after medieval thought disintegrated in the religious wars of the seventeenth century. Whereas earlier philosophies viewed human nature as sinful, requiring authority to keep it in check, liberalism empowered the individual. Authority does not come from God, according to liberal thinkers like Locke and Rousseau, but instead from a "social contract" conferring privileges and duties on everyone, both rulers and ruled (see Chapter 2).

The social contract preserves individual rights such as life, liberty, and property that are more fundamental than the hereditary privilege of the nobility or the religious privilege of the clergy. Having certain inviolable rights is necessary because liberal thinkers view altruistic sentiments—that is, the desire to "do good"—as too weak to provide a reliable basis for government. Human beings are willing to oppress (or at least mistreat) others if allowed, so rights are a necessary protection.[28]

Instead of viewing individuals as the product of political society, a view that goes back to the ancient Greeks, liberalism makes society the product of individuals. You might wonder what difference this makes. Consider Democratic President John F. Kennedy's famous exhortation: "Ask not what your country can do for you; ask what you can do for your country." Classical liberals shudder at these words. If society is nothing more than a collection of individuals, then any sacrifice demanded for the "greater good" is simply something taken away from one person for the benefit of another.[29]

What kind of political system follows from such a philosophy? A small government, one that treats everyone equally under the law and is limited by individual rights—rights to the exercise of religion, to free expression, and to their own property. Governments in such a system are merely instrumental, not ends or values in themselves. The political system exists to protect and serve individuals, and it may be retained or jettisoned depending on how well it meets these obligations.

The preceding words should have a familiar ring, for the ideas are the basis of America's political system. Indeed, the second paragraph of the Declaration of

Independence (see the Appendix at the back of this book) is little more than a summary of liberal ideals: political equality, natural rights, and instrumental government. The Constitution and its Bill of Rights form an elaborate statement of the limits under which government should operate. For this reason, the American constitutional tradition often is called a liberal tradition.

Writers sometimes exaggerate America's level of philosophical agreement. A competing tradition, often called **civic republicanism,** existed at the time of the Revolution.[30] Civic republicanism placed more emphasis on virtue and the public good, less emphasis on individual freedom. Over time it lost ground to liberalism, but the tradition certainly has not disappeared—as indicated by the positive response to President Kennedy's message of self-denial.[31] Modern advocates use the label **communitarianism,** which emphasizes their belief that freedom comes not from individuals making the best choices for themselves but rather, from community members working together to make decisions for everyone.[32] *like in Asian cultures...*

Other critics point out that the ideals exalted in the liberal tradition often did not extend very far in practice.[33] African Americans did not enjoy equal rights until a century after the Civil War. Full rights and privileges did not extend to women until even later, and the rights of other minority groups, such as homosexuals, remain matters of political controversy today. Nevertheless, there is plenty of evidence that Americans agree to certain basic liberal principles that set them apart from the citizens of other democracies.

AMERICAN INDIVIDUALISM

Perhaps the most striking difference between Americans and people elsewhere lies in the emphasis Americans place on individual responsibility. Figure 4.2 reports the results of a survey conducted in 14 democracies that asked respondents whether they "completely agree" that "It is the responsibility of the state ('government' in the United States) to take care of very poor people who can't take care of themselves." Note that less than a quarter of the American respondents opted for governmental responsibility, a proportion that is only half as large as that in the next closest country (Germany).

Another survey of six long-established Western democracies found Americans to be similarly uniform in their belief that individuals are responsible for their own welfare. Less than a quarter of Americans supported a government-guaranteed income, disagreeing with majorities of Germans, British, Italians, and Dutch (see Figure 4.3). Fewer than one in three Americans agreed with the notion that government should reduce income inequality. And little more than one-third of Americans, compared to an average of two-thirds in the four European democracies, believed that the government should guarantee a decent standard of living for the unemployed. Interestingly, Australia seems to occupy a middle position between the individual responsibility favored by Americans and

cause we're all stupid~

Since the 1970's our birthrate has been below the replacement rate... birth rate is usually a function of the population + standard of living... & death rate so now it is low because death rate has also been low

FIGURE 4.2

Americans emphasize individual responsibility much more than people elsewhere

Why would an immigrant society be more likely to embrace self-sufficiency?

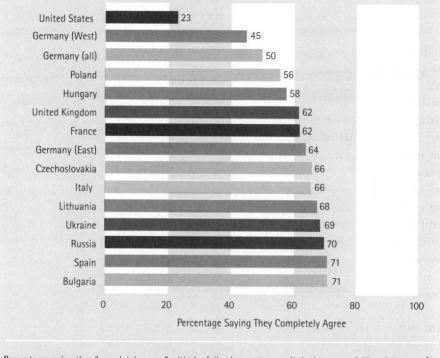

Country	Percentage Saying They Completely Agree
United States	23
Germany (West)	45
Germany (all)	50
Poland	56
Hungary	58
United Kingdom	62
France	62
Germany (East)	64
Czechoslovakia	66
Italy	66
Lithuania	68
Ukraine	69
Russia	70
Spain	71
Bulgaria	71

Percentage saying they "completely agree" with the following statement: "It is the responsibility of the state [in the United States, "the government"] to take care of very poor people who can't take care of themselves."

SOURCE: Everett Carll Ladd, *The American Ideology* (Storrs, CT: The Roper Center, 1994), p. 79.

the governmental responsibility favored by Europeans. Australia, too, is a society of immigrants.

The American preference for individual responsibility is not simple stinginess. Rather, Americans are suspicious of government (see Chapter 1). They fear its power and doubt its competence. In Samuel Huntington's view, "the distinctive aspect of the American creed is its anti-government character."[34] People skeptical of government naturally have qualms about letting the state take their money and hand it out to others. At the same time, Americans believe that individual responsibility works. They consider hard work the key to success, whereas people elsewhere are less likely to put faith in personal effort. As a consequence, an overwhelming majority of Americans are optimistic about getting ahead—again at a level approached only by Australians (see Figure 4.4).

FIGURE 4.3

Americans are far less supportive of policies to reduce inequality than people elsewhere

Why is Australia closer to the United States in this regard than European nations are?

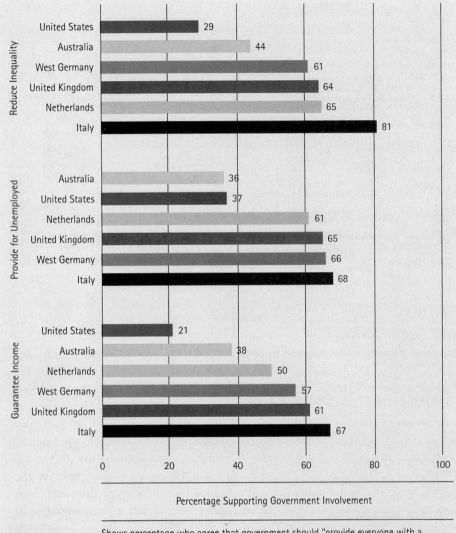

Percentage Supporting Government Involvement

Shows percentage who agree that government should "provide everyone with a guaranteed basic income," "reduce the differences in income between people with high incomes and those with low incomes," and "provide a decent standard of living for the unemployed."

SOURCE: Ladd, *The American Ideology,* p. 75.

FIGURE 4.4

Americans are much more optimistic the benefits of hard work

Are Americans more optimistic because of their political beliefs or because they genuinely have more opportunity to improve their conditions?

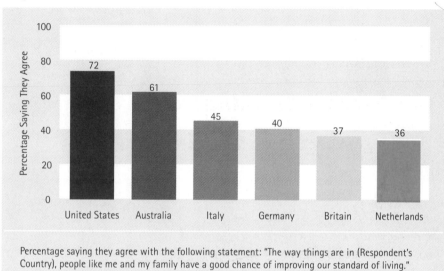

Percentage saying they agree with the following statement: "The way things are in (Respondent's Country), people like me and my family have a good chance of improving our standard of living."

SOURCE: Ladd, *The American Ideology*, p. 75.

One would think that those at the bottom of the economic ladder would be far less optimistic than those at the top. In fact, the American belief in individual achievement bears little relation to personal success. Even the poorest Americans reject a government-guaranteed income, and only the very poorest feel that the government should reduce income differences. Americans at all income levels believe in the importance of hard work.[35] Poor Americans are as likely as others to embrace the "work ethic" and as likely to take personal responsibility for their condition.[36] The poor dislike the progressive income tax almost as much as the rich.[37]

Perhaps the most powerful illustration of American individualism lies in the attitudes of minorities. African Americans and Hispanics clearly share in the American Dream less often than white Anglos do. On average they earn less, work in less prestigious occupations, and suffer discrimination in many forms. It comes as no surprise, then, that they are a bit less likely than whites to embrace the American Dream. But it does come as a surprise that they embrace it as often as they do. Black and Hispanic Americans are quite similar to white Anglos (see Figure 4.5). In sum, even those who face an extra burden in the American social order still support its basic premises.[38]

FIGURE 4.5

Even American minorities share the individualistic values of the larger society

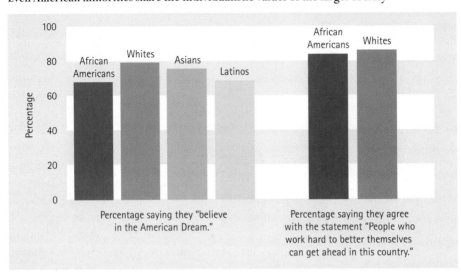

SOURCE: Adapted from data reported in "People, Opinions and Polls: An American Dilemma (Part II)," *The Public Perspective* (February/March 1996): 19–35.

ALL PEOPLE, CREATED EQUAL

Liberal philosophers once assumed that liberty and equality would reinforce each other, and they typically ranked equality right after liberty in their list of cherished values. They assumed that a free society would allow lots of people to generate wealth, therefore equalizing conditions compared to a society in which some of the people labored in chains. At the same time, a wide and nearly equal dispersion of wealth would spread political influence across the society, creating an independent population able to resist encroachments on their freedoms.

Early in American history, liberty and equality probably did go together. Citizens in the democratic United States enjoyed both more liberty and more equality than did their contemporaries in nations run by kings and queens. However, French observer Alexis de Tocqueville foresaw that a day was coming when Americans would have to choose between their two central values, and he was not optimistic that freedom could survive a clash with the leveling spirit. "Democratic peoples," he explained, "want equality in freedom, and if they cannot have that, they still want equality in slavery."[39]

The two ideals clashed after the Civil War, as a result of the Industrial Revolution. Technological developments raised the barriers to economic competition; the start-up capital for a factory greatly exceeded the resources needed to set up shop as a small-town craftsman. Changes in finance, such as the development of stock markets and large-scale banking, allowed greater concentrations of wealth. Farming and trade relied on government-supported railroads and storage facilities, usually run by corporations that spanned many communities and could use their clout to overpower independent enterprises. Under such conditions, the concepts of liberty and equality diverged. The only way to stop ambitious people from working to collect profit was to regulate their property—inhibiting their ability to compete, limiting their production, or taking away their earnings. Conversely, maintaining liberty required accepting inequality after the Industrial Revolution, a dilemma that only increased with time.

Thus far, however, Tocqueville's worst anxieties about the frailty of liberty seem to have been unwarranted. The United States has maintained support for most freedoms, even when faced with growing financial disparities, because American political culture mandates only a certain kind of equality: equal treatment before the law. One person has the same rights as another, regardless of heredity, religious faith, or the whims of public officials. By contrast, Americans are not committed to economic equality, believing that intelligence and hard work should bring special rewards. They celebrate entrepreneurs who become rich by providing consumers with products or services they want to buy, seemingly agreeing with Madison that "diversity in the faculties of men" inevitably produces inequalities.[40]

Today it is customary to talk about this distinction in terms of the difference between "equality of opportunity" and "equality of results." Americans strongly support equality of opportunity. Everyone should have a fair chance to *pursue* happiness or success. No one has a right to *attain* those things, though, without earning them. Government need not, and maybe should not, use its power to ensure equality of results: similar jobs, similar houses, similar clothes, similar bank accounts. The dilemma between liberty and equality therefore is a false one—public policy need not crack down on personal ambitions to produce the brand of fairness that Americans demand.

However, the global economy continues to challenge how Americans think about equality. Large-scale economic activity obscures whether someone's wealth has resulted from personal accomplishments or from unequal opportunities. Corporations may succeed because of their political pull rather than because of their successful competition in the marketplace. Appointment to plum corporate offices can open up a world of vast financial resources, complete with tax-shielded expense accounts and exorbitant compensation—opportunities that few Americans share. Nor is it clear that rising through the corporate ranks results from a process that rewards intelligence or hard work, the merits that have justified inequalities in the past. Some critics charge, for example, that executives revolve in and out of their well-paid positions on the basis of an irrational celebrity system that corporate boards do not scrutinize adequately. Hotshot executives receive generous compensation packages for joining companies that they did not create, to manage the sales of products whose development they did not oversee—and can rely on generous "severance" packages even if the companies end up performing badly.

Discomfort with the ostentatious display of wealth—including gas-guzzling vehicles, aristocratic lifestyles, and giant homes of oriental splendor—grew during the last decade. A 2001 survey by Pew Charitable Trusts found that an increasing number of Americans considered the country "divided into 'haves' and 'have-nots.'"[41] But these attitudes crystallized into an issue on the political agenda after scandals erupted in 2002. Right in the middle of a devastating stock market slide, the American public learned of a whole series of corporate officers who banked millions by selling overvalued stock as their companies secretly approached financial ruin.

Of course, the officers sometimes faced charges of fraud or insider trading (no one expects criminal activity to represent an "equal opportunity"). But particular traits of the new economy contributed to these abuses and therefore fell under critical scrutiny. For example, the same banking and investment companies that provided financing to corporations were the ones advising regular Americans to invest in the companies, a (legally permitted) conflict of interest. Corporations hired the accounting firms that audited their books, another conflict of interest that discouraged critical financial reports. Large portions of executive compensation came in the form of stock options, which need not appear in corporate accounts. Owning these options encourages corporate leaders to puff up the apparent success of their companies as a way of inflating stock prices.[42]

Not all of the newsworthy corporate excesses grew out of illegal or even unethical practices. Famed CEO Jack Welch left General Electric after a 21-year tenure, during which the company expanded from an appliance manufacturer to a $480 billion conglomerate, and he left GE on good terms. Yet his retirement compensation package, when disclosed during divorce proceedings, still caused quite a stir: a furnished Manhattan apartment, food and wine, a cook and wait-staff, a chauffeured car, travel and entertainment, as well as an office with administrative support.[43] The backlash against such corporate generosity may represent a change in American attitudes.

Great inequalities now exist in the United States, a situation that has not improved in six decades and in fact has worsened since the early 1970s.[44] Naturally, some Americans have become disillusioned with a political system that can tolerate such inequalities. It is not clear, though, whether public uproar will strengthen the future appeal of policies that equalize economic results. Reform movements typically focus on curbing the worst abuses of corporate power; they seldom attack the foundations of the economic system. So far, the financial scandals of 2002 have not produced a reform effort serious enough to threaten the current style of doing business.

TABLE 4.1

ALL POLICIES ARE NOT CREATED EQUAL

Americans share a basic belief in the importance of equality, but their support for using policy to equalize social resources varies sharply depending on the particular policy area. Are the policies with strong support for equalization distinct from those with lukewarm support?

QUESTION: Do you believe it is the responsibility or isn't the responsibility of the federal government to make sure minorities have equality with whites in each of the following areas, even if it means you will have to pay more in taxes?

POLICY AREA	PERCENTAGE SAYING YES	NUMBER OF RESPONDENTS
Courts/police	82.1%	983
Schools	79.0	983
Health care	74.8	981
Jobs	54.6	953
Housing	50.1	954
Income	46.2	949

SOURCE: Washington Post/Kaiser Family Foundation/Harvard Survey Project 1995 Race Poll. One subsample received the top three questions, another received the bottom three, but assignment was random so the percentages are comparable.

In sum, current events only underscore that Americans consider equality of opportunity sufficient and do not demand equality of results. Success is up to the individual. This belief shows up in government policy. The United States spends a smaller proportion of its national income on social welfare than most other democracies do. But the United States historically has spent a larger proportion of its national income on education than other democracies have. Education is a means by which individuals improve their skills and make themselves useful, a policy that enhances opportunity—so it is one of the few areas of society that Americans want government to equalize (see Table 4.1).

IDEOLOGY, AMERICAN STYLE

Readers whose primary knowledge of American government comes from observing current events may wonder how scholars can seriously propose that a philosophical unity governs national politics. News coverage constantly echoes with energetic, and sometimes vicious, attacks fired back and forth among political figures subscribing to different "ideologies." The clashes sometimes rise beyond personal squabbles, instead involving clear debates over the proper direction of government. These debates sometimes unite most members of one major political party against the other. If this is the sound of consensus, one reasonably might ask, what would real conflict sound like? How can we dismiss ideological disagreements that seem so real and so fundamental to the people participating in them?

Answering this challenge requires an understanding of political ideologies and how they operate. An **ideology** is the basic lens through which someone observes and evaluates government, the collection of orientations a person uses to impose order on a complicated political world. When a new conflict intrudes on the political agenda, citizens need some way to determine where they stand on the issue, and their individual ideologies can provide the shortcuts they needed to formulate a quick opinion. Furthermore, to the extent that a candidate for office can convey his or her ideology, it aids voters in predicting how the candidate will react to unanticipated issues that do not spring up until after the election.

This is all quite abstract, but usually it works in a fairly straightforward way. Consider one example of an ideology: a person's basic perspective on the meaning of human conception. Some people believe that human life begins when an egg becomes fertilized, others that it occurs at some later stage of fetal development. This ideological difference will divide people on a host of political issues. The obvious one is abortion, because someone who considers a fertilized egg to be human life will find the procedure more objectionable than someone who does not. But these ideologies also speak to a host of other issues related to the origin of human life, such as cloning, stem-cell research, surrogate parenting, and even prenatal care. Voters can evaluate that whole gamut of specific issues in terms of their ideology toward human life, and they may be able to anticipate a candidate's positions if they know whether the politician is pro-life or pro-choice.

Ideologies are not equally encompassing, however. Political philosopher Karl Mannheim distinguishes an ideology according to how fundamentally it shapes one's political thinking.[45] Some ideologies are "particular," a way of thinking about politics that grows out of a specific set of interests or personal preferences. Other ideologies are "total," in that they refer to the very basis of one's existence, the entire mental apparatus that determines how someone relates to the world. The liberal ideology that unites Americans is the all-embracing, total sort of ideology. It grew out of the religious, economic, and scientific changes that characterized the Enlightenment period of European thought, which roughly corresponded to the eighteenth century.

Liberals differed fundamentally from people who believed in rule by kings (that is, monarchists). Economically, liberals tended to emerge from the capitalist economy developing at the time, so they stood out for their belief in the importance of property rights, their faith in contracts, and their sense that commercial relations should take place with limited government interference. In terms of religion, liberals emphasized the dignity of the individual human soul and the importance of observing nature's rules as a means of getting closer to religious truth. They thought that education and spiritual development shaped a person's character, downplaying the significance of heredity. The Enlightenment period was also a time of great mathematical and scientific advances, which encouraged people's faith in logic and careful observation—as well as their sense that individuals could work together, without direct coordination by a higher governmental authority, to produce a vibrant society. These impulses combined into a comprehensive world view, one that early settlers to the American colonies usually brought with them.

The relatively distinct perspective that united philosophical liberals allowed Thomas Jefferson's Declaration of Independence to call it "self-evident" that all individuals are created equal and enjoy unalienable rights. Such ideas were hardly evident to King George III or his ministers during the war for independence. Nor are they necessarily obvious to some of the modern rivals to liberal political theory, such as Marxists (who view religion, science, and politics as subordinate to economic relations) or theocrats (who believe truth comes primarily through religious leaders with a close connection to a higher power). For the most part, though, liberal ideals *are* taken for granted by the bulk of Americans today, which is why the United States lacks strong communist or religious political parties in the European mold. Political debate in the United States operates largely within the bounds of liberal philosophy, with all sides, however strident, endorsing their policies by invoking similar ideas of freedom, fairness, and individuality.

Some Americans do endorse conflicting "liberal" or "conservative" or "libertarian" political ideologies. But these are examples of Mannheim's "particular" ideologies, growing out of specific interests and preferences. They usually revolve around the best method for achieving social goals, rather than around what the goals ought to be. **Libertarianism** most closely resembles the beliefs of liberal political philosophy, in that it gives individualism a central place in political life and permits only minimal use of government power. But liberals and conservatives do not stray far from this perspective. They both have areas of life that they think government ought to leave alone—and in the areas for which they do promote heightened government activism, their reasons tend to be stated in terms of promoting freedom, equality, or individual rights more actively.

Any generalization about the political system usually has exceptions, but it is possible to describe how modern liberals and conservatives differ (see Table 4.2). American **liberalism** supports an active government in the economic sphere but permits a high degree of autonomy when citizens make moral choices. Liberals endorse using political institutions to address widespread social inequalities, such as those associated with race or gender, but not to promote other forms of good behavior. They prefer more international cooperation to solve world problems and look to foreign policy as a way of promoting freedom and equality worldwide.

Conservatism, meanwhile, endorses less government regulation of economic matters but favors public policies that will shape the nation's culture in a moral direction rather than an amoral one. Conservatives shy away from allowing government to intrude on people's private spheres of life—such as families,

TABLE 4.2

TYPICAL ISSUE PREFERENCES BY IDEOLOGY

No ideological grouping is completely uniform, but it is possible to offer a profile of the issue positions typically held by a proponent of each political ideology. Are three ideologies adequate for capturing the issue preferences of most American voters?

ISSUE	CLASSICAL LIBERAL (LIBERTARIAN)	MODERN LIBERAL	MODERN CONSERVATIVE
Strong Federal Government	Against	For	Against
Higher Taxes, More Services	Against	For	Against
Aggressively Equalizing Wealth	Against	For	Against
Increasing Business Regulations	Against	For	Against
Affirmative Action	Against	For	Against
Gun Control	Against	For	Against
Generous Foreign Aid Payments	Against	For	Against
Legislation to Promote Morality	Against	Against	For
Incentives for Traditional Family Structures	Against	Against	For
Weakening Rights of the Accused	Against	Against	For
Strong, Aggressive Military	Against	Against	For
Religion in Public Schools	Against	Against	For
Subsidies to Help American Businesses	Against	Against	For
Laws to Regulate Internet Content	Against	Against	For
Removing Abortion Rights Guarantee	Varies	Against	For
Decentralizing Government Power to States	Varies	Against	For
Outlawing Capital Punishment	Varies	For	Against
Active Federal Judiciary	Varies	For	Against
Agricultural Subsidies	Against	Varies	Varies
Taxes on Imported Goods	Against	Varies	Varies
Ban on Flag Burning	Against	Varies	Varies
Greater Limits on Immigration	Against	Varies	Varies

churches, clubs, or businesses—and may endorse taking steps to strengthen private institutions weakened by prior government policies. On many issues, they favor decision making at the state and local level rather than at the national level. They see foreign and defense policy as a means for promoting the American way of life, so they endorse a strong military and an independent foreign policy focused on national security concerns.

In sum, liberals, conservatives, and libertarians all share a liberal political philosophy in the broader sense; they agree that freedom and equality are good things but differ on how best to protect and promote them.

WHY A LIBERAL POLITICAL CULTURE?

We now return to the question posed at the start of the chapter. How can we explain the apparent contradiction: a population that is strikingly diverse in its ethnic, racial, and religious makeup but surprisingly uniform in the beliefs and values that constitute its political culture? How has American political culture survived waves of immigrants bred in different social environments?

Part of the answer lies in the way the nation formed. Early settlers in the United States, although ethnically and religiously diverse, nevertheless originated from a relatively narrow economic slice of the European population. Impoverished peasants usually could not afford the costs and risks of transporting their lives to the American frontier, and the colonies held few attractions for European nobles.[46] Rather, the early settlers overwhelmingly came from what, looking back, we might call the middle class, the very group that embraced liberal ideas. They found nothing in the Americas to dispute such ideas because, as political scientist Louis Hartz emphasizes, the colonies lacked their own feudal tradition. There was no hereditary elite or established church to provide the basis for the kind of aristocratic conservatism that persists even today in Europe. Nor was there an oppressed peasant class that might form the basis for radical agrarian parties.

Perhaps as important as what the United States lacked, however, is what it had. In particular, it had a great deal of land. North America was a sparsely populated continent over which the United States steadily expanded.[47] Some historians suggest that the frontier operated like a social safety valve: Rather than revolt against intolerable conditions (the only option in the settled countries of Europe), struggling citizens found it easier to pack up their belongings, move west, and start again—as did many of the rural protestors in Shays' Rebellion (see Chapter 2).

A plentiful supply of land and a scarcity of labor meant that ambitious individuals could and did succeed. The individualistic values that the early settlers brought with them were reinforced by conditions in the new country. Generations of radical scholars have plaintively asked, "Why no socialism in America?"[48] The simplest answer is that Americans never saw much need for it. Why risk trying to change the political system, as a strategy for personal improvement, when more direct methods are readily available? Individual effort usually has been enough to provide an acceptable life for most people.

Still, questions remain. The frontier closed more than a century ago, and labor shortages have not been of much concern for more than half a century. Even if historical conditions reinforced the beliefs and values of the early settlers, of what relevance is that today? The millions of immigrants who arrived after the Civil War were not from liberal societies. Most of them came from authoritarian states with established churches, and most had lived their lives in communal peasant societies that *did* have feudal traditions. Habit cannot explain their embrace of American political culture, nor can simple lessons taught in books or in American schools.

One possibility is that American institutions teach liberal political philosophy indirectly rather than just directly. Political scientist Sven Steinmo argues that American government is so fragmented that it rarely acts in a positive way to improve society.[49] Often it is "gridlocked," or unable to address social problems at all—and when it does act, it often does so via the exchange of political favors among special interests (see Chapters 8 and 9). In consequence, immigrants to the United States pick up on the same wisdom already possessed by natives: Look to yourself because you cannot look to government, and best keep government limited because it will usually act against the public interest. In short, American institutions may preserve the ideas that gave rise to them.

Immigrants may even be healthy for the liberal tradition. Rather than posing a threat to American traditions, as many feared, the flow of diverse peoples to America may have reinforced and strengthened American traditions. How could that be? The answer lies in what social scientists refer to as *self-selection*. With the tragic exception of African Americans, immigrants came to the United States voluntarily. It is possible that the sort of person most likely to leave family, friends, and village behind is exactly the sort of person most likely to adopt the liberal tradition.

Remember that through most of history, immigration was not a matter of taking a train to Dublin, Frankfurt, or Rome and catching a flight to New York. Before the Civil War the journey usually took months, as immigrants walked to a port and then suffered through a long journey below deck on a sailing ship. Even after the Civil War, when steamships shortened the ocean voyage and railroads shortened the land journey, the trip still took weeks. Most of the people who booked passage knew that they would never see their relatives or their homes again.[50] What kind of people made such a decision?

In all probability, the people who migrated already were—relative to their own societies—unusually individualistic. They were willing to leave the communal order of their societies. They were more ambitious, more willing to run risks in the hope of bettering themselves. Bigoted as it was, even the Immigration Commission in 1911 recognized that "emigrating to a strange and distant country, although less of an undertaking than formerly, is still a serious and relatively diffi-cult matter, requiring a degree of courage and resourcefulness not possessed by weaklings of any class."[51] In short, although they had never heard of the liberal tradition, immigrants already displayed much of its spirit.

Today's immigrants seem no different. They have left their homes and families in Asia, Africa, and South America. They have endured hardships to come to a new land with a different culture and language. In some extreme cases they have risked life and limb to emigrate, as with the boat people of southeast Asia who braved pirates, sharks, and storms, and with the Cubans who swam from rafts to the Florida coast. Such people display a kind of individual initiative that can fairly be considered "American," regardless of their nationality.

True, many come to the United States after they are pushed off their land, when crops fail, or when unemployment takes away their jobs. Emigration under such circumstances may not seem to have occurred by choice, such that it would select for individualists. Nevertheless, not everyone in poor or troubled countries chooses to try life elsewhere. Many remain in their homelands, enduring miser-able conditions. The few who do emigrate, therefore, still exercise a politically meaningful choice. And those who dislike American values can always return to their home countries, as a third of all immigrants eventually do, so self-selection also shapes the ones who stay behind.

In sum, immigration and the resulting diversity should not threaten core American values. On the contrary, successive waves of immigrants should rejuve-nate those values. People who are willing to endure hardships, eager to work hard, and convinced that they can create a better life are unlikely to demand an intrusive government. Rather, whatever their skills or education, these immigrants will be the kind of self-sufficient people that Americans themselves seek to become.

AFTERSHOCK:
CLOSING THE DOORS AGAIN

Some Republican leaders have been at the forefront of defending new immi-grants. This may seem strange, given that immigrant groups lean toward the Democratic party and that Republicans often are construed as neglecting the dis-advantaged. Nevertheless, numerous high-profile GOP leaders have opposed anti-immigration policies. During the 1994 battle over California's Proposition 187, which would have denied government services to illegal immigrants and their children, prominent Republicans William Bennett and Jack Kemp opposed the initiative publicly.[52] Similarly, in 1996 Rudolph Giuliani, the Republican mayor of New York, made news by denouncing congressional attempts to limit immigrant eligibility for welfare and other governmental services.[53]

President George W. Bush began his administration in the style of these pro-immigrant Republicans. He campaigned actively for Hispanic, Middle Eastern, and other immigrant votes in the 2000 election. After taking office, Bush worked to cultivate an image of camaraderie with Mexican President Vicente Fox, inviting Fox to be the guest at his first state dinner. The White House floated a proposal in 2001 that, eventually, could have bestowed legal residency on as many as 3 million undocumented Mexicans living in the United States illegally.[54] Bush received roughly a third of Mexican votes in 2000, but his percentage topped that picked up by most Republicans. He seemed committed to building Hispanic support with his policies.

Why would Republicans stand back and allow hordes of likely Democrats to join the population? One cynical explanation is that business owners who support the GOP want more cheap domestic labor. More likely, though, these Republicans were betting on the long-term future of their party. By opening their arms to diversity, they were calculating that the Mexican laborers, Korean grocers, and Iranian service station operators of today are successors to the Irish laborers, Italian grocers, and Polish shopkeepers of generations past. They were betting that, eventually, such people would become middle-class Americans concerned about their tax rates, their schools, and their property values—and willing to consider Republican appeals. More generally, they presumed that these immigrants eventually would adopt American political culture, not threaten it.

New face of patriotism

Americans of Middle Eastern descent made special efforts to express their loyalty to the United States after 9/11. But the process of immigration ensures that most newcomers are fundamentally "American."

Evidence supports their gamble. Surveys show that although foreign-born immigrants differ from other Americans on some philosophical questions, their mainland-born children quickly adapt to American culture. Indeed, they embrace some liberal values at a level indistinguishable from that exhibited by other natives who find themselves in similar socioeconomic conditions.[55] They also assimilate quickly in other ways. One widely noted study reports that, judging on the basis of standard measures of assimilation (citizenship, home ownership, English acquisition, and intermarriage), today's immigrants "overwhelmingly do what immigrants have always done: slowly, often painfully, but quite assuredly, embrace the language, cultural norms and loyalties of America."[56] Other studies suggest that the use of English as a principal language is occurring *more* rapidly among the children of today's immigrants than among the children of past immigrants.[57]

What made the political flexibility of Republicans possible? The reason is that, even though not all Americans embrace immigration fondly, the American public tolerated high levels of immigration before September 11, 2001. Political leaders of both parties responded to that tolerance by proposing policies attractive to immigrant voters. The 9/11 tragedy sharply altered the debate, however, and not just among the Republicans who were experimenting with pro-immigration policies. American public opinion shifted rapidly against allowing foreigners to flow across national boundaries. A reporter with the *Washington Post* summarized the new situation this way: "After a decade of historic immigration, the United States slammed the gates on outsiders and began to reconsider those within its borders."[58]

The Bush administration stopped promoting the idea of granting amnesty to illegal immigrants. New lights and helicopters appeared on the Mexican border, making illegal immigration more difficult.[59] The federal government detained hundreds of foreign visitors for violations that once went ignored, such as overstaying their visas or taking unapproved jobs. Officials planned to deport most of them after questioning.[60] Attorney General John Ashcroft proposed legal changes to make deportation easier.[61] Procedures quickly tightened for foreigners attempting to receive identification cards or student visas. Even entertainers such as the Afro-Cuban All Stars and Iranian pop diva Googoosh had to cancel concerts in the United States because U.S. authorities would not allow their entry, leading former Grateful Dead drummer Mickey Hart to scoff, "I don't know any terrorist-musicians."[62]

It is unclear whether anti-immigration attitudes will persist at current levels. By 2002, many elected leaders were returning to their former ways. President Bush proposed restoring eligibility for food stamps to legal immigrants.[63] Several senators filed bills favorable to both legal and illegal immigrants, such as Utah Senator Orrin Hatch's proposal to encourage financial aid for illegal aliens at public universities and New Mexico Senator Jeff Bingaman's proposal to guarantee illegal immigrants access to Medicaid money for expensive procedures such as kidney dialysis and chemotherapy.[64] But regardless of whether public opinion remains hostile to immigration in the years that follow, the immediate government response to 9/11 anxieties illustrates how quickly policy responds to changing voter attitudes—a sudden response that had a long-lasting impact on the lives of foreign visitors who were already in the United States.

CHAPTER SUMMARY

For more than two centuries the United States has been a study in contrasts. On the one hand, the nation always has been diverse socially, containing a wider array of ethnic and religious groups than most other lands. On the other hand, the diverse citizenry of the United States has long shown a higher level of agreement on fundamental principles than is found in other democracies.

America's fundamental political principles grew out of a classical liberal political philosophy that stressed the rights and liberties of individuals, while giving much less emphasis to their duties and obligations to the community. Today, that philosophy is reflected in a greater emphasis on individual responsibility and hard work, as well as greater suspicion of government, than is found in other countries.

Throughout American history, many native-born citizens have feared that immigration threatened the distinctly American political culture. Yet American political ideals have proved surprisingly resilient. In all likelihood, immigrants reinforce rather than weaken the spirit of individualism in the United States. The very fact of their mobility suggests that they have an ambitious, individualistic outlook compatible with the American political culture.

KEY TERMS

civic republicanism, p. 102

classical liberalism, p. 101

communitarianism, p. 102

conservatism, p. 111

ideology, p. 110

liberalism, p. 111

libertarianism, p. 111

political culture, p. 91

SUGGESTED READINGS

Borjas, George. *Heaven's Door: Immigration Policy and the American Economy.* Princeton, NJ: Princeton University Press, 1999. Argues that immigration has hurt the poorest native-born workers, especially African Americans. Calls for restricting immigration and limiting it to better-educated and more highly skilled people.

Erie, Steven. *Rainbow's End: Irish-Americans and the Dilemma of Urban Machine Politics, 1849–1985.* Berkeley, CA: University of California Press, 1988. Interesting account of the Irish urban machines that played an important role in American political history.

Hartz, Louis. *The Liberal Tradition in America.* New York: Harcourt, 1955. This classic, if impenetrable, discussion of the liberal tradition argues that the absence of feudalism allowed liberal ideas to spread without resistance in the United States.

Kleppner, Paul. *The Cross of Culture.* New York: Free Press, 1970. This example of the "ethno-cultural" school of political history provides a detailed account of political conflict in the Midwest from the rise of the Republican party to the end of the nineteenth century.

Lipset, Seymour Martin. *American Exceptionalism.* New York: Norton, 1996.

The latest work on American political culture by an eminent senior scholar who has spent much of his career studying it.

Mills, Nicolaus, ed. *Arguing Immigration: Are New Immigrants a Wealth of Diversity . . . or a Crushing Burden?* New York: Simon & Schuster, 1994. This collection of essays provides a good overview of the contemporary debate.

Schlesinger, Arthur, Jr. *The Disuniting of America.* Knoxville, TN: Whittle, 1991.

An eminent senior historian complains about the contemporary influence of multiculturalism.

Simon, Julian. *The Economic Consequences of Immigration,* 2nd ed. Ann Arbor, MI: University of Michigan Press, 1999. Argues that the U.S. economy would benefit from an increase in legal immigration.

ON THE WEB

Immigration and Naturalization Service
www.ins.usdoj.gov
This comprehensive site, maintained by the U.S. Department of Justice, covers all facets of immigration in the United States. It provides statistical reports on the history of immigration to the United States, as well as information on the current guidelines for becoming an American citizen.

Diversity Inc
www.diversityinc.com
Sponsored by several major corporations and public interest organizations, this site provides original content on many groups in the American population, with a particular focus on diversity in the work force.

PUBLIC OPINION AND THE MEDIA

CHAPTER OUTLINE

A fter months of wrangling over oil, territorial boundaries, and war debts, the nations of Iraq and Kuwait descended into armed conflict on August 2, 1990. Iraqi troops surged across the Kuwaiti border and subjugated that small state in a single day.[1] Such open aggression in the Middle East posed a difficult challenge for Republican President George H. W. Bush, who had a reputation for foreign policy expertise to uphold.

Bush reacted without hesitation. He condemned the invasion in the strongest possible terms and on November 29 secured a United Nations (UN) resolution authorizing member states to expel Iraqi forces from Kuwait. It was an impressive diplomatic victory for Bush because the UN had not condoned member states going to war since the Korean conflict four decades earlier.

Bush's administration faced a tougher challenge convincing the Democratic Congress. Members began deliberating shortly after New Year's Day but waited until January 12, after an energetic televised debate in the Senate, to approve using military force. Democrats accounted for virtually all of the opposition. They charged that a war in the Middle East would be "about oil," and asked for additional time for economic sanctions to work. Nevertheless, in the end 86 Democrats in the House and 10 in the Senate joined Bush's effort, enough to assure victory. The vote in the House was 250 to 183, and in the Senate, a closer 52 to 47. Bush's presidential leadership seemed to win out over partisan squabbling, a impressive political victory.

By early 1991, a million UN troops lined the Kuwait border to face the invaders. The air war began a day after the January 15 deadline for Iraq's withdrawal. Broadcasting from downtown Baghdad during the bombardment, CNN showed Americans stunning military footage of technologically advanced weaponry. The ground offensive followed on February 24, and again the contest was almost completely one-sided. Allied forces outflanked the entrenched Iraqi troops and in four days drove them from Kuwait—with only 89 Americans dead and 38 missing in action.* By contrast, at least 50,000 Iraqis perished in the conflict. On March 6, more than a week after the shooting had stopped, President Bush was able to declare before Congress, "The war is over." The United States had achieved a impressive military victory under his leadership as commander-in-chief.

The evening news telecasts showed throngs of jubilant Kuwaitis parading through the streets chanting "Bush! Bush! Bush!" The reaction at home was more muted but no less favorable. In the aftermath of the war, President Bush's approval ratings soared, reaching unprecedented heights—as much as 90 percent in some polls. Most people regarded his reelection, only a year and a half away, as a foregone conclusion. Prominent Democrats who had been mentioned as likely opponents—

---

*Other physical illnesses experienced by soldiers, called the "Gulf War syndrome," probably resulted from exposure to burning nerve gases and toxins.

House Majority Leader Richard Gephardt, Senators Sam Nunn and Bill Bradley, and New York Governor Mario Cuomo—all thought better of taking on the seemingly unbeatable Bush. With the Democratic "first team" on the bench, the field of play was left to "minor leaguers" like Arkansas Governor Bill Clinton.

Yet even as his strongest opponents were conceding him the election, Bush's fortunes were slipping. The public forgot about the war as media reports harped on the troubles that Americans were facing with a stagnant economy.[2] The barrage of negative economic news did to President Bush's popularity what the Iraqi military could not. Bush's approval rating dropped by 50 percent within a year of his great success in the Persian Gulf. He went into the 1992 election as one of the least popular presidents of the past 50 years and lost to Clinton in a three-way race, a casualty of the public's fickleness.

BUSH'S TURBULENT RATINGS IN THE POLLS REFLECT A LARGER TRUTH about America's new democracy: Voters have very high expectations of their leaders, and they often use election time to express their displeasure. Leaders must be careful to anticipate public demands, or they will not lead for long. At the same time, public opinion can be terribly capricious, flitting from one issue to the next. It is difficult to measure accurately. The public, operating collectively, has limited knowledge, a short attention span, and rather sloppy methods for decision making.

Furthermore, most Americans derive their knowledge of government from media organizations that are themselves major players in both the U.S. economy and the U.S. political system. Although the media do not speak with one voice, the professionals who convey political news—and who disseminate news of public opinion to government officials—have their own interests and personal traits that influence how they carry out the critical function of keeping Americans informed.

For these reasons, elections capture the people's demands imperfectly. Elections drive American politics, but it is not always clear what drives voters.

SOURCES OF PUBLIC OPINION

The reason for public opinion's importance is captured aptly by political scientist V.O. Key's definition: "those opinions held by private persons which governments find it prudent to heed."[3] Democratic governments find it "prudent" to heed the opinions of private persons, of course, because of elections. Note that in Key's conception, public opinion can, but need not, be expressed actively. Even if public opinion is silent, or "latent," public officials may act or fail to act because they fear arousing it. This is the so-called law of anticipated reactions, whereby elections influence government even though they do so indirectly and passively.[4] The common phrase "Public opinion wouldn't stand for that" acknowledges that public opinion can exercise power subtly.

The opinions that people hold reflect numerous influences. Most of these sources are stable and personal: values, self-interest, education. But applying them to particular issues may not be straightforward. And some influences—such as the media—can shift rapidly. Thus even a politician who tries to "give the people what they want" may be surprised come election day.

Children begin to form political attitudes at an early age. Research carried out in the 1950s and 1960s generally concluded that the single most important socializing agent was the family, and that within the family the mother was most important—she spent far more time with the children in that era. Studies found that many children identify themselves as Democrats or Republicans well before they have any idea what the parties stand for. And older children are very likely to share the party affiliation of their parents. A few scholars concluded, however, that schools were more important than family.[5] And the influence of family may have declined in recent decades, given increases in single parenthood, in the divorce rate, and in mothers working outside the home.

Socialization often works indirectly, by forming the *beliefs and values* on which individuals act later in life. For example, a very young child may learn fear of, or comfort with, nudity—and this psychological orientation may shape adult attitudes about such political issues as strip clubs restrictions or pornography bans. But sometimes socializing agents consciously try to activate political attitudes. The Catholic Church officially opposes abortion, for example, and rank-and-file Catholics are indeed less accepting of abortion than are mainline Protestants and Jews.[6] Whether the influences lie in the distant past or in the present, differences among people with different socialization experiences emerge regularly on all kinds of issues.

Although people form many of their attitudes in childhood, their political views continue to develop over the course of their lifetimes. Childhood socialization can be reversed by adult experiences, and especially by one's *self-interest*.[7] For example, blue-collar workers are more sensitive to a rise in unemployment that throws them out of work, whereas professionals and managers are more sensitive to a rise in inflation that drives up interest rates and depresses the overall business climate.[8] In 1978 California homeowners were significantly more likely than renters and public employees to support Proposition 13, the famous initiative that rolled back property taxes.[9] People often evaluate public policy by asking, "What's in it for me?"

Education shapes public opinion, but it belongs in a separate category because it works in varied ways. Schooling shapes the interests people have, by determining their occupational choices as well as their tastes in entertainment. It shapes the beliefs people adopt, because teachers and college professors tend to hold political attitudes that differ from those of the general public and may consciously or unconsciously socialize students to see the world as they do.[10] Finally, the skills learned in colleges and universities may change how people think about

FIGURE 5.1

Higher education is associated with greater tolerance of diversity

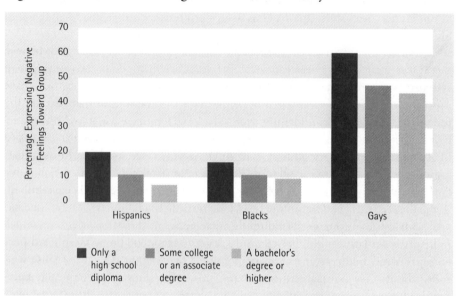

SOURCE: American National Election Study, 1994.

the political world. Highly educated people tend to be willing to tolerate minorities or deviant groups, for example, which may reflect how they analyze and adapt to diversity (see Figure 5.1).[11] Higher education also is associated with a greater sense of **political efficacy**—the belief that the citizen can make a difference by acting politically—which may be a result of the skills learned in school that make participation easier.

MEASURING PUBLIC OPINION

In the nineteenth century, measuring public opinion was an art form. Politicians looked at informal straw polls, consulted community leaders, or scanned the newspapers' editorial pages to understand the public mood. But the process was less like science and more like "reading tea leaves."[12] The advent of modern survey research in the 1930s (pioneered by George Gallup) clarified public opinion, making it a much more powerful political force. The key to this change was the scientific design and administration of randomized surveys, which has become a standard tool of the modern election campaign.

Most often researchers measure public opinion via telephone polls. Various firms and academic organizations contact individuals, ask them questions, and report the responses. Of these, Gallup is the most widely recognized name.

Newspapers, magazines, and TV networks also sponsor regular polls—NBC News/*Wall Street Journal,* CBS News/*New York Times,* ABC News/*Washington Post, USA Today*/CNN—and base major stories on them.[13]

SAMPLING ERROR

The general public is sometimes suspicious of survey research, refusing to believe that fewer than 2000 people can speak for an entire nation. They may be right to distrust polls, but the reason for skepticism is misplaced. Statisticians have demonstrated that the responses of a few thousand people usually mirror the opinion of 200 million adults quite well—so long as everyone has a roughly equal chance of being polled. That is, the small group needs to be a **random sample** of the population. For this reason, telephone surveys often use random-digit dialing; to equalize the odds of selection, a computer randomly selects which numbers to call within a given telephone exchange. People with unlisted numbers may be irritated when they answer their phones and hear pollsters, but no one has given out their numbers—the computer has found them by accident!

Even if an opinion poll based on a random sample could be conducted perfectly, it still would not get estimates of public opinion exactly right, because who appears in the poll would be a matter of chance. But the existence of such **sampling error**—the error that creeps into polls because of the necessity of taking a sample of the public rather than asking everyone—is not the reason why polls are sometimes unreliable. On average, relatively small random samples will yield a correct picture of political attitudes, and the sample need not be very large before those estimates are consistently precise.

Consider a simple example to illustrate. Suppose that every reader of this book flipped a coin 1500 times. The most likely result, the "right" answer in this instance, would be 750 heads—because a coin flip turns up heads half the time. But of course some of you would get a few more heads by chance, and some a few more tails—that's the sampling error. Statistical theory tells us precisely how much each experiment would bounce around the typical result. It is a statistical fact that 95 percent of the time, we would find between 705 and 795 heads (between 47 and 53 percent). This range is what pollsters mean when they report that surveys have a "margin of error" of plus or minus 3 percent: 95 percent of the time their survey method would turn up an estimate within 3 points of the right answer.

In the real world, though, the calculated sampling error captures only one source of inaccuracy, probably a relatively minor one—although it can make more of a difference in polls that sample places, such as voting precincts, rather than individual people (see the accompanying Election Connection, "The 2000 Florida Debacle"). The main dangers with random-sample surveys are instead the inaccuracies that do not result by chance but, rather, occur because the survey method is biased away from the truth—either because of *selection effects* or because of *measurement error.* We discuss those two sources next.

ELECTION CONNECTION

The 2000 Florida Debacle

Since the 1960s, the major networks have used election-day polls to project winners in national elections. These surveys are called *exit polls* because they catch voters leaving their precinct stations immediately after casting votes. In 1990, the networks agreed to pool their resources, creating an organization—Voter News Service (VNS)—to conduct exit polls for all the networks. The networks' track record was very impressive in the four elections of the 1990s. The only serious miscall occurred in the 1996 New Hampshire Senate race; the networks called it for the Democrat, but Republican Bob Smith actually won the seat.

At times, voters on the West Coast have complained that announcing results for the East depresses turnout in the West, a complaint supported by some studies but contradicted by others.[a] But the 2000 election night debacle (see Chapter 1) caused a much more serious debate over exit polls, because they misled the nation's top newscasters. Each major network managed to call the presidential race in Florida first for Gore around 8 P.M. EST, then for Bush around 2:15 A.M., and finally for neither at 3 A.M. By the end of the night, the network anchors appeared downright lost as they searched the set looking for guidance.

All the network calls were based on the VNS exit polls. The night's early call for Gore was made a little under an hour after the polls closed in most of Florida. This first miscall was based on several flaws in the exit poll methodology, including underestimating the number of absentee voters and sampling from a biased set of Florida precincts that inflated Gore's estimated lead.

Although the networks eventually corrected this mistake, a few short hours later they made another one, calling Florida for Bush. This miscall was based on a data entry error of 20,000 votes in Bush's favor. There was a secure line connecting VNS to each of the networks to permit quick correction of such mistakes, but the networks and VNS apparently did not communicate well enough to correct the error in time to prevent a miscall. By the time they corrected their mistake, Vice President Gore was in the car on his way to deliver his concession speech, a concession he withdrew only minutes later.

Commentator Ben Wattenberg called the exit poll system "idiotic." He pointed out that, although some exit polls were relatively accurate, some were off by as much as 20 points.[b] VNS promptly announced plans to use new models, rely more heavily on pre-election telephone polling, and institute reforms to prevent a recurrence of the "extra 20,000 votes." But VNS could not get its system repaired in time for the 2002 congressional elections, and shortly thereafter the networks suspended its operations (at least temporarily).

What do you think?

- Should networks conduct exit polls and then use them to "project" winners?
- The networks have argued that legislation outlawing the practice would interfere with the exercise of rights guaranteed by the First Amendment. Are there other feasible reforms?

[a]John Jackson, "Election Night Reporting and Voter Turnout," *American Journal of Political Science* 27 (1983): 615–635. Compare to Laurily Epstein and Gerald Strom, "Survey Research and Election Night Projections," *Public Opinion* 7 (1984): 48–50.

[b]Ben Wattenberg, "Network Arrogance," United Media Syndicated column, June 7, 2001.

SELECTION EFFECTS

The key to getting an unbiased sample is to make sure that individuals cannot affect whether they are in or out of the sample. If we were to poll attendees at a hockey game, an opera, or even a political science lecture, our sample would be suspect, because the members of each of these audiences share a common interest—in hockey, opera, or political science—that brought them together. This common interest differentiates them from the American population at large, and it might do so in ways relevant to the survey questions being asked.

Errors in survey estimates caused by an unrepresentative method of selecting respondents is called a selection effect. Just as immigrants to the United States are not representative of citizens in their home countries because they elect to migrate (see Chapter 4), survey respondents will not be representative of the general public if they have control (directly or indirectly) over whether to participate. Similarly, a survey will be biased, and will produce consistently inaccurate results, if the researcher's sampling method consciously or unconsciously selects a certain kind of participant.

Using random telephone samples certainly does not solve the problem with **selection bias.** Some of these selection effects are small. For example, most telephone polls leave out citizens of Hawaii and Alaska. And they all omit the small proportion of the U.S. population without telephones. Some selection effects are more serious, though. Typically, more than half the original sample either never answer the phone or refuse to be interviewed.[14] Regardless of whether unavailability results from personality traits or lifestyle differences, the people whom surveys fail to catch may differ in politically relevant ways from those who participate. For example, research shows that surveys tend to underrepresent men, young people, whites, and the wealthy—all traits that are related to one's political attitudes.[15] In 1996, for example, pre-election polls overestimated Bill Clinton's margin over Robert Dole. Some commentators claimed that this was because pro-Democratic groups were more likely to respond to the polls than pro-Republican groups.[16]

Selection bias will be even more severe for call-in surveys of the sort conducted by radio and TV stations. These may be good ways to generate listener or viewer interest, but they have no more scientific value than letters to the editor or the feedback heard by elected officials at town meetings. People who take the time and trouble to participate are those who care the most. They are not representative of the much larger population.

The latest rage is Internet polls. The problem with Internet polling was highlighted by a mildly embarrassing experience suffered by the Democratic National Committee (DNC) in January 2000. The DNC Web site includes a weekly opinion poll. The poll in question noted that the United States was enjoying a large budget surplus and asked people to vote for one of two ways to use the surplus: "saving

Social Security, strengthening Medicare, and paying down the debt," or "implementing George W. Bush's $1.7 trillion risky tax scheme that overwhelmingly benefits the wealthy." Surprisingly, when the results were tabulated, 72.2 percent of the respondents favored "risky" tax cuts for the rich. Mischievous Republicans monitoring the opposition had voted in the Democrats' poll![17] This amusing episode illustrates the problem with allowing the sample to determine itself. Thus survey researchers must be continually on guard against selection bias.

MEASUREMENT ERROR

Opinions are difficult to gauge using surveys, which makes them subject to **measurement error**—to being measured improperly. Part of the problem is that opinions are not physical facts that can be measured objectively like the length of a body part or the weight of a candy bar. Beliefs and judgments may be hard to quantify, and answers may depend on the options provided for a particular question.[18] Opinions often are expressed as casual answers to questions the respondent has never really thought about—especially if the respondent is not offered the chance to say, simply, "I don't know."

Also, people hold complex attitudes. Yet the speed necessary for opinion polls may not allow a detailed picture of those views. The questionnaire cannot take too long, or costs will be very high and respondents may stop cooperating. The answers have to be easy to code into a computer and summarize, or the results from a large sample will be too complicated to process and report to others. For these reasons, how people answer a poll depends very much on the wording of the questions: whether they are *confusing,* whether they are *value-laden,* and whether they are *too blunt* to capture the complex range of opinions people hold.

CONFUSING QUESTIONS The Holocaust Memorial Museum opened in Washington, DC, in the spring of 1993. Coincident with the dedication of the museum, the American Jewish Committee released startling data from a survey conducted a few months earlier by Roper Starch Worldwide, a respected commercial polling organization. The poll indicated that 22 percent of the American public believed it "possible . . . the Nazi extermination of the Jews never happened" and that another 12 percent were unsure. In total, one-third of all Americans apparently had doubts about whether the Nazis murdered 6 million Jews in World War II.

The news media jumped on the story, which fit the preconceptions of editorialists and columnists eager to find shortcomings in their fellow citizens. What was wrong with the American people? Had the educational system failed so miserably that in the short span of 50 years the worst genocide in history had become a matter of mere opinion? Was anti-Semitism so widespread and deeply ingrained in the population that Holocaust denials by the lunatic fringe were making headway? What did the Holocaust poll say about the American people?

Embarrassed by a poll

The 1993 opening of the Holocaust Memorial Museum was accompanied by a polling embarrassment that underscored the necessity of keeping questions on public opinion polls clear and simple. Explain why a person might have answered yes to the following question: "Does it seem possible, or does it seem impossible to you that the Nazi extermination of the Jews never happened?"

Very little, it turned out. The Gallup organization—a Roper business competitor—soon demonstrated that the Roper poll was gravely mistaken, because Roper had asked a confusing question. The exact wording of Roper's question was

> *Does it seem possible, or does it seem impossible to you that the Nazi extermination of the Jews never happened?*

One of the first rules of survey research is to keep questions clear and simple. The Roper question fails that test because it contains a double negative (*impossible . . . never happened*)—a grammatical construction long known to confuse people.

Gallup conducted a new poll in which half of the sample was asked the Roper question with the double negative and the other half was asked an alternative question,

> *Does it seem possible to you that the Nazi extermination of the Jews never happened, or do you feel certain that it happened?*

This seemingly minor difference in question wording made a great deal of difference indeed. In the half of the sample that was asked the Roper question, one-third of the respondents again replied that it was possible the Holocaust never happened or that they were unsure, but in the half that was asked the alternative question, less than 10 percent of the sample were Holocaust doubters. Roper eventually retracted its initial poll results after doing its own follow-up studies. The whole episode had been the product of a simple mistake.[19]

The point of the Holocaust poll example is that no one accused the Roper organization of choosing a bad sample or a sample that was too small. Roper asked a poorly constructed question, and the results gave a highly reliable indication of how Americans typically would respond to that question (something Gallup's follow-up survey confirmed).

VALUE-LADEN WORDING What look like minor variations in question wording can produce significant differences in measured opinion. This is especially likely when the variations involve the substitution of emotionally or politically "loaded" terms for more neutral terms. A classic example comes from the controversy over social spending. Consider the following survey question:

> *We are faced with many problems in this country, none of which can be solved easily or inexpensively. I'm going to name some of these problems and for each one I'd like you to tell me whether you think we're spending too much money, too little money, or about the right amount.*[20]

When the public was asked about "welfare" in the spring of 1994, the responses showed that a large majority of Americans believed that too much was being spent:

Too little 13%
About right 25%
Too much 62%

Conservatives might take heart from such a poll and use it to argue that public assistance to the poor should be slashed. But when the same people in the same poll were asked about "assistance to the poor," a similarly large majority responded that too little was being spent:

Too little 59%
About right 25%
Too much 16%

Liberals might take heart from such a poll and use it to argue that welfare spending should increase.

Looking at these two questions together, though, it's hard to tease out any real preference. Both invoke the same policy, but different stereotypes. "Welfare" carries negative connotations; it seems to prompt people to think of lazy and undeserving recipients, so-called welfare cheats. But "assistance to the poor" does not seem to evoke these negative images. Here is clearly a case where the careless (or clever) choice of question wording can produce contradictory findings on a major public issue.

OVERSIMPLIFIED QUESTIONS The Supreme Court handed down the *Roe* v. *Wade* decision in 1973, striking down restrictions on a woman's right to termi-nate a pregnancy in the first three months (and limiting restrictions on that right in the second trimester). Since then, the abortion issue has never left the national agenda, so most Americans probably decided long ago where they stand on it. The answers they give to specific questions about abortion are fairly constant, chang-ing little after a 1989 Court decision called *Webster* v. *Reproductive Health Services,* which opened the way for some state regulation of abortion, or after the 1992 *Planned Parenthood* v. *Casey* decision, which upheld some specific abortion restric-tions imposed by Pennsylvania.

Yet the results of polls on abortion vary widely. Some suggest that the United States is strongly anti-abortion, and others portray the United States as over-whelmingly pro-choice. If this variation does not result from uncertainty and does not result from variation over time, the difficulties must result from incon-sistent measurement. The main problem is that most survey questionnaires are too limited to capture the complexity of attitudes toward abortion.

Consider the effects of question wording shown in two surveys that brack-eted the 1989 *Webster* decision.[21] A *Los Angeles Times* poll asked,

> *Do you think a pregnant woman should or should not be able to get a legal abortion, no matter what the reason?*

By close to a 2-to-1 margin (57 percent to 34 percent), Americans thought she should not. As pro-life spokespersons claimed, Americans were pro-life. Should Democratic campaign consultants have advised their clients to flip-flop to the pro-life side in anticipation of the next election? Well, probably not. A few months later, a CBS News/*New York Times* survey asked,

> *If a woman wants to have an abortion, and her doctor agrees to it, should she be allowed to have an abortion or not?*

By more than a 2-to-1 margin (58 percent to 26 percent), Americans said yes. As the pro-choice spokespersons claimed, America had a pro-choice majority. Should Republican campaign consultants have advised their clients to flip-flop to the pro-choice side?

Which poll was right? Probably neither. Upon close examination, both sur-vey questions are suspect. Each contains words and phrases that predispose peo-ple to answer in one direction. The first question uses the phrase "no matter what the reason." Most Americans are not *unconditionally* pro-choice, any more than their other political ideals are unconditional. If forced to choose yes or no, some genuinely pro-choice people will say no, believing that there must be reasons for an abortion that even they would consider invalid. The CBS News/*New York Times* question leans in the opposite direction. A doctor's approval suggests a reasoned decision based on medically justifiable grounds. Some generally pro-life people might agree to permit abortion in such a case. Thus, even on an issue where many people have stable, considered opinions, variations in question wording can make a big difference in the answers they give.

A survey also can skew answers by how it frames an issue, encouraging the respondent to answer questions from one point of view rather than another. For example, a CBS News/*New York Times* poll asked the following question:

> *Even in cases where I might think abortion is the wrong thing to do, I don't think the government has any business preventing a woman from having an abortion.*[22]

By close to a 3-to-1 margin (69 percent to 24 percent), Americans agreed with that sentiment. Apparently, the country stands firmly in support of abortion rights. On the other hand, when another CBS News/*New York Times* poll asked people whether they agreed or disagreed with the stark claim that "abortion is the same thing as murdering a child," Americans were deeply split (46 percent agreed and 41 percent disagreed). Similarly, a plurality or majority of Americans regularly agrees that "abortion is morally wrong" (51 percent agreed, and 34 percent disagreed in the aforementioned CBS News/*New York Times* poll).[23]

The first question uses a *choice* frame. Individualistic Americans favor freedom of choice, especially when it involves freedom from governmental interference. The second and third questions use an *act* frame. Many Americans who favor choice nevertheless are troubled by the act of abortion. Hence even poll respondents with stable, well-defined positions on abortion might react differently to these variations in questions—depending on which values the interviewer seems to be asking them to endorse. It is no surprise that the pro-choice side of the debate consistently employs one frame, the pro-life side the other. Nor is it any surprise that an accomplished politician like then-President Clinton, recognizing the conflict felt by many Americans, announced that he was pro-choice and against abortion.

The National Opinion Research Center (NORC) uses an abortion question that illustrates clearly that the complicated relationship Americans have with abortion causes answers to be sensitive to what pollsters specifically ask:

> *Please tell me whether or not you think it should be possible for a pregnant woman to obtain a legal abortion if*
>
> 1. *the woman's health is seriously endangered?*
> 2. *she became pregnant as a result of rape?*

3. *there is a strong chance of serious defect in the baby?*
4. *the family has low income and cannot afford any more children?*
5. *she is not married and does not want to marry the man?*
6. *she is married and does not want any more children?*

For the most part, answers to each of these various conditions change little over time. After moving in a liberal direction in the late 1960s, opinion stabilized at the time of the *Roe* decision, stayed remarkably constant for two decades, and then moved slightly in a conservative direction in the late 1990s (see Figure 5.2). Yet answers vary widely across the conditions. On average, Americans favor legal abortion in half of the circumstances, with large majorities supporting abortion in the first three ("traumatic") circumstances but more people regularly opposing abortion in two of the second three ("elective") circumstances.[24]

Consistently inconsistent, Americans are pragmatic, not ideological, on the abortion issue. They favor the right to choose, but not an unconditional right to

FIGURE 5.2

Popular attitudes toward abortion have been remarkably stable since *Roe v. Wade* (1973)

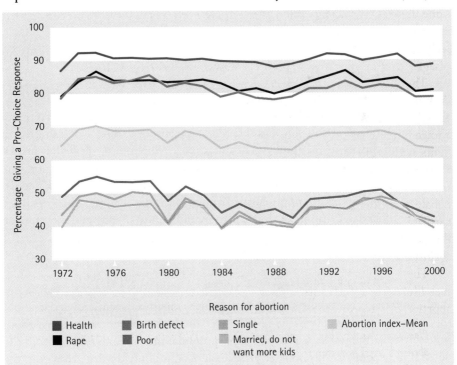

Reason for abortion

■ Health   ■ Birth defect   ▨ Single   ▨ Abortion index–Mean
■ Rape   ■ Poor   ▨ Married, do not want more kids

NOTE: Respondents who answered "don't know" are included in the calculation.

SOURCE: Calculated by the authors from the General Social Survey 1972–1998 Cumulative Data File.

FIGURE 5.3

Americans tend to favor abortion rights, but with restrictions

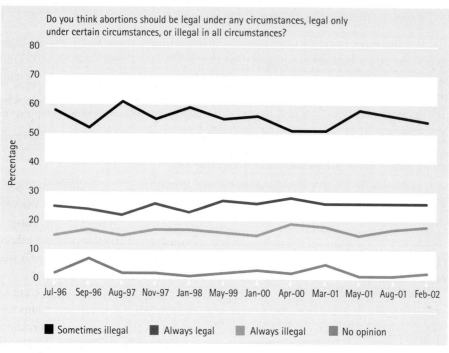

Do you think abortions should be legal under any circumstances, legal only under certain circumstances, or illegal in all circumstances?

■ Sometimes illegal   ■ Always legal   ▨ Always illegal   ▨ No opinion

SOURCE: Gallup, July 6–7, 1989.

choose in every conceivable circumstance—a complexity that the shorter, and more common, abortion questions fail to tap. Surveys show that rape, birth defects, and threats to the mother's health are overwhelmingly viewed as justifiable circumstances, but personal convenience and gender selection are not. The mother's age, financial condition, and marital status divide the population deeply. For this reason, Americans oppose overturning *Roe,* but as Figure 5.3 shows, they approve of state laws that make abortion more difficult to obtain, and they oppose public funding.

GOVERNING BY PUBLIC OPINION?

Public opinion is incredibly sensitive to how it is measured, but knowledge about survey techniques has increased greatly over time. The more leaders learn about precisely what the public wants, the more potential they have to respond to those desires. In general, as this book argues, leaders commonly do that. However, the limits on "governing by public opinion" do not all result from imperfection in how pollsters measure it. Leaders may choose to ignore public opinion polls for other reasons. Public attitudes may not be a reliable basis for choosing good policies—or even for choosing policies that will make voters happy in the long run. And most elected officials do not represent the nation as a whole; they represent a specific set of constituents whose opinions vary in their intensity.

THE LIMITS OF PUBLIC OPINION

Polls offer a snapshot of public opinion, but the demands that voters express at election time may not reflect the answers that they will provide a stranger who knocks on the door or who calls on the telephone. Poll results are vulnerable to how people approach political life—that, on most issues, people are *uninformed,* *unconstrained* by ideology, and *unpredictable* because of their inconsistency.

AMERICANS ARE UNINFORMED Americans are an accommodating people. If a pollster asks a question, many will cooperate by giving their best answer, even if they have never thought about the question or have no basis for deciding. A 1989 survey provides an extreme example. People were asked to rate 58 ethnic and nationality groups. Although one group included in the list ("Wisnians") was fictitious, 29 percent of the sample ranked them anyway.[25]

Most people have little or no information about public affairs. The extent of popular ignorance is most obvious when surveys pose "factual" questions. As shown in Figure 5.4, in 1995 only one-quarter of the voting-age population knew how long U.S. senators serve. Barely half could name the Speaker of the House (Newt Gingrich, who had been on the cover of *Time* magazine), and only 60 percent could recall the name of the vice president (Al Gore). Almost half had no idea which branch of government interprets the Constitution.

Elections are not standardized tests, of course; voting intelligently does not require knowing the answers to all sorts of factual questions. But widespread ignorance extends to important matters of government and public policy. During the 1995 federal government shutdown, 40 percent of Americans were unaware that the Republicans controlled Congress (and 10 percent did not know that the president was a Democrat). And by more than a 2-to-1 margin, Americans believed—absolutely wrongly—that the federal government spent more on foreign aid than on Medicare. In fact, the United States spends four times as much on Medicare as on foreign aid, and the ratio is growing.[26]

Why do people have so little knowledge of basic facts and issues? The answer is that most people seldom pay attention to politics. News magazines sell far fewer copies than entertainment and lifestyle magazines do. Far more Americans love *Raymond* than watch *NewsHour with Jim Lehrer.* Far more care about who becomes the next "American Idol" than care about who becomes their next U.S. senator. Upon learning the full extent of popular ignorance, some politically involved

FIGURE 5.4

Americans are not very knowledgeable about the specifics of American government

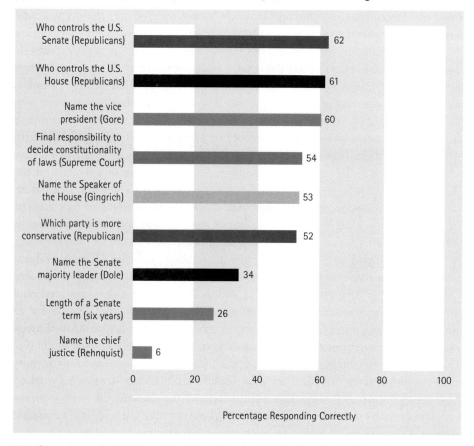

NOTE: This survey was conducted by Princeton Survey Research Associates in late November 1995 and early December 1995, after the Republicans took control of Congress for the first time in 40 years and during the federal budget impasse of 1995. Correct answers appear in parentheses.

SOURCE: "Why Don't Americans Trust the Government?" (Menlo Park, CA: The Kaiser Foundation, 1996).

students react critically, jumping to the conclusion that apathetic Americans are irresponsible people who fall far short of the democratic ideal. Such reactions overlook the reasons why people pay so little attention to public affairs.

The simple fact is that most people have little time for politics; it is something of a luxury interest. They work hard to take care of the "necessities"—paying the bills, caring for their families, and nurturing personal relationships. They may not have time or energy for the *New York Times* and *Nightline* after dropping off and picking up children, commuting, working, and housekeeping. The effort required to stay informed competes with human necessities like recreation and relaxation.

Those who criticize ordinary citizens for paying little attention to public affairs often have jobs that enable them to stay informed with little effort. For example, in a university environment, political conversation is a common diversion, and for many professors and students, being informed is relevant to academic pursuits. Likewise, many journalists have jobs that involve following politics: If they are not informed, they are not doing their jobs. But most Americans do not have these incentives, a fact that critics in academia and the media tend to forget. Nor is it clear what such people would do with their knowledge of public affairs if they were able to obtain it.

The general point is that gathering, processing, and storing information is neither effortless nor free. For most Americans, bearing such **information costs** brings them little tangible return.[27] Few citizens believe that they have enough power to influence how conflicts in Afghanistan, the Ivory Coast, or the next crisis spot will resolve. And when faced with a costly activity that has no obvious benefit, many of them quite rationally decide to minimize their costs. Thus, from a logical standpoint, the puzzle is not why so many Americans are ill-informed; the puzzle is why so many are as informed as they are.[28]

Of course, information costs do not fall equally heavily on all people. Education makes it easier to absorb and organize information; thus it comes as no surprise that more-educated Americans are better informed than less-educated ones (see Figure 5.5). In addition, the benefits of information are not the same for all people on all issues. Most people will be better informed on issues that directly affect their lives. Parents and teachers are more knowledgeable than other citizens about school operations and budgets. Human services providers are more knowledgeable about welfare and other public assistance policies. Steel workers have strong views on foreign imports. Such **issue publics** are different from the large mass of citizens in that their members' occupations make information cheaper to obtain, as well as more relevant, interesting, and valuable.[29]

In addition to varying across people and issues, the costs and benefits of being well informed may vary over time. When a tax revolt erupts or a debate over condom distribution in the schools flares up, information levels surge as people get caught up in the controversy. But after the burning issues are resolved and the controversy subsides, information levels also return to normal.[30]

Of course, some people consider it their duty as citizens to be informed, so they stay attuned to public affairs simply because they believe it is the "right thing" to do. Other people follow public affairs because they find it intrinsically interesting, in the same way that some follow sports or the arts. For such people, staying informed is a matter of taste or values, not the result of any tangible benefit from being informed. What others view as costs, they see as a source of satisfaction.[31]

Finally, we note that Americans are not unique in paying little attention to public affairs. Citizens in other countries are similarly inattentive and similarly lacking in knowledge. A 1998 British Gallup poll, for example, found that only

FIGURE 5.5

Higher education is strongly associated with greater knowledge of politics and government

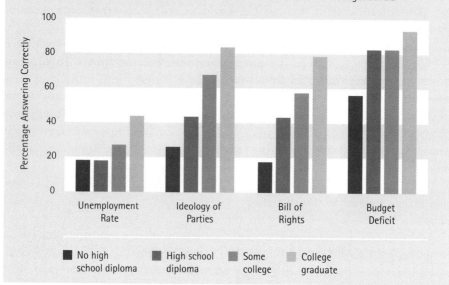

Columns indicate the percentage of people, by education, who correctly give the unemployment rate, identify the relative ideological (conservative–liberal) positions of the Republican and Democratic parties, give the name for the first ten amendments to the Constitution, and state whether or not the United States has a budget deficit.

SOURCE: Data are taken from Michael Delli Carpini and Scott Keeter, *What Americans Know About Politics and Why It Matters*, p. 189.

40 percent of Britons knew that the United States once was part of the British Empire! [32]

AMERICANS ARE UNCONSTRAINED   Another characteristic that makes it easy to misinterpret public opinion is that even when people have reasonably firm views on issues, those views often are surprisingly unconnected to each other. That is, the American people are not constrained by political ideology.

People who are deeply interested and involved in politics, whether as activists or as office holders—such people are traditionally called **political elites**—tend to have well-structured **ideologies** that unite their positions on policy issues. To know that such a person is a "liberal" or a "conservative" is to know a good deal, because underlying principles and political alliances mold their system of belief (see Chapter 4). Ordinary citizens—traditionally called the **mass public**—are another matter. [33] Rather than believing consistently in either activist or minimal government, an important trait that distinguishes liberals and conservatives, citizens generally favor federal spending in some areas but oppose it in others. They favor regulation in some areas but oppose it in others. They favor toleration for some groups in some situations, but not for other groups in other situations. When given the option, one-quarter to one-third of the population will not even classify themselves on a liberal–conservative scale, and another one-quarter put themselves exactly in the middle: "moderate, middle of the road."[34]

There is a common tendency to interpret the nonideological thinking of ordinary Americans in a negative light and to presume that preferences with little obvious interconnection are somehow less valid than those with a predictable structure. Here again, we disagree with such pessimistic judgments. In our view, American political ideologies are as much *social* as logical constructions, which is why they change in meaning over time. Personal views aside, can anyone explain the logical connection among supporting low capital gains tax rates, being pro-life, opposing gun control, and favoring high defense spending? Positions on such issues may go together for liberal and conservative elites, but why? Maybe political elites are the ones who should be viewed critically.

No time for hate

Most Americans favor "free speech for all" yet endorse suppressing the right of unpopular groups to give speeches. Does this inconsistency represent a wise practicality or a dangerous lack of understanding?

The American people have a strong pragmatic strain, often noted by international observers accustomed to a more ideological style of political discourse. Perhaps views unconstrained by ideology should be taken as evidence of American common sense. Whether you regard ideological thinking as good or bad, however, bear in mind one point: Because they presume that ideological thinking is the norm, party and issue activists, media commentators, and many public officials tend to conclude too much on the basis of opinion polls and voting returns. Support for one variety of government action may indicate nothing about support for another, seemingly similar government action. Support for a candidate's position on one issue may suggest little or nothing about that candidate's "mandate" to act on seemingly related issues. In short, the nonideological nature of people's issue preferences means that elites often hear more than the voters are saying.

AMERICANS ARE UNPREDICTABLE Given that people often have not thought about issues or the connections among them, it should come as no surprise that people's views often are also inconsistent and therefore unpredictable. Opinions with little basis are not likely to abide when survey questions change emphasis or as time passes. For example, in 1980, when Ronald Reagan defeated Jimmy Carter and the Republicans made striking gains in Congress, many in the media interpreted the election results as a "resurgence of conservatism" or a "turn to the right" in American politics. The evidence, however, was confusing.[35]

A poll taken in 1978 reported that an overwhelming 84 percent of the citizenry thought the federal government was spending too much money. A smaller majority thought that the federal government had gone too far in regulating business. Popular sentiments like these appear to foretell the Reagan victory that followed. Then again, the same poll asked the same people which domestic programs they favored cutting and which areas of business activity they favored deregulating. Surprisingly, majorities often indicated that most domestic activities deserved *higher* funding or *more* regulation—hardly a conservative resurgence! Similarly, after the Republican congressional victories in 1994, polls reported that large majorities wanted to balance the budget but not to cut specific programs, especially not the large entitlement programs causing the budget deficits.[36] Such contradictory views recall the old maxim that "everybody wants to go to heaven but nobody wants to die."

Obviously, such contradictory views confuse political debate, distorting whatever message voters try to send during an election. President Reagan claimed—with some justification—that he had been elected to cut government spending and deregulate the economy. Democratic leaders in Congress claimed—with some justification—that their party had been returned to power so that they could protect existing spending and regulatory programs. Both claims were plausible given the public opinion data. In 1994, Republican congressional leaders believed they had a mandate to balance the budget. But when they attempted to slow the growth of Medicare spending, they discovered that the mandate did not extend that far.

Why is public opinion so unpredictable? Obviously, ignorance is part of the explanation. People are unaware how little is being spent on programs such as welfare and foreign aid. Thus they believe, erroneously, that cutting such unpopular programs will free up sufficient funds to maintain popular ones. Some voters also believe that waste and inefficiency are so pervasive that simply streamlining government operations would allow painless spending increases.

Not all examples of inconsistency reflect insufficient and inaccurate information, however. Citizens are so consistently unpredictable when applying general principles to specific cases that other explanations must be at work. We have seen that people favor cutting spending in general but not specific programs. They also oppose amending the Constitution but favor amendments to require a balanced budget, limit congressional terms, and ban flag burning. And, perhaps most interesting of all, they support fundamental rights but regularly make numerous exceptions.[37] As Figure 5.6 shows, most citizens favor "free speech for all"—but then half refuse to agree that a member of their most disliked group should be allowed to give a speech. Similarly, they believe in the separation of church and state but favor prayer in schools!

It is easy to label such inconsistencies hypocrisy, and some do. Or such inconsistencies may indicate that ordinary people do not have a clear understanding of rights, and perhaps they do not. But there are other, more positive interpretations as well. To the law professor, the newspaper editor, or the political activist, rights may be viewed as absolutes. Letting government infringe on guaranteed protections leaves open the possibility that government will water them down until they are meaningless. But Americans tend to be pragmatists. Few distrust their elected government so much that they are unwilling to bend the rules once in a while. The absolutist language of rights is foreign to the problem-solving American way of thinking. Rights are good things, but they must be balanced against other values.[38] To adults familiar with life's conflicts and trade-offs, the legalistic language of rights belongs in the realm of theoretical argument, not the realm of real-world politics. They may feel no contradiction in advocating a right while simultaneously endorsing significant exceptions.[39]

THE ROLE OF REPRESENTATION

Never before have politicians been so well equipped to measure and interpret public opinion. Bill Clinton's White House, in particular, developed a reputation for "the way policy and politics were routinely interwoven in his decision-making process." Critics regularly complain that policy is too "poll driven." During the 2000 presidential campaign, George W. Bush promised that he would end the

FIGURE 5.6

Americans tend to endorse general principles but make numerous exceptions to them

The first three items show the percentage of people supporting the general principles indicated. The last four items show the percentage of people supporting specific civil liberties for the political or social group they dislike the most. The groups about which people were asked included members of the John Birch Society, the Ku Klux Klan, and the Black Panthers, as well as fascists, communists, socialists, atheists, anti-abortionists, and pro-abortionists.

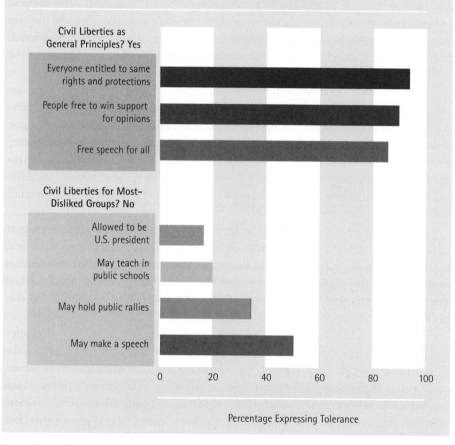

SOURCE: Data are taken from John Sullivan, James Piereson, and George Marcus, *Political Tolerance and American Democracy* (Chicago: University of Chicago Press, 1982).

permanent campaign. "A responsible leader . . . makes decisions based upon principle, not based upon polls or focus groups," he told an audience in Michigan. Six months into his presidency, though, observers noted that the Bush White House was polling about twice a month.[40] The permanent campaign seems inescapable. The presidency aside, however, there is no guarantee that public policy will follow public opinion even when preferences are fairly clear. The reason is that although individual politicians may be highly responsive to public opinion, the system of representation as a whole may not be.

One recent tragedy provides an illustration. On April 20, 1999, two male students at Columbine High School in Colorado killed 12 of their peers and wounded more than 20 others. The killers used two shotguns, a semiautomatic pistol, and a semiautomatic rifle in their murderous spree. This was the fourth school shooting in little more than a year. Other young males had shot teachers or students in West Paducah, Kentucky; in Jonesboro, Arkansas; and in Springfield, Oregon. Whether because of the cumulative impact or the sheer scale of the rampage, the Columbine shootings energized elected officials into action. In particular, antigun members of Congress decided to revive a stalled juvenile-crime bill so that they could use it as a vehicle for passing new gun control laws.

One controversial measure was a Senate proposal to require background checks on potential customers at gun shows. The measure initially had failed because many Republican lawmakers saw it as an undue burden on gun consumers, but the inflamed state of public opinion following the school shootings gave some of them second thoughts. After still another shooting (in Conyers, Georgia), the Senate reconsidered its earlier decision. The highly publicized debate reached its climax with a roll call vote in which senators divided equally for and against the proposal, allowing Vice President Al Gore to use his constitutional tie-breaking power to give the idea Senate approval. By much wider margins, the Senate adopted other provisions mandating trigger locks on or lock boxes with every handgun sold, outlawing imports of high-capacity ammunition clips, and raising the age at which juveniles could buy handguns and assault weapons. The amended bill passed the Senate by a comfortable margin and then went to the House of Representatives.

House Republican leaders also thought that the aroused state of public opinion required some response. Speaker Denny Hastert (R-IL) commented that "This is one of those rare times when the national consensus demands that we act" and promised that the House would pass a gun control measure.[41] But the issue was now thoroughly entangled in partisan politics. Vice President Gore obviously believed that his highly visible gun control stance would aid his presidential bid, and congressional Democrats hoped to use the issue to help regain control of the Congress in 2000. The key target group was suburban voters—especially women, whom polls showed favored gun control more than men did.[42] To appeal to them, Democrats framed the issue as one of protecting children.

The Democrats were not united, however. A senior Democrat, John Dingell of Michigan, was an avid hunter and a former National Rifle Association (NRA) board member. Dingell worked with Republican leaders to develop an amendment that would weaken the Senate's gun show restrictions. Forty-five Democrats followed Dingell and joined Republicans to pass the weaker provision. However, angry liberal Democrats who believed the legislation did not go far enough then joined with angry conservative Republicans who felt it still went too far and rejected the bill! The House adjourned, so no gun control provisions resulted from the furor over Columbine.

At first glance this story seems to be one of irresponsible or even corrupt behavior by the Congress. Certainly, that is the way the media portrayed it. The story line offered by the media was simple: Public opinion counted less than the campaign contributions and arm twisting of the NRA. But this account is too simplistic. Members of Congress do not get reelected by opposing an aroused majority of their constituents in exchange for an interest-group endorsement or a $5000 PAC contribution. Rather, the failure of the House to pass gun control measures shows the imperfect connection between aggregate public opinion and national public policy.

Members of Congress typically represent districts of 630,000 people, their **constituents.** These voters may hold opinions quite different from those of the country as a whole. The national distribution of opinion is of little importance to members of Congress unless they happen to be considering a run for the presidency; the distribution of opinion in their districts is what counts. And what counts even more is the distribution of opinion among the voters who elected them. So it is no surprise that the minority of Democrats who followed Dingell's lead came mainly from rural and mixed districts, where guns tend to be a more important part of daily life. Many representatives who voted against gun control followed the sentiments *in their districts.*

Still, given the high level of support for the gun control provisions, it is likely that some representatives did vote against district majorities. Was this the NRA at work? To some extent, probably yes, but remember that interest-group endorsements and campaign contributions don't vote. There have to be voters in the district who will act on the group's support. The problem for gun control activists is that their supporters are much less likely to act on their convictions than are their opponents, who see government attempts to limit access to guns as an attack on their way of life. Even Democratic Minority Leader Richard Gephardt (D-MO) conceded, "The 80 percent that are for gun safety just aren't for it very much. They're not intense."[43]

Indeed, although most polls registered a high level of support for gun control, the same polls indicated that the public did not regard it as one of the more important issues facing the country. One national poll indicated that gun control ranked twelfth in importance as a voting issue in the next election.[44] Not many supporters of gun control are intense, **single-issue voters** (if they vote at all), but the opponents of gun control certainly are. Dingell and the Democrats who followed him pointed out that popular support for gun control was at least as high earlier in the decade as it was after Columbine, but despite that fact, Democrats lost their congressional majority in 1994 in part because of the party's support for the ban on assault weapons.

DOES PUBLIC OPINION MATTER?

American voters often fail to provide clear and useful signals to politicians, because people's views are uninformed, unconstrained by ideology, and therefore unpredictable. Nor is it certain that a good politician should make decisions based on national opinion, even when it is clear—both because people's views vary in intensity and because no one except the presidential administration represents the entire nation. Despite all these limits, however, leaders do tend to "govern by public opinion" inasmuch as voters usually get what they want in the long run. Benjamin Page and Robert Shapiro, for example, analyzed a huge collection of surveys and concluded that American public policy follows public opinion. When trends in opinion are clearly moving in one direction, public policy follows. The more pronounced the trend, the more likely policy is to follow (especially when the public moves in a liberal direction).[45]

The reason why public opinion can serve as a guide, despite all its flaws, is that what individuals do is not directly connected to what groups do. People individually may serve as poor guides for policy making, but public opinion in the aggregate possesses many virtues that individual people's opinions lack. Public opinion as a whole operates in a fashion that is fairly rational and fairly consistent. This may seem like a difficult idea, but it makes sense intuitively, as indicated by the common maxim "The sum can be greater than the parts." Think of a grade school orchestra. Individually, the young musicians are so unsteady that it is difficult to identify the tune each is playing; but put them all together, and the audience can make out "Twinkle, Twinkle Little Star." So it is with public opinion.

Most of the public is not ideological, but the public at large certainly understands that the Democrats are to the left of the Republicans on most issues.[46] Moreover, the public knew that Ronald Reagan was farther to the right than Richard Nixon was and that George McGovern was farther to the left than Jimmy Carter was. So even if individual voters do not know a candidate's ideology or party affiliation, many people do know this, and even the less-informed voters will tend to back the appropriate candidate by taking advice from other voters or organizations that share their perspective.[47] The same process works with individual issue preferences. Any one person's opinions may contain some random elements caused by lack of information or lack of reasoning, but the general direction or "mood" of the public is easier to detect, and voters act on their shifting moods in a predictable fashion.

Political scientist James Stimson shows, for example, that if hundreds of survey questions are analyzed together, they indeed yield a portrait of an electorate that was turning to the right in the years leading up to Reagan's election.[48] Given these views, voters sensibly showed greater inclination to select a Republican. In the same vein, Page and Shapiro have argued that, viewed *collectively,* the public is reasonably "rational." Analysis of thousands of poll questions asked between 1935 and 1980 shows that, in the aggregate, public opinion is more stable than the opinions of individual members of the public. Similarly, recent research shows that when federal spending goes up, public preferences for continued increases go down, an effect that indicates some broad public recognition of the direction in which government policy has moved.[49]

In short, the process of aggregation may cancel out individual error and enable the central tendency to emerge. Any one voter may hold some haphazard views based on personal interest or lack of information, but those oddities will differ from the haphazard views of the next person—and when you put everyone together, those random personal quirks will cancel each other out. That is why, if one looks at the general direction of policy as shaped by the electoral system, public opinion emerges as a critical influence on the government.

MEDIA INFLUENCE ON PUBLIC OPINION

Public opinion on the whole responds predictably and rationally to the information available to it. For many critics of the American political system, though, this begs a very important question: How good is the information available to the overall public? A public that reacts sensibly to poor or distorted information could still be a hindrance in a democratic society. Following popular opinion might even be dangerous, because it would be open to manipulation.

Concern with the quality of the nation's information providers is a legitimate source of anxiety. Very few Americans experience national politics first hand. Most learn about the national government through **mass media**—affordable communications technologies capable of reaching an extensive audience. They rely on newspapers, magazines, broadcast stations (for television or radio), or at least on word-of-mouth political commentary from friends and relatives who form part of the mass-media audience. Yet the country contains a small and shrinking number of media organizations, so the sources for political information could be narrowing.

Furthermore, the men and women who staff these organizations do not form a random sample of the U.S. population. People choose whether to enter journalism, which creates another selection effect. The attitudes of people who enter the journalistic profession inevitably will be unrepresentative of what Americans typically believe.

On the other hand, news reporters and editors generally try to perform their jobs in as "unbiased" or "balanced" or "objective" a way as possible. They may fail on occasion, but news coverage is not as distorted as media critics customarily suggest—at least not in obvious ways, such as favoring one political party or ideology. And even if media organizations occasionally distribute a biased product, it is doubtful that these distortions make much difference for American attitudes.

Audience members are both sophisticated and stubborn; they recognize unfair news coverage and resist opinions different from their own.

WHICH INFORMATION SOURCES DO AMERICANS USE?

Communication is a two-way street. No one can make people read newspapers, listen to the radio, watch TV, or visit a Web page. Citizens are free to consume or ignore any message. These choices affect what information becomes available, because media companies are profit-making enterprises. Their growth or decline reflects the tastes of the popular audience.

Surveys show that TV supplanted newspapers as the public's principal source of information in the early 1960s. Nearly 50 percent of Americans today rely primarily on television (see Figure 5.7). Figure 5.8 shows that a comparable percentage reports TV to be the most credible source of information. In short, TV is America's dominant information provider, although people still turn to newspapers in large numbers when they wish to learn about state and especially local elections.[50]

Individuals vary in their absorption of information.[51] Well-educated or older individuals are particularly likely to rely on newspapers, as are whites. Newspaper

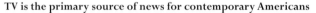

FIGURE 5.7

TV is the primary source of news for contemporary Americans

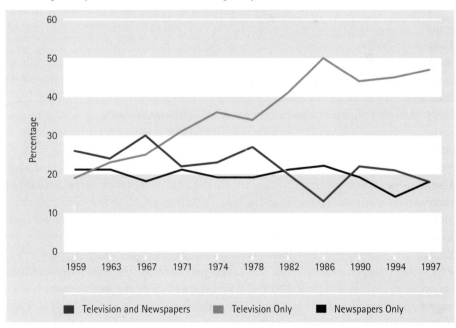

SOURCE: Data are taken from the Roper Organization, *America's Watching: Public Attitudes Toward Television* (1997).

FIGURE 5.8

Contemporary Americans consider TV their most credible source of news

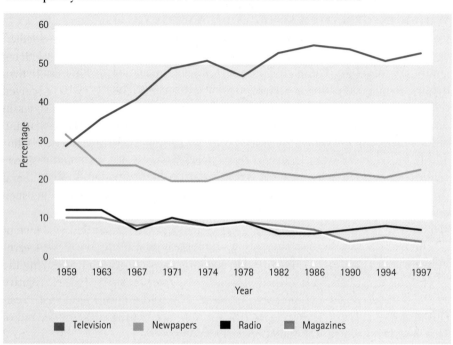

SOURCE: Data are taken from the Roper Organization, *America's Watching: Public Attitudes Toward Television* (1997).

supporters argue that print is more informative than TV, but research fails to uphold that argument once the characteristics of the audience (such as education) are taken into account.[52] That is, people of comparable background tend to learn about the same amount, whether they rely on print or television.

MEDIA BIASES

Modern journalists strive to be objective. They are supposed to report events and describe conflicts accurately so that voters can make informed judgments about their government. If reporters and editors usually lived up to this ideal, then the shrinking number of established news sources would not be much cause for concern. But news organizations and other media corporations represent an important player in the political system—essentially an institution with its own interests, values, and operating procedures. The people who staff these organizations differ from the general public. The mass media therefore might threaten democracy's operation by providing skewed information or even by trying to manipulate popular opinion.

Many observers believe that the media do skew the news. The most common charge is that the media show political bias, but most academic critics believe that other sorts of bias are even more serious.

IDEOLOGICAL BIAS   Conservatives often complain about the "liberal media." There is no doubt that liberal viewpoints are overrepresented among practicing journalists. Numerous studies report that journalists are more Democratic than the population at large: Even George McGovern and Walter Mondale received strong majorities of the vote among journalists, despite popular landslides in favor of their opponents. More recently, a survey of Washington bureau chiefs and congressional correspondents reported that, in 1992, 89 percent voted for Clinton, compared to the 43 percent of the electorate at large that did so.[53] More detailed analyses indicate that journalists hold views that are even more liberal than those of other college-educated professionals, especially on social issues such as abortion, crime, and gay rights.[54]

But do such biases show through in the news? Some studies find evidence of partisan bias on the part of reporters. For example, a team of researchers carefully watched tapes of the network evening news programs broadcast during the 1984 campaign. Their aim was to evaluate the spin—the positive or negative slant—that reporters and anchors put on their reports. They found that President Reagan, a Republican, received 10 seconds of bad spin for every second of good spin. In contrast, the Democratic candidate, Walter Mondale, had a 3-to-2 ratio of good spin to bad.[55] On a less serious note, a study of the jokes told by late-night TV talk show hosts during the 1988 campaign found that Republicans were skewered twice as often as Democrats.[56] As for the 2000 election, by mid-September George W. Bush had been the butt of 50 percent more late-night jokes than Al Gore.[57]

Lowest common denominator

As the public gets more reports of scandal, some worry that the electorate grows more cynical. Do feeding frenzies "packaged as a soap opera and a horse race" lead the public to distrust government?

Sometimes the journalistic hostility against Republicans shows through in small ways. During President Reagan's farewell address at the 1988 Republican National Convention, his speech followed a repetitive structure. Reagan would claim an accomplishment for the outgoing administration, one that Democrats might wish to deny, and end the item by admonishing, "But facts are stubborn things." Part way through the list, a loud crack shattered Reagan's concentration. The noise probably came from the stage sound system, or perhaps a balloon, but it resembled a gunshot enough to rattle Reagan, who had already survived one assassination attempt. The next time he returned to the refrain, Reagan flubbed the line, saying, "Facts are stupid things." A friendlier press corps might have described the speaker's mistake as a very human reaction to fear. Instead, national journalists did not even mention the loud noise; they portrayed Reagan's gaffe as symbolic of the conservative administration's scorn for truth.

Although journalists do deviate from objectivity and Republicans suffer more than Democrats, lapses are not as common as media critics imply. More than three-fourths of the presidential election coverage on television in 1984 had no spin at all. In the 2000 election campaign, Democrat Al Gore received a considerable amount of negative coverage, interrupted only during the couple of weeks immediately following his selection of Connecticut Senator Joseph Lieberman as a running mate. The media tend to be hard on incumbents, losers, and those caught up in scandals—even when they are Democrats. Similarly, late-night TV hosts usually focus on whoever offers the best material.

Although they are less vocal, critics on the left of the political spectrum also charge that the media are ideologically biased—only *they* see a conservative slant. Whatever the personal views of rank-and-file journalists, they work for profit-making enterprises that rely on corporate advertising. They cannot afford to emphasize ethical or environmental abuses perpetuated by business, because to do so would offend potential advertisers. Media celebrities also attract generous honoraria from corporate interests who invite them to give speeches, leading critics to call them "buckrakers" rather than muckrakers.

Some defenders of the journalistic profession point to the contradictory critiques as evidence that no real ideological bias exists. If one group says the news is too liberal and another says it is too conservative, they imply, then coverage must be just right. This response rules out the possibility that *both* criticisms may be correct. News professionals resemble others who share their social status: progressive reformers with left-wing social views who nevertheless reap the solid incomes and generous retirement benefits that go with being on a corporate payroll.[58] Just as Al Gore in 2000 could be both too left-wing for the Republicans and too comfortable with big business for the Greens, so it is possible for the typical journalist to be biased in a way that will prompt different critics to use different terminology.

The weakening of the dominance of the big-three networks should reduce any existing progressive bias. Local news and public affairs programs are more likely to reflect community sentiments and less likely to represent the biases of network news operations headquartered in New York, Washington, and Los Angeles. Cable channels broadcast programs produced by conservative and evangelical groups. Talk radio has a conservative slant. The Internet is open to all points of view, and libertarians are especially well represented there. In short, the communications channels of the future should be more open to alternative points of view than were the airwaves in the past.

BIASED STORY SELECTION Periodically, frustrated citizens write to editors to complain that all their newspapers ever print is bad news. These readers are criticizing the professional norms that journalists use to define what is "newsworthy."[59] People working hard and contributing to their communities are not news; the kidnaping of a little girl is. A government program that works well is not news; one that is mismanaged, corrupt, or a failure is. An elected official who works diligently and avoids conflict is not newsworthy; those who stoke controversy or become mired in scandal are. This negative tone has only become more prominent over time, with reporters today exhibiting what some media critics consider a "junkyard dog" mentality—attacking anyone who comes within range.[60]

Newsworthiness also favors things that are new, especially those that are exciting and unusual. Sudden events make better news than gradual developments or persistent conditions. A crisis lends itself to the kind of hit-and-run coverage favored by contemporary media. Heroes and villains, not abstract social and economic developments, form the ingredients of a good story. This bias is particularly characteristic of TV, which is even more fast-paced than print. TV needs dramatic events, colorful personalities, bitter conflicts, short and snappy comments (sound bites), and, above all, compelling pictures. A frequently heard maxim is "If it bleeds, it leads."

A media tendency to favor sudden, short-term developments can have serious political implications. Stories that do not fit media needs may receive insufficient, or at least distorted, treatment.[61] A favorite example is the largest economic policy debacle in recent American history: the savings and loan (S&L) disaster of the 1980s. This one event cost taxpayers a total of $200 billion.[62]

As early as 1981, accountants, prominent economists, and a top government regulator began to issue warnings about the troubled S&L industry—but media outlets paid little attention. As one journalist commented, "It was a 'numbers' story, not a 'people' story."[63] Most reporters lacked the training to handle such a complex issue, and anyway it was hard to cram into 30-second news segments. The government waited until 1989 to close down insolvent S&Ls, after years of reckless operation. At this point the crisis started generating catchy stories: indictments of executives, investigations of members of Congress, and housing developments auctioned off for a song. But the news coverage came a little too late for American taxpayers; they paid dearly for the S&L losses through the

Federal Savings and Loan Insurance Corporation. And even the stories that did emerge concentrated on a few instances of corruption rather than on the government policies that led to the crisis.[64]

PROFESSIONAL BIAS   A third kind of media bias arises from the demands of the journalism profession itself. A few journalists are experts who work specific beats—business reporters, education reporters, health reporters, Supreme Court reporters, and so on. But most reporters and journalists are generalists who lack specific substantive expertise. They operate on tight deadlines and must start from scratch on each new story. Thus, on many subjects more complex than scandals and conflicts, they are dependent on experts and other outside sources for information and interpretation.

Ironically, despite the familiar image of the investigative journalist, reporters uncover only a small fraction of the scandals they report—probably less than one-quarter.[65] Government agencies expose the lion's share, and they generally do so

Silence of the lambs

Journalists usually cluster together, following the same stories and relying on the same sources. This phenomenon may be called "pack journalism," but media critics suggest that the behavior more closely resembles that of sheep than a pack of wolves.

officially, not through surreptitious "leaks." Moreover, as journalists themselves recognize, the news media have increased their emphasis on entertainment.[66] Especially in the case of TV, looks and personalities are more important today than a generation ago, but even serious newspapers have become more like tabloids.

The lack of internal expertise and the competitive pressure for ratings and sales contribute to an unattractive feature of modern political coverage: "pack journalism," in which reporters unanimously decide something is The Big Story and stampede after it. When a scandal arises, the group mentality becomes even more extreme, leaping upon the victim like sharks tearing apart wounded prey in a "feeding frenzy."[67] Journalists enjoy safety in numbers, even if it means duplicating each other's efforts and obsessing over overblown, inconsequential stories. Editors cannot blame a reporter for working on the same topic or event as other prominent journalists, and in doing so, the reporter avoids the risk of missing a big story that the rest of the press corps catches.

POLITICAL NEWS

The mass media play an important role in democratic politics. Ideally, they transmit information about problems and issues, helping voters make intelligent choices among the candidates who compete for their votes. Many critics believe that the general biases we have just discussed can cause media coverage of elections and government to fall far short of the ideal.

EMPHASIS ON PERSONALITIES

The president is a single individual with personality and character; therefore, he (no woman has thus far been president) is inherently more interesting than a collective like Congress or an abstraction like the bureaucracy. The president receives the lion's share of evening news coverage.[68] And not only does Congress play second fiddle, coverage of the institution has declined in recent decades.[69]

The problem, of course, is that the president is only one part of the government, a part with fairly limited powers (see Chapter 10). Thus the media prime citizens to focus on the president to a degree that is disproportionate to his powers and responsibilities. The exception to this generalization is one that proves the rule. For six months after the 1994 elections, the media virtually forgot about President Clinton as pack journalists turned their attention to House Speaker Newt Gingrich, who led a new Republican majority in Congress. For once, the media could represent Congress via a single personality. If the Republican takeover of Congress had not been associated with a colorful individual like Gingrich, the media would undoubtedly have paid less attention.

This focus of the media on personalities seems to be a universal tendency. Note that it is similar to building sports coverage around superstars, such as baseball slugger Barry Bonds or ace pitcher Pedro Martinez. An effective governmental team, like a winning sports team, requires a strong group, but the media find individual heroics and failures more compelling. Unfortunately, this sort of personal coverage probably discourages teamwork, reinforcing grandstanding tendencies already present in the political system. Moreover, such media coverage primes citizens to think about government in terms of the heroic exploits and tragic failures of individuals rather than in terms of institutions and processes that are operating effectively or less well.[70]

EMPHASIS ON CONFLICTS, SCANDALS, AND MISTAKES Every time Speaker Gingrich made a controversial comment, he was assured of media coverage. Indeed, Gingrich's rise in national politics grew in part from his willingness to generate political conflicts of the sort reporters love and to offer his attacks on opponents in convenient sound bites. In 1995, though, Gingrich disappointed his fans in the press corps. He appeared with President Clinton on the same platform in New Hampshire, but rather than trade barbs, the two engaged in an intelligent, mature discussion. Citizens there were very receptive, and even Clinton and Gingrich seemed to enjoy it. Journalists found it dull. How could they report an intelligent discussion? And if they did, who would listen? Most reported little about it, except perhaps to note that it happened.

Reporters may focus on conflict, but they really swoop down on a story when it contains a whiff of scandal. In the first months of Bill Clinton's presidency, the public was bombarded with stories about the Whitewater land deal, aide Vince Foster's suicide, $200 haircuts, parties with actress Sharon Stone, turmoil in the White House travel office, Hillary Clinton's investments, and numerous other matters that you probably do not remember. The reason you most likely do not remember them is that, however important these matters were to the individuals involved at the time, they were not important for the overall operation of government. Hence they have been appropriately forgotten.

The focus of congressional coverage also has changed. From 1972 to the mid-1980s, policy stories outnumbered scandal stories by 13 to 1, but since then the ratio has plunged to 3 to 1.[71] It is doubtful either Congress or the White House has gotten that much worse.

CAMPAIGN COVERAGE Nowhere do critics of the mass media find more to criticize than in the media's coverage of political campaigns. The media provide little coverage of policy proposals, which voters might use to pick among candidates. Nor do they spend much time covering formal party events, such as the national conventions at which the major parties select their presidential nominees (see Figure 5.9). Instead, reporters focus on "character" issues that have little to do with the ability of candidates to govern—for example, whether a candidate was suspended from school, had an extramarital affair, or once worked for a company with interest in government contracts.

FIGURE 5.9

The networks increasingly ignore the national political conventions

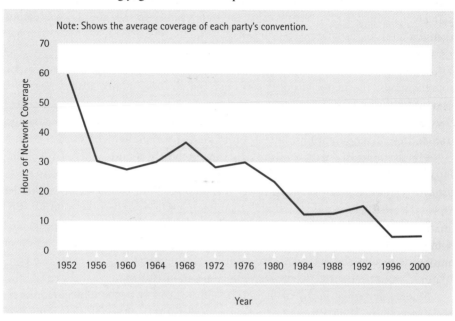

SOURCE: Adapted from Harold Stanley and Richard Niemi, *Vital Statistics of American Politics,* 5th ed. (Washington, DC: CQ Press, 1995), p. 69.

Journalists ignore policy positions because their main goal is to handicap the race. Coverage focuses on which candidate is leading, which candidate is dropping back, which one is coming up on the rail, what the latest polls say, who got what endorsement, and how a new announcement on a key issue will affect the polls. Candidate qualifications receive little attention, and issue positions are evaluated for their success as tactical moves. In short, reporters treat democratic elections as little more than horse races.

This tendency toward **horse-race coverage** has become much more pronounced over the past generation, and the attention devoted to substance has declined.[72] Increasingly, journalists interpret what candidates say rather than allowing candidates to speak for themselves. One study that compared network newscasts in 1968 with those in 1988 found that the average sound bite for presidential candidates who appeared on the news had fallen from 42 seconds to less than 10 seconds in length.[73] Even high-profile candidates receive little time to explain their positions on complex issues.

As a result, most candidates seek ways to communicate with voters directly, such as appearing on television talk shows, setting up Web pages, and paying for phone banks that contact potential voters. Establishment reporters complain that candidates are trying to insulate themselves from the hard questioning of seasoned political reporters. But if "hard questioning" is only going to produce snippets on the evening news, then it cannot be doing much for the democratic process. Candidates may simply value the opportunity to talk about issues rather than the trivia so fascinating to journalists.

THE PRESIDENTIAL DEBATES   Although political coverage exhibits many shortcomings, the material going out over the airwaves is not always negative. One of the high points of modern presidential campaigns is the series of debates between the two—sometimes three—major candidates. No other campaign events earn such high ratings. In fact, more people watch the debates than vote.

The first televised debates were held during the 1960 campaign between candidates Richard Nixon and John Kennedy. One of the surprising findings in studies of the debates was that people who listened to them on the radio evaluated Nixon's performance more favorably than people who watched them on TV did, an indication that visual images could influence voter perception.[74] No debates took place in 1964, 1968, or 1972, but they have been held in every election since. The format and arrangements continue to be matters of considerable controversy, but presidential debates have become an institution.

Studies show that performance in the debates can sway the undecided voter. For example, in 1984 President Reagan appeared tired and confused in his first debate with Walter Mondale. His unexpectedly poor performance raised the issue of his age (then 73) and resulted in a slight drop in the polls. Knowing how important the next encounter was, Reagan came in alert, prepared, and full of good humor. He dispelled the concerns raised in the first debate and gained 4 points in the polls.[75]

As in campaign coverage generally, the first question journalists raise about debates is "Who won?" Most observers agree that Vice President Gore flubbed *something* during the 2000 debates, although they disagree on exactly what and on how many votes it cost him. Several minor falsehoods, uttered in the heat of debate, attracted a journalistic feeding frenzy.[76] Gore also wavered between an arrogant and combative style (in the first and third debates) and smarmy ineffectiveness (in the second debate), some combination of which apparently alienated important swing voters.[77] But even his drop in the polls eventually dissipated.

PROSPECTS FOR CHANGE   Americans are not happy with the press corps. Popular evaluations of the media have declined sharply since the mid-1980s. Growing percentages believe that the media are unprofessional, uncaring, immoral, and even harmful to democracy (see Table 5.1). Yet the American public gets what it pays for. News executives use focus groups and other measures of audience interest to determine what impresses their consumers: what they will read, what they will watch, what they will buy.[78] News coverage may fall short of

TABLE 5.1

NEGATIVE EVALUATIONS OF THE MEDIA
ARE ON THE INCREASE

NEWS ORGANIZATIONS GENERALLY ARE	1985	1999
Moral	54%	40%
Immoral	13	38
Caring about people they report on	35	21
Uncaring about people they report on	48	67
Highly professional	72	52
Not professional	11	32
Protecting democracy	54	45
Hurting democracy	23	38
Caring about how good a job they do	79	69
Uncaring about how good a job they do	11	22

SOURCE: "Big Doubts About New Media's Values," The Pew Research Center for the People and the Press
http://www.people-press.org (posted February 1999).

what public-spirited critics would like to see, but only because it provides more of the sort of "news" that the audience wants. As humor columnist Dave Barry gently mocks, "You don't want to read about the economy. You love to read about sex. Everybody does."[79]

Perhaps the main hope of media critics is that executives underestimate their audience. People in the media were stunned by the ratings Ross Perot's "infomercials" earned during the 1992 presidential campaign—as many as 10 million households tuned in.[80] TV producers defend sound-bite journalism with the observation that the average voter has an attention span of less than 30 seconds, but Perot treated voters as intelligent adults and held the interest of many for 30 minutes with lengthy expositions accompanied by charts and figures!

MEDIA EFFECTS

Media organizations offer a biased product, but do the distortions in political journalism influence how Americans think about their government? Are advanced communications technologies something to worry about?

People once feared mass media as a great danger to democratic politics. The rapid spread of radio in the 1930s coincided with the rise of fascism in Europe. Some worried that this was more than coincidence. Before 1930, political leaders had communicated with constituencies indirectly, speaking and writing to lower-level leaders who in turn communicated with the grassroots. But demagogues like Hitler and Mussolini spoke directly to their audience, sparking fears that radio created a "mass society" of lonely individuals susceptible to charismatic hate mongers.[81]

Stimulated by such concerns, researchers conducted numerous studies of the media's ability to persuade. Contrary to expectations, though, research on the effects of mass communication turned up negative results. Americans were remarkably resistant to propaganda; media messages seldom altered the audience's views. Listeners apparently engaged in **selective perception,** absorbing information consistent with their predispositions and discounting the rest. Thus media exposure tended to reinforce what people already believed.[82]

By 1960, many scholars accepted the idea that mass media had a minimal impact on American public opinion.[83] Younger generations of researchers took a new look at the subject, however, after the rapid spread of TV. This newer research has documented important media effects, more subtle than the kind of mass persuasion that earlier studies had sought to discover.

AGENDA SETTING   The media set the agenda, even if they cannot determine how issues get resolved. By focusing on an issue or event and whipping up concern, news coverage induces people to think about a particular problem. Catastrophes in Third World countries, for example, go largely unnoticed unless the media—particularly television—turn their attention to such events. Famine struck Ethiopia in 1984, resulting in numerous front-page articles in powerful U.S. newspapers such as the *New York Times* and the *Washington Post.* The Associated Press (AP) wire service carried 228 stories.[84] But it was not until television stations beamed heartrending footage into their living rooms that a great number of Americans became aware of the problem and supported governmental efforts to help.[85] Similar responses followed media coverage of Somalia, Rwanda, and Kosovo. Media analysts have even given responses like these a nickname: the "CNN effect," after the tendency for a problem to be addressed once CNN covers it. In short, the media may not tell people *what* to think, but they do tell people what to think *about.*[86]

Agenda setting is well documented, although much of the evidence is inconclusive.[87] Researchers face a dilemma trying to sort out what causes what. Do worries prompt the coverage, does coverage instill the worries, or do real experiences produce both? Some careful studies suggest that the independent impact of the media has been exaggerated; astute government officials use the media to publicize problems that they already wish to address.[88] Nevertheless, experimental studies that raise viewer concern about subjects *not* high on the national agenda have been able to provide some evidence of agenda setting.[89]

PRIMING AND FRAMING   As we noted in the introduction to this chapter, President George H. W. Bush's approval ratings soared in 1991 after an American ground offensive drove Iraqi forces out of Kuwait. His popularity ratings reached unprecedented levels (near 90 percent). Yet within a year they had plummeted. What happened? Journalists turned to other stories after the war ended, chiefly the struggling economy. Gradually, Bush's ratings became dependent on his handling of the economy, which was viewed far less positively than his handling of the war.[90] His son also faced a foreign policy crisis, of course: the 9/11 attacks. The extended coverage of 9/11 allowed George W. Bush's popularity to improve rather than deteriorate while in office (see Figure 5.10).

The elder Bush's fall from favor is an example of **priming**—news coverage primed people to evaluate him according to his handling of the war in February 1991, but later coverage primed people to evaluate him in terms of the economy. Obviously, the media do not have full control over which criteria Americans use to evaluate their presidents. War pushes everything else off the agenda of public

FIGURE 5.10

Wartime presidents, father and son

George H.W. Bush's, extraordinarily high approval rating declined steadily after the media shifted its focus to the economy (rather than Desert Storm). His son George W. Bush saw an enormous jump in approval rating after September 11. It subsequently eroded, but not before the 2002 elections where the Republicans gained in both the House and the Senate.

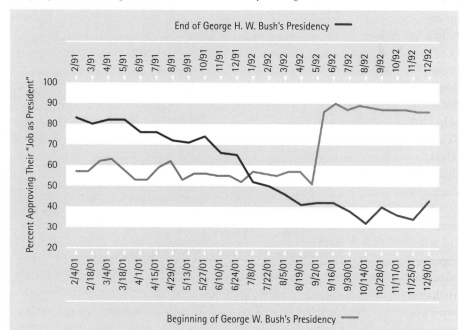

opinion: All other concerns seem minor when husbands and wives and sons and daughters are in danger. Still, studies suggest that the media overemphasized economic difficulties in the early 1990s, heightening public pessimism as well as the attention people paid to an issue on which President Bush was vulnerable.[91]

Framing and priming are related notions.[92] Earlier in the chapter, we explained that Americans tend to shift their reported issue preferences depending on how pollsters frame a question. How issues are framed shapes more than just survey results, however; it also molds how public opinion thinks about issues more generally. For example, if Wall Street scandals are portrayed as the sins of a few villainous characters, then voters are less likely to demand structural changes in the investment world than they would if the scandals were portrayed as a natural by-product of economic policy.

EVALUATING MEDIA EFFECTS   Media organizations can affect the political agenda—what people think about. They can prime people to think about certain issues and frame how they evaluate them. But the strength of these media effects depends on both the audience and the message. People who are uninterested in and uninformed about politics are most susceptible to agenda setting. For example, political independents are more likely to be uninformed, so their concerns shift from one issue to another with changes in the intensity of media coverage. On the other hand, partisans are already primed to think in terms of issues at the core of their party's concerns, so their attitudes prove more resistant to change.[93]

The characteristics of the information being communicated are at least as important. When a problem or event is far away—well beyond personal experience—the mass media provide the only information available. During the Vietnam conflict, for example, Americans supported the war early on, when journalists did not criticize it, but turned against the war when journalists started publicizing American failures. Media influence diminishes, though, when information is closer to home and people have some personal basis for arriving at opinions (see the accompanying Election Connection, "The Whole World Was Watching").[94] American voters are not mere slaves of the mass media when it comes to the domestic policies that most closely affect their daily lives.

MASS MEDIA AND
THE ELECTION CONNECTION

Mass media have existed for less than two centuries. The political news they provide does contain some bias, and sometimes the resulting distortions do sway public opinion. However, the overall trend in their development has not been to undermine democracy, but to strengthen it. Indeed, mass media are a critical

ELECTION CONNECTION

The Whole World Was Watching

More than three decades ago, hundreds of thousands of young Americans fought in the Vietnam War. More than 58,000 died, and ten times that number were wounded. Many Americans protested against the war, and especially against the military draft—the selection system that decided who would have to fight. Their protests sometimes won sympathy with journalists, but the public response was far more negative, a striking illustration of the way people resist media messages.

As the 1968 Democratic convention drew near, activists planned to gather in Chicago and protest the impending presidential nomination of the sitting vice president. Hubert Humphrey had not entered a single primary, but his influence within the Democratic party guaranteed that delegates would select him anyway. Most voters could not figure out exactly where Humphrey stood on the Vietnam conflict by 1968 (see Chapter 7), but his previous support for the administration still angered those committed to the antiwar movement.

The level of tension that existed at that time exceeds anything familiar to observers of contemporary politics. Mayor Richard Daley and the Chicago police force fully expected widespread violence on the streets. Rumors flew among the cops and National Guard troops stationed outside that activists might lace the Convention water supply with hallucinogenic drugs or pose as cab drivers to kidnap Democratic officials.

Daley refused to issue protest permits and warned that the city would deal harshly with those who spoiled the celebration. But some protest leaders were more than willing to provoke such reprisals. A group calling themselves yippies even floated the rumor that they would fill a nearby lake with 10,000 nude bodies. They never carried through on this threat, but they did help fill Chicago with roughly that number of demonstrators.

Many protesters flooded into Chicago's Grant and Lincoln parks, despite the lack of permits. They milled about on the grass, danced to provocative rock music, or chanted Buddhist mantras. After some preliminary skirmishes, Daley's storm troopers finally decided to flush them out of the parks. They bathed the assemblies with tear gas, forcing many into the streets, where more tear gas and more police waited. The harshest confrontation occurred outside the Hilton Hotel, where the convention delegates stayed. As a mostly college-age crowd gasped and choked, armored troops formed into attack wedges and surged into the crowd, flailing about with stout clubs. Other officers hid their identities and attacked news reporters. Ultimately, more than 500 victims needed medical attention. An investigative commission later described the explosion as a "police riot."

The attacks greatly disturbed many political elites. Inside and outside the convention, public figures used the harshest rhetoric. From the podium of the convention, on prime-time television, Senator Abraham Ribicoff of Connecticut accused Mayor Daley of using "Gestapo tactics" to quash dissent—eliciting a string of obscenities from Mayor Daley that media microphones could not pick up. Hard-bitten British reporters who had covered the civil war in Northern Ireland wrote that the Chicago police had gone berserk.

Media reporters clearly sympathized with the protesters. As Tom Wicker of the *New York Times* put it, "These were our children in the streets, and the Chicago police beat them

(continued)

(continued from previous page)

up."[110] Over the course of the evening, the media lost all semblance of balance. They allowed bleeding protesters to vent their anger over the airwaves. Longtime NBC anchor Chet Huntley condemned the police. Walter Cronkite choked back tears.

It was exactly the sort of shocked reaction that many of the protesters had hoped to provoke when they exposed themselves to attack. They had uncovered the bankruptcy of "the establishment," which could combat disagreement only through brute force. As tear gas floated hazily before the cameras and sirens filled the background, the news footage carried a continuous taunt from the demonstrators: "The whole world is watching! The whole world is watching!"

Indeed, much of the United States *was* watching. But what neither the protesters nor the journalists realized was that most in the audience were cheering on the storm troopers! Poll results that followed the Democratic National Convention stunned American elites: Popular majorities thought Chicago police had acted appropriately. In fact, more believed that the police should have used greater force than considered their actions excessive.

Protesters of the sort demonstrating in Chicago were familiar sights on college campuses, at public buildings such as draft offices, and in city streets. Many people had developed strong views about protesters; there was little opportunity for the media's interpretation of the events in Chicago to alter such predispositions. In other words, the American people had tuned out the chatter, stared at their TVs, and rooted for the cops. So much for the awesome power of television.

What do you think?

- If cops beat up student protesters today, would Americans find such treatment as acceptable now as they found it in 1968?

- If cops beat up student protesters today, would journalists be as upset now as they were in 1968?

SOURCES: Allen J. Matusow, *The Unraveling of America: A History of Liberalism in the 1960s* (New York: Harper & Row, 1984); Jules Witcover, *The Year the Dream Died: Revisiting 1968 in America* (New York: Warner Books, 1997); Todd Gitlin, *The Sixties: Years of Hope, Days of Rage* (New York: Bantam, 1987); Ronald Radosh, *Divided They Fell: The Demise of the Democratic Party, 1964–1996.* (New York: Free Press, 1996); Lewis Chester, Godfrey Hodgson, and Bruce Page, *An American Melodrama* (New York: Viking, 1969); John Robinson, "Public Reaction to Political Protest: Chicago 1968," *Public Opinion Quarterly* 34 (1970): 1–9.

component of America's new democracy. The more that voters know about the actions of their governmental leaders, the more they can exert popular influence. Knowledge is power, and more political information is available now than ever before. Politicians must adapt to the information-rich environment, part of a never-ending struggle to shape how their constituents perceive them.

NEWSPAPERS

At the time of the American Revolution, most of the colonies' newspapers were weeklies; the first daily paper in the United States began publication in Philadelphia in 1783.[95] These early papers were published by printers who, like Benjamin

Franklin, also published books, almanacs, and official documents. They reprinted material from European newspapers and from each other, as well as letters and essays from their readers.

As party politics developed, both fledgling parties realized the importance of having a means of communicating with their constituents. Hamilton and the Federalists established a "house" paper, the *Gazette of the United States,* and the Jeffersonians responded with the *National Gazette.* These newspapers were unabashedly one-sided: They printed the party line, viciously attacked the oppo-sition, and depended for economic survival on government printing contracts. Thus, although early presidents did not speak in their own voices, they have been "going public" to the extent that technology allowed since the beginning of the republic.[96]

Improvements in the manufacturing of paper and type and the invention of the steam-driven printing press made it cheaper and easier to publish papers. In 1833 the *New York Sun* began daily publication, selling for a mere penny. (Before that time the going price for a newspaper was an exorbitant six cents!) The rise of the penny press marks the birth of the mass media in the United States. Millions of ordinary people could purchase and read newspapers. Within two years the circulation of the *Sun* was third in the world, behind only the two largest London newspapers.

As readership expanded, newspapers began to acquire their modern charac-teristics. One is sensationalism. Then, as now, crime and sex sold newspapers. Politics and economics were left to the older weeklies. Still, the new penny papers were overwhelmingly partisan. According to the 1850 census, only 5 per-cent of the country's newspapers were neutral or independent.[97] Politicians worked hand in hand with the editors of friendly papers and withheld informa-tion from those allied with the opposition.

After the Civil War, an independent press began to develop. One-sided edito-rial positions remained common, but many publishers saw little point in alienat-ing a large portion of their potential audience. Nor did political leaders need party organs any longer. This was the heyday of the political machine, when party bosses used their own networks of volunteers to communicate with constituents (see Chapter 8). Patronage jobs and government contracts, not editorials, cemented political alliances.

The trend toward independence continued into the turn of the century, when many newspapers became large enterprises. Hearst, Scripps, and other compa-nies bought up independent papers and consolidated them into great chains. Thus the typical paper no longer was the voice of a lone editor. Journalists became more professional and even less partisan. Some newspapers were important participants in the Progressive movement, publishing "muckraking" exposés of shocking conditions in American industry and of corruption in government.

The most important development in the modern newspaper industry has been the decline in diversity. Afternoon newspapers have all but disappeared. Mergers have resulted in most cities being served by one or two papers, compared to several half a century ago, and chains such as Gannett have continued to gobble up independent newspapers. Moreover, some media conglomerates own TV and radio stations—even networks—not just newspapers. Some observers worry that the mass media are losing their value as they face increased pressure to generate corporate profit.

RADIO

In the 1930s, the print monopoly of mass communications began to erode. The first radio stations appeared in the 1920s, the first radio news agencies in the 1930s. Politicians quickly made use of this exciting new technology. President Coolidge (1924–1928) was known as "Silent Cal," but to reach voters he took to the airwaves. Franklin Roosevelt helped calm a worried nation in the 1930s with his famous "fireside chats." Radio demagogues, such as the hateful Father Coughlin, exerted a less calming influence during the same period.

Radio spread rapidly throughout the country. Today, more than 14,000 stations reach nearly 85 percent of the population at some time on an average day. Virtually every household has at least one radio; the average is more than five. And, of course, there are millions of cars on the road, nearly all of which contain radios. Because of its local orientation and because it is relatively cheap, radio continues to be an important way for lower-level public officials to reach people.

Probably the most important recent development in radio communications is the rapid increase in talk shows. Talk shows have existed for half a century, but until recently most were local productions. The development of satellite technology and the lowering of long-distance telephone rates removed the geographic limits on such shows, and today many of them are syndicated by large networks. Rush Limbaugh's show is perhaps the best-known example. This conservative commentator began broadcasting nationally in 1988, and as of 2000, his program was reaching about 20 million listeners on more than 600 stations.[98] Liberals have tried to compete in this medium as well, although conservative viewpoints continue to have a wide edge. The talk format is a very popular radio format, trailing only country–western and adult contemporary music programs.[99]

TELEVISION

To most people today, the term *mass media* means television. There are more than 1500 television stations in the United States, and about 99 percent of all households have at least one TV set, the average being four. Like radio, TV is close to being a universal medium of communication.

The first TV station went on the air in 1939, but TV grew very slowly during World War II. Afterward it spread rapidly; by 1960, 90 percent of all households had TVs. Three large networks initially dominated the industry: NBC, CBS, and ABC. The networks pay local affiliates to carry programs the networks offer. The affiliates, in turn, make advertising time available for the networks to sell. Of course, the profit that networks make from their advertising time depends critically on the popularity of their shows—which is why ratings are such an important consideration when it comes to programming decisions.

The Eisenhower campaign was the first to take advantage of TV for communicating political messages, producing simple commercials that seem silly when viewed today. But it was the Kennedy administration that elevated TV above the print medium and used it effectively. During his short presidency, Kennedy held regularly televised press conferences that enabled him to go over the heads of the media and communicate directly with voters. Kennedy once commented to a reporter, "When we don't have to go through you bastards we can really get our story to the American people."[100]

Network TV reached its height in the 1980s. About 85 percent of all the commercial TV stations in the country were affiliated with one of the big-three networks: ABC, CBS, or NBC. But the network system began to fray after government deregulated the cable industry in the 1970s. The percent of households with cable increased from 20 percent in 1980 to 67 percent in 2000. Prime-time network programming has lost more than a quarter of its audience, as cable stations have proliferated.[101] Still, although the combined ratings of the big-three evening news telecasts have fallen by 30 percent since the mid-1980s, they continue to draw an audience of about 70 million people on an average weekday.[102] Network TV remains the largest single source of information available to Americans.

NEW MEDIA

During the 1992 campaign, Bill Clinton and Ross Perot irritated the establishment media by appearing on nontraditional outlets, such as *Larry King Live!* and the *Arsenio Hall Show,* and even on cable station MTV. Clinton played his sax for Arsenio and discussed his underwear preferences on MTV. Perot virtually announced his candidacy on *Larry King Live!* Even President Bush felt compelled to appear on these shows to compete for attention. National politicians now avoid popular programs at their peril.

Cable TV is the most widespread example of the **new media,** although the term also includes VCRs, fax machines, cellular phones, satellite dishes, CDs, and especially anything connected with the Internet.[103] The Cable News Network (CNN) appeared in 1979. Aside from cable TV, few Americans use the new media for political information. Surveys indicate that only half of the American population had access to the Internet by the summer of 2000.[104] Few of those with Internet access pay much attention to political Web sites. One survey conducted during the height of the 2000 primary season found that only 11 percent of Internet users had ever visited a candidate's Web site, a figure far lower than the number who had seen a candidate on network TV's evening news or even CNN.[105]

But radio and TV also started small, and given the explosive growth of the Internet, it is likely that after another election cycle or two, the Internet will be a true mass medium. Consider that in 1992, neither presidential candidate had an official Web site; by 2000, Web sites were standard in campaigns as far down as the local level. Use of the Web for raising money grew rapidly in the recent primary campaigns as well. In absolute terms the amount raised was small: The four leading presidential candidates (Bradley, Bush, Gore, and McCain) raised a total of $139 million in 1999, less than 3 percent of which came from online contributions.[106] But the proportion that was raised online increased over the course of the year. Moreover, after McCain's upset victory in the New Hampshire primary, online contributions soared—he raised $5.6 million in the month after New Hampshire, a quarter of his total fund raising.[107] Given the ease of contributing online, especially after so-called e-check technology becomes widespread, such fund raising no doubt will grow.[108]

Network TV has a large, diverse audience. Thus it encourages politicians to make general appeals. In contrast, the newer media allow politicians to communicate more specific information to targeted audiences. Once again, an innovation in the media realm is altering the existing equilibrium between politicians and the media, this time apparently in favor of politicians. The new media give them a greater capacity to communicate to voters without having their messages constrained and edited by the traditional mass media. The struggle for control of information continues.

CHAPTER SUMMARY

Public opinion is a basic element of democratic politics, but measuring public opinion is an inexact science at best. The question wording, the sample, and the complexity of the issues make designing good public opinion polls very tricky. Public opinion exerts its influence largely through the calculations of public officials, who understand that they can be challenged in free elections and must consider the distribution and intensity of views on any issue. Elected officials clearly hesitate to defy the will of an aroused public, but even unexpressed public opinion may influence the actions of politicians who fear arousing it.

Despite the importance of public opinion, governing by opinion poll is difficult and perhaps undesirable. Citizens tend not to be well informed; their views are not firmly held, can change quickly, and often are not connected to other, seemingly related views. For these reasons, poll results often are misleading and often are misinterpreted by politicians and journalists. In the long run, American democracy follows public opinion, but public policy does not always respond to shifts in public opinion over the short term.

In recent years many people have expressed concern that *mass media* are increasingly shaping public opinion. Overall, little evidence supports the worst fears of media critics. For example, an extensive study of opinion change during the 1980 presidential campaign found that in the aggregate, TV and newspaper exposure had only marginal effects on preexisting views.[109] And more recently, despite the overwhelmingly negative coverage President Clinton received during the Lewinsky scandal, his job performance ratings scarcely budged. Nevertheless, under some circumstances, the media can move public opinion—if not directly, then by determining how values, interests, and education come together to shape individuals' political beliefs. Such effects depend on people's predispositions and on their outside sources of knowledge.

Frequently, critics charge the media with one or another form of bias. Journalists certainly appear to be establishment liberals, progressive reformers who support capitalism but endorse liberal social change. More important, norms of newsworthiness and pressures on the news-gathering process distort coverage of political issues, prompting critics to assail the way the news industry presents both elections and the process of governance. Nevertheless, the mass media are less than two centuries old, and the spread of political knowledge permits voters to use their influence more effectively. If knowledge really is power, then media organizations form an important political institution that has expanded popular influence in America's new democracy.

KEY TERMS

agenda setting,
  p. 158
constituents, p. 144
framing, p. 160
horse-race coverage,
  p. 155
ideologies, p. 138
information costs,
  p. 137
issue publics, p. 137
mass media, p. 146
mass public, p. 138

measurement error,
  p. 128
new media, p. 165
political efficacy,
  p. 124
political elites,
  p. 138
priming, p. 159
random sample,
  p. 125
sampling error, p. 125
selection bias, p. 127

selective perception,
  p. 158
single-issue voters, p. 144
socializing agent,
  p. 123

ON THE WEB

American Association for Public Opinion Research
www.aapor.org
An academic association interested in the methods, applications, and analysis of public opinion and survey research. This site offers access to the *Public Opinion Quarterly* index and its contents.

The Roper Center for Public Opinion Research
www.ropercenter.uconn.edu
An academic, nonprofit center for the study of public opinion that maintains the world's largest archive of public opinion data.

The National Opinion Research Center
www.norc.uchicago.edu
Based at the University of Chicago, this social science data site provides access to survey history, a library of publications, links, and information on general social survey methodology.

News Organizations
abcnews.go.com/sections/politics
www.cnn.com/allpolitics
www.latimes.com/news/politics/
www.foxnews.com/politics/
www.washingtonpost.com/ wp-dyn/politics/
These industry leaders provide thorough coverage of political news and do not require visitors to subscribe or log in before using.

The Pew Research Center for the People and the Press
www.people-press.org
This site reports on surveys of American public opinion, particularly as related to the media and the way they cover campaigns and government.

SUGGESTED READINGS

Cook, Elizabeth, Ted Jelen, and Clyde Wilcox. *Between Two Absolutes: Public Opinion and the Politics of Abortion*. Boulder, CO: Westview Press, 1992. Careful, disinterested description and explanation of American attitudes toward abortion.

Herbst, Susan. *Numbered Voices: How Opinion Polling Has Shaped American Politics*. Chicago: University of Chicago Press, 1993. An informative historical survey of the growth of opinion polling, with a critical exami-

nation of its impact on contemporary politics.

Iyengar, Shanto, and Donald Kinder. *News That Matters*. Chicago: University of Chicago Press, 1987. An exemplary experimental study that demonstrates the existence of agenda setting and priming.

Jacobs, Lawrence, and Robert Shapiro. *Politicians Don't Pander: Political Manipulation and the Loss of Democratic Responsiveness*. Chicago: University of Chicago Press, 2000. Provocative argument that today's politicians follow their own strongly held preferences and that polls are only a tool used to determine how best to frame the positions that the politicians personally favor.

Page, Benjamin, and Robert Shapiro. *The Rational Public*. Chicago: University of Chicago Press, 1992. Monumental study of public opinion from the 1930s to the 1990s. The authors argue that, viewed as a collectivity, the public is rational, however imperfect the individual opinions that members of the public hold.

Patterson, Thomas. *Out of Order*. New York: Vintage, 1994. A critical discussion of the way the print media define news when they cover presidential campaigns. Recommended by President Clinton.

Sabato, Larry. *Feeding Frenzy: Attack Journalism and American Politics*. Baltimore: Lanahan, 1991. New edition. Entertaining critique of the most extreme manifestations of "pack journalism."

Schuman, Howard, and Stanley Presser. *Questions and Answers in Attitude Surveys*. New York: Harcourt, Academic Press, 1981. A comprehensive study of the effects of question wording, form, and context on survey results.

Stimson, James. *Public Opinion in America: Moods, Cycles, and Swings*. Boulder, CO: Westview Press, 1991. Statistically sophisticated examination of American public opinion from the 1960s to the 1990s, in which the author finds that public opinion was moving in a conservative direction in the 1970s but reversed direction around the time of Reagan's election.

Zaller, John. *The Nature and Origins of Mass Opinion*. New York: Cambridge University Press, 1992. An influential reinterpretation of public opinion findings that argues that people do not have fixed opinions on many subjects. Rather, their responses reflect variable considerations stimulated by the question and the context.

INDIVIDUAL PARTICIPATION

I t is impossible to say who really won the 2000 presidential contest (see Chapter 1). The winner of Florida was the winner of the election, but that knowledge does not help much—the vote was too close and the state's method of balloting too messy for drawing any definitive conclusions. Election night left George W. Bush ahead of Al Gore by only 537 votes, so Florida law required a recount, but it left rather muddled instructions on how to carry out the process.

Counties in Florida used paper ballots, and numerous voters marked those ballots inadequately. Some did not register their choice cleanly, so electronic counting machines skipped them (undervotes). Others voted for two or more candidates, usually because of confusion about the ballot instructions; their choices were thrown out as well (overvotes). Determining a final vote count for Florida therefore depends on how one decides to treat overvotes compared to undervotes. It also depends on a subjective judgment about how clearly the undervotes had to be marked on the ballot for them to count. And it depends on whether one tallies the ballots in every Florida county or one chooses a subset based on the legal claims of Gore and Bush.

The U.S. Supreme Court ended the official counting, which ensured Bush's victory. But media organizations decided to conduct the recount that Florida was not permitted to see whether, as some disenchanted Democrats could be heard to state around the nation's water coolers, "the Republican Supreme Court stole the election." The recounts cost lots of money and took lots of time, and ultimately they produced a crystal-clear answer to the question of who won: "It depends."

A recount that only worked in the undervotes found that the outcome varied between a margin of 1665 votes for Bush and 3 votes for Gore, depending on the standard used.[1] Ironically, Gore's 3-vote victory resulted from using the recount standard urged by Bush's legal team! A second study included the overvotes as well as the undervotes (even though overvotes are routinely discarded by election authorities across the nation). It found that Bush won under almost any system of counting the undervotes. Gore could have won narrowly with the overvotes included—but again, that was a standard his legal representatives never requested.[2] Thus Gore would have lost even if the U.S. Supreme Court had granted his requests, but it is possible that he deserved to win anyway. Who really won in 2000? Who knows.

It may seem discouraging that so many Americans had their ballots rejected on election day. On the other hand, undervoters and overvoters were not the only two sorts of Floridians whose voting rights counted for nothing. A much larger pool of citizens also did not have their choice tallied, in Florida as well as across the United States. What sets this group apart, though, is that it never even tried to register a preference.

Barely more than half the eligible electorate turned out to vote, despite the closeness of the 2000 contest, which means that 100 million potential voters stayed home across the nation. In Florida, where the vote margin was less that

1000 under almost any recount scenario, nearly 6 million eligibles stayed away from the polls. Nonvoters were 400 times more numerous than Gore's margin in the country as a whole, and in every state nonvoters exceeded the difference between the Bush and Gore votes—typically many times over. The closeness of the race, combined with the large pool of untapped potential voters, underscores that electoral politics is not entirely about the candidates and parties that voters pick. People also must decide whether to vote in the first place, and that decision is critical to political outcomes.

VOTING IS WIDELY REGARDED AS THE FUNDAMENTAL FORM of democratic participation. If a bare majority votes, how representative are the public officials they elect, and how legitimate are the actions these officials take? Political theorist Benjamin Barber charges that "In a country where voting is the primary expression of citizenship, the refusal to vote signals the bankruptcy of democracy."[3] Not everyone is so concerned about low voter turnout, though. Unlike a century ago, some point out, there are no poll taxes, literacy tests, gender barriers, or property requirements to block access to the voting booth. Voters *choose* to stay away. Some are apathetic; some are ignorant; some are simply self-centered. Why badger such people? What would they bring to an election?[4]

Whether or not one is concerned about low participation, it presents a puzzle. The United States is a rich country, with citizens who have high levels of education. Usually democracy thrives in such a setting, and voting is the *only* form of democratic participation for the great bulk of the population. Yet turnout is low in presidential contests and even lower in other elections, even if they feature close contests. For example, approximately 40 percent of the voting-age population turned out in 2002, even though control of both the U.S. House and the Senate hung in the balance. It is intriguing that so few exercised their right to wade into a battle that would determine the future of their country.

Low voter turnout is interesting for one other reason. It threatens our claim that elections drive American politics. Why would voter participation be significantly *lower* if elections had a *greater* impact on politicians in America than in other countries? Americans presumably have enough common sense to decide whether an activity is worth their effort. Surely most would vote if they learned from observation that elections were important. Therefore, maybe Americans do not vote because their experience contradicts our interpretation.

Certainly some Americans stay out of politics because they doubt their ability to make a difference. But this chapter will show that most explanations for why Americans do not vote have very little to do with the importance of elections or who wins them. Americans actually vote at a higher rate than the statistics imply, and—leaving aside voting—they participate in politics at a *higher* rate than citizens in other countries. To the extent that voter participation is lower, it generally results from the laws governing elections and does not undermine the relevance of voting itself. Before defending these claims, however, we will review the history of the **franchise,** or right to vote, in the United States. Equipped with this background, you will be ready to understand why many people do not participate actively in America's new democracy.

A BRIEF HISTORY OF THE FRANCHISE IN THE UNITED STATES

A single political party, the Democratic–Republicans, dominated the United States in the early nineteenth century. The party's members in Congress met in a caucus before each presidential election to nominate their candidate, who invariably won. But in 1824 the caucus could not unite behind a single nominee. As a result, four candidates vied for the office; the main contenders were Secretary of State John Quincy Adams (son of the second president), War of 1812 hero General Andrew Jackson, and Speaker of the House Henry Clay of Kentucky.

Although Jackson received the largest share of the popular vote—50 percent more than his closest competitor—no one managed a majority in the Electoral College. The election went to the House of Representatives, as specified in the Constitution. There, Speaker Henry Clay delivered the victory to Adams, who in turn appointed Clay secretary of state, a position once considered the stepping-stone to the presidency. Jackson, the popular favorite, was shut out.

THE BIRTH OF MASS DEMOCRACY

Ironically, this instance of popular frustration produced one of the nation's most dramatic moves toward full democracy. Jackson's supporters were so outraged by the "corrupt bargain" between Adams and Clay that they redoubled their efforts for the next presidential election. They linked local political organizations together across the country, and they spread their campaign outward to the newly settled West. They pressured for change in election laws, sometimes successfully. For example, four states transferred the right to choose presidential electors from their legislatures to the voters. Turnout increased in all the other states. In total, more than three times as many men voted for electors in 1828 as had voted in 1824, and Jackson easily defeated Adams.[5]

Despite the tripling of voter turnout between 1824 and 1828, only about 56 percent of the adult male population voted in 1828. The problem was not necessarily lack of interest. Many men had no choice. Property qualifications for voting varied from state to state and were very unevenly enforced, but in various forms they continued into the 1830s. Most states restricted the franchise to taxpayers until the 1850s. Only upon the eve of the Civil War could it be said that the United States had universal white male **suffrage** (another term for franchise).

Not all voter qualifications were economic. Until the 1830s, a few states limited voting to those who professed belief in a Christian god. Jews were not permitted to vote in Rhode Island as late as 1830. Blacks generally could not vote until after the Civil War, and they lost their rights again a generation later by means of poll taxes, literacy tests, white primaries, and other discriminatory procedures (see Chapter 14). Only modern electoral reforms, such as the Voting Rights Act of 1965, effectively expanded the franchise to African Americans.

Women briefly enjoyed the right to vote in New Jersey after the Declaration of Independence. They lost it in 1807, though, and more than 60 years passed before another state granted women voting rights. Wyoming became the first state to extend the franchise to women in national elections in 1890. Eleven other states, mostly in the West, had followed by 1916. Finally, in 1920, the suffrage movement won its crowning victory when the Nineteenth Amendment was ratified (see Figure 6.1).

The last major extension of the franchise came with the adoption of the Twenty-sixth Amendment. Prior to 1971, most states did not grant the vote to

FIGURE 6.1

The right to vote in the United States has been steadily expanded

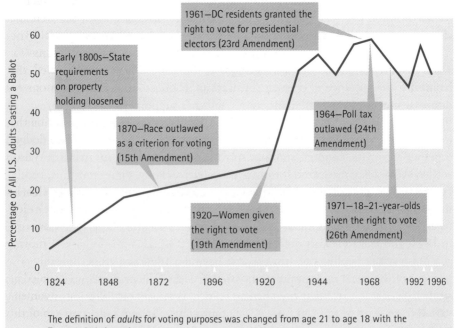

The definition of *adults* for voting purposes was changed from age 21 to age 18 with the Twenty-sixth Amendment.

NOTE: Extending the franchise to new groups does not always result in better turnout.

SOURCE: Adapted from Harold W. Stanley and Richard G. Niemi, *Vital Statistics on American Politics 1999–2000* (Washington, DC: CQ Press, 2000), p. 12.

those under age 21. This restriction became an embarrassment during the Vietnam War, however, because it implied that soldiers mature enough to die in Asian jungles were not mature enough to choose political leaders. Even Republican President Richard Nixon supported extending the suffrage to include those 18 and older, despite the certainty that young voters of the era would oppose both him and his party.[6]

WOMEN'S SUFFRAGE AND
THE IMPORTANCE OF ELECTIONS

The uneven expansion of the franchise illustrates the overwhelming power of free elections to make a society even more democratic over time. Elected leaders naturally want to expand the influence of social groups that support them. And once a few members of a social group achieve political power, no politician wants to explain why others like them should remain powerless. Promising to give a group more influence in future elections is a fairly cheap way to attract its support, or at least forestall its opposition. This dynamic operated to expand voting rights for blacks and the young, but it was most apparent in the case of women's suffrage.

Fewer than a dozen states allowed women to vote in 1916. Many influential Democratic politicians opposed giving them the franchise. They believed that women were more likely to support Republican reformers. Women would vote against labor unions, against liquor interests, and against machine politicians—all key Democratic constituencies. Moreover, southern Democrats worried that granting voting rights to women would raise African American aspirations for similar rights.

Democratic President Woodrow Wilson, who was running for reelection that year, did not have a clear position on women's suffrage. Indeed, he once dodged the issue by saying that the question had never come to his attention. But Wilson was in a difficult spot. He had won the 1912 election in a three-way race, receiving only 42 percent of the popular vote. His 1916 opponent, Republican Charles Evans Hughes, supported women's suffrage, and one-sixth of the country's electoral votes belonged to states where women could vote. If Wilson came out against a constitutional amendment to expand the franchise, he risked moving Hughes one-third of the way toward an Electoral College majority.

Thus Wilson decided to ignore the wishes of many Democrats and signaled his moderate support for the cause. He promised to vote in favor of a 1916 women's suffrage referendum in New Jersey, his home state. Partly on the strength of this moderate position, Wilson was able to carry 10 of the 12 women's suffrage states and narrowly win reelection. Politicians quickly jumped on the bandwagon, passing a constitutional amendment through Congress and the states in time for women to vote in the 1920 presidential election nationwide. Interestingly, the

United States was far ahead of most of the world in granting full rights of citizenship to women. France did not allow women to vote until 1945, and the last Swiss canton did not enfranchise women until 1990![7]

INTERNATIONAL COMPARISONS OF VOTER TURNOUT

The United States expanded the franchise more quickly than other advanced democracies. Today every mentally competent, law-abiding citizen who has reached the age of 18 may vote. Elections are a central institution of American politics. It is therefore puzzling (and perhaps a bit embarrassing) that Americans participate at particularly low levels (see Table 6.1). The truth is not quite as dire, however, as the statistical comparisons imply. Procedures for calculating turnout differ from country to country, and the differences systematically downgrade American turnout figures relative to those in other democracies.

COMPUTING TURNOUT

Turnout would seem simple enough to measure. It should be the proportion of those able to vote who actually do so. The U.S. Bureau of the Census calculates official turnout in presidential elections as the number of people voting for president divided by the number of people in the voting-age population. This definition seems straightforward, but it lowers American turnout as much as 5 percent relative to other countries.

Consider the numerator, the number of people voting for president. If an American believes that all the candidates are bums and either does not vote for president or does not pick a recognizable candidate, that citizen is not counted as having voted. Other countries are more flexible. In France, for example, unhappy voters have long scribbled an offensive suggestion across their ballots (the English translation has initials "F.Y."). French election officials count such ballots, whereas most American officials would not.[8] Furthermore, if someone casts a "frivolous" write-in vote (actual examples from U.S. elections include ZZ Top and Batman), election officials in many jurisdictions ignore that vote rather than tabulating it as "other." The decision to exclude some ballots lowers U.S. turnout figures by 1 to 2 percent per election.[9]

More important are factors that affect the denominator, the number of people in the voting-age population. The **voting-age population** is the number of people over the age of 18, a number that includes some groups legally ineligible to vote: felons, people confined to mental or correctional institutions, and (most important) noncitizens. Counting the entire voting-age population rather than only the eligible voting-age population lowers U.S. turnout figures by another 3 percent.[10] The underestimate is getting worse because the numbers of felons and immigrants are rising.[11]

TABLE 6.1

AMERICANS ARE LESS LIKELY TO VOTE
THAN THE CITIZENS OF OTHER DEMOCRACIES

The figures represent the average turnout (in percentages) in elections to the lower house of the legislature or parliament in 37 countries, 1960–1995. Why are some nations high on this list and others low?

COUNTRY	AVERAGE TURNOUT (%)	COUNTRY	AVERAGE TURNOUT (%)
Australia (14)[a]	95	Costa Rica (8)	81
Malta (6)	94	Norway (9)	81
Austria (9)	92	Israel (9)	80
Belgium (12)	91	Portugal (9)	79
Italy (9)	90	Finland (10)	78
Luxembourg (7)	90	Canada (11)	76
Iceland (10)	89	France (9)	76
New Zealand (12)	88	United Kingdom (9)	75
Denmark (14)	87	Ireland (11)	74
Venezuela (7)	85	Spain (6)	73
Bulgaria (2)	80	Japan (12)	71
Germany (9)	86	Estonia (2)	69
Sweden (14)	86	Hungary (2)	66
Greece (10)	86	Russia (2)	61
Lithuania (1)	86	India (6)	58
Latvia (1)	85	United States (9)	54
Czech Republic (2)	85	Switzerland (8)	54
Brazil (3)	83	Poland (2)	51
Netherlands (7)	83		

[a]Number of elections.

SOURCE: Adapted from Mark Franklin, "Electoral Participation," in Lawrence Le Duc, Richard Niemi, and Pippa Norris, eds., *Comparing Democracies* (Thousand Oaks, CA: Sage, 1996), p. 218.

Other countries use a different denominator in their turnout calculations: the registered population. More than 30 percent of the American voting-age population is unregistered. When turnout is measured as the number voting among **registered voters**—those who have signed up according to the requirements prevailing in their states and localities—U.S. figures jump to the mid-range of turnout in industrial democracies.

Since registered American voters turn out at levels typical of other democracies, it is tempting to conclude that registration requirements are part of the problem. Voter registration is automatic in most of the world, a function performed by the central government. American practice differs in making registration entirely the responsibility of the individual, and one-third of the eligible population does not bother to register. It is not clear whether simplifying registration would make a significant difference, though. A few states have no registration, and others let voters register at their polling stations on election day, yet turnout still falls well below the levels in many European countries.[12] Activists tried to increase voting by pushing 1993's "motor voter" law, which required motor vehicle offices to double as voter registration offices—but preliminary evidence suggests that this reform did not make much difference.[13] Statistical simulations suggest that liberalizing registration procedures would increase national turnout figures by only about 9 percent.[14]

HOW AMERICAN INSTITUTIONS HOLD DOWN TURNOUT

Registration requirements may not explain low voter turnout, but other legal differences between Europe and the United States do. Voting is compulsory in some countries.[15] Greek electoral law provides for imprisonment of nonvoters for up to 12 months. That penalty is never applied, but other democracies do penalize nonvoters, at least sometimes. Australian law allows for fines of up to $50 for not voting (without a valid excuse), and 4 percent of nonvoters apparently must pay. Belgium also imposes fines. In addition to having their identification papers stamped "Did Not Vote," Italian nonvoters have their names posted on community bulletin boards. Nonvoters risk the possibility of unsympathetic treatment at the hands of public officials or criticism from their friends.

Turnout is almost 15 percent higher in democracies with compulsory voting than in other democracies.[16] No doubt turnout in American elections would increase if the government punished those who abstained! But it is not clear that, to Americans, the ideas of democracy and forced voting go together.

Several additional institutional variations raise the costs of voting for Americans. Elections in America traditionally are held on Tuesdays, an ordinary workday. In most of the rest of the world, either elections are held on Sundays or election days are proclaimed official holidays. In Italy, workers receive free train fare back to their places of registration, usually their hometowns, so in effect the government pays for family reunions.

Also, keep in mind that the United States conducts more elections than other countries do (see Chapter 1).[17] In most European countries, citizens vote only two or three times in five years—once for members of Parliament, once for representatives to the European Union, and perhaps once for small numbers of local officials. The burden is much less than American voters face, so turnout statistics for a single American election are not comparable with those for a single European election. Some have suggested, not completely tongue in cheek, that turnout in the United States should be calculated as the percentage who vote at least once during a four-year period. This number would be closer to turnout figures for other countries.*

Finally, some states use voter lists to select people for jury duty. Although serving on juries is an important right, established to protect citizens from out-of-control government prosecutions, many Americans consider it an annoying disruption of their private lives; they will forgo voting to avoid the responsibility. One study concluded that turnout is 5 to 10 percent lower where jury selection targets voters.[18] And this calculation leaves out the many Americans who do not register because they mistakenly believe that they live in such jurisdictions!

All in all, both intentionally and accidentally, American practices raise the "costs" of voting relative to those in other countries. When some citizens understandably react to those costs by failing to vote, editorialists criticize them for their lack of public spirit. Scholars, meanwhile, are puzzled that turnout is so low in such a wealthy, educated country, where civic attitudes encourage popular participation. But the nation's laws are not equally encouraging. Political scientist Bingham Powell estimates that differences in electoral institutions, chiefly registration systems, depress American turnout between 10 and 15 percent relative to that in Europe.[19] In sum, it costs Americans more to vote, and they receive less support for voting than citizens in most other countries.

WHY AMERICANS VOTE LESS OFTEN THAN IN THE PAST

For many people the puzzle is not only that turnout levels are lower in the United States than in other advanced democracies, but also that turnout has fallen over time (see the accompanying Election Connection, "The Critical Election of 1896"). The declines have continued during the past generation, hitting a half-century low in 1996 (see Figure 6.2). In off-year elections, turnout has declined more erratically, but it is significantly lower now than it was a generation ago. Other forms of electoral participation—such as working in campaigns, attending political meetings, or signing petitions—may have declined over the last generation as well.[20]

To many observers, these declines in popular participation suggest that something is terribly wrong with American politics. Their concern was reinforced in the late 1970s when analysts noted that participation was declining at the same time that trust in government was declining—recall Figure 1.1. Many feared that declining trust threatened the entire political system and that declining turnout was

---

*Interestingly, Switzerland also asks voters to turn out frequently, and the turnout rate there is comparable to the American rate.

FIGURE 6.2

Turnout in the United States has declined since 1960

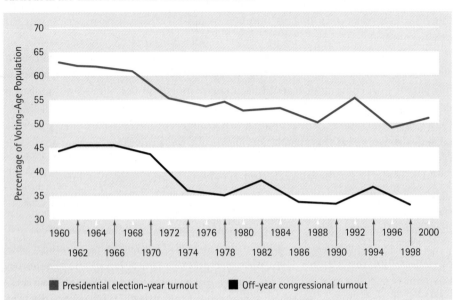

SOURCE: Norman Ornstein, Thomas Mann, and Michael Malbin, *Vital Statistics on Congress, 1999–2000* (Washington, DC: American Enterprise Institute, 2000), p. 48.

but an early symptom of a coming crisis. Research soon showed, however, that the two trends were largely unrelated. That is, turnout declined among the trusting and the cynical alike, and the former were no more likely to vote than the latter.[21]

What makes the decline in turnout all the more puzzling is that two other developments in the past three decades led to an expectation of *rising* turnout. First, court decisions, federal legislation such as the Voting Rights Act and its amendments, and the Twenty-fourth Amendment to the Constitution have removed numerous impediments to voting. For example, poll taxes and literacy tests were abolished, state and local residency requirements were shortened, registration was made simpler and more convenient, bilingual ballots were permitted, and absentee voting was made easier. Such reforms were especially effective in the South, where they helped overcome the legacy of racial discrimination.

Second, socioeconomic change should have raised turnout in the post-1964 period. Education is the single strongest predictor of turnout. Higher educational levels produce a keener sense of civic duty and help people deal with the complexities of registering and voting. Researcher Ruy Teixeira estimates that, other things being equal, the net effect of socioeconomic changes, chiefly education, should have been to raise national turnout by about 4 percent.[22]

The Critical Election of 1896

American turnout levels reached all-time highs in the late nineteenth century. Turnout averaged 80 percent of the male voting-age population in the five elections leading up to 1896. Behavior suddenly changed, though. In the five elections following 1896, turnout averaged just 65 percent. It has never returned to its former level.[a]

What happened in 1896? That year featured a critical election (see Chapter 8), one that altered voting alignments in significant and lasting ways. The decades from the end of the Civil War to the mid-1890s were the most electorally competitive in American history. The parties of this period were stronger than ever, almost like military organizations.[b] Supported by the patronage system (see Chapters 8 and 11), the parties had ample *resources* to mobilize the electorate. And given the intense competition, the parties had the *incentive* to do so—defeat would throw tens of thousands of party workers out of their jobs.

But political developments undercut the resources and the incentives fueling high turnout.[c] Civil service and other reforms ate away at the patronage system. And between 1888 and 1896, 90 percent of the states instituted some kind of personal registration system, raising the cost of voting and restricting opportunities for corruption such as voting the dead, voting people twice (or more!), and voting the ineligible.[d]

Meanwhile, the Democrats nominated William Jennings Bryan, a populist and religious fundamentalist who thundered that Republicans were trying to "crucify mankind on a cross of gold." After taking a look at Bryan, many voters decided to chance Republican candidate William McKinley or to stay home. It was more than a temporary victory. In many places outside the South, Democrats were no longer competitive.

With competition reduced, the parties no longer had the incentive to mobilize supporters. Meanwhile, reforms continued to sap the material resources the parties had relied on, and party organizations went into long-term decline. Although political historians continue to argue about the relative importance of the institutional and political factors that led turnout to decline, 1896 clearly was a watershed for American voting behavior.[e]

What do you think?

- Given the many questionable reasons why Americans before 1896 turned out at high levels, should we be concerned that numbers are lower now?

- If compulsory voting (the "stick") is unacceptable, why not pay people (the "carrot") to vote? For example, your ballot stub could be a ticket in a lottery with large cash prizes—which might encourage the poor to vote more often.

[a]Walter Dean Burnham, "The Turnout Problem," in A. James Reichley, ed., *Elections American Style* (Washington, DC: Brookings, 1987), Table 5.3.
[b]Richard Jensen, "American Election Campaigns: A Theoretical and Historical Typology," presented at the 1968 meeting of the Midwest Political Science Association.
[c]Walter Dean Burnham, *Critical Elections and the Mainsprings of American Politics* (New York: Norton, 1970), Ch. 4.
[d]Philip Converse, "Change in the American Electorate," in Angus Campbell and Philip Converse, eds., *The Human Meaning of Social Change*, (New York: Russell Sage, 1972), pp. 263–337.
[e]See the articles, comments, and rejoinders by Walter Dean Burnham, Philip Converse, and Jerrold Rusk in *American Political Science Review* (September 1974).

What, then, explains the decline in turnout? There is less agreement here than on the explanations for turnout differences between the United States and other democracies. Journalists often take voters to task for being lazy and uninvolved, while criticizing the candidates for being uninspiring and unworthy. But

Dilbert's philosophy of representation

Some Americans, like Dilbert in the accompanying cartoon, consider voting a duty rather than merely a right. Voting is the central act of participation, one these Americans find personally gratifying. Other Americans neglect voting and seek representation through protests or other focused activities.

the question of why some people vote while others abstain is certainly more complicated than newspaper editorials usually imply.

For one thing, although citizens of other democracies generally vote at much higher levels than Americans, turnout is on the decline elsewhere as well. In 17 of 19 advanced democracies around the world, turnout in the 1990s was lower than in the 1950s.[23] Hence the sources of declining turnout cannot be unique to the United States. Rosenstone and Hansen divide the reasons for voting into two general categories: individual motivations and outside mobilization.[24]

THE DECLINE OF INDIVIDUAL
MOTIVATIONS TO VOTE

Individual motivations reflect the personal costs and benefits associated with voting. If you are paid by the hour and you take time off in order to vote, you lose a portion of your wages. If you are a parent who cares for small children, you must pay a sitter or drag the kids along in order to vote. Even if you are a professional with flexible hours, you do less work on election day if you take the time to vote.

Moreover, not all costs are tangible. When you spend time on political activity, you have less time to spend on other, perhaps more attractive or fulfilling, activities. For some people with little education or information, the entire voting situation is confusing and uncomfortable; staying home enables them to avoid such discomfort. If you are surprised that such minor considerations could lower turnout, consider that turnout generally falls when the weather is unpleasant.[25]

There also can be benefits to voting, of course. One reason, though not the only one, why historical turnout levels were so high (sometimes more than 75 percent outside the South) is that many people were paid to vote. For example, scholars estimate that the going price of a vote in New York City elections in the 1880s was $2 to $5 (expressed in 1990 dollars) and that prices soared as high as $25 in particularly competitive circumstances.[26] Material rewards are a much rarer benefit of voting today, but direct payments for voting (sometimes called "walking around money") still surface here and there.

And for some citizens, elections still directly affect their material interests. For example, local government employees vote in low-turnout local elections at higher rates than people employed in the private sector, and government employees in general vote at higher rates, other things being equal.[27] For such individuals, elections give them influence at picking their own bosses.

Today, however, most of the material benefits of voting have faded. The incentives are primarily psychological. Some people take civic norms to heart and feel a duty to vote; they avoid guilt by voting. Others take satisfaction in expressing their preferences for candidates or positions on issues, much as they might enjoy cheering for athletic teams. These "psychic" benefits of voting are important, because it is very rare for elections to approach a tie.[28] With a small committee, every member has the potential to tip the scale, but in an election, any single voter is relatively insignificant. Almost 100 million Americans voted in the 1996 presidential election, despite the lowest turnout rate in 70 years. In the 1998 elections for the U.S. House of Representatives, an average of 141,000 citizens voted in each congressional race. A voter would have been unreasonable to think the outcome depended on whether he or she voted.[29] The personal benefits of voting can not exceed the costs, and this has dismal implications for turnout if an individual vote makes no difference.

Thus psychic benefits are critical. They do not depend on whether a voter affects the outcome. A voter with a strong sense of duty, who takes considerable satisfaction in expressing a preference, gets those benefits just by casting a vote. These incentives have declined over time, however. Americans once expressed their political preferences by marching around in uniforms or attending festivals. Now they do so in the privacy of a voting booth, simply pulling a lever or coloring in an arrow or punching out a chad. Such an anonymous manner of expressing preferences gives many potential voters little satisfaction. And, as we noted in Chapter 4, Americans are individualistic; they are unlikely to respond to civic duty alone. The result is that Americans today are disengaged from the electoral process.[30]

Another political factor that has lowered the benefits of voting is that elections have become less competitive. As we will see in Chapter 7, the advantage of incumbency in congressional elections increased greatly between the mid-1960s and the mid-1990s, and a similar process occurred more slowly in state legislative elections. Many presidential elections in the 1970s and 1980s were landslides, and gubernatorial elections became less competitive as well. Rosenstone and Hansen find that in states with competitive gubernatorial campaigns in presidential election years, turnout is 5 percent higher, other things being equal.[31] In a result consistent with such arguments, national turnout dropped 5 percent in 1996 when Bill Clinton led Bob Dole by a comfortable margin from start to finish.

Furthermore, with election polls so common, voters are more likely than ever to know when the outcome of a contest is a foregone conclusion. The notion that one's vote actually makes a difference must seem more outlandish than ever. The puzzle is not that turnout is so low in the United States but, rather, that turnout is as high as it is.

THE DECLINE OF OUTSIDE ENCOURAGEMENT TO VOTE

Parties, groups, and activists are often concerned about the **mobilization** of their potential supporters (although they are less so in uncompetitive elections). Campaign workers provide baby-sitting and rides to the polls, thus reducing the individual costs of voting. They apply social pressure by contacting citizens who have not voted and reminding them to do so. Various groups and social networks to which individuals belong also exert social pressures, encouraging the feeling that one has a responsibility to vote.

For a long time, parties neglected their mobilizing efforts, instead focusing on media strategies. Polling and advertising are probably not good substitutes for the kind of pound-the-pavement, doorbell-ringing workers who once dominated campaigns. Voters may be motivated by the coaxing of a campaign worker standing at the front door or telephoning late in the afternoon on election day, but those same voters may not be motivated by an impersonal TV spot or a taped telephone message urging them to vote. Thus, the shift from labor-intensive to high-tech campaigning may have indirectly contributed to declining voter turnout.

Late in the 2000 presidential campaign, however, intensive get-out-the-vote efforts helped Al Gore mobilize a large urban electorate and win the popular vote—a success that has prompted both parties to reconsider their priorities. Recent campaign-finance reforms should help revive mobilization practices as well, since they included a loophole allowing state and local parties to fund get-out-the-vote activities that assist candidates for federal office.[32]

THE DECLINE OF SOCIAL CONNECTEDNESS

A final explanation for declining turnout falls somewhere between personal and outside motivations. Stephen Knack raises the possibility that common thinking about voting is misconceived. Rather than voting being the fundamental political act, voting may instead be a social act—a way to be part of the community. Voters may take pleasure from having an excuse, once in a while, to gather in a local building and make contact with their neighbors. Voting is related to giving blood, donating to charities, doing volunteer work, and other forms of community involvement.[33]

Voters would respond to these incentives only if they felt connected socially to those around them. **Social connectedness** is the extent to which people are in fact integrated into society—their families, neighborhoods, communities, churches, and other social units. Social connectedness may well have declined over time. Older Americans grew up in a simpler age, when Americans were less mobile and more trusting of their fellow citizens. They may be more connected than are younger Americans, who have grown up in a highly mobile society where cynicism about their fellow citizens is widespread.

Certainly young people seldom vote, and not simply because of their stage in life. Rather, political scientist Warren Miller has shown that declining voter turnout is a result of what social scientists call a **compositional effect:** a change in the people who compose America's potential electorate, rather than a change in behavior.[34] Turnout is declining because of the simple fact that older Americans, who have always been accustomed to voting at high rates, are dying and being replaced by younger Americans who have never voted much.

It is less clear whether social connectedness explains turnout directly. Investigators have examined the possibility, but they are stuck using relatively crude indicators of social connectedness, such as marriage rates, home ownership, church attendance, and length of residence in a community. Nevertheless, such studies find that decreased social connectedness accounts for as much as one-quarter of the decline in presidential election turnout.[35] (Interestingly, although being married is associated with higher turnout, being *newly* married lowers the odds of voting. Voting is apparently not high on the priority list of newlyweds![36])

Is low turnout a problem?

Low voting rates probably would not stimulate as much discussion as they do if all social and economic groups in America exhibited the same rates. But people differ in their ability to bear the costs of voting, in the strength of their feeling that voting is a duty, and in how often they are the targets of mobilization. Consequently, turnout rates differ considerably across social groups (see Figure 6.3).[37]

Highly educated people are far more likely to vote than people with little formal education. Education instills a stronger sense of duty and gives people the knowledge, analytic skills, and self-confidence to meet the costs of registering and voting. Over and above education, income also has a significant effect. The wealthy are far more likely to vote than the poor. Affluence, too, reflects a set of skills and personal characteristics that help people overcome barriers to voting.

Studies of turnout in the 1970s concluded that once differences in education, age, and income were factored out, blacks were at least as likely to vote as whites.[38] But more recent research finds that blacks are still somewhat less likely to vote, even taking into account socioeconomic differences.[39] One suggestion is that African Americans were disillusioned by the failure of the Jesse Jackson's

FIGURE 6.3

Group differences in turnout, 1996

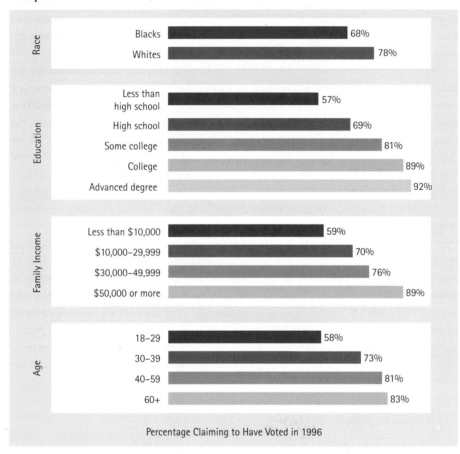

SOURCE: American National Election Studies.

campaigns in 1984 and 1988.[40] Other minorities, such as Latinos and Asians, face language barriers that depress their participation levels.[41]

Turnout increases with age until one becomes very old, when the trend reverses. People presumably gain experience as they age, experience that makes it easier for them to overcome any barriers to voting. They also become more socially connected, as well as more settled in a life situation that clarifies their political preferences. But at some point, poor health and limited mobility intervene.

Interestingly, the relationships between socioeconomic characteristics and turnout are consistently stronger in the United States than in other democracies. Indeed, in some countries there is almost no relationship between education and income on the one hand and voting on the other.[42] The reason is not that in other democracies education and income have effects different from those in the United States; it is that elsewhere parties are much more effective at mobilizing their supporters. In particular, European Social Democratic parties do a far better job of getting their less-advantaged potential voters to the polls than the Democratic party does in the United States.

Given who votes and why, should the relatively low turnout rate in the United States be a cause for concern? Quite a few answers have been offered on both sides of this question. Democrats generally decry low turnout whereas Republicans tend to be more complacent, because many people assume that the electorate is more conservative than the voting-age population at large. On the other hand, among scholars, differing views on turnout often hinge on different beliefs about the motives for voting. We briefly sketch three arguments on each side of the debate.

LOW TURNOUT IS NOT A PROBLEM: THREE ARGUMENTS

AN OPTIMISTIC ARGUMENT   Many of those concerned about low turnout implicitly assume that high turnout indicates enthusiasm about politics and commitment to making the political order work. Maybe that assumption is not correct. Some skeptics suggest that high turnout may indicate tension or conflict. People may vote because they believe losing would be unacceptable. Consider the experience of Austria and Germany as their democratic governments crumbled and the

Portrait of a Swing Voter

Critics often bemoan the infrequency with which American adults go to the polls. But nonvoters may simply be Americans who are content with their lives and have little interest in or knowledge about politics, people who would add a random element to elections by making ill-considered choices.

Fascist parties took power in the 1930s.[43] Turnout in those elections reached very high levels, but this reflected disillusionment and desperation more than commitment and enthusiasm. The 1992 presidential election is a less extreme case in point. Turnout rose, but did this indicate a healthier political system? On the contrary, by many indications people were "mad as hell"—frustrated and upset with their government. Low turnout therefore may be a sign of the health of a political system, a sign of stability. As political scientist Samuel Huntington puts it, "The effective operation of a democratic political system usually requires some measure of apathy and noninvolvement on the part of some individuals and groups."[44]

AN ELITIST ARGUMENT   On average, nonvoters are less educated than voters. Studies also show them to be less informed, less interested in politics, and less concerned about it. Such voters may be more susceptible to getting caught up in political fads. They may be vulnerable to deceptive political advertising, or even outright manipulation. Not voting may represent an admirable display of restraint, an awareness on the part of uninformed citizens that they should stay out of a contest they know little about. Social theorist David Reisman once remarked, "Bringing sleepwalkers to the polls simply to increase turnout is no service to democracy."[45] Columnist George Will is even more succinct. "Smaller is smarter," he says.[46] Of course, the process of encouraging people to vote might inform them at the same time. But the elitist argument has gained credence since the 2000 election, in which many voters apparently were incapable of following the instructions on their ballots, either voting for the wrong person or voting for multiple candidates.

A CYNICAL OR RADICAL ARGUMENT   Some radicals contend that it is not the nonvoters but the voters who are a cause for concern. According to this viewpoint, elections don't matter—they are charades. Real decisions are made by power elites far from the popular arena. If so, voting is merely a symbolic act that makes the masses feel content. Anyone who turns out has been duped. Of course, we disagree strongly with this argument. As we illustrate throughout this book, elections matter a great deal—in some cases, too much.

LOW TURNOUT IS A PROBLEM: THREE ARGUMENTS

LOW TURNOUT REFLECTS A "PHONY" POLITICS   Low turnout may reflect disgust with an American politics that does not address "real" issues of concern to minorities and the poor. What are real issues? Basically, they involve economics: jobs, health care, housing, income distribution, and education. Instead, the parties debate "phony" **social issues** relevant to the upper-middle class: rights of free expression, gun control, feminism, animal rights, capital punishment, and gay rights. This argument often is made by Democrats and other progressive thinkers nostalgic for the New Deal coalition (see Chapter 8). On the other hand, the decline of economic issues may simply result from a stronger national economy. When times are relatively good, voters worry less about their pocketbooks and more about the direction of society.

LOW TURNOUT DISCOURAGES INDIVIDUAL DEVELOPMENT   Classical political theorists from Aristotle to John Stuart Mill emphasized that political participation educates citizens, stimulating their individual development. Participants become better human beings, which in turn enables them to take society to a higher level. From the standpoint of this argument, low turnout signifies a lost opportunity. The argument is rather persuasive when applied to participation in intensive, face-to-face processes like local board or council meetings. It seems less relevant to impersonal processes like voting in a national election.[47] Nevertheless, it reminds us that voting may shape more than just an election. It may shape the voters themselves and help determine what manner of people they are.

THE VOTERS ARE UNREPRESENTATIVE   The most obvious concern arising from low turnout is that it produces an unrepresentative electorate. The active electorate is wealthier, whiter, older, and better educated than the potential electorate. However, numerous studies suggest that voting patterns do not bias election results. The policy views and the candidate preferences of nonvoters differ little from those of voters. Some studies have even found that at times the conservative candidate was more popular among nonvoters—Ronald Reagan in 1984, for example.[48]

How can this be? First, although minorities and the poor vote less often than whites and the affluent, the difference is only a matter of degree. Thus blacks are less likely to vote than whites, but only about one-eighth of all the nonvoters are black. Similarly, the more highly educated are more likely to vote, but 25 percent of the nonvoters have some college education. Nonvoters are not all poor, uneducated, or members of minority groups. Plenty of nonvoters are affluent, well educated, and white—particularly those who have relocated. According to the U.S. Bureau of the Census, nearly one in five Americans moves during the two-year interval between national elections.[49]

Second, few groups are as one-sided in their political inclinations as African Americans, who voted roughly 9 to 1 Democratic in the 2000 presidential election. If turnout among most other groups were to increase, the Democrats might get more than half the additional votes, but the Republicans would get a fair proportion as well. Teixeira calculates that, if all the Hispanics and African Americans in the country had voted in 1988 at levels 10 percent higher than whites and if all the white poor had voted at a level 10 percent higher than that of the white rich, Democratic candidate Michael Dukakis would still have lost by two and a half

Political protest

Americans may not turn out to vote quite as much as citizens in other nations, but protests are common in Washington, DC. Here, Kosovar Albanians march in front of the White House in support of American involvement in the Balkans. Protest is an often controversial form of participation. When should it be? Why or why not?

million votes.[50] Not all elections are so one-sided, of course, but given the improbability that minorities and the disadvantaged could ever be mobilized at such high levels, it is even more doubtful that realistic changes in turnout would produce a sea change in American politics.

Still, as a Marxist might point out, there could be an element of "false consciousness" here: Because present nonvoters are uninformed and uncommitted, they fail to understand or act on their true interests. The political or social changes necessary to increase their voting would also greatly increase their knowledge. That learning process might produce a different political outlook. This line of argument is purely speculative, though, and could be settled only by greatly increasing turnout and seeing whether the preferences of nonvoters changed.

DOES TURNOUT MATTER?

Our view is that nonvoters and voters have diverse motives. Some nonvoters are content while others are alienated, and the same goes for voters. High turnout can indicate either high approval of the political order or serious dissatisfaction with it. Nonvoters don't have much information, but as we saw in Chapter 5, neither do many voters. Low turnout does make the actual electorate somewhat less representative than the potential electorate, but not as much as critics often assume. Some potential voters undoubtedly are discouraged by a politics focused on social issues, but other citizens turn out to vote precisely because of their concern with such issues. And although participation fosters citizenship, we doubt that the impersonal act of casting a vote fosters it very much. In short, we find some validity in each of the arguments presented; we reject in its entirety only the argument that elections do not matter. Low turnout is a cause for concern, yes, a cause for despair, no.

OUTSIDE THE VOTING BOOTH

Americans turn out at lower levels than citizens in other democracies. Moreover, they are significantly less likely to participate in other ways than they are to vote. Only one-third of Americans report having signed a petition, and a similar number claim to have contacted a government official at one time or another. Substantially fewer have made financial contributions to a party or candidate, attended a political meeting or rally, or worked in a campaign. Two-thirds of Americans participate in no way beyond voting.[51]

It is a bit surprising, then, to learn that Americans are *more* likely to engage in these less common forms of participation than are the citizens of some countries where turnout is much higher. Even though only a small number of Americans work in campaigns or contact public officials, the numbers are even lower elsewhere (see Figure 6.4). Why would Americans vote less often, but participate frequently in other ways? Explanations vary.

- Because there are far more offices and government bodies in the United States, there are far more opportunities to contact officials, attend board meetings, and so forth. Even if Americans were less likely to take advantage of any particular opportunity, the sheer number of chances would result in a higher level of political participation than in other countries, where opportunities are more limited.
- America's individualistic political culture, with its emphasis on rights and liberties, encourages Americans to contact public officials and to protest government actions. In contrast, the political cultures of most other democracies are more deferential to authority and discourage ordinary citizens from taking an active role in politics. Citizens elsewhere are less likely to protest government decisions, and when they do, their governments are more likely to ignore them.
- Because American political parties are weaker today than in earlier eras, candidates construct numerous personal organizations, many of whose members are temporary. In other countries a small cadre of committed

FIGURE 6.4

Americans are more likely than citizens in other democracies to participate in ways more demanding than voting

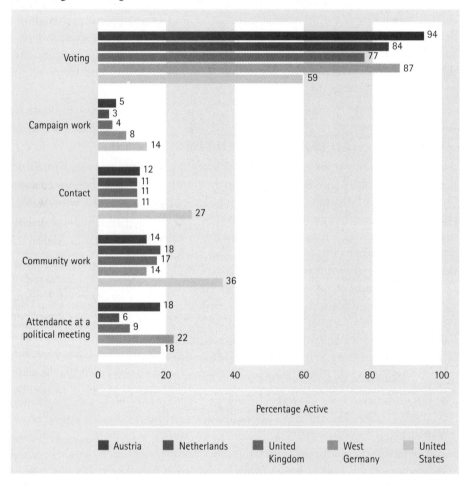

SOURCE: Adapted from Sidney Verba, Kay Lehman Schlozman, and Henry Brady, *Voice and Equality* (Cambridge, MA: Harvard University Press, 1995), p. 70.

party workers shoulders most of the burden of campaigning year in and year out, but in the United States campaigns are fought by much larger groups of "occasional activists." These are enthusiastic amateurs who drift in and out between protest and politics, depending on whether particular candidates or issues arouse their enthusiasm.[52]

- Finally, many Americans participate in politics indirectly by joining or supporting interest groups. These groups encourage activism by soliciting signatures or contributions from their members, sponsoring political meetings, and so forth. There are far more groups and associations active in politics in the United States than in other countries, so there are far more opportunities for participation through groups. Groups are particularly likely to be the source of "unconventional" or "contentious" participation: protests, demonstrations, and civil disobedience.

Chapter Summary

A majority of the American electorate stays away from the polls in most elections. To some extent this pattern results from barriers to participation. Registration is left to the individual, voting is less convenient than elsewhere, and citizens are called on to vote often. In addition, mobilizing agents, such as parties and unions, are weaker in the United States than in other modern democracies; hence Americans get less encouragement from larger organizations than do citizens of other democracies. Nevertheless, turnout statistics exaggerate the difference between the United States and other democracies—and Americans are more likely to engage in other forms of participation than citizens of democracies elsewhere.

The declining rates of participation in the United States are more difficult to understand, especially because other democracies have experienced a similar trend. Reforms have lowered the costs of voting, and educational levels have gone up, but Americans seem less interested in politics than ever. The explanations for such disenchantment are a matter of much debate. But for our purposes, low turnout appears to be irrelevant. Evidence is thin that low turnout alters the election results. Nonvoters are not all the same, and they do not differ from voters as much as is usually presumed. Elections do not matter less just because some voters choose to stay home.

Key Terms

compositional effect, p. 185	registered voters, p. 177	suffrage, p. 173
franchise, p. 173	social connectedness, p. 184	voting-age population, p. 176
mobilization, p. 184	social issues, p. 188	

Suggested Readings

Keyssar, Alexander. *The Right to Vote.* New York: Basic Books, 2000. A comprehensive history of the evolution of the suffrage in America.

Piven, Francis, and Richard Cloward. *Why Americans Don't Vote.* New York: Pantheon, 1988. This critical commentary on nonvoting in the United States contends that "have-nots" are systematically discouraged from voting.

Rosenstone, Steven, and John Mark Hansen. *Mobilization, Participation, and Democracy in America.* New York: Macmillan, 1993.

Comprehensive statistical study of electoral and governmental participation from the 1950s to the 1980s, with particular emphasis on the decline in turnout.

Teixeira, Ruy. *The Disappearing American Voter.* Washington, DC: Brookings, 1992. Comprehensive statistical study of turnout from the 1960s to the 1980s, with particular emphasis on the decline in turnout and the difference between turnout in the United States and that in other democracies.

Verba, Sidney, Kay Schlozman, and Henry Brady. *Voice and Equality: Civic Volunteerism in American Politics.* Cambridge, MA: Harvard University Press, 1995. Fascinating discussion of the development of political skills in nonpolitical contexts, such as churches. Strong on attention to differences involving race, ethnicity, and gender.

Wolfinger, Raymond, and Steven Rosenstone. *Who Votes?* New Haven, CT: Yale University Press, 1980. A statistical study that relies on huge Census Bureau samples and thus provides the best estimates of the relationships between demographic characteristics and voting, though in a limited number of elections (1972 and 1974).

On the Web

The League of Women Voters
www.lwv.org
A nonpartisan political organization, the League of Women Voters encourages the informed and active participation of citizens in government.

Project Vote Smart
www.vote-smart.org
This wide-ranging site is supported by a nonpartisan group that gathers and distributes biographical histories, voting records, campaign finances and promises, and performance evaluations of elected officials and candidates.

A History of the Suffrage Movement
www.rochester.edu/SBA/hisindx.html
An online history project with links dealing with the Nineteenth Amendment and the history of voting rights in the United States. This site is maintained by the University of Rochester.

NATIONAL ELECTIONS

emocratic Governor Bill Clinton of Arkansas survived a grueling contest to become president of the United States—one in which he had been savaged by accusations of extramarital sex, draft dodging, and pot smoking. Clinton entered office in 1992 as a "minority president," having received only 43 percent of the popular vote. It was not an auspicious start. Republicans presumed that Clinton's stay in the White House would be brief, since their party's candidates had won the presidency in five of the last six elections, three times by landslides.

Congressional Republicans quickly served notice that they would oppose the minority president's agenda. Party members in both chambers voted unanimously against Clinton's budget, which passed by one vote in the House and only by virtue of Vice President Gore's tie-breaking vote in the Senate.[1] Senate Republicans killed his economic stimulus program by refusing to allow it to come to a vote. Other defeats followed, including the national health insurance plan Clinton delivered to Congress (see Chapter 8).

Resistance seemed to be working. The public apparently did not blame those who obstructed Clinton's proposals. Indeed, voters began to perceive that Clinton was more liberal than they had originally thought. As opponents characterized his early record, Clinton favored gays and opposed guns; he had raised taxes and proposed a massive government takeover of health care; and he had broken his campaign promise by doing absolutely nothing about welfare. Republicans charged that Clinton was nothing more than a liberal sheep in a moderate wolf's clothing. These accusations resonated with the public. Polls indicated that many Americans resented taxes and had grown skeptical of ambitious government programs. They believed that Clinton and the Democratic party did not share their values.

Two years later, in the 1994 elections, the Democrats lost control of both House and Senate, giving their opposition control of the legislative branch for the first time in 40 years. Some congressional Democrats blamed the president for their electoral misfortunes, and many thought he would follow them down to defeat in 1996. Republicans began gearing up to oppose his reelection almost immediately. One GOP senator started campaigning in New Hampshire six days after the election, and another had filed a statement of candidacy.

But Clinton did not gain his reputation as "the comeback kid" for nothing. He hired a moderate, Richard "Dick" Morris, as his campaign adviser, and he began recasting himself as a centrist. He signed a welfare reform law opposed by liberals in his party and concentrated on balancing the budget without threatening popular middle-class programs for the elderly. By the time the 1996 campaign season rolled around, Clinton enjoyed a comfortable lead in the polls, and he stayed ahead of opponent Senator Robert Dole throughout the campaign. He coasted to an easy Electoral College victory, taking even Republican mainstays such as Florida.

The 2000 election produced another upset, this time on behalf of the Republicans. Clinton had held the White House for eight years and would leave it

[Handwritten annotation at top: most states used closed primaries to select candidates: partisans vote for party candidates. IN uses closed primaries (no card the)]

a popular president. He had fashioned an appealing, middle-of-the-road program. He had worked with Republicans to reduce the national deficit and had allowed respected Republican appointee Alan Greenspan to remain in charge of the Federal Reserve Board. Apparently as a result, the Clinton administration had presided over an unprecedented period of economic growth. His presidency was marred by scandal, most notably deceptions growing out of Clinton's extramarital affair with a young White House intern (see Chapter 10), but few in the administration shared blame for these personal peccadillos.

The gloves were off

Some critics charge that Gore ran a poor campaign in 2000, because he rarely mentioned the economic successes of the Clinton administration. His demeanor in presidential debates appeared aggressive and unappealing. Why do you think that Gore's theme was "I'm going to fight for you" instead of "You've never had it so good"?

Vice President Al Gore thus seemed guaranteed to retain the White House for the Democratic party. Like Clinton, he was a southerner with a moderate stance on many policy issues, and he was implicated in few of the White House scandals. The economy remained strong, and his campaign was well funded. He left his party's national convention with a solid showing in the polls. The standard statistical models that are used to predict presidential elections generally indicated that Gore would win handily.[2] And his opponent was a relatively inexperienced politician, Texas Governor George W. Bush, whose main advantages seemed to be his family's influence and a boyish charm.

Once again the underdog headed for the center. Despite an aggressive primary battle with Arizona Senator John McCain, Bush was able to unite with his rival. He also attracted the endorsement of billionaire Ross Perot, whose independent campaign in 1992 helped dethrone Bush's father. Bush was comforting to both business Republicans and cultural Republicans, because he spoke like an evangelist but offered economic proposals pleasing to corporate interests.[3] The fringes of his party did not demand that he take many unpopular policy stands to satisfy them.[4]

Gore, by contrast, faced repeated threats to his liberal base. Vanquishing respected New Jersey Senator Bill Bradley in the Democratic primaries required him to form ties with national labor unions early on. Then, in the general election he faced a serious challenge from the Green party candidate, activist Ralph Nader—a credible national figure who appealed directly to leftists upset with White House moderation when dealing with international corporations. Unlike Bush, therefore, Gore could not soften his message to appeal to wavering voters. He worked closely with liberal advisers and portrayed himself in a belligerent fashion—someone who would "fight for you."[5] The result? For the second presidential election in a row, the winner was someone who had been thought to have little chance two years before.

THESE TWO UPSET VICTORIES UNDERSCORE THE DIFFERENCE between how journalists approach elections and how political scientists understand them. Looking back, both sets of professionals can offer a story to explain why the 1996 and 2000 elections turned out the way they did, but the two stories have very little in common. Journalists emphasize personalities and short-term campaign strategies. They focus on how much money the candidates raised or how clever their ads were. They trace small shifts in the polls to recent campaign events— such as Gore's poor performance in the presidential debates[6] and his factual mistakes on the campaign trail (which critics interpreted as lies).[7] After each contest, reporters wipe the slate clean and start speculating on the next election.

Our story, though, emphasizes the long-term regularities that shape voting. Research indicates that much of electoral behavior is predictable in advance. The public enters an election period with attitudes and loyalties mostly in place (although it may take some time to sort out their priorities and apply them to the options at hand).[8] The most important question for voters is how close the candidates' values and preferences are to theirs, and this favors candidates who seek the political center.

Nor can candidates simply pick the message Americans want to hear. They enter an election constrained by their own political histories and by the alliances they have formed. Their prospects depend on the quality of the opponents they face—assuming that they face any opposition at all, since anticipation of inadequate voter support may convince a potential candidate not to run. Thus, once the cast of characters stabilizes, for most voters their choice is obvious. This predictability makes elections look less important than they are.

Some reformers seek radical change in the political system because they think elections do not give regular Americans much influence. They are discouraged by the performance of political institutions, and they suppose that legal changes to open up the electoral system—for example by limiting campaign spending or by making election laws fairer—would somehow correct the flaws. Our sense, by contrast, is that elections and public opinion matter more in the United States today than they ever have, so we are naturally skeptical of remedies based on the opposite diagnosis!

open primary - in some, anyone can vote
democratic or republican - some intentionally
vote for the weak candidate

The difference between how journalists and political scientists view national elections is not just a quibble between two sets of professionals. The journalistic approach helps explain why Americans would be cynical about the system, blaming bad candidates or unfair media coverage or campaign-finance abuses for results they dislike. But short-term election strategies matter less than people commonly think and rarely influence the final showdown.

Once one realizes that the main force guiding elections is the abiding dispositions of American voters, a different culprit for poor institutional performance emerges. The problem is not that Americans lack influence, but that their electoral system is oriented toward giving even a divided public what it wants.

VOTING BEHAVIOR:
THE IMPORTANCE OF ELECTIONS

Citizens exhibit considerable continuity in voting behavior. This "electoral inertia" explains why presidential candidates know ahead of time that they will probably lose some states and win others. It is also why some congressional districts feature hard-fought campaigns, while in others no one challenges the sitting representatives. Elections sometimes are uneventful not because voters are powerless but because they exercise their power in ways that political actors can plan around.

Many people decide how they will vote before a campaign begins. In presidential elections, typically one-third to one-half of the electorate decides how to vote *before the primaries.* According to American National Election Studies surveys, one-half to two-thirds of the electorate decides how to vote before the fall campaign gets under way. The figure was 54 percent in 2000, when no incumbent ran, and 64 percent in 1996, when Clinton sought reelection. Hence strategy cannot influence most voters.

How can people make up their minds before candidates debate their policies and programs? The answer is simply that Americans have a longer time horizon than the considerations that dominate news coverage. Voter preferences accumulate for years, long before a single contest gets under way. They emphasize party loyalties and government performance, not policy proposals or candidate personalities.

PARTY LOYALTIES

About two-thirds of the American electorate view themselves as Democrats or Republicans. Political scientists call this allegiance **party identification,** or party ID.[9] Party ID was once thought to be much like a religious affiliation: learned in childhood, resistant to change, and unrelated to the group's actual doctrines.[10] In fact, partisanship does respond to events and ideas, but only gradually.[11] Party ID thus ensures strong continuity from election to election.

For example, the Civil War and Reconstruction created many yellow-dog Democrats in the South—people who wouldn't vote for a Republican if the Democratic nominee were a yellow dog. Eventually white southerners began to vote Republican in national elections, but they took much longer to switch party labels. Similarly, the Great Depression left many northerners intensely committed to the New Deal Democratic party of Franklin Roosevelt.

Party ID makes most elections quite predictable, even before candidates decide whether to run or how to manage their campaigns. Certain groups consistently vote Democratic, others steadily Republican (see Table 7.1). African Americans, urbanites, and Catholics have traditionally been Democratic groups. The wealthy,

TABLE 7.1

GROUPS DIFFER IN THEIR SUPPORT FOR THE PARTIES

	PERCENTAGE VOTING REPUBLICAN				
POPULATION CATEGORY	BUSH 2000	DOLE 1996	BUSH 1992	BUSH 1988	REAGAN 1984
White	54	46	40	59	64
Hispanic	31	21	25	30	37
African American	8	12	10	12	9
Poor (< $15,000/year)	37	28	23	37	45
Affluent (> $50,000/year)	52	48	44	62	69
Union	37	30	25	42	46
White Protestant	63	52	47	66	72
Catholic	47	37	35	52	54
Jewish	19	16	11	35	31
Big-city resident (population > 500,000)	26	25	28	37	n/a
Suburban resident	49	42	39	57	61
Rural resident	59	46	40	55	67
Lives in the East	39	34	35	50	53
Lives in the Midwest	49	41	37	52	58
Lives in the South	55	46	43	58	64
Lives in the West	46	40	34	52	61

SOURCE: "Portrait of the 2000 Electorate," *New York Times* (December 20, 2000). Available at time of publication at http://www.nytimes.com/images/2000/12/20/politics/elections/nwr_portrait_education.html.

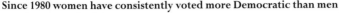

FIGURE 7.1

Since 1980 women have consistently voted more Democratic than men

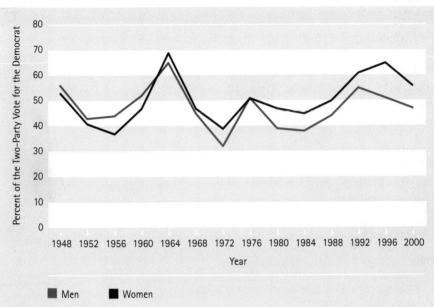

SOURCE: The Gallup Organization.

rural residents, southerners, and white Protestants—especially evangelicals—tend to vote Republican. The increase in political independents has not undermined this predictability. Even the growing number of self-professed independents usually find themselves closer to one party than to another. [12]

A "gender gap" has also sprung up, dividing the political preferences of men and women—a gap that has been growing stronger (see Figure 7.1). Robert Dole might have won the 1996 election if only men had voted! Gender differences in voting do not result from so-called women's issues, such as abortion, which men and women view similarly. [13] Rather, the gap appears to stem more from long-standing gender differences over the use of force and the responsibility of government to address social ills (see Table 7.2). [14] It is not clear whether such differences grow out of childhood socialization, biology, self-interest, or some combination of factors. [15] The political preferences of women are not all the same, though; married women tend to have preferences much closer to those of men. [16] The electoral gap flows naturally from each gender's political preferences. [17]

Politicians are aware of how various groups differ politically. For the strongest partisans, the campaign is irrelevant; come hell or high water, they will vote their party IDs. Because potential candidates know how many members of each group appear in a given state or congressional district, they can strategize

TABLE 7.2

WOMEN'S AND MEN'S ATTITUDES

	WOMEN	MEN
Role of Government		
Consider self conservative	29%	43%
Say government should provide fewer services	30	45
Rank poverty and homelessness as among the country's most important problems	63	44
Believe government should guarantee medical care for all	69	58
Favor affirmative action programs for blacks and other minority groups	53	41
Force/Violence		
Thought American bombers should attack all military targets in Iraq, including those in heavily populated areas	37	61
Say handguns should be illegal except for use by police and other authorized persons	48	28
Favor the death penalty	76	82
Approved the caning of a teenager in Singapore who committed acts of vandalism	39	61
Approve of the way the Justice Department took Elian Gonzalez from his Miami relatives	35	52

SOURCES: *The Public Perspective* (August/September 1996): 10–27; *The Public Perspective* (July/August 1994): 96; Gallup Tuesday Briefing, May 2, 2000.

around such data. They usually need not wait for the formal election to respond to known voter preferences.

GOVERNMENT PERFORMANCE

Not every voter consistently supports the same political party. Swing voters typically react to the performance of current elected officials, though, and not so much to personalities or campaign promises.[18] Assessing performance does not require hours watching C-SPAN or reading the *New York Times*. Rather, voters can judge economic conditions from their own experiences and from word-of-mouth stories. They can judge other social conditions by observing their communities, schools, and workplaces.

Sometimes voters are upset about a problem and eager for government to do *something* about it. Thus candidates talk about the need to "get tough on crime," or "fix the health care system," or "get guns out of the hands of children." These are important political issues, to be sure, but they do not evoke specific policy solutions. Such appeals merely tap into a general judgment of government performance.

The 1984 presidential election provides a classic illustration of how voters look toward past performance (this tendency is often called **retrospective voting**). Surveys showed that on many issues, voters were closer to the Democratic nominee, Walter Mondale, than to President Reagan. A majority considered tax increases inevitable (Mondale's position), were skeptical about "Star Wars" (the missile defense system dear to Reagan's heart), rejected Reagan's call for increased defense spending, and disliked Reagan's policies toward Central America.[19] Nevertheless, Reagan carried 49 states. Policy differences aside, most voters approved of the nation's overall direction since 1980.

Voters can hardly be blamed for adopting shortcuts like retrospective voting. They are not equipped to judge among policy proposals, and candidates may not keep their promises anyway. Good performance by government suggests competent leadership, so voters reasonably choose not to "fix something that ain't broke."[20] Bad times, on the other hand, add credibility to any claim that someone else ought to get a shot at running the government. A campaign can "spin" an administration's record creatively, but it is difficult to make virtues out of a bad economy or an unpopular war—no matter how clever the media experts or how expensive their advertisements.

Incumbents receive credit for good times because voters assume they will continue to do what they have done before. This brings up a puzzle: Why did the sitting vice president lose in 2000, when times were so good? The best guess is that Gore was not the incumbent, but his second in command. He distanced himself from the Clinton administration and its scandals. He had to counteract Bill Bradley's primary challenge, as well as Ralph Nader's Green party presidential bid, by emphasizing liberal policy reforms rather than maintenance of the status quo. As one critic sarcastically observed, Gore's theme was "You've never had it so good, and I'm mad as hell about it."[21] If anything, Bush ran as the incumbent, drawing from Clinton's moderate playbook more often than Gore did. Swing voters may have considered Bush likely to continue the pattern of compromise they associated with the outgoing administration and favored him as a result.

POLICY PROPOSALS

Policies and programs are the essence of elections for the most politically active citizens. These voters view campaigns as long-running debates—opportunities for candidates to educate the electorate about alternative paths the country might choose and to persuade voters to follow one of them. However, voters seldom use policy proposals to determine their choice among candidates.[22] One reason is that policy debates often are complex, and people have limited information. To cite one extreme example, President Clinton's 1993 health care plan required 1342 printed pages, and that was just one of the options! How could voters possibly be expected to evaluate such complex proposals?

Moreover, voters often are unsure where the candidates stand. Research on the 1968 election, for example, found that views on U.S. policy in Vietnam were mostly unrelated to the presidential vote. How could that be true, when disagreement about the war was tearing the country apart? The answer is that the candidates gave voters little basis on which to choose. The Democratic nominee, Hubert Humphrey, kept wavering. The Republican, Richard Nixon, refused to reveal his position, because to do so would undermine his "secret plan" to end the war. In the end, befuddled voters assessed both candidates as though they supported the same policy.[23]

One occasional exception is a social or cultural policy, such as gun control or abortion. Such issues are "easy" in the sense that voters generally know where they stand. Moreover, the desired outcome and the policy that achieves it are one and the same: allow gun ownership or ban it; stop abortions or permit them.[24] Yet even these "hot-button" issues allow candidates to equivocate. In 2000, Gore tried to distance himself from gun control, emphasizing gun licenses rather than weapons bans and espousing the rights of hunters. Bush gave mixed messages on abortion: He was unhappy with the Food and Drug Administration's decision to allow sale of the abortion pill, RU-486, but claimed uncertainty about whether the next president could reverse the ruling.

CANDIDATE QUALITIES

Not surprisingly, the individual candidates are a major source of *change* in how people vote from election to election.[25] In a country that exhorts voters to "support the person not the party," the nature of the candidates is a major influence on how people vote. But it is important to keep in mind several cautions.

First, personality is seldom the most important candidate quality. In fact, detailed analysis of what people like and dislike indicates that most of the traits they mention are relevant to governing: intelligence, integrity, experience.[26] Voters may admire a president open enough to smooch with his wife on national television. They may not relish the prospect of spending four years listening to a stumbling speaker or hearing lectures from an arrogant one. But these considerations sway few voters.

Second, after the election there is a tendency to downgrade the loser's personal qualities and upgrade the winner's. Journalists reinforce this tendency by

Public display of affection

Al Gore's aggressive kiss reportedly surprised wife Tipper at the Democratic National Convention. Whatever her reaction, "The Kiss" electrified some pundits, who gave it credit for Gore's bounce in the polls. But humorist Dave Barry thought Gore resembled an alien depositing an egg sac. Is it important to have an affectionate national leader, or is that relevant only to a personality contest?

habitually explaining politics in personal terms. Many Republicans dismissed Senator Robert Dole as a terrible choice after his defeat in 1996. Yet two years earlier during the Republican takeover of Congress, Dole was viewed as the rare "grown-up" in Washington, an admirable man possessing warmth and a quick wit. He was a mature, experienced public official who could fill the leadership vacuum. Did the election expose Dole as anything else? No, but his charisma was insufficient to unseat a moderate incumbent backed by peace and prosperity. Clinton's enemies preferred to blame Dole rather than credit the president. Similarly, Michael Dukakis received praise before the 1988 election and criticism afterward. Dukakis hadn't changed, but many in the Democratic party found it easier to blame their messenger than to admit that the electorate had rejected their message.

FIGURE 7.2

The Democratic advantage in party identification has eroded

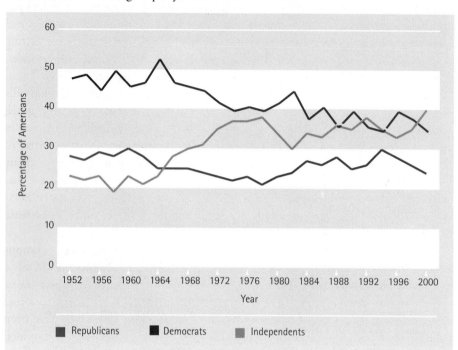

SOURCE: American National Election Studies.

There are some striking contrasts between what voters actually think of candidates during a given campaign and how popular history later views the combatants. John F. Kennedy is the best example, because he is now legendary as the charismatic king of a new Camelot, an inspiring leader who fell to a lone gunman's bullet. JFK was not loved half as much in life as he is in death. During the 1960 election, the public considered Kennedy's opponent, Richard Nixon, more experienced and better qualified than the young senator.[27] JFK owed his narrow victory primarily to the fact that he was the standard bearer of the majority party (see Figure 7.2).[28] What lives on in political folklore may have little connection to why people voted the way they did.

Finally, we should remember that what people think about a candidate is based partly on political compatibility—whether they belong to the same party, whether the politician has performed well, and whether the politician espouses similar values. Thus candidates are important, but there is a tendency to misunderstand how. Personality looks much more influential than it really is.

THE INCUMBENCY ADVANTAGE

It is not hard to see how presidential elections might ensure public influence. The contests are nearly always energetic ones, covered heavily in the media. Voters pay attention and participate at relatively high rates. The importance of congressional elections may seem less obvious, though, for they are seldom competitive. Sitting members of Congress, called **incumbents,** often do not face serious opposition. And even when they do encounter real opponents, incumbents rarely lose.

The true measure of voter strength is not how often they replace elected officials, however. Low congressional turnover is itself a symptom of how much voters matter. Party has long been and continues to be the dominant factor in winning House elections, just as it is in presidential elections. Partisan control of the House seldom changes, and House incumbents seldom lose, because many House districts are **safe seats.** Voter preferences are so one-sided that these districts are almost certain never to elect representatives of a different party. Serious candidates from the minority party rarely challenge the incumbent, because they know they will lose.

One reason why party remains the most important factor in House elections may be that many voters know little, if anything, about specific candidates. Only a third of the citizenry can recall the names of their incumbents, and even fewer can remember anything they have done for their districts. Only 10 percent or so can remember how incumbents voted on a particular bill. Challengers are even less known. Lacking information, many people simply pick the party with which they generally sympathize. The importance of partisanship explains why the Democrats could maintain unbroken control of the House of Representatives between 1954 and 1994, despite the departure of all but three of their 1954 incumbents during the period.[29] In House elections, 70 percent or more of all party identifiers typically stick with their party's candidate.[30]

Incumbents do win reelection at a very high rate, a trend that has increased while the effect of party has declined. Statistical studies of House elections have found that the **incumbency advantage**—the electoral benefit of being an incumbent, after taking into account other relevant traits—has grown from about 2 percent before 1964 to as high as 12 percent in some recent elections.[31] The increase has not been smooth; rather, the incumbency advantage surged in the late 1960s, bounced around that high level until 1986, and then slipped in the 1990s (see Figure 7.3). This development need not betray a decline in voter influence, however.

One reason why incumbents seem to do so well is that politicians have more information about voters than they did in the past. Incumbents usually know when they are in trouble, and endangered incumbents frequently decide against running for reelection—which pumps up the success rate of the ones who try to keep their seats.[32] Also, members of Congress work very hard to maintain good relations

FIGURE 7.3

The advantage of incumbency surged in the mid-1960s

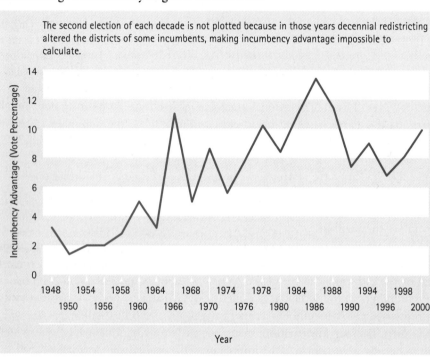

The second election of each decade is not plotted because in those years decennial redistricting altered the districts of some incumbents, making incumbency advantage impossible to calculate.

SOURCE: Calculated by the authors using the Gelman–King method. See Andrew Gelman and Gary King, "Estimating Incumbency Advantage Without Bias," *American Journal of Political Science* 34 (November 1990): 1, 142–164.

with their constituents. Their continued success in large part reflects their efforts at pleasing district voters (see Chapter 9). When members of Congress do not behave in the manner desired by their constituents, strong candidates rise to challenge them, and no automatic advantage of incumbency saves them from defeat (see the accompanying Election Connection, "The Political Death of MMM").

NATIONAL FORCES

Former Speaker of the House Thomas P. "Tip" O'Neill (D-MA) once commented that "all politics is local." O'Neill's remark partly reflected the parochial politics of Massachusetts, but it also is a reminder that members of Congress ultimately must answer to people in thousands of separate localities. Modern congressional elections have become less susceptible to national political forces generated by presidents, parties, and economic conditions.[33]

Presidential **coattails**—the tendency of presidents to carry their own party's candidates for Congress into office—have declined in strength.[34] More voters

ELECTION CONNECTION

The Political Death of MMM

The year 1992 was the so-called year of the woman. Four new female senators were elected, and the number of women representatives rose from 28 to 47. One of the newcomers to the House was Democrat Marjorie Margolies-Mezvinsky, commonly known as MMM, a popular local newscaster. She had defeated her Republican opponent in November by less than 1 percent of the vote, the first Democrat elected from Pennsylvania's thirteenth district in 76 years.

Normally, a member's first election is the hardest. Once in office, she can utilize the advantages of incumbency to expand her support. So long as she does not give potential challengers a damaging issue, she can anticipate reelection with very high probability. MMM gave her constituents such an issue—eight months after the election, when the House considered the final version of President Bill Clinton's deficit reduction plan.

It was a sweeping package of spending cuts and tax increases that would chart the course of economic policy for the next five years. Not a single Republican would support the plan; the income tax increases were unacceptable to them. Democratic leaders scrambled feverishly to muster a majority. President Clinton himself worked the phones, calling undecided Democrats and telling them that his presidency was at stake on the tax vote.

For MMM the situation was a political nightmare. She had consistently opposed Clinton's economic proposals, including the deficit reduction plan. In fact, she had reassured constituents that she would continue to oppose the plan. Now she was under intense pressure from the president and Democratic leaders to reverse her stand.

At the conclusion of electronic voting, the tally stood at 216 to 216. A majority of the full house (218 of 435) is needed to pass the budget. Pat Williams of Montana had agreed to support the president if necessary—so MMM's vote would decide the fate of the plan. Surrounded by supportive Democrats and "with the demeanor of someone being marched to her own hanging," she cast a written vote for Clinton's taxes. Gleeful Republicans chanted "Goodbye, Marjorie!"[a]

MMM may have saved the Clinton legacy, but the cost was her political life. Democratic leaders helped her raise more than $1,600,000 in campaign funds for the 1994 election, and Clinton appeared in her district, but it wasn't enough to save MMM. The Republican she defeated in 1992 returned for a second try. He raised less than two-thirds as much money, but MMM could not overcome the stigma of having cast that damaging vote. She was swept under the national Republican tide. MMM is the exception that proves the rule: Incumbents win regularly only because they usually do what constituents want.

What do you think?

• Does a representative who knowingly bucks the preferences of her district provide an inspiring example of political leadership, or does she betray the voters?

• To what extent does your answer to the last question vary depending on whether you agree with the elected official or with the official's constituents?

[a]Quoted in George Hager and David Cloud, "Democrats Tie Their Fate to Clinton's Budget Bill," *Congressional Quarterly Weekly Report*, (August 7, 1993): 2127, 2125.

FIGURE 7.4

Incumbent administrations do not lose as many House seats in midterm elections today as they did in the past

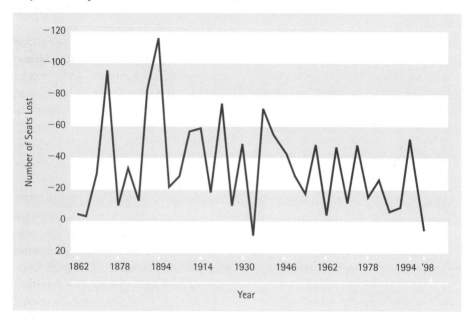

SOURCE: Norman J. Ornstein et al., eds., *Vital Statistics on Congress, 1995–1996* (Washington, DC: Congressional Quarterly, 1996), p. 55.

today split their tickets, voting for presidential and congressional candidates of different parties.[35] Moreover, fewer voters seem to treat voting in an election year without a presidential contest as a way to send the president a message. From the time of the Civil War until 1998, the president's party lost House seats in every off-year election except one (1934). But **midterm loss** has been declining (see Figure 7.4). The limited connection between presidential and congressional elections indicates the independent importance of each contest.

The 1994 elections challenged the prevailing view of incumbent insulation. Democrats lost 52 seats in the House, the largest rupture since 1946, and 8 in the Senate. A strong national tide apparently swept away the Democratic Congress.[36] However, even the 1994 surprise owes less to national forces than many supposed. Democrats did experience severe incumbent losses in 1994; yet 85 percent of the party's House incumbents who ran still won reelection, and a handful of Democratic losses in the early 1990s resulted from unique district changes intended to help elect minorities to office.[37]

Experts are uncertain whether national forces will continue to play a significant role in congressional elections. Many of the new Republicans retained their seats in 1996 by using the same time-honored localism once used by their Democratic predecessors: avoiding controversial stands and highlighting district activities.[38] In 1996, 91 Republican House candidates managed to win districts carried by President Clinton. The trend continued in 1998, when Democrats distanced themselves from Clinton by canceling fund-raisers where he was scheduled to appear,[39] and in 2000, when only 8 out of 412 House incumbents lost.

On the other hand, the 2002 congressional elections were a stunning success for George W. Bush and the Republicans. The GOP gained seats in the U.S. House and picked up enough seats in the U.S. Senate to return control of Congress to the president's party. Bush's aggressive pre-election travel schedule helped boost support for Republican candidates across the country, prompting analysts to argue that some of the candidates were riding into office on Bush's coattails. Among the winners were candidates recruited by Bush's political advisers, including Norm Coleman, who was able to beat former Vice President Walter Mondale in a battle for Minnesota's seat.

To the extent that national forces are regaining strength, it may be because political parties have become more active. Parties control more campaign resources that candidates wish to attract; the parties raised nearly $500 million in 2000.[40] The congressional parties are more unified than they were a generation ago, and the differences between Republicans and Democrats are greater.[41] Congress contains few moderates. Thus voters today usually are presented with a clear choice between two candidates who hold distinct positions on national issues. Such clear differences can overwhelm local factors or the candidate's personal traits.

Interest groups help link congressional elections through issue advocacy. In 1998, for example, the National Rifle Association spent $2.3 million on ads, and it is by no means the biggest spender. Indeed, in 1998, groups began running ads without the knowledge of (and sometimes in defiance of the wishes of) their candidates. In a spring special election in California, for example, pro-life groups attacked the Democratic candidate even though the Republican opponent did not want abortion to be an issue in the race. As the campaign progressed, groups supporting business, environmentalism, and the "Religious Right" jumped in.[42] Campaign-finance reforms passed in 2002 imposed some limits on how interest groups may advertise, but they hindered the parties even more—so interest groups might gain even greater ability to force candidates to address national issues.

THE SENATE PARADOX

The founders intended the House of Representatives to be highly sensitive to popular wishes. However, they viewed the Senate differently. The Constitution originally provided for senators to be chosen by state legislatures, not elected by the people. According to Madison, the insulated Senate would proceed "with more coolness, with more system, and with more wisdom, than the popular branch."[43]

FIGURE 7.5

Representatives get reelected more often than Senators

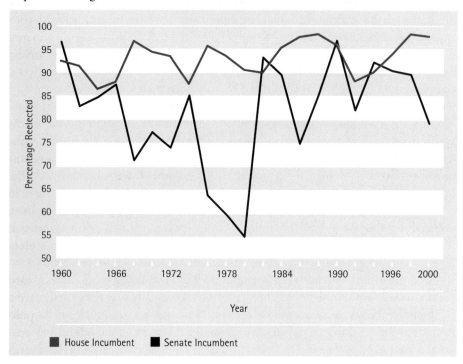

Year

■ House Incumbent   ■ Senate Incumbent

SOURCE: Norman J. Ornstein et al., eds., *Vital Statistics on Congress, 1995–1996* (Washington, DC: Congressional Quarterly, 1996), pp. 60–61.

Neither institution has evolved in the manner Madison and the founders expected. The House as a whole is not very responsive to changes in the national mood, because most members succeed at constructing political identities satisfying to their local constituencies. On the other hand, the Seventeenth Amendment (adopted in 1913) exposed senators to popular election.* Senators must stay sensitive to public opinion.

Of course, elections are never far from the mind of any member of Congress. Members of the House put their fates on the line every other November, not counting the primary campaigns that are under way scarcely more than a year after they take the oath of office. But if anything, the situation is worse for senators (see Figure 7.5). Not only are one-third elected every two years, but Senate campaigns are so expensive that typically incumbents must raise an average of

---

*Many states adopted various popular-voting procedures for their senators as early as the mid-nineteenth century.

just over $15,000 every week of their terms. This time-consuming, psychologically draining activity keeps all of them aware of their need to maintain political support. Plus senators represent more diverse constituencies, who are therefore harder to please. And because their offices are more powerful and have a higher visibility—with an average of 33 news appearances in a single session, compared to 5 for the average representative—senators are more likely to face strong opponents.[44]

EVALUATING THE IMPORTANCE OF CAMPAIGNS

The importance of the campaign is exaggerated. Contrary to what the media imply, many presidential elections are decided before the campaign begins. Conditions in the preceding four years and the government's response to those conditions generally determine the outcome. Political scientist James Campbell has calculated that between 1948 and 2000, the campaigns probably were decisive in 1948 and 1960, two exceedingly close elections. The campaigns may have been decisive in 1976, 1980, and 2000. In the other nine elections, the outcome was largely predetermined.[45] Certainly campaigns matter, but only when the electorate is otherwise closely divided.[46]

Campaigns are shaped by what takes place long before the election. A card game provides a good analogy. Who wins often depends on the deal of the cards. No matter how skillfully one plays, skill may not overcome a bad hand. In politics, some cards are dealt years, even decades, before the election. Good economic conditions are aces dealt to the incumbent party; poor conditions are aces dealt to the opposition. International embarrassments and costly wars also may serve as trump cards. Media coverage seldom mentions the luck of the draw, because most of this is "old news." Journalists praise and criticize campaigns, as though strategic decisions operate on a level playing field; they forget that social and economic realities often dictate how the game is played. In short, journalists generally neglect the main explanations for who wins, the topic on which they expend so many words and so much ink.

Did the fact that Massachusetts Governor Dukakis lost to Vice President Bush in 1988, while Arkansas Governor Clinton beat the same man four years later, indicate that Dukakis ran a poor campaign and Clinton a brilliant one? Dukakis surely could have done some things better, and Clinton certainly found his way out of a few tight spots.[47] But a recession made the Bush administration a much fatter target in 1992 than the Reagan–Bush administration was in 1988. As Clinton's adviser, James Carville, said, "It's the economy, stupid!" The 1996 Dole effort is another example; his campaign was lackluster because he had no chance to win.[48] The economy and the conservative image that the Republican party projected in 1995 and 1996 had Dole against the ropes before the fight even began.

The Ragin' Cajun
Bill Clinton's political consultant in 1992, a Louisiana native named James Carville, is known for his irreverence and wacky sense of humor. But he understood the science of politics enough to realize that an economic recession would bother voters more than the Arkansas governor's personal scandals.

The importance of the campaign emerges in close contests. If a race is about even when the election begins, then any minor event or clever ploy can tip the balance among the few swing voters. Biased media coverage or a few extra advertisements may make a difference. But then, so can any sort of happenstance—trying to pinpoint the "cause" of victory or defeat becomes futile. Nor does the rarity of such close contests justify the attention that campaign strategy receives in the news.

CAN REFORMS IMPROVE THE SYSTEM?

Thus far, we have been very optimistic about the importance of elections in American politics. Despite the media's emphasis on campaigns and character, these are mostly short-term, frivolous factors that operate at the margins. Most voters choose among candidates in a sensible manner, following their long-term party loyalties and medium-term evaluations of government performance. If elections seldom seem very close, this is partly because good candidates know how to anticipate voter behavior and adjust their own career decisions accordingly.

Despite this optimism, three topics worry many would-be reformers: (1) the role of money in national politics, (2) the apparent unfairness of some electoral institutions, and (3) the haphazard nature of the nomination process. In each case, critics exaggerate distortions in the nation's democratic process. Further, the practices and laws that most bother reformers sometimes provide underappreciated benefits. What would result after fixing specific flaws in the electoral system might not be better—and could be much worse—than what the United States has now.

CAMPAIGN FINANCE: THE ROLE OF MONEY

National officeholders generally must win two stages of election: a nominating campaign in which they become the standard bearer of a particular political party, and a general election in which they defeat other parties' nominees to win the office. The process usually requires large sums of money, some of which the federal government collects. The money comes from voluntary checkoffs on Americans' income tax returns and is distributed by the Federal Elections Commission (FEC).

FINANCING NOMINATION CAMPAIGNS Qualifying presidential candidates may have their fund raising matched, dollar for dollar, as long as they agree not to exceed a spending limit. In 2000, the FEC spending limit for the nomination campaign was $40.5 million. This limit was low enough that two candidates, Steve Forbes and George W. Bush, chose to forgo the **matching funds.** Bush had already raised $70 million without federal aid before the primary season began.[49] Experts anticipate that few serious candidates will accept public funding in the future, because changes in campaign-finance law have doubled the size of contributions that candidates may accept from individual donors.[50]

Eligibility for campaign subsidies is not automatic. To be eligible, a candidate must raise at least $5000 in each of 20 states, with no contribution larger than $250. Most serious candidates do not find this legal minimum very difficult to reach; even minor candidates have qualified. Staying eligible is harder. A candidate who fails to receive at least 10 percent of the vote in two consecutive primaries loses eligibility and can regain it only by getting 20 percent or more of the vote in a later primary. Thus a struggling campaign may find itself deprived of funds just when it most needs them. And once candidates become strong, government money helps ensure that they stay that way.

FINANCING PRESIDENTIAL CAMPAIGNS Under the terms of the 1974 Federal Elections Campaign Act (FECA), the general-election campaign is publicly funded. The FEC gives major-party candidates subsidies (Bush and Gore

FIGURE 7.6

In the 1990s reliance on soft money in presidential elections increased dramatically

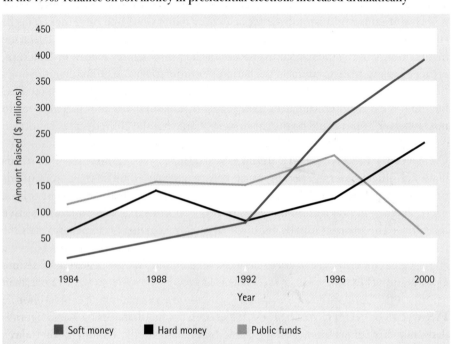

SOURCE: The Federal Election Commission. Note that the Federal Election Commission began requiring the parties to disclose their soft money in 1991. Figures for 1991 through 2000 are from the FEC. Figures for the 1984 and 1988 cycles are based on voluntary disclosures by the parties and on published estimates. Public funding declined in 2000 because Bush, Forbes, and the Republican party did not accept federal matching funds.

received approximately $67.5 million each in 2000), and in return the candidates agree not to raise and spend any more. Beginning in the 1990s, however, campaigns increasingly relied on funding that is not subject to federal regulation (see Figure 7.6). Unlike the hard cash provided to an individual candidate, this unregulated **soft money** never reaches the nominee's hands. Nor may the nominee coordinate how it is spent. So much soft money flows through the political system that reformers have focused their efforts on limiting its influence (see Chapter 8).

SPENDING IN THE GENERAL-ELECTION CAMPAIGN   Labor Day traditionally is the official start date for the fall campaign, although today's nominees take shorter breaks after the summer conventions than in the past. From the start of the campaign until election day (the first Tuesday after the first Monday in November), the candidates maintain an exhausting pace, and the campaign dominates the news.[51]

Campaign consultants oversee the expenditure of the large sums of money raised. These specialists in modern, candidate-based campaigns have replaced party leaders, who supervised strategy in earlier eras. Modern campaigns retain pollsters expert in measuring surges and slumps in public opinion. Media consultants schedule the candidate's time, design campaign ads (or spots), and stage media events that attract the interest of reporters. Derided by critics as "handlers" or "hired guns," some campaign consultants have become celebrities.

The most important category of general-election spending is for what the FEC calls electronic media—TV and radio advertising—and the lion's share goes to television. In 1996 over 60 percent of both Clinton's and Dole's general-election spending was for electronic media.[52] Although campaign advertising is widely criticized, studies have consistently found that it is informative; those exposed to ads know more about the candidates and where they stand. The issue content of ads actually has increased in recent years.[53] The emphasis on issues has come with a cost, however; ads are increasingly negative in tone. Rather than make positive cases for themselves, candidates offer memorable criticisms of their opponents.[54]

FINANCING CONGRESSIONAL CAMPAIGNS   House elections have become increasingly expensive: Average total spending in each House race was more than half a million dollars in 2000, with 91 candidates spending over a million.[55] Moreover, the gap between incumbents' spending and that of their challengers is wide and has grown wider since 1980 (see Figure 7.7). For many of today's reformers, the explanation for the advantage of incumbency is simple and self-evident: money.

Money certainly affects candidate visibility, and congressional challengers are seriously underfunded. Furthermore, attracting so much campaign cash requires extensive effort from elected officials, a chore they often dislike. Nevertheless, research on congressional election financing paints a surprisingly complicated picture. Although money contributes to the electoral advantage that incumbents enjoy, its contribution is less than is often supposed.

Researchers have found that campaign spending yields what economists call *diminishing returns:* The more a candidate spends, the less impact each additional dollar will have. For an incumbent who already has perquisites of office worth as much as a million dollars a year, an extra $100,000 has less impact than it would if it were spent by a challenger who lacked taxpayer-provided resources. For this reason, campaign-finance reform should lessen electoral competition by hurting challengers, who most need money so that they can compensate for the incumbents' name recognition and perks.[56]

Incumbents may receive so much money in part because they are so likely to win, rather than the reverse. The mid-1960s surge in the incumbency advantage *preceded* the explosion of congressional campaign spending. Moreover, the growth

FIGURE 7.7

The spending gap between incumbents and their challengers

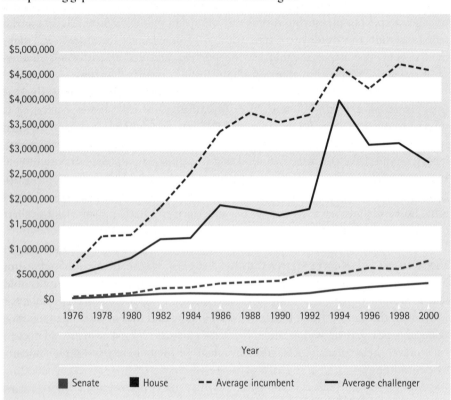

SOURCE: Norman J. Ornstein et al., eds., *Vital Statistics on Congress, 1999–2000* (Washington, DC: American Enterprise Institute, 2000), p. 81.

of political action committees (PACs) took place only after the adoption of campaign-finance laws in 1974, by which time incumbents had already developed a significant advantage. Heavy spending by an incumbent generally signals that the incumbent is in trouble.[57] Of the ten highest-spending representatives in 1998, four lost. The great majority of incumbents probably would still be reelected if campaign spending were slashed.

Perhaps the most discouraging impact of campaign spending today is one that is difficult to observe, let alone measure. Because it takes so much money for a challenger to mount a serious campaign—$600,000 in the estimation of political scientist Gary Jacobson—many potential challengers never enter the race. Why invest so much money for what is at best a long shot? Thus, amassing substantial campaign funds may be most important as a deterrent: Money can't buy the candidate love, but perhaps it can scare off rival suitors.[58]

In recent years the topic of campaign-finance reform has received enormous attention. Many citizens view the system as little more than bribery. Columnist Dave Barry writes, "Basically, our campaign finance system works this way: Donors give money to politicians, who then use the government to do favors for the donors."[59] Although this may exaggerate the current system's negative effects, there is no question that citizens are disgusted with it. They are cynical about government, suspecting that politicians care only about what wealthy interests have to say.

Even if the campaign-finance system is fundamentally flawed, however, it is not certain what sort of electoral reform would improve matters. Spending is heavily regulated in other democracies. In Britain, neither parties nor individual candidates for office are permitted to buy broadcast time to communicate directly with potential voters. They are limited to a small number of publicly financed addresses by national party leaders. In Germany the law restricts parties to the free air time provided by TV networks; they may not buy additional ads.[60] Such restrictions on campaign messages do not appear consistent with the First Amendment or with American values in favor of free expression.

Many other democracies provide at least some degree of public financing.[61] But using government money to subsidize campaigns requires some method of determining eligibility and deciding how much money to give. The country could not turn over millions of dollars to any person or party that chose to throw a hat into the ring. The typical solution is to look back at the previous election. For example, in many countries the parties receive public subsidies in proportion to the number of votes they received in the previous election or the number of seats they hold in parliament.* It is hard to see how a system geared toward rewarding past successes would make either incumbents or dominant parties any less secure than they are now.

THE ROLE OF ELECTORAL INSTITUTIONS

The United States operates on the principle that everyone should have equal influence over government. This commitment fuels widespread distaste for the role of money in national elections, for example, and undergirds the one-person–one-vote legal doctrine. Systems of representation never give everyone equal influence in practice, however. Full equality is impossible to implement, if for no other reason than the fact that an electoral system must accommodate other social goals—including efficiency, individual autonomy, protection of minorities, and fidelity to tradition.

Inequality may open election laws to criticism. Certainly alternative arrangements could equalize influence compared to the current system. On the other hand, reforms also often carry costs, including possible unanticipated consequences. Weighing the costs and benefits of political change requires analyzing

---

*Examples include Austria, Belgium, Denmark, Finland, Germany, Mexico, Sweden, and Turkey.

how current institutions actually work. We focus here on two institutions in the U.S. system that cause voter influence to vary—the Electoral College in presidential elections and legislative districts in congressional elections.

THE ELECTORAL COLLEGE   The presidential candidate who garners the most votes—the so-called **popular vote**—does not necessarily win. Four times in American history, the candidate who came in second became president, including George W. Bush in 2000.[*] The reason for this discrepancy is the Electoral College. Each state possesses a certain number of **electoral votes** and selects the rules that determine which candidate(s) will receive them. If a candidate wins more of the battles for electoral votes, then the total quantity of individual votes received nationwide is irrelevant.

The Electoral College distorts popular preferences by unequally distributing the electors who cast electoral votes. Each state picks one elector for each House and Senate seat in Congress (with an additional three electors assigned to the District of Columbia under the terms of the Twenty-third Amendment). Because every state has two senators, influence is not proportional to population; small states get a numerical advantage. The smallest states receive yet another advantage because of the guarantee that they will each get at least one House member no matter how small their populations. For example, with two senators but only one seat in the House, Wyoming has three electoral votes—approximately 1 electoral vote per 165,000 residents. With two senators but 53 seats in the House, California has 55 electoral votes, approximately 1 vote per 617,000 residents—a ratio only one-quarter as large as Wyoming's. Using 2000 figures, a candidate theoretically could become president with the electoral votes of states containing only 45 percent of the U.S. population.

Large states have tried to compensate for their disadvantage by assigning all of their electors to the candidate receiving the most votes. This **winner-take-all voting** system is used in all states except Maine and Nebraska. Because large states have so many electoral votes to distribute, they are often the most attractive targets for campaign activity. And because large states tend to be diverse, they are usually competitive electoral arenas, another trait that draws candidate attention.

Experts disagree about whether, on balance, the Electoral College favors large states, favors small states, or balances power. Their disagreements usually hinge on rather technical differences in how they evaluate influence.[62] But the small-state advantage helped President Bush tease out a victory over former Vice President Gore, because many Bush states were small ones. And the winner-take-all system explains why candidates often win big Electoral College majorities despite modest advantages in the popular vote. In 1996 Clinton won 49 percent of the popular vote but 70 percent of the electoral vote.

---

[*]The other three were John Quincy Adams in 1824, Rutherford B. Hayes in 1876, Benjamin Harrison in 1888.

FIGURE 7.8

The Republican "L"

The base on which GOP majorities were built in presidential elections in the 1970s and the 1980s was a wide swath of states called the Republican "L." It takes in the Rocky Mountain region, the Plains states, and the entire South. With Alaska thrown in, these states have a total of 233 electoral votes (270 are needed to win). Bill Clinton cracked the "L," but it reemerged in 2000.

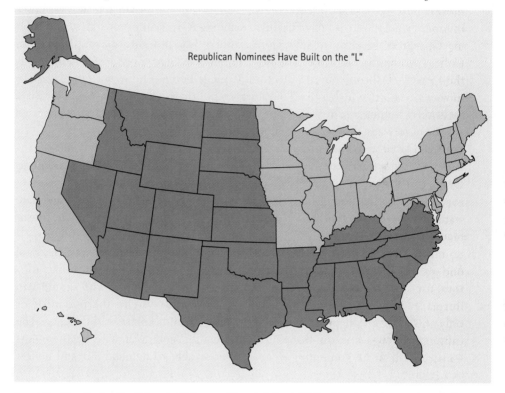

Republican Nominees Have Built on the "L"

SOURCE: "Republican Nominees Have Built on the "L," *Congressional Quarterly Guide to the 1996 Republican National Convention* (August 3, 1996): 9.

For more than a century the popular and electoral vote winners were the same, so the Electoral College received little attention. The 2000 election changed that. At first many observers thought Al Gore might win the presidency with a minority of the popular vote. Bush seemed quite strong in the Republican "L" (depicted in Figure 7.8), a cluster of heartland states that consistently vote for the GOP.[*] Yet Gore seemed capable of tipping the balance in enough swing states to win without a popular majority. Concentrating his efforts in rural states would have cost Bush the election. As it turned out, Gore's policy proposals played well in

---

[*]Between 1968 and 1988, 21 states with 191 electoral votes voted six consecutive times for the Republican candidate. Only the District of Columbia, with 3 electoral votes, was so loyal to the Democrats.

coastal areas, and urban voters mobilized heavily behind him, so that he trounced Bush in a handful of densely populated states. But he lost the electoral vote.

Norms of equal influence have become very strong. It seems unjust, in America's new democracy, for the majority to find its desires frustrated.[63] It is therefore worth considering what useful role the Electoral College might play. Breaking up votes by state requires that a candidate have broad appeal. Winning a state overwhelmingly is not as useful as winning lots of different states. The 2000 election illustrates this dynamic. Gore crushed Bush in California and New York, so he won the popular vote. (Remove either state and Gore lost handily.) But Bush squeaked through in the Electoral College because he won a larger variety of states. The system therefore discourages politicians from adopting a strategy that unites a minority of the country (whether Southerners or city dwellers or anyone else) while dividing the majority. Divisiveness does not pay off.

The Electoral College also may reduce the importance of money. It allows candidates to focus their resources on undecided states. Candidates still can choose to spend vast sums, blanketing battleground states with ads, but these excessive expenditures bring diminishing returns more quickly. The major-party candidate with fewer resources therefore does not suffer as much under the current, more-focused system.

Finally, the Electoral College may reduce corruption. Presumably electoral misbehavior is easiest in states where partisanship is most one-sided. Public officials are more likely to share interests, and citizen opinion on who should win the presidency is most uniform. Under the current system, the potential for statewide corruption peaks where it is least likely to make a difference. The Electoral College ensures that vote totals matter only as a state becomes less lopsided, when the competing sides are better able to demand fair and honest procedures.

Replacing the Electoral College with a popular-vote system certainly would equalize political influence (though probably less than people think). Yet doing so would change very few elections, judging from the past, and it could make a difference only in elections when the public does not clearly favor one candidate or the other. A popular-vote system, meanwhile, might bring costs: encouraging discriminatory campaign appeals, forcing candidates to find resources adequate to compete for votes nationwide, and rewarding states that can find ways (fair or foul) to pile up overwhelming majorities for their candidate of choice.

Whatever happens to the Electoral College, it is clear that the current system shapes campaign strategy. If you were a citizen of Kansas or Utah, of Mississippi or Massachusetts, you might scarcely have known the 2000 election was taking place. Your states were written off by one party and taken for granted by the other. But if you were a citizen of Florida, Pennsylvania, Missouri, West Virginia, or another "battleground" state, you were bombarded with campaign ads, and the

Duvergers Law

Fair weather for Republicans

Population growth in the heavily Republican Sun Belt has outpaced that in the North, causing congressional districts to migrate southward. The Detroit area of Michigan, where this cartoon was first published, has been especially hard hit. Do you think it is harder for a region to recover economically if it loses political power after a decline?

candidates visited your state numerous times. The candidates also recast their issue positions to appeal to the swing states, with Gore edging away from his strong antigun stance and Bush distancing himself from social conservatives.

APPORTIONMENT OF CONGRESSIONAL DISTRICTS   Using electoral districts to determine the nation's legislators also frustrates the will of the majority. This is obvious for the Senate. The Constitution gives every state two senators, regardless of population.[*] The House presents a more complicated picture, because representatives run in election districts that shift periodically. The Constitution requires a census every decade. After each census, the 435 seats in the House are apportioned among the states according to their populations, a process called **reapportionment.**

Currently, six states have populations so small that they get only one representative each, a minimum guaranteed by Article I. After the smallest states

_____
[*]This provision can be amended only with the consent of every state (Article 5).

receive their single representatives, the remaining congressional districts must be of almost precisely equal population. This provision applies both within states and, to the extent possible, across them. Nationally, the shift in congressional districts from state to state has favored the GOP. States in the Northeast and Midwest have lost House seats to the South and Southwest, as population has shifted to the predominantly Republican Sun Belt.

Once states learn their allotments, they set to work **redistricting**—drawing the boundaries of the new districts to equalize population. In most states the legislature does the work, but in five states bipartisan commissions do the job, and several others have a more complicated process. Redistricting is often highly contentious, because political careers depend on which voters get placed in which districts. Politicians often accuse each other of **gerrymandering**—that is, of drawing the lines to benefit a certain group. The courts may be pulled into the process. (See Chapter 14 for a discussion of gerrymandering intended to elect representatives of a certain race or ethnicity.) But every district still ends up with the same population.

Aside from voters in a few small states, therefore, everyone receives about the same amount of House representation. The prime source of inequality is the winner-take-all process of electing one member per district and granting the seat to the person who wins the most votes—called the **single-member, simple-plurality (SMSP) system.** The system disadvantages voting minorities. Candidates win nothing if they do not receive the most votes, even if the second-place finisher gets 49 percent. Any minority spread out over many districts will remain unrepresented unless it becomes dominant in at least one place.

Recognizing these realities, critics occasionally question the electoral system itself. Some suggest that the United States should shift to **proportional representation,** in which a party receives congressional seats according to its share of the vote. Certainly, such a system would equalize influence, compared to the current method. Yet it could undermine the ombudsman role served by legislators (see Chapter 9). The current system assigns each locality a particular member of Congress, responsible for defending that area's interests before the national government. An alternative system that pooled votes over a large geographic area or even over the nation as a whole would sever this direct link between legislator and voter.

Proportional representation systems also carry a risk. They might assist fringe parties dedicated to undermining the political system.[64] Even parties with few supporters could garner enough votes to win at least one seat, so the incentive to choose mainstream politicians would diminish. The party system might splinter enough that social conflicts would all have to be settled within the halls of government, among combative representatives, rather than through the coalition building that candidates often require to win elections in a district-based system.

THE NOMINATION PROCESS

The role that incumbent war chests play in chasing off qualified challengers is not the only problem with the manner in which candidates for office are recruited and nominated. If any segment of the electoral system dampens popular influence, and in a fashion that is difficult to justify, it is a nomination process that limits the range of choices voters can express.

PRESIDENTIAL NOMINATIONS   The United States is unusual among world democracies for its lengthy, participatory process of nominating candidates for chief executive. One British correspondent calls it "a bizarre ritual."[65] In most democracies, party activists and leaders choose nominees. But in the United States every citizen, whatever the depth of his or her commitment, may participate in selecting among possible candidates for the two major parties. Barriers are minimal for participation in a **caucus**—a meeting of candidate supporters—or a **primary election**—a preliminary election. At the presidential level, nearly three-quarters of the states choose their delegates in primary elections, and the remainder choose them in caucuses. Because caucus states tend to be smaller, most of the nation's delegates are chosen in primaries.

The caucus is a rather time-consuming process. Supporters of the respective candidates meet in each voting precinct to start the process of delegate selection. Generally, they gather in public places, such as town halls or public schools, but sometimes they meet on quasi-private property, such as restaurants. These precinct gatherings are only the beginning, however, because the process has a number of stages. For example, the Iowa caucuses are the first major test for candidates, because they occur very early in the election year. But these caucuses only choose delegates to the county conventions held in March, which then choose delegates to the May congressional district conventions, who move on to state conventions held in June!

Democratic caucuses are constrained by national-party rules that require proportional representation for the supporters of different candidates, as well as equal numbers of male and female delegates where possible. Any registered Democrat is eligible to participate. Republican caucuses are less open. Some limit participation to party officials and workers. Some use variants of proportional representation, and some continue to use winner-take-all voting procedures.[66]

Caucus turnout is extremely low—typically in single digits. About 6 percent of the voting-age population participated in the 2000 Iowa caucuses. This figure was not unusually low; the 12 percent turnout in the 1988 Iowa caucuses, when both parties had competitive contests, is believed to be the highest caucus turnout ever recorded. Caucus participants of both parties are unrepresentative of the general population in terms of income and education, and ideologically they tend to be more extreme than their party's broader base of party identifiers.

Primaries take many forms across the states. In **closed primaries,** only party members can vote—and only in the primary of the party in which they are registered. Some primaries are only "semiclosed" because they allow independents to select party primaries and vote as well. **Open primaries** allow any registered voter to select one party's primary and vote in it, even if that person is a member of another party. Most of the southern and upper midwestern states have open primaries. A few Pacific Coast states experimented with "blanket primaries," in which a voter selects a party primary for each office, but in 2000 the U.S. Supreme Court struck down the California law.

Variation in primary laws was significant in the 2000 election season because of the candidacy of John McCain. McCain won in New Hampshire, a semiclosed-primary state, because he received heavy support among independents. Then he scared George W. Bush in South Carolina and won in Michigan—both open-primary states. He was less successful in states where only registered Republicans could participate.

The parties generally would prefer to control participation in their primaries. Even third parties often prefer closed primaries, because they fear how easily an active group can take over a small party—as Pat Buchanan's supporters illustrated in the 2000 election, when they won control of the Reform party from Ross Perot's old allies (see Chapter 8).[67]

EVOLUTION OF THE NOMINATION PROCESS   The direct primary is an American invention, a Progressive reform that swept across the states in the early twentieth century. Despite their adoption at the state and local levels, however, primaries did not determine presidential nominations for another half-century.[68] As late as 1968, Vice President Hubert Humphrey won the Democratic nomination without entering a single primary. Primaries simply served as beauty contests used by particular candidates to show party leaders their popular appeal. These leaders—mayors, governors, and other public and party officials—actually controlled the delegates to national conventions.

The Republicans were the first to begin moving toward greater popular participation in their nominating process. In 1964 Senator Barry Goldwater, an insurgent from Arizona, won the nomination by edging out the party's establishment candidate in the California primary.[69] But the real push to openness came after Humphrey's presidential nomination. Many liberal activists had supported "peace" candidates Eugene McCarthy and Robert Kennedy, who opposed the war in Vietnam.[70] These candidates won most of the year's primaries, driving President Lyndon Johnson from the race in the process. Their supporters thus were outraged that the nomination went to Johnson's vice president. The party adopted its current process to mollify the antiwar movement.[71]

The past two decades have seen much tinkering with the rules, but the broad outlines of the system have not changed. In 2000, all of the Republican delegates and about 80 percent of the Democratic delegates were chosen in primaries and caucuses.* The general pattern today is for candidates to build extensive organizations in the states where the first caucuses and primaries are held. Here the emphasis is on "retail politics," face-to-face contact with voters.[72] An early victory can lead to greater support and more news coverage in the caucuses and primaries that follow.

STRENGTHS AND WEAKNESSES OF THE NOMINATION PROCESS   Despite its participatory nature, many observers are critical of the presidential nomination process.[73] Their concerns fall into two broad categories, one procedural, the other political.

The nomination process is sequential: Candidates organize and campaign in one state, then pack up and move on to the next. The problem, critics complain, is that the process starts before citizens are interested in the election and outlasts citizen endurance.[74] A poll taken in January 2000, as the candidates were gearing up for Iowa and New Hampshire, revealed that 58 percent of the respondents felt that the campaign is too long, and about 50 percent believed it starts too early.[75] A candidate debate that month, carried by NBC in prime time, drew an audience of 4.7 million. That was only a bit larger than the audience for reruns of *Buffy the Vampire Slayer* and only 60 percent as large as the audience for *WWF Smackdown!*[76] Many candidacies therefore die before voters are tuned in to the campaign.

The long process may bore ordinary voters and leave the nominees "damaged goods" when they finally emerge from the grueling process. Yet it shines a bright light on candidates, revealing a great deal of information about them that Americans choose to consider when they vote. Is it better for voters to be ignorant of personal shortcomings or the questionable activities of a public servant, flaws that often went unknown before the modern nomination process? Opinions differ. The scrutiny may expose bad leaders, but the lack of personal privacy also may drive away some good leaders. Indeed, some have suggested (jokingly?) that anyone willing to expose every aspect of his or her life to media scrutiny is not the kind of person who should be in power.

And so the procedural argument goes, back and forth. The structure of the nomination process has positive and negative qualities, and any change is soon criticized. For example, in 1996 and 2000 the primaries were "front-loaded"; many states moved their primaries to early dates in hopes that the nomination contests would be decided more quickly and the winners would have more time to unify their parties and plan for the fall election campaign.[77] As Figure 7.9 shows, these hopes were fulfilled. But then critics charged that this front-loading

---

*The Democrats generally reserve about 20 percent of their slots for elected officials and party leaders called *superdelegates*.

FIGURE 7.9

In 1996 and 2000, the presidential nominations were decided earlier than ever

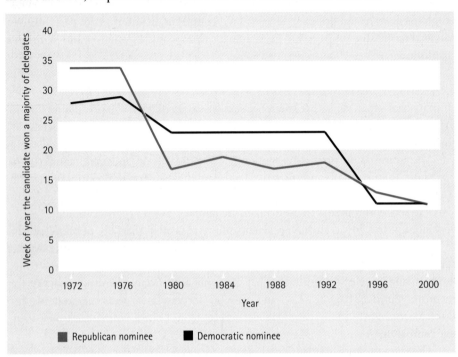

SOURCE: Data compiled by Sam Abrams through various news reports.

gave an advantage to well-known, establishment candidates who could raise large sums of campaign money quickly.

A second set of criticisms focuses on the *politics* of the nomination process. Reformers who instituted primaries claimed they were giving "power to the people"—the new procedure would empower ordinary citizens at the expense of the party bosses. In fact, other elites rose up to be the new bosses: political activists and the media.

Political activists have always exerted more influence than ordinary citizens, because they participate. Caucus turnout is extremely low, and although primary turnout is higher, it is still much lower than that in general elections. Of the 18 states that voted while the nominations were still undecided in 2000, 12 set turnout records, but the average turnout was only 13.6 percent![78] Even more important, activists work in campaigns and give money to candidates; they help mobilize others.

None of this would be cause for concern if the activists were like everyone else. But activists differ in politically relevant ways. Not only are their views more *intense,* but party activists' positions are more *extreme* as well (see Table 7.3). Candidates often must conform to these policy positions if they wish to win nominations. Consequently, the primary process may force candidates to take positions far from the center of the political spectrum where the mass of Americans are located.

TABLE 7.3

PARTY ACTIVISTS ARE NOT MODERATES

Surveys find that on most issues, Democratic activists tend to be more liberal than Democratic identifiers, and Republican activists more conservative than Republican identifiers. Here is how national convention delegates compared to their parties' supporters in 1996. Democratic delegates were more extreme than identifiers on eight of ten issues, and Republican delegates were more extreme on nine of ten issues.

ISSUE	DEMOCRATIC		REPUBLICAN	
	DELEGATES	IDENTIFIERS	IDENTIFIERS	DELEGATES
Government should do more to solve the nation's problems	76%	53%	20%	4%
Government should regulate the environment and safety practices of business	60	66	37	4
Government should promote traditional values	27	41	44	56
Abortion should be permitted in all cases	61	30	22	11
Assault weapons should be banned	91	80	62	34
It is necessary to have laws to protect racial minorities	88	62	39	30
Affirmative action programs should be continued	81	59	28	9
Organized prayer should be permitted in public schools	20	66	69	57
Trade restrictions are necessary to protect domestic industries	54	65	56	31
Children of illegal immigrants should be allowed to attend public school	79	63	46	26

SOURCE: From CBSNews/*NewYorkTimes* Poll results distributed by Michael Kagay at the Annual Meeting of the American Political Science Association, San Francisco, August 31, 1996.

Democratic candidates generally are more liberal, and Republican candidates generally more conservative, than the average voter.[79]

Another consequence of the enhanced influence of activists in the nominating process is that they skew the political debate. To someone following the process, it may seem that the most important issues facing the United States are so-called hot-button issues, such as abortion and gun control. Although issues like these are important, ordinary voters do not view them as crucial.[80] So they may prefer that the spotlight turn to bread-and-butter issues, such as education, medical care, and prosperity.

The media are the second group that gained influence from the nomination process, because journalists are the ones responsible for interpreting primary and caucus developments for the American people. Some critics claim that the press trivializes elections by emphasizing matters other than policy and performance (see Chapter 5). The press reports the horse race—who is ahead and by how far, who is "coming up on the rail," and who is fading from contention. This emphasis has increased over time such that, for the last couple of decades, four-fifths of election coverage focuses on the horse race aspect.[81]

The media warp public perception of elections in other ways. For example, Iowa, the first caucus state, and New Hampshire, the first primary state, receive a disproportionate share of news coverage. Some critics ask whether two sparsely populated, rural states should play such an important role in determining candidate viability or, indeed, in determining who is the front runner.[82]

Finally, some observers complain that the media no longer merely report the nomination process but also have become important players in it. News stories have grown overwhelmingly interpretive, rather than simply factual.[83] For example, in every campaign there is a widely publicized "expectations game." The question is not so much whether candidates win or lose but how they perform relative to "expectations." And who sets these expectations? The media.

The classic example occurred in 1972, when Senator Edmund Muskie's campaign never recovered from his showing in the New Hampshire primary. Muskie won the primary over George McGovern 46 percent to 37 percent. But New Hampshire was next to Muskie's home state of Maine, so the media expected him to do well. They thought that, comparatively, McGovern's showing was unexpectedly strong for a native of South Dakota and brought him extensive publicity as a result. The momentum that McGovern took out of his New Hampshire loss carried him to the Democratic nomination!

The media are more influential in the primaries than in the general-election campaign. Voters cannot use party cues to decide among candidates in primaries, because they all belong to the same party. Nor is presidential performance of any use. Normally, all the candidates in the incumbent party's primaries defend the president's record, whereas all the candidates in the other party's primaries criticize that record. Consequently, citizens use other information to choose among the candidates, and in most cases the media provide it. In particular, the electorate usually wishes to know which candidates are serious, and campaign coverage gives that signal. None of these sources of media influence appears in the general election.

Whatever your view of the pros and cons of the American nomination process, it is now well established and, therefore, unlikely to change except in marginal ways for the foreseeable future. Many of the problems that bother critics originate not in national law, but in the combined decisions of political parties, individual states, and media organizations. Even if reformers did succeed at changing the process, the alternatives might be worse than the current system.

Holding all primaries on the same day could increase the role of money and national stature. Trying to increase the amount of candidate information available or the number of candidates might result in overload and alienate citizens from the process. Opening up the nomination system might hinder the ability of party leaders to recruit and promote strong candidates able to build a national constituency. The only obvious possible enhancement would be if citizens became more attentive to their political decisions and more savvy about evaluating potential candidates—and that is the one thing that reformers probably cannot legislate.

WHO NOMINATES THE VICE PRESIDENT?   Before the establishment of the contemporary nomination process, the conventions chose the vice-presidential as well as the presidential candidates. Today, the choice is completely in the hands of the presidential nominees. The presidential nominees simply announce their choices, and the conventions accept them. Usually they attempt to select a nominee who will help the ticket (or at least not hurt it).[84]

Bush's choice of Dick Cheney offset his inexperience with national politics; Cheney was a widely respected former Cabinet secretary and congressman. Gore chose Connecticut Senator Joseph Lieberman, whose religiosity and early criticism of the Monica Lewinsky affair inoculated his ticket against contamination by the outgoing Clinton administration's scandals. Recent choices for vice president have, as often as not, been better respected nationally than the men who chose them.

THE CONGRESSIONAL NOMINATION PROCESS   The congressional nomination process is much simpler than the presidential one: A nominee for the House or Senate must win at most one primary election, not a sequence across many states. In a few states party conventions can nominate candidates, but in most states primary voters do the job.

The dates of **filing deadlines** and primary elections vary widely across states.[85] The filing deadline is the latest date on which a politician who wishes to be

The moral high ground

Al Gore's ticket surged in the polls after Connecticut Senator Joseph Lieberman joined it as Gore's running mate. Lieberman seemed an inspired choice. Not only did his Jewish faith attract lots of media attention, but his devoutness also set up a nice contrast with the sex scandals of the Clinton administration. More recently, though, critics have blamed Gore's loss on his decision to shut Clinton out of the 2000 campaign. Was Gore's decision to distinguish himself from Bill Clinton wise or foolish?

on the ballot must file official documents with, and/or pay fees to, state election officials. In 2002 the dates ranged from December 7 (2001!) in California to August 23 in Louisiana. The primaries started on March 5, and the last was held on September 21. Thus some candidates know whether they will have opponents, and who those opponents are, as much as nine months earlier than others.

The hardest-fought primaries occur when a seat becomes "open" because an incumbent dies, retires, resigns, or opts to run for another office. If both parties have strength in the area, the primaries in both parties are hotly contested. If only one party is strong, its primary will be a donnybrook, because the winner is viewed as the next member of Congress. **Open seats** are critical to political change within a party because few incumbents lose primaries. In the ten elections held since 1980, a total of 50 House incumbents and 6 Senate incumbents were defeated in primaries, and not many more faced tough races. This record does not prove that primaries are unimportant. Incumbent primary successes probably indicate the same thing as general-election successes do: Incumbents behave in such a way as to keep their constituencies satisfied and preempt a strong challenge.

CHAPTER SUMMARY

Many traits that reformers dislike about the American electoral system result from the quantity of popular input, rather than from the limits on it. For example, incumbency advantages in congressional elections largely result from the effort that incumbents put into satisfying voters back home. Even senators must campaign continually to retain their power, contrary to what the founders originally expected. They cannot simply ride national political forces to victory.

The American nomination process is far more open than the nomination processes of other democracies. It gives rank-and-file voters more influence in the United States than they have in other countries, and it gives "outsider" candidates a chance by enabling them to pull off upsets in early primaries and caucuses. If the system has any serious flaw, it is probably the way campaign finance, party activists, and the media can run off or shut out candidates before ordinary voters have had adequate time to consider them. But even this influence may be exaggerated, and at any rate no obvious reform is available to fix it.

Campaigning is often misunderstood. It is not an independent force that determines election outcomes. Rather, the campaign itself is shaped by events and conditions in the years leading up to the election. The reason why campaigns are limited in their impact is that most voters do not make up their minds on the basis of campaigns. People vote for the parties they favor, vote against leaders when they dislike the government's performance, consider policy differences when these are easy to compare, and weigh candidate traits relevant to governance. Only a minority decide how to vote late in the campaign, by using knowledge of particular candidates or the particular things they say.

KEY TERMS

caucus, p. 225
closed primaries, p. 226
coattails, p. 208
electoral votes, p. 220
filing deadlines, p. 231
gerrymandering, p. 224
incumbency advantage,
   p. 207
incumbents, p. 207
matching funds, p. 215

midterm loss, p. 210
open primaries, p. 226
open seats, p. 232
party identification, p. 199
popular vote, p. 220
primary election, p. 225
proportional representation,
   p. 224
reapportionment, p. 223
redistricting, p. 224

retrospective voting,
   p. 203
safe seats, p. 207
single-member, simple-
   plurality (SMSP) system,
   p. 224
soft money, p. 216
winner-take-all voting,
   p. 220

On the Web

The United States Electoral College
http://www.archives.gov/ federal_register/electoral_ college/electoral_college.html
A detailed explanation of the electoral college as well as an historical database of presidential election data. The site is maintained by the National Archives and Records Administration and has links to other government data sets pertaining to elections on all levels of government.

Common Cause
www.commoncause.org/index. html
Common Cause is a nonprofit, nonpartisan citizen's lobbying organization that promotes open, honest, and accountable government. This site contains a searchable database of special-interest soft-money contributions to the Democratic and Republican national party committees, as well as a database of materials that focus on the impact of big money in politics.

Presidential Election Statistics
www.multied.com/elections/
A graphical presentation on each of the U.S. presidential elections, providing both electoral and popular votes. This site is run by MultiEducator Incorporated, an online education company that offers free access to many of its files over the Internet.

American National Election Studies
www.umich.edu/~nes/
Probably the single most important source of data for students of American elections. This impressive collection of election surveys, conducted from the 1950s to the present, is the source of many of the figures and tables that appear in this book.

Federal Election Project
www.american.edu/academic. depts/spa/ccps/fepindex.html
A repository for year-2000 election statistics at the precinct level, compiled by David Lublin at American University and Steve Voss at the University of Kentucky. For many of these states, the election returns are matched with racial and ethnic population figures from the Census.

Suggested Readings

Brady, David. *Critical Elections and Congressional Policy Making.* Stanford, CA: Stanford University Press, 1988. Prize-winning account that ties together congressional elections, processes, and policy making.

Brown, Clifford, Lynda Powell, and Clyde Wilcox. *Serious Money.* Cambridge: Cambridge University Press, 1995. A detailed empirical study of who contributes to presidential campaigns and why.

Butler, David, and Bruce Cain. *Congressional Redistricting.* New York: Macmillan, 1992. Readable account of the redistricting process, with comparisons to practices in other democracies.

Campbell, James. *The Presidential Pulse of Congressional Elections.* Lexington: University of Kentucky Press, 1993. Detailed analysis of national forces operating in midterm elections.

Canon, David. *Actors, Athletes, and Astronauts.* Chicago: University of Chicago Press, 1990. Interesting study of how political amateurs run for and occasionally win seats in Congress.

Fenno, Richard. *Home Style.* Boston: Little, Brown, 1978. Influential study of how House members interact with constituents, earning their trust.

Fiorina, Morris. *Congress—Keystone of the Washington Establishment,* 2nd ed. New Haven, CT: Yale University Press, 1989. A critical look at the implications of constituency service for national policy making.

Hibbing, John. *Congressional Careers.* Chapel Hill: University of North Carolina Press, 1991. Detailed study of career development of modern U.S. representatives after their initial election.

Holbrook, Thomas. *Do Campaigns Matter?* Thousand Oaks, CA: Sage, 1996. A scientifically rigorous study of the impact of presidential campaigns.

Kahn, Kim, and Patrick Kenney. *The Spectacle of U.S. Senate Campaigns.* Princeton, NJ: Princeton University Press, 1999. Detailed study of how candidate strategies, media practices, and voter decisions interact in contemporary Senate campaigns.

Mayer, William, ed. *In Pursuit of the White House 2000: How We Choose Our Presidential Nominees.* Chatham, NJ: Chatham House, 2000. An informative collection of essays covering all facets of the contemporary nominating process.

Mayhew, David. *Congress—The Electoral Connection.* New Haven, CT: Yale University Press, 1974. Influential work that shows how much of congressional structure and behavior can be explained by the assumption that reelection is the most important goal of members.

POLITICAL PARTIES
AND INTEREST GROUPS

Americans entered the 1990s profoundly unhappy with the state of their medical care.[1] They were paying out far more of their economic resources per citizen than in other industrialized countries—twice as much as in the United Kingdom, for example. Yet health access and health outcomes in the United States were no better, and often worse, than in countries with lower costs. Life expectancy was shorter: 76 years compared to more than 78 years in Canada or France. Infant mortality was higher. Eight out of every thousand children born in the United States died in 1995, more than in comparable countries. Americans availed themselves of health care services less often than citizens in other countries. Almost 15 percent of the population lacked health insurance, which means that their level of care almost certainly fell below need.

Where was all the money going, then? A large part of the problem was that medical bills had to cover grave inefficiencies in the health care industry. Almost a third of hospital beds sat empty, compared to vacancy rates that seldom rose above a fifth of capacity in other advanced countries. About 14 percent of insurance costs went toward overhead and administration, more than in other countries. Studies suggested that as much as a quarter of the common tests and procedures run on American patients was unnecessary, presumably because physicians wish to avoid medical-malpractice lawsuits and because they receive more money when they provide lots of complex services. An American doctor's average salary greatly exceeded rates elsewhere: roughly $156,000 per year in 1990, compared to $85,000 in Canada and only $51,000 in Britain.

Americans made no secret of their dissatisfaction with the health care system. They reported their unhappiness to pollster after pollster. Only 10 percent of American respondents told the Louis Harris organization in 1990 that their system worked "pretty well," compared to more than a quarter of Brits, around a third of Swedes, and more than half of Canadians.[2] Americans were more likely than citizens in other advanced nations to think the health-care system needed "fundamental changes." And at first it seemed as though the political system was going to respond to their demands. President Bill Clinton promised to "take on the health care profiteers" after his election.[3] He appointed a task force, led by his wife Hillary, to propose an omnibus reform bill that could limit rising health care costs and expand coverage to the uninsured. The administration eventually suggested a massive reorganization of the health care system.

But interest groups descended on Congress and fought an all-out war over the reform bill—what Haynes Johnson and David Broder have called "the most expensive lobbying battle in history." Spending estimates for this effort ranged as high as $300 million, including $50 million in campaign contributions from interests both for and against the reforms. One opposition group ran an especially popular series of ads against the Clinton Plan, featuring two characters named Harry and Louise. The ad warned that Americans would have to "pick from a few health care plans designed by government bureaucrats" and then delivered the punch line: "There's got to be a better way."[4]

Health reform became a partisan weapon that Clinton and Republican House Speaker Newt Gingrich could use to bash each other. The Clintons ignored warnings from their own advisers that "We have won a mandate for change, but not one for any specific policy."[5] They proposed an aggressive plan that most Republicans and some moderate Democrats could not support and then blamed the opposition for failing to act. In turn, the opposition accused Clinton of proposing an objectionable plan that would limit health care choices, increase government bureaucracy, and force a tax increase to cover more health care for the poor—yet they showed no initiative at identifying and promoting a bill Clinton could sign. The Clinton Plan died, but so did every other proposal. No one managed to identify the "better way" that Harry and Louise claimed must exist. Americans did not receive the fundamental changes they wanted.

Fast forward a decade to the 2002 congressional elections. New health care issues dominated the political landscape. For example, the elderly were spending increasing sums of money on medicine. Pharmaceutical companies release new drugs every year, and sometimes these drugs represent significant advances in medical treatment over older alternatives. Naturally, the companies want to profit from the effort they spend walking drugs through the complicated and risky process of testing, patenting, and winning government approval. Seniors, in turn, demand government assistance to help them pay the price of these costly products, a demand that many younger Americans apparently endorse. Democrats in 2000 strongly advocated using taxpayer money to buy drugs for the elderly, a proposal so popular that George W. Bush felt it necessary to assemble his own plan.

Voters also did not like the way health insurance had evolved. Many Americans have joined what are called health maintenance organizations, and one tactic used by HMOs to limit their costs is to cut down on unnecessary medical procedures. Physicians have little incentive to help with this effort, though, so the HMOs need some means of "second guessing" medical decisions to determine when health providers are wasting insurance money. This role occasionally placed HMOs in the uncomfortable position of denying people medical care recommended by their doctors, which caused public opinion to turn against them. Politicians responded to this pressure by proposing a "patient bill of rights" that would limit how and when insurers could refuse to pay for a medical procedure.

These issues may seem distinct from the previous decade's. But the political pattern remained unchanged. In each case, Americans seemed to agree that the national government should "do something" to fix the problem, but neither the public nor the political parties nor the interest groups involved could agree on a solution. Indeed, in both cases, the system was slow to respond to public demands for reform for much the same reasons: interest-group clashes and partisan sniping. On prescription drugs, Republicans wanted to provide the assistance through private health insurers, whereas Democrats insisted on extensive coverage through Medicare.[6] On patients' rights, Democrats wanted to encourage patients to sue their HMOs as a means of ensuring medical coverage, whereas Republicans insisted on a plan that limited costly lawsuits. Interest groups lined up to oppose the policies offered by each party, strengthening the willingness of each party to block change. And the end result was that, as of early 2003, Congress had failed to address public unhappiness via concrete reforms.

JAMES MADISON WARNED AGAINST THE "MISCHIEFS OF FACTION"—against the danger of allowing self-interested pressure groups to take over the reins of government. Yet to many Americans, Madison's worst nightmares appear to have been realized. The decade-long saga of paralysis on health care reform graphically illustrates all the perceived ills of interest-group democracy. It shows special interests, both within parties and outside of them, using their powers of persuasion to prevent change. It demonstrates the extent to which American institutions neglect public demands because of their sluggishness. In short, it indicates why Americans think that the system does not listen to what voters have to say.

On the other hand, this chapter will show that the current political system does not stand out from the past as much as the American public might think. Interest groups did not rise up to take over a government that previously concentrated on promoting the public interest. Rather, the United States moved to the contemporary system of interest-group democracy from a system ruled by stronger political parties. The old parties did not give Americans equal influence; they simply created different sorts of inequalities. They worked at least as hard to promote their selfish interests. They excelled at creating gridlock, at suppressing political issues, and at limiting the choices of voters, just as they do in the health care area today. Indeed, interest groups rose up primarily because public unhappiness with those old political parties led to policies that weakened them. What stands out about modern parties and interest groups is not the extent to which they clog up the system, but the extent to which both sorts of organizations have opened up to public influence over time—even if that means paralysis when the public cannot agree on how to solve social problems. Because they have grown more responsive to public input, the factions in politics today resemble the rest of America's new democracy.

POLITICAL PARTIES: A NECESSARY EVIL?

When George Washington left office in 1796, he warned his fellow citizens away from forming political parties. "The spirit of party," he warned, "agitates the community with ill-founded jealousies and false alarms, kindles the animosity of one part against another, foments occasional riot and insurrection." Washington's warning came too late—the spirit of party already was loose, never to be confined again.

John Adams, Washington's vice president, won the presidency in that year. Thomas Jefferson, Washington's secretary of state, came in second in the Electoral College voting and thus became the new vice president. Over the course of the next few years, Jefferson and James Madison laid the foundations of a new electoral alliance against Adams. Jefferson, who regularly glorified the small farmer, began to reach out to urban interests. By the next presidential election, he and Madison had concluded an alliance with the New York Republicans and New York City political operative Aaron Burr, by all accounts a superb organizer, delivered the New York legislature, which chose the state's presidential electors. New York's 12 electors were the key to the 1800 election—Jefferson and Burr finished eight votes ahead of President Adams.

Thus, within eight years of the adoption of the Constitution, a two-party presidential race had been fought. Voters chose to cast out one party and replace it with another. The Constitution contains not a word about political parties, but they have been active in U.S. national politics ever since. Indeed, some historians claim that the individual colonies had parties even earlier.[7] It is hard to imagine a government without them.

All modern democracies have political parties. Traditionally defined as groups of like-minded people who band together in an attempt to take control of government, **political parties** serve as the main connection between ordinary citizens and the public officials they elect. Parties nominate candidates for office, shape the electoral process, and mobilize voters. And after elections have determined the winners, parties also coordinate the actions of elected officials in the government.

Despite the presence of parties almost since the country's founding, however, Americans have not always accepted the role they play in the political system. Periodically, voters have grown unhappy with the major parties available to them and have expressed their displeasure by supporting new organizations (see Table 8.1). Often these periods of instability caused significant changes in the political system or evoked demands for reforms that stripped parties of their organizational strength.

THE TWO-PARTY SYSTEM

Two major parties have dominated elections for national office throughout American history. Americans therefore understandably regard a two-party system as a natural state of affairs. Third parties regularly arise—most recently Ross Perot's Reform Party and Ralph Nader's Green Party. But they nearly all disappear quickly, either because they are a reaction to a particular problem that fades in importance or because one of the major parties co-opts their main issues (see the accompanying Election Connection, "Third Parties and the 2000 Election").[8] Only once has a new group risen to become a major political party: the Republicans in the 1850s.

TABLE 8.1

THIRD PARTIES IN U.S. HISTORY

CANDIDATE (PARTY, YEAR)	SHOWING	SUBSEQUENT EVENTS
Martin Van Buren (Free Soil party, 1848)	10.1% 0 electoral votes	Party drew 5 percent in 1852; supporters then merged into Republican Party
James B. Weaver (Populist party, 1892)	8.5% 22 electoral votes	Party supported Democrat William Jennings Bryan in 1896
Theodore Roosevelt (Progressive party, 1912)	27.4% 88 electoral votes	Party supported GOP nominee in 1916
Robert M. La Follette (Progressive party, 1924)	16.6% 13 electoral votes	La Follette died in June 1925
Strom Thurmond (States' Rights Democratic party, 1948)	2.4% 38 electoral votes	Democrats picked slate acceptable to South in 1952
Henry A. Wallace (Progressive party, 1948)	2.4% 0 electoral votes	Party disappeared
George C. Wallace (American Independent party, 1968)	13.5% 46 electoral votes	Wallace ran in Democratic primaries in 1972 until he was injured in assassination attempt
John B. Anderson (National Unity Campaign, 1980)	6.6% 0 electoral votes	Anderson withdrew from elective politics
H. Ross Perot (Independent, 1992)	18.7% 0 electoral votes	Perot formed new party (Reform) to take part in 1996 and 2000 presidential elections
H. Ross Perot (Reform party, 1996)	8.5% 0 electoral votes	Perot adopted a lower profile
Patrick Buchanan (Reform party, 2000)	< 1% 0 electoral votes	Buchanan appeared to be finished in national politics
Ralph Nader (Green party, 2000)	3% 0 electoral votes	Nader failed to qualify for federal funding in 2004

NOTE: The list excludes many third-party candidates who received less than 2 percent of the popular vote. Other third parties that won at least 2 percent of the vote include the Liberty party (1844); the Greenback party (1880); the Prohibition party (1888, 1892); and the Socialist party (1904, 1908, 1912, 1916, 1920, 1932).

SOURCE: Adapted from Kenneth Jost, "Third-Party Prospects," *The CQ Researcher* (December 22, 1995): 1148. Updated with 1996 and 2000 election returns.

Third Parties and the 2000 Election

George W. Bush won Florida by a mere 537 official votes in the 2000 presidential election. Ralph Nader, the Green party candidate, received 97,488 votes there. Had just over one-half of 1 percent of Nader's predominantly left-wing voters backed Vice President Al Gore instead, a Democrat would have moved into the White House. Bush also won narrow victories in New Hampshire, Ohio, and West Virginia; Nader's primarily left-wing voters could have saved Gore in those states as well. Although Nader won an unimpressive 3 percent of the popular vote—far less than the 19 percent attracted by colorful Texas billionaire Ross Perot in 1992—those liberal votes were critical in electing a conservative president.

Nader had known he might cost Gore the presidency but expressed little concern about the possibility, arguing that "the only difference between Gore and Bush is the velocity with which their knees hit the floor when corporations bang on their door." Democratic leaders could not ignore the enthusiastic crowds attending Nader events in progressive states such as Oregon and Washington. Web sites sprang up where Nader supporters in close states could trade their votes with Gore supporters in uncompetitive states. That way, Naderites would be able to promote their main goal—helping the candidate get 5 percent of the national vote and so qualify for 2004 campaign funds—without swinging the election to a Republican.

These efforts failed. Nader's campaign pulled in left-wing voters who otherwise would have preferred Gore to Bush, resulting in a more conservative administration than governed in the Clinton–Gore White House. Yet the Green party failed to qualify for 2004 campaign money. Looking back, Nader remains unapologetic for the damage he did to Gore's campaign. Nader voters, though, could be remorseful. They may be willing to back mainstream Democrats in 2004 who work to address the issues that concern them. If so, the Green party's days as a serious organization will be numbered.

If the Green party does fade, it will have followed in the footsteps of Perot's Reform

The number of political parties may result from how a country's laws translate popular votes into control of public offices.[9] The United States relies almost exclusively on the **single-member, simple-plurality (SMSP) system.** Elections for office take place within geographic units (states, congressional districts, city wards, and so on), and the candidate who wins the most votes wins the electoral unit. This system is typical of "Anglo-American democracies" (England and its former colonies). It is often called the first-past-the-post system; just as in a horse race, the winner is the one who finishes first, no matter how many others are in the race or how close the finish.

In the SMSP electoral system, winning is everything—finishing in any position except first gets nothing. Thus, if small parties have more in common with each other than with the largest party, they have an incentive to join together. Dividing the opposition simply plays into the hands of the largest party. Citizens,

party, which died during the same presidential election in which the Greens rose to prominence. After the 1992 election, Perot had tried to create a formidable political organization that could continue to push his policy goals. He transformed his campaign organization into a citizens' group called "United We Stand" that could speak out on national politics. Then, in late 1995, he backed the formation of an official political party—the Reform party. Perot's vote slipped when he ran again in 1996, but his party put up more than 180 candidates for a variety of offices and eventually elected a governor, former professional wrestler Jesse Ventura, in Minnesota.

The Reform party qualified for $13 million in public funds for the 2000 presidential election, but even these resources could not save it. Perot chose not to run again. Lacking Perot as a unifying figure, the party split badly over its presidential nomination. Conservative commentator Pat Buchanan brought in his troops from past campaigns for the Republican nomination, and they took over the ill-attended Reform party convention, even though

Buchanan shared few issue positions with Perot other than opposition to free trade. Perot refused to endorse him. Ventura left the party. And Buchanan ultimately attracted about half a percentage point of the national vote, despite his access to the Reform party's millions. By 2001, the party treasury contained only a few thousand dollars. The Reform party was dead, like so many third parties that preceded it.

What do you think?

- When does it make sense for voters to abandon the mainstream party closest to them and support a third party?
- Will Green party voters return to the Democratic fold in 2004, leaving their third party behind?
- Will Democratic candidates in 2004 try to satisfy Green party voters by taking left-wing issue positions?
- Will the concessions that Greens demand make Democratic candidates too liberal to win the 2004 general election?

SOURCE: Marianne Means, "Downfall of the Reform Party," Hearst Newspapers, August 3, 2001.

in turn, realize that voting for a small party is tantamount to "wasting" their votes—unless party sympathizers are so concentrated that they can win in a particular geographic unit.[10] Thus voters tend to support one of the two larger parties. These calculations work against third parties.

In most of the world's other democracies, however, the electoral system is some version of **proportional representation (PR).** In such systems, elections may (as in Germany) or may not (as in Israel) take place within geographic units, smaller than the nation as a whole, but either way voters elect a number of officials, with each party winning seats in proportion to the vote it receives. Multiple political parties are much more likely under a PR system, because votes for a third party seldom go to waste. One study found that the average number of parties in proportional representation systems was 3.7, whereas the average number in SMSP systems was 2.2.[11]

POLITICAL PARTIES IN U.S. HISTORY

The United States has always had two parties, but the system has not remained static throughout the country's history. When Washington issued his warning, parties were not unlike groups of scheming courtiers in a monarchical government who jockeyed for power by engaging in "palace intrigues." The electoral system has gone through numerous changes since then: the development of parties appealing to the masses, the collapse of a major party and birth of a new one, and wild fluctuations in the balance of power between Republicans and Democrats.

Realignment theorists view American political history as a succession of electoral eras, often referred to as party systems (see Table 8.2).[12] Within each era, elections are similar, in that each social and economic group consistently supports one party or another. The minority party rarely wins the presidency, unless it can find a military hero to nominate or identifies some other tempo-

---

TABLE 8.2

THE PARTY-SYSTEMS INTERPRETATION OF U.S. ELECTORAL HISTORY

First Party System (Jeffersonian): 1796–1824[*]
    7 Democratic–Republican presidential victories
    1 Federalist victory

Second Party System (Jacksonian Democracy): 1828–1856
    6 Democratic victories
    2 Whig victories

Third Party System (Civil War and Reconstruction): 1860–1892
    7 Republican victories
    2 Democratic victories

Fourth Party System (Industrial Republican): 1896–1928
    7 Republican victories
    2 Democratic victories

Fifth Party System (New Deal): 1932–1964
    7 Democratic victories
    2 Republican victories

Sixth Party System (Divided Government): 1968–??
    6 Republican victories
    3 Democratic victories

---

[*]Years are approximate.

rary opportunity. But at some point a crisis disrupts the tidy arrangement of voters. Rivals within the major parties may start fighting each other, or strong third parties may arise. Voter turnout surges in response to the excitement. Finally, a **critical election** (or realigning election) alters the existing electoral alignment altogether. New groups enter the electorate, or influential groups switch parties for good, solidifying the terms of political conflict for a generation or more.

THE FIRST PARTY SYSTEM (JEFFERSONIAN) Some historians date the first party system from the early 1790s to about 1824. The Federalist party of Washington and Adams opposed the Democratic–Republicans of Jefferson and Madison. The overriding issue during this period was the proper balance of power between national and state governments. Support for the Federalist program was strongest in New England. It was generally endorsed by commercial interests and by those in favor of centralized government under a strong executive. Opposition to the Federalists was strongest in the South and West, especially among agrarian interests (many of whom were particularly outraged by Treasury Secretary Alexander Hamilton's tax on whiskey). Those averse to a strong executive also gravitated to the opposition, which was centered in the Virginia congressional delegation.

Both embryonic parties had their own newspapers, which they used to revile each other.[13] Critics vilified the Federalists as monarchists and British sympathizers. The Democratic–Republicans were maligned as radicals and French sympathizers. The Jeffersonians were the dominant party, winning the presidency seven consecutive times from 1800 to 1824, but the system splintered when a "corrupt bargain" denied General Andrew Jackson the presidency in 1824—after he had won both the popular *and* the electoral vote.

THE SECOND PARTY SYSTEM (JACKSONIAN DEMOCRACY) After Jackson's defeat in 1824, he and his allies laid the groundwork for another presidential campaign. They sought to mobilize more potential voters—spreading the Democratic party outward from Washington and downward into the grassroots. They succeeded with a vengeance: Between 1824 and 1828, turnout in the presidential election tripled, sweeping Jackson into office. The Jacksonian Democrats were the world's first mass party; one of their efforts' principal architects, Martin Van Buren, is sometimes called the father of parties.[14]

Many conflicts from the previous alignment persisted in the second party system, especially those over the proper power of the federal government. The Jacksonians vigorously opposed having a national bank and otherwise limited the growth of federal power. As a charismatic military leader, "King Andrew" might have built up the presidency into a much stronger office, but he devoted most of his

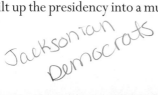

energies to other tasks—and the Democrats who followed Jackson showed little inclination to aggrandize their post. The opposition Whig party, led by Kentuckian Henry Clay, endorsed programs of internal improvement led by the national government. Forces also clashed over rates of taxation on imported goods.

Until it splintered in the 1850s, the Jacksonian Democracy lost only two presidential elections to the Whigs—in 1840 to William Henry Harrison and in 1848 to Zachary Taylor, both of whom were war heroes. The Democrats also controlled Congress through much of this period. But the party system could not contain sectional differences. Dissatisfied citizens began challenging the system under third-party banners. The Free Soilers opposed the expansion of slavery into the territories.* Then, from 1854 to 1856, a new Republican party rose to replace the Whigs. The badly split Democrats nominated both northern and southern candidates for president in 1860. Together with the Constitutional Union candidate, they received nearly 60 percent of the popular vote. But the Electoral College and the winner-take-all election system translated Abraham Lincoln's 40 percent of the vote into a victory—which ultimately sparked the Civil War.

THE THIRD PARTY SYSTEM (CIVIL WAR AND RECONSTRUCTION)

War seldom enhances democracy, but the Civil War realignment produced the most competitive electoral era in American history.[15] The Democrats maintained a base in the House of Representatives during the Civil War and then took control in 1874, following the South's readmission to the Union. The Republicans maintained control of the Senate, though, because the wartime government had admitted several sparsely populated western states that dependably elected Republican senators.[16]

At the presidential level, the third party system became known as "the period of no decision." From 1876 to 1892, no presidential candidate received as much as 51 percent of the popular vote. In two elections (that of Rutherford Hayes in 1876 and that of Benjamin Harrison in 1888), the Electoral College chose a president who had come in second in the popular vote. The dominant issue at the beginning of the period was Reconstruction, but after 1876 economic issues took center stage. Industrialization, the rise of large business organizations, and a long agricultural depression generated the political issues of this party system.

During this era, party organizations reached their high point. Bitter memories of the Civil War left many people committed to the party of the Union (Republicans) or of the rebels (Democrats), and these citizens voted a straight party line. Indeed, independents often were viewed as traitors. With feelings so strong and politics so competitive, the parties exerted tremendous effort in

---

*Another third party, the Know Nothings, opposed immigration, especially of Catholics.

campaigns.[17] Moreover, there were thousands of immigrants and former slaves to be fed, housed, employed, and marched to the polls. Parties reached such a high level of organization in many cities that they were referred to as **machines.**[18]

The depression of the 1890s plunged much of the country into misery. Agricultural protest, common throughout the period, gave rise to the Populist movement—which seriously challenged the major parties in the South and West. Eventually Populists fused with the Democrats at the national level; they attempted to form a worker–farmer alliance linking the down-trodden.* The new strategy was doomed from the start. Cultural issues sharply divided urban Catholics and rural Protestants, as did questions such as taxation and immigration. Many of the impoverished voters who might have joined the alliance were African Americans, who remembered their debt to the "Party of Lincoln." In 1896, the Democrats nominated William Jennings Bryan for president, a man who encapsulated the economic and social frustrations of rural America.[19] His nomination undermined Democratic support in urban areas. The "period of no decision" was over; Americans had decided.

THE FOURTH PARTY SYSTEM (INDUSTRIAL REPUBLICAN)   The critical election of 1896 inaugurated a period of Republican dominance.[20] The Democrats contracted to their base in the old Confederacy. The Republicans lost the presidency only twice during the fourth party system: in 1912, when Democrat Woodrow Wilson won a three-way race, and again in 1916, when Wilson narrowly held his post on a platform of keeping the United States out of World War I (which he did not do).

Wilson's unique success owed much to a factional split within the GOP. The Republican party included two wings, the old guard of pro-business conservatives and a progressive wing that wanted to reform American institutions. President William Howard Taft, elected in 1908, increasingly allied himself with the old guard, dismaying progressives. They convinced former Republican President Theodore Roosevelt to take up their banner. He hammered Taft in the 1912 primaries, but an alliance of professional party operatives and corrupt southern delegations gave Taft the nomination anyway.† Roosevelt's supporters therefore formed a new Progressive (or Bull Moose) party, and he ran in the general election. Not only did this split give Democrat Woodrow Wilson the White House, but Roosevelt also edged out Taft, so it marked the first and only time a

---

*At the local level, Populists sometimes fused with Republicans. The Fusion ticket in Louisiana linked Populists with South Louisiana Republicans, both blacks and sugar cane planters.

†By this time, African Americans could not vote in much of the South, and few whites were Republicans. GOP organizations in the region tended to be little more than patronage machines. The Republican leadership bought their loyalty with jobs and other resources.

third-party candidate has attracted more votes than a major-party presidential nominee.

This temporary rift within Republican ranks did not end the fourth party system, however. Ohio Senator Warren Harding, the Republican candidate in 1920, promised to quiet the turmoil of the World War I years. "America's present need is not heroics, but healing; not nostrums, but normalcy," he explained.[21] This message played well, not only to men but also to the millions of women who would be participating in their first presidential election. Harding won by an unprecedented landslide, and two more successful Republican presidential candidates followed him.

Two forces eventually undermined their dominance. One worked slowly. Rural and small-town Protestants increasingly allied with the Republican party, while urban populations increasingly preferred Democrats—a pattern that crystalized when Al Smith of New York won the Democratic presidential nomination in 1928, the first time a major party had run a Catholic for president.[22] Population trends sided with the urban vote. The disastrous stock market crash of 1929 was more sudden, and more damaging to the incumbent party. The Great Depression of the 1930s resulted in unemployment levels over 20 percent. A third of the nation's banks failed; a quarter of families lost their savings.[23] Voters no longer considered Republicans the party of prosperity. The Republican party lost the House in 1930, and the Democratic party established a new party system starting in 1932.

THE FIFTH PARTY SYSTEM (NEW DEAL)   The fifth party system was a class-based alignment like those found in modern European democracies. In 1936, after Franklin D. Roosevelt's first term, the Democrats became the party of the "common people" (blue-collar workers, farmers, and minorities), whereas the Republicans became, more than ever, the party of established interests. The former accounted for a lot more voters than the latter, leading to a period of Democratic dominance. Only Republican war hero Dwight D. Eisenhower was able to crack the Democratic monopoly on the White House, and only from 1952 to 1954 did the Republicans control Congress as well as the presidency.

The South formed a major component of FDR's coalition early on, but Democratic politicians struggled to reconcile the region's expectations with those of liberals and African Americans in northern cities. Gradually, party leaders began weaning themselves off the southern white vote. FDR won repeal of the 104-year-old **two-thirds rule,** which required that the Democratic nominee receive a two-thirds majority of delegates to the national convention. With that rule's elimination in 1936, southerners no longer could veto unacceptable presidential candidates—which meant that they could not could not resist the growing national pressure for racial change. In 1948 the Deep South bolted the party rather than vote for President Truman, who had begun taking steps toward racial equality. Then southerners—along with other voters upset with the pace of social change—left in droves when President Lyndon B. Johnson pushed an aggressive civil rights agenda through Congress in the mid-1960s.

THE SIXTH PARTY SYSTEM (DIVIDED GOVERNMENT) By 1968 the Democratic party was at war with itself, and Republican Richard Nixon won the presidency. For much of the past generation, scholars have debated whether Nixon's victory inaugurated a sixth party system. What puzzles them is that, although the Democrats lost all but one presidential election in two

Preaching to the converted

Vice President Al Gore made a strong effort to turn out African American voters late in the 2000 presidential campaign, including this appearance at a black church in Tennessee. His attempt continued a long party tradition of courting minority voters. Democrats locked up the black vote starting in the 1960s through aggressive appeals, including an ambitious social welfare agenda as well as support for race-conscious policies, such as affirmative action. But their strong civil rights stand may have ended the New Deal party system by driving away white southerners and the urban working class.

decades, they never lost control of the House during that time and held the Senate through most of it. And then, just when the White House changed hands, Republicans seized control of Congress. Voters display a high rate of **ticket splitting,** supporting the presidential and congressional candidates of different parties in the same election. This evidence leads some scholars to argue that American parties may have grown too weak to realign into a new party system.[24]

In retrospect, though, most scholars agree that the mid-1960s were another critical transition period. The third-party presidential campaigns of Alabama Governor George Wallace revealed just how much resentment racial activism had caused—even in the North. The Vietnam conflict also led to a popular reaction against the Democratic leadership. And as the first wave of baby boomers entered college, young people challenged conventional norms about drug use and sexual behavior. These social issues alarmed their more traditional elders, a struggle that took on political dimensions as both New Left and Religious Right groups gained influence. The GOP alliance with Middle America helped them dominate presidential elections for a generation.

EVALUATING AMERICAN POLITICAL PARTIES

American parties may have changed their issue alignments and even their names over time, but the two-party system has existed almost from the country's inception. This durability has done little to endear political parties to the American public. Americans do not regard parties as a fundamental institution of democratic governance. Mostly they are indifferent, but many Americans think government would be better off if no parties existed at all.[25] Political scientists typically challenge that conventional wisdom. E. E. Schattschneider devoted much of his life to that task, arguing that "modern democracy is unthinkable save in terms of the parties."[26] Professional organizations in political science at times have called openly for stronger parties.[27] What critical functions do strong parties carry out?

THE PLUS SIDE OF STRONG PARTIES   Without political parties to *organize political life,* it is likely that democracy would be too disorganized to operate except at the local level.[28] Parties coordinate the actions of hundreds, indeed thousands, of public officials. At each level of government, executives count on the support of their fellow partisans in the legislature, and legislators trust the information they get from their fellow partisans in the executive branch. Parties also coordinate activities across levels of government—as when, in 1995, Democratic governors convinced some Democratic members of Congress that they should support far-reaching welfare reform proposals. Parties need to maintain unity, or their "brand names" will not mean anything.

Party members correctly believe that they will be judged according to their collective performance.[29] This belief gives them an incentive to *fashion a party record worth defending* at the polls. Parties identify social problems, publicize them, and advance possible solutions. The competitive struggle for power motivates them to educate the public and fashion a policy agenda. Like predators, party leaders seek to identify vulnerable members of the other side and recruit strong candidates to challenge them.[30] Where parties are weak, as they were in the American South during the first half of the twentieth century, politics degenerates, taking on a more personal quality as factions contend for private benefits.[31]

Not all problems can be solved by clever policy proposals. Occasionally interests conflict, and some sort of compromise becomes necessary. And even if satis-

Hobgoblin of little minds

Political party leaders usually embrace distinct principles that set them apart from leaders of the other party but link them to other leaders in their own party. Democrats, for example, vocally oppose racial profiling; Republicans, for their part, oppose using government to perform social functions that businesses in the private sector can handle. But leaders need to promote the electoral interests of their party members, so they cannot afford to worry about consistency when the public demands action, as it did in the wake of 9/11.

fying every specific interest were possible, the end result might detract from the general interest. For example, granting every individual's spending demand can lead to deficits, inflation, high interest rates, and other national costs. Parties help *synthesize societal demands into public policy.* Because parties compete nationwide, they offer a mix of benefits and burdens to everyone. Yet they must do so in a way that appears beneficial to the general interest, or they suffer at the polls—as the Democrats did in 1984 or the Republicans in 1996.

Imagine that no parties helped *winnow the field of candidates.* Rather than choosing between two candidates for most offices, voters would be faced with many more. The candidates would lack party labels, so voters would have to learn about each set of candidates to determine their preferences. And if elections usually had more than two serious candidates, officials would frequently enter office with a minority of the vote. Politics thus would become much more complicated than it is now.

THE MINUS SIDE OF STRONG PARTIES   Americans hold political parties in relatively low esteem, despite the valuable functions they can perform, for two reasons. First, parties do not always provide the valuable services of which they are capable. Politicians do not form parties to promote the public good. They want to win elections and gain power; organizing politics happens to be a good way to do that.[32] Public officials devote real effort to maintaining their parties, but only because parties help them govern. A second and more important reason why Americans are suspicious of political parties is that party influence is a double-edged sword. Parties strong enough to organize politics are also strong enough to abuse their power. Each of the positive functions that parties can perform may be corrupted.

A strong party that controls its members can become the equivalent of an elected dictatorship, a charge the Progressives leveled at urban machines. They can force voters to select between two stark choices, even on issues for which more than two options (should) exist. They may recruit celebrities, or party hacks good at winning elections, rather than qualified people good at administering government.

Parties may choose to suppress issues rather than address them. For example, the parties avoided the slavery issue during the first half of the nineteenth century, and the Democrats suppressed issues of racial equality in the first half of the twentieth. Third-party candidate Ross Perot's support in the 1992 presidential election came disproportionately from voters concerned about the deficit who believed that neither the Republicans nor the Democrats would do much about it.[33]

The parties may attempt to confuse responsibility so that they can escape any blame for bad times and win undeserved credit for good ones. Worse, rather than helping to solve a public problem, opposition parties may concentrate on blocking the governing party's attempts to do so. The temptation to torpedo the other party's initiatives is especially strong when **divided government** exists—when one party holds the presidency but does not control Congress—because then voters will be unsure who is responsible for lingering social problems.[34]

THE BALANCE SHEET   On balance, then, are parties good or bad? Scholars value parties because they answer important political needs. Academics generally do not evaluate parties in isolation; their focus on institutional performance forces them to question the merits of a party-driven system compared to the available alternatives. Reformers, on the other hand, can emphasize the failings of political parties: that they often do not make useful contributions and, indeed, often abuse their power. Reformers can advocate reforms without specifying what alternative institution will evolve to take on the responsibilities once shouldered by parties. Regardless of which side is right, it is clear which side has won: The reformist impulse successfully spawned legal changes that have weakened the political parties over time.

"If we only had a spare . . ."

Republicans controlled every branch of the national government when George W. Bush took office, but they did not have any votes to spare in the U.S. Senate, which was evenly divided between the parties. Vermont Senator James Jeffords left the GOP in 2001, giving control of the chamber to the Democrats—an alteration that stalled Bush's main policy agenda until after the 2002 elections (see Chapter 9).

WHY ARE AMERICAN PARTIES SO WEAK?

Parties have never been as strong in the United States as they are in other industrialized countries. In most of the world, major parties are fairly unified organizations, more like third parties in the United States. People join parties the same way they join clubs: They pay dues, receive official membership cards, and have a right to participate in various party-sponsored activities (such as nominating candidates). Americans who travel abroad often are surprised to find that parties elsewhere have buildings, full-time staffs, and even newspapers and television stations. Party members in government are much more united than they are in the United States, and party candidates run much more coordinated campaigns than those seen in the candidate-centered politics of the United States.

Historically, the United States did not have true national party organizations. Rather, the state parties briefly joined together every four years to elect a president. Similarly, party members in government have not been terribly cohesive. Both parties (but especially the Democrats) have suffered from regional splits, and both parties have incorporated conflicting interests—agricultural versus commercial, and so forth.[35] Because parties lack unified memberships, modern American commentators often discuss parties primarily in terms of adherents to the parties in the electorate, ordinary citizens who identify themselves as Democrats or Republicans.

For most of the twentieth century it appeared that political parties in the United States—whatever concept of party one used—were in decline. Reforms wounded state and local organizations first; then changes after World War II undercut the national associations. Party cohesion and presidential support in Congress declined.[36] The number of adherents to the two parties began dropping in the mid-1960s as well, to be replaced by self-professed "independents." But by the mid-1980s, the first two of these trends reversed: Party organizations became more active again, and parties were becoming more important in government.

PARTY ORGANIZATIONS UNDER FIRE   Party organizations were at their strongest near the end of the nineteenth century. But a progressive reform movement arose, in the 1890s, in the wake of rapid industrialization and urbanization. Progressives sought to enhance fairness in the political system, boost the economy, and improve the standards of everyday living. Although Progressives accepted popular democracy in theory, they were outraged by some democratic practices. Progressives thus became active in government reform, notably the destruction of political machines in favor of a more intellectualized democracy. They combined elitist reforms, such as literacy tests to establish voting eligibility, with measures of direct democracy, such as primaries and citizen initiatives. As with most progressive reforms, this transformation originated on the local level and only gradually spread. But parties went into decline at all levels of government because of the reforms the Progressives promoted.

The two principal resources that parties depend on are control of **patronage**—the dispensation of government jobs and contracts—and control of nominations for office. Progressive reforms limited both of these. Patronage was gradually eliminated by regular expansions of civil service protection (see Chapter 11). After World War II, unionization of the public sector also gave government workers a layer of protection from partisan politics.[*] Today, the president controls fewer than 4000 appointments.[37] At the height of the spoils system—and with a much smaller federal government—presidents controlled well over 100,000.[38] Similarly, governors and big-city mayors who once controlled tens of thousands of jobs control only a few thousand today. Meanwhile, party control

---

[*]The largest union in the AFL-CIO today is the American Federation of State, County and Municipal Employees.

over nominations was greatly weakened by the spread of the direct primary, an important Progressive reform (see Chapter 7).

Deprived of their principal resources, modern American parties had few sticks and carrots with which to work. Electoral defeat did not mean that people would lose their jobs, so they were less inclined to support parties unquestioningly. Similarly, outsiders could challenge parties for their nominations—and if they won, the parties had no choice but to live with the result. Controlling neither the livelihoods of ordinary voters nor the electoral fates of public officials, party organizations atrophied.

However, deliberate political reforms are not entirely to blame for the weakening of American parties. Other factors also contributed to their decline. For one thing, the communications revolution lessened the need for traditional parties. Candidates could raise funds through direct-mail appeals and then reach voters directly with ads. Elections have become less labor-intensive; party workers are no longer critical to reelection.[39] And in the United States, political parties do not control communications outlets the way they do in some European countries.

The post–World War II increase in mobility—social, economic, and residential—also undercut parties. Better-educated voters have less need of parties to make sense of politics. And as the suburbs grew, the traditional, urban-based parties came to represent an ever-smaller proportion of the population—while the new, decentralized suburbs went largely unorganized.

Another development that may have weakened parties was the so-called reapportionment revolution set off by the Supreme Court's one-person–one-vote decisions in the 1960s.[40] Prior to these decisions, political jurisdictions tended to coincide with natural communities. In the lower houses of many state legislatures, for example, every county had a seat. Thus a natural association existed between legislators and their local parties. In the aftermath of the reapportionment revolution, however, legislative districts often cut across cities, counties, and other jurisdictions in the pursuit of numerical equality, racial balance, and other considerations. Today, a legislator's district may stretch across numerous counties, and a city or town may be divided into multiple districts. Such fragmentation broke apart the relationship between legislators and local parties.

THE REVIVAL OF PARTY ORGANIZATIONS?   The reforms did not kill political parties. Rather, it was clear by the 1980s that creative politicians had found new uses for the old organizations. Leading this effort were Republicans such as William Brock, chairman of the Republican National Committee (RNC) from 1976 to 1982. Brock and the Republicans first saw the possibilities of adapting parties to the modern age. They used direct-mail technology to raise large sums of money. They hired full-time political operatives who were campaign experts. They retained lawyers who knew how to exploit loopholes in the campaign-finance laws, as well as specialists skilled in computers and other technologies. They made these consultants and services available at low cost to Republican candidates nationwide. Congressional campaign committees began actively recruiting candidates for office, a level of national intervention that would have been unthinkable half a century earlier. For their part, the Democrats imitated the Republicans, although they did so later and less successfully until the Clinton presidency.

National organizations are no longer the weakest level of party organization, as they were through most of their 150-year history. Today, the national committees are active and well financed, and they have been joined by senatorial and congressional campaign committees. Together these national committees have helped rejuvenate lower-level party organizations, which had started rebuilding as early as the 1960s.[41] Most state parties, meanwhile, now have permanent headquarters and employ full-time staff. Many conduct statewide polls. They provide campaign aid and recruit candidates more actively than they did a few decades ago. The parties have built up some strength again, although not the same powers they once exercised.[42]

PARTIES VERSUS INTEREST GROUPS

Parties once served important functions. They provided the channel of communication between voters and their government. They brought like-minded citizens together into institutions that could work for their interests and their policy preferences. They gave candidates electoral resources and delivered votes. When reforms undermined the strength of parties, the basic political needs that caused strong parties to rise up in the first place remained. Voters still needed a way to communicate with government. Citizens still sought to unite in organizations that would promote their interests and policy preferences. Candidates still needed to find resources so that they could win elections. To fill the political void, therefore, citizens naturally created private associations to carry out the tasks for them.

Special-interest groups rose up from the ashes of the political parties. These groups differ from parties in that they seldom seek mass membership and they do not try to win political offices themselves. Rather, they tend to collect people according to relatively narrow political interests: by occupations, by industries, by leisure activities, by preferences on a single public-policy issue. Interest groups proliferated in the Progressive era, when reformers systematically attacked the parties. They surged again in the 1960s and 1970s, when American parties reached a nadir, before their recent recovery. For this reason, some political theorists suggest that there is a necessary trade-off between parties and interest groups.[43] If parties do not fill the political vacuum, interest groups must. Logically, then, the real alternative to party domination of the electoral process is not some ideal form of popular control, but a different system of skewed influence. As the next section shows, the contemporary political system that replaced party-dominated government is not clearly better or worse than the one it replaced.

INTEREST GROUPS: A BIASED CHORUS?

Many Americans participate in politics indirectly by joining or supporting private associations—organizations that are made up of people with common interests and that participate in politics on behalf of their members. Although only half the adult population votes in presidential elections, more than three-quarters of Americans belong to at least one **interest group.** On average they belong to two, and they make financial contributions to four.[44] Americans are joiners, more so than citizens in other nations.

Of course, not all the groups with which people are associated are political groups. Many are social clubs, charities, service organizations, church groups, and so forth. But there are literally thousands of groups that do engage in politics, and even seemingly nonpolitical groups often engage in political activity. For example, parent–teacher organizations often are active in school politics; neighborhood associations lobby about traffic, crime, and zoning policies; and even hobby or recreation groups mobilize when they perceive threats to their interests—witness the National Rifle Association!

DEVELOPMENT OF THE INTEREST-GROUP SYSTEM

Americans have a long-standing reputation for forming groups. In his classic book *Democracy in America,* Alexis de Tocqueville, the celebrated nineteenth-century French visitor to the United States, noted this tendency. "Americans are forever forming associations," he wrote. "At the head of any new undertaking, where in France you would find the government or in England some territorial magnate, in the United States you are sure to find an association."[45]

However natural and long-standing the American propensity to form associations, there are more political groups today than ever before. Nor has group formation in the United States been a steady process. Rather, it has occurred in several waves. The greatest wave of group formation in American history occurred in the 1960s and 1970s. In fact, one study found that 40 percent of the associations with Washington offices were formed after 1960.[46]

Before the Civil War, few national organizations existed. Life revolved around "island communities" unconnected by social or economic links.[47] Regions produced much of what they consumed themselves. As the railroads connected the country after the Civil War, though, a national economy developed—and national associations, such as labor unions, were not far behind.

Another major wave of group organization occurred during the Progressive era, roughly 1890 to 1917. Many of today's most broad-based associations date from that era; the Chamber of Commerce, the National Association of Manufacturers, and the American Farm Bureau Federation are examples. These associations often unite economic interests, but associations founded during the Progressive era had other goals as well. For example, the National Association for the Advancement of Colored People (NAACP) represented an effort to improve the fortunes of black Americans.

The wave of group creation from 1960 to 1980 is by far the largest and the most diverse. Thousands of additional economic groups formed, but they tended to be narrower than earlier ones; the American Soybean Association and the Rocky Mountain Llama and Alpaca Association are two examples. Similarly, in commerce and manufacturing, numerous specialized groups joined the older, more broad-based ones. "Government interest groups" formed to represent public-sector workers. All kinds of specialized occupational associations formed as well, such as the National Association of Student Financial Aid Administrators. One researcher estimated that almost 80 percent of the interest groups active in the 1980s represented professional or occupational constituencies.[48]

The other 20 percent consisted of shared-interest groups, many of which have formed in recent decades. Some are actively political, working for particular points of view. Liberal groups, such as the National Organization for Women (a feminist group) and People for the American Way (a civil liberties group), are deeply involved in politics, as are such conservative groups as the Christian Coalition (which promotes traditional morality) and Operation Rescue (an anti-abortion group). Many "citizens" groups, such as Common Cause (a political reform group), Greenpeace (an environmental group), and the National Taxpayers' Union (an antitax group) are less than a generation old. Such groups often have a narrow focus, in which case they are called "single-issue groups."

Other groups are not primarily political but have a political side. For example, the American Association of Retired Persons (AARP), established in 1958, is the largest voluntary association ever with more than 33 million members—and still growing! AARP is a major player whenever Social Security or Medicare is on the political agenda. Under the right circumstances, almost any group may become involved in politics. A sports association for snowmobilers and mountain bikers may seem as apolitical as a group can get, but when government threatens to restrict their use of public lands, then such organizations gear up for a political battle.

Not all active interest groups have elaborate formal organizations with membership dues, journals, meetings, conventions, and so forth. Some are little more than addresses for teams of lawyers to whom sympathizers send contributions. One study found that of 83 public interest groups examined, 30 had no membership at all.[49] Some large corporations maintain their own Washington offices, as do hundreds of state and local governments and even universities.*

The explosion of groups is partly reactive; the expansion of government activity has given people more reasons to form groups. Business groups, for instance, may form in reaction to governmental regulations or because they see opportunities to procure government subsidies. Group formation also responds to opportunities; groups expand whenever a change in communications or transportation technology enables them to do so. Computer databases, for example, permit the generation of all kinds of specialized mailing lists. People with common interests can communicate easily and cheaply via the Internet. And once a group forms on one side of an issue, its opponents usually need to get organized or lose the fight.

FORMING AND MAINTAINING INTEREST GROUPS

That so many Americans belong to so many associations often leads people to overlook the difficulties that groups face.[50] Women's groups contain only a small fraction of the female population. Few blacks join the NAACP. Most gun owners do not belong to the NRA. As these examples suggest, millions of people do not join or support associations whose interests they share.

Supporting a group requires the investment of personal *resources*. Contributing money or paying dues is the most obvious cost, but the time required for group activities can be significant too. One commits resources when the *incentive* to do so—the expected benefit—justifies the investment. Incentives take many forms, though, and different groups rely on different incentives. Political scientist James Q. Wilson divides incentives into three categories.[51] The first he calls *solidary*. Some people join a group for social reasons. They simply wish to associate with the particular kinds of people who join the group, so membership is an end in itself. Most of these groups are nonpolitical, though, such as Greek organizations on a college campus. Political groups rarely use solidary incentives. It is unlikely that people join the National Taxpayers Union to enjoy the company of other taxpayers!

A second category of incentives is *material*. Some people join a group because membership confers tangible benefits. IBM does not belong to various trade associations because its executives like to socialize with other computer executives.

---

*The term *interest group* may not suggest a college or university. But American universities, especially private institutions, are quite active in lobbying government.

FIGURE 8.1

Union membership has declined significantly since mid-century

Why do American workers find unions less attractive than they once did?

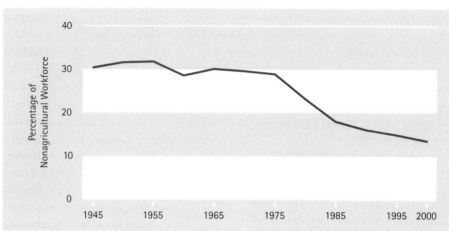

SOURCES: George Kurian, *Datapedia of the United States: 1790–2000* (Lantham, MD: Bernham Press, 1994), p. 80; *Almanac of the 50 States,* 1997 ed. (Palo Alto, CA: Information Publications, 1997).

They have plenty of other opportunities to do that. IBM belongs because the trade associations are seen as a way to protect and advance corporate interests. Material incentives also play a role in some political groups. Workers may join a politically active union because it gives exclusive access to some jobs. Interest groups oriented toward material benefits have declined in influence, as has happened with unions (see Figure 8.1).

Finally, some people join groups for *purposive* reasons. They are committed to the group's purpose, such as saving whales or ending abortion. But interest groups that work only to improve government policy often experience the greatest difficulty attracting active members. The **free-rider problem** hinders their efforts.

THE FREE-RIDER PROBLEM   Groups, no matter how popular their cause, find themselves struggling to attract members and contributions. They appeal for assistance in changing public policy, but most people who fully support an organization's goals nevertheless fail to help. The group's achievements may fall far short of what they could accomplish if everyone who believed in the group's purpose lent a hand. This unsupportive behavior can frustrate political activists. Why in the world, they ask, would people do nothing to promote a goal in which they really believe? Why would they accept results far less satisfying than what they could obtain, when all they would have to do is work together—that is, to engage in collective action? Something must be wrong with people. Their "apathy" seems so irrational.

What is rational for a group of like-minded people, though, is not the same as what is rational for an individual. If you donate $20 to Greenpeace, does your contribution guarantee the survival of some particular baby seal? If you donate several hours of your time to march for the end of hunger, does your contribution measurably reduce the amount of malnutrition in the world? Although most well-meaning people are reluctant to admit it, in each case the truthful answer is no. If you do not contribute, just as many baby seals will live or die, and world hunger will be no different. So if your personal sacrifice makes no measurable difference, why contribute?

Furthermore, most policy changes and social improvements are **public goods** rather than private ones. You cannot walk into a store, buy them, and consume them yourself—as you can pizzas or stereos. Individuals receive the benefit whether they contribute or not. When world hunger declines or more seals swim in the ocean, everyone lives in a better world, not just those who worked to make it happen. So if groups cannot deny you the fruits of their labor, why contribute?

The overwhelming temptation is for an individual to "free-ride" on the efforts of others. When a group works to change policies, people enjoy roughly the same level of benefits whether or not they contribute. Nor is it easy to punish, in other ways, those who refuse to help. Even if someone genuinely wants the world to change, therefore, inactivity is not irrational; political activism is. This logic applies to just about everyone who might participate in collective action, so it creates a free-rider problem for the group as a whole.[52]

Most interest groups suffer the free-rider problem in one form or another. But it is less likely to plague smaller groups and those promoting fairly tangible goals. If a few neighbors pool their efforts to clean up a nearby vacant lot, it is easy to identify the slackers and pressure them. It would be unthinkable, however, for a large city to rely on volunteers to maintain city parks. At the same time, cleaning up a vacant lot is more satisfying than cleaning the atmosphere. Feeding the poor in a soup kitchen is more satisfying than reducing world hunger. This is why bumper stickers often urge socially concerned individuals to "Think globally, act locally."

Material incentives can be public goods as well. If General Motors lobbies successfully for a tariff or quota on Japanese cars, Ford still enjoys the benefits (lower competition and higher prices). If members of the Corn Growers' Association pool their efforts to get a higher corn subsidy, even growers who are not members may reap the benefits. The free-rider problem therefore even affects groups seeking material improvements. Only those groups based on social incentives escape it. Hanging out with other members is the main benefit in this case, so most people outside the group customarily receive nothing.

The most important implication of the free-rider problem for democratic politics is that "special" interests will be able to overcome it more easily than "public" interests will. Other things being equal, small groups organized for narrow purposes have an organizational advantage over large groups organized for broad purposes. For example, a small number of agribusinesses seeking millions of dollars in farm aid will find it easier to organize an association than the millions of consumers whose grocery bills each might go up an extra dollar a month as a result.

OVERCOMING THE FREE-RIDER PROBLEM   The tactics that interest groups use to compel cooperation are not always pretty. Labor unions may rely on threats—and sometimes even outright violence—to enforce a decision among workers to strike, for example. Milder forms of coercion are widespread. For example, professional and occupational associations lobby governmental jurisdictions to hire, approve, or certify only their members, thus making membership a condition of working or practicing in that jurisdiction. Such requirements are ways of coercing potential free riders into joining the associations that represent their trades and professions.

Many groups develop **selective benefits** available only to their members. They may publish journals containing useful information. They may provide consulting services, giving members a place to call when they need help. The American Association of Retired Persons (AARP) offers the most notable example of this strategy for overcoming the free-rider problem. For a mere $12.50 per year, members gain access to the world's largest mail-order pharmacy (where volume buying keeps prices low); low-cost auto, health, and life insurance; discounts on hotels, air fares, and car rentals; and numerous other benefits. Even a senior citizen who disagrees with the AARP's political positions finds it hard to forgo membership!

Many groups owe their existence to **political entrepreneurs,** activists who take the lead in promoting collective goals.[53] Motives vary for why someone would allow others to free-ride on them. Sometimes being a leader offers personal advantages: power, excitement, money, sex appeal. Sometimes individuals do not experience the sense of powerlessness that encourages free-riding. Your $20 contribution to improve health care in the Third World may have no measurable impact, but if Microsoft founder Bill Gates contributes $6 million, he certainly will observe the effects of his sacrifice. Sometimes individuals, institutions, or corporations have such a large stake in the group goal that they are willing to bear more than their share of the effort. They let others free-ride on them to give the appearance of broad-based support. For such large actors, political activity is simply a good business decision.

One organizer that is often overlooked is the government itself. As the role of government expanded in the 1960s and 1970s, activists needed new ways to implement programs within a decentralized federal system. One strategy was to stimulate and subsidize organizations. Once formed, local groups could help develop standards and regulations, publicize them, and carry them out. To those trying to build a stronger welfare state, these groups were politically useful as well because, once established, they would be able to fight against shrinking government. Not surprisingly, associations that receive federal funds are more than twice as likely to support expanded government activity—and, by implication, elected officials who expand it—as groups that do not.[54] The government subsidized political groups who would then help it grow bigger.

Despite the prevalence of free-rider problems, people do not always evaluate their political activities from a self-interested standpoint. Sometimes individuals simply get caught up in a **social movement** and jump on the bandwagon. These broad-based demands for social change have a long history in American politics. The abolitionist movement is one of the best known. Dedicated to ending slavery, this movement forced the issue onto the national agenda. It played a role in the political upheaval of the 1850s and, ultimately, in the outbreak of the Civil War. The civil rights movement is another, more modern example of a social movement. Few abolitionists or civil rights marchers ever received benefits equivalent to the costs they paid.

Social movements build on emotional or moral fervor. Many activists dedicate themselves to what they see as a higher cause and receive satisfaction from being part of that effort. When individuals adopt a moral perspective, they may ignore the practical considerations that normally would lead them to free-ride. Still, social movements typically mobilize only small proportions of their prospective constituencies. Moreover, emotional and moral fervor are temporary social conditions, so movements have a tendency to lose momentum. For a social movement to exert continued influence, it must find a way to "institutionalize" itself—to spin off formal associations that face the same free-rider pressures as other interest groups.

HOW INTEREST GROUPS INFLUENCE GOVERNMENT

The groups, associations, and institutions that make up the interest-group universe engage in a wide variety of political activities.

LOBBYING Many interest groups attempt to influence government the old-fashioned way: by lobbying public officials. **Lobbying** consists of attempts by group representatives, known as lobbyists, to influence the decisions of public officials. Lobbyists draft bills for friendly legislators to introduce, testify before congressional committees and in agency proceedings, meet with elected officials and present their cases (sometimes at posh resorts where the officials are the guests), and provide public officials with information.

Corporations account for the lion's share of traditional lobbying, spending upwards of $1.5 billion per year.[55] There are federal and state laws that require lobbyists to register, but because of disagreement about what lobbying is and who is a lobbyist, as well as lack of enforcement, those who register are only a fraction of those engaged in lobbying.[56] For example, the *American Lobbyists Directory* lists 65,000 legally registered federal and state lobbyists, but estimates are that in Washington alone, there are upwards of 90,000.[57]

The profession labors under a negative image (we doubt many parents dream that their children will grow up to be lobbyists). Movies, novels, and even the newspapers often portray lobbyists as unsavory characters who operate on the borders of what is ethical or legal—and often step across them. This characterization is an exaggeration. Although there are examples of shady behavior by lobbyists, such transgressions are hardly the norm, and corrupt behavior by interest-group lobbyists is less widespread today than in it was previous eras of American history. Numerous conflict-of-interest laws and regulations, along with an investigative media ever on the lookout for a hint of scandal, make outright corruption in today's politics relatively rare.

For the most part, lobbyists supply public officials with information and arguments to support their political goals. They tend to deal with officials already sympathetic to their positions, providing them ideas and support. Lobbyists have little incentive to distort information or lie. To do so would mislead their allies and undermine their credibility. "One of the perceptions about lobbying is that you go out drinking, and the guy's your buddy so he does you favors," one lobbyist explains. "Those days are long gone. That sort of thing may work on tiny things like a technical amendment to a bill, but on big, important issues personal friendships don't mean a thing."[58] Many political scientists think that lobbyists serve a useful purpose, injecting valuable information into the legislative process.

GRASSROOTS LOBBYING   Interest groups supplement their Washington lobbying with public-outreach activities, trying to persuade the "grassroots." Whereas lobbying consists of attempts to influence government officials *directly,* grassroots lobbying consists of attempts to influence officials *indirectly* through their constituents, the "troops in the field." This sort of lobbying is not new. The Anti-Saloon League, a prohibition group, included more than 500,000 names on its mailing list nearly a century ago—long before dependable long-distance telephone service, let alone computers, the fax, and e-mail![59] But grassroots lobbying is especially effective now that Congress is decentralized (see Chapter 9). Inside-the-beltway strategies worked when only a few leaders required persuasion, but government is generally more open than in the past. It is not so easy for

A gift that brought little peace

The Federal Election Commission fined Democrats $719,000 as a result of fund-raising scandals from the 1996 presidential election, including steep fines for illegally accepting donations from Chinese nationals. Here Vice President Gore raises cash at a Buddhist temple. Should foreign citizens be able to contribute to American politicians?

Washington insiders to make private deals; it is more important than ever to show popular support for their groups' positions. Moreover, the availability of cheap communications technologies makes grassroots lobbying much easier.

ELECTIONEERING AND PACS Personal and grassroots lobbying try to influence public officials on specific matters. Another way to promote a group's goals is to influence who gets elected in the first place.

Political action committees (PACs) are specialized organizations for raising and spending campaign funds. Many are connected to interest groups or associations. They come in as many varieties as the interests they represent.[60] Some, such as the realtors' RPAC and the doctors' AMPAC, represent big economic interests. Others are smaller. Beer wholesalers, for example, have SixPAC. Not all PACs serve economic interests, and politicians sometimes form their own.[61]

There is widespread public dissatisfaction with the role of PACs in campaign finance (see the accompanying Election Connection, "Making Soft Money Harder to Use"). It is therefore ironic that the proliferation of PACs is partly an unintended consequence of previous campaign-finance reforms.[62] They sprang up in the early 1970s, as a direct response to reforms, and have enjoyed explosive growth in the past few decades. From a mere handful in 1970, they proliferated rapidly in the 1980s (see Figure 8.2).

PACs have played an increasingly prominent role in congressional campaign finance. They tend to give instrumentally, which means that they donate to incumbents regardless of party, especially to the members of key committees. When the Democrats were in the majority in Congress, some of their members became highly dependent on business contributions, and critics charged that this dependence affected their legislative judgment.[63] Notably, when Democrats

---

FIGURE 8.2

PACs formed rapidly after the 1974 Federal Election Campaign Act (FECA) reforms

Campaign-finance reform had unintended consequences unwelcome to reformers. Can you think of other reforms that may have backfired?

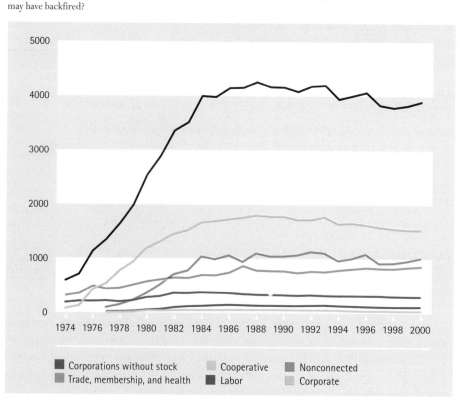

Source: Paul Herrnson, *Congressional Elections, 2nd ed.* (Washington, DC: CQ Press, 1995), p. 106.

TABLE 8.3

Business PAC Contributions Tend to Follow Political Power

	CONTRIBUTIONS TO REPUBLICANS JAN.–FEB. 1993 (DEMOCRATIC MAJORITY)	CONTRIBUTIONS TO REPUBLICANS JAN.–FEB. 1995 (REPUBLICAN MAJORITY)
American Dental Association	27%	90%
American Bankers Association	52	87
American Hospital Association	53	81
Ameritech	35	79
AT&T	36	79
American Institute of CPAs	45	87
Home Builders	45	71
Realtors	75	91
RJR Nabisco	69	81
United Parcel Service	55	78

Source: Jonathan Salant and David Cloud, "To the 1994 Election Victors Go the Fundraising Spoils," *Congressional Quarterly Weekly Report* (April 15, 1995): 1057.

became a minority after the 1994 elections and contributions began to favor their rivals (see Table 8.3), they became much more supportive of campaign-finance regulation that restricted PACs.

Like interest-group corruption in general, the PAC problem in particular may be somewhat exaggerated by the popular media. Most PAC contributions are small and are intended as a way to gain access to public officials. Most research has failed to establish any significant relationship between contributions and votes.[64] Evidence even suggests that politicians extort PACs, pressuring them to buy tickets to fund-raisers and otherwise make contributions as a condition of continued access. For example, a former congressional staffer told one of us the following story:

> *In our office we loved the FEC [Federal Election Commission] reports. We'd comb through them and list all the business groups who had contributed to our opponent. Then we'd call them up and say, "Hey, we noticed that you contributed to our opponent's campaign. The Congressman just wants you to know that there are no hard feelings. In fact, we're holding a fund-raiser in a few weeks; we hope you'll come and tell us your concerns."*

ELECTION CONNECTION

Making Soft Money Harder to Use

Campaign-finance reforms passed in the 1970s sharply limited the amount of money that individuals could contribute to political candidates. People hoping to influence the political system and help their favored candidates sought other means to inject funds into the political system. One option, although slow to develop, was the use of **soft money**—money that the candidates do not receive in hard cash, but that parties and interest groups spend on behalf of their candidates.

Soft money filters into the political system through varying channels. Often it is cash spent by political parties or interest groups to mobilize voters or to broadcast issue ads. Parties might use the money to register friendly citizens to vote or to place calls on election day asking likely supporters to turn out. Groups might run ads advocating a particular issue position and then identifying the candidate who supports or disagrees with that position. Both uses of soft money can make a difference in an election, so soft money regularly floods districts where there are close contests.

The increasing amount of soft money in politics concerns reformers. Until recently, parties could take contributions of any size and spend the money to promote their candidates for office. Such contributions exploded in the 1990s, exceeding the public election funds available to presidential candidates for the first time in 1996. Arizona maverick John McCain made hostility to soft money a centerpiece of his 2000 presidential campaign.

Criticism of soft money culminated with passage of the Bipartisan Campaign Reform Act of 2001. Known as the McCain–Feingold (–Shays–Meehan) bill, this law regulated the use of soft money in federal elections. It limited the amount of money that national parties and their congressional campaign committees could collect from donors to use for issue ads or for other election activities that might help party nominees for federal office. It curtailed the ability of candidates to solicit

PERSUADING THE PUBLIC In recent years a phenomenon called issue advocacy has grown in prominence. Groups conduct advertising campaigns designed to move public opinion in regard to some policy proposal. Estimates are that $150 million was spent on issue advocacy in the 1996 presidential campaign and $260 million during the 1998 congressional campaigns. Preliminary figures suggest that these amounts were greatly exceeded during the 2000 campaigns.[65]

Many groups communicate with citizens even when no specific election or regulation is at issue. Their goal is to build general support for the group and its interests. Thus, in the 1970s, the Mobil Oil Corporation began paying to have columns printed on the editorial page of the *New York Times*. Sometimes these were "advocacy ads" directed at specific government activities or proposed laws, but more often they were simply attempts to convey ideas favorable to the industry.

One technique allowed by modern electronic communications is **direct mail.**[66] Groups compile computerized mailing lists of people who may look

soft money for their parties. It restricted the use of soft-money issue ads in the days before an election.

Will these restrictions cause big changes in campaign finance? The national parties will have to change how they operate—but otherwise, probably not. The law says little about interest groups. Loopholes in the law protect, and could even enhance, the power of state and local parties, which often operate under looser campaign-finance regulations and can use their funds for mobilization efforts even if the party's federal candidates would benefit.[a] And, at least initially, neither the Federal Elections Commission nor the federal courts appear friendly to a rigorous application of the new rules.

Ironically, McCain–Feingold grew out of frustration with interest-group money in American politics, but the main outcome of the legislation may be to strengthen well-funded interest groups at the expense of political parties. The law mostly targeted the parties, leaving political action committees alone

aside from a few (possibly unconstitutional) regulations on the sorts of ads they may run. The stream of soft money once funneled through national parties probably will flow through issue groups instead.[b] If so, McCain–Feingold will be just another stage in the process through which interest groups have supplanted political parties as the main source of communication between voters and their government.

What do you think?

• Practically speaking, is soft money any less dangerous to the electoral system than hard money?

• Is it more important to limit soft money spent by political parties or that spent by interest groups?

[a]Susan Roth, "Campaign Finance Law's Loopholes Set Stage for Legal Wrangling, Political Posturing," *Gannett News Service,* September 29, 2002; Michael Scherer, "Campaign Finance Reform School," *Columbia Journalism Review* (September/October 2002): 54.
[b]Thomas B. Edsall and Juliet Eilperin, "PAC Attack II: Why Some Groups Are Learning to Love Campaign-Finance Reform," *Washington Post* (August 18, 2002): B02.

favorably on their leaders or causes and then send out printed or computer-generated materials soliciting contributions. Often, an attempt to scare or provoke recipients into contributing to the mailing exaggerates the threat the group faces. Some groups depend almost completely on direct-mail fund raising for their budgets. The citizens group Common Cause, for example, prides itself on its dependence on small contributions.[67] Once again, the rise of the Internet has made the direct-mail strategy both easier and cheaper.

Finally, any group likes to have favorable media coverage for its activities and points of view. Thus, groups are always on the lookout for opportunities to get such coverage—opportunities to plant stories, to associate themselves with popular issues and candidates, and to position themselves as opponents of unpopular issues and candidates. In sum, whether they call it public relations or education, communication with a wider audience is a significant concern for many interest groups.

LITIGATION   Many groups impatient for social change either do not wish to wait for the public to get behind them or doubt that they will ever persuade enough people. Instead, they file lawsuits and concentrate on persuading the legal community of th rightness of their causes.[68] Liberal groups tend to be more active in the courts, but conservative groups use litigation strategies as well. Not all legal tactics involve direct lawsuits. Some groups stage demonstrations in front of courthouses to influence judicial decision making. Others file *amicus curiae* (a Latin term meaning "friend of the court") briefs in cases in which they are not otherwise directly involved.

Naturally, legal action is not a strategy oriented toward democratic majorities. The growth of lawsuits may be the most significant limit on popular influence in America's new democracy. On the other hand, lawsuits are a way for individual citizens to challenge entrenched government officials and force them to be responsive. Thus the growth of litigation limits the popular will in some ways but enhances it in others.

DIRECT ACTION   The United States has a long history of citizens engaging in direct action to influence government policy. From the Revolutionary War itself, to abolitionist raids before the Civil War, to urban riots and violent strikes, protests are as American as apple pie.[69] Forms of direct action are often used by social movements, whose members previously have not been organized, who lack access to power, and who lack the resources to use other strategies. The media— TV in particular—find direct action newsworthy and thus communicate the protests to locales far beyond where they occur.

HOW INFLUENTIAL ARE INTEREST GROUPS?

The answer to this question is a matter of enormous disagreement. On the one hand, some critics believe that interest groups dominate American politics. One critic charges that the United States suffers from "demosclerosis," a condition in which interest groups clog the veins and arteries of the body politic.[70] Another claims that Americans have the best Congress "money can buy."[71] Certainly the volume of interest-group activity and their massive expenditures of resources amount to strong circumstantial evidence that groups are influential.

On the other hand, academic research yields less clear conclusions. Interest groups tend to cancel each other out.[72] There are so many groups, and so many *opposing* groups, that the efforts of one association offset the efforts of another. Also, it is likely that particular interests were more influential in the past than most individual interests are today. Changes in American politics have undermined the classic "iron triangles" that once governed areas of policy.

IRON TRIANGLES   Observers of American politics in the 1940s and 1950s noted that a collusion of congressional committees, executive agencies, and inter-

Ghosts of the sixties

Not since the 1960s have Americans seen these kinds of militant protesters, who disrupted the city of Seattle during a meeting of the World Trade Organization. How extensive must protests be before they are no longer simply free speech but instead lawless action instead?

est groups dominated many policy areas.[73] These three actors worked hand in hand to form a subgovernment that was almost entirely responsible for the particular policy in question. A congressional committee provided an agency with budgetary support. The agency produced outcomes favored by the interest group. The interest groups provided campaign support to the members of the congressional committee. Some of these three-way alliances were so tight, and therefore so hard to penetrate, that they received the name **iron triangles.**

The preconditions once necessary to sustain iron triangles are almost gone. Congress has changed, making the committees weaker. Interest groups have proliferated, so most associations have rivals who will not leave their influence unchallenged. In particular, citizens groups representing consumers, environmentalists, and taxpayers can oppose the excesses of special-interest politics. And the media are less likely to ignore examples of special-interest profiteering. In the spring of 1996, for example, an effort to help milk producers raise prices collapsed after CBS anchor Dan Rather called it an "attempted rip-off of the consumer" on his evening news program.[74] Iron triangles melt in the glare of publicity.

ISSUE NETWORKS   Many scholars believe that a new form of policy environment has arisen. The new **issue networks** are bigger, broader, and much looser
connections of interest groups, politicians, bureaucrats, and policy experts.[75]
Given the enormous variety of interest groups today, the proliferation of policy
experts, and the overlap among many policies, issue networks are much more
open than subgovernments and much less stable in their composition. Indeed, calling the collection of people in a policy area a "network" may exaggerate the actual
degree of organization that characterizes interest-group activity in Washington
today.[76]

The safest conclusion is that the influence of interest groups is conditional: It
ranges from weak to strong, depending on the conditions under which groups try
to mold policy. Groups are most capable when they act on low-profile issues,
when they attempt to block action rather than originate it, when no other groups
directly oppose them, and when they have plentiful resources.[77] Otherwise, they
face significant limits. The real world of American democracy is more complicated than many popular commentators suggest.

EVALUATING INTEREST GROUPS

Participation is easier for people who have more resources. Thus it is no surprise
that the affluent contribute more than the poor and that two-worker families with
small children participate less than those whose family situations leave them more
free time.[78] More generally, a large institution or corporation has more resources
to contribute than a solitary citizen. No doubt this is one reason why Americans
hold interest groups in such low regard.[79] They seem to violate the American
principle that everyone should enjoy equal influence on government.

On the other hand, equal influence can never be more than an ideal. Party-
dominated government did not give Americans equal influence either. Political
scientists thus have not held interest groups in as low regard as ordinary citizens
have. In fact, one mid-century school of thought assigned groups a central place
in American politics.[80] Pluralists held that American politics should consist of an
interplay of numerous interests, organized into associations. Under such a system, groups would exercise countervailing power, and public policies would
emerge from compromise. Policies would be moderate and would change
incrementally.

Pluralism is out of fashion today, because it overemphasizes how representative groups are. As critic E. E. Schattschneider once observed, "The flaw in the pluralist heaven is that the heavenly chorus sings with a strong upper-class accent."[81]
The free-rider problem gives an advantage to narrow interests. In particular, economic groups and funding recipients benefit, at the expense of the broader population of consumers and taxpayers. Furthermore, rather than check and balance
each other, interest groups often cooperate—demanding a mixture of higher
prices and tax breaks at the expense of the national economy.[82]

Perhaps most important, when groups clash, the result is a more negative politics than that which occurs when individuals deal with the political system directly. Ordinary citizens have multiple attachments and affiliations. A retired couple, for example, naturally favors higher social security and Medicare expenditures. But they might demand less for themselves, knowing that the result would be higher taxes on their children or lower government expenditures on their grandchildren's schools. Leaders of interest groups for the elderly, by contrast, typically see their job as maximizing group benefits. They have no incentive to be reasonable or to balance competing social goals.

This crowding out of moderate demands by more extreme ones is reinforced by the tendency of group activists and leaders to be more zealous in their views and more committed to group goals than nonmembers or even rank-and-file members (see Table 8.4). It is doubtful that most regular men and women who supported the Equal Rights Amendment (ERA) wanted to force female soldiers into combat. But activists pushing the ERA argued that "combat duty, horrendous as it might seem to all of us, must be assigned to persons on a gender-neutral basis."[83] Most Americans prefer a satisfactory compromise on abortion or the

TABLE 8.4

THE EXTREMISM OF GROUP ACTIVISTS AND LEADERS

One study compared the views of 100 top leaders in environmental groups with the views of scientific experts—in this case, cancer researchers. Both sets of people were asked to rate various cancer risks on a scale of 1 to 10, with 10 being the highest. Relative to expert judgments, environmentalists consistently overstated the risks of cancer from environmental causes.

| | RISK OF CANCER | |
CARCINOGEN	ENVIRONMENTALISTS	SCIENTISTS
Dioxin	8.1	3.7
Asbestos	7.8	6.5
EDB	7.3	4.2
DDT	6.7	3.8
Pollution	6.6	4.7
Dietary fat	6.0	5.4
Food additives	5.3	3.2
Nuclear power	4.6	2.5
Saccharin	3.7	1.6

SOURCE: Stanley Rothman and S. Robert Lichter, "Environmental Cancer: A Political Disease," *Annals of the New York Academy of Sciences* 775 (1996): 234–235.

environment, not the extremes posed by the organizations they may join to promote one side or the other. In the end, the general interests of a moderate population can get lost amid the bitter fighting of intense and extreme special interests.

But what can be done? As the critics look over the experience of democratic governments, they see only one means of controlling group demands that is both democratic and effective. Ironically, it is the institution that George Washington warned the country about—political parties. Americans thus may face a difficult choice: determining which is the lesser evil, particularized groups that give more weight to those with money or general groups that distort individual influence in haphazard and potentially dictatorial ways.

CHAPTER SUMMARY

Although the Constitution makes no mention of them, political parties have been part of American politics from the beginning. Indeed, American political history has exhibited a series of party systems, wherein each party has dependable support among particular social groups so that elections tend to be similar. Such electoral eras end with critical or "realigning elections" that alter the group alignments and usher in new party systems.

The basic reason why parties have played such an important role in American history—as well as in the histories of all modern democracies—is that they perform organizing functions that are essential in large-scale representative democracies. Yet most Americans do not hold parties in especially high regard. Parties struggle for power and, therefore, often act in self-interested ways contrary to the general interest. To prevent such behavior, the nation passed a series of reforms aimed at undercutting the power of political parties.

At present, the United States has a party system that is less stable and more confusing than most of those that have preceded it. Americans have turned to a different source of influence on government. They participate indirectly in politics by joining interest groups. In fact, compared to citizens of other democracies, Americans are more likely to participate indirectly and less likely to participate directly by voting. There has been a major increase in the number of interest groups since 1960. These groups overcome the free-rider problem by offering members selective benefits and relying on dedicated activists who keep the effort going. They are an important mechanism for increasing popular influence, because more than ever they use strategies of electioneering, grassroots lobbying, and public persuasion.

Although interest-group activity is constitutionally protected, many worry about its effects. Special interests seem better represented than general interests. No doubt the United States could choose to reverse course, strengthening the political parties and weakening interest groups. The result would not be a return to some golden era of individualistic politics; the parties did not give Americans equal influence any more than interest-group democracy does. But one thing is clear. Regardless of which mechanism for popular influence becomes dominant in the future, both sorts of groups have become better at representing popular demands than they were in the past. The need for formal institutions to communicate with government may be regrettable, but those organizations have opened up to greater citizen input, along with the rest of the political system, to help form America's new democracy.

KEY TERMS

critical election, p. 245

direct mail, p. 268

divided government, p. 252

free-rider problem, p. 260

interest group, p. 257

iron triangles, p. 271

issue networks, p. 272

lobbying, p. 263

machines, p. 247

patronage, p. 254

pluralism, p. 272

political action committees (PACs), p. 265

political entrepreneurs, p. 262

political parties, p. 240

proportional representation (PR), p. 243

public goods, p. 261

realignment, p. 244

selective benefits, p. 262

single-member, simple-plurality (SMSP) system, p. 242

social movement, p. 263

soft money, p. 268

ticket splitting, p. 249

two-thirds rule, p. 248

SUGGESTED READINGS

Aldrich, John. *Why Parties?* Chicago: University of Chicago Press, 1995. Wide-ranging rational-choice account of how and why politicians form and transform political parties.

Baumgartner, Frank, and Beth Leech. *Basic Interests.* Princeton, NJ: Princeton University Press, 1998. Comprehensive review, critique, and synthesis of literature on interest groups.

Epstein, Leon. *Political Parties in the American Mold.* Madison: University of Wisconsin Press, 1986. Capstone work by a prominent student of American parties. Argues that modern parties have adapted and continue to play an important political role but that their future prospects are limited by ambivalent feelings in the American electorate.

Heinz, John, Edward Laumann, Robert Nelson, and Robert Salisbury. *The Hollow Core: Private Interests in National Policy Making.* Cambridge, MA: Harvard University Press, 1993. A recent, major study of the Washington interest-group scene. Principal focus is on the characteristics and activities of group representatives and lobbyists.

Jewell, Malcolm E., and Sarah M. Morehouse. *Political Parties and Elections in the American States,* 4th ed. Washington, DC: Congressional Quarterly, 2000. Textbook on parties and elections at the subnational level.

Key, V. O., Jr. *Southern Politics.* New York: Vintage, 1949. A classic. The material is dated, but the theoretical arguments about the nature of politics in systems with weak or nonexistent parties remain relevant today.

Lowi, Theodore. *The End of Liberalism.* New York: Norton, 1969. Noted critique of "interest-group liberalism." Argues that a government of laws has been superseded by a process of bargaining between organized groups and public officials.

Mayhew, David. R. *Placing Parties in American Politics.* Princeton, NJ: Princeton University Press, 1986. Comprehensive study of state party organization in the twentieth century.

Moe, Terry. *The Organization of Interests.* Chicago: University of Chicago Press, 1980. Analyzes the internal politics of groups and the strategies used by political entrepreneurs for organizing and maintaining groups.

Sundquist, James. L. *Dynamics of the Party System,* rev. ed. Washington, DC: Brookings, 1983. History of national politics since the 1840s told from a party-systems perspective.

Walker, Jack. *Mobilizing Interest Groups in America.* Ann Arbor: University of Michigan Press, 1991. Describes the state of the Washington interest-group universe. Noted for discussion of outside support for the establishment of groups.

ON THE WEB

The Major Parties
www.democrats.org
www.republicans.org
The Internet home of the two major political parties. These sites offer information on virtually all aspects of the two parties—from their beliefs to their structure.

The National Committees
www.rnc.org
www.dnc.org
Party Web sites that solicit contributions, attack their opponents, and advocate party policies.

The Libertarian Party
www.lp.org
Home of the longest-lasting minor party in the United States and the one that has been most successful at winning ballot access for candidates around the country. The Libertarians advocate classical liberalism, opposing government intervention in both economic and social areas of American life.

National Lobbyist Directory
www.lobbyistdirectory.com/
This site provides a state-by-state directory of lobbyists, containing names, addresses, and phone numbers.

Part Three

THE INSTITUTIONS OF AMERICA'S NEW DEMOCRACY

9

THE CONGRESS

CHAPTER OUTLINE

Making public policy is a messy business. Side deals and legislative bargains—often known by the colorful terms "log rolls" and "horse trades"—are critical to the process. Sometimes the backroom deals complement the policy-making process, helping gather support for important public interest legislation. Occasionally, though, private interests gobble at the trough so greedily that they swallow the public good.

Such was the case with the farm bill passed by Congress and signed by President Bush in 2002, which commentators overwhelmingly criticized as a terrible boondoggle. The *New York Times* called the bill an "orgy of pandering to special interest groups." *USA Today* called it a "congressional atrocity." *The Economist,* a British news magazine, used the words *monstrous* and *lunacy* to describe the legislation. [1]

The problem did not start with this one bill. U.S. farm policy is an unmitigated disaster. Farmers have been subsidized and protected in various ways since the New Deal of the 1930s—when, in an effort to prop up prices, the national government began paying farmers to waste food at a time when city dwellers went hungry. They plowed fields under. They poured good milk into ditches and slaughtered pigs, leaving the meat to rot. Such policies were billed as "emergency measures," of course, but two generations later the entire industry remains addicted to unfair and wasteful handouts.

Crop limits, price supports, guaranteed loans, and other agricultural subsidies hurt consumers twice: once through higher taxes, and once through higher prices on household staples such as meat, produce, and dairy items. Similarly, restrictions on importing agricultural goods keep food prices higher than they otherwise would be and provoke retaliation against American exports by potential trading partners.

Moreover, farm subsidies primarily make a select group of farmers wealthy. A tenth of the nation's total farms receive more than two-thirds of the money. And because subsidies reward the growing of specific crops in each region of the country, they distort incentives, discouraging farmers from planting whatever is best for their lands or for the market. If you grow vegetables in California, the largest crop-producing state in the nation, you are out of luck. But California grows more rice than Japan. How can anyone profit from growing a swamp crop in desert conditions? Simple: California rice growers are among the 9 percent of farmers in the state who receive cash subsidies. They also get huge amounts of subsidized water, another public policy scandal.

Of course, economic critiques of farm policy have stimulated efforts to reform the system. Most of these attempts have been unsuccessful. In 1996, for example, the Republican congressional majority teamed up with a selection of Democrats to adopt a new farm policy, one that reduced federal payments and tried to equalize the distribution of benefits somewhat. Democratic President Bill Clinton quietly accepted the reforms. But they made little difference, because members of Congress quickly undermined them. In each of the next five years,

Congress passed "emergency" appropriations bills, arguing that farmers had suffered a bad year. The assistance was a paltry $5.8 billion in 1998, but by 2000 it had ballooned to more than $30 billion.[2]

Five years after the reforms first passed, farm-state legislators initiated a move to revoke them altogether, to be replaced by a new 10-year, $190 billion commitment. President Bush initially balked, concerned with the rising governmental costs associated with a war on terrorism. But both the Republican House and the Democratic Senate passed versions of the legislation enthusiastically.

In the conference committee, where legislators from both chambers met to reconcile House and Senate versions of the bill, subsidy opponents initially tried to cap the benefit amounts available to individual farmers, but House conferees walked out of the negotiations in response.[3] California senators Barbara Boxer and Dianne Feinstein decided that the agricultural subsidies could not be stopped, so they hastened to secure larger payoffs for their state's rice farmers before the bill went to President Bush. Bush reluctantly signed the bill in May 2002.

How is this possible, you might ask? How can agribusinesses use the force of government to take billions of dollars from American taxpayers, inflating their food prices and undercutting the economy? Well, for one thing, agricultural policy is not a sexy issue for most voters. Legislators are more likely to pander to special interests when voters are not paying attention. Also, the costs of farm subsidies are widely distributed; each person pays a few dollars here and a few dollars there, but no one loses enough to get worked up and start a crusade over it.

The farm population, on the other hand, pays close attention, because financial rewards are immense and benefits narrowly distributed. *Washington Post* reporter Dan Morgan provides one example: Westerfield Ranch, a farm three miles from President Bush's land in Crawford, Texas. That farm alone collected almost $1 million over five years, a third of all payments released to the Crawford area.[4] Beneficiaries of such a generous and focused program are going to feel intensely about it.

Humorist Dave Barry asks, "Wait a minute! Isn't this kind of like, I don't know . . . welfare?" But Barry decides the two policies are not quite the same. "Welfare is when the government gives money to people who produce nothing," he writes. "Whereas the farm-money recipients produce something that is critical to our nation: votes."[5] The Farm Security Act of 2002 was merely one act in the drama called the permanent campaign. Neither political party can count on the votes from agricultural areas, so legislators cannot afford to neglect their demands. Farm-state Democratic senators up for reelection in 2002 included nervous veterans like Max Baucus (Montana), Tom Harkin (Iowa), and Paul Wellstone (Minnesota), as well as vulnerable freshmen like Jean Carnahan (Missouri), Tim Johnson (South Dakota), and Max Cleland (Georgia).* All enthusiastically supported the bill, as did House colleagues in a similar situation.

---

*The Democrats ultimately lost half of these seats in 2002.

The Jolly Green Giant

A montrous payoff?

Congress passed an expensive farm assistance bill shortly before the 2002 congressional elections, helping some members keep their legislative seats. It was the kind of "monstrous" boondoggle that disgusts regular Americans with their legislative branch but immensely pleases those who benefit from the program.

Still, a majority of incumbents held safe seats in both chambers of Congress, and many members represent states or districts that receive almost no agricultural money at all. They did not need to endorse wasteful farm payments to save their own skins. What led Congress to pass the bill and President Bush to sign it was the struggle for control of Congress: Republicans controlled the House by only five seats, and Democrats controlled the Senate by a single vote. Neither party could afford to neglect rural districts if they wanted to remain on top. As one Bush aide commented after the president signed the bill, a veto would have been "political suicide in the November election."[6] Farm policy in 2002 not only affected farmers and their congressional representatives; it also affected the agendas of two major political parties who receive relatively few of their votes from those who collected the cash.

THE FARM BILL STORY REVEALS SEVERAL CHARACTERISTICS of the national legislature that are worth understanding. On the one hand, individual members are quick to "do something" when obvious national problems arise. On the other hand, they usually perceive social needs in terms of their own constituencies. Members generally use their influence to seek particular benefits for constituents;

they have little incentive to focus on the general interest or to cooperate when others try to reform a policy from which their supporters benefit. Sometimes the particular interests they serve may not even be their own, because they have to worry about the party's image with swing voter groups. This seemingly perverse behavior explains why so many Americans can be disenchanted with an institution that works so hard to please them. Dedication to satisfying key voters, as America's new democracy requires, need not produce results that will gratify the nation as a whole.

CONGRESS—THE FIRST BRANCH

Article I of the Constitution sets out the structure and powers of a national elected assembly, called the Congress. The U.S. Congress differs from elected assemblies in other advanced nations. Most world democracies are *parliamentary* in form, with the elected assembly choosing a chief executive from among its members.[*] In parliamentary systems, the assembly usually does little more than rubber-stamp proposals from the executive it has selected. Indeed, assemblies are rarely called legislatures, because they do little legislating; instead they are called parliaments, because they do a lot of talking. The United States is one of the few world democracies with a *presidential* form of government—a government in which the chief executive is elected directly by the people rather than chosen by the legislature. Legislatures are more independent, and therefore ultimately more powerful, in presidential systems.

Like many of the world's parliaments, Congress is **bicameral,** consisting of two chambers. The relative importance of the Senate and House of Representatives has fluctuated over time. In the decades prior to the Civil War, the country's most prominent statesmen—Henry Clay, John C. Calhoun, Daniel Webster, and Stephen Douglas—were members of the Senate. After the Civil War, political leadership moved to the House, where shifting party control more accurately reflected national sentiments. Presidents of the period were undistinguished, and the public image of the Senate was poor, partly because the membership included numerous party bosses and millionaire industrialists. In this unusual context, a series of strong House Speakers, starting with Maine Republican James G. Blaine (1869–1875), organized their party members into energetic, cohesive lawmaking majorities.[7]

For most of the twentieth century the two chambers were equally important. Regardless of the political circumstances that gave prominence to one chamber, the other chamber always had the ability to check it. For example, after Republicans took over Congress in 1994, fewer than half of the 21 Contract with America provisions passed by the House won final congressional approval—senators

---

[*]A few countries, such as France, have hybrid systems.

resisted the ambitious proposals advanced by their colleagues in the lower chamber. This balancing role creates a bit of a rivalry between the two chambers. A Speaker of the House once commented that "The Senate is a nice quiet place where good Representatives go when they die."[8] The Senate has a quick response to such jibes: Throughout the twentieth century, no one ever gave up a Senate seat to run for the House.

THE ORGANIZATION OF CONGRESS

The House and Senate are not undifferentiated collections of people who sit in their seats all day debating and voting as the urge strikes them. Like other large decision-making bodies, the two chambers have developed traditions that advance their work: (a) the committee system, which is an extensive division of labor; and (b) a party leadership structure, which effectively organizes large numbers of people to make decisions. Both are more important in the House than in the Senate. The House is much larger, so it needs more internal organization to facilitate its work. The smaller Senate can afford to operate less formally.[9]

THE CONGRESSIONAL PARTIES

Political parties organize the legislative branch, although they do not dominate Congress to the extent that they dominate parliaments in other democracies.

SPEAKER OF THE HOUSE   The Constitution stipulates that the House shall elect a Speaker. Although technically a constitutional officer, the **Speaker** in practice is always the leader of the House's majority party. Until the late nineteenth century, the Speaker was the only formal party leader in the House. Indeed, from the end of Reconstruction to the turn of the century, the Speaker often rivaled the president as the most powerful public official in the United States. Powerful Speakers made all House committee assignments, awarding the chairmanships of important committees to their close allies and punishing disloyal members by removing them from committees on which they had previously served.[10] Moreover, as the presiding officer of the House and chair of the Rules Committee—which determines legislative procedure—the Speaker controlled the **floor** of the chamber. Speakers ruled.

A folksy Republican called "Uncle Joe" Cannon was the last of the dictatorial Speakers. Cannon dominated the House in the first decade of the twentieth century, but he could not suppress the Republican party's growing progressive wing. He alienated various other political interests as well, such as western farmers, labor leaders, anti-liquor crusaders, and supporters of women's suffrage. Imposing party discipline on House members he considered "traitors" led Cannon to an increasingly punitive use of his powers.[11] Dissident Republicans who chafed under

Big boss men

Georgia Republican Newt Gingrich (on right) was the most powerful House Speaker since Progressives helped strip the influence of "Uncle Joe" Cannon (on left) in 1911. But Gingrich's power still did not come close to that of a nineteenth-century congressional boss.

the Speaker's iron rule eventually joined with Democrats in a revolt that stripped Cannon's office of its most important resources. From 1910 to 1911, the Speaker lost the power to make committee assignments and was removed from the Rules Committee. Procedural reforms also guaranteed ordinary members some right to have their proposals considered.[12] The office of Speaker has never regained the powers removed at this time.

PARTY LEADERSHIP: HOUSE   Next in line to the Speaker is the **majority leader,** who organizes the majority party on the floor. Majority leaders are elected by the members of their party. They are responsible for day-to-day operations: scheduling legislation, coordinating committee activity, and negotiating with the president, the Senate, and the minority. They play an important role in building the coalitions necessary to pass legislation, not simply by shoring up votes for a single bill but also by maintaining "peace in the family." Different points of view flourish within parties, and it falls to the leadership to prevent minor spats and quarrels from developing into destructive feuds.[13]

The minority counterpart of the majority leader is the **minority leader,** the floor leader of the minority party. Both party leaders are assisted by **whips,** whose jobs are to communicate regularly with the parties' rank and file. The whip explains positions and strategies, counts votes, and carries rank-and-file views back to the leadership. The whip offices are rather large, with 25 whips in the Democratic party and 20 in the Republican party. Their title conjures up an image of party leaders whipping their members into line (the title derives from whip-pers-in of the hounds in a fox hunt), but in practice these officers seldom rely on coercion.

Other party members participate in leadership via steering committees, which are forums for discussing issues, developing party programs, and identify-ing committee heads.* Finally, all members belong either to their party *caucus* (if Democrats) or party *conference* (if Republicans). These meetings of the full party membership elect the leadership and vote on committee slates recommended by the steering committees. In Woodrow Wilson's time, they sometimes adopted resolutions requiring party members to support particular policy proposals—but this power is rarely used today.

PARTY LEADERSHIP: SENATE With two members from each state—an even number—the Senate requires some tie-breaking mechanism, and the Con-stitution obliges by making the vice president the president of the Senate and giv-ing him a tie-breaking vote. The Constitution also provides for a **president pro tempore,** who presides in the absence of the vice president (which is most of the time). This office is mainly honorific, without real power. Ordinarily, it goes to the most senior member of the majority party.

The Senate too has majority and minority leaders and whips, but Senate lead-ers today are not as strong as those in the House. Indeed, one of the main jobs of the leaders is to hammer out **unanimous-consent agreements,** so called because they are agreed to by all senators with any interest in proposals. Gener-ally these agreements specify the terms of debate: what sort of amendments will be in order, how long they will be debated, when votes will be taken, and so forth.[14] Agreements specifying the terms of debate are necessary because of the Senate's tradition of careful deliberation.

According to present rules, a single senator can talk for as long as she or he desires. This right has been converted into a weapon that senators may use during the legislative process: the filibuster. When senators oppose a bill or a presidential nominee especially severely, but lack the votes to win a floor fight, they vow to **filibuster**—to keep talking until the other side gives up. Often the threat of a filibuster is enough to force a Senate majority to compromise. The Senate major-ity can end a filibuster, but only by adopting a **cloture** motion. A vote for cloture requires the support of 60 senators, so a coalition of 41 senators may stop the Senate from acting on any issue. The Senate's old-fashioned debating rules are one important reason why voting majorities often fail to get their way.

---

*The role of the steering committee differs depending on whether the Democrats or the Republicans control the House.

Ups and Downs of the Congressional Parties

Although the party leadership today is not as strong as it was in the period before the revolt against Uncle Joe Cannon, it is stronger than it was for half a century after the revolt. From the 1920s to the 1970s, Speakers were far weaker and less active than in the preceding half-century. Scholars refer to this period of weak party leadership as the era of "committee government," an allusion to the fact that committees operated much as they pleased with little constraint from the party leadership.[15] Beginning in the mid-1970s, however, a series of reforms and political developments strengthened the party leadership in general and the speakership in particular.

The Democrats picked up a large number of new seats in the wake of Watergate. The party caucus, fortified by this contingent of younger and more liberal members (the "class of '74"), deposed three standing committee chairmen. These older members were too moderate for the new party rank and file. Two of them were also known for overbearing and arbitrary styles of leadership that the newcomers found unacceptable. For example, when Armed Forces Committee chair F. Edward Hebert (D-LA) spoke before the freshmen, he reportedly insulted them—for example, by addressing them as "boys and girls."[16] Hebert's arrogance cost him his position.

Shortly thereafter, the party leadership regained influence. The power to make Democratic committee assignments was transferred to a steering committee in which the leadership was highly influential. Moreover, the Speaker was given the power to appoint Democratic members of the Rules Committee, making it virtually part of his office. Figure 9.1 shows how increased party unity in roll-call voting accompanied these institutional changes.

When the Republicans took control of Congress in 1994, partisanship surged. They had chafed under Democratic control for decades, and now the time for payback was at hand. Democrats personally disliked Speaker Gingrich and bitterly opposed his program. Republicans, in turn, united in support of the leader who had brought them majority status. The congressional parties looked stronger in the mid-1990s than they had looked at any time since the late nineteenth century.

Why does party power rise and fall? Recent scholarship suggests that one reason is the homogeneity of the parties. If all party members agree about some issue, anyone can make decisions for the group. Members are willing to give more power to party leaders because they have little fear that the leaders will endanger their reelection prospects. But when the parties are more diverse, members are reluctant to give power to party leaders, who may act in ways that are electorally dangerous to them.[17]

Historical evidence backs up this supposition. The strong congressional parties of the late nineteenth century were a product of a time in which the two parties represented quite distinct interests.[18] Only when the Republican party split into progressive and regular wings did the movement to weaken the Speakership

FIGURE 9.1

The congressional parties are more unified today than a generation ago

The graph shows the percentage of all recorded votes on which a majority of voting Democrats opposed a majority of voting Republicans. Numbers for each year have been averaged over each Congress. Is party unity in Congress good or bad?

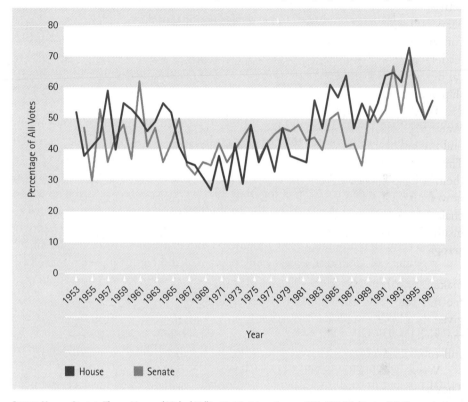

SOURCE: Norman Ornstein, Thomas Mann, and Michael Malbin, *Vital Statistics on Congress, 1999–2000* (Washington, DC: Congressional Quarterly, 2000), p. 201.

gain momentum. Conversely, the weak parties of the mid-twentieth century reflected their internal divisions. Numerous events undermined Democratic party cohesiveness. In particular, labor and liberal groups shaped presidential policy proposals during the New Deal, alienating moderates; civil rights split the party in the 1960s; and Vietnam and "social issues" continued dividing the party into the 1970s. Southern Democrats became especially unwilling to accept party leadership that would reflect the views of the northern majority.[19]

Parties are growing stronger again, in part because they are again fairly uniform. The civil rights revolution and the 1965 Voting Rights Act guaranteed everyone—particularly southern African Americans—the right to vote. Many southern districts eventually elected minority Democrats. As the electoral influence of southern African Americans increased, and as conservative whites started voting Republican, new Democrats elected in the South became much more liberal than their predecessors. Consequently, southern Democrats in the 1990s did not differ much from northern Democrats. Especially in the House, the Democrats are now a liberal, urban party, whereas the Republicans are a conservative, suburban and small-town party. Thus members have less to lose when they support strong leaders committed to particular national policies.[20]

Uniformity of beliefs may explain why strong leadership is less harmful to individual members, but it does not really explain why a member of Congress would accept it. What does a party member gain from cooperating with the team? Why are party switching and defections from the party line as rare as they are? Part of the explanation is that often strong leaders can help a party produce better outcomes than the party would get if they all worked independently. Passing an imperfect bill may be better than passing no bill at all, so members may sacrifice some influence over particular details.

Even when party members are unhappy with policies desired by their leaders, they have some incentive to stick together. Electoral success is partly linked to the successes of their political parties, the party images as a whole, and the performance of their presidential candidates. Congressional parties are also increasingly active in campaign funding, causing members to feel indebted to the leadership.[21] But members of Congress occasionally do tire of the compromises required by leadership, especially when the other party's beliefs seem more compatible (see the accompanying Election Connection, "The Jeffords Defection").

THE COMMITTEE SYSTEM

Congress does its work through its committees. Since 1980, for example, 6000 to 8000 bills have been introduced in each two-year session of the House of Representatives, but only 10 to 15 percent eventually passed. A few unsuccessful proposals died on the floor, but most of the 85 to 90 percent that failed never made it out of committee. Floor majorities can save a bill stuck in a recalcitrant committee via a rarely used "discharge petition," which requires 218 signatures, but in most cases favorable action by a committee is necessary for a proposal to become law.

To accomplish their work, both the House and the Senate utilize several kinds of committees. **Standing committees** have fixed memberships and jurisdictions, and they persist from one Congress to another. The Appropriations, Commerce, and Foreign Relations Committees are examples. **Select committees,** by contrast, are temporary committees created to deal with specific issues. For example, the House established a Select Committee on Homeland Security in June 2002. Both houses of Congress had standing committee systems in place by 1825.[22] More than half a century later, the Legislative Reorganization Act of 1946 gave the committee system the shape it largely retains today. In the 107th Congress (2001–2002) there were 19 standing committees in the House and 17 in the Senate (see Table 9.1). These "full" committees are subdivided into more

reconstruction
1870

The Jeffords Defection

Everyone suspected that GOP control of the U.S. Senate would not survive long after the 2000 elections. Democrats and Republicans split the seats 50–50, leaving Vice President Dick Cheney to break ties. The loss of only one GOP senator would give the Democrats organizational control over the chamber.

A handful of elderly Republicans seemed likely candidates for the first departure. Most commentators guessed that the first to retire would be Strom Thurmond, a South Carolina Republican born in 1902. No one suspected that Vermont moderate James Jeffords held the most vulnerable Republican seat—at least not before rumors started circulating that the rangy maverick was upset with his party's leadership. Jeffords had never fit comfortably within the GOP, voting as often as not with the other party—but as the Republican center of gravity drifted in a southwesterly direction, the New England native felt less and less at home.[a]

Jeffords fought hard to liberalize the 2001 tax bill and, as a swing vote, mostly got his way.[b] But Jeffords was still unhappy with the treatment he received from Republican leaders. Some say the final insult came when White House staffers neglected to invite Jeffords to a Teacher of the Year award ceremony, even though the guest of honor came from his state. Jeffords left the GOP in early June with a guarantee from Democratic leaders that he could lead the Environment and Public Works Committee. His decision to become an independent ended six months of unified Republican government.

Only rarely does one person exert so much influence. The Jeffords defection meant that the Judiciary Committee fell under the control of one of the Senate's most liberal members, fellow Vermonter Patrick Leahy, who was able to stall the president's judicial nominees. West Virginia's Robert Byrd, considered a champion of pork-barrel spending, regained the Appropriations chairmanship. Every committee except Ethics suddenly had more Democrats than Republicans. Jeffords also raised the political stock of several senators considered possible 2004 presidential contenders. The Jeffords defection reinforces the same message as the 2000 presidential election that preceded it: When the voting public is almost evenly divided between two parties, minor changes can make all the difference.

However, the Democrats did not enjoy their dominance for long. Bush campaigned actively during the 2002 elections, making speeches on behalf of his allies and raising money for their campaigns. His political adviser, Karl Rove, recruited successful candidates to run for office. And although the 2002 vote was very close, Republicans picked up enough seats in both the House and the Senate to enjoy undivided government again. Bush won another chance to work with, and protect, a slim congressional majority. And James Jeffords lost the committee chair that his defection had secured him.

What do you think?

- Would Jeffords have left the GOP if the Senate split had not been 50–50 or if the Democrats had not promised him an important committee?
- Who is responsible for keeping party members in Congress happy? Anyone?
- Do sitting members of Congress betray constituents when they change parties?

[a]Karen Yourish and Bonnie Scranton, "Who's a Rock—and Who Rolls." *Newsweek* (June 4, 2001): 30–31.

[b]John F. Harris and Dan Balz, "A Delicate Balance: The Steady Courtship of Senate Moderates Was Key to the Passage of the Tax Bill," *Washington Post Weekly Edition* (June 4–10, 2001): 8–10.

TABLE 9.1

STANDING COMMITTEES OF THE 107TH CONGRESS

COMMITTEE	SIZE	NUMBER OF SUBCOMMITTEES	MAJOR COMMITTEE?
Senate			
Agriculture	19	4	
Appropriations	26	13	✓
Armed Services	19	6	
Banking, Housing, and Urban Affairs	19	5	
Budget	18		✓
Commerce, Science, and Transportation	16	7	
Energy and Natural Resources	19	4	
Environment and Public Works	16	4	
Finance	14	5	✓
Foreign Affairs	16	7	✓
Governmental Affairs	15	3	
Health, Education, Labor, and Pensions	18	4	
Indian Affairs	13		
Judiciary	16	7	
Rules and Administration	15		
Small Business	16		
Veterans' Affairs	13		
House			
Agriculture	51	4	
Appropriations	61	13	✓
Armed Services	60	7	
Budget	43		
Education and Workforce	49	5	
Energy and Commerce	53	5	
Financial Services	60	5	
Government Reform	44	8	
House Administration	9		
International Relations	49	5	
Judiciary	37	5	
Resources	52	5	
Rules	13	2	✓
Science	47	4	
Small Business	36	5	
Standards of Official Conduct	10		
Transportation	75	6	
Veterans' Affairs	31	3	
Ways and Means	39	5	✓

SOURCE: Respective committee Web sites at the House homepage (www.house.gov) and the Senate homepage (www.senate.gov)

than 150 subcommittees. There also are 4 "joint" committees with membership from both houses, and a small number of select committees.

HOUSE COMMITTEES   House committees fall into three groups by level of importance. Both parties agree that the Rules, Appropriations, and Ways and Means Committees are highest in importance. The Rules Committee is the "right arm" of the Speaker. It controls the flow of legislation to the floor and the conditions of debate. The other two committees deal with spending and taxing, broad powers that enable them to affect nearly everything government does.

Committees at the second level of importance deal with nationally significant policy areas: agriculture, armed services, energy, and so forth. The least important committees include "housekeeping" committees, such as Government Reform and Oversight, and committees with narrow policy jurisdictions, such as Veterans' Affairs. The Budget Committee has a special status. Members can serve for only four years in any ten-year period, and its membership is drawn from other committees and from the leadership.

SENATE COMMITTEES   The Senate committee system is simpler than that of the House; it has only major and minor committees. Like their House equivalents, Appropriations and Finance are major committees, but the Senate Rules Committee is a minor committee with far less power than its House counterpart (the Senate leadership itself discharges the tasks performed by the House Rules Committee). Budget is also a major committee, as is Foreign Affairs, reflecting the Senate's constitutional responsibilities to advise on and consent to treaties and to confirm ambassadors.

Committee power in the Senate is widely distributed: Chairs of major committees cannot chair any other committee or subcommittee, and chairs of minor committees can chair only one other panel. Each senator serves on one minor and two major committees, and every senator gets to serve on one of the four major committees named above. On average, senators sit on more committees than representatives do. In part this reflects a simple size difference: The Senate has nearly as many committees as the House but less than one-fourth as many members to staff them. But in addition, senators represent entire states, so many more issues concern their constituents. As a result, senators' legislative lives are not so closely tied to particular committees as are the lives of representatives.[23]

HOW COMMITTEES ARE FORMED   The committee system is formally under the control of the chamber's dominant party. Party committees nominate members for assignment, and party members gather in caucus to approve those assignments. Each committee thus has a partisan balance at least as favorable to the majority as the overall division of the chamber. The more important committees are especially stacked in favor of the majority party. In the 107th Congress, for example, the Republicans had a 9-to-4 advantage over the Democrats on the House Rules Committee, a ratio far greater than their 223-to-210 edge in the chamber. In contrast, the party ratio on the less important Judiciary Committee was 21 to 16.

Party influence over committee membership actually does not prevent individual committees from exercising a considerable degree of independence. Part of the reason is the use of **seniority** to choose committee chairs. Members generally are not removed from committees after their initial appointments, and the majority-party member with the longest continuous service on the committee is usually its chair. This norm for selecting committee chairs evolved in the Senate in the 1880s and migrated to the House after the 1910 revolt; it gives the committee leadership some autonomy from the parties. Seniority is rarely violated, although in 1994 Speaker Gingrich did pass up the most senior committee members when he named the Republican chairs of the Appropriations, Commerce, and Judiciary committees.[24] The Republican conference also adopted a three-term limit on committee chairs that they first enforced in 2000, another means of weakening the seniority system.

COMMITTEE REFORMS By the 1950s, party leaders in Congress had become so weak that many observers believed committee chairs held the real power. A few of them behaved autocratically, closely controlling staff and budgets and even refusing to call meetings or to consider legislation they opposed. Some manipulated the subcommittee structure, creating and abolishing the smaller units, varying their jurisdictions, and monopolizing their chairmanships. To make matters worse, because members from safe southern seats had built up considerable seniority, Democratic chairs tended to be notably more conservative than their party's rank and file.[25]

Eventually, the Democratic party caucus injected more democracy into the system, weakening the chairs.[26] A caucus resolution passed in the early 1970s allowed House committee chairs to lead only one subcommittee. A "subcommittee bill of rights" protected the jurisdictions, budgets, and staff of the smaller units. The Senate moved in the same direction as the House, spreading power more evenly across the membership.

For more than a decade, political scientists debated the net impact of these reforms. Some questioned the wisdom of decentralizing power to 250 standing committees and subcommittees, many containing only eight or nine members. Today the prevailing view is that committees have been more subject to party influence in the last decade than they were a generation ago. An out-of-the-mainstream chair of an important committee or subcommittee would run a greater risk of being overthrown today than at any time since the revolt against Speaker Cannon. Moreover, when the Republicans took control in 1995, their leadership acted to restrict the independence of subcommittees.

THEORIES OF THE COMMITTEE SYSTEM

Why does the standing-committee system exist at all? Members of Congress are elected as equals. Why would the body give minorities—sometimes unrepresentative minorities–permanent influence over any policy area? Why not consider everything on the chamber floor (the so-called Committee of the Whole), where all members participate on an equal basis? And if the size of the membership would make that process too unwieldy, why not consider legislation in select committees specifically created for particular bills or resolutions? The various answers to these questions invoke different interpretations or theories of the committee system. We mention two here: the distributive theory and the informational theory.

The **distributive theory** notes that members choose committees relevant to their districts. For example, members from urban districts seek membership on committees that deal with banking, housing, or labor; members from rural districts opt instead for committees that deal with agriculture and natural resources. The committee membership gets first crack at legislation in their issue area, and other members of the chamber go along with the committee in exchange for similar deference on bills they have shaped. This **logrolling** ensures that Congress will deliver benefits to each participant's constituency.[27] Studies document that districts and states receive a disproportionate share of government grants if their representatives sit on the relevant committees.[28]

An alternative interpretation is that committees primarily serve a knowledge-gathering function.[29] This **informational theory** stresses that members frequently are uncertain about the outcomes that proposed laws will produce. Hence they wish some members to become experts in each subject area and to share their knowledge with the broader membership. One way to do this is to give committees disproportionate influence, subject to the condition that they do their job conscientiously and not abuse their power. Committee members can utilize their positions to gain a bit extra for themselves, but only to the extent that they specialize and give the chamber useful, reliable information.

These two theories are not incompatible. Each describes an important aspect of the committee system. Indisputably, members wish to serve their constituencies and regard committees as important means for doing so (although certainly not the *only* means). But just as certainly, members often are unsure exactly how they can serve their constituencies best, so they need and value information. If they adopt the wrong policy and the results are disastrous, it could come back to haunt them in a future campaign.[30] They need specialists in the relevant policy area to guide their choices.

The two theories probably apply differently to various committees. The distributive theory appears most relevant to committees responsible for straightforward matters, such as handing out money—subsidies, grants, and funding for projects. In these areas, members of Congress will allow interested colleagues to turn public institutions into private preserves, so long as they receive similar privileges in areas important to *their* constituencies. In contrast, where policy making involves great uncertainty or large costs and benefits—telecommunications regulation, for example—members will wish to have reliable information and will hold committees to a higher standard.

The distributive theory also seems somewhat less applicable today than in the period of so-called committee government. When government revenues were rising steadily and congressional party influence was weak, there was little to prevent members from using the committee system for their narrow ends. But with the budget deficits of the 1980s and 1990s, with stronger congressional parties, and with considerable uncertainty surrounding much of the policy agenda (including issues such as health care, environmental protection, and the Internet revolution), committee members are less free to pursue their narrow constituency interests. The incentives still are present, but the opportunities are more limited.

THE STAFF

The legislative branch is much larger than the 535 elected members of the House and Senate. The members have personal staffs that total more than 7000 in the House and 4000 in the Senate, and each chamber hires thousands of staff members to support the committees. Many of these staffers are clerical workers, and others are policy experts who play an important role in shaping legislation. Additional employees help coordinate partisan legislative proposals.

Thousands of other staff members work in various support agencies of Congress. The Library of Congress employs thousands. So does the General Accounting Office (GAO), the watchdog agency of Congress that oversees the operation of the executive branch. A smaller number of people work for the Congressional Budget Office (CBO). This agency provides Congress with expert economic projections and budgetary information. In total, the legislative branch of government consists of some 24,000 people.

HOW A BILL BECOMES A LAW

Every civics class teaches that Congress "makes the law" governing the United States. However, this tidy phrase is inadequate to describe the complex process by which a bill becomes a law. Passing a single statute requires steering it through two chambers, organized into more than 250 committees and subcommittees, and usually requires the support of members of two political parties and numerous interest groups. Although no flowchart could possibly convey the complexity of getting a major bill through Congress, we will outline the stages through which important legislation must pass (see Figure 9.2).

To start things off, a bill or resolution is introduced by a congressional **sponsor** and one or more cosponsors. The initial wording may be the legislator's own work or a proposal offered by a constituent, but most often it is provided by leg-

ex post facto – A bill that makes itself retroactive

congress can't do this

FIGURE 9.2

How a bill becomes a law

There's a bit more detail involved than passage by Congress and a presidential signature. With such a complicated process, can voters ever be sure that their representatives are working hard?

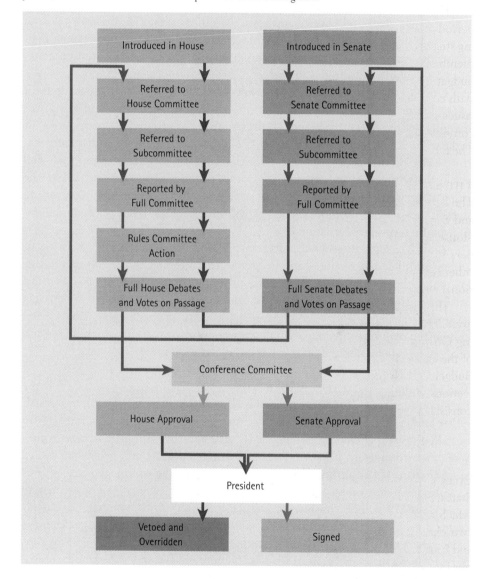

islative staff at the member's direction. The House Speaker or the Senate presiding officer, advised by the chamber's parliamentarian (an expert on rules and procedures), refers the proposal to an appropriate committee. Because legislation has become more complex and committee jurisdictions overlap, recent House

Speakers have used **multiple referrals,** sending the bill simultaneously to more than one committee or dividing it among several committees.

Once the bill goes to committee, the chair gives it to an appropriate subcommittee. In some cases, bills are dead on arrival. Multiple bills often try to do roughly the same thing, for example, so supporters may settle on the legislation with the best chance of passage and leave the others alone. The sponsor may not be serious about changing the law, having written the bill to please some constituency or interest group, in which case it may stagnate. The subcommittee may not take the bill seriously and so neglect to bring it up for consideration.

Otherwise, the staff schedules hearings at which witnesses will speak in favor of the bill or in opposition to it. Witnesses can be other members of Congress, members of the executive branch, representatives of groups and associations, or ordinary citizens. Sometimes hearings are genuine attempts to gather information. More often, hearings are carefully choreographed: The subcommittee staff stacks the witness list in favor of the position of the subcommittee chair. As one study observed, "committees neither seek nor receive complete information. Rather, they seek to promote certain views of their issues to bolster their abilities to produce favorable legislation."[31]

After hearings, the subcommittee begins **markup** of the bill—revising it, adding and deleting sections, and preparing it for report to the full committee (assuming that a majority of the subcommittee supports the final product). The full committee may repeat the process, holding its own hearings and conducting its own markup, or it may largely accept the work of the subcommittee.[32] If a committee majority supports the bill after committee markup, the bill is nearly ready to be reported to the floor—but not quite.

WHEN BILLS GO TO THE FLOOR

Let's consider first what happens in the House. Bills that are not controversial, either because they are trivial or because they have extremely narrow impact, can be called up at specified times and passed unanimously with little debate. Somewhat more important bills are considered under a fast-track procedure called **suspension of the rules.** Upon being recognized, the committee chair moves to consider a bill under suspension. If a two-thirds majority of those voting agrees, the bill will be considered. Debate is limited to 40 minutes, no amendments are in order, and a two-thirds majority is required for passage. There is some risk in considering a bill under suspension because it needs two-thirds support. Even if a majority backs the legislation, it might fail under the higher threshold. Indeed, opponents of a bill sometimes support the motion to suspend the rules precisely so that they can raise the required number of votes.

Legislation that is especially important, and therefore usually controversial, goes to the Rules Committee before going to the floor. The Rules Committee may hold its own hearings, this time on the type of **rule** it should grant. In these hearings only members of Congress may testify. The rule specifies the terms and conditions of debate. A rule specifies the time that the supporters and opponents will be allowed to speak. It also may regulate the introduction of amendments, prohibiting them (a *closed rule*) or specifying the amendments that are in order (a *restrictive rule*). In recent years three-quarters of all bills coming from the Rules Committee have been granted restrictive rules.

Assuming that the Rules Committee recommends a rule, the floor then chooses to accept or reject the rule. Rules rarely are rejected, but that does not mean the floor goes along with anything the Rules Committee proposes. Rather, in shaping the rule, the committee anticipates the limits of what the floor will accept. Sometimes committee members miscalculate and are embarrassed when a floor majority rejects their rule. Otherwise, the bill is finally under consideration by the chamber. After debating a proposal and voting on amendments, the floor then decides whether to adopt the bill.

In the Senate, the process is a bit simpler. For uncontroversial legislation, a motion to pass a bill by unanimous consent is sometimes all that is necessary. More important and controversial legislation will require the committee and party leaders to negotiate a unanimous-consent agreement, which is a complicated bargain analogous to a rule granted by the House Rules Committee. Assuming that they succeed and thereby avoid a filibuster, the bill eventually comes to a floor vote.

If a majority votes to adopt the bill, are we at the end of the process? Not at all. Before the bill can be sent for the president's signature, it must pass both chambers in identical form. The bill may have started in one chamber before going to the other, or it may have proceeded simultaneously through both. In either case, it is extremely unlikely that the House and Senate will pass exactly the same bill. In fact, their versions of the legislation may be in serious conflict.

For major legislation, each chamber appoints conferees to participate in a **conference committee** that tries to reconcile the two versions of a bill. In theory, each chamber's conferees are committed to their chamber's version of the legislation and will negotiate a compromise as close as possible to their chamber's desired solution. In practice, this is not likely. Conferences for some complex bills involve hundreds of members who support some parts, oppose other parts, and care little about still other parts. This context makes the situation ideal for bargaining. When a majority of each chamber's conferees agree to the final draft, the compromise bill is reported back to the parent chambers, where another floor vote in each chamber is required for passage.[33]

BUDGETARY POLITICS

Budgetary

Now, you may think that we have finally reached the end of the legislative process. Technically, this is true, but passage of a bill does not guarantee that it will be implemented. The reason is that we have been describing only the **authorization**

process. Before the government actually can carry out the activities that Congress authorizes, funding must be approved for them.

The Constitution grants Congress the power of the purse and makes the House the lead actor: All tax bills must originate in the House, and by custom and tradition, all appropriations bills do too. The **appropriations process** parallels the authorization process. Thirteen appropriations subcommittees in each chamber hold hearings and mark up a budget bill (the subcommittee chairs are commonly referred to as "the Cardinals of Capitol Hill").[34] The full committees may do the same, but usually they defer to their subcommittees.

In the House, appropriations bills are *privileged;* they take precedence over other legislation, and a motion to take up an appropriations bill can be offered at any time. But in practice, appropriations bills, too, usually pass through the Rules Committee. Thus appropriations subcommittees in both chambers must report bills, the rank and file in both chambers must pass them, and a conference committee must agree on every dollar before the government actually has any money to spend.

THE CONGRESSIONAL CAREER

Legislators are extremely sensitive to their constituents' wishes, more so than members of Congress from earlier eras. The reasons are straightforward: (1) Elected officials are more likely to think of politics as a job and wish to retain office. (2) Technological changes have made elected officials less able to hide their actions and better able to determine what voters want. (3) Electoral fortunes are less likely to rise or fall on the basis of ties to national political parties. (4) Elected officials remain in office longer if they cater to the tastes of local voters and provide the services that constituents demand.

THE GROWING ELECTORAL INCENTIVE

Until the late nineteenth century, many more congressional representatives quit than were defeated. Job conditions were not very attractive. The national government was weak, and the District of Columbia little more than a swamp.[35] Ambitious politicians, especially outside the South, often found state government a better outlet for their energies.[36] Even those members willing to serve multiple terms sometimes were prevented from doing so by rotation practices, whereby political factions in a congressional district "took turns" holding the congressional seat. Abraham Lincoln, for example, stepped down from the House of Representatives in 1848 after serving only one term.[37] Average service in the House did not reach three years until after 1900.

The early Senate was equally unstable. In the first ten years of the republic, more than one-third of the senators failed to serve out their terms. Before 1820, more senators resigned during their terms than were denied reelection by their state legislatures! Although they had the opportunity to stay longer than members of the House, many chose to leave.[38]

Today things are quite different. The Congress is the world's foremost example of what political scientists call a professional legislature. Its members are full-time legislators who stay for long periods. Relatively few members quit voluntarily, and many intend to remain in Congress indefinitely. This professional interest in retaining their jobs prompts representatives to be electorally sensitive, if not hypersensitive. Contemporary incumbents fare so well precisely *because* they are so electorally aware; they anticipate threats to their reelection and act to avoid them.

CHANNELS OF COMMUNICATION

More congressional decisions are public now than they were a generation ago. Until 1971, many House votes were cast by standing, speaking (aye–nay), or depositing colored cards (called tellers) into boxes—procedures that camouflaged each member's position. But rule changes that year made it easy to demand a **roll-call vote**—in which each member declares a vote on the record—and the number of roll calls in an average session more than doubled. Recorded votes are risky because they are available to interest groups or opposition researchers seeking campaign issues. Damaging votes need not be highly visible ones. Even an obscure vote can come back to haunt a member years later.[39]

Compensating for this increased scrutiny is the improved information that members of Congress have about their constituents. Not only do their offices have fax machines, e-mail, and World Wide Web pages—technologies undreamt of a few decades ago—but travel subsidies and other perks have expanded greatly.[40] Members were reimbursed for only three trips to their districts in 1960. By 1976 the yearly limit had increased to 26, and today there is no limit except the overall budget allocated to each member. Members travel to their districts 30 to 50 times a year! Important business is rarely scheduled for Mondays or Fridays, because so many members travel on those days. Moreover, members can afford to conduct surveys if they want a scientific way to learn the views of constituents. Today's representatives therefore probably make fewer mistakes based on bad information than their predecessors did and hence are better prepared than ever before to serve as "delegates" to the national government.[41]

Members of Congress also can compensate for increased scrutiny by communicating with constituents directly. Congressional use of the **frank**—free postage for official business—has grown, and computerized mailing lists make the tool more useful. Not surprisingly, congressional mailings to constituents are more frequent in even-numbered (election) years than in odd-numbered years. However, newsletters cannot be mailed within 90 days of an election, and members cannot include more than two personal photos per page.

THE DECLINE OF PARTY

At one time, parties were powerful enough to bully members of Congress into sticking with the leadership, even if it meant casting votes that would damage them in their districts. In modern times, fewer constraints exist to prevent legislators from acting on the electoral incentives they face and the information they have. Legislators can support the interests of their district—liberal or conservative, with the president or against, and so forth—except under unusual circumstances. This flexibility tends to make voters in a district happier with their representative (although it may make leadership in Congress more difficult). Thus, one reason why fewer incumbents are defeated is that fewer give their constituents reasons to defeat them.

Parties are also weaker in the electorate. Although these days 70 percent of voters select their parties' candidates, that figure is low by historical standards.[42] Voters are more open to diverse appeals, which encourages candidates to court voters of all parties.[43] Constituents often find good reasons to ignore partisanship. Since the late 1960s, the rate at which voters support incumbents of a different party has often been close to 50 percent.[44]

Meanwhile, representatives know that their own partisan constituencies are less secure. They cannot take votes for granted. It is seldom sufficient to vote for party proposals or stick with their leadership. They usually must offer district voters additional, more personal reasons to support them. Constituency service often fills this need.

CONSTITUENCY SERVICE

You may think of members of Congress primarily as *lawmakers*. Making laws is their principal business and main constitutional responsibility. But members of Congress do much more than legislate. The official title of House members is "representative," and most people's view of representation involves a wide range of activities.[45]

One chore that demands a great deal of the time and effort is district service—making sure that congressional districts get a fair share (or more) of federal programs, projects, and expenditures.[46] Some members of Congress are famous for their efforts to bring such economic benefits to their districts. Even Americans who disapprove of pork barrel legislation usually applaud when their representatives and senators bring home the bacon, and they reward them at the ballot box for it.

Another activity to which modern representatives devote a great deal of attention is constituent assistance, or "casework." Citizens, groups, and businesses frequently encounter difficulties in qualifying for government benefits or in complying with federal regulations. When their problems are not solved through normal channels, they appeal to members of Congress for assistance. About one in

Shoe on the other foot
Even members of Congress dedicated to the principle of smaller government are reluctant to give up money that might go to their own districts.

six voters reports having contacted a representative for information or assistance. In overwhelming numbers, they were satisfied with the resolution of their problems and, again, showed their gratitude at the polls.[47]

In many other countries, an administrative official called an ombudsman assists citizens when they must deal with the government bureaucracy. In the United States, members of Congress play this role, hiring large staffs to help with the chore.* Some observers compare members of Congress to CEOs (chief executive officers) of small businesses.[48] Each House member heads an office system—one part in Washington and one or more parts in the district—and directly employs an average of 18 personal staff assistants, more than 40 percent of whom are assigned to district offices.[49] Indeed, it has been said that Capitol Hill is the headquarters of 535 political machines.

Such was not always the case. In 1950 the average representative had three staff employees. And as late as 1960, nearly a third of the representatives did not have permanent district offices. The 1960s and 1970s were a period of unparalleled growth in congressional staffs. The ombudsman role has grown in importance because of the federal government's expansion.[50] More subsidies and more regulations resulted in more opportunities for members of Congress to engage in constituent assistance. The number of citizens who reported contacting their representatives for this purpose tripled between 1958 and 1978.[51] Thus, at the same time that strength of party affiliation was declining, an expanding federal government conveniently stimulated constituent demands that members of Congress were willing and able to meet.

District service and constituent assistance often are included together under the general term **constituency service.** Service takes up a growing amount of

---

*Senators have larger staffs than House members. The size depends on a state's population.

legislators' time, and for good reason: It helps them please voters and therefore makes reelection easier. When members of Congress take positions on issues, they please some groups and antagonize others. On controversial issues, their positions may lose them as many votes as they gain. But when incumbents provide valued services to constituents, nearly everyone approves. Small wonder that, by a 5-to-1 margin (judging from one survey), House administrative assistants consider constituency service the most important factor helping their employers stay in office.[52]

EVALUATING CONGRESS

It is easy to get so wrapped up in the detail of Congress and its operations that one loses sight of the reason for our interest in the institution. The reason, of course, is that Congress is the first branch—arguably the most powerful and most important of the three branches of government. It is the branch that bears primary responsibility for representing the needs and values of the American public and for developing legislation to improve their well-being. How well does Congress meet its responsibilities?

CRITICISMS OF CONGRESS

The most common criticism of the congressional process is obvious: *It is lengthy and inefficient.* Legislation may take months or even years to wend its way through the process, with lots of duplicated effort—both within and across the chambers. Moreover, after all is said and done, Congress often produces a compromise that satisfies no one. To those who want quick, decisive action, watching Congress is enough to put their teeth on edge. Of course, this is what the framers intended. They wished to ensure that laws would pass only after thorough deliberation.

But that raises a second criticism: *The congressional process works to the advantage of policy minorities, especially those content with the status quo.* Proponents of legislation must build many winning coalitions—in subcommittee, full committee, appropriations committee, conference committee, and on the floor—in both chambers. Opponents have it much easier. A minority that controls only a single stage of the process may be able to frustrate the majority. Of course, a determined majority cannot be stopped indefinitely, except by a Senate filibuster, but it can be held at bay for a long time. Moreover, potential majorities sometimes decide not to act, calculating that the costs of overcoming all the obstacles are not worth the effort. Making laws is hard work (see the accompanying Election Connection, "The Mystery of the Misspent Money"). Because changing the status quo requires positive action, the congressional process handicaps majorities who support change and helps minorities who are content to block change.

Given that members are trying to please constituencies, *they constantly are tempted to use their positions to extract constituency benefits,* even when important national legislation is at stake. President Jimmy Carter got so upset trying to deal with Congress on national energy policy that he wrote in his diary, "Congress is disgusting on this particular subject."[53] President Clinton's lobbying on behalf of the North American Free Trade Agreement (NAFTA) was likened to an "oriental bazaar." Members not only demanded special treatment for constituency interests but even traded votes for concessions on unrelated issues. Besides appearing unseemly (unless *you* are part of the constituency getting the concession), the process defeats, distorts, and otherwise damages national interests in pursuit of its members' parochial interests. Sometimes the very process of passing such legislation ensures that it will not work. The compromises necessary to get legislation through Congress may spread available resources too thin to make much difference.

Examples like these illustrate the charge that Congress regularly shows a distributive tendency—a tendency to spread program benefits widely. Every member wants a "fair" share of the federal pie for his or her district, and by *fair,* the legislators usually mean "as much as possible." Even if the district or state is relatively affluent or does not have the problem that a program addresses, its representatives and senators are reluctant to pass up an opportunity to deliver local benefits. Some federal programs distribute money on the basis of complex formulas that include population, economic conditions, and characteristics of the people and area. These formulas are of great importance to members of Congress; staff members use state-of-the-art spreadsheets to show how much their districts would gain or lose under alternative formulas. All too often, those estimates become the basis for supporting or opposing policies.

Taken to extremes, this tendency can be almost comical. Consider, for example, the Economic Development Administration created in the 1960s to subsidize the construction of infrastructure—roads, utilities, industrial parks, and so forth—in depressed areas. By the time the program was killed by the Reagan administration, it had been repeatedly expanded by Congress to the point where more than 80 percent of all the counties in the United States were officially classified as "economically depressed" to make them eligible for federal subsidies.[54]

Bashing federal programs is a popular sport. Sometimes it is warranted—programs may be badly designed, poorly implemented, or incompetently administered. But federal programs often fail because they were born to fail: They are not focused on where they will do the most good, and resources are not sufficiently concentrated to have a major impact. Consequently, money is spent, and the citizenry has little to show for it. But this is not because of incompetence or corruption. It is because members of Congress, ostensibly working in their constituents' interest, spread resources so broadly and thinly that they have little impact.

The Mystery of the Misspent Money

Gobs of money flow into congressional elections every two years, and most of that money goes to the Democrats and Republicans who already hold office. Interest groups consistently fatten the campaign coffers of senators and representatives at the same time that these politicians are voting on issues of public policy critical to lobbyists. Usually the favored legislators vote the way their contributors wish them to vote.

The whole system, when observed from a distance, reeks of political bribery. Humor columnist Dave Barry describes the way most popular observers view the campaign-finance system: "Sleazeballs who want government favors give money to politicians, who give it to consultants, pollsters, advertising agencies, and television stations, who get you to elect the politicians, who thus get more money from sleazeballs. Do you see what's morally wrong with this, voters? That's correct: Your government, the government that your Founding Fathers fought and died for, is being sold over and over like a used mobile home, and *you're not getting a cut.*"

This cynical interpretation may sound logical. "If lobbyists are spending tons of dough on Congress, they must be buying something that is not supposed to be for sale, right?" But political scientists who actually dig into the flow of cash often come away with a sharply different story. Neither the pattern of giving nor the pattern of accepting interest-group donations looks the way it should if cynics are right.

Take the suspicion that lobbyists buy votes with their weighty checks. "How in the world," one might wonder, "could politicians vote against people who have dropped thousands of dollars into their laps?" This logic seems persuasive—but if donors are trying to buy votes, their strategies are incredibly foolish. Interest groups do not give the bulk of their money to swing legislators. Rather, generous donations usually go to the members of Congress most likely to support a group in fair weather or foul. Agricultural associations favor rural representatives. Medical associations favor doctors. Trial-lawyer associations favor trial lawyers. Why would lobbyists try to buy the votes they could have had for free?

Perhaps contributors do not try to buy new votes but, instead, try to buy elections for their firmest supporters. Maybe money, in other words, disrupts the election connection between rulers and ruled. "If interest groups are doling out money to keep their friends in office," critics ask, "is that really democracy?" Problem is, the pattern of donations contradicts this straightforward logic as well. Interest-group money does not flow to the politicians most in danger of losing their jobs. Quite the contrary, often the biggest checks go to the most stable members of Congress, including some who expect no opposition at all

WHY DO AMERICANS DISLIKE CONGRESS BUT LIKE THEIR MEMBERS?

More than people in other democracies, Americans are proud of their political institutions. They revere the Constitution, honor the law, and respect the presidency and the courts. But the prominent exception to this generalization is the Congress. Congress is often the butt of jokes. Humorist Mark Twain once ob-

when they run for reelection. Money also flows to party leaders who have gained influence precisely because of their ability to hold on to power for many terms, leaders who enjoy so much influence that their constituents are unlikely to sacrifice it by voting them out of office. Smart contributors would not invest precious funds in elections where they were least likely to make a difference.

If they are not buying votes or elections, what do political action committees get for all that money? Political scientists Rick Hall and Frank Wayman propose a compelling answer. After interviewing staff members and probing the bill histories for three congressional committees, Hall and Wayman discovered that the main effect of campaign contributions is that special interests get extra work out of members. They are not buying legislative votes or legislative seats; they are just buying time.

Contributors reward those who perform important services to them in the halls and committees of Congress. Campaign cash helps mobilize legislators on a group's behalf, making up for the time they spend attending committee meetings, fine-tuning legal language, or marshaling votes before a congressional showdown. The money might lure legislators away from rival activities, such as working on other legislation or doing casework for constituents.

To reformers, this alternative story may evoke just as much cynicism as the more direct tale of political bribery. "Legislators are supposed to use their precious time working for the people," a critic might charge, "not for those with the deepest pockets!" True enough. But it is not exactly clear what a member of Congress would do if freed from the obligation of working to pay back supportive interest groups.

Legislators who lacked demanding contributors might choose to skip more meetings, pass the shaping of legal provisions off on unelected staff members, or let crucial votes shape up haphazardly—because these are the sorts of activities that voters back home seldom monitor. Lacking the money to buy advertisements, representatives might focus less time on legislating and more on campaigning or on scraping together smaller contributions. They might just work less! In short, special interests may have purchased "the best Congress that money can buy," but it is not clear they purchased anything that voters otherwise would have owned themselves.

What do you think?
- Is "buying time" as bad as buying votes or buying elections?
- What would members of Congress do with their time if they did not need to satisfy deep-pocketed contributors?

SOURCE: Richard Hall and Frank Wayman, "Buying Time: Moneyed Interests and the Mobilization of Bias in Congressional Committees," *American Political Science Review* 84 (1990): 797–820.

served that "it could probably be shown with facts and figures that there is no distinctly native American criminal class except Congress."[55] Congress has been defined as "a creature with 535 bellies, and no brain." Critics regularly remark that "the opposite of progress is Congress."

Disparaging quips like these reflect popular sentiments. Surveys report that only a minority of Americans trust Congress to do what is right or have confidence in Congress (see Figure 9.3), and they view members as having ethical standards only a bit higher than those who sell cars (see Figure 9.4). The reputation of Congress has been repeatedly tarnished by scandals. Ironically, this most electorally sensitive institution is the one whose image is the most negative.[56] Majorities of Americans doubt the competence and integrity of Congress.[57]

This negative perception of Congress contrasts with the generally positive view Americans have of their particular senators and representatives. After all, at the same time that popular majorities express doubts about the collective Congress, they reelect 90 percent or more of all the incumbents who run. This gap between electoral approval of individual members and unhappiness with the collective Congress is so striking that political scientists have given it a name: Fenno's paradox. Professor Richard Fenno first publicized the fact that citizens invariably rate their members of Congress far more favorably than they rate the Congress as

FIGURE 9.3

Public confidence in Congress trails confidence in many other institutions

Why might trust in the president and the military be so high in this poll?

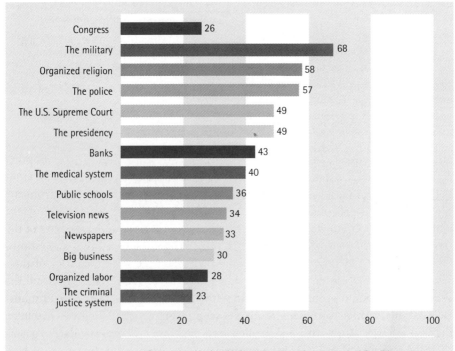

Percentage Having "A Great Deal" or "Quite a Lot" of Confidence

Source: The Gallup Poll, June 10, 2000.

FIGURE 9.4

The public rates members of Congress lower than those of other occupations

What do the occupations with low rankings have in common with politicians? What sets the ones with high rankings apart?

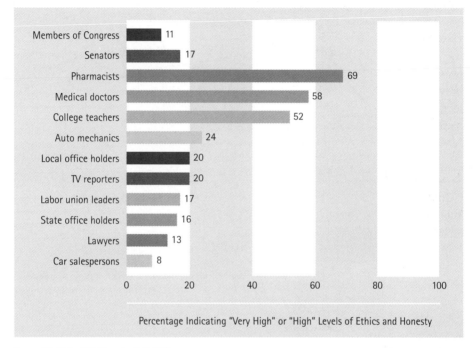

Percentage Indicating "Very High" or "High" Levels of Ethics and Honesty

SOURCE: The Gallup Poll, November 4–7, 1999.

a whole (see Figure 9.5).[58] Members take advantage of this disparity by adopting an unusual electoral strategy: "Members run *for* Congress by running *against* Congress."[59] They criticize the institution and claim that they are different from the members who cause problems.

Fenno's observations are not puzzling in light of a good understanding of the operation of Congress and the incentives underlying congressional operations. Americans dislike Congress but nevertheless reelect the great majority of their senators and representatives because they judge the collective Congress and the individual member by different standards.[60] They judge the Congress by how well it solves major problems and meets the serious challenges the country faces. Judging from opinion polls, Americans think Congress rarely discharges its collective responsibilities. Moreover, citizens take an equally dim view of how they think Congress operates—sluggishly, conflictually, inefficiently, and sometimes corruptly.

FIGURE 9.5

Americans rate their representatives much more positively than they rate the Congress

Approval of Congress varies more than approval of each incumbent. Why do you think that is?

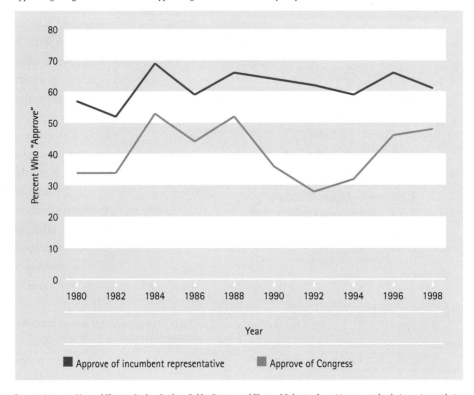

SOURCE: American National Election Studies Guide to Public Opinion and Electoral Behavior (http://www.umich.edu/~nes/nesguide/nesguide.htm).

But citizens judge their representatives and senators positively for doing the very things that make the collective Congress perform poorly. Members respond to narrow—special—interests that are part of their constituencies. They look for opportunities to channel benefits to constituents. They go to bat for constituents seeking exemptions from general policies and try to extract concessions from major legislative efforts. Even though many of these activities detract from the national good, voters back home appreciate the willingness of representatives to serve them.

The collective good may suffer. An old country maxim states that "if you want to make an omelet, you've got to break some eggs." Constituencies want the omelet, but they oppose contributing any of the eggs—and indeed, they reward members of Congress for stealing eggs from other henhouses. Widespread disgust with Congress, therefore, does not stem from a breakdown in the connection between constituents and representative; it grows from the responsiveness required by an especially strong connection.

CHAPTER SUMMARY

The United States Congress is the world's most powerful legislature. It has an extensive division of labor—the committee system—that is the envy of parliamentarians in other countries who have much less power and responsibility. The political parties structure congressional policy making, providing a relatively united legislative leadership that party members usually support in large numbers.

Members of Congress work as full-time professional legislators, and most (at least try to) serve for many terms. They have strong incentives to please the constituencies who must reelect them. This pressure shapes Congress itself. Members organize the committee system not only to deal efficiently and effectively with major national problems but also to enable them to concentrate on issues important back home. Members hesitate to give the party leadership enough power to mount efficient and effective responses to national problems, in part because that power might be used to prevent them from serving constituency interests or even to force them to oppose constituency interests. The structure of Congress is an uneasy compromise between what it takes to get the job done and what it takes to get reelected.

The result is that Congress is slow and inefficient, and the laws that emerge from the complex legislative process may not be very effective policy. Citizens hold Congress in much lower esteem than they hold their individual representatives and senators, whom they reelect regularly. Critics fail to see, though, that the problem is not a lack of democratic responsiveness—caused, for example, by large interest-group donations—but rather an excess of it. It is precisely the efforts of representatives to serve their supporters that make it so difficult for Congress as a whole to serve the national interest.

KEY TERMS

appropriations process, p. 298
authorization process, p. 297
bicameral, p. 282
cloture, p. 285
conference committee, p. 297
constituency service, p. 301
distributive theory, p. 293
filibuster, p. 285
floor, p. 283
frank, p. 299

informational theory, p. 293
logrolling, p. 293
majority leader, p. 284
markup, p. 296
minority leader, p. 284
multiple referrals, p. 296
president pro tempore,
    p. 285
roll-call vote, p. 299
rule, p. 296

select committees, p. 288
seniority, p. 292
Speaker, p. 283
sponsor, p. 294
standing committees, p. 288
suspension of the rules,
    p. 296
unanimous-consent
    agreements, p. 285
whips, p. 284

SUGGESTED READINGS

Arnold, R. Douglas. *The Logic of Congressional Action.* New Haven, CT: Yale University Press, 1990. An excellent discussion of how the incentives that motivate members interact with characteristics of public policy problems to shape legislation.

Deering, Christopher, and Steven Smith, *Committees in Congress.* Washington, DC: CQ Press, 1997. A thorough and up-to-date discussion of the congressional committee system.

Kingdon, John. *Congressmen's Voting Decisions,* 3rd ed. Ann Arbor: University of Michigan Press, 1989. Classic study of how representatives decide to vote on the floor.

Ornstein, Norman, Thomas Mann, and Michael Malbin. *Vital Statistics on Congress, 1999–2000.* Washington, DC: American Enterprise Institute, 2000. This biennial compilation of congressional statistics is to Congress watchers what *The Bill James Baseball Sourcebook* is to baseball fans.

Schickler, Eric. *Disjointed Pluralism.* Princeton, NJ: Princeton University Press, 2001. Focuses on the historical development of congressional rules and procedures.

Smith, Steven. *Call to Order: Floor Politics in the House and Senate.* Washington, DC: Brookings, 1989. Detailed study of the increasing importance of the chamber floors in the contemporary Congress.

ON THE WEB

Roll Call Online
www.rollcall.com
Roll Call is widely regarded as the leading source for congressional news and information both inside the beltway and beyond.

THOMAS Online: Legislative Information on the Internet
thomas.loc.gov
THOMAS is the most comprehensive congressional Web site. It posts the full text of all congressional proceedings and contains historical information on Congress from its inception to the present.

Congressional Quarterly
www.cq.com
Congressional Quarterly is extremely successful in its mission to "project the highest levels of accuracy, comprehensiveness, nonpartisanship, readability, timeliness and analytical rigor."

Capitol Advantage
www.congress.org
This alternative, private source of congressional information chronicles the daily activities of Congress in committee and on the floor and makes it easy to contact members who represent any given state or district.

10

THE PRESIDENCY

C ampaigning for the presidency in 1992, Democrats Bill Clinton and Al Gore needed to overcome the stereotype that characterized their party as champions of bureaucracy. To be tagged with a big-government label would have hurt their chances to oust the incumbent president, because some 95 percent of the public believes that the federal government wastes "a great deal" or "quite a lot" of taxpayer money.[1] Accordingly, Clinton and Gore emphasized their willingness to make changes. "We can no longer afford to pay more for— and get less from—our government," they declared to voters.[2]

The focus on streamlining federal agencies ended up being more than just campaign rhetoric; it produced what many call the longest sustained effort at institutional reform in the nation's history.[3] After the election, Vice President Gore spearheaded a Clinton administration initiative to "reinvent government." He gathered an initial staff of 250 career bureaucrats into the National Partnership for Reinventing Government in 1993, and they quickly produced a report brimming with more than 1200 proposals for change. The administration projected that the REGO efforts, as they are known, would save over $100 billion.

Gore worked hard to turn the complex policy issue into a political boon. It was precisely the kind of task that appealed to the scholarly former senator: highly technical, and yet something he might reduce into terms regular Americans could understand. The federal government would no longer order "designer bug sprays," he promised, or pay more for computer disks than those who buy at discount stores do.[4] When Gore's office needed a new electronic-mail program, employees did not go through a complicated procurement process; they simply drove to a nearby supplies store and bought the software. Gore appeared on David Letterman's talk show with a hammer and protective goggles to demonstrate the federally mandated procedure for safety regulators to test "ash receivers, tobacco desk type" (known to most of us as ashtrays). Gore eventually became so closely associated with the effort that he joked REGO was just "Gore spelled sideways."

President Clinton actively promoted the efforts of his second in command. "Make no mistake about this," Clinton said. "This is one report that will not gather dust in a warehouse."[5] Yet when the dust settled, the Clinton administration's efforts to make government "work better and cost less" returned little more than a mixed record. Only a third of federal bureaucrats surveyed in 1999 said their agencies treated reinvention as a priority. The federal workforce shrank by 300,000 employees, but only because of reductions attributable to the end of the Cold War. Otherwise, the federal bureaucracy grew. The General Accounting Office studied cost reductions reported by Gore's office and found that it could not document billions of the claimed savings. Rather, Gore's budget analysts had counted the same savings more than once, ignored expenses, and wrongly attributed savings created by other policy alterations to the REGO effort.

Civil servants and congressional power breakers felt most threatened by potential changes in employee policies or agency organizations, so these proposals saw the least progress. An illustrative example of the frustrations is Gore's proposal to "transfer law enforcement functions of the Drug Enforcement Administration [DEA] and the Bureau of Alcohol, Tobacco and Firearms [ATF] to the Federal Bureau of Investigation [FBI]." The missions of the three overlapped, and duplication of efforts was not just inefficient; it was dangerous. "It is not uncommon for agents from one . . . agency to believe the other to be the criminal element," claimed a draft version of the Gore study.[6]

Despite the president's commitment to consolidating law enforcement, Gore's proposal never got off the ground. Within days of its announcement, critics in Congress and in government agencies scuttled the idea. ATF was located within the Department of the Treasury, headed by Secretary Lloyd Bentsen, who let it be known he did not want to give up part of his turf. The DEA also had its supporters. Representative Charles Rangel, head of the House Caucus on Drugs, said the merger "would be a monumental mistake."[7] Many government employees, familiar with the cultures of the DEA and the FBI, also considered a merger between the two inconceivable. DEA agents often arrived at work in jeans, ponytails, and earrings, whereas their counterparts in the FBI dressed like Wall Street bankers. Said one DEA agent, "An FBI guy's idea of undercover is to loosen his tie."[8] In the end, the reorganization was abandoned.

EFFORTS TO REFORM THE STRUCTURE OF THE EXECUTIVE BRANCH are not new and have generally met with little success. This long record of failure at combating "unresponsive bureaucracies" often provokes frustration from regular citizens. The limited success of reform in the 1990s might appear to contradict the central claim of this book—that elections give the public more influence over government than ever before. But government's resistance to presidential control is not incompatible with electoral responsiveness. Most elements of the Clinton–Gore attempt to reinvent government—an ambitious presidential agenda that conflicts with vested political interests, executives with inadequate control over their policy areas, and a bureaucracy tied down by rules that hamper efficiency—grew directly out of America's new democracy.

These barriers to change generally result from public preferences expressed through elections and through other forms of participation. Voters, seeking more from their government, have required a more aggressive and politicized presidency to manage highly complex institutions. At the same time, they impose demands on Congress and the bureaucracy that make institutions resistant to change and insulate them from presidential reorganization efforts. The president lacks strong constitutional powers, relying on persuasion and negotiation to accomplish political goals. The chain of command is a loose one, and the president's administrative duties may exceed the capacity of an elected official. The resulting inefficiencies slow down government action backed by the president. Sometimes they make progress nearly impossible. As with so many institutions in the political system, therefore, the presidency may disappoint voters by failing to produce desirable results, but the cause of difficulty is not a desire to resist the popular will. Rather, the president often fails because the public got what it asked for.

THE PRESIDENT'S GROWING RESPONSIBILITIES

For most Americans, one person embodies the entire executive branch: the president of the United States. Certainly the president is an influential public official, perhaps the most powerful individual in the world. But very few of the changes in culture, society, nature, or even government trace back to the decisions of single people. Markets follow their own economic logic, dictated by the behavior of numerous consumers, firms, and countries. Cultures evolve new habits, new tastes, and new modes of family or religious life through the individual decisions of millions. Climates fluctuate, diseases develop, the earth's crust shifts without asking permission of any mortal. Even the most powerful person in the world faces severe limits.

It may seem that the national government should be different. The president is clearly at the top of any flowchart of power. Changes in government must be the ultimate responsibility of the "big boss," right? In theory, yes. But the federal government is a "12-million person operation," as executive-branch specialist Paul Light puts it. It is not just the combination of advisers, agency directors, and civil servants under a presidential administration, but also the "shadow government" of independent contractors and local government employees who carry out federally funded programs.[9] Such a massive and complicated executive branch would be beyond the close management of any one person, even if he or she did not have to share power with other public officials.

The president faces an unresolvable dilemma when trying to change government in response to public desires. Folk wisdom suggests, "If you want something done right, you'd better do it yourself." But of course, a president cannot do the work of millions. Someone else has to perform most governmental tasks, and the president's dilemma is finding a way to get good performance from employees who may not share the same values. With any effort to exercise authority, therefore, the president faces a difficult choice. The less detailed the instructions, the less likely government employees will carry them out exactly as desired. But more-detailed instructions reduce efficiency. Creating them requires the White House to spend lots of time and money gathering information about a policy area, so that rules passed down the chain of command provide clear guidance. And such rules may defeat their initial purpose, too, by preventing government employees who are trying to perform a job from using their own skills and judgment.

One way to increase the political responsiveness of government workers is to find employees who share a president's values or who subscribe to clear and predictable professional norms. The more someone thinks as you do, the more you can trust that person to perform a task the way you would do it. Within the executive branch, though, many employees can resist presidential pressure. The less control a president has over who holds a position, the less likely it is that a particular government employee will share the goals of the boss—and thus the less true control the president is likely to exercise. The president still selects and influences top-level appointees, but other administrators require an endorsement by members of Congress before they can take their jobs. Other rules, meanwhile, insulate rank-and-file government employees from a president's political desires, and many federal tasks are carried out by private companies, by independent government agencies, or by state and local governments that the executive branch controls indirectly if at all. The whole structure of the federal system sharply limits what the White House may accomplish.

Presidents do have a unique political asset: They fill the only position elected by a national constituency. Only presidents can claim to represent the country as a whole. This enhances their authority. On the other hand, this broad responsibility also creates problems. In the eyes of the voters, presidents are the focal point of the U.S. government. The public routinely blames presidents for events and conditions over which they have little control. Presidents are expected to conduct foreign policy, promote desired legislation, respond to disasters, manage the government, and address an endless variety of real and imagined social problems.[10]

Although presidents sometimes take credit for prosperity and success, they more often attract the blame when things go wrong. President George H. W. Bush, for example, enjoyed a succession of foreign policy triumphs equaled by few of his predecessors. His tenure saw the fall of the Berlin wall, the collapse of the Soviet Union, and a spectacular victory in the Persian Gulf War. Yet when the economy faltered, Bush was drummed from office (see Chapter 5). Clinton presided over one of the longest periods of economic expansion in history, but Vice President Gore felt compelled to emphasize the economy's shortcomings during his presidential campaign rather than risk appearing unaware of the difficulties that many Americans still faced (see Chapter 7).

Presidents also serve as the highest-ranking elected officials in their political parties. They must be sensitive to how their actions shape their parties' images. They must retain the support of their parties' most active members and contributors. If they do not satisfy their party constituencies, they may encounter difficulties with the party faithful in presidential primaries. In the 2000 primaries, when Democratic party activists considered Vice President Al Gore too moderate on health and environmental policies, many turned to Bill Bradley. This sort of defection is a common problem, because party activists are generally more extreme than typical voters are (see Chapter 8). Presidents have to find ways to balance the demands of their ardent supporters with those of the electorate at large.

THE PRESIDENT'S LIMITED POWERS

Even if presidents can balance their national and party constituencies, they usually cannot take action on their pledges without considering their level of support in Congress. Accommodating congressional demands is particularly important because of the fundamental division of power between the executive and legislative branches written into the Constitution. Those who wrote the Constitution ensured that presidents would govern only with the help of Congress. The result is a government of "separated institutions sharing powers."[11] Presidents are seldom in a position to force members of Congress to support them; they usually have to coax, beg, plead, and compromise to gain the necessary votes. Over 80 percent of the time, presidents either fail to secure passage of their major legislative agendas or must make important compromises to win congressional approval.[12]

Presidents find their position particularly exasperating because the public expects them to take decisive action. The expectations they face have increased much more quickly than the powers they have to meet such expectations. A thorough review of constitutional powers shows how little has changed to meet the increased expectations that presidents face in America's new democracy—and how many of the president's powers depend on congressional cooperation (especially in domestic affairs.)

THE POWER TO PERSUADE

Perhaps the most important presidential power receives no direct mention in the Constitution. Modern presidents rely on hundreds of public speeches each year to set forth their visions of the country's future. They use their high profiles, as well as their responsibility to spread information about the government, as an opportunity to persuade Congress and the public at large to support their policies. Congress cannot check presidential propaganda, only reply to it—and members of Congress risk incurring either public or presidential wrath if they ignore the message.

The power to persuade is used much more openly today than it was in the early years of the republic (see Figure 10.1). Early presidents seldom spoke in pub-

FIGURE 10.1

Growth in presidential speech making

Presidents started giving more public addresses with the Progressive Era presidencies, from Theodore Roosevelt to Woodrow Wilson, but a big surge followed the spread of broadcast media.

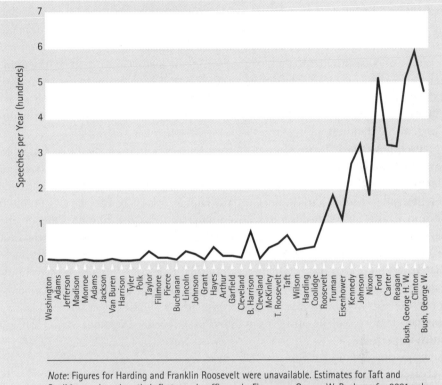

Note: Figures for Harding and Franklin Roosevelt were unavailable. Estimates for Taft and Coolidge are based on their first year in office only. Figures on George W. Bush are for 2001 only.

SOURCES: Data on Washington through McKinley are taken from Jeffrey Tulis, *The Rhetorical Presidency* (Princeton, NJ: Princeton University Press, 1987), p. 64; for Theodore Roosevelt, see Robert V. Friedenberg, *Theodore Roosevelt and the Rhetoric of Militant Decency* (New York: Greenwood Press, 1990); for Taft, see *Presidential Addresses and State Papers of William Howard Taft*, Vol. 1, 1910 (New York: Doubleday); for Wilson, see Albert Shaw, ed., *Messages and Papers of Woodrow Wilson*, Vols. 1 and 2 (New York: Review of Reviews Corporation, 1924); for Coolidge, see Claude M. Feuss, *Calvin Coolidge: The Man from Vermont* (Hamden, CT: Archon Books, 1965); for Presidents Truman through Reagan, see Roderick Hart, *The Sound of Leadership* (Chicago: The University of Chicago Press, 1987); for Hoover, Bush, and Clinton, information is taken from *The Public Papers of the President*, various years.

lic, and when they did, their remarks were of a general nature. The Constitution requires that presidents report on the state of the union annually, but Thomas Jefferson and his immediate successors met this obligation through written messages to Congress. Early presidents usually avoided open involvement in day-to-day politics, and when they did get involved, they seldom used public speeches to do so.[13] Jefferson, a master politician, invited members of Congress to the Executive Mansion (later called the White House) for dinners, at which he attempted to persuade them to support his political agenda.[14] He also communicated his views through friendly newspaper editors.

The first moves toward a vocal presidency came early in the twentieth century, during the Progressive Era. Perhaps more than any other president, Theodore ("Teddy") Roosevelt changed the definition of what was permissible in presidential rhetoric. Roosevelt liked to achieve results by using what he called the **bully pulpit.*** Roosevelt suggested that, like a preacher, the president could use his position to move his "congregation"—the public—to action. Early efforts at public persuasion often failed, of course. As one historian has noted, "the number of laws [Roosevelt] inspired was certainly not in proportion to the amount of noise he emitted."[15] Yet Roosevelt's popular appeal ran high—so high that a cartoon depicting the president sparing the life of a bear cub resulted in the widespread term "Teddy Bear."

Presidents since Teddy Roosevelt have increasingly used the bully pulpit to persuade others.[16] Woodrow Wilson addressed a joint session of both houses of Congress in 1913 to deliver a formal **State of the Union address,** a practice that has since become traditional in late January or early February.[17] Franklin Delano Roosevelt's "fireside chats" over the radio enabled him to sidestep the print media, which Republican publishers dominated. President Reagan, the first president with experience as a professional actor, used television more effectively than any of his predecessors. He understood that there is "a thin line between politics and theatricals."[18] Pictures were worth a thousand words, and body language spoke more convincingly than verbal formulations.[19] As Reagan once said, "I've wondered how people in positions of this kind . . . manage without having had any acting experience."[20]

THE POWER TO RECOMMEND

Presidents who served before the Civil War seldom developed or promoted policies of their own.[21] They stayed out of the explosive slavery issue—a principle of silence that extended to other issues as well, especially after deliberations started on Capitol Hill.[22] Yet the Constitution explicitly encourages presidents to recommend for congressional "consideration such Measures as he shall judge necessary and expedient." This power expanded rapidly after the end of the Civil War. The country was growing swiftly, and many social and economic problems broadened in scope.

The power to recommend gives presidents an ability to initiate debate, to set the political agenda.[23] Presidents can shut down old policy options, create new possibilities, and change the political dialogue. George W. Bush placed tax cuts and education reform on the policy agenda. Bill Clinton proposed broaden-

---

*Bully was nineteenth-century slang for "good" or "excellent," as in the old-fashioned phrase "Bully for you!"

ing health care coverage, reforming welfare, and reducing class sizes in public schools. Theodore Roosevelt made conservation a major public concern. Franklin Roosevelt persuaded Congress to pass dozens of bills within 100 days of his inauguration.

However, this power does not go unchecked. Congress can—and often does—ignore or greatly modify presidential recommendations. Congress rejected Clinton's health care proposals and greatly modified his proposals on welfare reform. It trimmed Bush's tax cuts. Nor is the power to initiate limited to the president. In 1994, congressional Republicans campaigned on what was called a Contract with America that set the policy agenda for the next two years, although only a small proportion of the proposals became law.

Presidents have the best opportunity to initiate policy in the first months after their election. For this reason, presidents make most new proposals at the start of their terms (see Figure 10.2). "You've got to give it all you can that first year," one of Lyndon Johnson's top aides noted. "You've got just one year when they treat you right."[24] The 75-day **transition** period between election day and the inauguration of a new president is critical. Incoming presidents do not yet have the burdens of office, but they have the time, resources, and importance to

FIGURE 10.2

The presidential legislative agenda

Presidents offer their largest agenda during their first terms. Why do presidents try to get the most done in their first year in office?

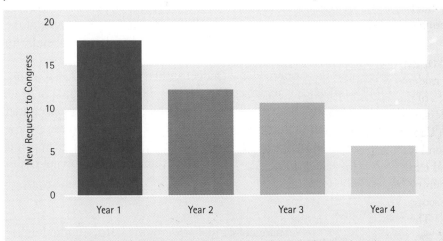

Note: Columns show the average number of new requests to Congress in each year across all administrations from 1949 to 1994, excluding requests made by Lyndon Johnson during his completion of John F. Kennedy's term.

SOURCE: Calculations are based on data drawn from Lyn Ragsdale, *Vital Statistics on the Presidency* (Washington, DC: CQ Press, 1996).

prepare for power. The transition period is typically followed by the presidential **honeymoon**—the first several months of a presidency, when reporters are kinder than usual, Congress more inclined to be cooperative, and the public receptive to new approaches.[25] Presidential popularity is at its peak, and public interest is high.

THE BUDGETARY POWER

Before 1921, every federal agency sent its own budget to Congress for examination by an appropriations subcommittee. No one, not even the president, knew whether agency requests exceeded government revenues. President Woodrow Wilson asked for a bureau to coordinate these requests, but Congress at first refused to create one, saying it would encroach on congressional authority. However, when federal deficits ballooned during World War I, Congress relented.

Originally known as the Bureau of the Budget, the agency is now called the **Office of Management and Budget (OMB),** a name that reflects its enlarged responsibilities. Although development of the president's budget is still its most important job, OMB also sets personnel policy and reviews every piece of proposed legislation that the executive branch submits to Congress to ensure that it is consistent with the president's agenda. Agency regulations, too, must now get OMB approval. One bureau chief claimed that OMB has "more control over individual agencies than . . . [the departmental] secretary or any of his assistants."[26]

OMB was once considered a professional group of technicians, who searched for budgetary savings. But OMB became more political as deficits took center stage in the electoral politics of the 1980s and 1990s (see Chapter 15).[27] Former Congressman David Stockman, Reagan's OMB director, led the fiscal side of the Reagan revolution.[28] Clinton's first OMB director, Leon Panetta, also came with congressional experience. The office has become a source of political power.

Congress created the Congressional Budget Office (CBO) in 1974 to counterbalance OMB's influence somewhat. The CBO evaluates presidential budgets as well as the budgetary implications of other legislation. The CBO's sophisticated analyses have enhanced its influence in Washington to the point where it now stands as a strong rival to OMB. In the health care policy debate, for example, it proved to be a "critical player in the game," whose estimates of the costs of health care reform doomed most proposals.[29]

THE VETO POWER

Perhaps the most important *formal* presidential power is the **veto,** a limited ability to prevent bills passed by Congress from becoming law. The Constitution declared that before any law "shall take effect," it must be "approved by" the president—whereas vetoed bills die unless "repassed by two-thirds of the Senate and House of Representatives." Before the Civil War, presidents seldom used the veto. President

FIGURE 10.3

Trends in presidential use of the veto power

Presidents today use the veto less than they did at mid-century but more than they did in the 1800s. Why did presidents become more assertive?

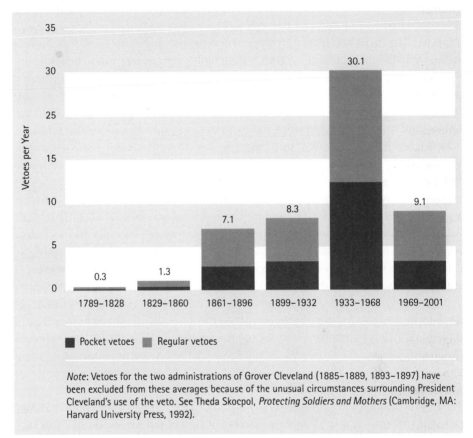

Note: Vetoes for the two administrations of Grover Cleveland (1885–1889, 1893–1897) have been excluded from these averages because of the unusual circumstances surrounding President Cleveland's use of the veto. See Theda Skocpol, *Protecting Soldiers and Mothers* (Cambridge, MA: Harvard University Press, 1992).

SOURCES: Figures from 1789–1996 are taken from Gary L. Galemore, "Presidential Vetoes, 1789–1996: A Summary Overview," Congressional Research Service Report for Congress, 97-163 GOV; figures from 1997–1999 are taken from Library of Congress, "Legislation: Bills, Amendments, and Laws," http://lcweb.loc.gov/global/legislative/bill.html accessed December 7, 1999.

Washington cast only two. The average number cast by presidents between Madison and Lincoln was slightly more than four. Presidents from Franklin Roosevelt on have been much more willing to use the veto power (see Figure 10.3).

Congress usually fails to muster the two-thirds vote that is necessary in each chamber to **override** a veto. Since the Kennedy administration, Congress has overturned approximately 1 out of every 10.[30] Only 1 of President Clinton's 32 vetoes was overridden. The main check on the veto is simply its negative nature; it can stop policy change but not initiate it. During the energy crisis of the late 1970s, President Carter wanted an energy policy that was the "moral equivalent of war," but when confronted with opposition from oil-state senators, he was forced to sign a law much altered from his original proposals. Carter could have vetoed the legislation, but his desire for action required him to take what Congress was willing to give.

The veto gives presidents leverage when negotiating with Congress. In late 1999, even though President Clinton was ineligible for reelection and had suffered the disgrace of impeachment, he was able to use the veto to force Republicans to compromise and allow him to achieve some of his policy objectives. Vetoes also enable presidents to define the terms of political conflict. Clinton both gained the upper hand in budget negotiations and increased his political support by vetoing a massive tax cut plan passed by Congress, for example. One GOP strategist acknowledged his advantages: "We've learned that it's nearly impossible to frame the national debate from the lower chamber of the legislative branch."[31]

If Congress enacts a law ten days before it adjourns, a president may exercise a **pocket veto** by simply not signing the bill into law. Nearly all of President Reagan's vetoes were pocket vetoes. Congress has no opportunity to override a pocket veto, so use of this power gave Reagan an aura of strength. The pocket-veto strategy works only at the very end of a congressional session, however; if Congress remains in session for more than ten days after passing a bill, the president must explicitly cast a veto to prevent the bill from becoming law. Congress remains in session virtually throughout the year, now that the lines between governing and campaigning have blurred, so the last few presidents seldom have had the chance to cast pocket vetoes.

THE APPOINTMENT POWER

The Constitution allows presidents to "appoint Ambassadors, other public Ministers and Consuls … and all other Officers of the United States." These appointments are subject to the "Advice and Consent of the Senate," which is taken to mean that a majority must approve the nominations. The appointment power enables presidents to place thousands of officials in positions of responsibility.

The president's **Cabinet** includes key members of the administration. Most are heads of government departments and carry the title "secretary." The terms are left over from the days when a *secretary* was a confidential assistant who kept secrets under lock and key in a wooden *cabinet*. Originally, the president's Cabinet had but four departments, and the secretaries met regularly with the president. It was in Cabinet meetings, for example, that Abraham Lincoln developed his strategy for fighting the Civil War.

Over the years, government began to perform a much broader range of functions. As the number of departments grew from 4 to 14 and interest groups gained influence over them (see Table 10.1), the Cabinet lost its capacity to provide confidential advice to presidents. "Cabinet government is a myth and won't work," President Richard Nixon explained. "No [president] in his right mind submits anything to his cabinet."[32] Today the Cabinet meets only occasionally, primarily for ceremonial purposes. But Cabinet jobs are still an excellent way for presidents to reward influential political supporters or to improve the administration's professional reputation by bringing in respected people.

TABLE 10.1

ESTABLISHMENT YEAR AND INTEREST-GROUP ALLIES OF EACH CABINET DEPARTMENT

Cabinet departments created after the nation's founding have specific issue domains and therefore fairly well-defined interest-group constituencies. Why would outer Cabinet departments form alliances with interest groups?

DEPARTMENT	YEAR	INTEREST-GROUP ALLIES
Inner Cabinet		
State	1789	
Treasury	1789	
Justice (attorney general)	1789	
Defense	1789 (as War)	
Outer Cabinet		
Interior	1849	Timber, miners, ranchers
Agriculture	1889	Farm bureau, other farm groups
Commerce	1913	U.S. Chamber of Commerce, other business groups
Labor	1913	Labor unions
Health and Human Services	1953	American Association of Retired Persons
Housing and Urban Development	1965	National League of Cities, Urban League
Transportation	1966	Auto manufacturers, truckers, airlines
Energy	1977	Gas, oil, nuclear power interests
Education	1979	Teachers' unions
Veterans Affairs	1987	American Legion, Veterans of Foreign Wars
Homeland Security	2003	State and local government, unionized public-safety providers
Environmental Protection Agency	Not an official department	Sierra Club, other environmental groups

TREATY POWER

Presidents may negotiate **treaties**—official agreements with foreign countries—but they do not take effect without approval by a two-thirds Senate vote. This supermajority requirement limits presidential flexibility when negotiating with foreign countries. Prior to 1928, the Senate did not endorse 14 percent of the treaties brought before it.[33] A president who cannot get Congress to approve a treaty after negotiations conclude loses credibility in international politics.

No president was more frustrated by this constitutional check on presidential power than Woodrow Wilson. During negotiations to end World War I, President Wilson pursued one objective above all others: establishment of the League of Nations, an international organization to settle international disputes. Wilson believed that such an organization could prevent future world wars. But the Senate perceived the League of Nations as a threat to U.S. sovereignty and voted against joining. Shocked and dismayed, Wilson lost both his political efficacy and his personal health.

Eighty years later, President Clinton faced similar difficulties with Congress. In October 1999, the Senate considered the Comprehensive Nuclear Test Ban Treaty, which had been negotiated three years earlier. The multinational agreement would have prohibited testing nuclear weapons and enacted more stringent monitoring systems to ensure compliance. Proponents of the treaty argued that it was essential to slowing the spread of nuclear weapons around the world. But critics, including many Senate Republicans, doubted its effectiveness and worried that it would hamper the nation's ability to modernize its armed forces. After negotiations broke down between Republican leaders and the Clinton administration, the Senate voted against ratification, 51 to 48.

Because a small number of senators can block a treaty, presidents often negotiate **executive agreements,** legal contracts with foreign countries that require only a presidential signature. Nothing in the Constitution explicitly gives the president power to make executive agreements, but the practice has a long history. President James Monroe signed the first executive agreement with Great Britain in 1817, limiting the size of both countries' naval forces on the Great Lakes.

The Supreme Court affirmed the constitutionality of executive agreements in 1937.[34] Since then, presidents have turned to the device regularly. Most executive agreements either are extensions of treaties ratified by the Senate or involve routine presidential actions otherwise permitted by Congress. But presidents sometimes use executive agreements to implement major foreign policy decisions. For example, President Clinton relied on an executive agreement to coax newly independent Ukraine into giving up its nuclear arsenal in exchange for economic aid.[35] In recent years, about 20 executive agreements have been signed for every treaty submitted to the Senate (see Figure 10.4).

FIGURE 10.4

Presidential use of executive agreements

Executive agreements are replacing treaties. Why have presidents increasingly turned to executive agreements? Does this behavior deny the Senate its constitutional role in foreign policy?

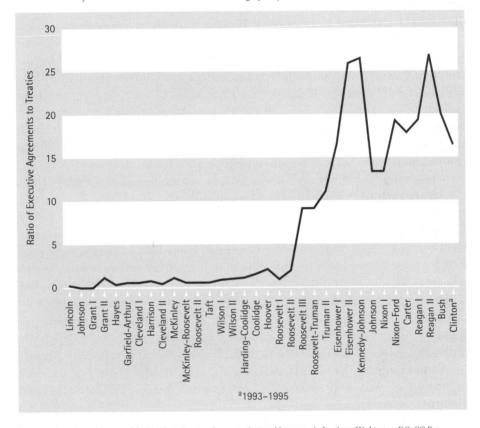

SOURCES: Gary King and Lyn Ragsdale, *The Elusive Executive: Discovering Statistical Patterns in the Presidency* (Washington, DC: CQ Press, 1988), pp. 131–140; U.S. Bureau of the Census, *Statistical Abstracts of the United States* (U.S. Government Printing Office, 1996), Table 1294, 792; and fax from Randall J. Snyder, Law Librarian, Office of the Legal Advisor, Department of State, Washington, DC, December 1996.

THE POWER AS COMMANDER-IN-CHIEF

The Constitution declares the president "commander in chief of the army and navy," a title that conveys significant authority over foreign affairs. Yet the Constitution gives Congress power to declare war and to govern the armed forces. It did not settle which branch ultimately would control the nation's war power. Prior to the Civil War, presidents seldom acted on their own in military matters. President James Madison refused to attack Great Britain in 1812 until Congress declared war. And in 1846, although President James K. Polk provoked a war by placing troops in disputed territory, he still waited for Congress before ordering troops into battle against Mexico.

Faced with a national emergency, Abraham Lincoln was the first to give an expanded interpretation to the role of commander in chief. When the southern states seceded from the Union, Lincoln proclaimed a blockade of southern ports and enlisted 300,000 volunteers before Congress convened. A few decades later, Theodore Roosevelt acted similarly, and in a much less urgent situation. He sent naval ships to Japan even though Congress refused to appropriate money for the trip. Congress, if it wished, could appropriate enough funds to get them back—which, naturally, members of Congress felt compelled to do! Following the lead of Lincoln and Roosevelt, modern presidents have often initiated military action without congressional approval. President Truman fought the Korean War without any congressional declaration whatsoever. More recently, President Clinton ordered the bombing of Kosovo without securing congressional approval.

Two major Supreme Court decisions have set the boundaries within which presidents exercise their authority as commanders in chief. In *U.S. v. Curtiss-Wright* (1936), the Court considered whether Congress could delegate power over arms sales to the president. Justice George Sutherland wrote that presidents were "the sole organ of the federal government in the field of international relations." The president has "a degree of discretion and freedom," he wrote, "which would not be admissible were domestic affairs alone involved."[36] This description seems to grant presidents wide latitude indeed.

The Court limited presidential power in a later case, *Youngstown Sheet and Tube Co. v. Sawyer* (1951). Trade unions in the steel industry had gone on strike during the Korean War. Claiming that the industry was crucial for national defense, President Truman ordered the federal government to seize control of the steel mills and commanded the strikers to return to work. In doing so, Truman ignored alternative procedures for handling strikes recently enacted by Congress, thereby attracting a constitutional challenge from the steel companies. Justice Robert Jackson wrote that presidents could not use their foreign policy authority to grab power at home. When a president "takes measures incompatible with the expressed or implied will of Congress, his power is at its lowest ebb," Jackson explained.[37]

The issue of executive authority arose again during the Vietnam War. In the summer of 1964, North Vietnamese torpedo boats attacked several U.S. destroyers stationed in Tonkin Bay off the coast of Haiphong, Vietnam's second-largest city. President Lyndon Johnson denounced the action as an unlawful attack on U.S. ships sailing in international waters.* Congress overwhelmingly passed the Tonkin Gulf Resolution, which effectively entered the United States into war

---

*Only much later was it revealed that Johnson had misled Congress; the destroyers had invaded North Vietnam's territorial waters.

with Vietnam by giving the president authority to "take all necessary measures" to repel any attacks and to "prevent further aggression."[38]

The experience of a long and discouraging war in Vietnam prompted Congress to rethink the president's authority over military action. In 1973 Congress passed, over President Nixon's veto, the **War Powers Resolution,** which required that a president formally notify Congress any time U.S. troops engage in military action. The resolution further specifies that troops must withdraw unless Congress approves the presidential decision within 60 days after receiving notification. Presidents generally question the War Powers Resolution's legal standing and sometimes ignore it. On five separate occasions, individual members of Congress sued in federal courts to enforce the resolution, but judges dismissed the suits, and Congress has never been willing to take more drastic steps while troops were in the field.[39] Nevertheless, recent presidents have sought congressional approval for their military actions, either formally or informally.

INHERENT EXECUTIVE POWER

The Constitution declares that "the executive power shall be vested in a President." Some claim that this statement adds nothing to presidential power; it simply summarizes the specific rights granted to the president. But many presidents have found in this clause the basis for a claim to additional rights and privileges. Presidential claims to inherent executive power have been invoked most frequently in making foreign policy, but presidents have asserted inherent executive power on other occasions as well.

One way in which presidents use their inherent executive powers is by issuing **executive orders**—directives to government employees that carry the weight of law unless they contradict acts passed by Congress. The Supreme Court ruled in 1936 that executive orders are constitutional, and since then they have increased in frequency and importance.[40] Truman used an executive order to desegregate the armed forces, Lyndon Johnson instituted the first affirmative action program, Ronald Reagan forbade homosexuality in the military, and George W. Bush sharply curtailed public access to the papers of former presidents.

Executive orders may not violate congressional legislation, and Congress may choose to overturn them after the fact. President Clinton decided not to issue an executive order removing the ban on gays in the military, for example, rather than face the threat of congressional action reversing him. However, presidents rarely worry about their executive orders being overturned, because passing a bill through Congress is so difficult and time-consuming (see Chapter 9). Figure 10.5 shows how sharply the use of executive orders has increased among modern presidents.

The most controversial invocation of inherent executive powers has been the doctrine of **executive privilege,** the right of the president to deny Congress

FIGURE 10.5

Significant executive orders, 1900–1996

A significant executive order is an order that receives mention in a Congressional hearing, on the floor of Congress, or in the pages of the New York Times. Why do you think modern presidents have issued more executive orders than earlier presidents?

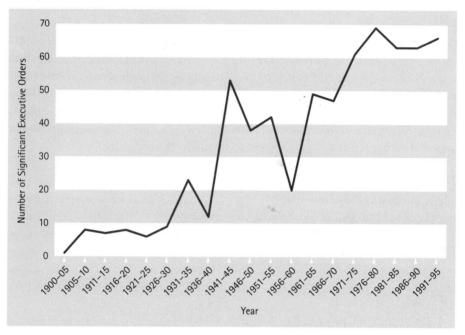

SOURCE: William Howell, "The President's Powers of Unilateral Action: The Strategic Advantages of Acting Alone." (Stanford University dissertation, 1999).

information it requests. George Washington was the first to invoke executive privilege when he refused to provide Congress information about an ill-fated military expedition on the grounds that "disclosure . . . would injure the public."[41] Ever since, presidents have claimed authority to withhold information on executive decision making from Congress.

The Watergate affair (see the section on scandals later in the chapter) brought this question before the Supreme Court. President Nixon had recorded extensive conversations with his aides and advisers. Prosecutors in the Watergate burglary case issued a subpoena to review the tapes, but Nixon refused to turn them over, arguing that executive branch policy discussions should be confidential. The case quickly rose to the Supreme Court, but the Court's posture was rather confused. The justices could not agree on how much extra confidentiality a president needed.[42] They sanctioned the doctrine of executive privilege, saying that confidential conversations between the president and his aides were "fundamental to the operation of government and inextricably rooted in the separation of powers under the Constitution."[43] Yet they ruled unanimously against Nixon after reviewing the communications, explaining that he lacked sufficient privilege to frustrate a criminal investigation.

THE POWER AS CHIEF OF STATE

Presidents often symbolize the United States to foreigners, including their political leaders. The Constitution anticipated this ceremonial role, indicating that presidents "shall receive Ambassadors and other public Ministers . . . and shall Commission all the Officers of the United States." This clause seems to say little more than that presidents may welcome visitors and administer oaths of office. Yet the words endow presidents with an invaluable resource: the capacity to act with all the dignity that countries accord heads of state.

Out of many, one
American presidents symbolize the United States around the globe, so foreigners upset with U. S. policies naturally express their opposition in terms of the nation's chief executive. These protesters are burning President George W. Bush in effigy. Can one person ever symbolize a democracy?

According to Walter Bagehot, a nineteenth-century analyst of British politics, governments have both "efficient" and "dignified" aspects.[44] The efficient aspect of government involves setting policy, administering laws, and settling political disputes. This is the nuts and bolts of policy making, the kind of activity performed by prime ministers in England or France. It is also hard work that often generates conflict. But government has a dignified aspect equally important to its long-term effectiveness. Governments must express the unity of the people, their values and hopes. Monarchs often symbolize their nation, as in England, whereas in France an elected president (separate from the prime minister) plays this ceremonial role. In the American system, the executive must perform both jobs—as seen by President Bush's activities after terrorists attacked the United States, comforting the nation and formulating antiterrorism measures at the same time.

The dignified aspect of the presidency has always seemed somewhat inconsistent with America's egalitarian ideals. One of the issues discussed in the very first Congress was how to address George Washington. A Senate committee recommended "His Highness the President of the United States of America and Protector of Their Liberties," whereas the House, objecting to royal language, pushed the simpler title preferred by Washington: "the President of the United States."[45]

Presidents differ in their level of comfort with the pomp and circumstance of office. Ronald Reagan emphasized the dignified aspect of the presidency—overseeing formal parties and appearing frequently at ceremonial events, but delegating day-to-day policy concerns to others. Bill Clinton initially took quite the opposite tack, becoming known as a "policy wonk." Eventually, however, he distanced himself from the efficient side of governing, cultivating a strong but sympathetic image during national tragedies. George W. Bush balances a formal image while in Washington against a more folksy image during retreats to his ranch in Crawford, Texas.

The balance presidents must seek between efficient and dignified activity changes with the times and with political events. Richard Nixon liked to listen to the presidential song, "Hail to the Chief," and to review ranks of marching soldiers at strict attention. His historical visit to China took on almost mythic proportions, leading composer John Adams to portray Nixon as an heroic figure in an English-language opera. After Watergate such pretensions began to look dangerous. Gerald Ford, a former college sports hero, distanced himself from his "imperial" predecessor by clowning on television. Jimmy Carter wore a sweater and carried his own suitcases; voters generally called him by his first name.

As presidents have become increasingly engaged in policy, they have found it harder to maintain dignity—especially given increased media scrutiny. Some have received assistance from their families. First Lady Jacqueline Kennedy invigorated

Men of the people

President Andrew Jackson was a war hero known for his plain speaking and rough-hewn appearance. President Jimmy Carter often dressed in comfortable sweaters, even when meeting world leaders. And while President George W. Bush usually maintains a formal appearance in the nation's capital, he dresses down for the cameras during retreats to his ranch in Crawford, Texas.

Washington art and culture and restored the White House. Barbara Bush's gray hair and unflappable demeanor gave her a matronly appeal that crossed political boundaries. Chelsea Clinton's maturity on trips to foreign nations, and her apparent devotion to her father even after the revelation of his affair with someone roughly her own age, may have helped Clinton survive his worst sex scandal.

But presidential family members can be a liability as well as an asset. George W. Bush's daughters, Jenna and Barbara, faced busts for underage drinking—resulting in embarrassment for both Bush and the Secret Service. First Ladies Eleanor Roosevelt and Hilary Clinton angered conservatives by working for left-wing social policies,[46] and Nancy Reagan often attracted the scorn of liberals. Clinton in particular may have redefined the role of first lady, parlaying

A mother's revenge

President George W. Bush's two daughters, Jenna and Barbara, created a minor scandal when they were accused of under-age drinking. First Mother Barbara Bush, who had to grapple with the president's own childhood disciplinary problems, quipped that "he is getting back some of his own."

her position into a successful run for one of New York's U.S. Senate seats.[47] If their spouses continue to use their posts as political offices and their family members continue to face intimate media scrutiny, presidents will have to maintain dignity in some other fashion.

The vice presidency once served a primarily ceremonial function, another potential source of dignity for an administration, but the job has become more politicized in the last several decades. Perhaps because of the greater awareness that the vice president may one day gain the highest office, the role of the vice president has steadily broadened. For example, Vice President Albert Gore played a key role in shaping the Clinton administration's environmental policy. Dick Cheney, George W. Bush's vice president, helps direct national security policy; he once served as Secretary of Defense.

THE IMPEACHMENT THREAT

Presidents may be impeached by a majority of the House for "high crimes and misdemeanors." The president leaves office if the Senate convicts by a two-thirds vote. Nothing better clarifies the subordination of presidents to Congress than the fact that legislators can remove the executive at will. Although seldom used, the constitutional power of **impeachment** is no dead letter—as indicated by a sex scandal that tarnished the Clinton presidency.

The president's misconduct became a political issue when Paula Jones, an Arkansas public employee, sued Clinton for sexual harassment. She claimed that, while Governor, Clinton had exposed himself to her in a Little Rock hotel room and requested sexual favors. Lawyers for Jones probed Clinton's romantic life while building their case, hoping to establish a pattern of inappropriate contact between Clinton and his employees and acquaintances. Under oath, Clinton denied having sexual relations with numerous women, including a young White House intern named Monica Lewinsky.

Evidence later appeared suggesting that Clinton and Lewinsky had indeed engaged in various forms of sexual conduct, including oral sex. Former solicitor general Kenneth Starr, who was investigating Clinton land deals, learned of this evidence contradicting the President's sworn testimony. Starr expanded his investigation to include possible charges of perjury and obstruction of justice, and he eventually issued a report for Congress to use in hearings. The House voted (along mostly partisan lines) to impeach Clinton on December 19, 1998, making him only the second U.S. chief executive to face possible conviction.

The Senate decided in early 1999 to acquit Clinton after his trial. The president eventually owned up to deceiving investigators but claimed his denial was not technically perjury because the Lewinsky affair did not include "sexual relations" as he understood the term. Public reaction to the explanation was hard to read. Clinton remained popular, and some attributed Republican losses in 1998 congressional contests to a perception that the GOP had tried to overturn the 1996 election. At the same time, Democrats apparently suffered in the 2000 elections because of the administration's poor image.

The Lewinsky scandal illustrates that Congress's impeachment power operates under an implicit check. The Constitution requires a two-thirds vote to remove a president after impeachment, so it would nearly always require bipartisan effort. That effort will not arise in politically motivated impeachments, because members of Congress will not vote to remove an executive from their own party unless they feel they must. Impeachment is feasible only when a president's actions fundamentally violate the norms of American politics, as Richard Nixon's apparently did during the Watergate scandal.

Yet Clinton's scandals altered the American presidency in one important respect: They may have ended the use of **independent counsels** (also known as special prosecutors), investigators appointed to look into reports of executive-branch wrongdoing. Starr was able to spend huge sums of money investigating Clinton's sexual misdeeds because a judicial panel had appointed him in 1994 to look into an unrelated controversy. Many observers decided afterward that giving roving investigators so much power and resources threatened the independence of the executive branch. The law authorizing use of special prosecutors expired in 1999, with few members of Congress favoring renewal and even Starr testifying against it. Ethics investigations are now the province of the attorney general's office, part of the executive branch.[48] This change may make high-profile investigations less likely.

THE PRESIDENTIAL ADVISERS

The modern president's closest advisers are White House aides who deal in matters of utmost confidentiality. At one time the president's personal staff was small and informal. Abraham Lincoln had just two young assistants. Even President Franklin Roosevelt originally had only a handful of personal assistants.

To address organizational problems caused by the growing size of the federal government, Roosevelt in 1936 asked a committee of three specialists in public administration (headed by Louis Brownlow) to consider ways to improve federal government organization. Saying "the President needs help," the Brownlow Committee recommended sweeping changes throughout the government, including additional appointments to the president's personal retinue.

Congress rejected most of the Brownlow recommendations, but did agree to enlarge the White House staff.[49] The president's staff has steadily evolved in size and complexity.[50] The number of aides has grown from 48 in 1944 to over 400 today. These aides generally fill the **White House Office,** part of a much larger collection of presidential advisers and coordinating agencies called the **Executive Office of the President (EOP)** (see Table 10.2).

SELECTING ADVISERS

In Franklin Roosevelt's day, no single person headed the White House staff. Even as late as the Carter administration, White House aides worked together as "spokes in a wheel," each having direct access to the president. But today presidents usually place one person in charge.[51] This person, the **chief of staff,** meets with the president several times a day and communicates decisions to other staff, Cabinet officers, and members of Congress.

The best chiefs are usually Washington insiders. Although seldom acclaimed, Ronald Reagan's chief from 1987 to 1988, Howard Baker, was one of the most powerful and effective. A former Senate majority leader and presidential aspirant, Baker served at a time when he had forsaken all political ambition. Baker's skill at reaching compromises helped boost Reagan's popularity, despite the fact that the aging president had lost much of his former vitality.

Newcomers to Washington are usually less successful. Typically, they become lightning rods—people to be blamed when things go wrong. John Sununu, for-

TABLE 10.2

EXECUTIVE OFFICE OF THE PRESIDENT,
BUDGET AND STAFF LEVELS

	BUDGET (MILLIONS)*	STAFF*
Office of Management and Budget	$70.7	490
White House Office	54.6	369
Office of National Drug Control Policy	25.2	109
Office of Administration	46.9	182
Office of the U.S. Trade Representative	30.1	173
White House Residence/Operating Expenses	11.6	90
National Security Council	7.5	47
Office of Policy Development	4.1	31
Office of Science and Technology Policy	5.3	19
Council of Economic Advisers	4.2	30
Office of the Vice-President	3.9	15
Council on Environmental Quality	2.9	22

*As of 1999.

SOURCE: Executive Office of the President, *Budget of the United States Government, Fiscal Year 2003*, Appendix.

mer governor of New Hampshire, was forced to leave the job of chief of staff when he was blamed for urging President George H. W. Bush to sign an unpopular tax increase.[52] Thomas McLarty from Arkansas resigned when he was blamed for the Clinton administration's poor start.[53]

Although Brownlow expected White House aides to have "no power to make decisions," modern presidents regularly use their staffs to shape their public policy proposals.[54] Within the White House staff, more than anywhere else, presidents can count on the loyalty of those around them simply because, unlike the careers of other bureaucrats (see Chapter 11), those of staff members are closely intertwined with those of the presidents.

The White House staff is more potent than ever in part because presidents have more need for political help. Presidents today need pollsters and consultants who can keep them in touch with changes in public opinion. Many observers criticized George W. Bush's early reliance on domestic policy adviser Karl Rove, whose primary experience was in campaign politics. They attributed Bush's decision to halt Navy bombing on the Puerto Rican island of Viecques and his proposal to grant amnesty to as many as 3 million illegal Mexican immigrants (see Chapter 4) to Rove's ambition to attract more of the Hispanic vote.[55]

Presidents also need assistants who can help them communicate with the media, interest groups, and members of Congress. Once a major bill arrives for consideration on the chamber floor, White House aides are in regular contact with many legislators. In 1992, as part of the White House effort to enact legislation that would engage young people in a national service program, one aide personally contacted 67 Senate offices.[56] So intense is the work inside the White House that most staff jobs demand 7-day, 100-hour work weeks. In short, presidential advisers are indispensable if the president hopes to exercise agenda-setting powers such as recommending policies, proposing budgets, persuading legislators, sustaining vetoes, and attracting support for nominees.

Quite apart from the president's genuine need for lots of political help, the White House staff is an excellent place to reward loyal supporters. Those who carry a candidate into office expect something in return after their candidate wins. The White House Office is a convenient place for the president to put campaign volunteers, because the president has exclusive control over appointments to his personal staff. None needs Senate confirmation, not even the chief of staff.

The number of people working at the White House sometimes provokes strong criticism from the opposition party, especially during presidential election years. When running for president, Bill Clinton promised to cut the White House staff by 25 percent. But when it came time to make the cuts, Clinton found his White House Office too valuable to be the target of cost-cutting efforts. Thus the president made staff cuts elsewhere in the Executive Office of the President. The public's limited understanding of executive branch organization prevented Republicans from getting much mileage out of Clinton's broken campaign promise.

SCANDALS IN THE WHITE HOUSE OFFICE

The highly personal and partisan nature of the White House staff can be a weakness as well as a strength. A White House full of personal friends and fellow partisans has at times so shielded presidents from external criticism that chief executives have lost touch with political reality. And sometimes staff members have used the power of the presidential office for improper, even illegal, purposes—paving the way for momentous scandals that tarnished both the sitting president's reputation and that of the presidency as an institution.

Scandals are hardly new to American politics. When lawmakers discovered that Abraham Lincoln's wife and her assistants outspent housekeeping funds, Lincoln successfully pleaded with Congress to appropriate more money secretly rather than to carry out an investigation.[57] But the intensity and significance of

White House scandals have escalated in recent decades.[58] In addition to the Lewinsky scandal, two major and many more minor scandals have captured the attention of the nation and carried the potential for impeachment.

The most serious was the Watergate scandal during the Nixon administration. In 1972, at the instigation of members of the White House staff, five men broke into Democratic party headquarters at the Watergate condominium complex in Washington, DC, apparently to obtain information on Democratic party campaign strategies. They were caught. Nixon's chief of staff, Bob Haldeman, knew that the burglars had received "hush money" so that they would not reveal White House involvement. When tapes of Nixon's own conversations indicated that the president himself had been involved in the cover-up, the House initiated impeachment proceedings, which convinced the president to resign.

In the Iran–Contra scandal, staffers in the Reagan White House illegally sold arms to the Iranian government and gave the profits, also illegally, to a group of guerrillas known as Contras who were fighting to overthrow a left-wing government in Nicaragua. White House aides faced prosecution and some Democrats talked of impeachment, but no direct evidence implicating the president turned up. Both scandals illustrate that presidents insulated from policy making by their advisers are often at risk.

THE TWO PRESIDENCIES

Put foreign affairs first, the sixteenth-century Italian thinker Nicolò Machiavelli advised his prince. If you fail at foreign policy, nothing you do in the domestic sphere will matter. American presidents often wish to ignore foreign affairs, because voters pay more attention to domestic policies that influence their daily lives. Yet international politics has a way of forcing itself onto a president's policy agenda, and domestic successes generally will not save a president who flubs a foreign policy crisis. Machiavelli's advice still holds in America's new democracy.

Just as the public demands a strong economy and punishes the president for failing to provide one (see Chapter 7), the public also expects the president to keep the nation strong internationally. These policy areas differ in one important respect, however. The president clearly must share power with Congress on fiscal policy (see Chapter 15) and must work through the Federal Reserve Board to influence monetary policy (see Chapter 11), but in foreign affairs the president exercises more personal influence. The main limits on presidential action in this arena come from foreign leaders and global trends, not from U.S. politicians.

For this reason, foreign and defense policies provide a rare opportunity for presidents. They exercise more authority when dealing with other nations than when dealing with domestic policy. Many foreign policy duties are ceremonial and therefore give the executive chances to look presidential—while avoiding the political squabbles that often plague domestic policy. Foreign affairs allow an executive to tap into deep-seated patriotic emotions, to inspire deep loyalty in voters with military ties, and to gain respect worldwide. The government's international performance can play a significant role in electoral calculations.

In a classic essay, political scientist Aaron Wildavksy developed the **two-presidency theory,** which explains why presidents usually will exert greater power over foreign affairs.[59] Foreign policy requires fast action and focused responsibility, and neither interest groups nor members of Congress conflict as much over foreign affairs.

Foreign policy questions often require a rapid response, and not only because voters demand it. Sometimes options disappear as a crisis develops. Sometimes, sluggishness at resolving a conflict can allow disputes among nations to escalate—for example, if foreign powers misunderstand the American position. Moreover, foreign policy success often relies on secrecy. Military operations may be more successful when they are surprises, and sometimes ignorance of a nation's strategic position can lead foreign negotiators to give up more than necessary. Presidents are better equipped to streamline decisions for speed and secrecy. Partly for this reason, members of Congress sometimes follow a "self-denying ordinance" on foreign policy. They may not think it is their job to determine the nation's defense posture.[60] This was particularly true in the years immediately after World War II.[61]

Special interests occasionally influence American foreign policy. For example, the United States has refused to recognize the legitimacy of Cuba's regime, in part because hundreds of thousands of people who live in Florida come from families who fled Castro's revolutionary government in the 1950s. The conflict between Israel and Palestine is "a perpetual fixture of domestic politics," according to former Secretary of State James Baker, in part as a result of "the political power of the American Jewish community."[62] Israel receives 20 percent of all U.S. foreign aid.[63] Yet few areas of foreign policy contain such strong and vitally interested domestic constituencies. Most nationality groups are not large enough, concentrated enough, or sufficiently attentive to events overseas to have a decisive effect on U.S. foreign policy. The interest-group structure is "weak, unstable, and thin."[64] This makes the policy environment easier for a president to negotiate.

EVALUATING PRESIDENTS

Presidents are expected to be strong, yet presidential powers are limited. As a result, presidents seldom satisfy the hopes and aspirations of the voting public. Presidential successes are quickly forgotten, whereas their failures are often magnified by time. Presidents thus must work hard and exhibit impressive political acumen to convert their position into a source of continuing influence. Presidents add to their effectiveness by building up a strong professional reputation and extensive popular support—both of which are more difficult to achieve because the intrusive nature of presidential news coverage.

Presidents who are competent and reliable are more likely to gain the cooperation of Congress and other **beltway insiders,** the politically influential people who live inside the highway that surrounds Washington.[65] Presidents also need to maintain their popularity with the general public. As Abraham Lincoln shrewdly observed, "With public sentiment, nothing can fail; without it, nothing can succeed."[66] Popularity is now quite easy to assess; pollsters ask respondents about presidential performance every week!

All presidents experience fluctuations in their popularity over the course of their terms. Their support rises and falls with changes in economic conditions and in response to foreign policy crises. But in addition to these external factors, presidential popularity tends to decline over time as public expectations go unfulfilled.[67] A study of the first term of eight recent presidents indicates that, apart from any specific economic or foreign policy events, their popularity on average fell by nearly 8 points in the first year and by 15 points by the middle of the third (see Figure 10.6). Their popularity recovered in the fourth year, when a presidential campaign was under way—either because presidents worked to communicate positive news about their administrations or because presidents start to look better when compared to their competition. Presidents regain popularity when reelected, but those bounces soon trail off.

If presidential leadership is so difficult—requiring a strong professional reputation, robust public popularity, and the cooperation of numerous self-interested individuals—why are some past executives remembered as "Great Presidents"? What allows some presidents to succeed, even in periods of crisis, when most fail? The simplest answer is that past presidents did not face the same expectations as today's executives, nor did they have to manage a mammoth government whose policies extend into all areas of public and private life. The federal government has, as the saying goes, "bit off more than it can chew."

Journalists typically discuss presidential performance in terms of personality traits: how clever the officeholder is, prior experiences in other political offices and the lessons those experiences taught, or how upbringing shapes the executive's world view. This emphasis on the identity of the president does receive support from some scholars. Political scientist James Barber, for example, proposes that effective presidents will be the ones who both like their job and readily adapt their policies to changing circumstances.[68] Presidents Lyndon Johnson and Richard Nixon failed, Barber suggests, because they saw the office as a burden rather than a blessing, and hence were willing to stick with failed

FIGURE 10.6

Decline in presidential popularity over the first term

The president's popularity typically declines until the year before the next election.

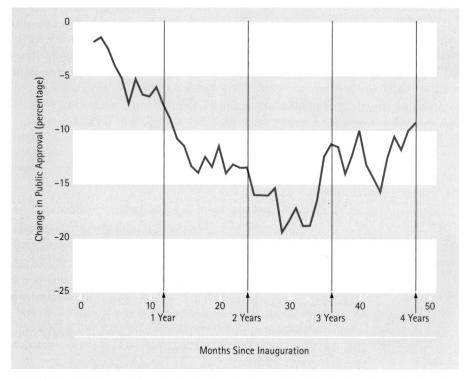

Months Since Inauguration

SOURCE: This figure is taken from Paul Brace and Barbara Hinckley, *Follow the Leader: Opinion Polls and the Modern Presidents* (New York: Basic Books, 1992), p. 33, Fig. 2.3.

policies even after public opinion turned against them. President Eisenhower missed the list of top presidents because, although he enjoyed the job, he waited for others to propose solutions for the nation's problems and so was too passive as a policy maker.

As tempting as explanations based on personality might be, they ignore the extent to which presidential performance depends on the conditions under which the officeholder must act (see the accompanying Election Connection, "Political Time"). We cannot say what Jimmy Carter would have achieved with the overwhelmingly Democratic Congress that Franklin Delano Roosevelt enjoyed, or how FDR would have grappled with the conservative Congress that his successor Harry Truman had to face. We do not know how FDR might have extracted himself from the Vietnam quagmire into which circumstances thrust Lyndon Baines Johnson, or what greatness LBJ might have achieved if faced by the evil of Nazi Germany. But the most recent evidence of how chance events can

Political Time

Franklin D. Roosevelt swept into the White House at a time of crisis. The Great Depression had eaten up savings and investments once possessed by American families, and breadwinners could not win much bread because they could not find jobs. FDR quickly set about trying to help the "forgotten man" after taking office. He guided dozens of bills through Congress in his first 100 days and followed those initial successes with other innovative programs.

Europe descended into an earthshaking world war during FDR's later years. Japan, unhappy with U.S. policies such as expansion in the Pacific Ocean, brought the battle to American shores with a surprise attack on naval bases at Pearl Harbor. FDR thus changed his administration's focus. He placed the nation on the warpath, regulating the economy and building up the military so that the United States could join forces allied against the Axis powers of Germany, Japan, and Italy. During this time, FDR negotiated a close alliance with Britain's prime minister, Winston Churchill, as well as a working alliance with Soviet leader Josef Stalin. Ultimately, the Allies prevailed.

FDR's stunning success fighting both an economic crisis and a military crisis endears him to Americans, and he is remembered as the last "great" American president. His aristocratic profile adorns the nation's dime. What Americans who fondly remember FDR seldom recognize, though, is that this "great president" worked with an extremely helpful Congress. FDR's power and success did not depend on his constitutional privileges, but on the willingness of legislators to pass his many proposals. They did so regularly, but not just because of FDR's shrewd political insights or the merit of his ideas. Rather, they did so because most were Democrats. During FDR's first two years, his

party controlled 73 percent of the House and 63 percent of the Senate. Until the very end of his administration, FDR's party never fell below 61 percent of the House and 63 percent of the Senate. Roosevelt held power in large part because he governed among friends.

Americans also express a fondness for FDR's successor, plain-speaking Harry S. Truman, but few claim he was a "great president." They admire his common sense. They admire his willingness to fight for the common American, urging him to "Give 'em hell, Harry." But the judgment of Truman's administration is not so positive. One drawback was the way Truman conducted foreign policy. Americans feel a certain discomfort with his decision to drop two atomic weapons on Japan, even if they ultimately think he made the right choice. He fought a war in Korea and failed to lessen tensions during America's "Cold War" with the Soviets. He fired popular General Douglas MacArthur after a highly publicized spat. And although Truman championed the idea of providing aid to war-torn nations trying to resist communism, arguing for a policy "to assist free peoples," U.S. efforts to rebuild the European continent are called the Marshall Plan after his secretary of state.[a]

But equally important in explaining Truman's diminished reputation is that he enjoyed few domestic policy successes. Instead, he squabbled with Congress regularly, and important pieces of legislation passed over Truman's veto. The reason why Harry had to give them so much hell is that, unlike FDR, he faced a hostile set of legislators—a coalition of Republicans and conservative southern Democrats. Later in his presidency the House was 57 percent Republican and the Senate was 53 percent Republican.

(continued)

(continued from previous page)

Americans also admire President Jimmy Carter, a Democrat who took executive office in 1976. But Carter's popularity stems from his charitable and diplomatic activities since leaving office. As a president, Carter showed little ability to attract and maintain popular support, and almost no one considers him one of the nation's "great presidents." Yet the cards were stacked against the former Georgia governor before he ever arrived at the White House. The late 1970s were not a time of widespread support for the Democratic party or its principles. Rather, Carter was part of a temporary wave of opposition to the Republicans that grew out of the Watergate scandal, and even then he only barely defeated opponent Gerald Ford. Democrats did control Congress during his tenure, but it was a slim lead, and the Democratic party was sharply divided between rural and urban wings.

Awareness of how the electoral environment shapes presidential success has led some scholars to emphasize that the limits executives face depend on the "political time" in which they serve. According to presidential scholar Stephen Skowronek's influential book *The Politics Presidents Make* (see the list of suggested readings at the end of this chapter), most presidents are so hemmed in by the checks placed on them that they simply cannot satisfy public expectations. As a result, presidents become "great" only when political circumstances allow them to move in a sharply different direction—usually in periods of crisis or right after a critical election upsets the balance of political power (see Chapter 8).

Some presidents do manage to succeed despite attaining office at an unfortunate time. Many people think Theodore Roosevelt was one of the country's most successful presidents; his face towers over visitors to the Mt. Rushmore monument in South Dakota, alongside three nineteenth-century presidents. Yet Roosevelt did not become president through a pivotal election. And some people think other presidents—Eisenhower (for managing the Cold War) or Johnson (for initiating the Great Society and promoting civil rights)—deserve inclusion at the top of the list of presidents. But, dramatic presidential leadership generally seems to require strong party majorities in Congress. Members of a president's party vote with their leader as much as 80 percent of the time. Opposition-party members vote with presidents less than half of the time. Nearly all the "great" presidents enjoyed an imbalanced Congress favoring their party.[b]

Recent events provide a clear illustration of the importance of congressional majorities. During the first two years of President Clinton's administration, he enjoyed a Democratic party majority in both chambers. During this time Congress approved significant components of Clinton's platform: easing voter registration requirements, providing family leave for new parents, and reducing the budget deficit. After Democrats lost their majority in 1994, Clinton was forced to scale back his agenda and accepted welfare proposals that he disliked. To a lesser extent, Vermont Senator James Jeffords's defection from the GOP forced President Bush to curtail his own ambitions (see Chapter 9).

What do you think?

- How can Americans judge the success of a president, if not by the amount of legislation passed through Congress?
- Should voters favor presidential candidates who are likely to get along with Congress, so that they might rise to greatness?

[a] George B. Tindall, *America: A Narrative History.* New York: Norton, 1984, p. 1192.
[b] Charles O. Jones, "Separating to Govern: The American Way," in Byron E. Shafer, ed., *Present Discontents: American Politics in the Very Late 20th Century.* Chatham, NJ: Chatham House, 1997, pp. 56–59.

shape a presidency comes from President George W. Bush, as discussed in the section that follows.

AFTERSHOCK:
UNIFIED IN THE FACE OF TERROR

Americans initially were divided over George W. Bush's presidency, with little more than half approving of his performance. Television comics regularly ridiculed the nation's leader, implying that he lacked intelligence. Other critics were less humorous. They dismissed Bush as an illegitimate leader, one who rose to wealth using family connections and shady stock manipulations, who rose to political prominence based on his father's name, and who rose to the land's highest office in a coup staged by Republican justices on the Supreme Court (see Chapter 1). Democrats in Congress seemed determined to resist him, especially after the Senate switched to their party's control early in Bush's presidency (see Chapter 9). The prospects of a long and successful Bush White House seemed rather dim.

On 9/11, though, the political environment changed and—despite no alteration having occurred in either the president's personality or the congressional balance of power—George W. Bush became a new sort of chief executive. All of a sudden everyone seemed happy with President Bush. Almost 9 out of 10 Americans reported to pollsters that they were satisfied with the job he was doing, a bounce in his ratings that lingered for at least a year.[69] Only two modern presidents have attracted such widespread popularity: Truman after World War II and Bush's father during the Gulf War. Nor was the wave of good feeling limited to regular folk. Democratic and Republican congressional leaders jointly pledged support for Bush, passing legislation giving him significant powers and significant funding to pursue those responsible for 9/11 and to rebuild New York City.

This wave of support may seem odd. President Bush played no role in the emergency efforts that immediately followed the terrorist strike. Nor was his initial response extraordinary—he bounced around a few command centers before returning to the nation's capital to give a brief speech expressing his condolences and vowing to fight back. Why would Bush be so popular all of a sudden? Americans responded to the terrorist attack much as they respond to any other foreign policy crisis: They rally around the flag. In the early days of a foreign affairs crisis, voters usually fall in behind the commander in chief and ignore those who criticize presidential actions. This tendency, often called the **rally 'round the flag effect,** shows up in opinion polls in almost every foreign policy emergency.[70] Between 1950 and 1999, public support for presidents increased by an average of 8 percentage points in the month after a crisis (see Figure 10.7). But President George W. Bush experienced the largest popularity increase ever recorded after the 2001 terrorist attacks; his ratings rivaled Roosevelt's after Pearl Harbor. Americans instinctively pull together to maintain a unified front against a hostile world.

FIGURE 10.7

"Rally 'round the flag" effects

Presidents' gains in popularity average 8 percentage points in the months following crises. Why do you think President Clinton did not experience as large a boost in public support as his predecessors after foreign policy crises?

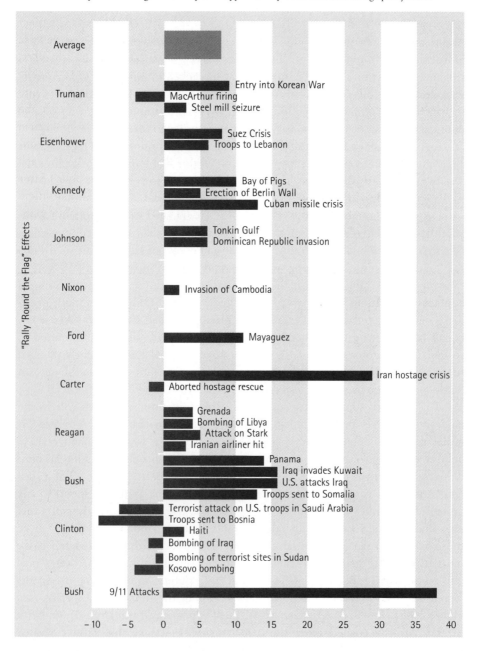

For this reason, a national security threat can present the defining moment in any presidency. It allows leadership at a time when passions run high and political obstacles are minimal. The Bush presidency after 9/11 looked nothing like it had the day before because the political environment, and especially voter support for the president, shifted so dramatically in response to the crisis.

With the new popularity comes a serious price, though: Americans expect to see quick performance. Failure to resolve the crisis can erase or even reverse this initial sympathy.[71] President Carter's popularity dropped significantly when he could not get American hostages back from Iran (see Figure 10.8). The public seems especially ready to hold presidents accountable when war breaks out and American casualties mount. The public supported U.S. entry into both the Korean and Vietnam wars. But when the conflicts dragged on, both Harry Truman and Lyndon Johnson lost so much public support that they decided against running for reelection. The opposition party won the next election in each instance.[72] The Clinton administration provides a more recent example. After Clinton kept troops in Somalia for more than a year, the deaths of 18 soldiers (later dramatized in the book and movie *Black Hawk Down*) cost the president public support, resulting in troop withdrawal.

FIGURE 10.8

Shifts in Carter's popularity during the hostage crisis

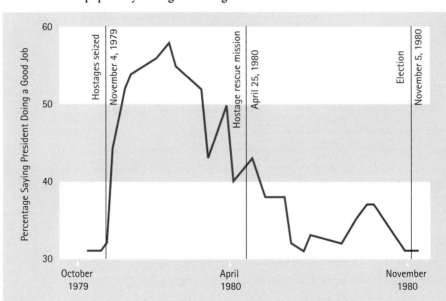

SOURCE: Michael Nelson, ed., *Congressional Quarterly Guide to the Presidency, 1989,* (Washington, DC: CQ Press), 1471.

Presidents may suffer for inaction, not just for their actions. Media coverage shortens the time presidents have to respond to a crisis and increases the number of international events that demand attention in the first place. Satellite television and the Internet supply details about international events to a broader public audience than ever before. Struggles that might have been unknown or ignored in the past are now served regularly on the nightly news. Americans can view intense images of conflict and suffering from anywhere on the planet.

President George H. W. Bush sent troops to Somalia to end internal warfare there, in part because television stations confronted American voters with "the sight of the suffering of the starving people."[68] Similarly, President Clinton felt responsible for resolving the political disorder that was causing widespread suffering in Haiti. He sent in troops to enforce a plan to restore democracy. In the words of one commentator, decisions such as these are "less the result of a rational weighing of need or what is remediable than . . . of what gets on nightly news shows."[73]

President Bush, therefore, faced overwhelming expectations after the 9/11 tragedy, including consoling the bereaved, increasing protections at home, exacting revenge abroad, shoring up the economy, and building international coalitions. He initiated wars with Afghanistan and Iraq—two harbors for terrorists—that pinched the budget and therefore prevented ambitious domestic policy initiatives. Such demands are almost certain to swamp other policy goals.

Yet, after a crisis is over, unity dissolves rapidly, and public attention wanders. Voters implicitly ask, "What have you done for me lately?" Presidents rarely profit from disaster. The increased power that Bush enjoyed after 9/11 only underscores that, however much presidential personality and congressional party balances might shape what a president can do, public opinion is the real power behind the throne in America's new democracy.

CHAPTER SUMMARY

Americans often wonder forlornly why the United States no longer elects great presidents who meet public expectations. They seem to believe that the failure is somehow one of insufficient public control over the political system. Yet most sources of frustration with the executive branch trace back to the demands of the public, or at least to the demands of elected officials who are then rewarded by voters for their behavior.

One reason why modern presidents fail is that they are expected to do so much. The institutions presidents must run and the problems they must solve have grown, yet their formal powers have changed very little. They still rely on cooperation from Congress. Passive presidents receive little praise but much scorn, and a president who preaches patience in the face of social problems risks reprisal from voters at the polls—even though presidents lack the opportunity to leave much of a stamp on government unless they are elected at the right political time.

Electoral considerations help account for the fact that presidents dominate policy making in foreign affairs more than on domestic issues. Voters expect presidents to take the lead, and they support presidents early in a crisis regardless of the actions taken. Only later, if things do not turn out well, do voters penalize poor choices. Voters defer to the president on foreign policy for good reason. The president has an expansive array of analysts and advisers from whom to draw advice (see Chapter 11). Having so much help allows the president to move quickly and secretly to resolve a crisis. If a president seems less capable in domestic policy, it is not due to disregard for public desires and is probably not due to personality quirks. Rather, the limits are imposed primarily by legislators closely tied to diverse voter preferences, the people with whom a president must share power.

KEY TERMS

beltway insiders, p. 339

bully pulpit, p. 318

Cabinet, p. 322

chief of staff, p. 334

Executive Office of the
 President (EOP),
 p. 334

executive agreements,
 p. 324

executive orders,
 p. 327

executive privilege,
 p. 327

honeymoon, p. 320

impeachment, p. 333

independent counsels
 (originally called
 special prosecutor),
 p. 333

Office of Management and
 Budget (OMB),
 p. 320

override, p. 321

pocket veto, p. 322

rally 'round the flag effect,
 p. 343

State of the Union address,
 p. 318

transition, p. 319

treaties, p. 324

two-presidency theory,
 p. 338

veto, p. 320

War Powers Resolution,
 p. 327

White House Office,
 p. 334

SUGGESTED READINGS

Barber, James. *The Presidential Character: Predicting Performance in the White House,* 4th ed. Englewood Cliffs, NJ: Prentice-Hall, 1992. Argues that presidential character affects presidential success.

Jones, Charles O. *The Presidency in a Separated System.* Washington, DC: Brookings, 1994. Examines the role of the president under divided government.

Kernell, Samuel. *Going Public: New Strategies of Presidential Leadership,* 3th ed. Washington,

DC: CQ Press, 1997. Describes the increasing tendency of presidents to use popular appeals to influence legislative processes.

Korn, Jessica. *The Power of Separation: American Constitutionalism and the Myth of the Legislative Veto.* Princeton, NJ: Princeton University Press, 1996. Identifies the many ways in which power is shared between Congress and the executive.

Mayer, Kenneth. *With the Stroke of a Pen: Executive Orders and Presidential Power.* Princeton,

NJ: Princeton University Press, 2001. Study of how presidents use executive orders to make policy.

Neustadt, Richard E. *Presidential Power and the Modern Presidents.* New York: Free Press, 1990. Modern classic on the limits to presidential power.

Silverstein, Gordon. *Imbalance of Powers: Constitutional Interpretation and the Making of American Foreign Policy.* New York: Oxford University Press, 1996. Argues that the president's constitutional authority over foreign policy has not been ceded to Congress.

Skowronek, Stephen. *The Politics Presidents Make: Leadership from John Adams to George Bush.* Cambridge, MA: Harvard University Press, 1993. Provocative analysis of the historical development of the presidency.

Tulis, Jeffrey. *The Rhetorical Presidency.* Princeton, NJ: Princeton University Press, 1987. Contrasts modern presidential rhetoric with that of early presidents. Argues against a rhetorical presidency.

ON THE WEB

The White House
www.whitehouse.gov
The official Web site of the White House offers current and historical information about U.S. presidents.

Center for the Study of the Presidency
www.thepresidency.org
The Center for the Study of the Presidency publishes *Presidential Studies Quarterly* and showcases academic information and links.

National Archives and Records Administration
www.nara.gov/nara/president/address.html
The National Archives and Records Administration provides information about and links to presidential libraries.

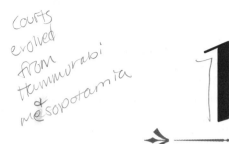

(handwritten:) courts evolved from Hammurabi + Mesopotamia

11

THE BUREAUCRACY

(handwritten:)
Commissions
NRC
FCC federal communications commissions
ITC
EEOC equal opportunity commission
FTC Federal Trade commissions

Amtrak created by gov't -always received subsidies

(handwritten diagram:)
President
→ Department of Justice
    — Bureau eg FBI
→ dpt.
→ dpt.
independent agencies — report directly to presidents e.g. EPA NASA CIA
gov't corporations — self sustained — can sell stock e.g. USPS Sallie May

The Constitution's framers justified their effort to centralize government power by pointing to the threat of enemy attacks. In fact, the first *Federalist Papers* promoting the new Constitution focused almost exclusively on national security, predicting that a strong federal government would deter outsiders from initiating violence. "One government can . . . avail itself of the talents and experience of the ablest men," Publius explained. "It can move on uniform principles of policy. It can harmonize, assimilate, and . . . extend the benefit of its foresight and precautions."[1] No one would wish to oppose such a capable and efficient government, so it would offer "the best security that can be devised against hostilities from abroad."[2]

The framers successfully created their strong federal government, and its power has only grown more vast with time (see Chapter 3). Indeed, it has expanded well beyond its prime responsibility—defending Americans against external threats—to influence a wide-ranging set of domestic social policies and economic conditions (see Chapter 15). It spends well over $1 trillion every year and directly employs 2 million people. Yet in 2001 this massive enterprise known as "the federal government" failed spectacularly at carrying out its most basic purpose: keeping Americans safe. An enemy force of 19 young men penetrated the nation's borders and, equipped only with bladed weapons, managed to murder thousands of civilians on September 11 (see Chapter 1).

When Americans finished reeling from the initial shock of the 9/11 tragedy, they quickly asked how federal officials could have allowed something so terrible to happen. Was the slaughter unavoidable, or did the feds commit a colossal blunder? Seeking answers, government agencies probed their internal records and reports. Congress initiated various investigations. Journalists began probing their government sources and their media archives. The soul searching is still unfinished and the conclusions undeveloped. Yet it is already clear that federal officials were horribly unprepared for terrorism—not only the specific kind the United States experienced, but other possible assaults as well—despite having every reason to suspect that some sort of terrorist violence was coming. Government agencies failed to exhibit the level of ability, experience, unity, and foresight that the framers promised. Indeed, numerous federal policies directly or indirectly contributed to the vulnerability of Americans by (1) being too passive when dealing with those who organized the attacks, (2) permitting foreigners to roam around the United States illegally, and (3) failing to maintain sufficient vigilance that they might have noticed the activities of terrorist cells operating in the United States.

Let's start with the planning. Just about everyone accepts that Osama bin Laden, leader of the terrorist network Al-Qaeda, masterminded the 9/11 attacks. Bin Laden had already been blamed for several other violent attacks on Americans, so why was he available to carry out another one? Because the United States missed several opportunities to end the man's career. For example, Sudan offered to arrest bin Laden in 1996 and hand him over to the United States or a U.S. ally. U.S. intelligence services lacked sufficient evidence to prosecute him domestically, though, and American diplomats could not or would not persuade Saudi Arabia's royal family (who had a legal basis for incarcerating or even executing bin Laden) to do their dirty work for them.[3] Later, after hard evidence of bin Laden's violent activities built up, the Central Intelligence Agency funded and trained at least three foreign commando teams to capture or kill the terrorist leader—but they never got a crack at him. Indeed, the team stationed in Pakistan had be disbanded prematurely because an unanticipated military coup overturned the Parkistani government.[4]

The Clinton administration was never willing to send American special forces after bin Laden, which would have been militarily, diplomatically, and perhaps politically risky. Instead, it kept two submarines in the Persian Gulf waiting for intelligence information pinpointing where Osama bin Laden would be six to ten hours later—so that they could fire cruise missiles at him. The intelligence had to be incredibly precise, though, since such missiles may not kill people standing within 100 yards of where they strike. The subs only fired once, at a spot near the Afghan town of Khost, and missed bin Laden by a few hours. The attack not only put the terrorist leader on alert to be more careful, it was so ineffectual that it turned him into an Arab folk hero and came to be regarded "as the greatest foreign policy blunder of the Clinton presidency."[5]

Nor was the United States particularly effective at dealing with the nation that harbored bin Laden after he was exiled from Sudan: Afghanistan. The United States originally funded the militant Islamic groups and *mujaheddin* religious warriors who created Afghanistan's hard-line Taliban government. Americans provided them with weapons and helped build their fortresses because they were anti-Russian. After the Taliban seized power, State Department spokesman Glyn Davies reportedly found "nothing objectionable" in their decision to impose strict Islamic law—which included castrating and killing the nation's former president.[6] The Clinton administration eventually demanded that Taliban leaders stop sheltering Osama bin Laden's activities, but it never backed up the threats and "was not serious about this whole thing."[7] For example, the United States never added Afghanistan to its list of terrorist sponsors. Clinton's secretary of state, Madeleine Albright, explains why the administration was so passive even after intelligence services traced bin Laden to specific terrorist attacks: "Those were happening overseas and while there were Americans who died, there were not thousands and it did not happen on U.S. soil."[8]

Now let's turn to what happened when enemy combatants finally did bring violence to American soil. Investigators still do not know how all of the 19 terrorists penetrated national borders. One reason for their uncertainty is that the border contains so many holes that it is hard to narrow down the possibilities. For example, 15,000 universities, colleges and vocational schools sponsor foreign students, yet the Immigration and Naturalization Service did not keep track of those visiting on student visas and completely ignored second-tier schools (including those that taught aviation!). One 9/11 hijacker had a student visa but never showed up for class. The level of scrutiny for tourist and business visas was even scantier. As a result, the INS in 2001 could not track more than 3 million foreign nationals who were illegally overstaying their visas in the United States, including three of the 9/11 hijackers. Two of the terrorists, including Mohamed Atta (see Chapter 1), were able to study in flight schools even thought they possessed tourist visas rather than student visas—because the law did not require anyone to check their status.[9] Indeed, six months after the attacks the INS managed to embarrass itself again by sending out visa approvals for two of the long-dead hijackers.[10]

What if one of the terrorists had not bothered to obtain a visa? Reports indicate that, in 2001, he would have faced little difficulty crossing the border from Canada (where an estimated 50 terror groups operate).[11] Apparently only 334 agents policed America's entire northern border, which represented about one agent per each 12-mile stretch. The only physical barrier in place at some entry points, between midnight and 8 am, was a string of orange cones to alert drivers that they were illegally crossing a boundary line. "The nice ones will put the cones back after driving through," explains U.S. Senator Byron Dorgan of North Dakota.[12] Much of the stretch contains cameras, but these would not stop a determined or well-trained terrorist. As one former Border Patrol agent put it, "I've never known a camera that can go down a pole and catch somebody."[13] And as horrible as the 9/11 attacks were, Americans may be lucky that the terrorists only used jetliners as their weapons of mass destruction, rather than infiltrating the United States with chemical or biological agents—because a federal commission estimated that the Customs Service only checks around 2 percent of the cargo shipments and vehicles crossing the border.[14] The end result of these policies? "Lord knows who is getting through and what is getting through."[15]

Once the terrorists penetrated the American border, they had to hide from law-enforcement agencies. This, too, was not terribly hard given the way federal bureaucracies operated. The INS, for example, opened a counterterrorism office in 1997, after the first terrorist attack on the World Trade Center—the agency only employed a few thousand agents for "internal enforcement" of immigration laws. Of course, the terrorists did not try to slip weapons directly into a federal building; they steered jetliners at them. But if they had tried to smuggle a weapon into a federal building, the task would have been rather easy. Although the federal government spent more than $1.2 billion to make workplaces safer after the 1995 Oklahoma City bombing (see Chapter 13), the effort fell far short. Undercover

Under Friendly Fire
More than any other agency, the Federal Bureau of Investigation faced withering criticism in the wake of 9/11 for being sluggish and antiquated. But poor government performance is not the same thing as unresponsiveness. Did the FBI's 1990s focus on stopping drugs lack popular support?

agents successfully slipped weapons past guards at 19 federal buildings, including guards at the CIA, the Justice Department, and the Pentagon. Perhaps the government should have spent more than $1.2 billion on security, but not all of the ineffectiveness came from inadequate funds. The national government's largest real-estate holder, the General Services Administration, reportedly spent $900,000 earmarked for security upgrades on unrelated programs. An audit found that dozens of detection tools remained unpacked two years after they had been purchased.[16]

The National Security Agency, meanwhile, has an operational budget twice as large as that of the CIA: $7 billion per year. Yet the funding is overwhelmingly dedicated to electronic snooping. An NSA listening post apparently processes 2 million communications in an hour, yet the NSA falls far short on the number of analysts who would be needed to sift through the data. It only employs linguists in 115 of the globe's 6500 languages, and it cut personnel during the 1990s. "We don't come close to processing, analyzing, and disseminating the intelligence we collect right now," a former congressional staffer claims. Perhaps the greatest irony: The NSA possessed all this expensive hardware to keep Americans secure, and yet the terrorists who took out one side of the Pentagon apparently lived right outside the agency's gates in Maryland, and patronized the same health clubs and groceries as NSA agents.[17]

Nor was the Federal Bureau of Investigation much more of a threat. Indeed, the FBI came in for the harshest criticism in the wake of 9/11, because it quickly became clear that the nation's chief law-enforcement agency did not have the capacity to protect Americans from terrorism. The FBI's offices were antiquated, using computers that were more than four years old with low-speed Internet connections. Lots of important FBI data appeared only on paper.[18] The FBI lacked the staff to translate Arabic documents or recordings, causing evidence to disappear into files without being analyzed.[19] It engaged in political turf wars with the CIA, which limited the flow of information between agencies. It was primarily oriented toward investigating crimes after they had already been committed, and it was obsessed with politically popular initiatives such as the drug war.

Perhaps most demoralizing, the FBI exhibited excessive bureaucratic caution when investigating potential terrorists. More than one field agent noted suspicious activities before 9/11 that indicated a possible terrorist hijacking plot, but no one followed up on their warnings. One Phoenix agent's report languished in the FBI chain of command. The FBI's Minnesota branch learned that Moroccan Islamic extremist Zacarias Moussaoui had paid cash to a flight school to learn how to pilot passenger jets, but they did not take him into custody. Indeed, supervisors at FBI headquarters there reportedly suppressed investigator requests for a search warrant that would have given them access to Moussaoui's laptop and belongings.[20] Two of the actual 9/11 hijackers—men known for years by the CIA to be potentially dangerous—lived with an FBI informant in San Diego while they took their flight lessons. The informant reported their presence, but his FBI case officer never investigated the identity of the mysterious Saudi visitors living with his informant.[21] FBI Director Robert Mueller eventually acknowledged that, had it put together more adeptly all of the information it possessed, the FBI probably would have identified at least some of the 9/11 hijackers.[22]

THINK ABOUT THE COMPLEX ORGANIZATIONAL EFFORT that was necessary to carry out the 2001 terrorist attacks. Someone had to plan for and bankroll the expedition without tipping off American intelligence officers. The 19 hijackers needed to enter the country in a way that would not raise suspicion and would not link them together as a terrorist cell. Some had to live in the United States and learn to pilot transcontinental jets without attracting attention. They needed to board four separate planes, at multiple airports, armed with enough knives and box cutters to take control of each jetliner. Finally, they needed to commandeer those jets and steer them toward important landmarks without being noticed and intercepted.

It's a complex process, fraught with risk because so many things could go wrong. Yet nothing went wrong. Three of the hijacker crews succeeded, while the fourth failed only because of heroism on the part of their victims. Why? All indications are that the mission succeeded because America's government failed. Even those loyal to federal law-enforcement agencies have agreed that they botched the key task of protecting Americans from attacks from abroad. One former FBI official called the incident "the greatest counterterrorism screwup in U.S. history." The NSA, the CIA, and the FBI "are all tasked with getting this kind of information," he argued. "Billions and billions of dollars are spent on this. And if we can't get it, there's something very, very wrong."[23]

Americans might have reacted to this litany of failures on the part of the federal law-enforcement bureaucracy by becoming more cynical about the national government. They might have asked why national officials spend so much time trying to regulate domestic affairs that the states used to manage on their own. They might have challenged federal law-enforcement officials for expending so much effort prosecuting "victimless" or nonviolent crimes. They might have demanded angrily to know what happened to the trillions of dollars that, in the 1990s, the federal government either taxed from citizens or borrowed in their name. Yet the American public did none of these things.

Rather, support for the national government grew. The proportion of Americans saying that they trusted the federal government jumped upward.[24] Conservatives once known for demanding smaller government suddenly altered their tone. "September 11 has changed everything," explained the president of one conservative think tank.[25] Progressives crowed victory in their battle to increase the size of government. As one *Washington Post* commentary, by a Democrat serving in the U.S. Senate, declared, "Big Government Looks Better Now." Senator Charles Schumer wrote that "those who believe the federal government should shrink have had the upper hand [since 1980]. Sept. 11 changed all that. For the foreseeable future, the federal government will have to grow." In language reminiscent of the appeal for centralized government that appeared in the *Federalist Papers*, Schumer promised, "Unity of action and purpose is required, and only the federal government can provide it."[26] Recognizing the new public demands, President Bush proposed spending more than $2 trillion in his 2003 budget.

Why didn't Americans react with shock and outrage against the law-enforcement bureaucracy that failed them? Some of their passive acceptance may reflect the general tendency of nations to withhold internal criticism and pull together when they are under attack (see Chapter 10). More likely, though, Americans instinctively recognized the core point that this chapter will develop in detail: They should not be surprised when government institutions fail to accomplish their missions, because that is the nature of bureaucracy. Government institutions tend to be inefficient because of how they are organized, and the U.S. government is even less effective than usual.

Is our argument, then, that Americans should shrink the national government and "stop throwing good money after bad"? Not necessarily. Our point is that both the successes and disappointments of American institutions come from the same source: the responsiveness of government to elections, to public opinion, and to political pressures. The same responsiveness to political goals that causes American institutions to fail also allows them to respond quickly when the public is aroused—as illustrated by the massive reorganization of American law-enforcement and security agencies that followed the 9/11 attacks. Americans may not always like the performance of their government, but they nonetheless usually receive the type of government they ask for.

STRUCTURE OF THE
FEDERAL BUREAUCRACY

The president of the United States serves as the chief executive of the government, the person who bears primary responsibility for implementing the nation's laws. However, the nation's legal code is incredibly complex, and the tasks necessary to execute those laws are far more complicated than one person could hope to carry out—or even to oversee. Nor could the president's few immediate advisers do an adequate job. Carrying out the country's rules and regulations requires an extensive network of employees living in every state, as well as a giant concentration of employees in Washington, D.C. The name for this structure of employees is the federal **bureaucracy.**

The federal government encompasses hundreds of agencies, most grouped under 1 of 15 **departments,** collections of federal agencies that report to a secretary who serves in the president's Cabinet. Some 63 **independent agencies,** such as the Central Intelligence Agency and the Environmental Protection Agency, are free-standing entities that report either to the president or to a board.[27] Finally, there are 27 **government corporations,** independent organizations that fulfill business-related functions.[28] Examples of government corporations include the Federal Deposit Insurance Corporation, which insures bank deposits, and the National Railroad Passenger Corporation, which runs Amtrak.

Bureaucrats, the people who staff government bureaus and agencies, do not run for election, nor does the Constitution grant them any formal authority. Yet the decisions they make in applying laws to real-life circumstances give them a unique political power, to the point where scholars often treat the bureaucracy as though it were a separate branch of government. An exasperated President Harry Truman once said, "All the president is, is a glorified public relations man who spends his time flattering, kissing, and kicking people to get them to do what they are supposed to do anyway." He was especially frustrated "when it comes to these bureaucrats."[29] Presidents have a difficult time managing the bureaucracy because it is filled with inexperienced political appointees and low-prestige civil servants.

Two other barriers also stand in the way of presidential influence over the bureaucracy. First, by law many policy-making agencies in the executive branch need not answer directly to the president. Second, the president is seldom the only "boss" that bureaucrats have. They also answer to Congress, to special interests, and (at least indirectly) to the voting public. Dividing responsibility in this fashion means that bureaucrats often can ignore the boss or play one boss off against the others.

WHY THE BUREAUCRACY IS UNRESPONSIVE

Bureaucracies are essential to governmental action. Laws become effective only when an agency implements them. Without some kind of organization, government cannot build roads, operate schools, put out fires, fight wars, distribute social security checks, or do the thousands of other things Americans expect. Ideally a bureaucracy is organized to carry out assigned tasks efficiently. Staff members are selected for their ability to do their jobs. Each reports to a superior, and ultimate authority is exercised by the head of the agency. The bureaucracy provides each worker with the supplies necessary to get the job done. When all works perfectly, that is, bureaucracies exhibit unity, focus, and power.[30]

Yet Americans often express frustration that the federal bureaucracy is arrogant and unresponsive. Three-fourths of all Americans think "people in the government waste a lot of money we pay in taxes" (see Figure 11.1). The bureaucracy is the big-government monolith that many disparage and some fear: the regulators, the tax collectors, and the social engineers. It is the villain of novels, movies, and television shows. Several presidents won office by campaigning against the government, promising to get the bureaucracy under control. Ronald Reagan's message was perhaps the most stark, as in this oft-quoted line: "Government is not the solution to our problem. Government *is* the problem."[31] But the size and power of government almost never shrinks; the sense of public vulnerability seldom diminishes.

Ironically, the public is partly to blame for their own sense of helplessness. The number of functionaries has greatly increased with the expansion of federal government responsibility, but few of these workers answer directly to elected national leaders. Most employment growth has occurred at state and local levels (see Figure 11.2). Because these positions often grow out of federal mandates or programs, the bureaucrats are not fully answerable to elected officials at any specific level of government. Many private contractors also perform tasks funded by government agencies. The decision to construct this "shadow government," over which elected federal officials exert only indirect influence, is a policy choice resulting from conflicting public demands. The voting populace opposes growth in the federal bureaucracy but still expects national leaders to accomplish an increasing number of tasks.

FIGURE 11.1

The public thinks there is a lot of waste in government

Survey respondents were asked the following question: "Do you think that people in the government waste a lot of money we pay in taxes, waste some of it, or don't waste very much of it?" What do you think? Is the public justified in its belief that the government wastes a lot of money?

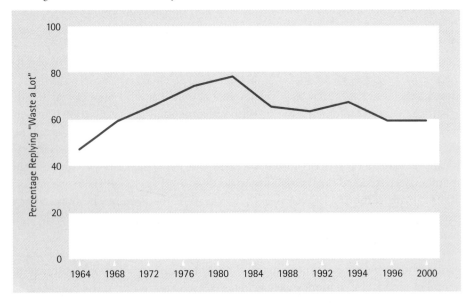

SOURCE: National Election Study, 1948–1998 Cumulative Data File, conducted by the Center for Political Studies at the University of Michigan.

THE BUREAUCRACY PROBLEM

Although the ideal bureaucracy has tremendous potential, many forces inhibit perfection. Some of these flaws are inherent in all bureaucracies: They are slow to change, they have a tendency to expand, and performance is difficult to measure by outsiders. Other flaws, however, reflect the demands imposed on government bureaucrats through democratic elections: They often work under impossible expectations or debilitating limits. Taken together, these flaws create what is known as the "bureaucracy problem."[32]

SLOW TO CHANGE   Any large governmental organization has standard deci-sion-making procedures. Standardization is essential if large numbers of people are to coordinate their work toward some common end. Otherwise, staff would be so confused they soon would be unable to do anything. Institutional habits are hard to break, though, so bureaucracies are slow to adapt.[33] The U.S. Customs Service issued forms in the 1970s that "have not changed to any great extent since

FIGURE 11.2

Government employment, 1946–1997

The number of state and local employees has increased, but the number of federal employees has remained about the same. Note that federal government employment figures include civilians only. Active-duty military personnel appear in a separate category.

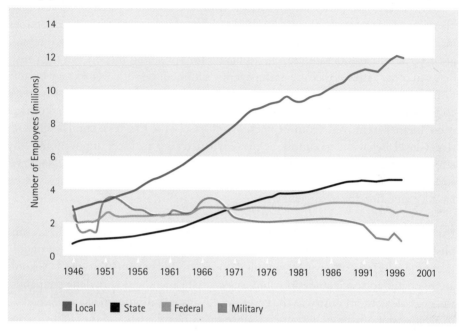

SOURCES: U.S. Bureau of the Census, *Historical Statistics of the United States: Colonial Times to 1970* (Washington, DC: GPO, 1975), pp. 1100, 1141; Advisory Commission on Intergovernmental Relations, *Significant Features of Fiscal Federalism, 1994* (Washington, DC: ACIR, 1994), Table E; Harold W. Stanley and Richard G. Niemi, *Vital Statistics on American Politics,* 4th ed. (Washington, DC: CQ Press, 1994), pp. 359–360; *Statistical Abstract of the United States, 1999,* Tables 534 and 578.

1790, and merchant vessels today are required to report on the number of guns mounted."[34] As one humorist observed, "Bureaucracy defends the status quo long past the time when the quo has lost its status."[35]

EXPANSIONARY TENDENCIES Once bureaucracies are created to address problems, they generally try to expand so they can address them better. Government agencies nearly always feel they need more money, more personnel, and more time to perform effectively.[36] The head of the Forest Service once exclaimed to a congressional committee: "Mr. Chairman, you would not think that it would be proper for me to be in charge of this work and not be enthusiastic about it and not think that I ought to have more money, would you? I have been in it for thirty years, and I believe in it."[37]

DIFFICULTY MEASURING PERFORMANCE   Measuring the performance of government agencies from the outside is difficult, sometimes almost impossible.[38] One might observe the social conditions agencies must address, but it is hard to know either (1) what conditions would be like without the agency's actions or (2) what an agency reasonably could accomplish given its resources.

The streets and parks may be strewn with litter, but are garbage collectors to blame for performing badly? Is City Hall to blame for funding garbage collections inadequately (and if so, is the problem low taxes or waste elsewhere in the budget)? Or are inconsiderate citizens to blame for spreading more trash than residents in other cities do? Not even an agency's immediate supervisors may be able to make these sorts of judgments without expensive studies, perhaps of garbage collection in other cities or of the citizenry's sanitation habits. An elected official even further removed from collection efforts, who has less familiarity with street-level behavior, is almost helpless when trying to force innovations. Any attempt likely would anger employee unions and politically connected supervisors more than it would please inattentive voters. As a result, bureaucracies often have a reputation for inefficiency.

IMPOSSIBILITY OF TASKS   Most governmental tasks are difficult to accomplish. If they were easy, someone other than the government would have undertaken the job! Tasks are usually complex, funds limited, and goals vague.[39] Schools are expected to teach students—but as society changes and knowledge expands, the possible content outpaces the resources. Transportation agencies are expected to achieve smooth-flowing traffic—but so many people demand the right to drive that avoiding bottlenecks would require paving almost everything. The Environmental Protection Agency is supposed to combat pollutants—but nearly all human activity pollutes, and citizens resist inconveniences that limit their own waste. With such conflicting responsibilities, agencies may have no hope of satisfying everyone.

RED TAPE   British bureaucrats once bound government and legal documents in a sticky, reddish tape, so that anyone who wanted to access a file would have to cut through the wrapping first. Today, the phrase *red tape* refers to any delay imposed by a government agency, the proverbial "forms filled out in triplicate" and "bureaucratic runaround" about which so many people complain.

Obviously, individual customers experience numerous delays and must surmount numerous barriers when they seek assistance from government. These inconveniences often lead regular citizens to conclude that agencies are unresponsive to the public, and perhaps even malicious. To an extent this perception may be correct. Certainly, there are times when an agency creates red tape to limit the number of people who take advantage of a program or so that individual officials can "cut through the tape" quickly in exchange for rewards ranging from gratitude or flirtations all the way to political favors or even bribes.

But this sort of chicanery is almost certainly the exception rather than the rule. Complaints overlook the fact that most red tape comes from elected officials, who require detailed documentation to explain spending and who force elaborate agency practices to promote political goals. As one analyst has observed, "One person's red tape may be another's treasured procedural safeguard."[40] Bureaucracies seem unresponsive to individual members of the public precisely because they are excessively responsive to public demands expressed through elected officials.

People often complain, for example, that it takes forever to get a bridge repaired. But bridge repair can be politically complicated. The design of the replacement bridge must be acceptable to neighbors. If the bridge has been designated an historical landmark—as have a surprising number of bridges—the local historical commission must approve. The agency, when letting contracts, must advertise the job and allow time for the submission of bids. To avoid accusations of political favoritism, published criteria must guide the choice of contractors. And regulators must supervise the repairs themselves—not only to ensure quality, but perhaps also to ensure worker safety or avoid environmental damage. Once again, a common bureaucratic problem is caused not by malice but by political demands that trace back to the public.

BUREAUCRACY IN AMERICA

The bureaucracy problem exists in all countries, but American bureaucracies have special problems that are rooted in the country's unusual political history. U.S. bureaucracies had a difficult beginning. They were built with patronage and modernized slowly through "bottom-up" civil service reforms.

DIFFICULT BEGINNINGS American bureaucrats lack the noble heritage of their counterparts in other industrialized countries, where government departments evolved out of the household of the king, queen, or emperor. The lineage of federal bureaucrats in the United States is far less distinguished. Few American parents dream of the day when their children will grow up to be bureaucrats! The framers could not even agree on where to put the people who would run the new national government. Finally, as part of a compromise, they agreed to locate the home of the federal government, the District of Columbia, on the Maryland–Virginia border. The land Congress had chosen was swampy and miserable. Visitors complained that it was thick with "contaminated vapour," which produced "agues and other complaints."[41] If the government were to attract quality workers, location would not be its main selling point.

MOUNTAINS OF PATRONAGE President Andrew Jackson's administration pioneered the use of federal jobs as a political reward, or source of **patronage.** The practice of hiring workers on the basis of party loyalty became known as the

spoils system when New York Senator William Marcy attacked Jackson for seeing "nothing wrong in the rule that to the victor belong the spoils."[42]

Politicians in both parties quickly saw that the spoils system suited their needs, because it allowed them to use tax revenue as an indirect payment to campaign workers who took on arduous jobs such as passing out pamphlets, organizing rallies, and getting people out to vote.[43] The New York machine politician George Washington Plunkitt explained the logic in this way: "You can't keep an organization together without patronage. Men ain't in politics for nothin'. They want to get somethin' out of it."[44] Patronage also made it easier for parties to raise large amounts of cash to fund campaigns. Government workers would receive open requests for political donations, knowing that failure to contribute their share could result in dismissal.[45] Politicians considered these practices a natural and legitimate part of politics.

Looking back on American political history, many scholars have found much to praise in the old spoils system.[46] For one thing, it helped immigrants adjust to the realities of urban life in the United States. "I think there's got to be in every ward somebody that any bloke can come to—no matter what he's done—and get help," said one Boston politician. "Help, you understand; none of your law and your justice, but help."[47] Some help took the form of jobs. Irish immigrants were particularly good at using politics to get ahead. In Chicago, the percentage of public school principals of Irish background rose from 3 percent in the 1860s to 25 percent in 1914. In San Francisco, it climbed from 4 percent to 34 percent over a similar period.[48] Affirmative action programs work much the same way; they allow disadvantaged groups to use their political leverage to gain a toehold in the economic and social mainstream.[49]

The spoils system nonetheless undermined the image of American bureaucracies. Education, training, and experience counted for little, and jobholders changed each time a new party came to power. As one Democratic leader joked after his party had been in power for years, a bureaucrat was "a Democrat who holds some office that a Republican wants."[50] The many decades of patronage politics have left an antibureaucratic legacy that continues to the present day. Not only do Americans consider government wasteful, they also do not grant federal workers much credibility.

BOTTOM-UP REFORM   Civil service reformers gradually eroded the spoils system. In the 1880s, these reformers—a group of professors, journalists, clerics, and business leaders—went under the unflattering name ***mugwumps***.* The reformers argued that government officials should be chosen on the basis of merit,

---

*Originally a sarcastic term of abuse, the name is a modification of a Native American word meaning "great man" or "chief."

not political connections. Mugwumps refused to back either political party, preferring to endorse reformers in both—leading to the quip that their "mugs" peered over one side of the fence while their "wumps" stuck out over the other.

The mugwumps won a succession of victories that gradually changed the system. Their first major breakthrough came in 1881 when President James Garfield was assassinated by a mentally disturbed man said to be a disappointed office seeker. Public scrutiny focused on the new president, Chester A. Arthur, who had once served as New York's customs collector and seemed to personify the spoils system. But the demand for reform swept the country, so Congress passed in 1883—and Arthur signed—the **Pendleton Act,** creating a Civil Service Commission to set up qualifications, examinations, and procedures for filling jobs.

Civil service reform occurred from the bottom up. Requirements initially applied mainly to lower-level, less-skilled jobs—those who swept the floors and typed government forms. Gradually, higher-level positions fell under the civil service system. Such additions were especially plentiful when the party in power expected defeat in the next election. By making a job part of the civil service, soon-to-be-ousted presidents blanketed in the position, making it impossible for their successors to replace an unsupportive employee. Reform became nearly complete when, in 1939, Congress passed the **Hatch Act** barring federal employees from campaigning and solicitation. The mountains of patronage were all but worn away.

Patronage still survives in the American political system, but primarily among the most prestigious jobs. Those include most members of the White House staff, the heads of most departments and agencies, and the members of most government boards and commissions. Political appointees also predominate in the upper levels of individual agencies and departments, inhabiting offices that bear such titles as deputy secretary, undersecretary, deputy undersecretary, assistant secretary, deputy assistant secretary, and special assistant. The estimated number of these top-level agency appointees grew from less than 500 in 1960 to nearly 2500 in 1998. Add the White House staff, and the total number of high-ranking patronage positions is estimated to be close to 3000.[51]

The president's ability to recruit political allies for the top levels of government has both advantages and disadvantages. On the positive side, it allows newly elected presidents to enlist people with innovative ideas, people who embrace their values and will lead agencies with these political goals in mind. For example, think-tank experts and business leaders helped design President Reagan's dramatic budget plans.

Yet the simultaneous arrival of so many new faces complicates the coordination of government. European and Japanese governments are marked by close, informal, long-time associations among leading administrators. In the United States, the average presidential appointee leaves office after only a little more than

2 years; almost a third leave in less than 18 months.[52] By the time they learn enough about an agency to lead it well, political appointees usually leave for other government posts or for better-paying jobs in the private sector. As public administration expert Leonard White once observed, "The previous experience of federal Secretaries does not usually prepare them to exercise quick and effective leadership."[53]

With rapid change in personnel, governmental memory becomes as limited as that of an antiquated computer. One Japanese trade specialist who negotiated with the United States observed that "in the case of the United States, almost all of their negotiators seem like they came in just yesterday."[54] At one point in 1994, the differing styles of top Japanese and U.S. bureaucrats created a relationship so abrasive that the two countries broke off trade negotiations on the eve of a summit meeting.

Worst of all, the denial of most top-level positions to regular civil servants makes government work an unattractive career for intelligent, ambitious young people. In Japan, many of the top students graduating from the country's most prestigious law schools know that eventually they can reach the highest levels of government through bureaucratic service. But the upper echelons of the U.S. government are not part of the career ladder.

OUTSIDE INFLUENCES ON THE EXECUTIVE BRANCH

The federal bureaucracy is difficult to control from the White House because of the way it was and is structured. However, presidents also struggle to direct the bureaucracy because political actors outside the executive branch influence agency behavior. In particular, government employees are also responsive to members of Congress, to influential interest groups, and to public expectations.

CONGRESS AND THE BUREAUCRACY

Everyone knows that no one should have more than one boss. When two or more people can tell someone what to do, signals get confused, delays ensue, and accountability suffers. It also becomes possible for employees to play one boss off against the other. However, the separation of powers ensures that every federal bureaucrat has many bosses. Presidents may appoint federal employees and otherwise execute policies, but Congress formally creates and funds government agencies. With Congress divided into House and Senate, and each chamber divided into many committees, bureaucrats often find themselves reporting to multiple bosses, each demanding and politically astute. This clamor for responsiveness from so many quarters means that the bureaucracy need not always give in to presidential demands or to congressional ones.

THE CONFIRMATION PROCESS Congressional influence begins with the selection of executive department officers. The Senate's advice-and-consent power has long given Congress a voice in administrative matters. One mechanism for exercising influence is the practice of **senatorial courtesy,** an informal rule that sometimes allows senators to block potential nominees for positions within their states or regions. This practice allows senators to protect their political bases by controlling patronage and gives them indirect control over administrative practices.

Confirmation battles sometimes receive extensive media attention and so have become a new form of electioneering. Little-known senators can rise to national attention through their advocacy or opposition exhibited in confirmation hearings. Votes on whether to confirm a particular nominee also can become a campaign issue. For this reason, senators demand greater influence than that permitted by traditional courtesies. Senators now want public assurances that presidential nominees will take acceptable policy positions, do not have conflicts of interest that will prevent successful performance of their public duties, and have not acted contrary to laws or conventional moral norms.

The Senate rejected George H. W. Bush's nomination of John Tower as secretary of defense because of an acknowledged drinking problem. It forced Bill Clinton to withdraw the nomination of Zoe Baird as attorney general because she had not paid the required social security taxes for her housemaid. It denied confirmation of Henry Foster as Clinton's surgeon general because he had performed 39 abortions. George W. Bush's appointee for attorney general, former Missouri Senator John Ashcroft, endured intense scrutiny for exercising his senatorial courtesy power to slow the advancement of an African American judge he considered soft on capital punishment. Ashcroft also had to convince pro-choice senators that his strong pro-life stance would not prevent him from honoring the constitutional protections enjoyed by abortion clinics and their clients.

The Senate still rarely rejects presidential nominees. Yet the new, more election-driven confirmation process has had important consequences for administration. To decrease the likelihood of rejection, the White House must interview potential nominees at length, ask the FBI to undertake extensive background checks, and defend nominees against exhaustive senatorial scrutiny. When John Kennedy was president, the average nominee was confirmed in less than two and a half months. The confirmation of Bill Clinton's nominees required, on average, more than three times that long (see Figure 11.3).

AGENCY REORGANIZATION Congress often interferes with agency organization—for example, by opposing presidential proposals to reorganize executive departments. Congress resists change because each agency reports to a specific congressional committee, and these committees are frequently protective of their

FIGURE 11.3

Average time it takes presidential appointees to be confirmed

It has taken longer in recent years for presidential appointees to be confirmed. What role might elections have played in this trend?

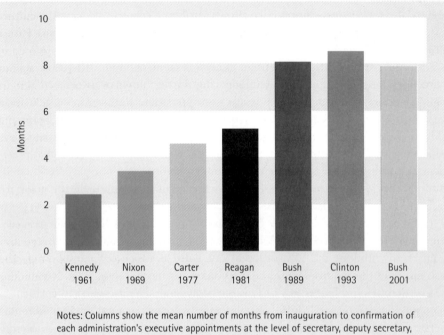

Notes: Columns show the mean number of months from inauguration to confirmation of each administration's executive appointments at the level of secretary, deputy secretary, undersecretary, and assistant secretary.

SOURCE: Paul Light, *Thickening Government* (Washington, DC: Brookings, 1995) p. 68; and Brookings Institution Presidential Appointee Initiative Press Release, "Critical Posts in the Bush Administration Remain Vacant as Congressional Session Nears End," December 18, 2001.

power, which allows them to serve constituencies back home. They therefore typically resist reorganization, no matter how redundant or antiquated existing organizational structures might be.[55] For example, Jimmy Carter proposed shifting worker training programs from the Department of Labor to the newly created Department of Education. But powerful senators defeated the proposal because they wanted to keep the programs within their committee's jurisdiction.[56] As seen at the beginning of Chapter 10, the same thing occurred when Vice President Gore proposed to move the DEA and ATF to the FBI.

LEGISLATIVE DETAIL   Congress sometimes writes detailed legislation outlining an agency's specific legal responsibilities. Even legislation proposed by the president or by a specific agency will be revised extensively by Congress, mainly by the relevant committees.[57] Sometimes Congress invites an agency's clients to sue if they are discontented with their treatment. American bureaucracies therefore have limited authority over the jobs they do.

Legislative politics can produce absurd results. For over a decade, critics have ridiculed laws that give the Agriculture Department authority to regulate sausage pizzas but give the Food and Drug Administration authority to regulate cheese pizzas. Agriculture receives its mandates from the House and Senate Agriculture committees, while the FDA operates under legislation authored by the House Commerce Committee and the Senate Human Resources Committee. No committee wants to give up its slice of the pizza pie, so the odd division of agency responsibilities remains unresolved. The result, according to one report, "hinders the government's efforts to efficiently and effectively protect consumers from unsafe food."[58] The confusion also makes it rather difficult for a voter to figure out whom to blame if she gets sick after ordering a pan pizza with sausage and extra cheese!

BUDGETARY CONTROL Every year each agency prepares a budget for the president to submit to Congress. That budget can go up or down at any stage in the legislative process, and with limited revenues, the fear is that it will drop substantially. One or two powerful congressional enemies can make an agency's experience unpleasant, and an agency whose budget request ignores the desires of important players in the appropriations process may jeopardize its funding. Congress therefore indirectly influences agency spending decisions.

Sometimes Congress influences agency policies more directly. To ensure that agencies spend monies in ways consistent with congressional preferences, significant portions of many agency budgets are subject to an earmark, a very specific designation for how to spend funds. Some legislation even specifies particular congressional districts.

Earmarking seems to be on the increase. At one time Congress let the scientific community decide national research priorities, but between 1980 and 1995, the amount of research dollars earmarked for specific projects skyrocketed from $11 million to $875 million, often for pet projects at a representative's home university.[59] The greatest "earmarker" of all time may be the former chair of the Senate Appropriations Committee, Robert Byrd of West Virginia, beloved by constituents for his generosity with federal funds. For example, he once slipped into an emergency bill a provision that shifted the 2,600-employee FBI fingerprinting center from downtown Washington to Clarksburg, West Virginia.[60]

LEGISLATIVE OVERSIGHT Committees sometimes hold hearings to ensure that agencies are not straying from their congressional mandates. In recent decades the increase in such oversight hearings has expanded committee control over administrative practice. The number of days each year that committees hold

The industrial age's poison sniffers
The Environmental Protection Agency (EPA) faces the difficult task of protecting the environment from pollutants. What kinds of groups and individuals do you think might exert pressure on the EPA?

oversight hearings nearly quadrupled between the 1960s and the 1980s.[61] At these hearings, members of the administration must testify about agency experiences and problems. Witnesses representing outside groups either praise or criticize the bureaucrats. Through the oversight process, committees decide whether to revise existing legislation or modify agency budgets.

Yet congressional influence is limited. Congress can enact general policies, but it cannot construct specific rules for every possible circumstance. Congress may decide to provide benefits to the disabled; but it is up to a bureaucrat to decide whether a particular handicap precludes employment, and it is up to the courts to determine whether the bureaucrat made the decision lawfully.[62] Often the difficulties of passing legislation will produce a compromise bill even vaguer than the policy area required. Thus Congress and the president both face the same problem when dealing with the federal bureaucracy: Exercising formal power can be terribly difficult. Bureaucracies will always exert substantial influence over policy because of the need to grant them administrative discretion, the power to interpret mandates from elected officials.

INTEREST GROUPS AND THE BUREAUCRACY

The purpose of many Cabinet agencies is to provide interest-group access to the executive branch of government.[63] The Interior Department's job was originally to regulate the use of federal land, particularly in the West. Today, it maintains close ties to ranchers, timber companies, mining interests, and others who depend on federal lands for their livelihood. The Agriculture Department serves farmers; the Commerce Department helps business and industry, especially firms with overseas contracts; Labor defends unions; Health and Human Services heeds the American Association of Retired Persons; and Education pays attention to teacher organizations.

Presidents exercise their control over the Cabinet departments primarily by appointing political allies to top positions. But once they become agency heads, allies often identify more closely with their turf than with the president's program. This tendency to "go native" is particularly pronounced when appointees already have close ties to interests connected to the department and hence are part of the issue network over which they suddenly gain responsibility (see Chapter 8).

ELECTIONS AND THE BUREAUCRACY

For more than a century, reformers have tried to separate politics from administration. Government should serve the people, they argue, not the special interests. Departments should make decisions according to laws and regulations, not in response to political pressure. Agencies should treat every applicant alike, not respond more favorably to those who contribute to political parties.

These reform principles are worthy of respect. When politics interferes, agencies can be inefficient and ineffective. The post office, long a patronage reserve, is said to deliver "snail mail." The Department of Housing and Urban Development, always a political thicket, has at times so badly mismanaged property that it had to blow up buildings soon after constructing them. Turf battles between the FBI and CIA may have prevented them from sharing critical information that could have prevented the September 11 terrorist attack.[64]

Many of the more effective federal bureaucracies are less politically charged.[65] The National Science Foundation, protected from political pressures by an independent board, is known for the professional nature in with which it allocates dollars among competing scientific projects. Compared to many state agencies, the Federal Bureau of Prisons does a better job maintaining security without depriving prisoners of rights; it has succeeded in part because members of Congress, respectful of prison leadership, have left the agency alone.[66]

But even though agency autonomy has worked in some instances, electoral pressures also have played a positive role and, in any case, are an essential feature of modern bureaucracies.[67] Public pressure exerted through elections has affected the way bureaucracies keep secrets, enforce the law, manage their budgets, and make decisions. In the end, elections create pressures that force many agencies to balance competing interests by striking compromises.

BUREAUCRATIC SECRECY   Bureaucracies like to protect their secrets. Inside knowledge is power. Secrecy can cover mistakes. Electoral pressures have sharply curtailed the amount of secrecy in American government. In the view of one specialist, "secrecy has less legitimacy as a governmental practice in the United States than in any other advanced industrial society with the possible exception of Sweden," in large part because "Congress has done a great deal to open up the affairs of bureaucracy to greater outside scrutiny."[68] Under the Freedom of Information Act of 1967, citizens have the right to inspect unprotected government documents. If the government believes the requested information needs to be kept secret, it must bear the burden of proof when arguing its case before a judge. The "sunshine law," passed in 1976, required that federal government meetings be held in public, unless they involve military plans, trade secrets, or personnel questions.

BUREAUCRATIC COERCION   Bureaucracies are often accused of using their coercive powers harshly and unfairly. Police officers stop young drivers for traffic violations that are often ignored when committed by older drivers. Bureaucratic zealots trick sales clerks into selling cigarettes to heavily bearded 17-year-olds. Landowners cannot drain puddles off their property because environmental authorities have declared the soggy mud a "wetland." Although such abuses occur, they happen less frequently because agencies are held accountable to the electorate.

In 1998, for example, Republican senators sensed popular discontent with the Internal Revenue Service (IRS), the government's tax collection agency. The agency's approval rating was an embarrassingly low 38 percent.[69] The Senate Finance Committee held a series of hearings that brought to light a litany of agency failings. The IRS had lost $150 billion in 1995 because of mistakes, unreported income, or improper deductions. Taxpayers were overbilled an average of $5 billion per year.[70] The technology the agency used was so outdated that even IRS Commissioner Charles Rossotti admitted, "I have never seen a worse situation in a large organization."[71] As a result of the hearings, Congress enacted a law restructuring the agency, making it harder for the IRS to accuse taxpayers of wrongdoing and bringing its tax collection systems up to date.[72]

AGENCY EXPANSION   Although agencies generally try to increase their budgets, elections brake such tendencies, if only because politicians get blamed for raising taxes. "As a general rule," says analyst Martha Derthick, "Congress likes to keep bureaucracy lean and cheap."[73] The number of people working for the federal government, as a percentage of the workforce, has declined (review Figure 11.2), in good part because elected officials are under public pressure to cut bureaucracy.

ADMINISTRATOR CAUTION Federal agencies are sometimes accused of going beyond their legislative mandates. But most federal agencies err on the side of caution. The worst thing any agency can do is make a major mistake. As one official explained, "The public servant soon learns that successes rarely rate a headline, but government blunders are front-page news. This recognition encourages the development of procedures designed less to achieve successes than to avoid blunders."[74]

In 1962 doctors discovered that thalidomide, a sedative available to pregnant women in Europe, increased the probability that their babies would be born with serious physical deformities. Congress immediately passed a law toughening the Food and Drug Administration's procedures for regulating prescription drug distribution.[75] Two decades later, in keeping with this policy, the FDA refused to approve the sale of several experimental drugs to terminally ill people suffering from AIDS. When the FDA's refusal to allow experimentation became a public issue, the agency began to allow AIDS patients to try the untested drugs, this time loosening regulations in response to potential electoral pressures.

COMPROMISED CAPACITY Agency effectiveness is often undermined by the very terms of the legislation that created it. For legislation to pass Congress, a broad coalition of support is necessary. To build this support, proponents must strike deals with those who are at best lukewarm to the idea. Such compromises, demanded by members of Congress to shore up their electoral support, can cripple a program.[76]

POLICY IMPLEMENTATION

Bureaucrats possess no independent constitutional authority. Instead, bureaucrats are employees who fall under laws passed by Congress, executive orders distributed by the president, and demands articulated by voters through elections and through the interest groups they join. In practice, however, government employees are the ones who must decide exactly how to enforce specific laws or presidential orders. They also are the ones who deal face-to-face with American voters and who decide when it is necessary to accommodate public demands. Because they exercise so much discretion, the bureaucracy as a whole possesses significant power.

It is not feasible to talk about bureaucratic policy making as conducted by every agency and in every policy area. Nor is it straightforward to determine, for any one policy area, where some influences on government programs stop and other influences start. The reality is complex, with different contexts shaping each policy area. Thus, this chapter selects three particularly important areas of policy and sketches out the bureaucratic structure in each: (1) regulation, (2) foreign policy, and (3) monetary policy. The discussion of each case illustrates the way bureaucracies ultimately set policy within the bounds placed on them by the public and by the elected branches of government.

REGULATION

Not all domestic policy involves redistributing tax dollars (see Chapter 15). The national government imposes numerous rules—called regulations—on private companies (as well as on lower levels of government). Regulations are attractive to politicians because their costs do not come out of the federal budget. They usually come indirectly, through higher prices paid by consumers (or through taxes paid to state and local governments). Voters reward elected officials for promoting social goals and blame someone else for the costs.

Regulations illustrate the important role of both bureaucracies and popular influence on domestic policy. Congress passes many regulations because they are a cheap way to curry favor with voters. When an industry's performance becomes unpopular, Congress can respond by adding rules for which consumers must pay. But most laws expanding the government's regulatory power are vague enough that Congress need not take responsibility for their implementation. Someone else has to give them teeth, and that unsavory task usually falls to bureaucrats who need not face reelection.

The breadth of regulations often outpaces what federal bureaucrats can enforce. Members of Congress are more eager to approve rules than they are to fund regulatory agencies. The result can be a false sense of security. Americans think that government is protecting them from a particular catastrophe when, practically speaking, their only guarantee consists of rules on paper. The 110 people who boarded ValuJet's Flight 592 from Miami to Atlanta on May 11, 1996, offer one example. These customers, many of them students returning from spring break, boarded a craft that regulations did not allow to carry hazardous materials.[77] Yet they were sitting on top of a potential bomb: 100 oxygen generators, mislabeled as empty, that had been loaded into the cargo hold. Shortly after takeoff the jet exploded and nose-dived into the Florida Everglades, killing everyone aboard. A Federal Aviation Administration (FAA) regulator was fired and ValuJet's 51 aircraft grounded. Congress launched a massive investigation. But this activity after the fact no doubt provided little consolation for the tragedy.

THE HISTORY OF REGULATION   The basis for federal regulation is found in the U.S. Constitution, which gives Congress authority "to regulate Commerce." The first commerce clause regulations targeted the railroad industry. They expanded briskly during three periods in the country's history: (1) the Progressive Era, from the 1890s to the early 1900s, when muckraking journalists aggressively exposed the abuses of industrialization; (2) the New Deal period, when the national government targeted practices thought to have caused the

Great Depression; and (3) the Great Society period, when the national government expanded its scope to influence numerous areas of American life.

Since the New Deal, the Supreme Court has almost always found regulatory policies constitutional.[78] Regulations now influence everything from civil rights to national insurance standards. Three situations frequently motivate policy makers to regulate industries: (1) when small numbers of companies provide products or services and could take advantage of their market dominance at the expense of consumers; (2) when companies might be tempted to engage in undesirable actions that would not cost them anything, such as polluting the environment to reduce production costs; and (3) when evaluating the quality of products or services would require more time or expertise than regular consumers are likely to bring to the task.

THE POLITICS OF REGULATION   Electoral pressures influence when and how regulations are imposed. Members of Congress often create regulations or regulatory agencies to escape criticism when things go wrong. For example, the *Exxon Valdez* oil spill in 1989 polluted the pristine waters of an Alaskan sound. Congress responded with the Oil Pollution Act of 1990, which established rules for avoiding future oil spills and requiring a rapid cleanup when spills do occur. The need to respond to each high-profile crisis often results in overlapping or even contradictory regulations.[79]

Because telling people what to do can upset or anger them, members of Congress usually try to disguise their actions. Congress may not write a detailed set of rules, instead passing the job to an agency. The Clean Air Act of 1990, for example, did not raise gasoline taxes or alter emissions standards for high-pollution vehicles; it simply stated goals for reducing pollution levels and let the Environmental Protection Agency (EPA) figure out how to get there. Forcing agencies to determine regulations lets legislators distance themselves from rules that prove unpopular.[80]

The autonomy afforded to regulatory agencies is not limitless. There exists a zone of acceptance—a range within which Congress will accept that whatever an agency decides is the correct interpretation of the statutes.[81] When an agency extends beyond what Congress will permit, political opposition arises, and Congress forces the agency to backtrack. The courts also may help determine how far regulations go. Although regulatory policies are enacted by Congress and executed by agencies, federal courts interpret the meaning of congressional statutes and decide whether agencies apply them properly (see Chapter 12). Courts exercise considerable discretion when performing this role, because they are often asked to interpret vague laws.

Court interpretations of the 1973 Endangered Species Act illustrate how federal judges influence public policy. The law protects any species on federal lands

ELECTION CONNECTION

The Spotted Owl Dispute

One of the most controversial examples of statutory interpretation involved the northern spotted owl. This small creature lives in the Pacific Northwest's old-growth forests. Some 3,000 pairs remain. The species can be saved from extinction only by preserving a habitat dark enough to allow it to evade its main predator, the great horned owl.

Environmentalists demand protection for the spotted owl partly because they can, at the same time, preserve old-growth forests from logging. Only 10 percent of the original forests remain, with their marvelous redwoods, cedars, and Douglas firs. To safeguard these, environmentalists asked the Fish and Wildlife Service to declare the spotted owl an endangered species. After extensive investigation, the Fish and Wildlife Service announced that logging on federally owned ancient forests would have to be reduced by 50 percent.

Timber interests prized these great trees for the quality of their wood. The industry saw little need to protect an owl that few had ever seen. "There are millions of owls in the world," said their political ally, Oregon Republican Representative Denny Smith. "This little puppy just happens to be a passive kind of owl that's being run over." The thousands of workers in the industry cherished not only their jobs but also the logging way of life. Bumper stickers appeared, calling on the reader to "Save a Logger. Kill a Spotted Owl." Local taverns advertised "Spotted Owl Stew" for dinner.

The dispute went before a federal judge, William Dwyer, who issued an injunction halting all logging on federally owned, old-growth forests until the government offered a clear plan that would protect the spotted owl. This became a major campaign issue in the 1992 presidential election, in part because Washington and Oregon were important swing states. Bush called the Endangered Species Act a "broken law," asserting "it's time to put people ahead of owls." Governor Clinton sought votes from both environmentalists and loggers by criticizing the Bush administration for failing to resolve the conflict.

After Clinton won the presidency (and both Oregon and Washington), officials in his administration reduced logging operations by two-thirds and restricted logging entirely in over 3 million acres of ancient forests. At the same time, the federal government allocated more than $1 billion to retrain loggers and to stimulate the economy of distressed logging communities. Both sides found it difficult to accept the compromise. Environmentalists condemned loopholes in the plan, and timber interests claimed the aid was simply a way of paying off displaced loggers. But Judge Dwyer found the compromise consistent with the requirements of the Endangered Species Act.

Subsequently, a Republican Congress voted in favor of allowing the timber industry to carry out a two-year program that salvaged fallen trees. Despite the intense opposition of environmentalists, who said fallen trees were part of the ecology, Clinton signed the bill—a decision he later reported regretting.

What do you think?
- Should courts have the power to safeguard a small animal in danger of extinction? Or should such issues be left to Congress?
- How would regulations change if Congress had to approve each regulatory decision?

SOURCES: Timothy Egan, *The Good Rain* (New York: Random House, 1991); *New York Times* (June 23, 1990): A1; *New York Times* (January 9, 1992): A14; *New York Times* (May 22, 1990): A20; and *New York Times* (September 15, 1992): A25. See also Kathie Durbin, *Tree Huggers* (Seattle, WA: Mountaineers Books, 1996).

that the U.S. Fish and Wildlife Service considers at risk of extinction. The natural habitats of species must be safeguarded from threatening human activity, no matter what the economic consequences. The push for this legislation grew from fear for politically popular animals, such as wolves, whooping cranes, and eagles. However, the Fish and Wildlife Service declared nearly 1000 species to be in danger of extinction, including such little-known species as desert kangaroo rats, tiny snail darters, and spotted owls—an interpretation that federal courts have upheld (see the accompanying Election Connection, "The Spotted Owl Dispute".

DEREGULATION   Regulation is expensive. Salaries for bureaucrats, lawyers, and investigators generate an annual price tag that runs to billions of dollars. Regulatory policies also may limit the ability of businesses to compete effectively. The additional paperwork, inspections, procedures, and mandates imposed by regulatory agencies can make the difference between a business that thrives and provides good jobs to Americans and one that cannot compete with foreign firms.

Regular voters usually do not connect higher costs and business failures to government action, but sometimes policy analysts do—and they frequently join businesses in calling for a reduction in regulation. Congress sometimes responds to their calls by backing off from rules that govern industries. It has systematically authorized the partial deregulation of the trucking, banking, and communications industries.[82]

Perhaps the most celebrated deregulation occurred in the airline industry. At one time, a government agency oversaw the airfare set for every route commercial planes flew. Critics charged that the regulators used their authority to limit price competition for customer fares, driving up profits for the few carriers in the industry. Alfred Kahn pushed the issue forward when President Carter appointed him chair of the Civil Aeronautics Board. Kahn stripped away many of the pricing regulations that had governed the airline industry for decades.[83] His initiative led to enactment of the Airline Deregulation Act. Many of the policy outcomes were favorable: lower fares, more service to remote areas, and fewer deaths per passenger mile.

INDEPENDENT REGULATORY AGENCIES   Not all agencies are part of Cabinet departments. Some of the most important, the independent agencies, have quasi-judicial regulatory functions meant to be carried out free from presidential interference. These agencies are generally headed by a board or commission appointed by the president and confirmed by the Senate. Independence from the president, which is considered desirable to insulate such agencies from partisan politics, is achieved by giving board members appointments that last for several years (see Table 11.1). For a number of agencies, a president may be unable to appoint a majority of board members until well into the second term.

TABLE 11.1

Independent Agencies and Their Interest-Group Allies

INDEPENDENT AGENCY	BOARD SIZE	LENGTH OF TERM (YEARS)	INTEREST-GROUP ALLIES
Federal Reserve Board	7	14	Banks
Consumer Product Safety Commission	5	5	Consumers Union
Equal Employment Opportunity Commission	5	5	Civil rights groups
Federal Deposit Insurance Corporation	5	3*	Banks
Federal Energy Regulatory Commission	4	4	Oil/gas interests
Federal Maritime Commission	5	5	Fisheries
Federal Trade Commission	5	7	Business groups
National Labor Relations Board	5	5	Unions
Securities and Exchange Commission	5	5	Wall Street
National Credit Union Administration	3	6	Credit unions
Tennessee Valley Authority	3	9	Regional farmers and utilities

*One member, the comptroller of the currency, has a 5-year term.

Congress established most independent agencies in response to widespread public pressure to protect workers and consumers from negligent or abusive business practices. The Federal Trade Commission (FTC) was created in 1914 in response to the discovery of misbranding and adulteration in the meat packing industry. The FTC was given the power to prevent price discrimination, unfair competition, false advertising, and other unfair business practices. Congress formed the Securities and Exchange Commission in 1934 to root out fraud, deception, and inside manipulation on Wall Street after the stock market crash of 1929 left many Americans suspicious of speculators and financiers.

When originally formed, most regulatory agencies aggressively pursued their reform mandates. But as the public's enthusiasm for reform faded, many agencies found that their most interested constituents were members of the very community they were expected to regulate. Thus the independent commissions have tended to become connected to organized interest groups.[84] In one instance, a regulator's legal fight to keep his job was financed by those subject to his regulation![85]

Slanted to the right . . . or is that to the left?

Not all government commissions are independent. Some, especially temporary ones, are appointed by presidents to accomplish political goals (such as to delay or promote reforms). Democrats criticized the Commission to Strengthen Social Security for pushing Republican policy ideas—but faced ridicule when, to accommodate them, the panel called Social Security "financially unsustainable" rather than "broken."

REGULATION OF THE ELECTRONIC MEDIA Freedom of the press is closer to being an absolute doctrine in the United States than in other countries. In theory the press has wide latitude in its ability to report on and even criticize government. For this reason, regulating media business poses different sorts of problems than regulating other sorts of businesses. Politicians do not routinely dictate policy to any significant media outlet—unlike the situation in some democracies.

Radio and TV, however, lack some press freedoms because they use the public airwaves. Government has used its power to regulate broadcast media, embodied in the Federal Communications Commission (FCC), as a justification for weighing in on media content—an argument accepted by federal courts. One outgrowth of this regulatory power is that politicians have ensured that media owners cannot use their property to favor some candidates over others. Legislation creating the FCC established an **equal-time rule** specifying that if a station sells time to a legally qualified candidate, it must be willing to sell time to all such candidates. Later, the rule was expanded so that, for example, when the networks carry the president's State of the Union speech, they also must carry a reply from the opposition.

From 1949 to 1987, the FCC also enforced a **fairness doctrine** that required stations to devote a reasonable amount of time to matters of public importance and to air contrasting viewpoints on those matters. Eventually, the doctrine also required stations to give public figures who were attacked an opportunity to reply. But communications technologies expanded so much that they undercut some of the rationale for government regulation. In 1987 an FCC staffed by Reagan appointees repealed the fairness doctrine. And more deregulation was to come, as Congress encouraged competition between telephone and cable television companies. Despite this general trend toward deregulation, though, the fact remains that FCC regulations determine what American media organizations may do or say, and in much the same ways that laws or policies from Congress have.

Recent years have seen a rise in the number of proposals for regulation of the Internet, a technology that does not use the public airwaves but does use electronic connections built up with assistance from government. Some people would like to regulate content, for example by banning pornographic, hate-filled, violent, or otherwise objectionable Web sites. The courts probably will rule against most such attempts to restrict content transmitted over the Internet. Various others would like to regulate so-called e-commerce. For example, many state governors are unhappy that purchases made over the Internet are often not subject to state sales tax, which has the effect of denying their states revenue and putting state merchants at a competitive disadvantage. Congress has been slow to tax Internet transactions, however.

FOREIGN POLICY INSTITUTIONS

The institutions responsible for American foreign policy took shape at the onset of the **Cold War** (1946–1989). This conflict between the United States and the Soviet Union sprang up in the wake of World War II. The Soviets first took over East Germany. In short order, they also converted Poland, Hungary, Bulgaria, and Romania into satellite nations. Finally, in 1948, Soviet-backed communists seized control of Czechoslovakia. Together, these East European countries formed a buffer between the Soviet Union and Western Europe. Armed barriers prevented movement across borders—a line that came to be called the **iron curtain.**

President Truman mobilized bipartisan support for a strategy of **containment.** This policy, designed by a State Department specialist named George Kennan, called for stopping the *spread* of communism but otherwise allowing the ill-considered system to collapse on its own.[86] The Truman administration therefore greatly modernized and expanded America's diplomatic and espionage capabilities. Truman also assembled an impressive team of foreign policy advisers to help the United States resist Soviet expansion.

Berlin remained a sticking point. After the Third Reich fell, the Allies divided Germany's former capital into four quadrants ruled by different countries: France, Britain, the United States, and the Soviet Union. People passed freely across quadrants, so East Germans wishing to flee communist tyranny could do so very easily. Approximately 2.7 million people made this choice between 1949 and 1961. One night in 1961, the East German government closed this last gap in the iron curtain, erecting fortifications through the center of Berlin. A huge concrete rampart, known as the Berlin Wall, eventually replaced the temporary partition. It dramatically symbolized the world's division into communist and Western spheres of influence.

STATE DEPARTMENT   The Cold War forced the United States to modernize its diplomatic institutions. Ever since then, the secretary of state usually has been the president's central foreign policy adviser and chief diplomat. For example, the secretary of state during the first term of the Clinton administration, Warren

Rockin' in the Third World

State Department employees bear the primary burden of U.S. diplomacy, but many other government officials and even private citizens sometimes act as informal national ambassadors. Former Treasury Secretary Paul O'Neill (on right)—affectionately called the Bush administration's "mad uncle" in his hometown newspaper—toured Africa with rock singer Bono (of the band U2) as part of a fact-gathering mission to investigate Third World debt.

Christopher, played a major role in negotiating a peace agreement between Israel and the Palestinians.

Reporting to the secretary of state are **ambassadors,** who head the diplomatic delegations to major foreign countries. Ambassadors manage U.S. **embassies,** which house diplomatic delegations in the capital cities of foreign countries. Consulates are maintained in important cities that are not foreign capitals. Although embassies and consulates help American tourists and businesses, their most important political responsibility is to gather detailed information on the government, politics, and social conditions of the host country. The ambassador also conveys to the host country the views of the U.S. government, as instructed by the State Department.

Negotiating with foreign powers is extremely challenging. As former Secretary of State George Marshall once commented, "In diplomacy, you never can tell what a man is thinking. He smiles at you and kicks you in the stomach at the same time."[87] Or as one pundit worded it, "Diplomacy is the art of saying 'nice doggie' until you can find a rock."[88] Because the diplomatic corps is critical to American foreign policy, the staff managing U.S. embassies and consulates is organized into the **foreign service.** Dean Acheson, President Truman's secretary of state, worked hard to improve the service's professional caliber. A reporter at the time declared, "For the first time in the memory of living man, the American foreign office comes somewhere near being adequate to the needs of the country."[89]

DEFENSE DEPARTMENT   Since the first decades of the country's independence, Americans have worried about the ill effects of a large military. Congress and the president have always made certain that the military was controlled by civilian appointees. As one analyst puts it, freedom "demands that people without guns be able to tell people with guns what to do."[90] The Cold War posed new challenges for this ideal of civilian control. To ensure the country's continued international leadership and carry out the policy of containment, Congress provided for the largest military establishment in the nation's history.

The military went through several major organizational changes. The 1947 National Security Act created a single Department of Defense that contained within it the departments of Army, Navy, and Air Force, each with its own civilian secretary appointed by the president. The secretaries for the army and the air force are responsible for their respective branches of the armed services. The secretary of the navy is responsible for both the naval forces and the marines. All three secretaries report to the secretary of defense, the president's chief civilian adviser on defense matters and overall head of all three departments.

Subordinate to the civilian leadership of the secretary of defense and the other three appointed secretaries, military professionals direct the armed forces.

At one time, each armed force had its own leadership, and they acted more or less independently of each other. To achieve better coordination, Congress formally created the **Joint Chiefs of Staff** in 1947. The Joint Chiefs consist of the heads of all the military services—the army, navy, air force, and marine corps— together with a chair and vice chair nominated by the president and confirmed by the Senate.

The end of the Cold War offers a number of serious challenges for the Defense Department. Some experts worry that the military has become so large and institutionalized that it is slow to adapt to the changing world. Most of the armed forces are operating with weapons systems and technology designed to battle the Soviet Union rather than to engage in smaller regional conflicts or to protect the United States against global terrorist networks.[91]

In part, the military has been slow to change because of congressional resistance. Many military facilities appear in key congressional districts. These key members of Congress resist any change that might mean a loss of jobs. With increasing frequency, the Defense Department is in the awkward position of receiving ample funds for projects that no longer need the money and of getting insufficient resources for important new weapons systems. At a congressional hearing in 1998, Chairman of the Joint Chiefs of Staff Henry Shelton scolded Congress for not closing enough military bases.[92] Defense Secretary Donald Rumsfeld met severe congressional resistance when he tried to reorganize the military early in George W. Bush's administration.

Accentuating these specific funding issues is the fact that the overall military budget declined significantly in the 1990s. At the beginning of the Cold War, the United States invested heavily in its armed forces. Throughout the 1950s, approximately 10 percent of the nation's productivity was devoted to defense. The figure reached as high as 14 percent during the Korean War and was 6 percent as recently as the mid-1980s. After the fall of the Berlin Wall, Congress began to cut the defense budget, responding to a decline in public concern. In 1998 and 1999, defense expenditures plummeted to 3.2 percent of economic activity (see Figure 11.4).

CENTRAL INTELLIGENCE AGENCY   Spying is an ancient and honorable practice, but its organization into an independent agency that reports directly to the president is of fairly recent vintage. The need for better-organized intelligence became clear during World War II, but it was not until the Cold War began that Congress established a systematic, centralized system of intelligence gathering. The National Security Act of 1947 created the Central Intelligence Agency (CIA)—the institution primarily responsible for gathering and analyzing information about the political and military activities of other nations—as a separate agency, independent of both the Department of State and the Department of

FIGURE 11.4

Budgets after the Cold War

Defense expenditures declined as a percentage of GDP from 1950 to 1999.

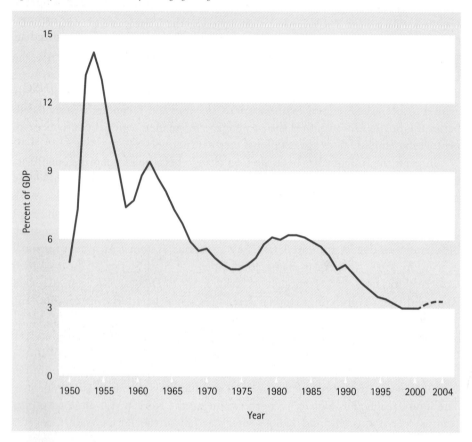

SOURCE: *Statistical Abstract of the United States, 1999* (U.S. Government Printing Office, 1999), Tables 574 and 1444.

Defense. Although State and Defense (as well as other departments) continue to have their own sources of intelligence, the 1947 law made the CIA the main intelligence collection agency.

It also gave the CIA the authority to conduct secret operations abroad at the request of the president, a controversial mandate. One especially notorious covert operation was an ill-fated attempt to dislodge communist leader Fidel Castro from Cuba.[93] In an effort to overthrow Castro, the CIA helped Cuban exiles plan a 1961 invasion on the shores of Cuba's **Bay of Pigs.** President Kennedy approved the invasion, hoping that it might foment a popular insurrection, but refused to give it naval or air support. The effort failed, leaving in doubt the CIA's ability to conduct large-scale military operations. CIA covert operations in Chile in the early 1970s and in Nicaragua in the 1980s also drew criticism.

Nevertheless, the CIA has become one of the pillars of the foreign policy establishment.[94] The agency helps identify and squelch potential terrorist operations, assesses the threat of nuclear proliferation, and helps monitor other nations' compliance with arms control agreements. In 1999, the CIA even assisted in efforts to document war crimes committed by the Serbian military in Kosovo.[95]

NATIONAL SECURITY COUNCIL   The National Security Council (NSC), created by Congress in 1947 and placed inside the Executive Office of the President, is responsible for coordinating foreign policy. Meetings of the NSC are generally attended by the president, the vice president, the secretaries of state and defense, the head of the CIA, the chair of the Joint Chiefs of Staff, the president's chief of staff, and such other persons as the president designates.[96] They help resolve competing foreign policy viewpoints.

Orchestrating Foreign Affairs

National Security Advisor Condoleezza Rice is neither the first woman nor the first African American to call the tune in a major policy area. Yet, as a black woman, Rice has broken ground for her virtuosity conducting foreign affairs—an issue whose leadership historically has been composed of whites and males. Has Condi Rice's commanding performance in international relations been instrumental in changing how Americans view women and minorities in government service?

The council is assisted by a staff located in the White House under the direction of the National Security Adviser (NSA). The NSA has often played a coordinating role, reconciling interagency disagreements or, if that proves impossible, reporting them to the president. But inasmuch as the NSA has more access to the president than any member of the foreign policy team, the adviser can wield great influence. During the Nixon administration, National Security Adviser Henry Kissinger even overshadowed the secretary of state.

The NSA has not escaped controversy. The most notorious scandal is called the **Iran–Contra affair.** The NSA office attempted to conduct a covert operation, selling arms to Iran and then diverting the funds to rebels in Nicaragua known as the Contras. Because Congress had forbidden such aid, the Iran–Contra affair developed into a bitter confrontation with President Ronald Reagan, who had privately asked National Security Adviser Robert McFarlane to "assure the Contras of continuing administration support."[97] Hearings and investigations followed, although no convictions withstood court appeals.

SETTING MONETARY POLICY

The **Federal Reserve System** (or "the Fed") manages the government's monetary policy. Created in 1913, the Fed is headed by a board consisting of seven governors appointed by the president and confirmed by the Senate. Each Fed governor holds office for 14 years. The chair of the system serves a four-year term. The Fed acts on the economy through the operations of its 12 regional banks, each of which oversees member banks in its part of the country.

The agency is formally independent of both politics and external pressure groups.[98] Long terms ensure that presidents may not appoint majorities of the board until they have been in office six years. Members of Congress also seldom get a crack at the Fed's board members. Furthermore, monetary policy is too arcane to engage the general public, so Fed-bashing is not a very effective campaign tactic. The Fed maintains a professional image, not a political one—a self-preservation tactic enhanced by the tendency to hire qualified specialists to staff the agency.

Because the Fed is small and relatively independent of other government officials, it can change monetary policy quickly—interest rates can fluctuate on a monthly, weekly, or even daily basis if the need arises (although the policy outcomes may take months to appear). The most important decisions affecting the day-to-day workings of the economy are made by the Fed's Open Market Committee (FOMC). This committee considers whether interest rates are too high or too low and what adjustments should be made. The committee consists of the 7 governors, all of whom vote, and the 12 regional bank presidents, only 5 of whom have votes (the New York bank president always has a vote; the remaining 4 votes rotate among the other 11 banks). When the national economy

Second most powerful man in America?
Alan Greenspan's role as chairman of the Federal Reserve Board gives him great independent influence. What are the sources of his sway over economic policy?

slowed early in 2001, and then confidence collapsed after the September 11 terrorist attacks, the FOMC responded with a series of nine interest-rate cuts by October 2.[99]

The chair of the Federal Reserve Board ranks among the most powerful persons in government. The chair's great power derives from close ties to the president, direct access to up-to-date economic information supplied by Fed staff, and the power to approve the appointment of the 12 presidents of the Federal Reserve banks (upon the recommendation of the member banks in each region). The current Fed chair, Alan Greenspan, has been particularly successful at wielding power and improving his reputation. Greenspan's management of the economy during the Clinton administration won him such universal acclaim that 2000 presidential candidate John McCain quipped, "If Mr. Greenspan were to die, God forbid, I would . . . stuff him and prop him up."[100]

WHO CONTROLS THE FED? Buying Treasury bonds is a necessary part of the Fed's job. It is one way the Fed influences the amount of money in the economy. Fed investments earn billions of dollars (nearly $27 billion in 1998). The Fed keeps about a tenth of this money for its own operations, turning the rest over to the Treasury.[101] This economic independence means that Congress cannot pressure the Fed by using its budgetary powers. Once the Senate approves nominees to the Fed, they become insulated from electoral pressures expressed through the legislative branch.[102]

The president—who appoints or reappoints the Fed's members, including the chair—has a great deal more influence than Congress.[103] The Fed must not stray too far from presidential demands, or it might tarnish its apolitical image. Ironically, this sensitivity to appearances allows politics to influence monetary policy. Republicans tend to dislike inflation, so the Fed attacks it more aggressively when Republicans hold the presidency. Democratic constituencies include lots of working-class voters whose jobs are insecure, so the Fed combats unemployment more aggressively when Democrats sit in the White House.[104]

Nevertheless, few citizens like either inflation or unemployment, so Fed behavior does not fluctuate very much with the party of the president. Presidents particularly dislike economic troubles during an election year. Some skeptics even argue that presidents deliberately manipulate the economy to engineer their reelections. They tolerate slow growth, even recessions, early in their terms of office so they can step on the gas and "rev up" the economic engine when payoffs are greatest. Richard Nixon's 1972 reelection campaign provides the classic example; his administration pulled out all the stops to achieve a huge increase in household income that year.[105] Yet neither Jimmy Carter nor George H. W. Bush presided over active economies during their reelection campaigns. At best, economic growth picks up only slightly in an election year, calling into question the extent to which presidents really manipulate monetary policy.

Many liberal critics argue that the banking industry controls the Fed and leads its members to fight inflation much more vigorously than they combat unemployment.[106] When jobs are plentiful and people are spending freely, the Fed typically responds by raising interest rates and slowing down the economy. As one critic put it, "Just when the party gets going, the Fed takes away the beer."[107] Certainly bankers enjoy some influence over monetary policy. They influence the appointment of the Board of Governors, and they nominate the Federal Reserve bank presidents, who cast five votes on the FOMC. But the Fed has not consistently fought inflation, as indicated by the 1970s, when it mistakenly allowed inflation to get out of control.

THE FED'S HOLD ON MONETARY POLICY The Fed is able to operate with a considerable amount of independence, in large part because it tries to achieve what nearly everyone desires: steady, stable economic growth. The president, in particular, requires solid economic performance and therefore usually can afford to leave the Fed alone. A case in point is the relationship President

Clinton had with Fed chair Alan Greenspan. Ronald Reagan first appointed Greenspan as Fed chair, but Clinton retained him in 1996 to reassure financial markets.[108] Members of Congress also know that they would undermine confidence in the U.S. economy if they encroached too much on the Fed's domain.

The position of the Federal Reserve System in America's new democracy therefore is a rare case in which popular moods play little role in determining policy. Yet it is "the exception that proves the rule" of public opinion's influence. The election connection usually does not sway monetary policy precisely because of a conscious choice to insulate the money supply from the tides of political fortune. Just as a dieter might padlock the refrigerator as a defense against moments of weakness, Americans apparently do not trust themselves to weigh in on monetary policy. They respect—and even revere—the distant body of experts who try to fine-tune the economy without giving in to shortsighted impulses.

POLICY ENVIRONMENTS: A SUMMARY

Scholars usually divide public policy into three areas: domestic policy, economic policy, and foreign and defense policy (see Chapter 15). We have now reviewed three rough policy areas, one in each category. Regulation is an important domestic policy. Monetary policy is the main approach to adjusting the U.S. economy. And the foreign policy apparatus provides the president with information to use when dealing with other nations. Although each topic is unique—with its own policy environment, its own bureaucratic organization, and its own direct or indirect connection to public opinion—the main purpose of the discussion was to illustrate what they have in common.

First, the president may sit at the top of each bureaucratic flow chart, but numerous other political actors and outside influences shape institutional behavior and so limit what a president may accomplish. Second, Congress is seldom far from the bureaucracy. Lawmakers set the regulations, fund the defense and intelligence agencies, and confirm most of the various appointees. Third, orders from Congress and the president are seldom so clear that bureaucrats lose their discretion; they still usually set the precise rules and regulations under which Americans must operate, and in some instances they are protected by rules that explicitly establish their independence when setting policy. But, finally, each policy area ultimately responds to public opinion. The government regulates an industry after high-profile scandals, accidents, or abuses of public trust—and then deregulates when the rules become too costly. The government shifts the money supply to find a proper balance between inflation and unemployment—but sometimes allows monetary policy to float so that it corresponds with the needs of elected leaders. And different portions of the foreign policy apparatus gain and lose power depending on the needs of elected legislators as well as the expectations for foreign affairs that members of the public hold. In short, policy implementation does not stray far from the pressures of elections and public opinion in America's new democracy.

AFTERSHOCK: HOMELAND SECURITY

The unprecedented 9/11 terrorist attacks provoked feelings of shock, anger, and vulnerability that many Americans had never experienced before. But in the aftermath of the attacks, some channeled their reaction into a much more familiar argument: U.S. government agencies had failed to do their jobs well. Such criticism contained more than just an element of truth (as the beginning of this chapter clearly indicates). American leaders knew that they had to take immediate steps to prevent another serious terrorist attack.

George W. Bush proposed reforming the way law-enforcement agencies conduct the business of domestic security. In doing so, the president moved to implement recommendations of a blue-ribbon commission that in February 2001 had called for greater coordination and planning among dozens of government organizations. His plan was different from that of the commission in one respect, however: Whereas the panel had called for a "significant organizational redesign"—namely, a new Cabinet-level agency charged with securing the U.S. from terrorism[109]—Bush's plan was much more modest. He created a new White House Office of Homeland Security, headed by former Pennsylvania Governor Tom Ridge.

Ridge, with his small staff of 100 operating from a corner of the executive mansion, was expected to coordinate the activities of agencies as diverse as the FBI in the Justice Department, the U.S. Customs Service in the Treasury Department, the Federal Aviation Administration (FAA) in the Department of Transportation, and the Federal Emergency Management Agency (FEMA), an independent entity. These agencies—and dozens of others that Ridge was supposed to keep track of—all had separate budgets, separate directors, and separate organizational cultures. One national security expert likened the task to "getting a 40-mule team . . . pulling in the right direction."[110] In his public appearances, Ridge admitted that the job was as large as "building the transcontinental railroad, fighting World War II, or putting a man on the moon."[111]

The new security director often appeared to be overshadowed by other administration officials. When authorities discovered that the deadly disease anthrax had been mailed to members of Congress and media outlets, Secretary of Health and Human Resources Tommy Thompson took center stage. When a would-be terrorist was arrested after attempting to set off a bomb hidden in his shoes on a trans-Atlantic flight, FBI officials in Boston fielded media enquiries. And Transportation Secretary Norman Mineta was charged with ensuring that aviation screening met tough new federal standards. Ridge's most visible accomplishment, one that brought him more ridicule than praise, was his invention of a color-coded national terrorism alert system. But even under this system, it was the attorney general—not Ridge—who would decide whether to raise or lower the nation's state of alert.

After eight and one-half months of trying to manage the domestic security apparatus from the White House, and as members of Congress and the public expressed alarm at new revelations about pre-9/11 intelligence failures, the president confessed that he needed to do more. In June 2002, Bush asked Congress to create a Cabinet-level Department of Homeland Security that would have direct authority over nearly 170,000 government workers from eight departments. The Border Patrol, the Coast Guard, the Transportation Security Administration, and even the Secret Service were all slated to be moved to the new organization. In a televised address to explain his reversal of course on this issue, Bush admitted that a more effective, unified structure was needed: "Right now, as many as a hundred different government agencies have some responsibilities for Homeland Security, and no one has final accountability."[112]

As obvious as their decision to reorganize might have been, Bush and Ridge faced a difficult task if they really wished to create a new department. The last time the United States had undergone a significant national security reorganization was in the late 1940s, after what President Truman called a "long hard battle" that lasted at least four years.[113] In other words, Bush and Ridge were attempting to win approval for the largest federal government shakeup in more than 50 years.

The eventual White House proposal was not the first one that administration officials tested. Ridge circulated two modest proposals before the final draft, both of which attracted vigorous objections from the agencies and interest groups involved. President Bush knew that the real proposal would need some method of overcoming "bureaucratic inertia."[114] He settled on secrecy. The final plan emerged from clandestine meetings conducted by Ridge with three high-ranked presidential aides: the top budgetary officer, the chief legal advisor, and the White House chief of staff. Few administration officials even learned of the real plan until days before its public debut, so potential opponents could not nibble it to death with minor complaints.

The Bush administration's proposal called for the creation of a huge new agency, with 169,000 employees and a $37.5 billion budget. It would be the third largest federal department, behind Defense and Veteran's Affairs. But Bush's advisers selected the agencies to incorporate into the department very carefully, choosing those with little political clout. Examples included (1) the Federal Emergency Management Agency (FEMA), which hires few employees; (2) the new Transportation Security Agency, which lacked deep roots in its department; and (3) the Coast Guard, which had moved departments before. Bush did not try to touch the politically influential agencies—such as the Federal Bureau of

Investigation (FBI), with its long history inside the Department of Justice. The stronger bureaucracies thus did not marshal their resources against Bush's plan.

Congress still could have blocked the sweeping Bush proposal. The White House estimated that 90 congressional committees and subcommittees exerted some jurisdiction over national security, a system of oversight that eventually would have to be simplified to deal with the consolidated department. But both chambers streamlined the legislative process—the House by creating a special committee of leaders to deal with the issue, the Senate by debating Bush's proposal on the floor of the chamber itself. Former senator Warren Rudman explained congressional cooperation this way: "Are you going to tell 280 million American people, if something bad happens, that you voted against this reorganization because you wanted to be sure that you had your subcommittee on carrots and lettuce?"[115]

One obscure provision did end up creating controversy. It allowed the secretary of homeland security to bypass ordinary civil-service rules and use a promotion system based on merit. Ridge argued that he would need such flexibility to assemble a "motivated, high-performance, and accountable workforce."[116] But leaders of the public employee unions strongly opposed giving department management so much influence over employees, many of whom enjoyed greater insulation from their bosses under the status quo. Democrats, the unions' usual allies, initially vowed to delay Bush's plan until Homeland Security employees received stronger job guarantees in the legislation.

Yet the 2002 elections were rapidly approaching. Critics claimed that a Democrat-controlled Senate was holding public safety hostage on behalf of their corrupt union allies. Bush himself charged that Senate Democrats who were opposing his executive reorganization were "not interested in the security of the American people." Senate Majority Leader Tom Daschle denounced Bush's remarks as outrageous,[117] but his copartisans rightly feared the result of a popular president appearing in their states questioning their patriotism. According to one observer at the time, "Bush is positioned to inflict grave political damage."[118]

The Democratic party may have paid a grave price for the delays. Homeland security played a significant role in several Senate elections. Democratic Senator Max Cleland of Georgia, a wheelchair-bound Vietnam veteran, especially seemed to suffer from claims that he did not have the will to support aggressive security measures; a Republican picked up Cleland's Senate seat. Democrats stood aside after their repudiation at the polls, allowing the Homeland Security bill to move swiftly toward passage. Tom Ridge took over the newest Cabinet-level government department.

Some political scientists believe that, in the United States, major governmental changes are no longer possible. Entrenched bureaucracies, allied with interest groups and key congressional committees, can block any comprehensive changes that would threaten their power or their resources.[119] Admittedly, Bush's pro-

FIGURE 11.5

Americans supported the Bush plan

Voters also believed the department would be a clear improvement over the present system. Was Bush's popularity the decisive factor in winning congressional passage of the proposal?

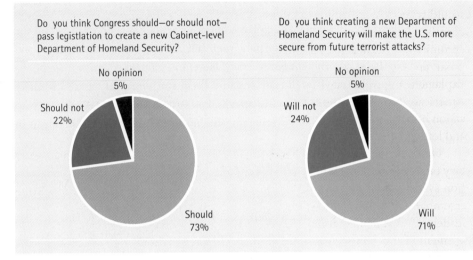

Do you think Congress should—or should not— pass legistlation to create a new Cabinet-level Department of Homeland Security?

No opinion 5%
Should not 22%
Should 73%

Do you think creating a new Department of Homeland Security will make the U.S. more secure from future terrorist attacks?

No opinion 5%
Will not 24%
Will 71%

SOURCE: *Statistical Abstract of the United States, 1999* (U.S. Government Printing Office, 1999), Tables 574 and 1444.

posal succeeded in part because it offended few powerful or entrenched interests. But being inoffensive is not enough to propel major bureaucratic reorganizations through the difficult legislative process described in Chapter 9.

The battle over creating a new Department of Homeland Security in 2002 proved that, under certain conditions, major change is possible. One important condition, of course, is public dissatisfaction. Voters need to believe that something is wrong with government. The 9/11 attacks left few doubts about that. But, of course, voters also said that American medicine needed dramatic changes when President Clinton offered his unsuccessful health-care proposals (see Chapter 8). Something more than dissatisfaction is required.

Voters also need to have a fairly clear idea what sort of changes would improve government's problems. As Figure 11.5 shows, the public exhibited special unity on Bush's proposal. Less than a quarter of the American public apparently opposed consolidating the agencies. Most Americans believed that the Department of Homeland Security would make them safer. Such unified opinion allowed Democrats little leverage to demand technical changes in the legislation. They still dragged their feet, but the unavoidable result was that opponents could brand them as opponents of change. Like any elected official who does not give voters what they want, Senate Democrats suffered for their unresponsiveness in the elections that followed.

CHAPTER SUMMARY

All bureaucracies exhibit certain operational flaws, but American bureaucracies have specific troubles that can be attributed to the electoral climate in which they have evolved. Moreover, the president must share influence over the bureaucracy with numerous other players, including Congress, interest groups, and the voting public. Bureaucracies do enjoy some discretion in implementing laws, but their actions generally fall within the bounds of what elected officials and the public demand of them. Both the inefficiency and the responsiveness of government bureaucracy, therefore, ultimately derive from political impulses—as illustrated by the failure and subsequent reform of national security agencies at the time of the 9/11 terrorist attacks. In short, the unelected employees who manage the day-to-day affairs of government respond to the elections so prominent in America's new democracy.

KEY TERMS

ambassadors, p. 380

Bay of Pigs, p. 382

bureaucracy, p. 356

civil service, p. 363

Cold War, p. 378

containment, p. 378

departments, p. 356

equal-time rule, p. 377

embassies, p. 380

fairness doctrine, p. 378

Federal Reserve System, p. 384

foreign service, p. 380

government corporations, p. 356

Hatch Act, p. 363

independent agencies, p. 356

Iran–Contra affair, p. 384

iron curtain, p. 378

Joint Chiefs of Staff, p. 381

mugwumps, p. 362

patronage, p. 361

Pendleton Act, p. 363

senatorial courtesy, p. 365

spoils system, p. 362

SUGGESTED READINGS

Leffler, Melvyn P. *A Preponderance of Power: National Security, the Truman Administration, and the Cold War.* Stanford, CA: Stanford University Press, 1992. Historical account of Cold War strategy.

Light, Paul. *Thickening Government: Federal Hierarchy and the Diffusion of Accountability.* Washington, DC: Brookings, 1995. Identifies and explains the growth in higher-level governmental positions.

Melnick, R. Shep. *Regulation and the Courts.* Washington, DC: Brookings, 1983. Case studies of the central role the courts play in interpreting government regulations.

Niskanan, William A. *Bureaucracy and Representative Government.* Chicago: Aldine-Atherton, 1971. Develops the argument that government bureaucracies seek to maximize their budgets.

Wilson, James Q. *Bureaucracy:What Government Agencies Do and Why They Do It.* New York: Basic Books, 1989. Comprehensive treatment of public bureaucracies.

Young, James. *The Washington Community 1800–1828.* New York: Harcourt, 1966. Engaging, insightful account of political and administrative life in Washington during the first decades of the nineteenth century.

ON THE WEB

Public Citizen
www.publiccitizen.org
Ralph Nader's Public Citizen lobbies for consumer protection regulations. The site contains facts and figures and links to papers and other publications.

The Federal Reserve
www.federalreserve.gov
The Federal Reserve System maintains an informative Web site, complete with publications, congressional testimony, and economic data.

FedWorld
www.fedworld.gov
Most U.S. government agencies and departments have informative Web sites that can be reached through FedWorld.

Office of Management and Budget
www.whitehouse.gov/OMB/
The Office of Management and Budget offers copies of budget documentation, testimony before Congress, and regulatory information.

Congressional Budget Office
www.cbo.gov
The Congressional Budget Office provides copies of its reports on the economy, the budget, and current legislation.

General Accounting Office
www.gao.gov
The General Accounting Office, the investigative arm of Congress, assists Congress in its oversight of the executive branch.

12

THE JUDICIARY

[handwritten marginalia: IN: 7th Circuit based in Chicago / 9th circuit in CA in Nevada etc / Federal supreme court is an appellate court for both state & fed courts. / Power is drawn from article 3]

394

Thurgood Marshall, the Supreme Court's first black justice, once jested, "I have a lifetime appointment and I intend to serve it. I expect to die at 110, shot by a jealous husband."[1] He nonetheless resigned in June 1991, reluctantly concluding that at age 83 he could no longer continue a civil rights struggle he had fought for decades. Asked by reporters why he was stepping down, an impatient Marshall declared, "I'm old! I'm getting old and coming apart."[2]

Marshall's retirement placed President George H. W. Bush in a bind. The Constitution allows presidents to appoint federal judges, but a majority of the Senate must confirm their choices. Most observers understood that, for symbolic reasons, President Bush would need to nominate an African American judge to replace Marshall. He could not afford to lose a confirmation battle in the Democrat-controlled Senate. But the pool of black conservatives from whom Bush might select was small, and almost any choice acceptable to a Republican president was bound to attract ire.

After days of media speculation, President Bush nominated Clarence Thomas, an African American with solid conservative credentials from his time as chair of the Equal Employment Opportunity Commission (EEOC). In stark contrast to the man he would replace, Thomas opposed affirmative action programs giving preferential treatment to minorities because "they assume that I am not the equal of someone else, and if I'm not the equal, then I'm inferior."[3] His general philosophy of constitutional interpretation also resembled that of the bench's most conservative members.

Democratic senators viewed the nominee with great suspicion, but at first it seemed that Thomas's political savvy would allow him to escape much criticism. For one thing, he had not publicly expressed his views on controversial constitutional issues, which made it more difficult for opponents to criticize his legal opinions. Thomas also realized that silence was golden during the nomination process. At the traditional confirmation hearings, members of the Senate Judiciary Committee asked Thomas his opinion on the constitutionality of abortion bans no fewer than 70 times—but his replies were studiously vague.[4]

Liberal senators initially went easy on Thomas for another reason. Civil rights groups had mixed feelings, disliking the nominee's views but encouraged that even a Republican president had heard their call for more blacks on the federal bench. They hesitated to oppose Thomas, whose defeat might give Bush an excuse to appoint a second judge of a different race. Moreover, opinion polls indicated that three-quarters of the black population, untroubled by his conservative opinions, supported Thomas's appointment.[5] Massachusetts Senator Edward Kennedy, opposed as he was to the Thomas nomination, had to admit, "In many ways he exemplifies the promise of the Constitution and the American ideal of equal opportunity."[6]

But Thomas ended up being the center of a political uproar after all—as the result of testimony by a soft-spoken young woman named Anita Hill. An attorney who once worked with the EEOC, Hill had left Washington politics to assume an academic position at the University of Oklahoma. She had left Washington, she told a friend, because Thomas had sexually harassed her.

Judiciary Committee staffers approached Hill, who told them her story. Within days, her accounts of sexual harassment leaked to the media. Liberal senators now had a legitimate justification for opposing Thomas, and they pounced. The committee scheduled televised hearings in which Hill described lewd and suggestive phrases she claimed to have heard from the mouth of a future Supreme Court justice. Thomas angrily denied all charges and called the televised Senate exploitation of Hill's allegations nothing less than a "high-tech lynching."[7]

The confirmation battle spilled out of the Washington beltway to involve men and women across the country of all races and creeds. For the 14 Judiciary Committee senators forced to listen to the sensational testimony, it was a political nightmare. They were bound to offend someone during the confirmation process: women, African Americans, maybe both. In the end, the Senate confirmed Thomas by a close vote. More Americans believed Thomas than believed Hill, and a clear majority continued to favor Thomas's confirmation.[8] The strong support Thomas received from black voters was particularly significant, because both Thomas and Hill were African Americans.[9]

Yet the process had a dramatic effect on the next election. The more women thought about the outcome, the unhappier they became. The percentage of women who believed Thomas had harassed Hill increased from 27 to 51 percent over the following year, despite a lack of new information.[10] Their anger led some women to run for Congress, and many others to support them. The number of women elected to the House of Representatives increased by almost 70 percent in 1992, from 28 to 47, and 4 new women were elected to the Senate. In the presidential election, Bush's support among women fell 5 percentage points lower than his support among men, enough of a difference to deny Bush reelection.[11] It was the costliest Supreme Court nomination a president had ever made.

IN RECENT DECADES, THE JUDICIARY HAS BECOME TIED more closely to electoral influences. Presidents are more likely to consider policy goals when selecting their nominees. If Senate committee chairs dislike a president's choice, they are more likely to delay or even refuse to schedule confirmation hearings. Individual senators openly ask nominees about their likely rulings on various types of issues, even though no specific cases sit before the potential justices. If the nominee takes a clear position on a particular issue, or has written on the topic in law reviews and judicial rulings, senators mobilize opposition based on their policy disagreements.

None of this maneuvering to influence the judiciary fits with how the framers viewed courts. They hoped that judges would remain free from public pressures, relative to other political institutions, so that they could interpret written law neutrally. Judges were to protect individual citizens from governmental tyranny, even when an electoral majority endorsed restricting freedoms. But if current practices violate how the founders envisioned the political system functioning, they are fully consistent with trends in America's new democracy—which have spread public influence to even the most insulated institutions.

THE FEDERAL COURT SYSTEM

The Supreme Court provides the linchpin for the nation's judicial system, resolving difficult questions of federal law. (States have their own legal systems, which we discuss briefly at the end of this chapter.) Most of the day-to-day work of the federal judicial branch takes place at lower tiers. Indeed, the Supreme Court generally hears fewer than 100 cases per year, and the vast majority of those cases start in lower federal courts or in the state courts. These lower courts are less visible institutions, but they are no less affected by political and electoral forces. Thus, understanding how elections influence the federal judiciary, as well as how they impact civil liberties (see Chapter 13) and civil rights (see Chapter 14), first requires understanding how the federal court system works.

ORGANIZATION OF THE FEDERAL COURTS

The Constitution established a Supreme Court but allowed Congress to decide on the shape of any lower courts (see Chapter 2). The first Congress enacted the Judiciary Act of 1789. That legislation still provides the basic framework for the modern federal court system, which is divided into three basic layers: trial courts, appeals courts, and the Supreme Court.

TRIAL COURTS   Most federal cases initially appear in one of the 94 **district courts,** the lowest tier of the judicial system. There are also two specialized courts with nationwide jurisdiction over particular issues. The Court of International Trade handles cases concerning customs and global commerce. And the U.S. Court of Federal Claims hears suits concerning federal contracts, monetary damages against the United States, and other issues that involve the federal government. Most federal cases end in these district courts, which are also called trial courts (see Figure 12.1).

As this name suggests, the main responsibility of district courts is to hold trials. In all trials there are two sides: the **plaintiff,** the party bringing the suit, and the **defendant,** the party against whom the complaint is made. Trials settle alleged violations of the civil and criminal codes.

The **civil code** regulates the legal rights and obligations of citizens with regard to one another. Individuals ask the court to award damages and otherwise offer relief for injuries they claim to have suffered. Medical malpractice suits are one example of a civil action; the patient sues a hospital or a doctor for improper

FIGURE 12.1

Federal and state court systems

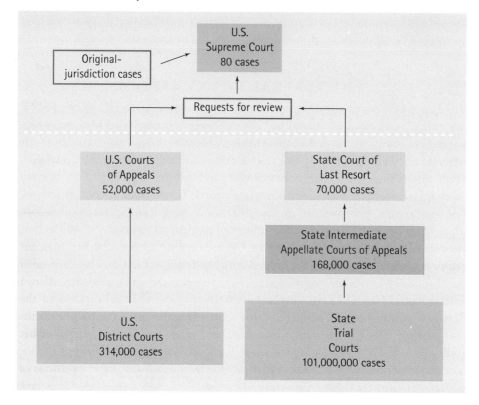

treatment. People cannot be imprisoned for violating the civil code (although they can be imprisoned for not complying with a court order growing out of a civil suit).

Violations of the **criminal code** are offenses against society as a whole. The government enforces criminal law, acting as plaintiff and initiating charges against suspects. If convicted, the criminal owes a debt to society, not just to the injured party. The debt may be paid by fine, imprisonment, or, in the case of capital crimes, execution. Table 12.1 summarizes the differences between civil and criminal cases.

The same action can violate both codes simultaneously, so the defendant may have to fend off accusations more than once. After a jury acquitted former football star O. J. Simpson in the murder of his ex-wife, Nicole Brown Simpson, her relatives filed a civil suit seeking compensation for pain and suffering caused by her wrongful death. Their tactic might sound foolish. Why should Simpson pay Nicole's family for their loss if he was not guilty of her murder? The plaintiffs were hopeful that they might win a civil suit, despite losing the criminal trial,

TABLE 12.1

DIFFERENCES BETWEEN CIVIL AND CRIMINAL TRIALS

	CRIMINAL TRIAL	CIVIL TRIAL
Plaintiff	The government	Private person or group
Issue	Duty of citizens to obey the law	Legal rights and obligations of citizens to one another
Type of wrongdoing	Transgression against society	Harm to private person or group
Remedy	Punishment (fine, imprisonment, etc.)	Compensation for damages
Standard of proof	Beyond a reasonable doubt	Preponderance of the evidence
Can defendant be forced to testify?	No	Yes

because the burden of evidence is weaker. In a criminal trial, one is "innocent until proven guilty" beyond a reasonable doubt, but in a civil suit the jury need only to decide whose case has the preponderance of supporting evidence. Also, a plaintiff cannot compel the accused to testify in a criminal trial because of the Fifth Amendment, but the accused in a civil action cannot refuse to respond without suffering consequences. The plaintiffs thus were able to secure a guilty verdict in the civil suit and a monetary award against Simpson of $33.5 million.

The Federal Bureau of Investigation usually looks into suspected violations of the federal criminal code, although other federal agencies (such as the Secret Service and the Bureau of Alcohol, Tobacco and Firearms) also exercise investigative powers. They turn over evidence to prosecutors in the office of a **U.S. attorney,** one of 93 litigators appointed by the president and confirmed by the Senate. If persuaded that a prosecution is warranted, the U.S. attorney asks a grand jury (consisting of 16 to 23 citizens) to indict, or bring charges against, the suspect. This stage is not a formal trial, just a decision to proceed with one, so the grand jury usually follows the U.S. attorney's advice. As one wit observed, "Under the right prosecutor, a grand jury would indict a ham sandwich."[12]

U.S. attorneys have a particularly high political profile. They usually share the president's party affiliation and may be sensitive to the needs of their own political careers. U.S. attorneys do not handle routine law enforcement. Often they concentrate on attention-grabbing activities that can lead to a candidacy for higher office. Former New York Mayor Rudolph Giuliani achieved prominence as a federal attorney after successfully prosecuting Wall Street inside-trader Ivan Boesky and tax-evading hotel magnate Leona Helmsley. Thomas Dewey may have turned the office of U.S. attorney to greatest political advantage. After winning fame by prosecuting labor racketeers, he became governor of New York and, in

1948, won the Republican presidential nomination. He narrowly lost the election to Harry Truman.[13]

APPEALS COURTS Federal district courts are organized into 13 circuits, including 11 regional circuits, a District of Columbia circuit, and a federal circuit (which includes the specialized courts). Each has a **circuit court of appeals,** the court empowered to review all district rulings (see Figure 12.2).[*] Appeals courts contain between 6 and 28 judges, depending on the size of the circuit. The senior appeals court judge assigns 3 judges, usually chosen by lot, to review each case. In exceptionally important cases, the appeals judges may participate in a **plenary session,** which includes all of them. Courts of appeals ordinarily take as given the facts of the case, as stated in the trial record and decided by district judges. They do not accept new evidence or hear additional witnesses but, rather, confine their review to points of law under dispute. Most appeals court decisions are final.

THE SUPREME COURT IN ACTION

The Supreme Court sits atop a massive pyramid of judicial activity. Each year prosecutors and private citizens bring more than 27 million criminal trials and civil suits before the state and federal courts.[14] Yet in the 1999–2000 term, the nation's high court heard only 80 cases. Through these few cases, the Court's chief justice and eight associate **justices** exert substantial influence.

CERTS At one time the Supreme Court was, by law, forced to review many appeals. The workload became so excessive that, in 1925, Congress gave the Court power to refuse almost any case it did not want to consider. Today, nearly all cases argued before the Court arrive because at least four justices have voted to grant what is known as a **writ of** *certiorari* (or "cert").[†] When a cert is granted, it means the Court has agreed to consider the case and requests to be informed of the details.[15] The Court receives around 7000 petitions each year, denying approximately 95 percent of them. Reviewing these petitions is a lot of work. "You almost get to hate the guy who brings the cert petitions around," a Supreme Court clerk once explained. "He is a really nice guy, but he gets abuse all the time."[16]

The number of certs granted by the Supreme Court has fallen markedly in recent years. In the 1970s the Supreme Court decided as many as 400 cases annually, including many controversial rulings.[17] The current Court seems to want to reduce its visibility in American politics; certs are granted only for those cases that raise the most important legal or constitutional issues.

---

[*]Originally, appeals court judges literally traveled a circuit, going by stagecoach from district to district to hear appeals—hence the name.

[†]*Certiorari* is a Latin phrase that means "to be informed of."

FIGURE 12.2
Courts of appeals circuit boundaries

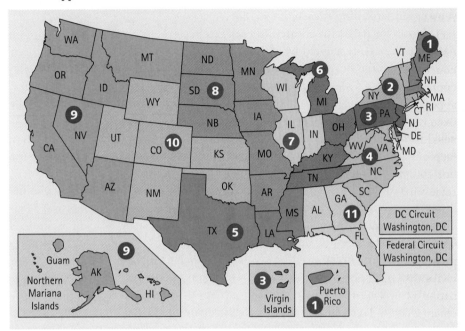

SOURCE: Robert A. Carp and Ronald Stidham, *The Federal Courts,* 2nd ed. (Washington, DC: CQ Press, 1991), p.18.

The case for cert is strongest if two lower courts have reached opposite conclusions on similar cases. The Supreme Court feels a responsibility to clarify and therefore standardize the law. In 1998, for example, the Supreme Court granted cert in a case involving media "ride-alongs" with law enforcement officials. The Fourth Circuit Court of Appeals had ruled in a Maryland case that police did not violate criminal defendants' privacy by bringing reporters along to witness an arrest. In a similar Montana case, however, the Ninth Circuit Court of Appeals ruled that the press should not be present when law enforcement officials search a private home. The Supreme Court eventually resolved the apparent contradiction between these two decisions: Police may not invite the press into private homes, but filming officers and suspects in public places is permissible.[18]

THE DECISION-MAKING PROCESS Before reaching a decision, the Supreme Court considers **briefs**—written legal arguments submitted by the opposing sides. (Unfortunately for the justices, briefs are seldom really brief!) The justices then listen to oral arguments from contending attorneys in a plenary session, attended by all nine justices, the chief justice presiding. Open to the public, these plenary sessions are held on Mondays, Tuesdays, and Wednesdays from October through May. During a controversial hearing, the courtroom over-flows, and outside "protesters square . . . off at the courthouse steps, chanting, singing and screaming at each other."[19]

During the half-hour allotted to each side to present its case, attorneys often find themselves interrupted by searching questions from the bench. Former law professor Antonin Scalia is especially known for his willingness to turn the ple-nary session into a classroom seminar. Court reporters usually analyze the ques-tions asked by justices to find clues indicating how each intends to vote on the case. Yet it is not always clear how closely the justices attend to the responses. As Chief Justice John Marshall said many years ago, "The acme of judicial distinction means the ability to look a lawyer straight in the eye for two hours and not hear a damned word he says."[20]

Justice William O. Douglas customarily brought books and paperwork to the plenary session, and did not try to hide his lack of attention during oral argu-ments. Soon after joining the high court, Justice Harry Blackmun noticed Douglas writing furiously during one of these meetings. He sent Douglas a note. "Bill, what are you doing, writing another opinion?" Douglas scribbled back, "Yes, this lawyer was done 20 minutes ago, but he didn't know it."[21]

After hearing oral arguments, the justices usually reach a preliminary deci-sion that same week in a private conference presided over by the chief justice. There are "three levels of elbow room about the conference table." The most ample is for the chief justice and senior associate justice, who sit at opposite ends. The next best is grabbed by the three most senior justices sitting on one side, leaving the four most junior crowded together across from them. No outsiders, not even a secretary, are permitted to attend. The only record consists of hand-written notes taken by individual justices.

Justices use the private conferences as opportunities to signal where they stand on each case—which way they are leaning and which points of law or poli-tics decided their position. The justices usually formalize their preferences in a vote, taken in order of seniority. When in the majority, the chief justice assigns authors to cases; otherwise, the senior associate justice in the majority does so.[22]

That the justices "vote" on the case does not mean they decide policy issues the same way a legislature might. Indeed, both clerks and justices become uncomfortable when their colleagues openly approach a decision with political considerations in mind.[23] Instead, courts are expected to follow the principle of **stare decisis.** The phrase is Latin for "let the decision stand." Judges should adhere to **precedents**—prior decisions—including the written justifications known as **opinions of the court** that explained past decisions.

Stare decisis is a powerful judicial principle, ignored only at the risk of the legal system's stability and credibility. Consistent court decisions enable a country to live under a rule of law, because then citizens know what they are expected to obey. "We cannot meddle with a prior decision," one judge explained, unless it "strikes us as wrong with the force of a five-week-old unrefrigerated dead fish."[24]

The principle also helps maintain the almost-sacred relationship between Americans and their Constitution. It preserves the image of judges as impersonal specialists applying a tangible body of law, rather than a tiny, unelected elite telling legislatures what they may or may not do. But having to follow precedent can annoy judges who dislike the choices of their predecessors. One Utah judge got a bit carried away expressing his frustration: "We feel like galley slaves chained to our oars by a power from which we cannot free ourselves."[25]

When reaching a decision that seems contrary to a prior decision, courts try to find a legal distinction between the case at hand and earlier court decisions, usually by emphasizing how the facts of the current case differ. As one wit has put it, the Supreme Court "could find a loophole in the Ten Commandments."[26] The process at times can strain credibility. An attorney once bragged, "Law school taught me one thing: how to take two situations that are exactly the same and show how they are different."[27]

The justice assigned responsibility for preparing the court opinion circulates a draft version among the other eight. Comments received from them usually lead to revisions. Sometimes the comments are only suggestions, but sometimes they are demands; the justice will refuse to join the opinion unless certain changes appear in future drafts. On rare occasions, the justice writing the opinion has "lost a court"—that is, so many justices change their minds that the initial author no longer has a majority. To keep a majority, the justice writing the opinion may produce an extremely bland statement that gives little guidance to lower-court judges. In a 1993 sexual harassment case, *Harris* v. *Forklift Systems,* for example, the majority hardly created any precedent at all, saying only that courts should look at the "totality of the circumstances" to decide whether harassment has occurred.[28]

Justices who vote against the majority may prepare a **dissenting opinion** that explains their disagreement. Any member of the majority who is unhappy with the Court opinion may write a **concurring opinion** that provides different reasoning for the decision. Two hundred years ago, when John Marshall was chief justice, the Court usually issued unanimous judgments and Marshall wrote most opinions. Today, the Court is seldom unanimous in its judgments; justices are sufficiently concerned with public policy that they choose to write either dissenting or concurring opinions explaining their own preferences. Often a case produces so many separate opinions that it is difficult to ascertain exactly what the majority has decided (see Figure 12.3). It is not uncommon for the Court's opinion to describe the full judgment of only one justice, with everyone else either dissenting or concurring.

FIGURE 12.3

Number of Supreme Court dissents

This graph shows the rising number of dissenting opinions written by members of the Supreme Court over the decades. Why do you think dissents have increased? Do dissenting voices make the Court look more or less useful in your view?

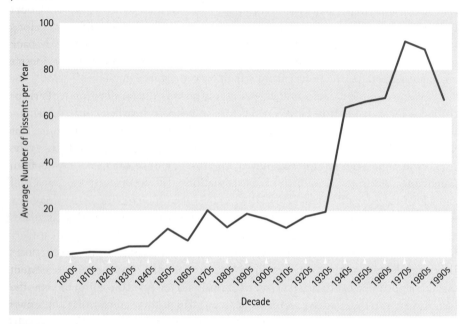

SOURCES: Data from Gregory Calderia and Christopher J. W. Zorn, *Of Time and Consensual Norms on the Supreme Court,* Inter-University Consortium on Political and Social Research, Study No. I01142; see Gregory Calderia and Christopher J. W. Zorn, "Of Time and Consensual Norms on the Supreme Court," *American Journal of Political Science* 42:3 (July 1998): 874–902.

Once the Court reaches a decision, it usually sends, or **remands,** the case to a lower court for implementation. Because the Supreme Court regards itself as responsible for establishing general principles and an overall framework, it seldom becomes involved in the detailed resolution of particular cases. This procedure leaves a great deal of legal responsibility in the hands of lower courts.

If a court finds that an injury has been suffered, it is up to the court to fashion a **remedy,** the compensation for the injury. Often the remedy simply involves monetary compensation to the injured party. But a judge may also direct the defendant to alter future behavior. To overcome racial segregation in schools, courts have ordered school boards to institute magnet schools, to set up special compensatory programs, or to bus children from one part of a city to another. As a Nixon appointee, Justice Lewis Powell, once put it, courts have the right, if racial segregation is sufficiently severe, to "virtually assume the role of school superintendent and school board."[29]

THE ROLE OF THE CHIEF JUSTICE The chief justice has only one vote, and many of the chief's tasks are of a ceremonial or housekeeping nature. For this reason, leading the court provides limited additional power. It may not even guarantee any special respect from the other justices, who may be arrogant and temperamental people. Chief Justice Charles Evans Hughes received a rude awakening on this score when he attempted to convene a session of the Court and noticed that Justice James C. McReynolds was absent. He sent a note along summoning McReynolds, but the independent-minded judge sent a reply back via the same messenger: "Justice McReynolds says to tell you that he doesn't work for you."[30]

Certain responsibilities do give the office added influence, however. Perhaps the most important power is the one mentioned earlier: the power of the chief justice, if voting with a majority, to decide who will write the majority opinion. This assignment power can have far-reaching consequences, because it influences the explanations given for a ruling and the tone of the Court's judgment. The chief can frustrate a particular justice by refusing to give him or her important cases. Chief Justice Warren Burger often angered his colleagues by switching to the majority side late in a case, presumably so that he could choose the opinion author.[31]

THE ROLE OF THE SOLICITOR GENERAL A powerful figure who appears before the Supreme Court regularly is the **solicitor general,** a government official responsible for airing the presidential administration's views before the Court. The solicitor general presents the government's case whenever it is party to a suit and, in other cases, may submit *amicus curiae* briefs—literally, briefs submitted by a "friend of the court" explaining its position.*

Involvement of the solicitor general is a signal that the president and attorney general have strong opinions on a subject, raising its visibility and political significance. Some call the occupant of this office "the tenth justice," because the Court accepts 70 percent of the solicitor general's cert petitions.[32] When the office of the solicitor general files an *amicus curiae* brief, its position is on the winning side approximately three-quarters of the time, a batting average envied by even the most successful private attorneys.[33] Some solicitor generals eventually join the Court, as did four during the twentieth century.

THE ROLE OF CLERKS Much of the day-to-day work within the Supreme Court building is the job of **law clerks**—young, influential aides hired by each of the justices. Recently out of law school, most will have spent a year as a clerk with a lower court before being asked to help a Supreme Court justice. Each justice employs between two and four law clerks.[34]

Amicus curiae briefs can also be submitted by others who wish to inform the court of a legal issue presented by a particular case.

The role of the law clerk has grown in recent years. Not only do clerks initially review certs, they also draft many opinions. Clerks have become so important to the Court's routine that some view the true "Supreme Court" of today as nothing more than a junior collection of bright but unseasoned attorneys, unconfirmed by the Senate or anybody else. The clerks' defenders reply that well-trained graduates of the country's most prestigious law schools may be better judges than aging titans who refuse to leave office well beyond the age of normal retirement. The truth probably lies between these two extremes: The enthusiasm of the young clerks and the experience of the justices are probably better in combination than either would be alone.[35]

LITIGATION AS A POLITICAL STRATEGY

Interest groups increasingly use the federal court system to place issues on the political agenda, particularly when elected officials have not responded to group demands. Civil rights groups pioneered this strategy (see Chapter 14), but the technique has since spread.[36] Alexis de Tocqueville anticipated as much over a century and a half ago. He wrote that "there is hardly a political question in the United States which does not sooner or later turn into a judicial one."[37]

To advance an issue, advocacy groups often file **class action suits** on behalf of all individuals in a particular category, whether or not they actually participate in the suit. For example, in the late 1990s groups of former smokers in several states filed class action suits against the major tobacco companies for lying to consumers about the harms caused by smoking. In the first such case to reach a verdict favorable to plaintiffs, a jury ordered the five major tobacco companies to pay millions of dollars in damages to up to 500,000 ill Florida smokers.[38] More recently, attorneys have filed class action suits against fast-food chains, alleging that they have contributed to the obesity and poor health of diners.

Class action suits are justified on the grounds that the issues affect many people in essentially the same way. It should not be necessary for each member of the class to bring an individual suit to secure relief. But the main motive may be less to benefit the supposed clients than to profit the attorneys, because the amount won by each member of the class may be relatively small whereas the lawyers' fees approved by the court may be astronomical. Critics of the judicial system's power also fear that lawsuits have become a tactic for circumventing the democratic process.[39] Lawyers can use the courts as an indirect way to punish unpopular groups or to ban controversial products such as cigarettes or handguns—driving up their costs or driving their manufacturers out of business.

THE POLITICS OF JUDICIAL APPOINTMENTS

The judicial system is supposed to be politically blind. Justice, like the rain, is expected to fall equally on rich and poor, on Democrat and Republican, on all ethnic groups, and so forth. Judges are appointed for life so that they may decide

Losing their own private Idaho

Political groups can use lawsuits to undermine other organizations with whom they disagree. Litigation is especially powerful when the target is an unpopular political minority. The right-wing Aryan Nations lost their entire Idaho compound in a lawsuit after one of their guards killed a man.

each case without concern for their political futures. Chief Justice Warren E. Burger expressed this ideal when he claimed that judges "rule on the basis of law, not public opinion, and they should be totally indifferent to pressures of the times."[40] At one level these ideals are clearly a myth in America's new democracy.

Political influences play a major role in the selection of federal judges. Most share the same partisan identifications as the presidents who nominate them; 94 percent of Ronald Reagan's nominees were Republicans, and 90 percent of Jimmy Carter's nominees were Democrats (see Figure 12.4).[41] The convention known as **senatorial courtesy** requires that a judicial nominee be acceptable to the senior senator of the state or region involved who shares the president's political party.

Judicial decisions reflect the political orientation of the president who appointed each judge. According to one study, Reagan's district court appointees were significantly tougher toward those accused of crime than were Carter-appointed judges.[42] More generally, judges appointed by Democratic presidents

FIGURE 12.4

Partisan affiliation of district judges

Republican presidents usually appoint Republican judges, and Democratic presidents usually appoint Democratic judges.

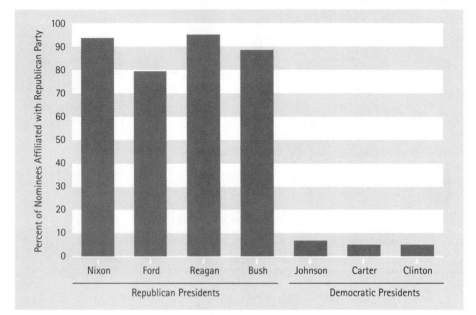

SOURCE: Sheldon Goldman, "Reagan's Judicial Legacy: Completing the Puzzle and Summing Up," *Judicature* 72 (April–May 1989): 321–322.

are more likely than those appointed by Republican presidents to hand down liberal decisions (see Figure 12.5).

For at least the first half of the twentieth century, the idealistic view of judicial decision making guided the process through which the Senate confirmed nominees. Senators approved presidential selections as a matter of course. Most nominees did not even testify before congressional committees first. One of Harry Truman's nominees declined an explicit invitation to testify but was confirmed anyway.[43] Earl Warren, an Eisenhower appointee who dramatically changed the tenor of the Supreme Court as chief justice, also avoided testifying before confirmation.[44]

This long-time separation of Supreme Court nominations from political disputes owed a great deal to the efforts of William Howard Taft. Taft was the only person ever to serve both as president (1909–1913) and as chief justice of the Supreme Court (1921–1930). Before Taft, political factors openly affected the confirmation decisions; the Senate rejected a third of the presidents' nominees in the nineteenth century.[45] But Taft worked hard to enhance the quality of nominees,

FIGURE 12.5

Decision making by Democratic and Republican judges

Judges appointed by Democratic presidents make more liberal decisions.

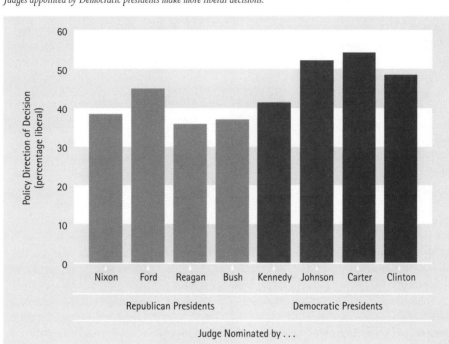

SOURCES: Robert A. Carp and Ronald Stidham, *The Federal Courts,* 2nd ed. (Washington, DC: CQ Press, 1991), p. 116; *U.S. News and World Report* (May 26, 1997): 24.

minimize the significance of confirmation procedures, and elevate the prestige of the Court. He also made sure that the new Supreme Court building, eventually completed in 1935, was designed to resemble a Greek temple, so that Americans would respect their laws with the same reverence with which the ancient Greeks venerated their gods.

Taft was so successful that until 1968, the Senate confirmed every twentieth-century nominee except one, most without significant dissent. The Senate has regained some of its power in the past 50 years, however, and the judicial-selection process has become increasingly political (see the accompanying Election Connection, "The Birth of Borking"). Justices are nominated by the president, evaluated by the Senate Judiciary Committee, and confirmed by a vote of the full Senate largely on the basis of their policy views. The procedure guarantees a voice in who holds judicial office to numerous politicians, interest groups, and the media—few of whom are equipped to evaluate the nominees for their legal

ELECTION CONNECTION

The Birth of Borking

Lewis F. Powell was the definitive moderate Supreme Court justice. Upon his retirement in 1987, he told a reporter what many court observers already knew: "I never think of myself as having a judicial policy. . . . I try to be careful, to do justice to the particular case, rather than to try to write principles that will be new, or original, or whatever."

This sentiment was without question alien to Robert H. Bork, the man President Reagan nominated to replace Powell. A gruff, chain-smoking ex-Marine, Bork professed an unapologetic conservatism. Liberal interest groups vowed to stop him from joining the high court. They waged a grassroots campaign the likes of which had never been associated with a judicial nomination. At first it seemed that they faced an uphill struggle—Bork was undoubtedly qualified, so the attack had to be based on his beliefs.

Controversial Supreme Court Nominee Robert Bork

The very writings that established Bork's scholarly ability proved to be his Achilles' heel, however. In the mid-1960s, he had criticized civil rights laws. In 1971, he questioned free-speech rights for scientific or literary publications. In the early 1980s, he argued that courts should not create rights, as they did in legalizing abortion, because such behavior was "imperialistic" and "inconsistent with the democratic form of government."

In confirmation hearings before the Senate Judiciary Committee, Bork argued that his present views were more moderate than his past pronouncements. But interest-group media advertisements, telephone calls, and direct mail convinced many voters that Bork was a dangerous extremist. Senators were flooded with thousands of letters, postcards, and telegrams urging

expertise. Instead, these players pay close attention to the electoral and policy consequences of judicial appointments. The Senate's propensity to reject presidential nominees has increased.

Most lower-court nominees win confirmation. Rejections usually result from financial or personal problems uncovered during the confirmation process. However, in recent decades even lower-court confirmations have become politicized. Opposition-party senators are most likely to exert their power by refusing to bring nominations to a vote. In the late 1990s, partisan conflict over judicial nominations became bitter and vocal, as President Clinton complained of congressional foot dragging and Republicans criticized his judicial nominations as too liberal. The Senate approved only about 45 percent of Clinton's 1997 nominees (a 20-year low) and delayed action on the rest. Most early reports indicate that President George W. Bush's nominations proceeded even more slowly while Democrats controlled

them to vote against the nominee. "We didn't anticipate this would be conducted like a federal election," one Reagan aide grumbled near the end of the battle.

Judiciary Committee chairman Joseph Biden, a Democrat, saw the nomination battle as a political opportunity—one that might give him enough momentum to win the Democratic nomination for president in 1988. He used his position as chair to hold a series of hearings that dramatized Bork's most unpopular views. Too many factors converged against Bork, and his hopes for a seat on the high court perished on October 23 by a Senate vote of 42 to 58.

The defeat shocked the Reagan administration. Reagan had just won the 1984 election in a landslide, so he expected that Congress would bow to his wishes. As one Reagan staffer put it, when asked about opposition from Biden, "Last time I looked, Ronald Reagan carried 49 states. It was in all the papers. How many states did Joe Biden carry?" What the administration did not realize was that the 1984 campaign was ancient history. The senators were looking forward to the next election, as they typically do

in America's new democracy—and for that purpose, Biden's main task was to please Democrats who would be voting in the presidential primaries. Bork's loss was just another symptom of the permanent campaign.

What do you think?
- Since the Bork nomination, presidents have avoided nominating controversial judges. Does this harm the judiciary by robbing it of superior intellects?
- What are the positive and the negative consequences of interest-group involvement in the confirmation process?
- Should the Senate reject nominees on the basis of ideology?

SOURCES: Stuart Taylor, Jr., "Powell on His Approach: Doing Justice Case by Case," *New York Times* (July 12, 1987): 1; Dale Russakoff and Al Kamen, "A Trip Across the Political Spectrum: After Flirting with Socialism, Bork Became a Conservative," *Washington Post* (July 26, 1987): A1; Lou Cannon and Edward Walsh, "Reagan Nominates Appeals Judge Bork to Supreme Court," *Washington Post* (July 12, 1987): A1; David Lauter, "Forthcoming Battle Over Bork Will Weigh Issue: Is Senate Rejection for Ideology Proper?" *Los Angeles Times* (July 3, 1987): 1; Gloria Borger with Kenneth T. Walsh, "Going . . . Going: How the White House Booted the Nomination of Judge Robert Bork," *U.S. News & World Report* (October 12, 1987): 20.

the U.S. Senate. The Democratic Senate Judiciary Committee refused to hear one Bush appointee to the Fifth Circuit, Charles Pickering of Mississippi, and stalled on hearing several other appeals court nominees.[46]

Presidents sometimes avoid confirmation battles by choosing moderate judges or nominees with unknown views. In 1990 President Bush nominated David Souter, a New Hampshire state supreme court justice; Souter had never written an opinion or treatise on any major constitutional question. Most Supreme Court nominees also tell senators that they cannot comment on specific issues that might come before the Court. Legal scholars lament such conflict avoidance. One law professor protested that to sidestep a political firestorm, "no president will nominate anyone who has written anything very interesting."[47] Yet the strategy works. Washington insiders could not identify Souter's opinions, so the Senate confirmed him easily.

Sacred justice
*Originally conceived by President and Chief Justice William Howard Taft to instill public respect for the judicial branch,
the Supreme Court building resembles a Greek temple built to house ancient gods or goddesses.* Why did Taft not design
the courthouse in a Gothic style, which many churches use to instill respect?

The United States is unlikely to go back to the apolitical way of selecting federal judges. Modern methods of communication—televised hearings, fax
machines, toll-free numbers, radio talk shows, and the Internet—ensure that
senators and interest groups can conduct detailed evaluations of each appointee.
Presidents have no choice but to select judges with an eye to the public controversies they might create. Electoral considerations will continue to affect judicial
selections.

THE POWER OF JUDICIAL REVIEW

Policy-oriented senators scrutinize nominees closely because the Supreme
Court's vast political authority includes the power of **judicial review.** Federal
courts regularly declare laws of both Congress and the state legislatures unconstitutional, meaning that they are null and void. The Supreme Court is the court of
last resort on such judgments. Exercising this power is controversial because it

gives judges, appointed for life, the authority to negate laws written by elected representatives. Senators hesitate to surrender so much power, and the public seems to share their caution. By a margin of 5 to 1, Americans agree that the "Senate should carefully scrutinize a presidential nominee."[48]

Although the Constitution claims to be the "supreme Law of the Land," it says nothing explicit about judicial review. From what little they said at the Constitutional Convention, it seems the delegates did not expect the Court to be powerful. Alexander Hamilton, writing as Publius in the 78th *Federalist Papers* essay, initially seemed to claim review powers for the judiciary, but then he backed off his aggressive posture three essays later. "The United States began its history," political scientist Robert McCloskey once observed, "with a Supreme Court whose birthright was most uncertain."[49]

ORIGINS OF JUDICIAL REVIEW

The Supreme Court first asserted judicial-review powers in 1803, as part of the ***Marbury* v. *Madison*** judgment. Many consider this opinion the most significant Supreme Court decision ever rendered, so it is worth understanding how the case evolved and why even those skeptical of judicial review tolerated the ruling.[50]

Marbury v. *Madison* followed one of the most contentious elections in U.S. history and the first peaceful transition of power from a president of one political party to that of another. Federalist President John Adams lost the 1800 election to Thomas Jefferson, candidate of the arch-rival Democratic–Republicans (see Chapter 8). Congressional elections that year also produced widespread Federalist losses, costing them control of both chambers. Adams and his supporters feared that the Jeffersonians would usher in a period of dangerous radicalism. They were determined to leave their mark on the U.S. government before stepping down.

The best means of resistance seemed to be to stock the judiciary with Federalist sympathizers, who would enjoy lifetime appointments. So in the last days before Adams left office, he nominated numerous judges, including 42 new justices of the peace for Washington, D.C. The Senate approved the appointments a day afterward, and that evening, as the skies grew dark in the nation's capital, Secretary of State John Marshall stamped their official commissions with the Great Seal of the United States. The appointments had been arranged so hastily, however, that administration officials failed to deliver the commissions. Jefferson's supporters found them when they arrived.

The Jeffersonians decided that appointees had no right to their posts until they received commissions—and so refrained from delivering them. But appointee William Marbury did not believe that the Jefferson administration could deny him a position simply because the official notification had not gone out. A law passed by Congress in 1789, the Judiciary Act, specified how jilted appointees might challenge denial of their posts. They could request a writ of

Transfer of power

When government authority changes hands in many countries, it is a source of anxiety. Election "upsets" sometimes result in the end of democracy when leaders refuse to surrender power. Americans take for granted how casually power changes hands in their political system, even when rival leaders dislike or disrespect each other. Judging from the facial expressions and body language in this picture, what kind of relationship do you think President Bush and former President Clinton have with each other?

mandamus (a court order) directly from the U.S. Supreme Court. Accordingly, Marbury sued Jefferson's secretary of state, future president James Madison.

Ironically, John Marshall, who had prepared Marbury's commission, was the Court's chief justice by 1803. Indeed, it was a Federalist-dominated court. Marbury seemed certain to win. Yet Marshall saw a rare opportunity in the case. Installing a few extra justices of the peace might offer the Federalists a short-term victory, but nothing more. And there was no guarantee that Madison would honor a Court ruling on Marbury's behalf. For Jefferson's administration to ignore the Court would weaken the judiciary over the long term. Instead, Marshall decided to give the administration its way, but to do so by declaring a constitutional principle that Jefferson opposed.

Marshall read his opinion to an anxious, crowded audience on February 24. His initial statement chastised the Jeffersonians for denying Marbury his rightful position. But then Marshall asked a crucial question: Was the Supreme Court the proper place to address Marbury's complaint? His stunning conclusion was that it was not. The Judiciary Act of 1789, Marshall explained, had violated the Constitution by giving the Court original jurisdiction over judicial appointments. Marbury lost on a technicality.[*]

Marshall asserted the power of judicial review to explain why the Supreme Court could overturn offending portions of the Judiciary Act and deny Marbury's appeal. His reasoning was simple and straightforward: The Constitution is the highest law of the land, established by the people in convention before the national government even existed. No entity, not even Congress itself, can enact legislation that contravenes this higher law. Federal judges, who are responsible for interpreting the Constitution, are the ones who must declare when a law runs afoul of its restrictions. They could void unconstitutional laws.

Marshall's brilliant decision had transformed a situation sure to sap the Court's power into one that strengthened it tremendously. Madison and Jefferson could not refuse to win their own case simply because they disliked the reasoning used to decide it! They would have looked ridiculous and would probably have lost credibility. Marshall had gained more power for the Court—a Federalist goal—through his willingness to lose a minor political battle. By invoking the power of judicial review for the first time, and in a manner that insulated it from challenge, Marshall ensured that the judiciary would always be an authoritative force.

THREE THEORIES OF CONSTITUTIONAL INTERPRETATION

The justification for judicial review makes sense when one views a court's role as a technical one. If someone must examine laws and compare them to a higher written law, reconciling situations in which two rules plainly contradict, then judges seem a logical choice for the task. They have the training to interpret legal phrasing and the political independence to do it fairly if they wish. However, very few judgments of constitutionality are simple, because few provisions are precise. What should justices do when a law seems as though it might violate the meaning of the Constitution but does not do so in a manner so plain that anyone schooled in the law would see it?

To address this dilemma, judges have developed three distinct theories of constitutional interpretation: the plain meaning of the text, the original intent of the text, and the living-constitution approach. The approach most appealing to common sense is to go by the *plain meaning* of a constitutional provision's words. The law is whatever the written law says. After all, the words are what people voted on, not anything else, so only they can lay out the law. Plain meaning has two clear advantages: (1) it is the approach least open to judicial abuse, because courts must restrict their attention to the laws before them, and (2) it calls upon

---

[*]One of the great mysteries of American history is why Marbury never tried to go through proper judicial channels to attain his commission. Marshall left no doubt that Marbury would win if he followed legal procedures.

judges to perform the task for which they are best trained, which is to decipher the meaning of legal language.

But plain-meaning theory has limitations. The Constitution is a very short document that left many issues undecided and many phrases unexplained. For example, the First Amendment bars Congress from passing any law "respecting an establishment of religion." Legal experts disagree over how to give teeth to this prohibition—since to do so requires figuring out what the framers actually banned. What makes something a "religion" or not? At what point has a law moved too close to "an establishment" of one? And what does the "respecting" forbid that the word "establishing" alone might have allowed? The phrase is hardly plain, and the confusion it engenders is not just a rare exception.

Furthermore, words do not always have a clear legal definition. Vocabulary changes over time, and words that persist often alter in meaning. This transformation occurs regularly and swiftly in conversational English. The word *jazz* once served in New Orleans brothels to describe the transaction between prostitutes and their clients; now an interior decorator might offer tips to help you "jazz up" a bedroom. A "cool" teacher may be friendly or laid back, not coldly formal and aloof as once was the meaning of the term. Words used in legal terminology change in the same way, though perhaps more slowly. The word *man* at various times has referred to a male of any age, to an adult male, to an adult of any gender, or to humankind. The House may impeach a president for committing "high Crimes and Misdemeanors," but the Constitution did not intend that phrase to include the minor legal violations we call misdemeanors today.

Sometimes social changes take the law outside any context anticipated by those who first wrote the provisions. The Second Amendment may grant a "right to bear arms," but does this include nuclear bombs and tanks or only hunting rifles? The word *arms* provides little guidance about which sorts of weapons citizens have a right to possess. Those who write laws often leave out details because they assume readers will understand what they mean, not anticipating that one day Americans will lack their cultural perspective. Early Americans may have understood what the Bill of Rights meant by "unreasonable" searches or "excessive" fines or "cruel and unusual" punishments, but today's readers lack the same point of reference.

A second approach, the theory of *original intent,* also tries to remain true to inherited law—but helps the authors a bit by filling in the meaning of words. Judges who take this approach must perform historical research to ascertain the intentions of those who approved constitutional provisions. Very little solid evidence exists to determine what the typical voter believed, but at least scholars can assess the intentions of the framers. Judges may examine such documents as the notes that James Madison wrote down at the Constitutional Convention, the *Federalist Papers,* and the speeches made during the ratifying campaign in 1787 and 1788. They also look at the laws commonly in effect when an amendment originated. Justice Thomas, for example, favors overturning *Roe* v. *Wade* because the words used to justify a right to abortion joined the Constitution at a time when many states outlawed the practice.

Original-intent theory has its own problems. Those who wrote the Constitution did not contemplate many issues now before the courts. Nor could they anticipate the many social complexities added, for example, by advances in travel and communications. Judges can abuse the practice of determining intent. They may sift through the evidence selectively to find examples or arguments supporting their political preferences, and even a sincere judge is not trained in social science or historical methods. Furthermore, those who supported provisions often did not agree on the meanings themselves, so even trained historians cannot settle what voters thought they were endorsing in these instances.

Faced with the difficulty of figuring out what inherited words mean, or were supposed to mean, some judges prefer to assess the law according to the sentiments of their own time. Societies evolve, and even fundamental law can evolve with them. This *living-constitution* theory allows judges to update the meaning of laws in light of the entire history of the United States as a nation. They can go beyond the literal meaning of laws or the opinions expressed at the time of their passage and incorporate the moral lessons Americans have learned since then. In the words of Justice Oliver Wendell Holmes, Jr., constitutional questions must be "considered in the light of our whole experience and not merely in that of what was said a hundred years ago."[51] Presumably, the passage of another century since Holmes served the Court only makes his logic more compelling.

The living-constitution theory is practical in one important way: It gives the political system extreme flexibility when adapting law to situations alien to the framers. Laws, especially constitutional provisions, are slow to change through the democratic process. Judicial interpretation is a quicker method of adaptation. However, it is also the approach most susceptible to judicial abuse. Reading history's moral lessons is a highly personal endeavor. It takes judges farthest from their area of expertise, requiring as it does insights drawn from numerous fields (including sociology, political science, psychology, history, theology, and perhaps natural science). Many question the wisdom of giving this power to judges, who are appointed for life almost solely from the legal profession.

These three approaches—plain meaning, original intent, and living Constitution—are useful conceptually. A justice occasionally will develop the reputation for espousing a particular view of constitutional interpretation. The late Justice Hugo Black endorsed a literal reading of the Constitution, refusing in principle either to read rights into the language or to water down those stated starkly in the document. The late Justice William O. Douglas emerged from the "realist" school of law, which endorsed incorporating a judge's observations of the real world when interpreting legal phrases.

The labels are also useful as a form of shorthand in political discussion. During the 2000 presidential election debates, President Bush promised to appoint "strict constructionists" to the bench—meaning judges who would stick to the plain meaning of written law. Listeners attuned to the political buzzwords knew that most judges fitting this description would oppose abortion rights and loosen constitutional restrictions on government accommodation of religion. Vice President Gore, by contrast, said he would appoint judges likely to support abortion rights because they would believe in a living Constitution.

Concepts break down somewhat when describing the actual voting behavior of particular judges. Outsiders often point to Justice Antonin Scalia as the prime example of a strict-constructionist judge, but Scalia rejects the label. "I am not a strict constructionist," he told a law school audience in Wisconsin. "You shouldn't be a strict constructionist—you should be reasonable."[52] He does tend to read the religious-freedom clauses of the First Amendment narrowly, in that he allows the government wide latitude before finding a violation of either clause (see Chapter 13). But he allows occasional flexibility in the same amendment's free-expression clauses; for example, he includes symbolic gestures, such as flag burning, as instances of protected "speech." He considers free-speech rights to include an unwritten, but understood, "right to associate" with like-minded people in groups that exclude those who disagree. This principle led Scalia, in 2000, to forbid California's flexible party primaries and to permit the Boy Scouts of America to exclude homosexual scout leaders. And Scalia interpreted the guarantee against unreasonable searches broadly enough to include high-tech snooping devices from outside the home, not just investigations in which law enforcement authorities physically "search" the premises.

VOTING ON THE SUPREME COURT

The three legal approaches to constitutional interpretation are useful conceptually, but few justices have ever fit cleanly and consistently into one category or another. Nor do justices reveal a consistent and predictable allegiance to or disregard for precedents—another legal criterion for choosing sides in a case—although, of course, justices vary in their levels of caution. This flexibility leads some court watchers to question whether judicial opinions really derive, first and foremost, from legal criteria.

Scholars have proposed a variety of alternative explanations for judicial decision making, criteria that are personal and political rather than legal. Judges might vote according to their political ideologies, their policy attitudes, their party affiliations, or their personal backgrounds. It can be difficult to parse these various explanations out from each other, because they overlap so much. Conservative judges usually prefer conservative policies, for example, and may have a personal background that would cultivate a conservative orientation. What the explanations have in common is a sense that judicial decision making will be predictable based on information about who the judges are, not just about their relationship with legal interpretation. In short, the Supreme Court is largely a political entity.

PREDICTABILITY   Most of the time, justices vote along lines anticipated by those who nominated and confirmed them. By the time lawyers rise in prominence sufficient to warrant Supreme Court appointments, they usually have a track record of opinions, speeches, law review articles, and political activism to indicate likely future voting patterns. According to one study, information about the political views of Supreme Court justices at the time they were being confirmed allows one to anticipate the justices' decisions in civil liberties cases over 60 percent of the time.[53] This predictability enables elected officials—both presidents and senators—to shape the future direction of the Supreme Court, thereby maintaining some degree of popular control.

Not every prediction of future behavior is correct, however. Justices Felix Frankfurter and Robert Jackson, both New Deal insiders appointed by President Roosevelt, bitterly disappointed liberals by refusing to continue their progressive activism from the bench. President Nixon appointed Justice Harry Blackmun, expecting him to follow in the footsteps of his conservative fellow Minnesotan, Warren Burger. Instead, Blackmun shifted decidedly to the left over the course of his career, and by 1992 he was the Court's most liberal justice.[54] On the present Court, Justice Souter also has disappointed conservatives, compiling a record as liberal as that of Clinton appointee Breyer.[55]

POLICY MAKING   Justices of the Court fall into quite predictable voting blocs. Even Justice John Paul Stevens, "long . . . considered a maverick," has found himself almost constantly on the left in recent years. The most liberal justices, Stevens and Clinton appointee Ruth Bader Ginsburg, favor a certain amount of **judicial activism,** meaning that they are willing to overturn precedents to advance a vision of what the Constitution has come to mean (or ought to mean). Souter and the other Clinton appointee, Stephen Breyer, usually join the liberal bloc, especially when it comes to continuing the enforcement of activist judicial precedents from the Warren and Burger eras.

A second bloc of conservative restorationists—Thomas, Scalia, and Chief Justice William Rehnquist—also frequently endorse overturning earlier court decisions. They think liberal judges have undermined the original meaning of the Constitution, and they will strike down precedents to restore older legal traditions. Although Scalia in particular often favors deferring to elected representatives, the conservative bloc also shows a certain willingness to strike down liberal-minded legislation that they see as invasive of the private spheres of American life: family, church, club, and neighborhood.

Sandra Day O'Connor and Anthony Kennedy usually serve as crucial swing votes on the Court. Unlike the conservative and liberal activists, they often promote **judicial restraint,** forcing the majority to soften written opinions or weakening those opinions by writing a softer concurrence. They also write more than their share, because often the only way a majority can hold together is to conform to the preferences of its least enthusiastic members. One outgrowth of

O'Connor's and Kennedy's restraint is that they avoid overturning prior court decisions, sometimes sticking with precedents contrary to their conservative inclinations. They emphasize the importance of maintaining the Supreme Court's integrity as a judicial body rather than a legislative one. "Do I make policy?" Justice Anthony Kennedy once asked. "Was I appointed for life to go around . . . suggesting answers to the Congress? That's not our function."[56] If the law should change, that responsibility falls on the people's elected representatives or on the constitutional amendment process.

Ironically, it is often the moderates (and in particular O'Connor) who produce the decisions most frustrating to those who must stay within the bounds of constitutional law. "Ruling from the center" often requires rather fine legal distinctions. O'Connor allows government bodies to erect Christmas holiday displays—but only if they do not appear to endorse Christianity.[57] She considers nude dancing a protected form of expression—but allows a requirement that strippers wear partial covering as a means of limiting the negative social effects that crop up around strip clubs.[58] Sometimes the twists and turns of a moderate voting record can produce such a complicated body of constitutional law that it creeps disturbingly close to the type of policy detail customary in legislation.

Nevertheless, it is also striking how closely the Court's swing voters track the preferences of public opinion and how much their reasoning carries the flavor of common sense (although dressed up in a legalistic vocabulary). The moderate judicial position on abortion, for example, matches the ambivalent opinions expressed by the American public surprisingly closely (see Chapter 5). The moderates do not mind some religious influences in schools, as long as schools are not

The justices of the Supreme Court
In this composite, the justices of the 2003 Supreme Court are pictured from left to right according to their judicial philosophies. On the left are John Paul Stevens, Ruth Bader Ginsburg, Stephen Breyer, and David Souter. The two moderates are Sandra Day O'Connor and Anthony Kennedy. On the right are Chief Justice William H. Rehnquist, Antonin Scalia, and Clarence Thomas. Where do you think the next justice's picture will be positioned?

pushing religion on students. They do not mind if government considers race when shaping university admissions policies or designing legislative election districts, as long as the process does not resemble racial quotas or produce bizarrely shaped districts for which race was obviously the predominant factor determining their makeup (see Chapter 14). These are the sorts of compromises that one often hears proposed by regular voters.

EVALUATING JUDICIAL REVIEW

Disagreements about theories of judicial review or judicial activism are not just academic, despite the occasional inconsistency of particular judges. The manner in which a court interprets the Constitution can have serious consequences. The second time the Supreme Court declared a law of Congress unconstitutional, the 1857 case *Dred Scott* v. *Sandford,* it helped precipitate the Civil War.

Liberals unhappy with the active application of judicial review like to point to the Supreme Court's role at blocking reform early in the twentieth century. *Lochner* v. *New York,* decided in 1905, struck down a New York state law limiting the number of hours bakers could work. A string of such decisions around that time helped limit state governments as a force for social change. After Franklin Delano Roosevelt became president in 1933, several conservative Supreme Court decisions helped slow the New Deal. *Schechter Poultry Corp.* v. *United States* (1935), for example, struck down the National Industrial Recovery Act, which managed labor and competition in the private sector.[59] Called the "sick chicken" case, it placed the Supreme Court squarely at odds with the president and Congress, creating a constitutional crisis (see the Election Connection, "FDR's Court-Packing Plan").

FDR's Court-Packing Plan

Alexander Hamilton wrote that an independent judiciary was necessary, in part, to guard against "dangerous innovations in government." In the 1930s, as the Supreme Court considered the constitutionality of the programs making up Franklin Delano Roosevelt's New Deal, a majority of the Court considered FDR's new programs to be such dangerous innovations. They struck down numerous federal programs and regulations.[a]

The Roosevelt Democrats were furious at decisions that seemed to deny the country's elected officials their right to govern. Never before had judicial review placed the Supreme Court in such direct conflict with the president and Congress. But Roosevelt overplayed his hand. Instead of changing Court views gradually by appointing justices who shared his philosophy, he tried to "pack the Court" by adding six new justices over and above the nine already on the Court (one for each of those over 70 years old who refused to retire).

Although the Constitution does not specify the number of justices that shall serve on the Supreme Court—its actual size has varied between five and ten—many believed the Court should not face such direct political manipulation. FDR's popularity did not ensure that, as he confidently told White House visitors, "The people are with me." Instead, FDR's court-packing scheme cost him some public esteem. Members of Congress from his own party accused him of threatening democracy. The plan went nowhere in Congress.

Although Roosevelt lost the battle, he won the war. Shortly after his great reelection victory in 1936, Chief Justice Charles Evans Hughes and Justice Owen Roberts, who had previously voted to restrict federal power, changed their views. This time the issue involved the recently passed Wagner Act, a New Deal law that protected union organizers.[b] A Court majority, in a 5-to-4 vote, declared it constitutional.

Although judicial scholars note that the change of heart by Hughes and Roberts started before FDR challenged them, certainly the justices knew of the anger their rulings were causing. For this reason, the alteration in their jurisprudence has been called "the switch in time that saved nine." The New Deal majority that emerged on the Court was soon augmented and solidified by Roosevelt's own appointees.

What do you think?
- Should the Court respond to changing political conditions?
- Is it possible to alter the number of federal judges without engaging in political manipulation?

[a]For example, *Schechter Poultry Corp.* v. *United States* 295 U.S. 495 (1935). Another rule, that Congress could not delegate its power over the executive branch without giving clear standards, also later fell.
[b]*NLRB* v. *Jones & Laughlin Steel Co.* 301 U.S. 1 (1937).

If anything, conservatives unhappy with an aggressive judiciary find even more to criticize. Earl Warren's tenure on the Supreme Court, from 1953 to 1969, offers numerous controversial applications of judicial review—especially in criminal justice and federalism. Many critics blame the 1973 abortion case, *Roe v. Wade,* for igniting a political controversy that has plagued American politics ever since and wreaked havoc in both electoral and judicial politics.

The many examples of failure and controversy have led some voices in both politics and academia to argue that the country should abandon judicial review as undemocratic. Despite the debate, however, judicial review has become a well-established practice in American government. It survives in part because it is seldom used to defy the strongly held views of national leaders. Between 1803 and 1999, the Supreme Court decided that a federal law was unconstitutional on only 143 occasions.[60] Most of these decisions affected old laws that were no longer supported either by a majority of Congress or by the president. The Supreme Court spends much more time striking down state laws unpopular with a large segment, if not a majority, of the American public.

Research indicates that changes in Supreme Court policy generally parallel swings in national public opinion. These policy shifts are not so pronounced as those in Congress, but justices still seem to pay "attention to what the public wants."[61] Unpopular decisions are the exception, not the rule. Bartender Mr. Dooley, an Irish cartoon figure, was not wide of the mark when he observed years ago that "th' supreme court follows th' illiction returns." Federal judges are key players in the election-driven political system.

STATUTORY INTERPRETATION

Judicial review is only the most sweeping and controversial of judicial powers. The courts also engage in **statutory interpretation,** the application of the laws of Congress to particular cases. American courts have great discretion in exercising this power. For example, in 1973 Congress passed a vague and general law protecting endangered species. It was the Supreme Court that gave this law sharp teeth, by saying that Congress intended to protect all species, the tiny snail darter as well as the eagle. Similarly, the precise requirements of 1991's Americans with Disabilities Act have emerged in the federal courts rather than through the legislative process itself.

Approaches to statutory interpretation parallel those for constitutional interpretation. Judges may stick to the written law, because this is what a legislature formally approved. They may use congressional speeches, the claims of a bill's authors, and the record of amendments accepted or rejected to determine a bill's intent. Or they may read legislation expansively, to keep the meaning current with modern sentiments. This latter approach is often as controversial as the parallel theory of constitutional interpretation; it means that a bill can clear Congress with few members endorsing the sweeping application to which federal courts will put it.

CHECKS ON COURT POWER

Although court decisions have great impact, their consequences can be limited by other political actors. "Judicial decision making is one stage, not the only nor necessarily the final one," political scientist Jack Peltason explains.[62] Other branches of government can alter or circumscribe court decisions in two important ways: by changing the laws that courts interpret or by neglecting to implement their rulings.

Changing the law is difficult in constitutional cases. It requires amending the U.S. Constitution, which is an arduous process (see Chapter 2) Troublesome statutory interpretations are easier to address, because Congress can simply change the law or clarify it. In the case of *Wards Cove Packing Co.* v. *Antonio,* for example, the Supreme Court narrowly interpreted a law banning race and gender discrimination—requiring those bringing a complaint to prove they suffered mistreatment. Congress responded in 1991 by passing a law shifting the burden of proof to the accused, effectively overturning the Court's judgment. Even this approach to constraining court power is a limited one, however, since passing laws through Congress is so hard. Statutory interpretation favoring one side in a dispute gives that side the political advantage, because it is easier to block a bill than to pass one (see Chapter 9). The difficult process for passing new legislation may allow faulty statutory interpretations to persist for decades.[63]

The political branches also can check court decisions by ignoring them. When told of a Supreme Court decision he did not like, President Andrew Jackson reportedly replied, "Justice Marshall has made his decision, now let him enforce it."[64] Although outright refusal to obey a judicial decision is unlikely today, legislatures may drag their feet on enforcing rulings. After the Supreme Court declared Bible reading in public schools unconstitutional, for example, the practice continued unchanged in many southern school districts.[65]

STATE COURTS

Every U.S. state has its own judicial arrangements. In most states the basic structure follows the same three tiers found in the federal system: trial courts, courts of appeals, and a court of last resort, usually called the state supreme court. State courts perform the same basic tasks as federal courts: interpreting state laws and determining when they contradict the state constitution. Decisions of state supreme courts may be appealed to federal courts, but generally only when a question of federal law appears in the case.

TRIAL COURTS: THE JUDICIAL WORKHORSES

Most judicial activity takes place within state trial courts under the control of state and local governments, which go by many different names in the various states (district courts, county courts, courts of common pleas, and so forth). In fact, 99 percent of all civil and criminal cases originate in these courts.

GOING TO TRIAL   The process of bringing civil and criminal cases before state and local courts is comparable to the federal process. In civil cases, most states follow rules similar to the federal code of civil procedure. Criminal cases, meanwhile, rely on state attorneys and law enforcement officers to bring perpetrators to justice.

Upon receiving information from the police on criminal wrongdoing, prosecutors in the office of the local **district attorney** determine whether the evidence warrants presentation before a grand jury for prosecution. In large cities the district attorney has enormous responsibilities. In Los Angeles, for example, the district attorney's office prosecutes 300,000 cases a year. Many prosecutors earn recognition that wins them election or appointment to the judiciary. About 10 percent of all judges once worked in district attorneys' offices.[66] Many local district attorneys are interested in moving to other elected offices as well.

In early 2000, Paul Howard, a Georgia district attorney, was up for reelection. He pressed for the arrest and trial of Baltimore Ravens football star Ray Lewis after two murders outside a suburban Atlanta bar. But prosecutors could find no evidence linking Lewis to the crime, and Lewis's attorney criticized them for "indicting before investigating."[67] After prosecutors dropped charges and released Lewis, some observers blamed the botched investigation on the district attorney's desire for notoriety. "Because Howard tried to ride to fame on the back of Ray Lewis," one critic wrote, "he has damaged—not enhanced—his chances for reelection."[68]

ELECTED JUDGES   State courts are influenced by political factors at least as much as are federal courts. In 37 of the 50 states, both appellate and trial judges are subject to election. In the remaining states, judges are appointed by the state legislature, the governor, or a governmental agency. Exactly which judges are elected varies from state to state. In New York, trial court judges are elected but appellate judges are appointed.[69] In Georgia, it is the reverse.

Although many state judges are subject to election, most judicial campaigns "are waged in obscurity, with the result that most voters are unfamiliar with the names, not to speak of the issues, involved in the campaign."[70] As a result, judicial elections have traditionally been dominated by organized groups and party politicians interested in controlling court patronage. During the 1960s, 73 out of Chicago's 80 circuit court judges were active in Democratic party politics.[71]

Interest groups have also had a growing influence on judicial elections, especially as the cost of running campaigns for judgeships has increased. In 1996, for example, the candidates for two Alabama supreme court seats spent a combined total of over $2 million on the race, nearly ten times what they likely would have spent only a decade earlier.[72] Much of the money to fund judicial races is donated by single-issue groups that may have an interest in the way certain cases are decided.

RELATIONS BETWEEN
STATE AND FEDERAL COURTS

For the first few decades under the Constitution, the relationship between state and federal judicial systems remained vague. Then, in an early key decision, *McCulloch v. Maryland* (1819), the Supreme Court made it clear that the power of judicial review applied to state laws (see Chapter 3).[73] However, federal courts usually defer to how states choose to interpret their own laws and constitutional provisions. They rule only on whether the state's approach squares with federal requirements.

Over the decades, the Supreme Court has found more than 1100 state statutes and state constitutional provisions contrary to the federal Constitution.[74] It is not hard to see why the Supreme Court would have an easier time overturning state laws than it does tossing out congressional acts. Congressional legislation generally enjoys the support of a national majority, or at least a majority among national political leaders. Court action casting out a recent law will anger a large segment of elites in the other branches of government. By contrast, state laws reflect the tastes or preferences of a state majority, but the nation as a whole may not think much of regional opinion. The Supreme Court can undo such laws without angering most of the country and, indeed, may even please those outside the region in question. One reason why the Supreme Court could take an active role promoting civil rights, for example, was that they primarily angered opinion leaders in the South; most of those elsewhere felt little attachment to the southern system of race relations (see Chapter 14).

The same act can simultaneously be a violation of both state and federal laws. Although the Fifth Amendment to the Constitution forbids **double jeopardy**—being tried twice for the same crime—something very close to double jeopardy can occur if a person is tried in both federal and state courts for the same action. In 1897 the Supreme Court permitted dual prosecutions, saying "an act denounced as a crime by both national and state sovereignties is an offense against the peace and dignity of both."[75] In recent years the chances for such prosecution have been rising, because Congress, under pressure to do something about crime, has passed new laws essentially duplicating state laws.

Most of the time, federal and state officials do not prosecute a case simultaneously; rather, they reach an agreement allowing one or the other to take responsibility for prosecuting a crime. (From this comes the popular phrase "Don't make a federal case out of it.") For example, the 1995 bombing of a federal building in Oklahoma, which killed 168 people, constituted a violation of both state and federal laws. Although state officials began the investigation, federal investigators quickly took charge, and Timothy McVeigh and Terry Nichols were convicted in federal courtrooms for the crime. State prosecutors jumped back on the Nichols case only when he failed to receive the federal death penalty. The 2002 "Tarot Card Sniper" case that terrorized people around Washington, D.C., set off a legal battle between the federal government and two states (Maryland and Virginia) over who would get to prosecute the arrested suspects, John Allen Muhammad, 41, and John Lee Malvo, 17.

CHAPTER SUMMARY

The courts are the branch of government most removed from political influence. Federal judges are appointed for life. They are expected to rely on legal precedents when reaching their decisions. Nevertheless, the courts are not immune to electoral pressures. The day-to-day work of the judiciary is carried out by state and lower federal court judges. Many state judges and district attorneys are elected officials.

Political factors even influence the way Court justices use their powers of constitutional and statutory interpretation. When justices are selected for the bench, both presidents and Congress closely evaluate their judicial philosophies. Once appointed, most Supreme Court justices decide cases in ways that are consistent with views they were known to have at the time of their selection. If court decisions challenge deep-seated political views, they may be modified by new legislation, stalled at the implementation stage, or even reversed by legislators. For all these reasons, popular influences reach even the most insulated branch of government in America's new democracy.

KEY TERMS

briefs, p. 401

circuit court of appeals,
  p. 400

civil code, p. 397

class action suits, p. 406

concurring opinion,
  p. 403

criminal code, p. 398

defendant, p. 397

dissenting opinion, p. 403

district attorney, p. 425

district courts, p. 397

double jeopardy, p. 426

judicial activism, p. 419

judicial restraint, p. 419

judicial review, p. 412

justices, p. 400

law clerks, p. 405

Marbury v. *Madison,* p. 413

opinions of the court,
  p. 402

plaintiff, p. 397

plenary session, p. 400

precedents, p. 402

remands, p. 404

remedy, p. 404

senatorial courtesy,
  p. 407

solicitor general, p. 405

stare decisis, p. 402

statutory interpretation,
  p. 423

U.S. attorney, p. 399

writ of *certiorari,* p. 400

SUGGESTED READINGS

Agresto, John. *The Supreme Court and Constitutional Democracy.* Ithaca, NY: Cornell University Press, 1984. Makes a powerful case against judicial review.

Bronner, Ethan. *Battle for Justice: How the Bork Nomination Shook America.* New York: Norton, 1989. Fascinating case study of the Senate refusal to confirm Robert

Bork's nomination to the Supreme Court.

Massaro, John. *Supremely Political: The Role of Ideology and Presidential Management in Unsuccessful Supreme Court Nominations.* Albany: State University of New York Press, 1990. Engaging account of the politics of Supreme Court nominations.

Melnick, R. Shep. *Between the Lines: Interpreting Welfare Rights.* Washington, DC: Brookings, 1994. Insightful analysis of the Court's role in the interpretation and elaboration of statutory law.

Perry, H. W., Jr. *Deciding to Decide: Agenda Setting in the United States Supreme Court.* Cambridge, MA: Harvard University Press, 1991. Comprehensive explanation of the process by which the Supreme Court decides whether to review a case.

Simon, James F. *The Center Holds: The Power Struggle Inside the Rehnquist Court.* New York: Simon & Schuster, 1995. Describes the recent split between conservative and moderate justices.

ON THE WEB

Supreme Court
www.supremecourtus.gov
The official Web site of the U.S. Supreme Court contains information on the Court's docket, the text of recent opinions, the rules of the Court, and links to related Web sites.

Legal Information Institute
www.law.cornell.edu
The Legal Information Institute at Cornell Law School includes information on federal and state laws, rules of civil and criminal procedure, and a searchable database of Supreme Court decisions.

Legal Information Site
www.findlaw.com
This all-purpose legal-information site includes various searchable databases and links.

Federal Judiciary
www.uscourts.gov
The Federal Judiciary home page provides a concise guide to the federal court system, a regular newsletter, and annual reports on the state of the judiciary written by Chief Justice William Rehnquist.

Department of Justice
www.usdoj.gov/osg/
The Solicitor General's Office in the U.S. Department of Justice offers copies of briefs it has filed in federal court cases.

National Center for State Courts
www.ncsconline.org
The National Center for State Courts showcases statistical information on the caseload of state court systems, as well as links to state-level legal associations.

Part Four

OUTPUTS FROM AMERICA'S NEW DEMOCRACY

CIVIL LIBERTIES

Timothy McVeigh drove up to the Alfred P. Murrah Federal Building in a bright yellow Ryder truck. A 7000-pound bomb sat just two feet behind him, fuses already burning. The 26-year-old McVeigh did not hesitate. He parked beside the structure's north side and then walked swiftly but steadily into the streets of Oklahoma City to escape the imminent blast.[1]

It was 9 A.M. on a busy workday. This was no accident; the Gulf War Army veteran had planned his arrival with military precision to ensure an impressive number of victims. Lights already burned inside office windows. Pedestrians already coursed the sidewalks. Parents were already arriving to leave their children at America's Kids Day Care Center, which sat one floor above the smoking weapon.

The date—April 19, 1995—was also no accident. Exactly two years previously, federal law enforcement agents had ended an armed standoff with the Branch Davidian cult by storming their compound in Waco, Texas. Eighty-six cultists, including children, had died in fires linked to the assault. Like many fringe activists, McVeigh blamed the carnage on federal agents intoxicated by power. He viewed his own lethal mission as a sensible counterstrike, a "legit tactic." McVeigh's target was not the individuals who happened to fall within his blast radius, whom he had never met, but the government offices that many of them staffed.

The explosion struck a couple of minutes, after McVeigh had jogged to safety. It ripped off the Murrah Building's concrete face, reducing most of the offices to rubble. Surrounding buildings shuddered, sending plate glass cascading into the streets. Automobiles crumpled and caught flame. Even people hundreds of yards away felt the concussion.

It was the "worst act of domestic terrorism in American history" to date (although dwarfed by the terrorist strikes in 2001). Rescue workers would spend more than a month ministering to the living and extracting the 168 dead, sometimes battling cold wind and rain. The debris that remained behind would require even longer to clean up. So would the nation's emotional wounds. Gory photos of dead infants—19 children perished in the attack—shocked and horrified viewers across the United States. Americans cried for swift justice. They wanted the culprit identified, tried, and punished. Most wanted him executed.[2]

Catching the perpetrator, at least, did not take very long. An Oklahoma highway patrolman nabbed him just 90 minutes after the explosion. The officer stopped McVeigh's Mercury Marquis as it was speeding north on an interstate highway 75 miles from Oklahoma City. The vehicle bore no license plate, and McVeigh had stuffed his unregistered Glock pistol in a shoulder holster where it was visible, so the patrolman took him in to the station.

Investigators closed in on McVeigh's identity while he sat in jail on charges stemming from that traffic stop. Witnesses in Kansas described his face to a police sketch artist as the man who had rented the Ryder truck, and a former co-worker identified the terrorist from his sketch. Just before McVeigh was due for release, law enforcement officials realized that his name matched that of the suspected bomber.

Once McVeigh's name rose to the top of the suspect list, numerous indicators pointed to his guilt. His reported political obsessions and his loose affiliation with right-wing militia groups indicated a strong dislike for the federal government. Agents found bomb residue on McVeigh's clothing. His fingerprint appeared on a receipt for ammonium nitrate fertilizer, one of the bomb ingredients. A former associate and even McVeigh's sister provided damaging testimony against him. Thus, detailed evidence abounded that the feds already had their man.

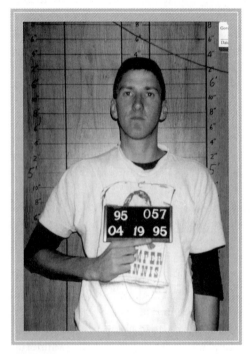

Dead man talking

The federal government's effort to execute Timothy McVeigh for blowing up a federal building in Oklahoma City took more than six years and cost millions of dollars. McVeigh thus encapsulates the American debate over civil liberties: Some thought he was able to abuse his rights, and others considered his trial and execution an abuse of the government's law enforcement powers. McVeigh's T-shirt, worn at the time of his arrest, ironically pictured Abraham Lincoln over the Latin phrase for "Always there will be tyrants."

Resolution of the atrocity was far, far slower in coming. The Justice Department could not afford to fail in its prosecution of such a sensitive case, so the FBI launched an investigation (code-named OKBOMB) that assembled millions of documents. FBI computers contained 26 separate databases to keep track of an effort that, by December 2000, had compiled 23,290 pieces of evidence, 28,000 interview transcripts, and 238,000 photographs. U.S. attorneys eventually compiled this record into what ABC anchor Tom Brokaw called "the single most effective prosecution case I've ever seen."[3] McVeigh's defense team requested that the trial be held outside Oklahoma so that they might find impartial jurors, but in June 1997, a federal jury in Denver finally convicted McVeigh on 11 counts of murder and conspiracy. They sentenced him to die.

McVeigh might have dragged the case on even longer with numerous appeals.[*] Instead, he soon shut down the legal maneuvering, admitted his guilt openly, and claimed sole responsibility for the explosion. "I bombed the Murrah Building. It was my choice, and my control, to hit that building when it was full," he boasted. "It was just me." McVeigh's celebrity status transformed his death-row

---

[*]State-level capital crimes generally take 8 to 12 years to resolve, although the federal process is more streamlined.

cell into a soapbox. He granted two reporters with the *Buffalo News* 75 hours of interview time so that they could write a book telling his story. The quotes they attributed to McVeigh revealed a remorseless murderer who dismissed the young casualties as "collateral damage" in a battle that he had won 168 to 1.[4]

Neither McVeigh's decision to suspend legal appeals nor his taunting confessions ended the Oklahoma City saga. While awaiting execution, McVeigh sat contentedly in Colorado's Supermax facility, holed up in a 9-by-12-foot concrete bunker with reading material and a simple television.[*] Prison officials loosened regulations so that he could exercise outdoors with cell-block mates as well as talk with them across cages.[5] McVeigh reportedly traded "smut books" with a New York City gangster, discussed religion with a Muslim terrorist, and analyzed the criminal justice system with Unabomber Theodore Kaczynski.[6]

Just days before McVeigh's scheduled demise, yet another obstacle slowed the process. The FBI suddenly revealed that roughly 4500 pages of documents from their OKBOMB investigation had gone unreported. Attorney General John Ashcroft had to postpone the execution yet another month while McVeigh's lawyers reviewed the allegedly inconsequential paperwork. His defense team appealed to the federal courts for even more time, but McVeigh instructed them to give up after the Tenth Circuit Court of Appeals judged that they had "utterly failed to demonstrate substantial grounds" why the execution should not immediately take place.

Finally, on Monday, June 11, 2001—more than six years after he had wrecked hundreds of lives—the Oklahoma City bomber ate his last meal: two pints of mint chocolate chip ice cream. He walked into an Indiana execution chamber and cooperated calmly as executioners prepared him for lethal injection, strapping him to a table and inserting an intravenous needle into his right leg. Timothy McVeigh spoke no last words.[†] He stared at the ceiling. Tubes emerging from a slot in the wall soon fed the needle and a toxic cocktail of three chemicals pulsed into his bloodstream, and the life passed out of Timothy James McVeigh at 7:14 A.M. central daylight time. For the first time in almost 40 years, the U.S. government had executed a criminal. Patti Hall, whose injuries from the bombing required repeated operations and extensive physical therapy, sighed before the cameras on the day of the execution, "People have been waiting for this for so long."

THE CRIMINAL JUSTICE SYSTEM'S SLUGGISHNESS, even when faced with an individual clearly responsible for a terrible atrocity, exemplifies why many Americans are impatient with their country's approach to civil liberties. They dislike the tendency to "coddle" criminals who face justice, and they fear that the

---

[*]The prison is hardly a luxury resort. Inmates call it the "Hellhole of the Rockies." But McVeigh apparently was content there.

[†]McVeigh allowed a poem to speak for him. It was "Invictus," by William Ernest Henley, which he had copied by hand.

presumption of innocence makes proving guilt so difficult that many dangerous criminals go free. The American system sets such a high barrier against tyranny that even the easy cases exact serious costs—whether measured in time, money, or emotional trauma. During the six years between McVeigh's crime and his punishment, he was able to publicize his beliefs widely, issuing several statements that were painful and offensive to his living victims. Some descended into depression, lost their marriages, or took their lives. The cost of protecting McVeigh's civil liberties was high indeed.

At the same time, other critics draw the opposite conclusion: The United States no longer respects civil liberties adequately. Constitutional rights no longer seem to inhibit governmental abuse of police powers. Critics point to the blunders committed by overzealous federal agents in the so-called drug war as well as during the crackdown on right-wing groups that spurred McVeigh to violence. They point to the federal government's growing role in law enforcement, which has taken authority away from state officials. Only eight of McVeigh's victims were federal agents, but it was for their deaths that the national government executed him, not for the other 160.

Both conspiracy theorists and death-penalty opponents interpreted the temporary loss of 4500 pages of FBI documents as an indication of how the criminal-justice system can tyrannize people caught in its web.[7] "The FBI proved his case for him—that the system is hopelessly corrupt," argued Bob Papovich, one of McVeigh's friends. Many Europeans and some Americans consider the reactivation of America's death penalty as a sign of its commitment to violent barbarism.[8]

This debate over one aspect of liberty—the treatment of the accused—mirrors the debate over civil liberties more generally. Some critics complain that judges undermine popular will by abusing the Constitution's freedoms. They allow individuals to exploit their rights. By contrast, this chapter argues that constitutional rights seldom protect individuals from a committed majority. Rights can deteriorate in response to political demands. Federal judges often shift the meaning of constitutional guarantees to suit the times. Especially in America's new democracy, courts seldom step far out of line from what voters expect from their government.

ORIGINS OF CIVIL LIBERTIES IN THE UNITED STATES

The U.S. Constitution never mentions the concept of **civil liberties**—fundamental freedoms that protect a people from tyranny. Nor did those who drafted the Constitution include explicit protection for most individual liberties. When delegate Charles Pinckney offered a motion at the Constitutional Convention to guarantee freedom of the press, a majority voted the measure down—on the grounds that states should be responsible for regulating speech and the press.[9] Federalists only later agreed to protect civil liberties, when ratification of the Constitution seemed in danger (see Chapter 2).

Conversational English sometimes refers to these fundamental freedoms as "rights." Indeed, the first ten amendments to the U.S. Constitution—which list some of the most cherished civil liberties—are called "The Bill of Rights." Do not confuse these freedoms with *civil rights* (considered in Chapter 14). Civil liberties promise *freedom from government interference,* whereas civil rights guarantee *equal treatment by the government.* The Supreme Court has shaped the scope and meaning of both civil rights and civil liberties over time, as have political debates and election outcomes.

SELECTIVE INCORPORATION

Initially, the Bill of Rights did not apply to state governments (or to the local institutions that states establish). Sometimes the limitation was explicit. The First Amendment, for example, focused solely on the national government, saying that "Congress shall make no law" restricting speech or religious freedom. State governments could do whatever their voters permitted. As a result, the Episcopal Church remained the official state church in Virginia, and the Puritan religion remained the established religion in Massachusetts.

Many other provisions failed to mention the level of government to which they applied. For example, the Fifth Amendment said that "no person shall . . . be deprived of life, liberty, or property, without due process of law." But deprived by whom? Chief Justice John Marshall ruled, in *Barron v. Baltimore* (1833), that "These amendments contain no expression indicating an intention to apply them to the state governments. This court cannot so apply them."[10] The city of Baltimore had harmed Barron's Wharf by filling the water around it with debris, but Marshall declared that the **due process clause** of the Fifth Amendment only protected Barron's property from the national government.

Civil liberties expanded over time. The first step came in the aftermath of the Civil War, when the Constitution picked up three new **civil rights amendments:** the Thirteenth, which abolished slavery; the Fourteenth, which redefined civil rights and liberties; and the Fifteenth, which guaranteed voting rights to all adult, male citizens.* Most important for civil liberty was the due process clause of the Fourteenth Amendment. This clause applied the language of the Fifth Amendment to the states, saying that they could not "deprive any person of life, liberty, or property, without due process of law."

---

*Southern voters likely would not have passed these amendments given the choice; but ratification was one condition for rejoining the union, and occupation governments controlled many southern states.

Of course, the due process clause is rather vague. States cannot take away freedoms "without due process," but does this mean they can do so "with due process"? In other words, can states restrict freedom as long as they follow a fair procedure? Or does the due process clause contain political substance, such that a fair procedure may never revoke certain natural privileges?

Most federal justices have hedged on these questions. Initially, the Supreme Court limited the impact of the new due process clause, ruling that it restricted only state actions that were fundamentally unfair. Starting in the 1920s, however, the Supreme Court began "incorporating" various liberties into the meaning of the due process clause. The Court has never accepted the theory, promoted by justices such as John Marshall Harlan of Kentucky and Hugo Black of Alabama, that states must respect all civil liberties mentioned in the Bill of Rights. But over time it has applied most of those guarantees to state governments anyway, an approach known as **selective incorporation.**

States may still ignore a few provisions of the Bill of Rights, such as the Second Amendment's right to "bear arms." But the due process clause gave federal courts a strong new weapon to wield against state laws unpopular elsewhere in the country. In particular, federal courts have limited what state governments may do in the areas of (1) *free expression,* (2) *religious freedom,* (3) *privacy,* and (4) *criminal justice.*

FREEDOM OF EXPRESSION

Of all the liberties listed in the Bill of Rights, one trio is paramount: freedom of speech, press, and assembly. These three rights, although distinct, are closely intertwined. They all promise that Americans may express political ideas freely.

Free expression is vital to conducting elections in a democratic society, since vibrant campaigning is impossible without it. Free expression is also necessary for social change, since otherwise citizens cannot present their visions of the good life or debate where society should go. Yet even elected governments sometimes infringe on free expression, especially if voters are intolerant themselves. The First Amendment therefore protects free expression against the intolerance of both ruler and ruled.

The classic defense of free speech was provided by English civil libertarian John Stuart Mill, who insisted that in the free exchange of ideas, truth eventually would triumph over error. But must society tolerate the spread of offensive or hateful views? Even in such cases Mill defends free expression, both to prevent scurrilous ideas from gaining strength under the cloak of secrecy and to remind people why they believe what they do. Mill's logic has not convinced everyone, though—Americans often have been punished, directly or indirectly, for expressing controversial thoughts.

THE EVOLUTION OF FREE SPEECH DOCTRINE

The Supreme Court generally has not protected speakers and writers from political majorities. Instead, the Supreme Court's view of what free speech entails has moved along at about the same speed as—or perhaps a little slower than—that of the rest of the country. Initially, free expression guaranteed only that a speaker or writer could deliver a message without officials censoring it first (the **prior restraint doctrine**). Nothing prevented the government from punishing messages after the fact. Indeed, the source of a hostile message could be convicted for bringing the government's "dignity into contempt," even if the criticisms were true!

CLEAR AND PRESENT DANGER   The first major Supreme Court decision affecting freedom of speech arose when the United States started conscripting soldiers to fight in World War I. Socialist Charles Schenck distributed a mailing urging draft-age men to resist their conscription into the armed forces. A jury convicted Schenck of violating the 1917 Espionage Act, which made it illegal to obstruct military recruitment. A unanimous Supreme Court accepted Schenck's conviction in *Schenck* v. *United States* (1919). Justice Oliver Wendell Holmes explained that free speech did not extend to messages posing a "clear and present danger" to the U.S. war effort. To justify speech restrictions, Holmes drew a famous analogy: No person, he explained, has the right falsely to cry "Fire" in a crowded theater.

Although the **clear and present danger doctrine** initially developed to justify censorship, it also implicitly limited what government might do. Congress could not regulate speech *unless* it posed a clear and present danger. The doctrine thus provided a foundation on which a tradition of free expression could build. Indeed, after facing widespread criticism for *Schenck,* Holmes was one of the first to liberalize his views. The Court heard a parallel case called *Abrams* v. *U.S.* (1919) less than a year later. Left-wing protesters, angry at the United States for intervening in Russia's revolution, had thrown antiwar leaflets to munitions workers from an upper-story window. This time Holmes split with the majority, no longer seeing sufficient danger in a "silly leaflet by an unknown man."

During the 1930s, when the public became more tolerant of dissenting opinion, the Supreme Court changed with the political climate. Two cases decided in 1931, *Stromberg* v. *California* and *Near* v. *Minnesota,* were particularly important in this regard. Yetta Stromberg had encouraged children attending a camp operated by the Young Communist League to pledge allegiance to the flag of the Soviet Union, a violation of California's "red-flag" law.[11] And the Minnesota legislature had shut down a newspaper for publishing "malicious, scandalous and defamatory" material. In both cases the Court endorsed free expression. Neither Stromberg nor the Minnesota newspaper constituted a clear and present danger, the Court explained.

Modern witch hunt

Senator Joseph McCarthy (at right) built a career in the 1950s on investigating alleged Communist sympathizers. His methods outraged many and frightened many more, but should civil liberties be balanced against other important governmental interests, such as national security?

BALANCING DOCTRINE   The toleration that emerged during the 1930s did not survive World War II. Congress responded to public outrage against fascism by enacting a new censorship law in 1940, the Smith Act. Instead of acting as a bulwark against majority tyranny, the Supreme Court again started endorsing limitations on free speech. Nor did the end of World War II automatically restore civil liberties. Instead, the nation went through a second "Red Scare" (see Chapter 4 for a discussion of the first one). People regarded as pro-Soviet suffered harassment by government officials. Senator Joseph McCarthy of Wisconsin gained political popularity by accusing artists, teachers, and government officials of having ties to the Communist party. Anyone who wished to receive a student loan or work for the federal government had to take an oath swearing loyalty to the United States.

It was not judges, but elected leaders, who resisted the threat that McCarthyism posed to the country's civil liberties. A disgusted President Eisenhower refused to act on McCarthy's most outrageous accusations, and McCarthy's Senate colleagues finally inquired into the senator's methods of operation, later censuring him for his inappropriate conduct. The courts, on the other hand, showed little interest in protecting minority dissidents. Instead, the Supreme Court enunciated a **balancing doctrine,** which allowed courts to "balance" freedom of speech against other public interests. In *Dennis v. United States* (1951), 11 nonviolent Communist party leaders faced prison sentences for spreading writings that espoused the revolutionary overthrow of government. The Court ruled their convictions constitutional, arguing that the "balance . . . must be struck in favor" of the governmental interest in resisting subversion.

FUNDAMENTAL FREEDOMS DOCTRINE   Public opinion eventually became more supportive of free-speech rights, even for radicals and communists (see Figure 13.1). Reflecting these changes in public opinion, the Supreme Court gradually developed the **fundamental freedoms doctrine,** the principle that some civil liberties are basic to the functioning of a democratic society and require vigorous protection.

FIGURE 13.1

Percentage opposed to allowing communists to make a speech

The public has become more willing to grant rights even to extremists. Do you believe that this is a sign that people are becoming more tolerant? Or is their changed attitude merely a reflection of the end of the Cold War?

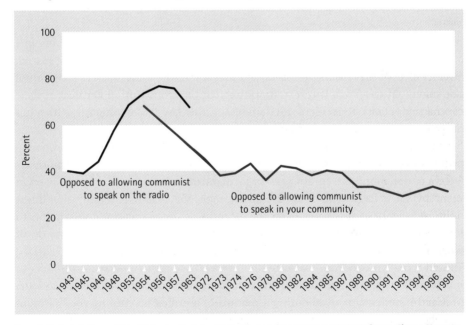

SOURCES: Benjamin L. Page and Robert Y. Shapiro, *The Rational Public: Fifty Years of Trends in Americans' Policy Preferences.* (Chicago: University of Chicago Press, 1992), p. 87; National Opinion Research Center, General Social Survey.

With enemies like these, who needs friends?

The federal government enjoys wide latitude if it declares military information as "classified" and keeps it from the public. Nonetheless, many Americans worry that journalists take freedom of the press too far when their war news outlines U.S. military strategies. How can citizens learn what a democratic government is doing abroad in their name without exposing important national security secrets to the enemy?

The doctrine had rather modest origins. It appeared, almost as an aside, in a footnote to an unrelated 1938 Supreme Court opinion written by Justice Harlan Stone. His *Carolene Products* footnote said that some freedoms, such as freedom of speech, might deserve a "preferred position" in the Constitution because of their central importance to an electoral democracy. Any law threatening these liberties should receive strict scrutiny from the Supreme Court.[12]

The fundamental freedoms doctrine became the Supreme Court's governing principle during the Vietnam War. Under its guidance, the Court was more effective at defending dissenters against government repression than it had been in any previous war. As one civil libertarian wrote in 1973, "The truly significant thing in recent years has not been the attempt of the current administration to suppress criticism, but rather the marked inability of the administration to do so effectively."[13]

In virtually every case that came before it, the Court ruled against efforts to suppress free speech. For example, it would not allow the University of Missouri to expel a student for distributing a picture of a policeman raping the Statue of Liberty. Said the Court, "The mere dissemination of ideas—no matter how offensive to good taste—on a state university campus may not be shut off" in the name of decency.[14]

The Nixon administration inadvertently helped expand civil liberties by trying to grab too much power. It tried to justify censoring publication of a Defense Department report criticizing the war effort, but it could not convince a single Supreme Court justice that national security required prior restraint of the document.[15] Commonly called the *Pentagon Papers case,* this decision greatly advanced freedom of the press. In subsequent years, the Nixon administration's entanglement in the Watergate scandal served to reinforce both public and judicial support of civil liberties.

SYMBOLIC SPEECH Nothing better illustrates the contemporary Supreme Court's strong commitment to fundamental freedoms than its flag-burning decisions, which have enjoyed the support of both liberal and conservative justices.[16] During the 1984 Republican national convention in Dallas, a young radical named Gregory Johnson was arrested for burning an American flag to protest Reagan administration policies. Five years later, Johnson's case came before the Supreme Court. The Court, in *Texas* v. *Johnson* (1989), overturned his conviction, saying the principal purpose of free speech is to invite dispute; the mere burning of the flag was "expressive conduct" that did not breach the peace.[17]

Unlike earlier court decisions, the Supreme Court in the flag-burning case went well beyond popular opinion of the day. President George H. W. Bush angrily called for a constitutional amendment to prohibit flag desecration, and over 70 percent of the public supported him. Almost immediately, Congress passed a law making it a federal offense to burn the flag, but within a year the Supreme Court had reaffirmed its defense of symbolic protest by striking down the new law.[18] The proposed constitutional amendment, meanwhile, never made it out of Congress.

LIMITATIONS ON FREE SPEECH

Although free speech has now been firmly established as one of the country's fundamental freedoms, this does not mean that all speech is free of government control. Government certainly may regulate the time, place, and manner in which one speaks. One does not have the right to express political views with a bullhorn at 3 A.M. in a residential neighborhood. Three particular types of speech also lack full protection: commercial speech, libel, and obscenity.

Government may regulate advertising to protect consumers from false or misleading information, or to discourage the consumption of harmful products such as cigarettes. False speech defaming someone's reputation also lacks constitutional protection, although the standard depends on whether the victim is a private or a public figure. For public figures, a **libel** conviction requires that the source made false statements knowingly or with reckless disregard for the truth—a strong protection of free expression announced in *New York Times* v. *Sullivan* (1964).

And the Court gives relatively little protection to sexual expression—which American culture finds more disturbing than, for example, violent images. Often sexual expression falls under the Supreme Court's 1973 definition of **obscenity**—offensive communications with no redeeming social value other than titillation. This determination, according to *Miller* v. *California* (1973), depends in part on local community standards.[19] Constitutional law provides at best minimal protection for obscenity.

But the Court frequently finds other legal justifications for allowing government to regulate indecency. For example, Justice O'Connor decided in *Erie* v. *Kandyland* (2000) that cities could ban nude dancing by requiring strippers to wear "pasties" and G-strings—even though dancing naked is not obscene. Her justification was that cities might choose to target the "secondary effects" that spring up around strip clubs, such as drug use and prostitution.

On the other hand, the Court does not accept government regulations simply because they target sexual expression. Congress often tries to halt the proliferation of sexually explicit material by using minors as the justification, but the Court resists censorship that goes beyond what is necessary to protect children. For example, when Congress targeted Internet pornography by passing the Communications Decency Act of 1996, the Supreme Court ruled that the law was too broad; it regulated adult behavior more than necessary. Another ruling prevented Congress from banning depictions of youthful sexuality that did not use real minors, because no child was victimized during production.[20]

FREEDOM OF RELIGION

Two clauses in the First Amendment guarantee religious freedom. Both appear in the same sentence: Congress shall make no law (a) respecting an establishment of religion, or (b) prohibiting the free exercise thereof. The **establishment clause** denies government the power to push religious practices on the citizenry. The **free exercise clause** protects the right of individuals to practice their religion. How the Supreme Court interprets these guarantees often depends on the political and electoral context in which it makes decisions.

THE ESTABLISHMENT CLAUSE

Few constitutional phrases have caused more difficulty than the ban on laws "respecting an establishment of religion." As discussed in Chapter 12, the language simply does not convey a clear meaning; judicial interpretation is necessary for the words to offer any protection at all. Perhaps for this reason, the relationship between church and state reveals numerous inconsistencies, sometimes allowing religion and government to mingle, sometimes not.

Federal judges cannot settle on a specific rule for determining when laws cross the line. Liberal judges generally embrace Thomas Jefferson's call for a strict separation of church and state. They prefer to keep government as far away from religion as possible, believing that to overlap the spheres would (1) corrupt churches by introducing political ambitions and (2) invite public officials to legislate moral codes, bullying those of different faiths.

THE LEMON TEST   In the late 1940s, when the Supreme Court first began probing the meaning of the establishment clause, liberals dominated the bench. Over the next 25 years the Court evolved a particular test for determining whether laws violate the Constitution. It is usually called the **Lemon test** after a 1971 case, *Lemon v. Kurtzman,* although the heart of the rule dates from earlier decisions. The Court (a) required all laws to have clear secular (that is, not religious) purposes, (b) did not permit laws to advance or inhibit either one religion or religion in general, and (c) considered it one sign of a religious establishment if the law entangled public officials with religious institutions or activities.[*]

Few people openly endorse the Lemon test these days. Even those who prefer a strong division between church and state recognize that federal courts have not done a very good job applying *Lemon.*[21] Furthermore, conservatives have long argued that "traditional family values" are disappearing from American society because federal courts will not allow communities to protect and promote morality—a concern that especially influenced Reagan administration judicial appointments in the 1980s. Liberals have become a minority on the Court; most justices disparage their approach as overly hostile to religion. Yet no ruling has ever cast out *Lemon* entirely, because its detractors cannot agree on a replacement. Instead, the evolution of case law has forced repeated modifications to how and when federal courts use the test.

THE COERCION TEST   Conservative judges generally read the establishment clause very narrowly: Government may not coerce citizens into pursuing religious practices. Permitting, encouraging, or even indirectly rewarding religion does not "establish" anything, so the Constitution does not forbid it. Some conservatives, such as Justice Antonin Scalia, openly embrace a government's use of moral judgments to construct law.[22] But religious conservatives have never been able to form a solid Court majority, so they win establishment clause cases only when they are willing to compromise with more moderate justices.

The closest conservatives have ever come to replacing the Lemon test may have been a 1992 case called *Lee v. Weisman.* Deborah Weisman's middle school, like so many public schools around the nation, permitted a prayer at the beginning of its graduation ceremony. Deborah objected to the practice, because it required her (1) to skip the ceremony, despite having earned her place there; (2) to rise and pray with everyone else, contrary to her religious beliefs; or (3) to opt out of the

---

[*]The significance of the Lemon test's third "prong" has varied over time. Recent modifications have demoted it from the Court's central approach to the establishment clause.

ceremony's prayer, in full view of her fellow students. She argued that the Constitution did not allow public schools to place students in such a position.

Conservatives seemed poised to win their long-running battle to constrict the establishment clause. So many schools featured graduation prayers, and had been doing so for such a long time, that public opinion weighed heavily against Deborah's complaint. Furthermore, Thomas, a strong conservative, had recently joined three committed opponents of the Lemon test: Rehnquist, Scalia, and White. And just three years before, Justice Anthony Kennedy had written that "policies of accommodation, acknowledgment, and support for religion are an accepted part of our political and cultural heritage." Any establishment clause test that consistently "would invalidate longstanding traditions cannot be a proper reading of the clause," he wrote.[23] Conservatives apparently had the votes lined up.

Imagine their dismay when Kennedy decided to abandon his conservative allies and write a 5-to-4 opinion against them! Kennedy ignored the Lemon test, explaining that Deborah's middle school had failed even if he applied a narrower reading of the establishment clause, one that required coercion. Avoiding the religious exercise would bring damaging peer pressure down on her, either because she skipped graduation or because she did not pray. Kennedy explained that a public institution could not bully a young girl using the force of local opinion.

Justice Scalia could hardly restrain his bitterness in the dissenting opinion: "In holding that the Establishment Clause prohibits invocations and benedictions at public school graduation ceremonies, the Court—with nary a mention that it is doing so—lays waste a tradition that is as old as public school graduation ceremonies themselves."[24] He dismissed Kennedy's concern with peer pressure as "psychology practiced by amateurs." Establishing religion requires *physical* punishment of dissenters, he argued, not simply hurt feelings. But no amount of bile could erase the fact that religious conservatives on the Court had lost their chance to unite behind a **coercion test** to replace *Lemon*. Justice White retired, replaced by a Clinton appointee, and in 2000 another longstanding American tradition fell to the establishment clause in a 6-to-3 vote: the practice of school-sponsored prayer at athletic events.[25]

RELIGION IN SCHOOLS   Public education especially aggravates the controversy surrounding church–state relations. Those who demand a strict wall between church and state generally fear that allowing religion in public schools will become an invitation for communities to promote their preferred faiths.

This fear is not ungrounded. Massachusetts passed the nation's first compulsory-schooling law in 1852 as a response to waves of Catholic immigrants pouring into Boston. The Boston School Committee openly declared that its purpose was to free Catholics from their "moral darkness."[26] As recently as 2000, the Supreme Court prevented a school district in Texas from hosting prayers before sporting events, in part because the District reportedly had worked to convert students by "promoting attendance at a Baptist revival meeting, encouraging membership in religious clubs, chastising children who held minority religious beliefs, and distributing Gideon Bibles on school premises."[27]

On the other hand, mandatory school attendance forces children out of their homes for much of the day. Many religious people believe that worship should be an ongoing part of a child's life, rather than just a diversion compartmentalized to evenings or weekends. They view education as going beyond reading and arithmetic to include teaching morality and values. Public institutions do not permit the type of values-based upbringing that some parents prefer, but often they cannot afford to take their children out of public schools, where children of diverse faiths must mingle. No one has found a feasible way for public schools to accommodate religious exercises without favoring particular forms of religion, nor is it clear that they could provide adequate spiritual guidance.

Evangelical religious groups, concerned by the growing secularization of society, have reacted to Court decisions by advocating an amendment to the Constitution that would allow prayer in schools. A majority of the public have said they support such an amendment,[28] and Republican presidential candidates have generally campaigned in favor of its adoption. But supporters have been unable to win the necessary two-thirds vote in Congress. The Supreme Court has been more responsive, ruling in 1990 that students may form Bible-reading or school prayer clubs if other clubs are allowed to use school property.[29] Banning religious groups while allowing secular ones to organize infringed upon students' rights to free exercise of their religion, a subject to which we now turn.

THE FREE EXERCISE CLAUSE

If the establishment clause seems to bar state involvement in religion, the free exercise clause seems to instruct states to accommodate religious practices. This mandate is equally hard to apply, however, for three rough reasons: (1) Someone has to decide when a set of beliefs qualifies as a "religion" rather than just a personal preference. (2) Someone has to decide when a law really infringes on core religious exercises rather than just on customs. (3) Someone has to decide what to do when religious beliefs interfere with governmental efforts to protect other constitutional values.

Sorting out these three dilemmas places federal courts in an impossible position. They are not qualified to define religions. Yet allowing elected officials to pick them could undercut constitutional protections: Popular faiths would be "religions," while unpopular faiths would be "cults" or merely "philosophies." Allowing individuals to define their own religions, meanwhile, could turn every disagreeable law into a constitutional violation. Imagine the religions that would appear! The Church of No Taxes, the Church of Marijuana Smoking, the Church of Running Red Lights—the possibilities are endless. And the same difficulty arises when determining a religion's core practices. Courts are not qualified to define the central tenets of a faith, but they cannot trust elected officials, church leaders, or individual worshipers to do so either.

THE SHERBERT TEST   On the matter of balancing religious free exercise against other governmental interests, liberals and conservatives once again differ on how stringently to apply the First Amendment. Around the same time they developed the core of the Lemon test, liberals formulated another three-prong formula—the **Sherbert test**—to determine when a law unconstitutionally violates the free exercise clause. The test took formal shape in *Sherbert* v. *Verner* (1963), a case that focused on whether laborers could apply for unemployment benefits if they gave up work because it fell on a holy day. Limits on religiously motivated action, or compulsions to engage in religiously prohibited action, had (a) to promote a secular (that is, nonreligious) goal that was (b) a compelling governmental interest and to do so (c) in the manner least restrictive to religious practices. [30]

THE NEUTRALITY TEST   Conservatives have been more successful at narrowing the free exercise clause than the establishment clause. Writing for a conservative majority in *Oregon* v. *Smith* (1990), Justice Scalia threw out *Sherbert* to rule that the free exercise clause did not protect ritual use of the drug peyote by members of the Native American Church. When government passes a neutral, generally applicable law to prevent criminal behavior, Scalia explained, individuals cannot claim a religious exemption. Scalia recognized that his **neutrality test** places minority religions "at a relative disadvantage," because laws will seldom interfere with mainstream religions. But he preferred to accept that unfairness as "an unavoidable consequence of democratic government" rather than contemplate the alternative: "a system in which each conscience is a law unto itself."

FREE EXERCISE AND PUBLIC SCHOOLS   Once again, religious freedom often arises in the context of education policy (see the accompanying Election Connection, "The Politics of School Vouchers"). The Court protects private religious schools from hostile action by state legislatures. But popular impulses sometimes push the Court to allow interference with religious practices.

Two flag-salute cases provide a good example of how the Court shifts with the times. In 1940, with war breaking out in Europe and patriotic fervor on the rise, the Court upheld a Pennsylvania statute requiring that Jehovah's Witnesses salute the American flag in public school ceremonies, even though their religion forbids revering a government symbol. The Court said that schools could interfere with religious liberty in this case, because saluting the flag promoted "national unity, [which] is the basis of national security."[31] Only one justice dissented. [32]

Just three years later, times had changed. Not only did the earlier flag-salute case stir up extensive mob violence against Jehovah's Witnesses, which brought

The Politics of School Vouchers

Parents who want religion to play an important part in the day-to-day lives of their children find themselves in a quandary because of the public education system. These families may feel unhappy with the public schools, because of the social environment they create, but may not have enough money to send their children to private institutions after paying taxes to support the public system they dislike. Even those who can afford private tuition suffer, because they are forced to pay for a school system they find objectionable.

School choice programs, which have been implemented by some cities and states, give parents yearly vouchers to pay for the education of school-age children, allowing them to shop among different schools as a customer. Some of the programs permit enrollment at religious private schools, a solution to the dilemma faced by religious families. These programs appear to reinforce the First Amendment's guarantee of religious free exercise. Such flexibility summons up a dilemma of another sort, however, which is that critics of school choice charge that it runs afoul of the First Amendment's establishment clause.

The supporters offer two main arguments on behalf of voucher plans: (1) Public schools implicitly teach that matters of the spirit deserve no place in education, which is itself a religious message, so parents should be allowed to choose the religious teaching they prefer for their own children. (2) The main purpose of school choice is educational, not religious, because vouchers force schools to improve their product as a way of attracting business.

Opponents respond with two basic arguments against these flexible voucher plans:

(1) Government stipends indirectly promote the activities of religious groups, which breaches the wall between church and state. (2) Vouchers will undermine the public school system, which already lacks sufficient resources, and divide America by encouraging schools identifiable by the race, ethnicity, and social class of students.

This debate played out in the 2000 presidential election. Republican candidate George W. Bush favored giving families vouchers that would allow parents to opt for religious private schools. Democrat Al Gore argued that choice should be limited to public schools. The Supreme Court weighed in on the debate in 2002, when asked to assess the constitutionality of Cleveland's voucher program for low-income families. The court divided 5–4, with the majority backing President Bush's position. Chief Justice Rehnquist's opinion in *Zelman v. Simmon-Harris* ruled that Cleveland's system passed constitutional muster, even though it applied to Catholic schools, because parents could decide where the money would go and they had a wide range of choices. The program did not favor religion.

What do you think?

- Do public schools unify Americans, such that the growth of private schools would undermine an important governmental interest?
- Do public schools violate the free exercise clause by creating an environment free of religious expression that children by law must attend?
- How would most parents choose schools for their children if everyone received educational vouchers?

shame on the Court, but experiences with Nazism lessened American ardor for forced patriotism. "Compulsory unification of opinion," wrote Justice Robert Jackson, when reversing the previous flag-salute ruling, "achieves only the unanimity of the graveyard."[33] Behind him were three justices who had ruled on the opposite side just three years before. Like guarantees of free expression, the religious freedom clauses evolve with public opinion.

THE RIGHT TO PRIVACY

The civil liberties discussed so far in this chapter—freedom of expression and freedom of religion—trace back to a specific provision in the Bill of Rights. Not all freedoms recognized by the courts appear in the Constitution, however. Indeed, the Ninth Amendment explicitly recognizes that the people retain rights not listed in the document. The most controversial unlisted right recognized by the Supreme Court is the **right to privacy.**

Privacy, as a legal concept, has evolved over time. Originally, the right to be "left alone" represented an ability to prevent others from spreading details about one's private life. A famous 1890 essay by Samuel Warren and Louis Brandeis publicized the need to protect people from "the evil of invasion of privacy by the newspapers."[34] The word's meaning changed as judges sought a concept to defend personal autonomy, which Americans increasingly valued after World War II. Privacy now means the right to be free of public interference in personal life choices.

CONTRACEPTION

The modern right to privacy owes its genesis to the Supreme Court's ruling in *Griswold* v. *Connecticut* (1965).[35] Estelle Griswold, executive director of Planned Parenthood, was fined $100 for violating a Connecticut law prohibiting the use of contraceptives. Justice William O. Douglas did not see any way for government to enforce such a law without intruding on the relationship between husbands and wives, so he declared the law unconstitutional on the basis of "a right of privacy older than the Bill of Rights." His approach to privacy was similar to the old-fashioned concept, because it emphasized keeping personal details out of the public eye. "Would we allow the police to search the sacred precincts of marital bedrooms for telltale signs of the use of contraceptives?" asked Douglas. "The very idea is repulsive to the notions of privacy surrounding the marriage relationship."[36]

A second contraceptives case represented a bigger conceptual leap. This time the Court faced a Massachusetts law that banned the sale of contraceptives rather than their use. The old notion of privacy could not apply here. Governments may not be able to regulate the personal relationships inside a family, but they regulate what businesses sell all the time. So Justice Brennan, who was assigned the case, sought a new reason for striking down laws against contraception. His solution in *Eisenstadt* v. *Baird* (1972) was to adapt the "right to be left alone": It no longer merely prevented government from exposing private details, but actually prevented government from trying to influence those details. Privacy had changed to mean personal autonomy rather than just secrecy.[37]

ABORTION RIGHTS

When Brennan wrote his *Eisenstadt* opinion, he was thinking about more than just condoms and the pill. He also had his eye turned toward a related set of cases on the Supreme Court docket: those dealing with abortion. Chief Justice Warren Burger had assigned the abortion cases to newly appointed Justice Harry Blackmun, an expert in medical law thought to be mildly conservative. Brennan did not wish to steal the chore away from Blackmun; as the Court's high-profile Catholic justice, he knew that someone else had better announce abortion rights. But Brennan did want to help steer Blackmun to a strong ruling in favor of the right to choose. Brennan's approach to privacy in *Eisenstadt* was tailor-made for the abortion issue.[38]

Before the remorse

Shown here in 1973, when Roe v. Wade *was decided, Norma McCorvey (whose privacy at the time was protected via the pseudonym Jane Roe) in 1995 made the surprise announcement that she had become a pro-life advocate.* Why would McCorvey's attitudes on abortion matter more than 20 years after the Supreme Court decision she instigated?

Blackmun's *Roe* v. *Wade* (1973) decision appeared the next year, guaranteeing at least a partial right of abortion. The case arose out of a request from Norma McCorvey, who used the pseudonym Jane Roe. She asked for a judgment declaring Texas anti-abortion laws unconstitutional. Blackmun grouped the decision whether to give birth to a fetus under the privacy rubric created by Douglas and Brennan, and allowed state interference only when public interest in the potential life became compelling—that is, when the pregnant woman was close to term.

The *Roe* decision arrived near the end of America's "sexual revolution" and so enjoyed substantial support from parts of the U.S. population. Many others ardently opposed the Supreme Court's decision, which had struck down anti-abortion laws across the nation. *Roe* v. *Wade* launched a powerful political crusade, the right-to-life movement, dedicated to banning abortion again. Supporters became actively engaged in state and national politics, lobbying legislatures and courts to impose as many restraints on abortion as the courts would allow.

Responding to right-to-life groups, Congress in 1976 enacted legislation preventing coverage of abortion costs under government health insurance programs, such as Medicaid. In 1980 the Republican party promised to restore the "right to life," and in subsequent years, Republican presidents began appointing Supreme Court justices expected either to reverse *Roe v. Wade* or to limit its scope. The Court began accepting restrictions on abortion. For example, in 1980 the Court upheld the congressional act prohibiting abortion funding.[39] In 1989 it ruled that states could require the doctor to ascertain the viability of a fetus before permitting an abortion, if the woman were 20 or more weeks pregnant.[40] By 1990 judicial observers believed that four justices on the Supreme Court were prepared to overturn *Roe* and that any new appointment by a Republican president would create the majority needed.

As the right-to-life movement gained momentum and it became more likely that *Roe v. Wade* would be overturned, the right-to-choose movement also gained strength and aggressiveness. By 1984 it was able to secure the Democratic party's commitment to the right-to-choose principle. Both sides of the controversy waited anxiously for the 1992 court decision in *Planned Parenthood v. Casey*.[41] Planned Parenthood had challenged a Pennsylvania law restricting abortion in numerous ways. Right-to-life groups hoped and right-to-choose groups feared that the Court would return authority for abortion law to the states. The majority ultimately decided against taking such a dramatic step, however. Justice O'Connor's opinion explicitly refused to overturn *Roe v. Wade*, although she allowed numerous restrictions on and regulations of the abortion procedure, as long as they do not place an "undue burden" on women trying to exercise their constitutional right. In 2000, the Court reaffirmed its position when it ruled that states could not simply ban a particular type of abortion, in this case the so-called partial-birth abortion procedure.[42]

Either by accident or by design, the Court majority once again adopted a position very close to that of the average American voter. It permitted restrictions endorsed by a majority of voters (such as a requirement that a teenager obtain parental consent) but rejected those most people consider unwarranted (such as a requirement that a married woman obtain the consent of her husband). Even in matters as sensitive as the right of privacy, the Court seems to be influenced by majority opinion.

Gay rights

There is little doubt that most Americans thought a married couple should be able to use contraceptives, and a large chunk of the U.S. population wanted to liberalize abortion laws. Early privacy cases therefore did not require the Court to stand alone against a large popular majority. In 1986, however, *Bowers v.*

Hardwick presented a more difficult constitutional claim: the claim that privacy rights prevented Georgia from prohibiting sodomy between two consenting homosexuals.

The Court declined to buck popular hostility to homosexuality, even though the privacy logic used to allow contraceptives and abortions seemed to apply to intercourse between same-sex adults. Noting that laws against sodomy—that is, anal or oral sex—existed at the founding, the Court majority found no reason to think that privacy rights exempted homosexual behavior from regulation. Not every state took advantage of the Court's weakened stance on privacy rights; many ruled that their state constitutions offered a stronger right to privacy than that found in the U.S. Constitution.[43] But the Court's decision did allow various sexual regulations to stand on the law books, including bans on sodomy of any sort (even between married couples) in 13 states.

Public opinion eventually intervened. In 1986, when *Bowers* was decided, a majority of those surveyed believed that homosexual relations should be outlawed. But by 2001, polls found that Americans favored legalizing homosexual behavior by a margin of 54 to 42 percent. Similarly, 85 percent of people thought gays and lesbians should have equal rights in the workplace—a figure up more than 25 percentage points from the early 1980s. The *Bowers* precedent could not last long. In fact, a 2003 decision extended privacy rights to include sodomy. The Court only achieved a consistent privacy doctrine when the public permitted it.[44]

CRIMINAL JUSTICE

We end where we began: with the criminal justice system. Elections also affect court interpretations of the procedural rights of the accused. Rights of the accused vary with social currents, with the dictates of public opinion. Barriers to criminal arrest and prosecution emerged during a period in which Americans were terribly suspicious of authority, but then they broke down again as the American public tired of the impositions that criminal behavior inflicted on their lives.

RIGHTS OF THE ACCUSED

The way the criminal justice system treats suspects underwent radical alteration during the 1960s. The Supreme Court, under the leadership of Chief Justice Earl Warren, issued a series of decisions that substantially extended the meaning of the Bill of Rights. It specifically broadened the interpretation of five constitutional provisions, discussed in this section: (a) protection from unreasonable search and seizure, (b) immunity against self-incrimination, (c) right to an impartial jury, (d) right to legal counsel, and (e) protection from double jeopardy. Eventually the Warren Court provoked a backlash among voters, who were angry about criminals "getting off on technicalities." An increasing number of voters began to favor rigorous enforcement of laws and harsh punishments for criminals (see Figure 13.2).

FIGURE 13.2

Most people think courts should be tougher on criminals

Although still strongly in favor of law and order, Americans no longer support tough criminal penalties at the rate they did a decade ago. Why has support for the death penalty dropped in recent years?

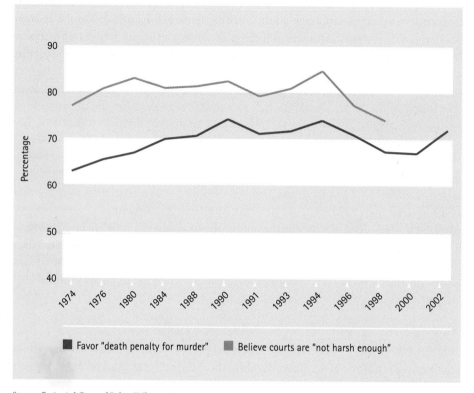

Favor "death penalty for murder"   Believe courts are "not harsh enough"

SOURCE: Benjamin I. Page and Robert Y. Shapiro, *The Rational Public: Fifty Years of Trends in Americans' Policy Preferences.* (Chicago: University of Chicago Press, 1992), p. 92; National Opinion Research Center, General Social Survey.

Court procedures soon became a campaign issue, and many who sought office called for tougher law enforcement. Richard Nixon's successful 1968 campaign was the first to provoke what has become known as a "law and order" election. Since then, the issue has arisen in both national and local campaigns. In the 2000 presidential race, both George W. Bush and Al Gore campaigned as law-and-order candidates. Bush, as governor of Texas, allowed the execution of a number of death row inmates during the presidential campaign, including born-again Christian Karla Faye Tucker and great-grandmother Betty Lou Beets. Although activist groups denounced Bush's failure to grant clemency in these cases, Gore did not. The Supreme Court has responded to changing political circumstances, tempering its decisions on the rights of the accused without actually overturning them. One side effect of this stance has been an exceptionally high incarceration rate in the United States (see Figure 13.3).

SEARCH AND SEIZURE   Police may not search homes without a court first granting them a search warrant based on evidence that a crime has probably been committed. The Warren Court established an **exclusionary rule** in *Mapp v. Ohio* (1961): Improperly obtained evidence cannot appear during a trial.[45] Conservatives on the Court have limited the scope of the exclusionary rule,

---

FIGURE 13.3
A "lock 'em up" mentality?

The United States imprisons a far larger proportion of its citizens than most other industrialized countries do. Arrests in the so-called drug war are a major source of America's large prison population; even limited drug possession can lead to years of incarceration. Does the United States imprison so many people because law enforcement officials catch more criminals or because the United States is less tolerant of deviant behavior?

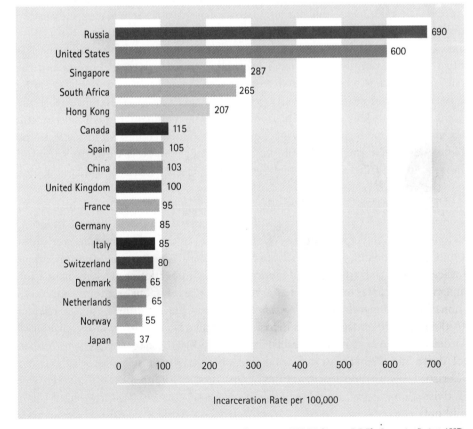

Incarceration Rate per 100,000

Country	Rate
Russia	690
United States	600
Singapore	287
South Africa	265
Hong Kong	207
Canada	115
Spain	105
China	103
United Kingdom	100
France	95
Germany	85
Italy	85
Switzerland	80
Denmark	65
Netherlands	65
Norway	55
Japan	37

SOURCE: Marc Mauer, *Americans Behind Bars: U.S. and International Use of Incarceration, 1995* (Washington, DC: The Sentencing Project, 1997).

however. For example, the Court exempted college dormitories from the rule's protection in 1982.[46] Lacking an official warrant may not invalidate police searches conducted in "good faith," according to a line of cases starting with *U.S. v. Leon* (1984). The Court has relaxed the exclusionary rule when officers use a warrant based on the wrong paperwork and when they accidentally apply a warrant to the wrong person or the wrong apartment.[47]

On the other hand, the Supreme Court has interpreted the guarantee against warrantless searches fairly broadly, to include electronic surveillance such as wiretaps. One recent 5-4 decision, surprising in light of the Court's general sympathy with the war against drugs, defended home owners against sophisticated technologies that can "search" their homes from the outside. The Supreme Court ruled, in *Kyllo* v. *U.S.* (2001), that police needed a warrant to scan someone's house with thermal imaging equipment, which is used to detect the presence of halide lamps needed to grow marijuana plants indoors.[48]

SELF-INCRIMINATION People often confess to crimes they have not committed. The reasons for this puzzling behavior no doubt vary: fear or exhaustion during interrogation, the desire to avoid more serious accusations, uncertainty about the implications of an accusation, the desire for attention or publicity. The most famous example comes from centuries of witch trials in Europe and the Americas, during which accused women would confess to sins such as eating dozens of babies, successfully casting powerful spells and curses, and repeatedly copulating with the devil.* The tendency to incriminate oneself falsely still appears in the modern era, though. Several young men confessed, in 1989, to the highly publicized rape and beating of a young jogger in New York City's Central Park—but scientific evidence analyzed in 2002 clearly established that someone else had committed the crime.

The Fifth Amendment recognizes the dangers of self-incrimination. It exempts accused persons from testifying against themselves. For this reason, defendants in courtroom dramas often "take the Fifth," refusing to answer questions on grounds of possible self-incrimination. At one time, law enforcement officials could take advantage of ignorance of civil liberties by tricking or scaring suspects into confessing after their arrests. The Warren Court therefore put teeth into the Fifth Amendment in *Miranda* v. *Arizona* (1966), requiring police officers to alert suspects to their rights before questioning them. This decision produced the **Miranda warning** so familiar in cop shows: "You have the right to remain silent . . . ." Courts exclude evidence obtained from suspects who are not informed, before questioning, of their constitutional rights.

---

*Even if one believes that such acts are possible, it seems safe to assume that few of the estimated 48,000 women and 12,000 men executed during witch trials in Western Europe actually enjoyed such privileged access to the demon world, especially given how these trials were conducted.

Father of a new right

Ernesto Miranda, namesake of the warning that is read to all suspects before questioning. The Supreme Court ruled that Miranda's confession was inadmissible in court because he had not been advised of his right to remain silent. Is the Miranda warning now part of American culture?

After Richard Nixon made the *Miranda* decision an issue in his 1968 presidential campaign, the Supreme Court softened the ruling. It decided, in *Harris* v. *New York* (1971), that information gathered in violation of the *Miranda* decision may be introduced in evidence when defendants testify on their own behalf. But the Supreme Court declined to throw out *Miranda* in a 2000 decision authored by Chief Justice Rehnquist, usually a hard-liner against rights of the accused. Rehnquist's 7-to-2 decision pointed out that "*Miranda* has become embedded in routine police procedure to the point where the warnings have become part of our national culture."

IMPARTIAL JURY The requirement that a jury be impartial is difficult to meet when crimes become newsworthy, because most potential jurors witness media accounts of the alleged crime before and during the trial. The Warren Court considered these issues in *Sheppard* v. *Maxwell* (1966), a case in which police accused an influential medical doctor of murdering his wife. (The story became the basis for two television shows and a movie, all called *The Fugitive*.)

Sam Sheppard complained about the excessive news coverage jurors witnessed. Journalists even sat in the courtroom, where they could listen in on Sheppard's conversations with his attorneys.[49] The Supreme Court overturned his conviction and provided guidelines to ensure impartial juries in the future. Judges can postpone trials or transfer them far away from the initial crime to lower public awareness. Timothy McVeigh's trial, for example, changed "venue" from Oklahoma to Colorado. Judges can "sequester" juries during a trial, keeping them from away external sources of information, as happened with jurors in the O. J. Simpson murder trial. Jurors also should be questioned to screen out those with fixed opinions and should be instructed to rule out any prejudices in the case derived apart from evidence presented in a trial.[50]

Although the Supreme Court has never reversed these constitutional safeguards designed to prevent a biased jury, some later decisions weakened them.

The Court's decision in *Nebraska Press Association* v. *Stuart* (1976) is just one example of how criminal justice law has reflected the country's more conservative mood, as well as a recognition that excluding citizens who stay informed of current events may not be healthy for the jury system. It ruled that "pre-trial publicity—even pervasive, adverse publicity—does not inevitably lead to an unfair trial."[51]

LEGAL COUNSEL   The Warren Court ruled in *Gideon* v. *Wainwright* (1963) that all citizens accused of serious crimes, even the indigent, must have access to proper advice. When the accused are too poor to hire attorneys, then the Sixth Amendment right to counsel requires courts to appoint legal representation.

It was easier to enunciate this right than to put it into practice. At one time, courts asked private attorneys to donate their services in order to defend the poor (so-called "pro bono" work). But donating time to help suspected crooks was not popular among members of the legal profession. As a result, states have created the office of **public defender,** an attorney whose full-time responsibility is to provide for the legal defense of indigent criminal suspects.

This solution has its own problems, though. For one thing, the job of a public defender is thankless, pay is low, and defenders must deal with "rotten case after rotten case."[52] From the perspective of the police, defenders simply throw up roadblocks to prevent conviction of the guilty. The public trend toward strong anticrime views therefore undercuts the right to counsel directly by influencing the budgets and prestige that accompany the job. Talented and ambitious lawyers usually will avoid the job, since defending the accused is politically unpopular. One of the public defenders' biggest problems is winning respect from those with whom they work—including from the suspects they represent. Defendants, like most other people, think that anything free is probably not worth much. One felon, when asked by a judge whether he had been represented by an attorney, replied, "No, I had a public defender."[53]

DOUBLE JEOPARDY   The Warren Court ruled in *Benton* v. *Maryland* (1969) that states cannot try a person twice for the same offense, thereby placing the defendant in **double jeopardy.** The purpose was to prevent law enforcement officials from wearing someone down by repeated prosecutions.

This rule does not prevent prosecution in both federal and state courts for the same act, as long as it violates multiple laws. Prosecution by both levels of government is most likely in high-visibility cases, in which political considerations may play a role. For example, when the state of California could not win a conviction of four police officers charged with beating a young black man named Rodney King, federal prosecutors went after the officers and won two convictions. Oklahoma courts tried to pin murder charges on Timothy McVeigh's co-conspirator, Terry Nichols, because a federal jury gave him only life imprisonment for his lesser role in the Oklahoma City bombing.[54]

CAPITAL PUNISHMENT

The Eighth Amendment prohibits "cruel and unusual punishment." Convicted criminals may not face torture, grotesque forms of execution such as crucifixion and burning at the stake, or sentences grossly disproportionate to the legal violations committed.

Starting in the nineteenth century, the morality of capital punishment itself came under question. This movement gained widespread support in the 1960s, resulting in a push by various interest groups (such as the American Civil Liberties Union and the National Association for the Advancement of Colored People) to classify executions of any sort as "cruel and unusual."

No Supreme Court majority has ever declared capital punishment, in and of itself, a violation of the Eighth Amendment. On the other hand, at various times the Court has thrown out death penalties when they resulted from a system that imposed capital punishment unfairly or arbitrarily. Executions in the United States virtually halted for 15 years as states grappled to find a constitutional means of applying the death penalty (see Figure 13.4). The Court's opinions

FIGURE 13.4

Executions in the U.S. 1930–2001

Why do you think executions were more common in the 1930s than they are today?

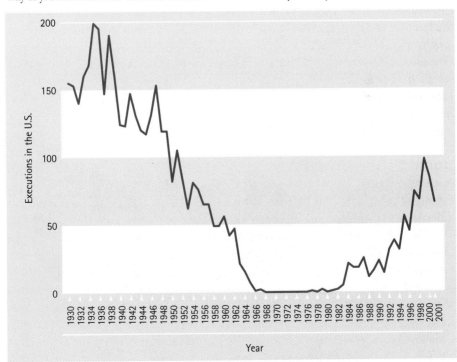

SOURCE: U.S. Department of Justice, Bureau of Justice Statistics, Capital Punishment 2000 (December 2001).

initially provided little guidance because justices could not unite behind a majority opinion. The five justices who threw out Georgia's system of capital punishment in 1972, for example, wrote five separate opinions! But the states eventually found capital-punishment procedures that the U.S. Supreme Court would allow.

Executions picked up again in the 1980s. The federal courts reflected public support for law and order, as well as for the death penalty itself (see Figure 13.5), by refusing to block as many capital sentences. The Court also issued various rulings that helped speed up the application of capital sentences. But the issue has never been settled, and public opinion leaves officials with some room to maneuver. The Supreme Court handed down one or more decisions related to the death penalty every year during the 1990s, sometimes upholding and sometimes overruling death penalties.[55] In 2002 it gave opponents of the death penalty cause for hope by ruling in *Atkins* v. *Virginia* that states cannot execute the mentally retarded in keeping with public opinion (see Figure 13.5). The Court also ruled that only juries may issue death sentences; judges may not.

The future of capital punishment remains in doubt. Many influential Europeans consider the death penalty barbaric, which hurts U.S. foreign relations. Poor people and minorities receive the death penalty at disproportionate

---

FIGURE 13.5

Most Americans favor the death penalty, with reservations

Should public opinion about the death penalty influence how the Supreme Court rules on the issue?

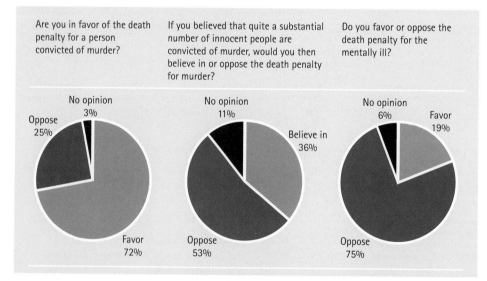

SOURCES: Gallup Poll, May 6–9, 2002; and Harris Poll, July 20–25, 2001.

rates, a disturbing echo of eighteenth-century debtor hangings or twentieth-century lynchings. And public support for the death penalty evaporates under certain circumstances (see Figure 13.5). Evidence occasionally surfaces suggesting that innocent people may be facing execution at an unacceptable rate. One *Chicago Tribune* study convinced the Republican governor of Illinois, George Ryan, to suspend executions and eventually to commute the sentences of everyone on Death Row in his state. Maryland Governor Parris Glendening, a Democrat, imposed a moratorium on executions in his state as well.

RIGHTS IN PRACTICE: THE PLEA BARGAIN

Although those accused of crimes enjoy numerous rights on paper, it is important to realize that these civil liberties often do not exist in practice. If a case is newsworthy, prosecutors and courts generally observe proper constitutional procedures: The public is looking on, and those participating in the trial must take political pressures into account. But the reality of justice in most criminal cases is very different. Hardly anyone accused of a crime is actually tried by a jury, and nearly all those convicted of a crime testify against themselves. The accused have their rights, to be sure, but most of the time invoking them would do more harm than good.[56]

Trial court judges depend on the willingness of prosecutors and defenders to settle cases before going to trial. The number of people accused of crimes is high, the list of cases on court dockets is seemingly endless, court personnel resources are limited, and court time is precious. Judges must preside over efficient courtrooms, settle cases quickly, and keep dockets short. To speed the criminal justice process, a defender and a prosecutor usually arrange a **plea bargain**—an agreement between prosecution and defense that the accused will admit to having committed a crime, provided that other charges are dropped and a reduced sentence is recommended. That is, most suspects "cop a plea."

AFTERSHOCK:
THE PATRIOT ACT OF 2001

Freedom customarily declines during wartime, even in democratic countries. The United States persecuted Germans and Eastern Europeans during World War I and concentrated Japanese Americans in detention camps during World War II. Congress cracked down on free speech during both world wars. Income taxes surged during the Korean War and never returned to their modest prewar levels. Protests against the Vietnam War led to a heightened concern for law and order, one that stalled a trend toward greater rights for the accused, and also prompted the Nixon administration to experiment with restrictions on press freedom. Civil libertarians therefore naturally fear the sound of rattling sabers.

The "war on terrorism" initiated by the Bush administration after 9/11 is different from past American wars. It involved attacking the Taliban government in Afghanistan and toppling Saddam Hussein's regime in Iraq, but it is not primarily a war that the U.S. can win militarily by pulling down a few governments. The enemy is less tangible: lawless organizations with no clear base of operations, roving cells of operatives who murder innocent civilians to panic an entire population. Terrorism feeds off civil liberties because the killers infiltrate a democratic society and exploit cherished freedoms—such as fluid national borders, privacy, freedom of movement, and the availability of consumer goods that may be converted into deadly weapons.

A war against terrorism therefore differs significantly from other wars, because armed forces cannot fight the enemy alone. The enemy is just as likely to be within the nation as to be outside it. Domestic law enforcement authorities must be a critical part of any antiterrorist effort. But these are the same authorities who have the power to investigate, arrest, and jail citizens. Expanding police powers to combat terrorism could do more damage to civil liberties than any wartime measure of the past.* It also could constitute an implicit act of surrender—a voluntary sacrifice of the democratic way of life that terrorists targeted in the first place. "If we allow our freedoms to be undermined," one civil libertarian warns, "the terrorists will have won."[57]

There is no easy way to determine when wartime regulations pass the boundary of what should be acceptable. The Bush administration requested a series of new powers for law enforcement officials after 9/11, in a bill intended to "Provide Appropriate Tools Required to Intercept and Obstruct Terrorism." The PATRIOT proposal granted federal agents much greater power and allowed them to exercise it with minimal court supervision. It included numerous provisions increasing the ability of law enforcement officers to spy on people in the United States through wiretaps, through their computers, and through secret searches of homes.

Critics from across the political spectrum rose up to oppose the effort, claiming that the requested powers crossed the line of acceptability. "This bill should worry Americans more than it should worry terrorists," claimed Steve Dasbach, national director of the Libertarian party.[58] Attorney General John Ashcroft is "waging a relentless assault on civil liberties," accused Ralph Neas, president of the liberal People for the American Way Foundation. "Terrorism isn't the only threat to our way of life." A conservative Republican in Congress concurred: "I'm not sure we can ever satisfy the federal government's insatiable appetite for more power."[59]

Civil libertarians had turned back many of the Patriot Act's provisions in the past. But opinion changed drastically after 9/11, leaving large majorities explic-

---

**Newsweek columnist Fareed Zakaria properly notes, however, that the United States has had to worry about internal enemies many times before (July 8, 2002, p. 27).

itly willing to trade their privacy and their liberties for increased safety.[60] Critics of the Bush administration could not sway the public. The Patriot Act of 2001 passed Congress with minimal hearings or debate. Within a year, federal agents were monitoring financial transactions in American banks. The Federal Bureau of Investigation had contacted 83 public libraries to investigate patrons.[61]

Executive departments scaled back other civil liberties, but public opinion supported these changes as well. For example, Ashcroft told the FBI that it could eavesdrop on communications between attorneys and the suspected terrorists that they represented, a rule supported by perhaps three-fourths of the American public.[62] President Bush issued an order decreeing that noncitizens suspected of terrorist links could be declared potential "enemy combatants" and tried in military tribunals—which would allow the Department of Defense to detain suspects indefinitely, admit secret evidence into their trials, and determine the necessary level of proof for establishing guilt. A two-thirds vote by the tribunal would be enough to authorize execution, a decision the accused could not appeal.[63] An estimated 60 percent of the American public supported the idea.[64]

As with so many of the changes in American government since 9/11, the full ramifications for civil liberties are not yet known and may not be known for some time. The new investigative powers established by the government ultimately may see little use against law-abiding Americans; they may do nothing more than aid in the pursuit and capture of serious criminals. Even if important freedoms *were* sacrificed, the war against terrorism could abate or the worst fears could subside, allowing those liberties to be restored. But the main lesson of 9/11, as regards civil liberties, is the same as the lesson that emerges in other parts of the American political system: When public opinion shifts, policy quickly follows.

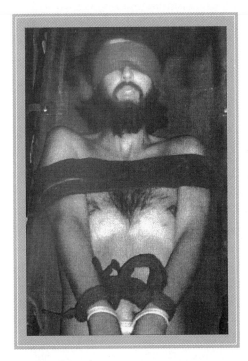

Privileged Captive

American soldiers captured John Walker Lindh, a U.S. citizen, while he was serving under the fundamentalist Taliban regime in Afghanistan. Lindh's treatment, as captured by this photo, may look harsh—nothing we would wish on ourselves. Yet the American government ultimately took it easy on Lindh. They tried him in a federal court, where he would enjoy due process rights, rather than prosecuting him in a military tribunal. Should Americans who serve a foreign flag face different treatment than other enemy combatants do?

CHAPTER SUMMARY

The Bill of Rights remained a dead letter until the Civil War ended slavery, because state governments did not have to honor the Constitution's civil liberties protections. Eventually, though, federal courts used the Fourteenth Amendment's due process clause to protect civil liberties in the states.

Although the founders hoped courts would protect individual rights against majority tyranny, most of the time the Supreme Court follows public opinion. This is true in most areas of constitutional law: free expression, religious freedom, privacy rights, and protection of the accused. Some examples of Court sensitivity to public opinion date back to the early twentieth century, including the Court's fluctuations on the clear and present danger doctrine between war time and peace time and its rapid reversal in the flag-salute cases. But sensitivity to public opinion seems heightened in America's new democracy.

The Warren and early Burger Courts responded to America's postwar liberalism by expanding civil liberties in many areas. The Court embraced free expression as a fundamental freedom central to the democratic system. It evolved three-prong tests to determine when laws violated the First Amendment's establishment clause or free exercise clause. It altered the meaning of privacy to increase personal autonomy and to protect individual decisions from public intervention. And it sought mechanisms to give teeth to constitutional provisions protecting those accused of criminal behavior.

The public has since become more conservative in various respects, and the Court has responded by pulling back somewhat from Warren Court precedents. This retreat is least pronounced for free speech, because several prominent Republican appointees (especially Scalia and Kennedy) continue to defend political expression. But current law on religious freedom no longer follows the Warren Court approach, perhaps most easily remembered as the "Lemon Sherbert" era (after the two tests that dominated the period). Now the United States is stuck with the Lemon, and a modified one at that. Privacy rights provide less protection for abortion than they once did, and they did not shield consenting adults who engaged in sodomy until 2003. Finally, law enforcement officials enjoy increasing power over those suspected of criminal behavior. The country's definition of civil liberties seems to depend as much on the thinking of its citizens as on judicial principles.

KEY TERMS

balancing doctrine,
   p. 439
civil liberties, p. 434
civil rights amendments,
   p. 435

clear and present danger
   doctrine, p. 437
coercion test, p. 444
double jeopardy, p. 456
due process clause, p. 435

establishment clause,
   p. 442
exclusionary rule, p. 453
free exercise clause,
   p. 442

ON THE WEB

American Civil Liberties Union
www.aclu.org
The sometimes controversial American
Civil Liberties Union has a detailed Web
site outlining its agenda for promoting
civil liberties, as well as describing the history and present status of the law.

Freedom Forum
www.freedomforum.org
The Freedom Forum is an international
foundation that promotes freedom of the
press and of religion.

Electronic Frontier Foundation
(EFF) and Center for Democracy
and Technology (CDT)
www.eff.org
www.cdt.org
Both groups are a useful source of information about free speech and privacy in
the computer age.

SUGGESTED READINGS

Friedman, Lawrence M. *Crime and Punishment
in American History.* New York: Basic Books,
1993. Readable overview of the changing
nature of the American system of criminal
justice.

Garrow, David J. *Liberty and Sexuality.* New
York: Macmillan, 1994. Comprehensive
account of the legal debate over abortion
before and after *Roe.*

Goldstein, Robert. *Saving "Old Glory": The
History of the Desecration Controversy.* Boulder,
CO: Westview Press, 1995. Authoritative
political and constitutional history of the
flag-burning controversy.

Lewis, Anthony. *Make No Law: The Sullivan Case
and the First Amendment.* New York: Random

House, 1992. Excellent case study of the
politics of the *Sullivan* decision and the evolution of the free-speech doctrine.

Macedo, Stephen. *The New Right v. The
Constitution.* Washington, DC: Cato
Institute, 1987. Thoughtfully asserts the
responsibility of the courts to protect all liberties, not just fundamental freedoms, from
legislative intrusion.

McIntyre, Lisa J. *The Public Defender: The Practice
of Law in the Shadows of Repute.* Chicago:
University of Chicago Press, 1987. Careful
sociological study of this little-appreciated
courtroom player.

Rehnquist, William H. *All the Laws But One:
Civil Liberties in Wartime.* New York: Knopf,

1998. The Supreme Court chief justice considers instances in which civil liberties were sacrificed to security needs.

Rosenberg, Gerald N. *The Hollow Hope: Can Courts Bring About Social Change?* Chicago: University of Chicago Press, 1991. Casts doubt on the proposition that the courts play a major, independent role in shaping policy.

Sandel, Michael J. *Democracy's Discontent: America in Search of a Public Philosophy.* Cambridge, MA: Belknap Press of Harvard University Press, 1996. A readable but sophisticated book arguing that the Supreme Court's approach to civil liberty overemphasizes individual autonomy at the expense of republican principles favoring a community's right to self-government.

Wilson, James Q. *Thinking About Crime.* New York: Basic Books, 1975. Makes a persuasive, realistic, and conservative case for ways of controlling crime.

CIVIL RIGHTS

ormer Senate Majority Leader Trent Lott matured politically just as Mississippi was passing through the worst throes of racial conflict. A young black man named James Meredith attempted to enroll at Ole Miss in Lott's senior year there, setting off a battle between federal troops and a segregationist mob. Lott apparently urged his Sigma Nu fraternity brothers to stay away from the violence, but his advice did not grow out of a desire for racial mixing. Lott at the time endorsed keeping blacks and whites separated from each other—and, according to another Sigma Nu leader, helped lead the fight to prevent his fraternity from integrating.[1]

It would have been exceptional, and self-defeating, for a politically ambitious college student in 1960s Mississippi to have held any other views. Lott was born in Mississippi hill country, perhaps the most violently racist section of the United States, and he grew up on the racially troubled Gulf Coast. Lott was 7 years old when his home state bolted the Democratic party to protest President Truman's civil rights record. Four years before Lott left his law practice to begin serious political work, Mississippi supported conservative presidential candidate Barry Goldwater, whose most-attractive trait to southern voters was opposition to government-led integration efforts. Lott's congressional representative in 1968, for whom he worked as a staff member, was a segregationist southern Democrat. Nothing about Lott's racial attitudes was extraordinary, given his context. Lott recognizes as much. "I am a product of my times and my state and my family."[2]

What is remarkable about Trent Lott, though, is how successfully he was able to maneuver up the national political ladder without making any real effort to communicate that he had changed with the times or with the state of Mississippi. If anything, from the 1970s straight through to the early 1990s Lott repeatedly signaled his continuing fidelity to the beliefs and symbols of strict racial conservatism. Lott championed a 1979 constitutional amendment proposal to prohibit busing children from one school to another as a means of obtaining racial balance. He supported tax breaks for a racially segregated religious college in 1981. He voted against Martin Luther King Day in 1983. In 1992, he praised the Council of Conservative Citizens, a group with its origins tied to the fight against desegregation, for containing people who "stand for the right principles."

Lott repeatedly expressed his admiration for the Confederate side in the Civil War, the southern government that fought in part to preserve slavery. Indeed, in 1984 Lott called that conflict the "War of Northern Aggression," a label favored by those who romanticize the Confederate effort. Of the Confederacy's president, Lott once said, "I sometimes feel closer to Jefferson Davis than any other man in America." He fought to restore (posthumously) Davis' U.S. citizenship in 1979. In 1984, he praised the Republican party platform for keeping alive "the spirit of Jefferson Davis." In short, Lott rose to his position of leadership over the U.S. Senate—which he held for the first months of the second Bush presidency—despite giving every sign that he was still "living in 1862 or, at the latest, 1948."[3] There was little if any questioning of whether someone with his legacy deserved to lead the upper chamber of Congress.

Lott's easy rise to power is exactly the sort of evidence social critics use to illustrate the inadequacy of America's racial progress. Lott "seems to hold a decidedly rosy view of the system and the times that gave rise to the butchery of the [Ku Klux Klan, or] KKK," writes columnist and scholar Ellis Cose. "Why is a man so willfully ignorant of history serving in the Senate at all—much less preparing to become its leader? How could a man on record for championing the ideas of the Confederacy become part of America's ruling power elite?"[4] University of Buffalo Adjunct Professor Wes Carter echoes the thought, asking "how our society could have allowed this individual to rise to such an elevated post."[5]

Notably, both of those published comments came after Republicans retook the Senate in 2002 (see Chapter 9), just as it was becoming clear that Lott might never regain his command of the upper chamber. At a birthday party for U.S. Senator Strom Thurmond, who once led the 1948 southern rebellion against President Truman, Senator Lott tried to give a "tip of the hat to the old man," as one journalist put it.[6] This is what he said:

> *I want to say this about my state. When Strom Thurmond ran for president we voted for him. We're proud of it. And if the rest of the country had followed our lead we wouldn't of had all these problems over all these years, either.*[7]

No doubt Lott thought that these were fairly innocent words, with minimal political content. You're supposed to heap lavish and exaggerated praise on the honoree at a birthday party. No one really takes such comments seriously. It was not as though Lott explicitly embraced the platform of Thurmond's 1948 campaign or explained which social problems Thurmond's leadership would have averted. It was not as though Lott intentionally or accidentally communicated a continuing intention to separate the races by law. He felt comfortable, while "winging it" before the birthday audience, to praise Thurmond's political career—saying words that, after all, he had spoken without cost years before.

But those listening to Senator Lott knew that the context had changed, that few people would hear his birthday party banter as empty words. Americans could not ignore praise from the incoming Senate Majority Leader, one of the last congressional power brokers to grow up in the segregated Deep South, for a presidential campaign fueled by racial hatreds and fears—too much history was wrapped up in those innocent-sounding words. Lott's comments would be especially incendiary given the Republican party's efforts to be racially and ethnically inclusive, as well as given Lott's own checkered past on racial issues. By all reports, the audience gasped audibly, knowing or at least sensing that they were watching a lengthy political career collapse before their eyes.

Griswald
vs
CT

Lott's political support evaporated rapidly. He issued repeated apologies, each one more self-critical and more respectful of civil rights. He disavowed his old support for segregation as immoral and asked forgiveness. But suddenly Americans, especially journalists and political leaders, no longer felt they should ignore all of Lott's racial baggage. News pieces on Lott's meltdown dismissed him as, at best, an unthoughtful man who "had not really re-examined some of the assumptions he had long taken for granted." *Newsweek* explained that "Lott is not a racist in the nightriding sense, but his paper trail of comments and votes on race strike many people as inappropriate to the high office he holds in a multiracial democracy."[8] Lott's leadership position did not survive the winter holidays. He was forced to resign. U.S. Senator Bill Frist of Tennessee eventually assumed command of the Republican majority, having served fewer years than any previous recipient of that honor.

Just as Lott's silent rise to power illustrated how America's racial problems still linger, his rapid collapse reveals why many people see so much cause to be optimistic about the future of civil rights. Lott lost his position of authority for vague words praising a man who was just ending a record-breaking career in the U.S. Senate, and who had served as the body's President Pro Tempore. He was cast out by a political party criticized for a tendency to "play the race card" as a means of attracting racially conservative voters, a party with few black officials who might have taken personal offense at a display of racism.[*] Ellis Cose, in his column, recognized the sign of hope provided by these anomalous events. "The very fact that so many are so upset at Lott may mean things are beginning to change."[9]

THE RISE AND FALL OF TRENT LOTT IS JUST ONE PIVOTAL EVENT in the story of America's battle for civil rights, albeit a recent and politically significant one. That being said, this one story invokes a much broader question about America's new democracy. Popular influence may have surged in the U.S. political system, but what does the change mean for people who are members of a minority because of their race, ethnicity, primary language, or sexuality? On the one hand, when elections drive policy, voters decide the nation's future. Minorities are, by definition, smaller than majorities—and so elections could place them at a political disadvantage.[†] For example, voters as a whole may have little concern with the racial credentials of the leaders they elect; people may be able to rise to power without anyone probing whether they can truly represent a diverse population.

---

[*]This wording assumes that African Americans logically would take "personal offense" at anti-black prejudice, while other races and ethnic groups would not. But there is an alternate way to view Trent Lott's story. Perhaps so many Americans have become committed to the goal of improved race relations that, regardless of race, they generally take "personal offense" when a leader violates those norms.

[†]This generalization refers to a *minority* in a statistical sense. Sometimes people use the term *minority* in a political sense, to mean a "disadvantaged or less-powerful group," in which case women are a "minority" with greater numbers than men.

On the other hand, elections can favor tightly knit groups whose common concerns prompt them to participate as a bloc. Politicians usually construct their electoral coalitions from multiple factions; they seldom appeal to voters as an undifferentiated mass. Minority-group leaders who can sway the behavior of a large chunk of voters receive disproportionate influence. They are valuable allies and worrisome enemies. Party leaders, from presidents on down to the smallest precinct organizers, cannot afford to keep around a politician who damages their party's reputation with a distinct voting bloc. For candidates and policy makers, it may be easier to accommodate the passionate demands of a unified and vocal minority than to worry about the mild or divided preferences of a numerical majority. America's new democracy therefore could expand minority influence, compared to a system more insulated from voters.

This chapter grapples with the difficult puzzle of where minorities stand in a system that enhances popular influence. Our ultimate answer is not entirely straightforward, though, because the reality is complex. Sometimes minorities thrive in election-driven politics, and sometimes their political goals suffer when the majority rules. Elected officials and ballot-box policies sometimes reflect the preferences, interests, and prejudices of those who enjoy strength in numbers. But sometimes the sensibilities and values of common voters prove friendlier to minorities than what elites or interest groups might have endorsed. And sometimes minorities can operate as swing voters in elections and single-handedly force public officials to pay heed.

By contrast, the least election-driven American institution—the judicial branch—occasionally stands up for minority groups against discriminatory policies. But in most cases the Supreme Court's approach to civil rights follows trends initiated by the public debates and coalition building that make up electoral politics. As Justice Ruth Bader Ginsburg once observed, "With prestige to persuade, but not physical power to enforce, and with a will for self-preservation, the Court generally follows, it does not lead, changes taking place elsewhere in society."[10] Usually, the Court does little more than codify existing policy preferences into constitutional doctrine. Sometimes it even lags behind the times.

CIVIL RIGHTS:
MORE THAN JUST A RACE THING

The terms *civil rights* and *civil liberties* are similar but not identical. Civil liberties are fundamental freedoms that preserve the rights of a free people. **Civil rights** embody the American guarantee to equal treatment under the law—not just for racial groups, as people often assume, but more generally. In Chapter 13 we emphasize how important the due process clause of the Fourteenth Amendment has been to the protection of civil liberties in the United States. An equally important provision in the Fourteenth Amendment guards civil rights. According to the **equal protection clause,** states must give everyone "equal protection of the law."

The equal protection clause is no plainer in meaning than the due process clause. Choice of the word *protection* might suggest that the language applies only to the justice system, requiring that law enforcement officials and the courts defend everyone equally. Yet most interpreters emphasize the word *equal* instead. They read the clause to imply that laws should not make categorical distinctions. Everyone must receive equal *treatment* when government formulates public policy.

But even given this wider understanding, it is not clear exactly how "equal" everyone must be. Almost every law treats some people in one way and others in a different way. Laws regularly distinguish among people on the basis of age, income, health, wealth, criminal history, or place of residence. Some distinguish among people on the basis of race, gender, or sexuality. Obviously, some sorts of categories are acceptable some of the time, and federal judges are the ones who decide (sometimes receiving indirect guidance from civil rights legislation).

Generally, the courts rank various sorts of unequal treatment according to the level of "scrutiny" they deserve. Most forms of inequality need only pass a *rational basis test*—the legal distinction between two types of people must offer a reasonable way to promote some legitimate government purpose. Laws receive *strict scrutiny* when they distinguish among people according to a **suspect classification**—which is to say, according to some grouping that has a long history of being used for purposes of discrimination, such as race. State governments or federal agencies responsible for unequal treatment must provide a compelling reason for the differentiation and must explain why their goals were unreachable using less group-conscious legislation. Certain groupings, such as gender, fall between these two extremes. Compared to regular laws, laws distinguishing among people according to these categories receive *heightened scrutiny,* but they need not clear the steep hurdle that suspect-class legislation does. In all three instances, though, the process is the same: Judges decide whether government has good reasons for the categories it uses.

Few voices criticize either the loose interpretation of the word *protection* or varying application of the word *equal* (although the three-tiered "scrutiny" system does have its detractors).[11] Two other questions about how to interpret the Fourteenth Amendment generate much more controversy.[12] The first is over how actively laws must distinguish among people before they fall under scrutiny. A government policy with no direct reference to race—say, for example, a performance test for police academy recruits—might impact two races differently. How should courts decide when indirect sources of unequal treatment represent unconstitutional discrimination? Answers differ.

The second major controversy over the equal protection clause is how to deal with a law that distinguishes among people according to a suspect class but does so to favor rather than harm a minority group. It may be unconstitutional to establish university scholarships available only to Asians or whites.* But can a public university offer money only for blacks, Hispanics, or Native Americans? It may be unconstitutional to shut minority businesses out of receiving government contracts. But can a state government set aside some of its projects exclusively for minority contractors? People clash angrily over whether equal treatment must go both ways when American society itself contains deep inequalities.

The stakes are high in these debates over the equal protection clause. Many minority group members rely on constitutional guarantees to ensure that they obtain equal opportunity. Those outside a minority group, meanwhile, must be on guard to ensure that the claim to equal treatment does not become an excuse for special interests to encroach on their liberties or their own rights to equality before the law. Elected leaders, although sensitive to the demands of minorities, also cannot forget that they are elected by majorities.

Because minorities seldom control the outcome of elections, they have often pursued a legal strategy, bringing apparent civil rights violations to the attention of the courts. But litigation does not always work. Judges, too, are concerned about preserving credibility with majorities. If judges defy public opinion regularly, they may undermine confidence in the courts—and eventually elected officials will replace them.

AFRICAN AMERICANS AND THE IMPORTANCE OF VOTING RIGHTS

At the end of the Civil War, some southern states passed "black codes," restrictive laws that applied to newly freed slaves but not to whites. "Persons of color . . . must make annual written contracts for their labor," one of the codes said, adding that if blacks ran away from their "masters," they had to forgo a year's wages.[13] Other codes denied African Americans access to the courts or the right to hold property, except under special circumstances.

Northern abolitionists urged Congress to override these black codes, which they considered thinly disguised attempts to continue slavery. Congress responded by passing the Civil Rights Act of 1866, which gave all citizens "the same right . . . to full and equal benefit of all laws." Both the sentiment and some of the words carried over to the equal protection clause of the Fourteenth Amendment, which won final ratification two years later.

The federal government promoted its civil rights stance during **Reconstruction,** a period after the Civil War when the federal military still occupied southern states. During this period, blacks exercised their right to vote, a right many white Confederate veterans lacked. In addition, Congress established a

---

*The term *white* has no basis in genetic traits such as skin, hair, or eye color. Anglo-Saxons, Nordics, Slavs, Arabs, Jews, and many other groups all fall into the "white majority" of the U.S. population.

Under the shadow of Jim Crow
Within a generation after the end of Reconstruction, southern states erected strict social barriers between blacks and whites, as did many states outside the South. People of different races could not attend the same schools, use the same public transportation, or mingle in the same public facilities (such as theaters). Would Jim Crow laws have been more diffi-cult to maintain if blacks had been able to vote?

Freedman's Bureau, designed to provide the newly freed slaves with education, immediate food relief, and inexpensive land from former plantations.[14]

The close election of 1876 brought Reconstruction to an end. Republican presidential candidate Rutherford B. Hayes claimed victory, but the outcome depended on fraudulent vote counts reported by several states, including three in the South. Politicians trying to resolve the disputed election worked out a com-promise. Republicans won the presidency; Democrats won removal of federal troops from the South and control of future southern elections.

BLACKS LOSE ELECTORAL POWER

Within a generation the South had restored many of its old racial patterns.[15] One critical change was that black citizens lost their voting rights, a process that dis-turbed the electoral connection between African Americans and their govern-ment. State legislatures enacted laws requiring voters to pass literacy tests, meet strict residency requirements, and pay poll taxes to vote. Although the laws them-selves used general words, and therefore did not seem to violate equal protection of the law, they clearly targeted blacks and the poor whites who might have allied with them in elections.

These laws became even more discriminatory once local officials began applying them. As the chair of the suffrage committee in Virginia bluntly admitted, "I expect the [literacy] examination with which the black men will be confronted to be inspired by the same spirit that inspires every man in this convention. I do not expect an impartial administration of this clause."[16] States also enacted what became known as a **grandfather clause,** a law that exempted men from voting restrictions if their fathers and grandfathers had voted before the Civil War. Of course, only whites benefited from this exemption.

The most successful restriction on the right to vote was the *white primary,* a nomination election held by the Democratic party that excluded nonwhites from participation. Republicans almost never won southern elections at the time, because of the party's tie to Reconstruction, so Democratic primary winners nearly always took office.[17] This practice, combined with the various voting restrictions, denied former slaves and their descendants a meaningful vote. Only 10 percent of adult African American males were registered in most states of the old Confederacy by 1910.[18]

After they lost voting rights, African Americans faced a series of **Jim Crow laws,** state laws that segregated the races from each other.[*] Jim Crow laws required African Americans to attend segregated schools, sit in separate areas in public trains and buses, eat in different restaurants, and use separate public facilities. These laws were almost universal in the South but appeared in numerous states outside that region as well. Thus those of African descent entered the twentieth century cut off socially and politically from other Americans.

The Supreme Court initially took a very restrictive view of the Fourteenth Amendment's equal protection clause, and so permitted Jim Crow segregation. Two rulings held particular significance. In a decision given the ironic title the *Civil Rights Cases* (1883), the Court declared the Civil Rights Act of 1875 unconstitutional.[19] This law abolished segregation in restaurants, train stations, and other public places. But the Supreme Court ruled that only government policies must comply with federal equal rights law, not the actions of private individuals (a position called the **state action doctrine**). Congress had no constitutional authority to tell private individuals who could use their property.

The second major decision by the courts, *Plessy* v. *Ferguson* (1896), had even more sweeping consequences. It developed the **separate but equal doctrine,** the principle that segregated facilities passed constitutional muster as long as they were equivalent. Homer Plessy had challenged Louisiana's law requiring racial segregation in buses, railroad cars, and waiting rooms. Plessy argued that his inability to use white facilities denied him equal protection before the law. But the Supreme Court upheld Louisiana's statute, explaining that separating the races did not stamp either with a "badge of inferiority." Only one justice, a Kentuckian,

---

[*]The name comes from a stereotypical, belittling characterization of African Americans in minstrel shows popular at the time.

dissented. Justice John Marshall Harlan protested that "our Constitution is color-blind, and neither knows nor tolerates classes among citizens." Laws enforcing segregation, Harlan argued, clearly violate this ideal.[20]

BLACKS REGAIN ELECTORAL POWER

Legally sanctioned segregation remained intact well into the twentieth century. During that time, however, African Americans gained electoral clout by migrating north, to states where they could vote (see Figure 14.1). During both world wars, in particular, northern industrial cities filled labor shortages with blacks from the rural South. Northerners were not much more tolerant of blacks than were southerners. But machine politicians who dominated big-city politics were not fussy about the color or religion of the voters they organized. Any warm body who could walk into a voting booth was worth courting.[21]

By the 1930s, African Americans had used their votes to win small places in the politics of a few big cities. But the biggest political breakthrough for African Americans occurred in 1948, when they appeared to cast the decisive votes elect-

FIGURE 14.1

Percentage of African Americans living outside the South, by decade, 1910 to 1999

The northern migration of African Americans greatly increased their electoral clout. What explains the northern migration of blacks from 1910 to 1970? What explains their recent return to the South?

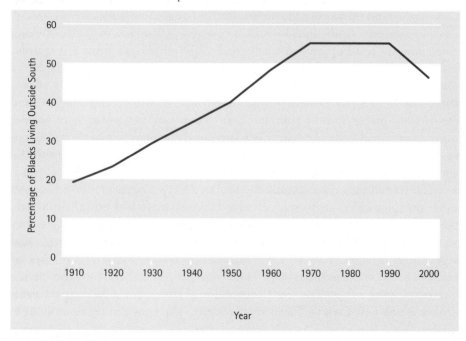

SOURCE: U.S. Bureau of the Census, *Current Population Survey Reports.*

ing Harry Truman president. This clout, and the increased rhetorical support Truman gave to civil rights, lent added force to lawsuits that activists began bringing before the federal courts.

REDEFINING STATE ACTION   The legal case against segregation was developed gradually by the National Association for the Advancement of Colored People (NAACP). Formed in 1909, the NAACP chose a courtroom strategy because its leaders feared the inadequacy of black electoral strength. Only 12 percent of the southern black adult population could vote in 1947.[22] Yet a legal strategy without electoral leverage could not be very effective. The NAACP's lead attorney, Thurgood Marshall (who later became the first black Supreme Court justice), initially had few successes.

The NAACP's efforts gained potency as blacks moved north. Their earliest advances involved the state action doctrine. The Court was willing to expand its definition of state activity to protect the political and legal rights of African Americans. In an important 1944 case, *Smith* v. *Allwright,* the Court outlawed the white primary, saying parties were not private organizations but integral parts of a state electoral system.[23] After this decision, black voting in the South gradually increased.

In 1948, the same year blacks helped elect Harry Truman, the Supreme Court took a major step against residential segregation. One tool that whites used to keep African Americans out of their neighborhoods was the **restrictive housing covenant;** a home buyer would sign a contract promising not to sell the property to a black household later. The Court ruled in *Shelley* v. *Kraemer* (1948) that states could not treat such private agreements as legally binding without violating the equal protection clause.[24]

TAKING THE "SEPARATE" OUT OF "EQUAL"   The Supreme Court moved much more slowly against the separate but equal doctrine, which helped preserve social inequalities, not just political ones. As late as 1950 the Court passed up several opportunities to overrule the *Plessy* precedent, sensing that the time was not right to take such a controversial stand.[25] The problem was not a lack of sympathetic justices. Rather, the Court feared stepping too far beyond public opinion and losing the policy battle.

NAACP attorneys continued seeking cases that might prompt the Court to overturn *Plessy.* Of the handful they moved to the Court's docket in 1952, one from Kansas eventually took center stage: ***Brown* v. *Board of Education of Topeka*** (1954). Oliver Brown had filed a suit arguing that his daughter Linda's all-black school denied her equal protection of the law. The fact that Topeka funded white and black education equivalently made no difference, NAACP lawyers argued; separation was inherently unequal. The Justice Department's Civil Rights Division backed the NAACP's claim, using strategies developed in collaboration with Justice Felix Frankfurter, a former director of the NAACP.* The Court agreed to hear their arguments and did so in December 1952.

The Supreme Court was still skittish, though. Chief Justice Fred Vinson, a conservative Democrat, did not consider *Plessy* a bankrupt precedent. Three other justices also hesitated to overturn it. The Court delayed the final decision, scheduling a second round of arguments in 1953. Before they could take place, however, Vinson died of a heart attack. Frankfurter called Vinson's death "the first indication I have ever had that there is a God."[26] President Eisenhower turned to a popular former governor, Earl Warren, to lead the Court.

Dramatic changes followed Warren's appointment. The Californian approached his appointment not as a former attorney or judge concerned with refining points of law, but as a politician determined to set public policy.[27] To Warren, the South's racial caste system represented an evil that most American voters were willing to exorcize; the Court should not hesitate to alter constitutional law as a means of promoting this moral goal. He decided to write the *Brown* opinion himself.

Warren realized how risky it was for the Court to abolish segregated institutions with long histories. To give the ruling additional authority, he wanted a unanimous judgment. He delayed voting on the issue for four months while he worked to persuade reluctant justices. He made compromises: limiting the judgment to schools and leaving flexibility in the ways a school district might remedy a segregated system. Eventually, every justice agreed to sign on—no dissents and no concurrences.

Warren's opinion in *Brown* built less from law than from social science. Warren cited psychological studies claiming that segregation created a sense of inferiority among black children. One study showed, for example, that black children favored white dolls over black ones.[28] Warren therefore overturned *Plessy* only in the field of education and did not embrace Harlan's *Plessy* dissent declaring the Constitution "color-blind." The Court still hesitated to take on social arrangements that dated back to the earliest colonial settlements.

THE MODERN BATTLE FOR CIVIL RIGHTS

The *Brown* decision energized civil rights activists around the country. The impact on young people and church leaders was particularly noticeable; they formed numerous civil rights organizations and adopted more militant techniques.[29] NAACP activist Rosa Parks, of Montgomery, Alabama, engaged in an extraordinarily successful act of **civil disobedience**—a peaceful violation of a law, designed to dramatize that law's injustice. She refused to vacate her seat in a seg-

---

*For a justice to collaborate with interested parties in a Supreme Court appeal clearly violates today's ethical standards, but there is no indication that Frankfurter saw any problem with sharing notes on an important case. See Howard Ball and Phillip J. Cooper, *Of Power and Right* (New York: Oxford, 1992), p. 177.

Civil rights workers
Tear-gas clouds, laid by the Mississippi Highway Patrol, rained confusion on early civil rights marchers in Canton, Mississippi. Did these marchers or the courts contribute more to the end of formal segregation?

regated bus when the driver attempted to expand the white section past her spot. The standoff prompted a bus boycott led by a young Baptist minister, Martin Luther King, Jr., who had recently earned his Ph.D. in theology. He was only 27 years old at the time, but he had the resourcefulness necessary to give the event national significance.[30]

The civil rights movement won overwhelmingly sympathetic coverage in the northern press, but it met intense opposition from regional officials.[31] In March 1956, nearly every southern member of Congress signed the Southern Manifesto, committing each official to resist implementation of the *Brown* decision by "all lawful means."[32] Southern resistance was so consistent and complete that, in the states of the Old Confederacy, few schools desegregated. In the fall of 1964, ten years after *Brown,* only 2.3 percent of black students in former Confederate states attended integrated schools.[33]

Yet the protests and demonstrations gradually had their effect. For one thing, southern blacks were registering to vote. From 1947 to 1960, the percentage more than doubled from 12 percent to 28 percent. At the same time, African Americans were becoming a more powerful political force in the large industrial

Content of his character

Martin Luther King, Jr., delivers his "I Have a Dream" speech at the 1963 March on Washington. Why did the civil rights movement lose support just a few years later?

states of the North. Presidential candidates had to balance southern resistance against their need for black votes.

John Kennedy's victory over Richard Nixon in the breathtakingly close election of 1960 owed much to his success attracting the black vote. When the 1960 election campaign began, Kennedy realized that he needed to improve his civil rights credentials, especially because he had won the Democratic nomination by defeating two candidates with stronger records: Hubert Humphrey and Adlai Stevenson. A golden opportunity arose when Birmingham authorities jailed Martin Luther King, Jr. Kennedy placed a well-publicized phone call to Coretta Scott King, expressing sympathy for the plight of her husband. That phone call took on great symbolic significance and helped mobilize Kennedy's supporters in the black community. He captured enough black votes to win such crucial states as Ohio and Michigan.

Once in office, Kennedy introduced civil rights legislation. To support his efforts, 100,000 black and white demonstrators marched on the Washington Mall in the summer of 1963. Others organized the event, but King emerged as the star, delivering his moving "I Have a Dream" oration from the steps of the Lincoln Memorial. Suddenly, a plurality of Americans viewed civil rights as the country's most important problem.[34] A few months later, Kennedy's assassination generated an unprecedented outpouring of moral commitment to racial justice (see Figure 14.2).

Elected political leaders responded quickly to this transformation in the nation's mood. The new president, Lyndon Baines Johnson (LBJ) of Texas, knew that he had to dispel public doubts about his commitment to racial change. The southerner called upon Congress to memorialize his dead predecessor by enacting civil rights legislation stalled in the Senate since the previous summer. After intense

FIGURE 14.2

Evaluation of civil rights as the country's most important problem

Many people saw civil rights as an important problem in the wake of the Kennedy assassination and civil rights demonstrations. Today (not shown) only around 3 percent view race relations as the most important problem. Does this change reflect real progress or a lack of attention to current problems?

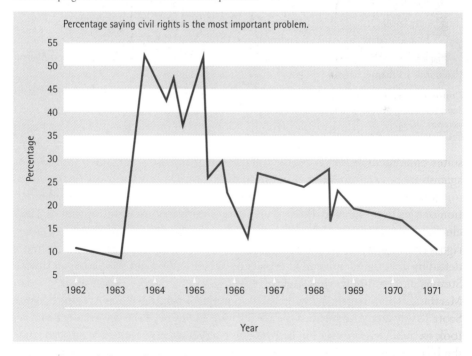

SOURCE: Gerald Jaynes and Robin M. Williams, Jr., eds., *A Common Destiny: Blacks and American Society* (Washington, DC: National Academy Press, 1989), p. 224.

debate, majorities of both Republican and Democratic members of Congress voted to pass the legislation in 1964. The act banned segregation in all places of public accommodation, prohibited the use of federal money to support segregated programs, and created the Equal Employment Opportunity Commission (EEOC) to guard against employment discrimination. From 1964 to 1972, the percentage of black students in southern schools that included whites increased dramatically from 2.3 percent to 91.3 percent.

Buoyed by economic prosperity and his civil rights achievements, LBJ won a sweeping election victory in the fall of 1964. He followed this success by engineering congressional passage of the Voting Rights Act of 1965, which guaranteed that more black voters would be able to turn out for Democratic candidates in the future.[35] The percentage of voters among southern black adults jumped upward; by 1992 they were as likely to vote as northern blacks.[36] From 1965 to 1998, the number of black elected officials rose from less than 500 to over 8800.[37]

THE PUBLIC MOOD SHIFTS

Segregation and discrimination did not stop at the South's borders. Most northern blacks lived in racially isolated neighborhoods, sent their children to predominantly black schools, and struggled to get good jobs. Martin Luther King shifted his focus northward after the successes in 1964 and 1965 by mounting a series of demonstrations in Chicago.[38] King broadened his issue concerns, protesting poverty and criticizing the Vietnam War. At the same time, new black leaders such as Malcolm X took a more militant position, affirming black culture and denying the value of integration.

Increasing assertiveness by black leaders changed how the public viewed civil rights. Support for protests dwindled.[39] At the same time, African Americans grew increasingly disenchanted with the slowness of racial change. Leaders began calling for **affirmative action** policies, which are programs designed to enhance opportunities for race- or gender-based groups by giving them special consideration in recruitment or promotion decisions. Destructive riots broke out in minority neighborhoods, beginning in Los Angeles in 1964 and spreading to other cities over the next three years. King's assassination in the spring of 1968 again set off violent racial disturbances in dozens of cities throughout the country. National guard and army units had to quell wholesale theft and property destruction. The civil rights movement lost its moral authority, and whites began to lose interest in the cause (review Figure 14.2).

Racial issues began to divide the two political parties. When Arizona Senator Barry Goldwater voted against the Civil Rights Act of 1964, he was among a minority of Republicans to do so. But by 1968, his party started pursuing a "southern strategy" by appealing to those who thought civil rights legislation had gone too far. Meanwhile, blacks solidified their allegiance to the Democratic party.[40] Between 1968 and 1972, the percentage of delegates attending the Democratic convention

Defending Dixie

Symbolizing Southern pride to some and racial hatred to others, South Carolina's practice of flying a Confederate flag over the statehouse became an issue in the 2000 presidential campaign. The flag was later moved elsewhere. When people battle over symbols, is compromise ever really possible? Or must one side necessarily lose?

who were black grew from 6.7 to 14.6 percent (see Figure 14.3).

African American leaders hoped the federal courts would remain a bulwark against popular sentiment, but they did not. The Supreme Court distinguished between two types of segregation: **de jure segregation,** the separation of races by law as practiced in the South, and **de facto segregation,** separation occurring as the result of private decisions made by individuals. The Court decided that the equal protection clause forbade only southern-style segregation.

In *Milliken* v. *Bradley* (1974), for example, the Supreme Court considered the constitutionality of the *de facto* segregation that plagued northern urban school districts.[41] A ring of all-white suburban districts surrounded the heavily black city of Detroit, leaving school systems racially distinct. No law required these racially segregated schools—they were a product of (1) district borders drawn with no apparent discriminatory intent and (2) residential decisions made by private individuals. Four justices tried to persuade their brethren that the state of Michigan still held responsibility for district borders; federal courts could force them to consolidate urban and suburban school systems to promote integration. But the Court majority, led by Nixon appointee Warren Burger, would not expand the definition of state action to include *de facto* social conditions. The chief justice wrote that the Constitution forbids discriminatory policy but "does not require any particular racial balance."

FIGURE 14.3

Percentage of African American delegates to the national party conventions

The shifting racial characteristics of party activists reflect similar changes in voter loyalties. Why has African American participation in Democratic party politics risen dramatically?

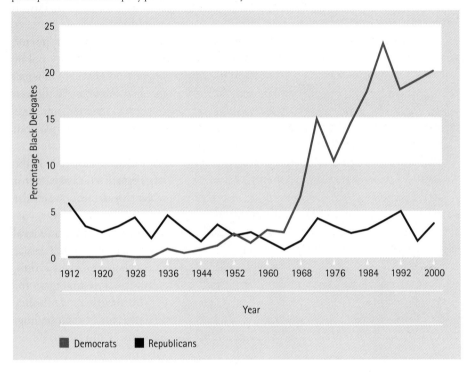

SOURCES: "The Democratic Delegates," *San Francisco Examiner* (August 27, 1996): A9; Robert Zauser, "Small Number of Black Delegates Illustrates Problem for Republicans," *Philadelphia Inquirer* (August 16, 1996): A22.

The Supreme Court also considered the constitutionality of affirmative action programs in a 1978 case, *Regents of the University of California* v. *Bakke*. Recruitment policies favoring minorities or women vary in their size and significance. In some cases, these programs consist of nothing more than special advertising and counseling designed to inform disadvantaged groups about available opportunities. At the opposite extreme, some policies establish inflexible **quotas,** or specific numbers of positions reserved for members of disadvantaged groups. The policy under review in *Bakke* was a quota system; the UC–Davis medical school required 16 percent of its entering class to be minority students. Allen Bakke, a Norwegian American, sued after falling just short of admission two years in a row—despite a stronger record than some of the minority applicants who were admitted.[42]

The Supreme Court could not agree on an opinion. Four justices rejected Bakke's claim, arguing that institutions with no history of discrimination could still formulate policies to remedy "societal discrimination." Four other justices would not allow policies that judged applicants differently on the basis of race—whether to help or hurt disadvantaged groups. They declared all forms of affirmative action illegal, a violation of either the equal protection clause or the Civil Rights Act of 1964. This left the Court in a 4-to-4 tie, with Justice Lewis Powell sitting in the middle.

Powell, a moderate southerner appointed by President Nixon, supported active attempts to create diversity but knew that explicit quotas lacked public support. He ended up writing an opinion fully supported by no other member of the Court, yet one that has defined constitutional doctrine to this day. It allowed race to play a role in university admissions decisions, with minority applicants favored over others, but forbade unseemly quota systems. Bakke won his case, but universities retained strong affirmative action programs across the nation.

Affirmative action has faced increasing criticism for decades. In 1995, the University of California Board of Regents voted to end the use of race as a factor in its admissions policies, a decision that took on broader significance when the state later passed Proposition 209 banning affirmative action. That same year, voters in Washington State passed a similar measure, and two years later, a federal court ordered Texas to eliminate race-based preferences from its state university admissions system. But the Court reaffirmed Powell's *Bakke* precedent in 2003, striking a rigid race-based point system used by the University of Michigan for undergraduate admissions but accepting a less formal affirmative action policy implemented by Michigan's law school. The need for diversity is so compelling, the Court ruled, universities need not treat everyone equally.

EVALUATING RACIAL PROGRESS

Significant problems still beset U.S. blacks. Chief among them is the persistence of unemployment,[43] which creates a high poverty rate in the black community.[44] Teen pregnancy and infant mortality rates are far higher among African Americans than among others.[45] But there is reason for increasing optimism. The percentage of black men and women in professional and managerial positions increased markedly in the decades following the civil rights acts.[46] From 1975 to 1997, the percentage of blacks between the ages of 18 and 24 who have dropped out of high school fell from 27 percent to 17 percent. And between 1980 and 1990, the test scores of black high school seniors improved by 9 percent (compared with negligible gains among whites).[47] Blacks have also made electoral gains, winning an increasing number of political offices—sometimes with the direct assistance of electoral laws (see the accompanying Election Connection, "Affirmative Action Redistricting") and sometimes without it.[48] Half a century is a long time to allow injustices to persist in a democratic society, but few nations have moved so quickly to address deep-seated social inequalities.

Affirmative Action Redistricting

Civil rights laws guarantee minority-group access to most jobs. One important exception is elected office. Neither Congress nor the courts may throw out election results by claiming that voters "discriminated." No one has a "right" to hold office without winning the most votes. Nevertheless, activists claim that the electoral system does not give minority candidates a fair shake. They seek a form of affirmative action for public service so that the country will not suffer from a lack of diversity in the halls of government.

Policy makers have targeted legislative offices as the best opportunity to increase minority representation. District borders change regularly—changes driven in part by political motives. The right district borders can virtually ensure the election of African American or Hispanic politicians by grouping voters according to race or ethnicity. Furthermore, the Voting Rights Act of 1965 (VRA) gives the Justice Department influence over how some states draw their legislative maps, so the national government is in a position to push affirmative action districts. And 1982 amendments to the VRA have been interpreted by the courts to require creation of districts dominated by a minority wherever possible.

The Bush administration Justice Department aggressively promoted affirmation action districts after the 1990 census, and the strategy worked. In the 103rd Congress, for example (the first Congress after that redistricting),

32 of the 39 black members came from districts in which African Americans had a majority, and in 5 of the remaining 7 districts, African Americans plus Hispanics made up a majority. Similarly, 15 of the 17 Hispanic members in the 103rd Congress came from majority-Hispanic districts; none came from a district with a white Anglo majority. Similar successes occurred in state legislatures around the country.

It may seem puzzling that a Republican administration would promote minority representation, when most minority legislators are Democrats. But the costs were low. Creating majority-minority enclaves requires pulling hordes of Democratic voters from surrounding districts, leaving the remainder much more favorable to the GOP. Many Democratic politicians found themselves defending new legislative districts filled with conservative suburban voters. The Democratic party lost around 11 seats in Congress as a result of the 1990 redistricting round, contributing to their minority status in the House. They also lost seats in almost every Southern state legislature, including control of two lower chambers.[a]

Some voters asked the courts to declare race-conscious map making a violation of their equal protection guarantees. Conservative federal judges ended up less interested in the practical political advantages of racial redistricting than other conservative public officials were.

THE CIVIL RIGHTS
OF ETHNIC MINORITIES

Congress framed 1960s civil rights legislation to redress unique historical grievances growing out of slavery and the Jim Crow system, and so it dwelt on the position of African Americans. Meanwhile, the Supreme Court has never specifically delineated requirements for a minority group to be eligible for government pro-

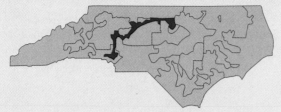

North Carolina's I-85 congressional district

They reacted negatively to the unseemly district shapes necessary to pack minority voters into single legislative districts.

The U.S. Supreme Court first faced the question in a case from North Carolina. One congressional district followed Interstate 85 across the state to pick up black residential areas in the state's major cities (see the accompanying graphic). A splintered Court ruled in *Shaw* v. *Reno* (1993) that creative electoral maps had limits: A district created on no basis other than to include a majority of minorities might raise constitutional questions. The Court went further in *Miller* v. *Johnson* (1995). By a 5-to-4 majority, the Court forbid plans that use race as a "predominant factor" when picking district borders.[b]

Changes mandated by federal courts initially had little effect. Both minority and Republican legislators who were first elected because of affirmative action districting usually were able to survive despite changes in their district borders. In particular, southern white voters proved as willing to vote for black Democrats as they were to support other candidates from that party. Sanford Bishop, a member of Congress from Georgia, was able to hold on to his heavily rural district despite a new constituency that was only 26.8 percent black.[c] Less clear is whether minorities will continue to be competitive in such districts after the current incumbents step down.

What do you think?

- Could election districts that were intended to increase minority representation actually harm their interests?
- How does the equal protection clause of the Constitution support arguments both for and against majority-minority districts?

[a]David Lublin and D. Stephen Voss, "Racial Redistricting and Realignment in Southern State Legislatures," *American Journal of Political Science*, 2000, 44 (October): 792–810; David Lublin and D. Stephen Voss, "Boll-Weevil Blues: Polarized Congressional Delegations into the 21st Century," *American Review of Politics*, 2000, 22 (fall/winter).

[b]Holly Idelson, "Court Takes a Harder Line on Minority Voting Blocs," *Congressional Quarterly Weekly Report* (July 1, 1995): 1944–1946.

[c]D. Stephen Voss and David Lublin, "Black Incumbents, White Districts: An Appraisal of the 1996 Congressional Elections," *American Politics Research*, 2001, 29 (March): 141–182.

tection. But after the civil rights movement altered equal protection law, groups representing other ethnic minorities began to make similar civil rights claims. Both Congress and the courts often gave recognition to these groups.

Not all ethnic minorities enjoy the same political standing in American law. For much of U.S. history, Jews faced virulent prejudice and crippling discrimination, including lynchings and synagogue bombings in the twentieth century.[49] Yet

Jewish people receive no affirmative protections from government. The degree to which each ethnic minority gains political clout depends in large part on how effectively it mobilizes members in elections. Hispanics and Asian Americans represent influential voting blocs in several large states that are crucial during presidential elections and, accordingly, can exert disproportionate influence on national politics. Only Native Americans rely on their legal position to issue demands on government.

HISPANICS

Hispanics (or Latinos) are the fastest-growing minority group in the United States.* In 1980 they made up only 6.4 percent of the U.S. population, but by 2000 they had grown to 12.5 percent, for the first time surpassing the 12.3 percent who are African American.[50] Yet Hispanics are only starting to make a significant political impact. Previously, language barriers and the large number of immigrants without citizenship limited their influence. Many new Hispanic immigrants also plan to return to their countries of origin and, therefore, stay out of U.S. politics.[51]

Hispanic voters are much less likely than African Americans to vote as a bloc. Whereas 85 percent of blacks consider themselves Democrats, only 55 percent of Hispanics do.[52] This political diversity is a natural outgrowth of real social and cultural diversity within "the Hispanic nation."[53] Some Hispanics have been Americans for many generations; others are recent arrivals speaking little English. Some are affluent and respected members of their communities; others are migrant laborers living on a pittance. Hispanics come from many different countries. Mexican Americans concentrate in the Southwest, from California to Texas. Puerto Ricans concentrate in northern industrial cities, such as New York. Cuban Americans concentrate in Florida. These disparate groups have little in common, so they share few political concerns.

Activists have worked hard to construct an Hispanic identity. One of the earliest groups to do so was the Mexican American Legal Defense and Education Fund (MALDEF), which has focused on voting, education, and immigration issues. In 1974, in response to MALDEF complaints, the Supreme Court interpreted the 1964 Civil Rights Act to mean that schools must provide special educational programs for those not proficient in the English language.[54] MALDEF and other advocacy groups also argued that voting materials discriminated against linguistic minorities because they appeared only in English. Congress responded in 1982 by requiring foreign-language ballots for any linguistic minority constituting more than 5 percent of a county's population.[55]

---

*Following author Geoffrey Fox, we opt for the less politicized term *Hispanic* rather than *Latino*, although we realize the imperfection in either label. See Geoffrey Fox, *Hispanic Nation: Culture, Politics, and the Constructing of Identity* (Secaucus, NJ: Birch Lane, 1996), pp. 9–14.

Courting the Hispanic vote

George P. Bush, whose mother is of Mexican descent, campaigned for his uncle, George W. Bush, in the Latino community in 2000. Why has the importance of the Hispanic vote lagged behind that of the black vote?

Cuban politics took center stage in 1999 when fishermen off the Florida coast rescued six-year-old Elian Gonzalez and brought him to Miami. Elian had escaped Cuba with his mother, but she had perished in an accident at sea. Elian's uncle and other relatives in Miami embraced the boy and sought to become his legal guardians. But the U.S. Immigration and Naturalization Service (INS) insisted that Elian return to his father in Cuba, a position the Justice Department enforced aggressively—angering activists who have long fought the island's dictatorial Castro regime. This event underscored the strength of Cuban voters in an important swing state: Vice President Gore broke with the Clinton administration position and took the side of Elian's Miami relatives, rather than risk giving south Florida to George W. Bush.

Both presidential candidates worked hard to court the Hispanic vote in 2000. George W. Bush repeatedly repudiated anti-immigration laws and cited his moderate record on immigration in Texas (Chapter 4). He also stressed his support for some bilingual education programs and his opposition to English-only mandates. Bush's Hispanic nephew, George P. Bush, made pleas on his uncle's behalf. Both Al Gore and George Bush peppered their speeches with Spanish while campaigning in such key states as California, Florida, and New York.

Asian Americans

Asian Americans only recently gained a voice in national electoral politics. They constitute just 4 percent of the population, and over 60 percent are foreign-born.[56] Like Hispanics, they represent many different nationalities and have differing, even conflicting, foreign policy concerns. Asians vote Republican more often than other minorities do, and they are more likely to oppose affirmative action programs that promote other ethnic groups at their expense.[57]

In 1996 activists in the Asian American community flexed their political muscle by mounting a coordinated fund-raising and voter registration drive.[58] That year, Gary Locke of Washington was elected the first Asian American governor of a state other than Hawaii. Yet many Asian Americans worry about anti-immigration sentiment among U.S. voters. Initiatives to require English for government business or to cut off immigrant welfare benefits frequently appear on state ballots. In 1996 a Chinese American scientist was jailed, and even placed in isolation, for alleged spying—even though the government eventually dropped all serious charges against him. Activists worry that a growth in stereotyping could produce a "chilling effect" on Asian American political participation.[59]

Native Americans

The Bill of Rights does not protect the rights and liberties of Native Americans. At the time of the Constitution's ratification, descendants of indigenous tribes were considered citizens of foreign nations. As one authority on Indian rights put it, "No constitutional protections exist for Indians in either a tribal or an individual sense."[60]

Instead, relations between Native Americans and the government operate under federal laws and treaties signed with American Indian tribes. Over the long course of U.S. history, the government, facing political pressure from those migrating westward, ignored or broke many of the treaties it made with these tribes. Still, the Supreme Court today interprets some of these treaties as binding.[61] As a result, tribal members have certain rights and privileges not available to other groups. For example, Court rulings have given tribes in the Pacific Northwest special rights to fish for salmon.

One economically significant right recognized in recent years has been the authority to provide commercial gambling on tribal property. The Court has said that tribal grounds are governed by federal, not state, law. Federal law does not disallow gambling on tribal grounds except if it is forbidden everywhere within a state. In several cases, tribes have secured political influence using proceeds from gambling operations.

Congressional legislation has applied most of the Bill of Rights to tribe members. To protect religious freedom, for example, Congress passed the 1978 American Indian Religious Freedom Resolution. Tribal leaders have argued that the resolution gives them special access to traditional religious sites in national parks and other government lands. But the federal courts have interpreted the resolution narrowly, saying it does not make indigenous Americans "supercitizens." Rather, it gives them religious freedoms comparable to those granted other citizens.[62]

GENDER, SEXUALITY, AND CIVIL RIGHTS

"It is in the very nature of ideas to grow in self-awareness, to work out all their implications over time," one constitutional scholar writes. "The very content of the great clauses of the Constitution, their coverage, changes."[63] So it has been with the equal protection clause of the Fourteenth Amendment. Although gender is not mentioned anywhere in the clause, its meaning has evolved to include equal rights for women. But these changes did not take place entirely within the confines of federal courtrooms. They were part of a broad struggle for women's rights, played out as much among the electorate as in the legal arena.

GENDER EQUALITY

The first struggle for women's rights focused on voting. Once the Nineteenth Amendment passed in 1920, the women's movement fell dormant for nearly 50 years.[64] Women's groups grew more active in the 1960s, and since then they have achieved three civil rights objectives: equal treatment before the law, protection against sexual harassment, and access to state-funded military academies.

EQUALITY BEFORE THE LAW   As unlikely as it may seem, a conservative southerner, Howard Smith of Virginia, proposed amending Title VII of the Civil Rights Act of 1964 to prohibit discrimination on the basis of sex as well as race, religion, or national origin. The amendment passed overwhelmingly, but activists formed the National Organization for Women (NOW) to ensure that courts would enforce it. They also pushed to ensconce equal treatment in the Constitution, backing the **Equal Rights Amendment (ERA),** a failed amendment that would have banned gender discrimination.

At first, the ERA seemed destined to sail through the ratification process; it appeared to be an easy way for politicians to secure female votes. Overwhelming congressional majorities passed the ERA in 1972. Within a year a majority of states voted to ratify it.[65] But just before the ERA could join the U.S. Constitution, a resistance movement led by groups of conservative women derailed the effort. Aware of unpopular policies mandated by federal courts in the name of racial equality, the ERA's opponents warned that judges would do the same with constitutional language promising gender equality. They would require government funding of abortions, coed bathrooms, and women in combat.[66] The ERA fell three state legislatures short of the three-fourths required to ratify a constitutional amendment.

As discouraging as the ERA defeat was for its supporters, in retrospect it seems that they achieved their objections despite losing the ratification fight. The Supreme Court had done little, if anything, to prevent gender discrimination before the ERA campaign. Court opinions changed after Congress voted overwhelmingly in favor of the ERA's passage. Gender equality gained recognition.

Categorizing people by their sex does not receive the same strict scrutiny that racial categories do. Nevertheless, the Supreme Court has ruled that gender discrimination violates the equal protection clause, so gender distinctions receive heightened scrutiny compared to most other legal categories.[67] The Court will rule against a law unless its gender distinctions have "a substantial relationship to an important objective."[68] In part, the Court's cautiousness reflects mixed public feelings about feminism.

The Supreme Court accepted gender distinctions within the military in *Rostker* v. *Goldberg* (1981). Congress holds broad constitutional powers in military matters, Justice William Rehnquist explained, and "the lack of competence on the part of the courts is marked."[69] The ruling was consistent with the view of a majority of the voters, who favor restricting female participation in combat.[70]

The Supreme Court also has allowed firms some latitude when they do not recruit and retain women, as long as a "business necessity" explains their imbalanced personnel practices.[71] The Court initially required those claiming discrimination to disprove the business-necessity argument. Justice Byron White argued in *Ward's Cove Packing Co.* v. *Antonio* (1989) that Title VII of the Civil Rights Act gave claimants the burden of proof.[72] Women's organizations opposed the ruling, because it is hard for plaintiffs to characterize conclusively what a business needs. The Civil Rights Act of 1991, signed by President George H. W. Bush, shifted the burden of proof to businesses. It was elected officials, not the Court, who took the lead on this issue.

SEXUAL HARASSMENT   The Supreme Court did not rule on the meaning of sexual harassment in the workplace until *Meritor Savings Bank* v. *Vinson* (1986).[73] In this case, Michelle Vinson said that sexually abusive language used in her presence had left her psychologically damaged. Justice Rehnquist decided in Vinson's favor, but he wrote a narrow opinion implying that harassment would be considered illegal only if it caused real harm. Afterward, sexual harassment became a major political issue, resulting in a large crop of new female elected officials in 1992, the "year of the woman" (see Chapter 12). Responding to the change in the political atmosphere, the Supreme Court expanded its definition of sexual harassment in the unanimous decision *Harris* v. *Forklift Systems* (1993).[74]

Teresa Harris worked at Forklift Systems, Inc., a heavy equipment rental firm. Her employer called her derogatory terms, such as "dumb ass woman." Although Harris complained and her boss promised to restrain his remarks, he subsequently suggested in front of other employees that Harris had slept with a client to obtain a contract. She quit and sued. Although Harris could not show serious psychological damage, Justice Sandra Day O'Connor wrote that Title VII of the Civil Rights Act "comes into play before harassing conduct leads to a nervous breakdown." Justice Ruth Bader Ginsburg went further, arguing in her concurring opinion that discrimination exists whenever it is more difficult for a person of one gender to perform well on a job. Once again, the Supreme Court moved forward in the wake of public pressure.

SINGLE-SEX SCHOOLS   Single-sex schools have long been a significant part of American education. As late as the 1950s, well-known private colleges, such as Princeton and Yale, limited their admissions to men. Although these colleges now admit approximately equal numbers of men and women, single-sex education survives at many private women's colleges. These colleges assert that women learn more in an environment where many can assume leadership roles. Hillary Rodham Clinton, who graduated from a Massachusetts women's college, once said: "I am so grateful that I had the chance to go to college at a place where women were valued and nurtured and encouraged."[75] All-male education also has supporters, especially for African American boys who frequently have low attendance and low test scores in conventional school programs.[76]

Despite the claims of those who favor single-sex education, many believe that education separated by gender cannot be equal. The Supreme Court cast doubt on its constitutionality in 1996. In *United States* v. *Virginia,* the Court ruled that women must be admitted to Virginia Military Institute (VMI), even though the state had recently established a separate military training program for women. The Court said the newly established program for women did not match the history, reputation, and quality of VMI. Justice Scalia, in his dissent, recognized the importance of public opinion on the Court's ruling. He lambasted "this most illiberal Court" because it had "embarked on a course of inscribing one after another of the current preferences of the society . . . into our Basic Law."[77]

EVALUATING WOMEN'S RIGHTS   Despite many gains, the women's movement has not yet realized all of its civil rights agenda. Sexual harassment remains a burning issue within the military and in many business firms. Only a few women have broken through what is known as the glass ceiling—the invisible barrier that has limited their opportunities for advancement to the highest ranks of politics, business, and the professions. Very few women serve as college presidents, as corporate heads, or as partners in major law firms. Women do hold many important political posts. In 2002, they held 2 Supreme Court appointments, 13 Senate seats, and 60 districts in the House. Republican electorates in 2002 supported numerous women, including Elizabeth Dole, elected to the Senate for North Carolina, and Katherine Harris, elected to the House for Florida. Women took several governor's mansions that year as well. However, no woman has yet received a major-party nomination for president.

GAYS AND LESBIANS

Some of the most contentious political debates in the late 1990s surrounded the rights of gays and lesbians. It is no accident that, at the same time, homosexuals engaged in electoral politics more than ever before—especially as campaign contributors. Gay and lesbian donors gave an estimated $3.5 million to the 1992 Clinton campaign, leading Clinton to flirt with ending a ban on gays in the military.[78] Since the early 1990s, according to one estimate, the number of openly gay government officials has tripled.[79]

At the same time, the country is undergoing an increasingly vocal debate over gay rights, a debate being fought in election and referendum campaigns. The American public believes that gays should have equal rights and in particular equal job opportunities, a belief that is a recent development (see Figure 14.4).

Faces of changing values

Openly affectionate homosexuals may trouble straight America, making public a way of life whose existence many would prefer to ignore. On the other hand, witnessing attractive same-sex couples, such as these couples at a gay pride parade, may lessen the extent to which American citizens view homosexual relationships as unhealthy or abnormal. Will gays and lesbians escape discrimination faster if they try to be as discreet as possible, or if they become a common sight on America's streets and in American towns?

FIGURE 14.4

Public opinion on gay rights has changed as gay and lesbian political activism has increased

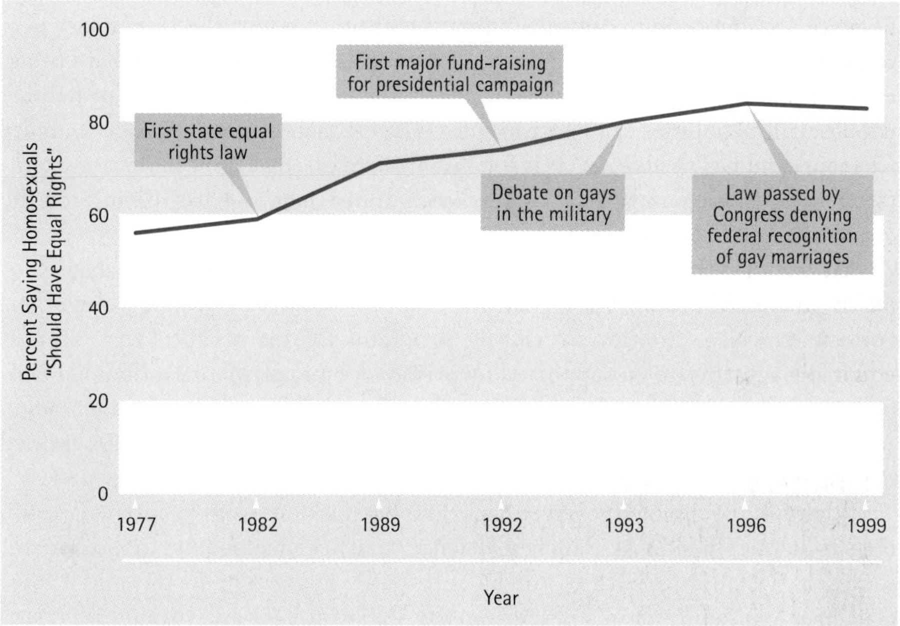

SOURCE: The Gallup Poll, www.gallup.com, accessed April 12, 2000.

Laws barring employment discrimination on the basis of sexual orientation have passed in 11 states and have bipartisan support in Congress.[80] In 2000 Vermont became the first state to recognize same-sex civil unions. Finally, the Supreme Court ruled in 2003 that privacy rights prevent states from outlawing sodomy. Justice Kennedy wrote that the decision ensured gays could live their lives with dignity.

But public opinion remains conservative on other issues regarding homosexuality. Large majorities disapprove of same-sex marriages, and 32 states have passed laws banning them. In Hawaii, where a state court decision had legalized such unions in 1993, voters overwhelmingly passed a constitutional amendment five years later outlawing them again. Americans also have serious reservations when asked whether gays should be allowed to serve as teachers or youth leaders. The Supreme Court ruled in 2000 that the Boy Scouts had a right to dismiss gay scout leaders because their presence undermines moral and cultural values that the organization seeks to convey to children. Elected officials must struggle to reconcile the confusing signals public opinion sends on the place of homosexuals in American society.

Rights of Americans
with Disabilities

Disabled people constitute about 9 percent of the working-age population.[81] They have an important political advantage that other minorities lack: Every person risks becoming disabled someday, so the rights of disabled people have broad appeal. Yet a troublesome drawback offsets this advantage: The cost of helping people with disabilities can be exorbitant. The estimated annual cost of disability payments and health care services for this group exceeds $275 billion, for example.[82] Even those sympathetic to the handicapped may not like paying for the expensive services needed to help them "live normal lives."

Government began concerning itself with the quality of life for disabled people in the 1960s, around the same time that other minority groups gained their voice in American politics. Previously, programs for the disabled were seen as charitable activities to be supported by private donations. Mentally disabled people were closeted away in "insane asylums" and "homes for the incurable." Americans held many stereotypes about the extent to which handicaps limited one's abilities.

Rights of the disabled received their first big push not from an interest group, but from one individual. Hugh Gallagher, a wheelchair-bound polio victim, served as a legislative aide to Alaska Senator E. L. Bartlett in the mid-1960s. Gallagher constantly faced difficulty using public toilets and gaining access to buildings such as the Library of Congress. At his prodding, Congress in 1968—just four years after the Civil Rights Act—enacted a law requiring that all future public buildings constructed with federal money provide access for the disabled. Similar language appeared in a transportation act in 1970.[83]

Once elected officials responded to the demands of the disabled, the courts became more sensitive. Previously, school officials had denied "retarded" children access to public education on the grounds that they were not mentally competent. But in the early 1970s, federal courts in Pennsylvania and the District of Columbia required that states provide disabled children with equal educational opportunity.[84] These decisions generated a nationwide movement for disabled children, culminating in the passage in 1975 of federal legislation that guaranteed all handicapped children educational access.[85]

Encouraged by both judicial and legislative victories, groups representing the physically and mentally disabled became increasingly assertive. They discovered that politicians did not wish to appear insensitive; guarantees of rights for the disabled were much less controversial than those for other minorities. A series of legislative victories in education, transportation, and construction of public buildings culminated in the Americans with Disabilities Act of 1991, signed by President George H. W. Bush. This act made it illegal to deny someone employ-

Forbidding dissent

Congress left federal courts to determine precisely what the Americans with Disabilities Act of 1991 really means. Golfer Casey Martin, disabled by a circulatory disorder in his leg, asked the Supreme Court to exempt him from PGA Tour rules that required all other golfers to walk each 18-hole course. Justices Scalia and Thomas faced withering criticism for insensitivity because they dissented from the seven-justice ruling in Martin's favor. Why are rights for the disabled so popular?

ment because of a handicap. Workplaces must adapt to the capacities of disabled persons, when feasible.

These legislative and judicial mandates have produced a sharp change in American society. Twenty years ago, public toilets for the disabled hardly existed. Sidewalks and staircases had no ramps. Buses and trains were inaccessible to those in wheelchairs. College and university campuses did not accommodate attendance by the physically challenged. Unlike President Franklin Roosevelt, who 50 years ago avoided being photographed in his wheelchair, Robert Dole referred constantly to his disabled arm during his 1996 presidential campaign. Meanwhile, Georgia voters elected wheelchair-bound Vietnam veteran Max Cleland to the Senate, and President Clinton appointed David Tatel, who is blind, to a federal appeals court.

Yet the disabled rely on goodwill from other voters to enhance their political strength, and resistance is growing as Americans gain a sense of the social costs. Educators complain that the investment required to teach a handful of disabled students extracts too many dollars from pinched school budgets. Architectural changes in public buildings and adaptations in transportation are said to be far too expensive to justify the limited amount of usage they receive. Ordinary citizens grumble as they drive past empty handicapped spots in parking garages filled to capacity. The disabled soon could lose their leverage over elected officials.

AFTERSHOCK:
THE NEW RACIAL PROFILING

All of the 19 hijackers directly responsible for the 9/11 tragedy were from Arab countries. None of the terrorists was American. Yet Arab Americans began to face widespread persecution immediately afterward. An estimated one-fifth of Arab Americans reported experiencing some form of discrimination in the month after the attacks.[86] Some incidents were as minor as school children fighting at recess. Many others were dangerous, even deadly. One attacker shot a sleeping Yemeni American citizen in the back 12 times, shouting his desire for revenge. A shopkeeper was murdered. Attacks sometimes resulted from cases of mistaken identity, as when an ignorant American gunning for Muslims shot down a Sikh in Arizona. California alone generated 73 incidents officially designated as hate crimes in 2001, more than half of them violent, directed against people perceived to be Arabs—compared to 3 such incidents the year before.[87]

These sad tales of misguided aggression prompted President George W. Bush to issue public appeals for tolerance a week after the terrorist strike. He appeared at a D.C. mosque to tell Americans that terrorism is "not what Islam is all about. Islam is peace."[88] Bush's sympathy is not hard to explain. Arab Americans were part of his constituency. They reportedly backed Bush over Democrat Al Gore in the 2000 presidential election. They disproportionately adopt conservative issue positions, such as support for school vouchers and capital punishment, and they tend to oppose abortion.[89]

But critics say that, at the same time Bush was asking Americans not to take their fears out on ethnic or religious minorities, his administration was gearing up to implement its own, official forms of discrimination. Federal authorities planned to detain 800 people, most of Middle Eastern descent, without releasing their names or offering any evidence connecting the detainees to terrorism. They also planned a dragnet to interrogate 5000 young men, mostly Muslims.

Basing an investigation on a person's ethnicity is called *racial profiling*. Americans generally hold it in low regard. Both Bush and Gore criticized the practice severely during the 2000 presidential election debates. But that was before 9/11, back when most voters associated racial profiling with indignities that African Americans sometimes face for the simple act of "driving while black."

After the attack, voters lost their squeamishness about racial profiling. Survey respondents overwhelmingly supported subjecting those of Arab descent to special security checks at airports, for example—a proposal that was at least as popular with blacks as it was with whites. A majority favored requiring Arabs to carry special identification cards, and more than a third supported placing them under "special surveillance."[90] Even Arab Americans accepted the practice in surprisingly large numbers.[91] Public opinion compelled the president to act swiftly and surely, even if the cost of protecting order included tactics that voters normally would not support. Bush's formal policies—by accommodating the fears of the majority—were just as consistent with the pressures of America's new democracy as were his speeches defending an important voter group.

Chapter Summary

African Americans achieved most of their advances through electoral politics—either directly by exercising their voting rights or indirectly by attracting political support through nonviolent demonstrations.[92] The most notable progress toward racial desegregation occurred as the result of legislation passed in the mid-1960s by bipartisan majorities in Congress. In contrast, the Supreme Court has usually followed the nation's popular moods: denying rights claims late in the nineteenth century, recognizing them after blacks moved north and acquired voting rights, and then pulling back after the civil rights movement lost public support (see Figure 14.5).

Warren Court decisions redefined the equal protection clause, which eventually led to a stronger legal position for Hispanics, Asians, and members of other minority groups. Yet getting courts to enforce legal rights relies in part on a group's clout. In general, these groups have only begun to exert their strength in national elections, so they have been slower than blacks to achieve recognition. Often congressional measures, such as the ERA and the Americans with Disabilities Act, signal to the courts when the political mood has changed. So, even civil rights respond to public opinion in America's new democracy.

Key Terms

affirmative action, p. 480

Brown v. *Board of Education
of Topeka, Kansas,*
p. 475

civil disobedience, p. 476

civil rights, p. 469

de facto segregation,
p. 481

de jure segregation,
p. 481

equal protection clause,
p. 470

Equal Rights Amendment,
p. 489

grandfather clause,
p. 473

Jim Crow laws, p. 473

quotas, p. 482

Reconstruction,
p. 471

restrictive housing covenant,
p. 475

separate but equal doctrine,
p. 473

state action doctrine,
p. 473

suspect classification,
p. 470

FIGURE 14.5

Important events of the civil rights and women's movements

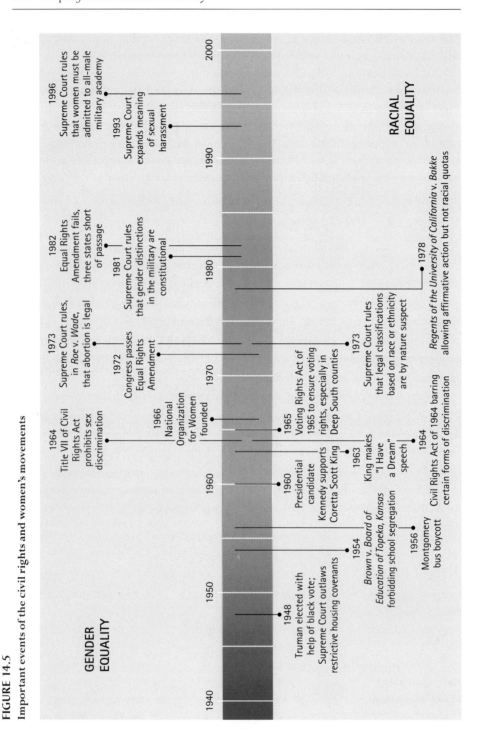

ON THE WEB

U.S. Department of Justice
www.usdoj.gov

The U.S. Department of Justice's Civil Rights division provides information on its enforcement of existing civil rights law.

U.S. Commission on Civil Rights
www.usccr.gov

Established in 1957, the U.S. Commission on Civil Rights monitors discrimination in many sectors of American society.

Martin Luther King, Jr., Papers Project
www.stanford.edu/group/King/

The Martin Luther King, Jr., Papers Project at Stanford University maintains a Web site with many of King's speeches and sermons, as well as several scholarly articles and book chapters.

National Association for the Advancement of Colored People (NAACP)
www.naacp.org

The NAACP is the nation's oldest civil rights organization.

National Organization for Women (NOW)
www.now.org

The country's largest feminist organiza-tion, NOW seeks "to take action to bring about equality for all women."

National Council of La Raza
www.nclr.org

The National Council of La Raza monitors issues of concern to Hispanic Americans.

Human Rights Campaign
www.hrc.org

This is the official Web site for the Human Rights Campaign (a leading gay rights organization).

Leadership Education for Asian Pacifics, Inc.
www.leap.org

Leadership Education for Asian Pacifics, Inc. (LEAP) houses the Asian Pacific American Public Policy Institute, which authors numerous reports on Asian Americans.

National Council on Disability
www.ncd.gov

The National Council on Disability is an independent federal agency that makes recommendations to the president and Congress regarding Americans with dis-abilities. The agency's site provides links to other relevant federal agencies, press releases, and in-depth reports.

SUGGESTED READINGS

Browning, Rufus, Dale Rogers Marshall, and David H. Tabb. *Protest Is Not Enough: The Struggle of Blacks and Hispanics for Equality in Urban Politics.* Berkeley, CA: University of California Press, 1984. Excellent analysis of the importance of electoral politics for black advances.

Deloria, Vine, Jr., and David E. Wilkins. *Tribes, Treaties, and Constitutional Tribulations.* Austin, University of Texas Press, 1999. Discusses the constitutional status of the rights of indigenous peoples.

Higgenbotham, A. Leon, Jr. *Shades of Freedom: Racial Politics and Presumptions of the American Legal Process.* New York: Oxford University Press, 1996. A sharp critique of racial bias in the legal system.

Key, V. O., Jr. *Southern Politics.* New York: Random House, 1949. Classic study of the effects of racial conflict on southern politics.

Rosenberg, Gerald N. *The Hollow Hope: Can Courts Bring About Social Change?* Chicago: University of Chicago Press, 1991. Argues that courts are generally unable to act contrary to majority opinion.

Skocpol, Theda. *Protecting Soldiers and Mothers: The Political Origins of Social Policy in the United States.* Cambridge, MA: Harvard University Press, 1992. Analyzes the way women's groups have influenced policy.

Wolbrecht, Christina. *The Politics of Women's Rights: Parties, Positions, and Change.* Princeton, NJ: Princeton University Press, 2000. Shows how divisions between Democrats and Republicans have been affected by debates over women's rights.

PUBLIC POLICY

For decades the United States government spent much more than it earned in tax revenue. Controversy swirled around tough political questions, such as how much to raise taxes and which program budgets to limit. But suddenly, in 1998, a budget surplus appeared—almost out of nowhere. The growing economy had allowed expected resources to outpace planned spending. By the summer of 2000, the projected 10-year surplus topped $2 trillion!

Unanticipated revenues are a true bonanza for elected officials, because of the possibilities they open up. Politicians quickly began jockeying to hand out the future trillions even though they existed only on paper. Some advocated helping the needy, arguing that national prosperity had left too many people behind. They wanted to increase welfare funding and expand health care coverage for the indigent. Others recommended shoring up programs oriented toward senior citizens before the "baby boom generation" retired. Those concerned with the severity of past defense cuts advocated investing in military supplies and equipment. Yet another group interpreted the excess revenue as a sign that early-1990s tax hikes had gone too far. They called for returning some of the largesse to taxpayers before the economy slowed down. "Let's give this money back to the people who earned it," they said.

By the time politicians aired all of their various proposals, not a single area of public policy had been overlooked. Every political interest entered the ring to get a piece of that $2 trillion prize—and the 2000 elections served as their arena. Presidential and congressional nominees committed their support to particular proposals, which voters and interest groups could use to help identify their candidate selections. The differences between Democrats and Republicans offered useful grounds for choosing a party. Democrats wanted more spending, Republicans more tax cuts. Democrats talked more about increasing welfare, promoting health care, and protecting the environment. The GOP talked more about quality education, military preparedness, and improving the transportation infrastructure. Leaving aside foreign policy, which played a minimal role in the campaign, both parties agreed on only one major policy: the importance of protecting and expanding programs for the elderly.

Republicans won the White House in 2000, held the House of Representatives, and temporarily controlled the Senate. They quickly began converting their priorities into law. President George W. Bush pushed an aggressive tax cut plan, although Democrats and moderate Republicans in Congress succeeded in limiting the magnitude of the reductions. Bush backed a bipartisan education reform initiative that also passed into law. The elderly, who already receive the lion's share of federal spending, looked likely to benefit from expensive proposals to cover their prescription drugs.

But then, suddenly, the policy environment changed. The 9/11 terrorist attack focused American voters on foreign and defense policy—even though they were the same voters who, a year before, had selected a president with limited experience in that area. To add to the difficulties, it became clear that the United States was mired in a recession; tax revenues were not meeting projections. The surplus rapidly turned into a deficit as new policy demands forced themselves onto the public agenda.

THE RISE AND FALL OF THE $2 TRILLION SURPLUS ILLUSTRATES how quickly policy environments can shift. At first, the 2000 elections seemed to produce clear winners: the elderly, taxpayers, and families. Suddenly, new groups took priority: the military, law enforcement agencies, and the intelligence community. How can things change so quickly? The answer lies in the growing importance of popular attitudes, and especially of elections. Leaders cannot afford to take a patient, deliberative approach to solving a crisis. When terrorists are murdering civilians, when public officials are receiving packets of anthrax in the mail, leaders must show that they are responding immediately—even if, as the old saying goes, haste makes waste.

Once fears faded after 9/11, however, the policy environment started shifting back to domestic issues—so politicians could return to their old interests. The

Wall Street petrified

U.S. policy priorities changed after the 9/11 terrorist attacks. Foreign and defense policy required special attention, but the tragedy also left New York City's economically influential Wall Street district devastated—both physically and financially. Congress quickly passed legislation to help dig the city out from under its rubble but could not dust off the nation's sluggish economy so swiftly. What hurt America more: the damage terrorists did, or the fears they stirred up?

2002 elections did not revolve around foreign policy (although some candidates did criticize the possibility of a war with Iraq). President Bush started promoting additional tax cuts. Congressional candidates, meanwhile, focused on a particular group of influential voters: the elderly. Not only do seniors vote in large numbers, but opinion supports their claims on the public till, whereas other policy areas must struggle to attract voter sympathy. The demand for senior drug benefits (see Chapter 8) and the debate over social security returned to the forefront. Elections mold policy in America's new democracy—and when emergencies do not demand immediate attention, the elderly reign supreme in the electoral arena.

SETTING PUBLIC POLICY

All government programs and regulations are examples of public policy so we have discussed numerous specific policies in previous chapters (see especially Chapters 3 and 11). Policies generally fall into one of three types: (1) domestic policy, which consists of all government programs and regulations that directly affect those living within the country; (2) economic policy, which indirectly affects those within the country by changing government budgets and the value of a nation's currency; and (3) foreign and defense policy, which involves relations with other nations to preserve national security. However, the distinctions among these three areas of policy are not always sharp and clear. Some domestic policies, such as immigration policy, affect relations with other countries. Some foreign policies, such as trade regulations, have major domestic consequences.

Policy making is a complex, never-ending round of events. To clarify what is often a very messy process, political scientists have divided the policy-making round into six stages (see Figure 15.1):

- *Agenda setting,* deciding which issues government must address.[1] Issues enter the agenda when they reach the notice of public officials. Those issues serious enough to influence voters are most likely to grab attention.
- *Policy deliberation,* the debate over how government should deal with an issue on the agenda.[2] At this stage, groups try to convince leaders that their proposals will win favor with the electorate.
- *Policy enactment,* the passage of a law by public officials at the national, state, or local level. Elected officials who support a law usually expect that doing so will enhance their popularity, although there are celebrated instances when political leaders have knowingly sacrificed their careers to take an unpopular stand.
- *Policy implementation,* the translation of a law into specific government programs.[3] Most laws are flexible, but bureaucrats seldom stray far from the intentions of the legislative branch when doing so might evoke a public backlash.

FIGURE 15.1

Policy-making stages

Political scientists break the policy process into six stages.

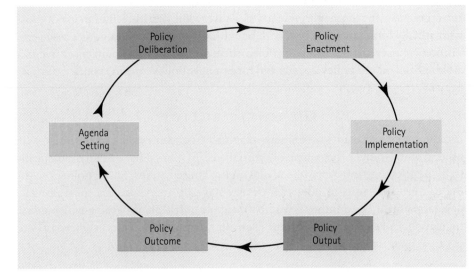

- *Policy outputs,* the rules and regulations growing out of a program. Beneficiaries usually think well of those responsible for helpful outputs and support them politically. Those who are hurt or neglected by a program may punish the elected officials responsible.
- *Policy outcomes,* the effect of a policy on American society, the economy, or the international sphere.[4] These outcomes often give rise to new issues, which in turn join the policy agenda.

The political forces at work differ from one policy to the next, but electoral incentives nearly always influence how policies pass through the six stages of development. The enactment of the 1996 welfare reform law, **Temporary Assistance for Needy Families (TANF),** provides one example of the policy process at work.

Bill Clinton placed reform on the policy *agenda* in his 1992 presidential campaign by promising to "end welfare as we know it." Interest groups, policy experts, members of Congress, and the media began *deliberating* how the United States might redesign welfare policy. Congress then *enacted* a law shifting responsibility for welfare policy to state governments, and President Clinton signed the bill. State governments *implemented* new welfare programs in early 1997. As one *output* of the new programs, many families left or were removed from the welfare rolls.

The *outcome* of welfare reform is only now becoming clear. Welfare rolls have declined dramatically; about half as many people received assistance in 1999 as in 1994. Many of these former welfare recipients found jobs because the economy was growing rapidly at the time. Others shifted to programs serving the disabled. However, many of those with few job skills were left destitute, and many of those who initially found jobs left or lost them within a year.[5] These numbers may grow as the economy falters. If this problem becomes severe, it could place welfare reform back on the policy agenda and force a new policy-making round.

DOMESTIC POLICY

Although the national government originally concentrated on relations with other countries, over the course of more than 200 years it has grown dramatically to influence more and more of daily life in the United States. Social policies set by the national government now affect every stage of American life, from prenatal development in the mother's womb (through nutrition programs and medical regulations) all the way to death (or even after death if one counts survivor's benefits and inheritance taxes).

A HEALTHY PLACE TO GROW OLD

The generosity of national social policies varies significantly over the course of a lifetime. The primary focus of domestic policy has been to enhance the income and medical care enjoyed by senior citizens, while relatively little money has gone to benefit Americans in the youngest age ranges. The effect of this policy choice shows up in the nation's poverty statistics. From 1970 to 1988, poverty among senior citizens fell from 25 percent to 10.5 percent (see Figure 15.2). During the same period, poverty among families with children increased from 15 percent to 20 percent, a rate twice as high as that in most other advanced industrial societies.[6]

Poverty is not just a matter of money; it is a matter of life and death. Of the seven countries with the largest economies, the United States has the highest infant mortality rate but the longest life span among senior citizens. As one analyst put it, the United States is the "healthiest place to grow old but the riskiest [in which] to be born."[7]

BENEFITS FOR SENIOR CITIZENS   The national government has not always worked so hard to finance retirement and medical care for seniors. Poverty among the elderly was so acute during the Great Depression that Congress enacted the Social Security Act of 1935. This legislation created a broad range of social policies, including a welfare program for senior citizens generally known as social security.[8]

Social security initially cost the government very little. Benefits were low and life expectancy short. Those reaching age 65 lived, on average, only another 12.6 years. Over time both medical improvements and policy changes caused the costs

FIGURE 15.2

U.S. poverty rates for senior citizens and children, 1970–1998

Poverty rates have fallen for seniors and risen for children.

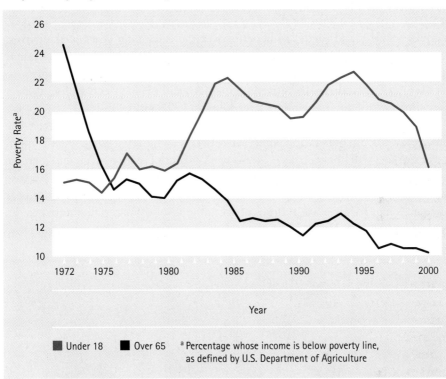

SOURCE: U.S. Census Bureau, *Historical Poverty Tables—People,* Table 3: Poverty Status by Age, Race and Hispanic Origin, www.census.gov/hhes/poverty/histpob/hstpov3.html, accessed July 24, 2000.

to leap upward. A typical worker retiring at 65 today lives more than 17 years. Congress expanded the number of people covered. Benefits have increased in size and cost, including a large hike in 1972 that linked future benefits to the inflation rate. If inflation goes up 10 percent, so does the paycheck.[9] And the national government took another substantial step in 1965 by setting up **Medicare,** a program to subsidize health costs for social security recipients.

The result is that spending on the elderly has grown to dominate the nation's domestic budget. From 1960 to 1995, the amount spent on social programs for senior citizens quadrupled after adjusting for inflation.* Nor do these benefits go only to the needy. Upon reaching the age of 65, even billionaire Microsoft founder Bill Gates will be eligible to receive a social security check.

---

*Spending grew from under $4000 per senior citizen to more than $16,500 in 1995 (based on 1999 dollars).

Many Americans believe that social security is an insurance program, taking money from able-bodied workers and returning it to them if they live long enough to need it back. This is a myth. Social security operates at a loss, giving far more to the elderly in benefits than they have ever contributed in payroll taxes. Typically, a couple who retired in 1995 could expect to receive about $471,000 in social security and Medicare benefits over the remaining years of their lives, even though the family's worker contributed only $184,000.[10] How is this magic possible?[11] It is possible because of a workforce that (1) has been increasingly productive, (2) outnumbers the retired population, and (3) has been willing to bear increasing payroll taxes, including large hikes in 1977 and 1982.[12]

The nation's approach to old-age insurance is probably not sustainable. The massive baby boom generation will reach retirement age after 2010, and the number of workers will not keep pace. Nor is worker productivity expected to increase much. Thus the only way to maintain retirement programs would be to increase payroll taxes substantially. But will the workers of the future be willing to bear taxes sufficient to subsidize retirees at the same level of material comfort as the

High stakes policy

One explanation why aid to the poor receives less public support than aid to senior citizens is that welfare subsidizes sins such as sloth, crime, and extramarital sex. Yet many Americans consider gambling a sin, and the elderly are known for their disproportionate presence in casinos. Indeed, some casinos park transports where seniors are known to exchange their social security checks. Why, then, are the elderly considered so deserving of government handouts?

FIGURE 15.3

Projected cost of social insurance for senior citizens

Costs of programs for senior citizens will rise rapidly in the coming years.

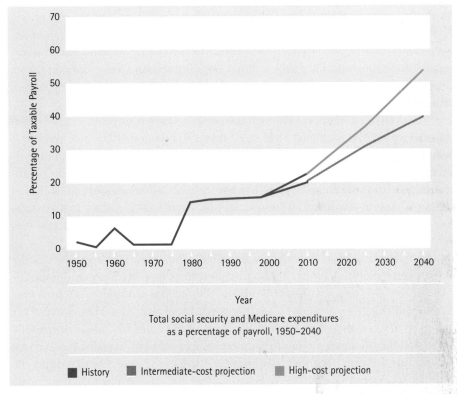

Total social security and Medicare expenditures
as a percentage of payroll, 1950–2040

■ History ■ Intermediate-cost projection ■ High-cost projection

SOURCE: Neil Howe and Richard Jackson, *The Graying of the Welfare State* (Washington, DC: National Taxpayers Union Foundation, 1999).

United States does today? Figure 15.3 illustrates how improbable that is. It projects the payroll tax rates that would be required to sustain current benefits into the future. By 2040, years before today's college students will be old enough to retire, benefits already would demand around 40 percent of taxable payroll. Pessimistically, the price tag could rise to more than half of all payroll money. Will the workers of 2040 give up half of their potential salaries just to take care of the elderly? Not likely.

And the outlook for the future may only be worsening. Analysts projected budget surpluses in the late 1990s—money that might have been saved for future retirement needs or returned to the economy in the form of tax cuts. However, those surpluses have turned into deficits, starting with a recession that began at the end of the Clinton administration. Security and reconstruction needs after the 2001 terrorist attacks have also laid claim to social resources.[13]

THE ELDERLY AND THE PERMANENT CAMPAIGN   Most public officials know better than to question the social security program, even though it is the most costly single item in the entire federal budget. In the early 1980s, President Ronald Reagan suggested offhandedly that Congress might need to place limits on the program's growth. The public backlash was swift and angry, prompting every single senator to condemn the president's idea two days later. Even so, Reagan's remark contributed to his party's loss of the U.S. Senate. For this reason, both Democratic President Clinton and Republican House Speaker Newt Gingrich insisted that social security would be "off the table" when they started imposing massive budget cuts in 1995.

The politics of Medicare is much the same, making it difficult to hold down program costs. Medicare cost little more than $30 billion in 1970, but by 1999 it had grown to nearly $212 billion.[14] It pays for cutting-edge medical techniques— such as magnetic resonance imaging, bone marrow transfusions, and other high-tech, high-cost procedures. Soon it may pay for an extensive range of prescription drugs. Adding to the financial burden are the exorbitant penalties that lawsuits extract when health care providers make mistakes, penalties that drive up the fees doctors must charge to cover their insurance.

Congress contained costs in the late 1990s, but costs will rise again as the baby boom generation ages—leading many to fear that Medicare is doomed.[15] Recognizing this concern, Republicans in 1995 proposed raising insurance premiums and requiring patients to pay a larger share of the costs. They suffered for the attempt. President Clinton and his Democratic allies in Congress gleefully noted that the Medicare savings Republicans wanted roughly equaled the cost of a tax cut "for the rich" that they also proposed.[16] Clinton was able to exploit the issue so successfully in the 1996 elections that he carried Florida, a normally Republican state to which many retirees have migrated.

Politicians avoid provoking senior citizens because the electoral cost of pleasing them is much lower than the cost of resisting. At a time when overall voter turnout has been declining, senior turnout rates are high and have been climbing. Sixty percent of Americans over 65 said they voted in the 1998 congressional elections, but only 17 percent of those between the ages of 18 and 24 reported voting.[17] Children cannot vote at all. Senior citizens are also much more likely than young people to back up their votes with other political actions, such as writing letters to officials and contributing money to campaigns.[18]

Upon reaching the age of 50, any person can become a member of the American Association of Retired Persons (AARP) for $12.50 per year. Members qualify for a wide range of discounts worth much more than their annual dues, so more than 33 million people have joined—making AARP the largest interest group in the United States. AARP employs more than 1100 people, works with over 160,000 volunteers, and has an annual budget that exceeds $500 million.[19]

FIGURE 15.4

Both young and old support senior citizens' programs

Why do the young support programs for the elderly even though they do not yet receive benefits from such programs?

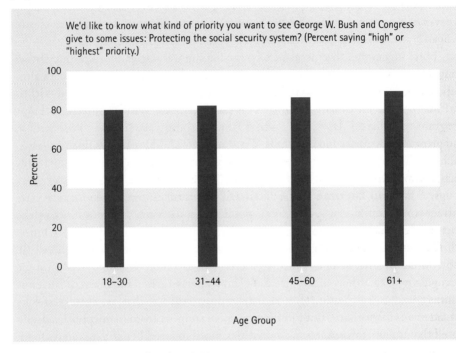

We'd like to know what kind of priority you want to see George W. Bush and Congress give to some issues: Protecting the social security system? (Percent saying "high" or "highest" priority.)

SOURCE: Washington Post/ABC News Poll, April 19–22, 2001.

Few voters punish elected officials for accommodating AARP demands. In fact, young people are just about as likely to support social security as those over the age of 65. They know others who are receiving benefits and hope to do the same some day. Many figure that the elderly are simply receiving funds they originally contributed—and they think that the government is saving their own contributions for them. Only 7 percent of younger adults say that the elderly are getting more than their fair share of government benefits, and 48 percent think the elderly are getting less than their fair share. Americans of every age category want political leaders to defend social security (see Figure 15.4).[20]

A RISKY PLACE TO BE BORN

Poor families with children do not receive very good representation in America's new democracy. No association comparable to AARP defends their interests, and neither political party shows much concern for programs that assist them. As a result, government aid to poor families is neither as lavish nor as easy to obtain as that intended for the elderly.

BENEFITS FOR THE POOR   More programs assist households with limited income than assist the elderly, but these programs are rarely as generous. Public assistance programs include TANF, food stamps, the Earned Income Tax Credit (EITC), rent subsidies, and Medicaid.

TANF maintains the incomes of poor families. It varies by state but always limits aid to no more than two years in a row and to no more than five years altogether. It took the place of a costlier, and highly unpopular, program called **Aid to Families with Dependent Children (AFDC),** which most Americans knew simply as "welfare." After the end of AFDC, some beneficiaries switched to Supplemental Security Income (SSI). Created in 1972, SSI provides financial assistance to disabled people of low income. As of January 2000, the average monthly benefit for SSI's 6.6 million recipients was $377.27.

The **Earned Income Tax Credit (EITC)** returns taxes to those who have little income. Initially proposed by Republicans in the early 1970s as a tax rebate that would reward the working poor, EITC was expanded early in the Clinton administration so that even those who have not paid taxes can receive checks. In 1999, a family of four could receive a credit of as much as $3800 a year. Some critics suggest that the Clinton-era EITC improperly turned the Internal Revenue Service into a mechanism for redistributing wealth—that is, into a sneaky replacement for welfare. But EITC enjoys firm support from many politicians.[21]

The national government also provides more focused benefits to needy families. **Food stamps** are coupons that can be used to purchase edibles. Enacted by Congress on an experimental basis in the early 1970s, the program has expanded gradually—in part because it is popular with agricultural interests who grow American produce. Low-income families also may receive rent subsidies if they live in designated residences, a program that has helped many minority families leave crime-ridden inner cities and move to the suburbs.

Medicaid covers medical services for the poor. A person becomes eligible only if he or she has no more than a minimal income and few assets other than a home. Medicaid costs have risen almost as rapidly as those for Medicare—from around $12 billion in 1970 to $108 billion in 1999. Because the program covers poor families regardless of age, however, the elderly benefit from Medicaid too. More than one-quarter of all Medicaid costs go to low-income seniors.[22]

WELFARE AND THE PERMANENT CAMPAIGN   The general public varies over time in its support for social welfare policies. Generally, when the economy is strong, people are more likely to blame the poor for their condition and less likely to attribute poverty to circumstances beyond the individual's control.[23]

Public opinion also shifts with the current policies. In particular, the welfare issue has become less controversial since the end of AFDC.

Political parties fluctuate on welfare policy in step with public opinion. When the country was building the Great Society in the 1960s and 1970s, Democrats took the lead, but Republicans were not far behind. Republican presidents signed into law several welfare programs for children. President Nixon proposed the food stamp and SSI programs. Republicans proposed, and President Ford signed, the law creating EITC. Republicans in Congress initiated the Medicaid program. As the public mood shifted in a conservative direction, the positions of both parties changed accordingly. In 1995 it was the Republicans who took the lead, proposing cuts in many of the programs they had once sponsored.[24] Although some Democrats opposed the cuts, a majority voted in favor of welfare reform, and President Clinton signed the bill.

SENIORS VERSUS CHILDREN: A COMPARISON

The list of public assistance programs helping poor families seems impressive, but actual expenditures are only one-tenth as much as what is spent on the elderly. Federal social programs for the elderly amounted to over $13,000 per person in 1990, whereas public assistance programs for families with children amounted to little more than $1300 per capita (see Figure 15.5). Government has committed itself to extending the last years of life rather than to enhancing capacities in the first years of life.

Programs for families with children are also more restrictive than programs for senior citizens.[25] They are less likely to provide flexible cash benefits and more likely to provide inflexible goods and services. In 1990 the elderly received nearly 67 percent of their benefits in cash,[26] whereas poor families received only 41 percent that way.[27] Nearly all benefits to the elderly are tied to changes in the cost of living. By contrast, welfare spending generally fails to keep pace with inflation. Between 1975 and 1993, AFDC benefits fell by 43 percent, on average, across the states. Following welfare reform and the switch to TANF in 1996, average benefit levels dropped another 7 percent.[28]

The benefits that families receive vary from one state to another. Only EITC benefits are uniform throughout the country. For the other major programs— TANF, food stamps, SSI, housing assistance, and Medicaid—eligibility rules and benefit levels vary from state to state. Variation makes using the programs more confusing and may limit the mobility of the poor.[29] For example, TANF benefits can be eight times as much in one state as in another.[30] Senior citizens, by contrast, can move from New Jersey to Florida (or even overseas) without jeopardizing the amount or delivery of their social security checks.

The benefits that poor families with children receive are substitutes for other income. In most states, a family is not eligible for assistance if it has savings of

FIGURE 15.5

Federal entitlement expenditures by beneficiary age group, per capita, 1960–1996

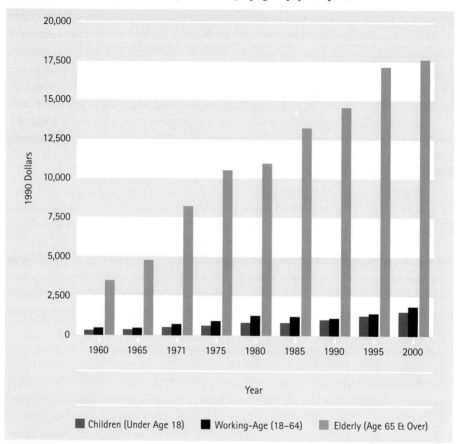

NOTE: Figures in constant 1996 dollars.

SOURCE: Neil Howe and Richard Jackson, *1998 Chartbook: Entitlement and the Aging of America* (Alexandria, VA: National Taxpayers Union Foundation, 1998), Chart 3-3, p. 35.

more than $1000, a car worth more than $1500, or anything other than a very modest home. The head of the household must visit a government agency and reveal to a government official the family's complete fiscal record. Benefits drop swiftly as a family starts to climb from poverty.[31]

By comparison, senior citizens' benefits supplement the recipient's own resources. Senior citizens may receive their Medicare and social security benefits even if they are working full-time, have savings, earn dividends and interest on their investments, and are homeowners. Before the year 2000, social security recipients between 65 and 69 years old lost some benefits if they earned more than

$17,000 per year. But Republicans and Democrats in Congress, eager to please elderly voters in an election year, repealed this "earnings penalty" unanimously.[32]

Historically, Americans have supported a large, well-financed education system. This solicitude seems to contradict their relative stinginess toward other programs for young people. Part of the explanation, of course, is that education differs in many ways from other programs oriented toward children. It is primarily funded by local taxes and governed by local leaders, so voters feel closer to the policy's beneficiaries (see Chapter 3). It is not restricted to the poor and so attracts middle-class support. It promotes "equal opportunity" rather than a "culture of poverty" and so coincides with America's political values (see Chapter 4). It cultivates good workers who generate profits and who are less likely to become criminals and so it benefits society as a whole.

To the extent that public schools fall short of expectations, however, the weaknesses in the educational system reflect the same handicaps that hold back other programs intended to help the young: limited growth in funding, low flexibility, and few budgetary assurances. Like other programs for children, educational policies do not provide cash benefits. Parents must send their children to the school provided for them; they usually cannot choose schools the way Medicare recipients may choose their doctors or hospitals.[33] The public programs available will not supplement family resources, only substitute for them. Citizens lose all the taxes they pay into the school system if they choose to send their children to private schools. In short, public policy strongly favors seniors.

ECONOMIC POLICY

The U.S. economy is one of the strongest in the world, allowing Americans good wages and a high standard of living. Nevertheless, even wealthy countries experience **business cycles**—periods of economic expansion and rising prices alternating with occasional slowdowns in economic activity called **recessions** (see Figure 15.6). Governments seek economic policies that minimize disruptions such as inflation and unemployment.

Inflation—a rise in the price level—makes consumers pay more money for an equal amount of goods and services, thereby undermining the value of personal savings. **Unemployment,** which occurs when people willing to work at prevailing wages cannot find jobs, harms a smaller number of people—but in ways that can be severe. For a long time, economists thought the two conditions were closely related; lower unemployment eventually created higher inflation, and vice versa.[34] But economists no longer believe the relationship is so close. In fact, President Carter had the misfortune to run for reelection at a time of stagflation, when both inflation and unemployment (stagnation) were high. He suffered a humiliating defeat.

FIGURE 15.6

Long-term growth and the business cycle in the United States

Although the general economic trend may be upward over the long run, expansions and recessions that characterize the business cycle can—in the short term—harm both citizens and elected officials.

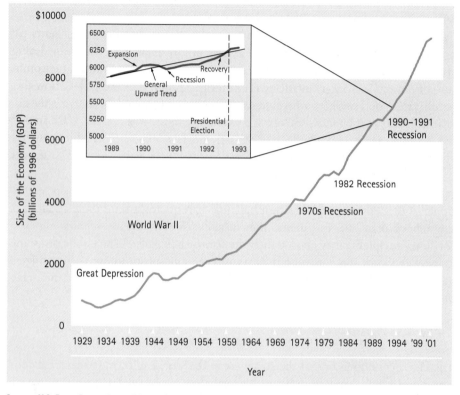

SOURCES: U.S. Census Bureau, *Statistical Abstract of the United States, 1999*, p. 881, Table 1434; U.S. Department of Commerce, Economics and Statistics Administration, "National Income and Product Accounts," www.bea.doc.gov/bea/dn/gdplev.htm, accessed July 27, 2000.

People tend to blame those in charge when times are hard. President George H. W. Bush's popularity ratings plummeted 40 percentage points over two years because of unemployment increases (see Chapter 5). Eisenhower, Nixon, and Reagan all lost public support when recessions struck on their watches.[35] Terrible economic times produce massive election losses for the president's party. The depression of the 1890s ushered in an era of Republican dominance, and the Great Depression of the 1930s did the same for the Democrats. Indeed, Republican President Herbert Hoover (1929–1933) became one of history's most unpopular presidents simply because he was in office when the Great Depression began.

Prosperity, in contrast, strengthens a president's position for reelection (see Figure 15.7). Riding booming economies, Lyndon Johnson trampled Barry

Goldwater in 1964, Richard Nixon crushed George McGovern in 1972, and Ronald Reagan trounced Walter Mondale in 1984. Of course, a healthy economy does not guarantee presidential popularity. For example, prosperity in 1968 did not protect Johnson from the Vietnam War's unpopularity. Nonetheless, presidents usually do better electorally when the economy is strong—results that spill over to influence both congressional and state elections.[36]

Because so much rides on national economic performance, presidents pay close attention to economic policy. Presidents enjoy little flexibility in dealing with the economy, though. One reason, of course, is that they must compromise with Congress; legislators scrutinize economic proposals closely to see how they would affect voters back home. But another limit on presidential power is the rise of a school of economic thinking called **monetarism,** which stresses the importance of the money supply. Responsibility for fine-tuning the money supply falls to the Federal Reserve Board, an independent entity at best indirectly influenced by the White House (see Chapter 11).

FIGURE 15.7

Retrospective voting

How Americans feel about the economy influences what they think about the president. When does the economy not have a major impact on the public's view of the president?

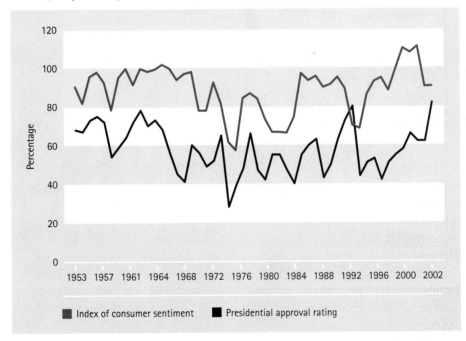

NOTE: The figure displays data for the first quarter of each year.

SOURCES: Index of Consumer Sentiment, Surveys of Consumers, University of Michigan; and Gallup polls, various years.

Monetary policy—whereby the Fed adjusts interest rates and varies the supply of money—is now the government's most important economic tool. When money is cheap, with low interest rates, people borrow more. They invest or spend the money, spurring new productivity and lower unemployment. The weak dollar attracts foreign spending and investments. Conversely, when money is expensive, with high interest rates, people hold on to their money and borrow less. Inflationary pressures ease. Foreign goods become cheaper for American consumers, siphoning cash out of the overheated economy.

FISCAL POLICY

Traditionally, presidents have tried to influence the economy more directly through the federal budget, a policy tool more amendable to political maneuvering. A government's **fiscal policy,** the sum total of taxation and spending in its

Runnin' on empty?

Although a democracy, the United States maintains close ties to Arab nations ruled by unelected royal families. This cartoon implies that raw self-interest—in the form of cheap fuel—motivates American ties to Saudi Arabia. Critics similarly charged that the American war against Saddam Hussein's Iraq was "about oil." But of course most foreign-policy decisions invoke a complicated mix of national ideals, as well as numerous economic and security interests. Would American voters accept significantly higher gas prices as a cost of promoting democracy in the Middle East?

budget, influences how money passes through a nation's economic system. Government spending usually exceeds revenue, producing a *deficit*. Occasionally, revenue outpaces spending, producing a *surplus*. In either case, fiscal policy influences the speed at which a nation's financial resources change hands.

According to an influential English economist of the 1920s and 1930s, John Maynard Keynes, budget deficits can lift an economy out of a recession. Government spending jump-starts the economy by giving consumers extra money with which to buy goods and services. Following this line of reasoning, which came to be called **Keynesianism,** Franklin Delano Roosevelt broke with the traditional belief in a balanced budget and embraced large deficits during the Great Depression. The flip side of Keynesianism is that, if government grabs up more money than it spends, then consumers lack sufficient cash to drive up prices and fuel inflation. Congress passed a tax increase in 1968 intended to limit inflation, although the tactic failed.[37]

Administrations today are much less likely to use fiscal policy as a tool for managing the economy than they were immediately after FDR's New Deal. Aside from the rise of monetarism, three reasons explain the movement away from using fiscal policy: the slowness of the budgetary process, the tendency of elected officials to put off unpopular choices, and the impotence of fiscal tools in the face of a globalized economy.

THE BUDGETARY PROCESS   The federal budgetary process is long and complicated. It starts within the executive branch a year and a half before the beginning of the fiscal year.* Federal agencies submit their budget requests during the summer to the Office of Management and Budget (OMB). During the fall, the OMB reviews requests and modifies them through negotiations with the departments (perhaps under the president's supervision). The Budget and Accounting Act of 1921 requires that Congress receive the president's budget no later than the first Monday in February.

No law requires Congress to pay any attention to what the president recommends. To construct its own budget, Congress generally follows the procedures laid down in the 1974 Budget and Impoundment Control Act. Two budget committees—one in the Senate, one in the House—collect budget proposals from the other congressional committees and construct a resolution specifying the overall amount that the government will raise and spend in each of the next five years. This stage can be quite controversial, because since 1990, Congress has operated under a pay-as-you-go rule; any proposal to cut taxes or increase spending must show where the money will originate. Congress has met the April 15 deadline for approving a budget resolution only once since the deadline went into effect in 1974.[38]

---

*By law, fiscal years and calendar years do not overlap completely. Fiscal year 2000, for example, started on October 1, 1999.

Once the budget resolution is enacted, appropriations subcommittees use its funding targets as a framework for writing 13 detailed appropriations bills. Congress has until October 1, the start of the new fiscal year, to pass these bills. In practice, passage almost never happens on schedule, and parts of the government must operate under continuing resolutions, temporary funding measures passed by Congress to keep the government operating.

In 1999, the Republican Congress had passed only 5 of the 13 appropriations bills by October, and Clinton vetoed one of these. The president also rejected a Republican-sponsored $800-billion, 10-year tax-cut bill. In addition, congressional Republicans wanted to delay payment of the earned income tax credit, a benefit for lower-income families (although they backed off after Republican presidential candidate George W. Bush objected to their proposal).[39] Resolving these differences of opinion required weeks of continuing resolutions and late-night negotiations over budget targets, producing serious partisan acrimony. Clinton signed the bill into law on November 29, 1999—two months after the fiscal year started.

This example may seem extreme in the amount of bickering that occurred, but in reality it is about average. Worse conflicts and delays occurred in 1985, 1987, and 1990. In 1995, partisan battles forced two extended government shutdowns and left the nation without a budget for nearly four months. In 1998, Congress skipped the budget resolution stage, technically violating the law.

Given this complicated process, it is not difficult to understand why fiscal policy is a blunt tool for addressing economic troubles. Fiscal policy changes slowly, especially when different political parties must agree on a budget, whereas economic conditions can fluctuate rapidly.[40] For example, in 1990 the national government approved a tax increase to check inflation, but it did not take effect until the country faced just the opposite problem: unemployment growing out of a recession.

SHORT-SIGHTED BUDGETING Fiscal policy operates under long-term limits. Several years of deficit spending can run up a serious *debt*—the total quantity of money a government owes. Not only does a large debt tie up lots of borrowed money that otherwise might go toward productive investments, it also commits the government to increasing interest payments on the loans. These sorts of obligations limit how much flexibility the government has to pump up the economy with direct spending. The more debt a nation carries, other things being equal, the higher interest rates that investors demand before they will lend more.

Furthermore, elected officials are quick to spend money they do not have, but they are much less eager to take away taxpayer money without a better justification than the need to slow down the economy! As a result, beginning in the

Sympathy for the dragon

Elected officials are slow to use fiscal policy when faced with an overheated economy, since Keynesian economics prescribes raising taxes or cutting spending. By contrast, politicians show great enthusiasm for distributing more money than they receive in tax revenue, especially when economic slowdowns provide sufficient justification. These gallant knights, gaily bedecked, mourn losing their excuse to wield a financial stimulus bill on behalf of voters in distress. Do elected officials really profit from troubles that they can attack aggressively?

early 1950s, the U.S. government ran up higher and higher deficits, and it did not reverse the trend until a brief period in the 1990s when the national debt's economic impact became too serious to ignore (see Figure 15.8). Policy makers cannot turn to deficit spending to help the economy if they are already running up a large deficit before the economy sours.

GLOBALIZATION Fiscal policy rarely seems to work in a globalized economy. Budgetary changes cannot compensate for swings in the value of a nation's currency. The value of money determines the exchange of goods across national borders. When the dollar is particularly valuable, Americans import more. Deficit spending cannot increase the circulation of money if the cash it pumps into the economy leaks across national borders. When the dollar is weak, foreigners buy more American goods. High taxes cannot limit inflation if consumers in

FIGURE 15.8
The federal deficit or surplus, 1950–2005

The last several decades witnessed unprecedented deficit spending for peacetime, a pattern that was reversed during the Clinton administration. What accounts for the large deficits of the 1980s and the sudden surpluses of the late 1990s?

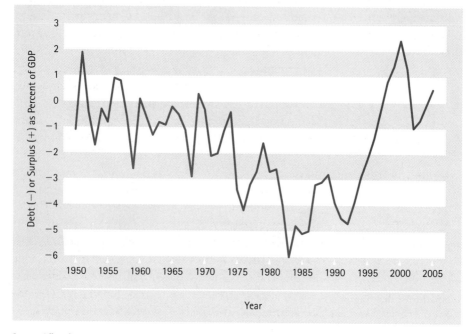

SOURCE: Office of Management and Budget, *The Budget of Fiscal Year 2001, Historical Tables,* p. 22, Table 1.2.

other countries pump their own assets into the U.S. economy. Investors can shift their assets back and forth in a similar fashion, using their knowledge of a country's economic policies. This sort of behavior dampens the economic impact of fiscal policies.

Globalization also limits the options available to a national government trying to set economic policies independently. Over time, the United States has participated in numerous international agreements that have increased the country's exposure to economic trends outside its borders, creating an "interdependence" among national economies. This trend received its first big push during the Truman administration. International banks were created to lend money to needy countries, United Nations organizations handled world health and refugee problems, and international trade agreements reduced tariffs around the world. In late 1947, for example, 23 countries founded the General Agreement on Tariffs and Trade (GATT). Under the current system, both the tax code and patterns of government spending influence trade with foreign countries—which can result in intense external pressure on national leaders not to implement swift and dramatic policy changes.

During the Cold War, most of the public saw trade policy as arcane and uncontroversial. But in the 1990s, trade became a much more contentious issue, further limiting what the national government could do in the area. First came the 1993 battle over the North American Free Trade Agreement (NAFTA), which eliminated trade barriers among the United States, Canada, and Mexico. Negotiated by President George H. W. Bush and promoted by President Clinton, NAFTA won only a narrow majority in Congress after fierce lobbying by all sides. It pitted Republican business groups and Democrats active in international affairs, who supported NAFTA, against Republican isolationists and such Democratic special-interest constituencies as labor unions and environmental groups.

The battle over NAFTA proved to be only the beginning of a very public debate over the status of world trade. In 1994, negotiators from 104 nations officially transformed GATT into the World Trade Organization (WTO), a more powerful trade body. Opposition to the organization was led by the same groups that opposed NAFTA. Tens of thousands of protesters disrupted a meeting of WTO trade ministers in Seattle in 1999, blocking streets and preventing delegates from attending the meetings. World trade shows signs of creating new political coalitions and invoking new conflicts in the political system—which makes it less of an international issue and more like the other domestic and economic issues that divide American public opinion. Policy makers must consider how trade policies will affect electorally important states or voter groups (see the accompanying Election Connection, "George W. Bush and U.S. Steel Policy").

THE POLITICS OF TAXATION

During the 1980s and most of the 1990s, the budget deficit was a major issue in American politics. Voters wanted to reduce the deficit without raising taxes or cutting spending—contradictory demands that elected officials struggled to reconcile. The task suddenly seemed possible thanks to surprisingly high economic growth, which produced a surge in expected government revenue.[41] The projected surplus grew so large that President George W. Bush was even able to convince Congress to cut taxes in 2001, carrying out one of his campaign pledges.

The drive to cut taxes puzzled many observers. After so many years operating on lean budgets, why wouldn't Americans use their sudden windfall to bolster national programs or start new ones? The answer lies in the popular preference for limited government in the United States, a core part of the nation's political culture (see Chapter 4). Most people think that their tax bills are too high. As a result, tax policy is a major topic of public concern that provokes heated debate.[42]

The total level at which Americans are taxed by the federal government, called the federal tax burden, has risen substantially since World War II. At the beginning of the war, only the wealthiest American families paid income taxes, whereas afterward only the poorest third of the workforce escaped the tax collector.[43] Federal individual income tax receipts rose by over 60 percent between

George W. Bush and U.S. Steel Policy

Most economists oppose barriers to international commerce, arguing that the free flow of goods across national borders enables world markets to function more efficiently and therefore promotes economic growth. For most of the last century, Republicans (aside from a few protectionists such as right-wing presidential candidate Patrick Buchanan) have accepted this argument and embraced free trade. Traditional Democrats, by contrast, have sided with labor unions wishing to erect trade barriers as a way of protecting the current jobs held by their members (although an increasing number of "New Democrats," such as President Bill Clinton, also endorse free trade).

Because of the historical connection between free trade and the GOP, it surprised some observers when, in 2002, President George W. Bush approved a new system of tariffs on imported steel, affecting up to $8 billion of imports annually from around the world. Under the three-year plan, steel entering the country could be taxed at a rate of up to 30 percent. Steel industry officials praised the new tariffs as necessary to enable U.S. manufacturers to compete with foreign producers, many of whom had benefited from past subsidies from their own governments. But others scoffed at these justifications.

Surprise at the Bush actions was muted by a recognition of the electoral facts, however. The list of major steel-producing states reads like a list of the most hotly contested states in presidential elections: Pennsylvania, Ohio, Indiana, Maryland, West Virginia, Michigan. Three of these six states voted for Bush in 2000; three voted for Democrat Al Gore. Furthermore, in four of these states, the margin of victory was 6 percentage points or less. Bush and his advisers clearly recognized the potential benefits of paying attention to steel workers in these states. In one appearance at a steel plant in Pennsylvania, Bush assured an assembly of plant personnel that their product constituted "an important national security issue."

What do you think?

- Do electoral considerations lead to distorted economic policies, or are elected officials just doing a good job of representing their constituents?

- Would the government's steel policy have differed if Al Gore had been elected in 2000?

SOURCES: "Romancing Big Steel," *The Economist*, February 16, 2002; Federal Election Commission 2000 election data.

1950 and 1970, relative to the nation's productivity, after which personal income stagnated.[44] Many Americans came to feel that they were paying too much, even though their combined tax burden is still low by international standards (see Figure 15.9).

Nor is opposition to taxation simply a matter of values. For some it is a matter of good sense. Free-market economists, as well as many regular Americans, believe that taxes damage economic performance over the long term. Taxes lessen the incentive that workers and businesses have to increase productivity. Taxes draw wealth out of productive sectors of the economy and distribute it according to political considerations that may have nothing to do with efficiency, logic, or

FIGURE 15.9

The U.S. tax burden is less than that in many other democracies

No one likes taxes, but low rates in the United States reflect the American political culture.

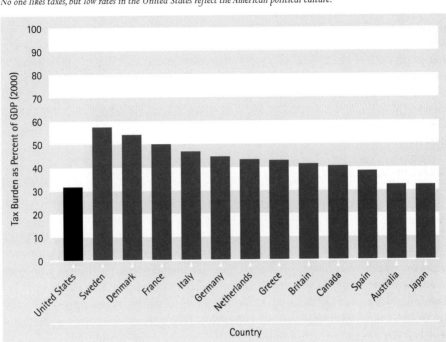

SOURCE: U.S. Bureau of the Census, *Statistical Abstract of the United States, 1999*, Table 1372.

fairness. To antitax thinkers, then, the best way for government to improve social conditions is to stand out of the way of economic progress.

On the other hand, few Americans endorse cutting national taxes altogether. The debate revolves instead around which taxes to permit and which to scale back or abolish. Organized groups work hard to convert public opinion over to their pet causes. They call on elected officials to use the tax code to encourage some behaviors and discourage others. In response to these pressures, national and state legislators have enacted thousands of **tax preferences**—special treatment that exempts particular types of activity from taxation. These tax loopholes cost the government billions of dollars in forgone revenue.

Many economists argue that taxes are less intrusive if they are broad-based— that is, imposed on all economic activity at the same rate. Thus, these theorists maintain, the amount one pays in income taxes should depend only on the amount of one's income, not on its source. Nor should sales taxes vary depending on whether one buys groceries, cars, beer, or medical insurance. If everything is taxed alike, then the policy will not distort economic decisions or otherwise sway the choices people make. Special interests will not be able to manipulate the tax code.

However, broad-based taxes are difficult to defend in the political arena. Tax preferences are extremely popular with the public or with attentive interest groups. Popular tax preferences include credits for college tuition and deductions for home mortgages and charitable contributions. Analysts have pointed to problems with each of these credits. They fault tuition credits for driving up education costs at the expense of the poor, mortgage deductions for funding oversized homes at the expense of the environment, and charitable deductions because it is hard to tell when a "charity" in fact is providing donors with some kind of hidden product or service. Yet no amount of criticism has dampened enthusiasm for these sacred cows of the tax code.

Furthermore, tax preferences are the classic "slippery slope." Once government grants one to any group, it abandons the principle of neutral taxation and confuses tax law. The policy encourages other groups to lobby for their own preferences, sometimes outside the view of public scrutiny. Moreover, granting preferences to some activities requires higher taxes on everyone else. This dynamic played out in the 2000 presidential campaign. Vice President Al Gore proposed extensive tax breaks for favored activities, leading George W. Bush—who preferred lowering overall tax rates—to dismiss him as "a picker and a chooser." Yet Bush's budget proposals included a fair sprinkling of tax breaks as well.

Not all special treatment is favorable. The government also sometimes imposes **sin taxes,** taxes intended to make money from people who engage in unpopular behavior. The most prominent sin taxes target cigarettes and alcohol. Critics of such measures argue that they fall primarily on the poorest segments of the population and fail to have a significant impact on the consumption of addictive products. But governments scrambling for revenue seldom pass up sin taxes as a politically popular source of money.

Dogbert's tax plan
Elected officials curry favor and influence social behavior by raising taxes to high levels and then exempting particular constituencies with tax preferences.

One more general form of unequal taxation is the *progressive tax*—any tax that affects people more severely as they become more affluent. The most important progressive tax is the federal income tax, which applies different rates depending on family income. Like other tax inequalities, progressive taxation attracts criticism for distorting economic behavior. Conservatives claim that progressive rates punish the investments and the hard work contributed by the most productive members of society. Liberals, by contrast, oppose narrowing differences in rates because to do so lessens the tax burden borne by the affluent.

Other taxes are *regressive,* hitting low-income people harder. The payroll tax in 2000 applied only to the first $76,200 a person earned, so the overall tax rate actually decreased as income climbed past that limit. For this reason, when all taxes levied by federal, state, and local governments—including numerous exceptions and exemptions—are taken into account, it is difficult to say whether the tax structure in the United States is progressive or not.[45]

EVALUATING AMERICA'S ECONOMIC POLICIES

People care whether they can find jobs and what they have to pay for the things they buy. When times are bad, the president takes the blame. When times are good, the president usually—but not always—gets the credit. National economic conditions significantly influence the president's popular standing. To a lesser extent, this is also true of members of Congress and even state-level officials.

Given these political facts of life, presidents accord economic policy top priority. They give the agency responsible for monetary policy, the Federal Reserve, a good deal of independence (see Chapter 11). For half a century, presidents also tried to use fiscal policy to manage the economy. But this approach has lost popularity, in part because it is hard to manipulate, but more so because it seldom works.

The American tax system generally reflects American political culture. The tax system includes numerous progressive taxes as well as tax breaks for individuals who pursue politically popular or influential activities. Yet candidates who push equalizing income attract limited support. Americans seem pleased with the balance in their system between rewarding success and eliminating inequalities—which has helped produce an adaptive economic system with less debt and lower unemployment rates (see Chapter 4).

Compared to other democracies, the United States is doing a decent job of dealing with its economic difficulties. Five and one-half trillion dollars, the size of the national debt in 2000, may be almost unimaginable. Relative to the size of the economy, though, the public debt in the United States is moderate. For example, relative to their productivity, France, Germany, and Japan all have larger national debts than the United States. Italy's debt is more than twice as large (see Figure 15.10).

The United States has done a better job than most countries of incorporating new workers into the economy. In 2000, for example, the unemployment rate in

FIGURE 15.10

U.S. debt is smaller than the debt of other countries

The U.S. debt exceeds $5 trillion, but this figure (as a proportion of national productivity) is moderate by international standards.

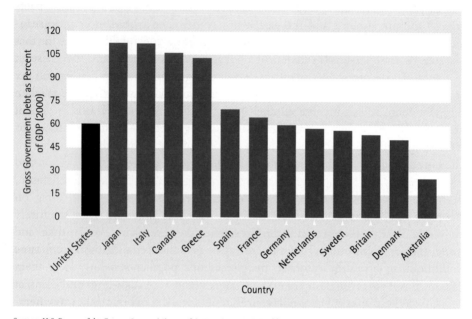

SOURCE: U.S. Bureau of the Census, *Statistical Abstract of the United States, 1999,* Table 1372.

Western Europe hovered around 10 percent—more than twice the U.S. rate. European countries kept their unemployment rates as low as they did only by using policies that would be unacceptable in the United States. For example, Germany and Switzerland induced so-called guest workers to return to their countries of origin. The United States, by contrast, increased immigration during the 1980s. Limited regulations and low taxation combined to encourage innovation—including development of the high-tech industries that fueled prosperity in the 1990s.

The price of limited government seems to be greater social inequality than is found in other advanced democracies. After declining between 1930 and 1970, inequality rose until, in the 1990s, it was higher than at any time since the 1930s. Yet public demand for income redistribution is low.[46] The explanation may lie in the necessary trade-off between encouraging prosperity and mandating equality. Americans do not wish to kill the goose that lays the golden eggs. At some point, being relatively poor in a strong economy becomes better than being equal in a weak one.

FOREIGN AND DEFENSE POLICY

America's founders initially set up a strong federal government so that the United States could coordinate relations with other nations (see Chapter 2). They thought that the states would create economic chaos if they negotiated trade pacts and treaties individually with other countries, or if they continued printing separate currencies and erecting trade barriers against each other. They thought that the nation would be unable to defend itself if it did not have the ability to raise an army rather than construct one from state militias, and if it did not have the tax powers to fund the military. Americans needed to speak in a unified voice when negotiating with other countries, including those who threatened the borders of the United States. In short, external relations seemed the proper function for national institutions.

Over time the federal government has concentrated less of its attention and its resources on protecting Americans from outside threats. Spending on defense, international relations, and foreign aid has declined relative to spending on domestic and economic programs, for example. National leaders are not entirely to blame for neglecting their primary responsibility, however. Foreign and defense policy is a difficult balancing act. If national leaders spend too much time on it, because they want to protect American interests, then no one rewards them for their preparedness. They suffer on election day for "ignoring problems at home." But if an international crisis develops and leaders have not prepared themselves to deal with it quickly and successfully, then they suffer on election day for being unprepared. In short, national leaders face a double standard: They must protect voters from foreign threats, but they must not spend much time doing it. Under the circumstances, it may make most sense for national leaders to give defense inadequate attention and hope for the best—knowing that if something bad happens, voters may blame the enemy instead of them.

In other ways, though, foreign and defense policy is easier for politicians to negotiate than other types of policies. Americans might disagree angrily about which social problems the national government should address, and they may have sharply divided interests on the economic policies that the nation might pursue. But most Americans share the same rough goals and interests for foreign and defense policy. They want a country that is prosperous, safe, and strong. They want enemies defeated and threats averted. They want access to the world's goods and resources. They want international allies, not international enemies.

This basic agreement across Americans of all ideologies and all political parties makes foreign and defense policy less troublesome than other sorts of policies because it is possible to take a stand that pleases just about everybody. It has encouraged Congress to defer to the president, the nation's commander in chief (see Chapter 10), and to create a large foreign policy bureaucracy that enhances the chief executive's ability to gather international intelligence and act on it (see

Chapter 11). Most of the policy battles in foreign and defense policy result not from disagreement over basic ideals and interests but, rather, from international decisions that actually affect domestic or economic policy.

Most, but not all. Occasionally Americans do find themselves sharply divided over how their country should deal with outsiders, and not simply because of what might happen back home as a result. A large antiwar movement rose up during the Vietnam conflict, and another peace movement surprisingly appeared as the Bush administration considered war with Iraq. But even on these rare occasions, Americans do not express differing ideals or differing interests. Rather, sometimes ideals and interests clash in international affairs, and Americans may not be able to decide whether their values or their self-interest should win out.

NATIONAL IDEALS

American foreign policy is shaped by a long-standing tension that exists between American philosophical ideals and the country's practical need to protect its interests. Alexander Hamilton, in the *Federalist Papers,* made the best case for placing the highest priority on practical interests: "No Government [can] give us tranquility and happiness at home, which [does] not possess sufficient stability and strength to make us respectable abroad."[47] The idealist point of view was best expressed by Abraham Lincoln, who reminded his fellow citizens that one purpose of the American experiment was to spread liberty throughout the world "for all future time."[48]

Over the course of its history, the United States has not been so naïve or innocent that it ignored underlying national interests. The country acquired land and possessions when opportunities were ripe. But more than most nations, the United States has expressed its international goals in missionary language. Liberty, democracy, and inalienable rights are so important to the country's self-definition that they cannot be ignored when framing its relations with other nations. America's early presidents spoke out against European expansion.[49] A century later, the United States fought in two world wars in the name of freedom. When asking Americans to enter World War I, President Woodrow Wilson claimed it was necessary because "the world must be made safe for democracy."[50] He promised, rather idealistically, that it would be the war to end all wars. When World War II broke out, President Roosevelt asked Americans to fight for four freedoms: free speech, religious freedom, freedom from want, and freedom from fear.[51]

NATIONAL INTERESTS

Ideals may structure American foreign policy, but that policy also reflects the country's practical self-interests. One of the oldest U.S. foreign policy principles, **isolationism,** is in fact explicitly self-centered. According to this principle, the United States should remain apart from the conflicts taking place among other nations. Isolationists often quote a phrase from George Washington's Farewell

Address, made when he retired from the presidency: "Tis our true policy to steer clear of permanent alliances."[52] For more than a century after Washington made this speech, the United States was, in the words of Winston Churchill, "splendidly isolated."

Isolationism is not so much a philosophy of weakness or of fear as a lack of concern. The United States has always sat an ocean away from the world's major powers. Wars take place far away. The U.S. mainland last faced foreign invasion in 1814—unless one counts recent terrorist attacks. Limited interest in international affairs has been fed by the country's wartime successes, which have fostered a sense of invincibility. After the War of 1812 and until the Vietnam conflict, the United States had an impressive military record. Most wars ended in overwhelming victories. The United States has suffered few casualties in foreign wars (see Figure 15.11).

FIGURE 15.11
United States lucky in war

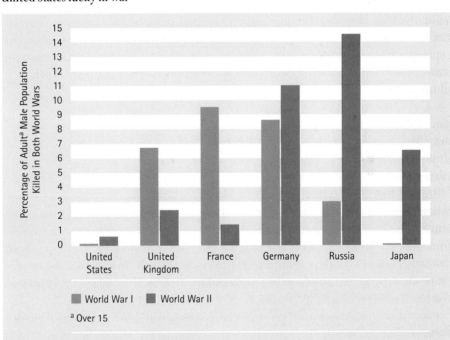

Note: Population figures are from the following years; France, 1911, 1936; Germany, 1910, 1939; United Kingdom (including Scotland), 1911, 1931; United States, 1910, 1940; Russia, 1913 (estimated), 1939; Japan, 1913, 1940.

SOURCES: R. Ernest Dupy and Trevor N. Dupuy, *The Harper Encyclopedia of Military History: From 3500 b.c. to the Present* (New York: HarperCollins, 1993); Y. Takenob, *The Japan Year Book: 1919–1920* (Tokyo: Japan Year Book Office, 1921); B. R. Mitchell, *International Historical Statistics: Europe 1750–1988* (New York: Stockton Press, 1992); B. R. Mitchell, *International Historical Statistics of the Americas: 1750–1988* (New York: Stockton Press, 1993); B. R. Mitchell, *International Historical Statistics: Africa and Asia* (New York: New York University Press, 1982); and Raymond E. Zickel, ed., *Soviet Union: A Country Study* (Washington, DC: U.S. Government Printing Office, 1991).

Such a large proportion of Americans sympathized with the isolationist argument that the United States became involved in World Wars I and II only reluctantly and belatedly. World War I broke out in August 1914, but the United States stayed out of it for more than two years. In language reminiscent of Washington's, President Wilson initially called for the United States to be "neutral in fact as well as in name."[53] The United States did not declare war until well after the Germans began torpedoing U.S. commercial ships.

At the beginning of World War II, the United States once again declared its neutrality. In his 1940 campaign for reelection, President Roosevelt promised "mothers and fathers" that the country's neutrality would be preserved: "I shall say it again and again and again: Your boys are not going to be sent into any foreign wars."[54] But soon after the election, Roosevelt began preparing for war, declaring "we must be the great arsenal of democracy."[55]

In sum, both idealistic and realistic factors help shape American foreign policy. On the one hand, the United States feels responsible for promoting the democratic experiment abroad. Voters do not appreciate presidential sluggishness when children are starving or people are being massacred. On the other hand, the United States, like any other country, has its own interests to protect. Voters become unhappy when the nation enters unnecessary conflicts or appears weak on the world stage. They reward elected officials who, because of their foreign policy activities, achieve important goals—not the least of which is prosperity.

AFTERSHOCK:
THE BUSH DOCTRINE

Presidents usually place their personal stamp on American foreign relations because the political system allows them an exceptional amount of influence over that policy area (see Chapter 10). These days, when a president articulates a personal vision of how the United States should interact with other countries, watchers across the globe take notice. Odds are that U.S. foreign policy will grow out of the president's guiding philosophy for America's role in the world—as, for example, George W. Bush's world view culminated in wars against Afghanistan and Iraq following the 9/11 attacks.

At one time, the major powers cared less about how Americans viewed international relations. Perhaps the most commonly discussed presidential proclamation of American intent, offered as part of President James Monroe's 1823 message to Congress, received little attention at the time. Monroe warned European nations against interfering with politics in the Western hemisphere, and explicitly forbade them from establishing any more colonies that would spread their form of political system into the region. In exchange, Monroe offered a similar passivity on the part of the United States: no intent to intervene in existing European colonies or in continental affairs. Other nations might have taken umbrage at receiving implied threats from such a young country, had leaders there taken much notice. Monroe's message did not draw enough European interest to warrant condemnation.

Sometimes presidents either intentionally or unconsciously communicate foreign policies that deviate sharply from previous approaches. Presidents may announce a more active or more passive orientation. They may embrace a pragmatic policy driven by national interests or favor a moral course consistent with national ideals. They may place heavy emphasis on cooperation through treaties and international organizations, or they may intend for the United States to keep its own counsel when formulating foreign policy. Later historians customarily identify significant changes in American doctrine with the chief executives who communicated them. For example, starting in 1852 the American stand against Europe's "new world" ambitions became known as the **Monroe Doctrine.**[56]

U.S. policy has fluctuated over time, but observers note a general trend toward more foreign involvement. The Monroe Doctrine represented a sort of "live and let live" policy, a unilateral insistence that nations would stay out of each other's way. As the United States gained power, though, it began to exhibit a sense of responsibility for international conditions—if not an aggressiveness on behalf of American interests and ideals.

Americans in the Progressive era, for instance, perceived a duty to spread their way of life to other regions of the world. Both Teddy Roosevelt and Woodrow Wilson, although quite unlike each other in many respects, nonetheless shared this sense of righteousness when dealing with international relations. President Roosevelt claimed a continued allegiance to the Monroe Doctrine, but his foreign-policy statements suggested a clear break with how that principle would be interpreted. For example, Roosevelt informed Congress that Americans must protect the welfare of "barbarous and semi-barbarous peoples" living in the vicinity of the United States. "Wars with uncivilized powers are largely mere matters of international police duty, essential to the welfare of the world," he explained in his second annual message. He repeated the theme two years later, claiming that "in the western hemisphere the adherence of the United States to the Monroe Doctrine may force the United States, however reluctantly, . . . to the exercise of international police power." This new impulse, Roosevelt's corollary to the Monroe Doctrine, drove U.S. expansion to less-developed places, including island nations in both the Pacific and Atlantic oceans.[57]

President Woodrow Wilson carried the sense of American mission further by making it appear even more idealistic. He promised to seek "peace without victory" in World War I—in essence to force the war's end without conquering the enemy, without profiting from the violence. In 1918, as the war wound down, Wilson outlined a fourteen-point peace plan that would guide ongoing American involvement in the conflict's resolution. The overall message communicated by the Fourteen Points was more important than the specifics: The United States would fight for a noble cause, even on other continents.

Most subsequent presidents if anything expanded the U.S. commitment to involvement overseas. President Franklin Delano Roosevelt, for example, broadened the scope of American responsibilities by promising to promote rather open-ended "freedoms." His successors, starting with President Harry Truman, carried out a Cold War of espionage and military skirmishes as part of their effort to contain communist expansion (see Chapter 11). The United States, under such leadership, began maintaining a large military bureaucracy. If other nations descended into civil war and risked "going communist," American leaders were prepared to intervene.

Many observers believe that the U.S. government has reshaped its foreign-policy stance yet again. The new orientation, already called the **Bush Doctrine,** developed rapidly in the wake of the 9/11 attacks. President Bush announced before a joint session of Congress that U.S. policy would not permit neutrality in the war on terrorism. "Every nation in every region now has a decision to make," he proclaimed. "Either you are with us or you are with the terrorists." Governments would be held responsible for tolerating or ignoring the actions of terrorists living within their borders. The United States might even attack a "failing" government preemptively, might strike first, rather than wait for open aggression.[58]

Bush's 2002 State of the Union address declared that three governments—those of Iraq, Iran, and North Korea—were part of an "axis of evil" in the world war on terrorism. This stark language, coming as the United States prepared for battle against Iraq, set off a storm of criticism. Many world leaders rejected the moralistic, good-versus-evil perspective as provocative and probably dangerous. More important, Bush's various statements seemed to justify a string of U.S. conquests around the globe, which made many world leaders uncomfortable. Bush backed off from that extreme implication, especially in his next State of the Union speech—but the Bush Doctrine nonetheless contains few traces of Washington's desire to avoid foreign entanglements or Wilson's focus on national self-determination. The public sense of vulnerability following 9/11 changed Bush's foreign policy options. It allowed, and may have forced, Bush to endorse a militarism quite in contrast with his 2000 presidential campaign, during which he criticized attempts at "nation building" and questioned whether President Clinton's foreign interventions had stretched the U.S. military too thin.

CHAPTER SUMMARY

The elderly enjoy disproportionate influence in the United States, partly because they participate more in American politics, and partly because younger voters endorse the demands that senior citizens place on government. The result is a national budget that, aside from times of crisis, spends ten times more on the elderly than it spends on other Americans. Furthermore, old-age welfare policies give senior citizens an unmatched amount of privacy and flexibility as they collect their benefits. Domestic policy is not the only policy area influenced by popular preferences, though. Fiscal policy does not work in part because politicians often do not believe they can raise taxes or cut programs to eliminate national debt without suffering electorally. Tax law reflects basic American values, including a preference for prosperity over equality. Presidents must attend to foreign affairs even when they wish to concentrate on domestic policy. A prime example is the way the September 11 terrorist attacks forced President Bush to put his domestic agenda on hold and prompted him to wage a war on terrorism. In sum, the whole scope of public policy illustrates quite starkly this book's central theme: In America's new democracy, elections (or at least the anticipation of them) matter more than they do in most countries—and more than they have for most of the nation's history.

KEY TERMS

Aid to Families with
  Dependent Children
  (AFDC), p. 512
Bush doctrine, p. 534
business cycles, p. 515
Earned Income Tax
  Credit (EITC), p. 512
fiscal policy, p. 518

food stamps, p. 512
inflation, p. 515
isolationism, p. 530
Keynesianism, p. 519
Medicaid, p. 512
Medicare, p. 507
monetarism, p. 517
monetary policy, p. 518

Monroe Doctrine, p. 533
recessions, p. 515
sin tax, p. 526
tax preferences, p. 525
Temporary Assistance
  for Needy Families
  (TANF), p. 505
unemployment, p. 515

SUGGESTED READINGS

Birnbaum, Jeffrey H., and Alan S. Murray. *Showdown at Gucci Gulch.* New York: Random House, 1987. Fast-paced case study of the passage of the 1986 tax reforms.

Bradford, David F. *Untangling the Income Tax.* Cambridge, MA: Harvard University Press, 1986. Everything you ever wanted to know about income taxes, presented in a reasonably comprehensible fashion.

Howell, William, and Paul E. Peterson, with Patrick Wolf and David Campbell. *The Education Gap: Vouchers and Urban Public Schools.* Washington, D.C.: Brookings, 2002. Analysis of school choice initiatives by scholars sympathetic to vouchers.

Huntington, Samuel. *The Clash of Civilizations.* New York: Simon & Schuster, 1996. Argues that future world conflicts will occur between clusters of nations that share a common cultural heritage.

Kingdon, John. *Agenda, Alternatives and Public Policies.* Boston: Little, Brown, 1984. Discusses the policy-making process, paying special attention to how problems become issues on the political agenda.

Koh, Harold Hungju. *The National Security Constitution: Sharing Power After the Iran–Contra Affair.* New Haven, CT: Yale University Press, 1990. Analyzes the distribution of constitutional authority in foreign policy.

Pierson, Paul. *Dismantling the Welfare State? Reagan, Thatcher and the Politics of Retrenchment.* New York: Cambridge University Press, 1994. Insightful analysis of political battles over cuts in welfare expenditure.

Weaver, R. Kent. *Automatic Government: The Politics of Indexation.* Washington, DC: Brookings, 1988. Explains policy changes that have allowed government entitlements to become increasingly expensive.

Weir, Margaret. *Politics and Jobs: The Boundaries of Employment Policies in the United States.* Princeton, NJ: Princeton University Press, 1992. Broad historical and political analysis of government efforts to guarantee jobs.

On the Web

Social Security Administration
www.ssa.gov
The Social Security Administration (SSA) Web site provides information on the characteristics of the social security program.

Health Care Financing Administration
www.hcfa.hhs.gov
The Health Care Financing Administration (HCFA) administers the Medicare and Medicaid programs.

American Association of Retired People
www.aarp.org
The American Association of Retired People (AARP) maintains a large Web site describing its volunteer programs and lobbying efforts and offering health and recreation tips for seniors.

Council on Foreign Relations
www.cfr.org
Founded in 1921, the Council on Foreign Relations promotes understanding of international politics and publishes the journal *Foreign Affairs*.

Senate Committee on Foreign Relations
www.senate.gov/~foreign/
The U.S. Senate's Committee on Foreign Relations provides information on treaties presented to the Senate for its approval, as well as on nominations and hearings on foreign policy.

APPENDIX

The Declaration of Independence
In Congress, July 4, 1776

The Unanimous Declaration
of the Thirteen United States of America

WHEN IN THE COURSE of human events it becomes necessary for one people to dissolve the political bonds which have connected them with another, and to assume, among the powers of the earth, the separate and equal station to which the Laws of Nature and of Nature's God entitle them, a decent respect to the opinions of mankind requires that they should declare the causes which impel them to the separation.

We hold these truths to be self-evident, that all men are created equal, that they are endowed by their Creator with certain unalienable Rights, that among these are Life, Liberty and the pursuit of Happiness. That to secure these rights, Governments are instituted among Men, deriving their just powers from the consent of the governed. That whenever any Form of Government becomes destructive of these ends, it is the Right of the People to alter or to abolish it, and to institute new Government, laying its foundation on such principles and organizing its powers in such form, as to them shall seem most likely to effect their Safety and Happiness. Prudence, indeed, will dictate that Governments long established should not be changed for light and transient causes; and accordingly all experience hath shown that mankind are more disposed to suffer, while evils are sufferable, than to right themselves by abolishing the forms to which they are accustomed. But when a long train of abuses and usurpations, pursuing invariably the same Object evinces a design to reduce them under absolute Despotism, it is their right, it is their duty, to throw off such Government, and to provide new Guards for their future security.

Such has been the patient sufferance of these Colonies; and such is now the necessity which constrains them to alter their former Systems of Government. The history of the present King of Great Britain is a history of repeated injuries and usurpations, all having in direct object the establishment of an absolute Tyranny over these States. To prove this, let Facts be submitted to a candid world.

He has refused his Assent to Laws, the most wholesome and necessary for the public good.

He has forbidden his Governors to pass Laws of immediate and pressing importance, unless suspended in their operation till his Assent should be obtained; and when so suspended, he has utterly neglected to attend to them.

He has refused to pass other Laws for the accommodation of large districts of people, unless those people would relinquish the right of Representation in the Legislature, a right inestimable to them and formidable to tyrants only.

He has called together legislative bodies at places unusual, uncomfortable, and distant from the depository of their Public Records, for the sole purpose of fatiguing them into compliance with his measures.

He has dissolved Representative Houses repeatedly, for opposing with manly firmness his invasions on the rights of the people.

He has refused for a long time, after such dissolutions, to cause others to be elected; whereby the Legislative Powers, incapable of Annihilation, have returned to the People at large for their exercise, the State remaining in the meantime exposed to all the dangers of invasion from without, and convulsions within.

He has endeavored to prevent the population of these States; for that purpose obstructing the Laws of Naturalization of Foreigners; refusing to pass others to encourage their migration hither, and raising the conditions of new Appropriations of Lands.

He has obstructed the Administration of Justice, by refusing his Assent to Laws for establishing Judiciary powers.

He has made Judges dependent on his Will alone, for the tenure of their offices, and the amount and payment of their salaries.

He has erected a multitude of New Offices, and sent hither swarms of Officers to harass our people, and eat out their substance.

He has kept among us, in times of peace, Standing Armies without the Consent of our legislatures.

He has affected to render the Military independent of and superior to the Civil power.

He has combined with others to subject us to a jurisdiction foreign to our constitution, and unacknowledged by our laws, giving his Assent to their Acts of pretended Legislation:

For quartering large bodies of armed troops among us:

For protecting them, by a mock Trial, from punishment for any Murders which they should commit on the Inhabitants of these States:

For cutting off our Trade with all parts of the world:

For imposing Taxes on us without our Consent:

For depriving us in many cases, of the benefits of Trial by Jury:

For transporting us beyond Seas to be tried for pretended offences:

For abolishing the free System of English Laws in a neighboring Province, establishing therein an Arbitrary government, and enlarging its Boundaries so as to render it at once an example and fit instrument for introducing the same absolute rule into these Colonies:

For taking away our Charters, abolishing our most valuable Laws, and altering fundamentally the Forms of our Governments:

For suspending our own Legislatures, and declaring themselves invested with power to legislate for us in all cases whatsoever.

He has abdicated Government here, by declaring us out of his Protection and waging War against us.

He has plundered our seas, ravaged our Coasts, burnt our towns, and destroyed the lives of our people.

He is at this time transporting large Armies of foreign Mercenaries to compleat the works of death, desolation and tyranny, already begun with circumstances of Cruelty and perfidy scarcely paralleled in the most barbarous ages, and totally unworthy the Head of a civilized nation.

He has constrained our fellow Citizens taken Captive on the high Seas to bear Arms against their Country, to become the executioners of their friends and Brethren, or to fall themselves by their Hands.

He has excited domestic insurrections amongst us, and has endeavored to bring on the inhabitants of our frontiers, the merciless Indian Savages, whose known rule of warfare, is an undistinguished destruction of all ages, sexes and conditions.

In every stage of these Oppressions We have Petitioned for Redress in the most humble terms: Our repeated Petitions have been answered only by repeated injury: A Prince, whose character is thus marked by every act which may define a Tyrant, is unfit to be the ruler of a free people.

Nor have We been wanting in attention to our British brethren. We have warned them from time to time of attempts by their legislature to extend an unwarrantable jurisdiction over us. We have reminded them of the circumstances of our emigration and settlement here. We have appealed to their native justice and magnanimity; and we have conjured them by the ties of our common kindred to disavow these usurpations, which would inevitably interrupt our connections and correspondence. They too have been deaf to the voice of justice and consanguinity. We must, therefore, acquiesce in the necessity, which denounces our Separation, and hold them, as we hold the rest of mankind, Enemies in War, in Peace Friends.

We, therefore, the Representatives of the United States of America, in General Congress, Assembled, appealing to the Supreme Judge of the world for the rectitude of our intentions, do, in the Name, and by Authority of the good People of these Colonies, solemnly publish and declare, That these United Colonies are, and of Right ought to be Free and Independent States; that they are Absolved from all Allegiance to the British Crown, and that all political connection between them and the State of Great Britain, is and ought to be totally dissolved: and that as Free and Independent States, they have full power to levy War, conclude Peace, contract Alliances, establish Commerce, and to do all other Acts and Things which Independent States may of right do. And for the support of this Declaration, with a firm reliance on the protection of divine Providence, we mutually pledge to each other our Lives, our Fortunes and our sacred Honor.

JOHN HANCOCK

NEW HAMPSHIRE
  Josiah Bartlett,
  Wm. Whipple,
  Matthew Thornton.

MASSACHUSETTS BAY
  Saml. Adams,
  John Adams,
  Robt. Treat Paine,
  Elbridge Gerry.

RHODE ISLAND
  Step. Hopkins,
  William Ellery.

CONNECTICUT
  Roger Sherman,
  Samuel Huntington,
  Wm. Williams,
  Oliver Wolcott.

NEW YORK
  Wm. Floyd,
  Phil. Livingston,
  Frans. Lewis,
  Lewis Morris.

NEW JERSEY
  Richd. Stockton,
  In. Witherspoon,
  Fras. Hopkinson,
  John Hart,
  Abra. Clark.

PENNSYLVANIA
  Robt. Morris,
  Benjamin Rush,
  Benjamin Franklin,
  John Morton,
  Geo. Clymer,
  Jas. Smith,
  Geo. Taylor,
  James Wilson,
  Geo. Ross.

DELAWARE
  Caesar Rodney,
  Geo. Read,
  Tho. M'kean.

MARYLAND
Samuel Chase,
Wm. Paca,
Thos. Stone,
Charles Caroll of
Carollton.

VIRGINIA
George Wythe,
Richard Henry Lee,
Th. Jefferson,
Benjamin Harrison,
Thos. Nelson, jr.,
Francis Lightfoot Lee,
Carter Braxton.

NORTH CAROLINA
Wm. Hooper,
Joseph Hewes,
John Penn.

SOUTH CAROLINA
Edward Rutledge,
Thos. Heyward, Junr.,
Thomas Lynch, jnr.,
Arthur Middleton.

The Constitution of the United States of America

PREAMBLE

WE THE PEOPLE of the United States, in Order to form a more perfect Union, establish Justice, insure domestic Tranquility, provide for the common defence, promote the general Welfare, and secure the Blessings of Liberty to ourselves and our Posterity, do ordain and establish this Constitution for the United States of America.

ARTICLE I
Section 1

All legislative Powers herein granted shall be vested in a Congress of the United States, which shall consist of a Senate and House of Representatives.

Section 2

The House of Representatives shall be composed of Members chosen every second Year by the People of the several States, and the Electors in each State shall have the Qualifications requisite for Electors of the most numerous Branch of the State Legislature.

No person shall be a Representative who shall not have attained to the Age of twenty five Years, and been seven Years a Citizen of the United States, and who shall not, when elected, be an Inhabitant of that State in which he shall be chosen.

Representatives and direct Taxes shall be apportioned among the several States which may be included within this Union, according to their respective Numbers which shall be determined by adding to the whole Number of free Persons, including those bound to Service for a Term of Years, and excluding Indians not taxed, three fifths of all other Persons. The actual Enumeration shall be made within three Years after the first Meeting of the Congress of the United States, and within every subsequent Term ten Years, in such Manner as they shall by Law direct. The Number of Representatives shall not exceed one for every thirty Thousand, but each State shall have at Least one Representative; and until such enumeration shall be made, the State of New Hampshire shall be entitled to chuse three, Massachusetts eight, Rhode-Island and Providence Plantations one, Connecticut five, New-York six, New Jersey four, Pennsylvania eight, Delaware one, Maryland six, Virginia ten, North Carolina five, South Carolina five, and Georgia three.

When vacancies happen in the Representation from any State, the Executive Authority thereof shall issue Writs of Election to fill such Vacancies.

The House of Representatives shall chuse their speaker and other Officers; and shall have the sole Power of Impeachment.

Section 3

The Senate of the United States shall be composed of two Senators from each State chosen by the Legislature thereof, for six Years; and each Senator shall have one Vote.

Immediately after they shall be assembled in Consequence of the first Election, they shall be divided as equally as may be into three Classes. The Seats of the Senators of the first Class shall be vacated at the Expiration of the second year, of the second Class at the Expiration of the fourth Year, and of the third Class at the Expiration of the sixth Year, so that one third may be chosen every second Year and if Vacancies happen by Resignation, or otherwise, during the Recess of the Legislature of any State, the Executive thereof may make temporary Appointments until the next Meeting of the Legislature, which shall then fill such Vacancies.

No Person shall be a Senator who shall not have attained to the Age of thirty Years, and been nine Years a Citizen of the United States, and who shall not, when elected, be an Inhabitant of that State for which he shall be chosen.

The Vice President of the United States shall be President of the Senate, but shall have no Vote, unless they be equally divided.

The Senate shall chuse their other Officers, and also a President pro tempore, in the Absence of the Vice President, or when he shall exercise the Office of President of the United States.

The Senate shall have the sole Power to try all Impeachments. When sitting for that Purpose, they shall be on Oath or Affirmation. When the President of the United States is tried, the Chief Justice shall preside: And no Person shall be convicted without the Concurrence of two thirds of the Members present.

Judgment in Cases of Impeachment shall not extend further than to removal from Office, and disqualification to hold and enjoy any Office of honor, Trust or Profit under the United States; but the Party convicted shall nevertheless be liable and subject to Indictment, Trial, Judgment and Punishment, according to Law.

Section 4

The Times, Places and Manner of holding Elections for Senators and Representatives, shall be prescribed in each State by the Legislature thereof; but the Congress may at any time by law make or alter such Regulations, except as to the Places of chusing Senators.

The Congress shall assemble at least once in every Year, and such Meeting shall be on the first Monday in December, unless they shall by Law appoint a different Day.

Section 5

Each House shall be the Judge of the Elections, Returns and Qualifications of its own Members, and a Majority of each shall constitute a Quorum to do Business; but a smaller Number may adjourn from day to day, and may be authorized to compel the Attendance of absent Members, in such Manner, and under such Penalties as each House may provide.

Each House may determine the Rules of its Proceedings, punish its Members for disorderly Behaviour, and with the Concurrence of two thirds, expel a Member.

Each House shall keep a journal of its Proceedings, and from time to time publish the same, excepting such Parts as may in their judgment require Secrecy; and the Yeas and Nays of the Members of either House on any question shall, at the Desire of one fifth of those present, be entered on the Journal.

Neither House, during the Session of Congress, shall, without the Consent of the other, adjourn for more than three days, nor to any other Place than that in which the two Houses shall be sitting.

Section 6

The Senators and Representatives shall receive a Compensation for their Services, to be ascertained by Law, and paid out of the Treasury of the United States. They shall in all Cases, except Treason, Felony and Breach of the Peace, be privileged from Arrest during their Attendance at the Session of their respective Houses, and in going to and returning from the same; and for any Speech or Debate in either House, they shall not be questioned in any other Place.

No Senator or Representative shall, during the Time for which he was elected, be appointed to any civil Office under the Authority of the United States, which shall have been created, or the Emoluments whereof shall have been encreased during such time; and no Person holding any Office under the United States, shall be a Member of either House during his Continuance in Office.

Section 7

All Bills for raising Revenue shall originate in the House of Representatives; but the Senate may propose or concur with Amendments as on other Bills.

Every Bill which shall have passed the House of Representatives and the Senate, shall, before it become a Law, be presented to the President of the United States; If he approves he shall sign it, but if not he shall return it, with his Objections to that House in which it shall have originated, who shall enter the Objections at large on their journal, and proceed to reconsider it. If after such Reconsideration two thirds of that House shall agree to pass the Bill, it shall be sent, together with the Objections, to the other House, by which it shall likewise be reconsidered, and if approved by two thirds of that House, it shall become a Law. But in all such Cases the Votes of both Houses shall be determined by Yeas and Nays, and the Names of the Persons voting for and against the Bill shall be entered on the Journal of each House respectively. If any Bill shall not be returned by the President within ten Days (Sundays excepted) after it shall have been presented to him, the Same shall be a Law, in like Manner as if he had signed it, unless the Congress by their Adjournment prevent its Return, in which Case it shall not be a Law.

Every Order, Resolution, or Vote to which the Concurrence of the Senate and House of Representatives may be necessary (except on a question of Adjournment) shall be presented to the President of the United States; and before the Same shall take Effect, shall be approved by him, or being disapproved by him, shall be repassed by two thirds of the Senate and House of Representatives, according to the Rules and Limitations prescribed in the Case of a Bill.

Section 8

The Congress shall have Power To lay and collect Taxes, Duties, Imposts and Excises, to pay the Debts and provide for the common Defence and general Welfare of the United States; but all Duties, Imposts and Excises shall be uniform throughout the United States;

To borrow Money on the credit of the United States;

To regulate Commerce with foreign Nations, and among the several States, and with the Indian Tribes;

To establish a uniform Rule of Naturalization, and uniform Laws on the subject of Bankruptcies throughout the United States;

To coin Money, regulate the Value thereof, and of foreign Coin, and fix the Standard of Weights and Measures;

To provide for the Punishment of counterfeiting the Securities and current Coin of the United States;

To establish Post Offices and post Roads;

To promote the Progress of Science and useful Arts, by securing for limited Times to Authors and Inventors the exclusive Right to their respective Writings and Discoveries;

To constitute Tribunals inferior to the supreme Court;

To define and punish Piracies and Felonies committed on the high Seas, and Offences against the Law of Nations;

To declare War, grant Letters of Marque and Reprisal, and make Rules concerning Captures on Land and Water;

To raise and support Armies, but no Appropriation of Money to that Use shall be for a longer Term than two Years;

To provide and maintain a Navy;

To make Rules for the Government and Regulation of the land and naval Forces;

To provide for calling forth the Militia to execute the Laws of the Union, suppress Insurrections and repel Invasions;

To provide for organizing, arming, and disciplining, the Militia, and for governing such Part of them as may be employed in the Service of the United States, reserving to the States respectively, the Appointment of the Officers, and the Authority of training the Militia according to the discipline prescribed by Congress;

To exercise exclusive Legislation in all Cases whatsoever, over such District (not exceeding ten Miles square) as may, by Cession of particular States, and the Acceptance of Congress, become the Seat of the Government of the United States, and to exercise like Authority over all Places purchased by the Consent of the Legislature of the State in which the Same shall be for the Erection of Forts, Magazines, Arsenals, dock-Yards, and other needful Buildings;—And

To make all Laws which shall be necessary and proper for carrying into Execution the foregoing Powers, and all other Powers vested by this Constitution in the Government of the United States, or in any Department or Officer thereof.

Section 9

The Migration or Importation of such Persons as any of the States now existing shall think proper to admit, shall not be prohibited by the Congress prior to the Year one thousand eight hundred and eight, but a Tax or duty may be imposed on such Importation, not exceeding ten dollars for each Person.

The Privilege of the Writ of Habeas Corpus shall not be suspended, unless when in Cases of Rebellion or Invasion the public Safety may require it.

No Bill of Attainder or ex post facto Law shall be passed.

No Capitation, or other direct, Tax shall be laid, unless in Proportion to the Census or Enumeration herein before directed to be taken.

No Tax or Duty shall be laid on Articles exported from any State.

No Preference shall be given by any Regulation of Commerce or Revenue to the Ports of one State over those of another; nor shall Vessels bound to, or from, one State, be obliged to enter, clear, or pay Duties in another.

No Money shall be drawn from the Treasury, but in Consequence of Appropriations made by Law; and a regular Statement and Account of the Receipts and Expenditures of all public Money shall be published from time to time.

No Title of Nobility shall be granted by the United States: And no Person holding any Office of Profit or Trust under them, shall, without the Consent of the Congress, accept of any present, Emolument, Office, or Title, of any kind whatever, from any King, Prince, or foreign State.

Section 10

No state shall enter into any Treaty, Alliance, or Confederation; grant Letters of Marque and Reprisal; coin Money; emit Bills of Credit; make any Thing but gold and silver Coin a Tender in Payment of Debts; pass any Bill of Attainder, ex post facto Law, or Law impairing the Obligation of Contracts, or grant any Title of Nobility.

No State shall, without the Consent of the Congress, lay any Imposts or Duties on Imports or Exports, except what may be absolutely necessary for executing its inspection Laws: and the net Produce of all Duties and Imposts, laid by any State on Imports or Exports, shall be for the Use of the Treasury of the United States, and all such Laws shall be subject to the Revision and Control of the Congress.

No State shall, without the Consent of Congress, lay any Duty of Tonnage, keep Troops, or Ships of War in time of Peace, enter into any Agreement or Compact with another State, or with a foreign Power, or engage in War, unless actually invaded, or in such imminent Danger as will not admit of delay.

ARTICLE II

Section 1

The executive Power shall be vested in a President of the United States of America. He shall hold his Office during the Term of four Years, and, together with the Vice President, chosen for the same Term, be elected as follows.

Each State shall appoint, in such Manner as the Legislature thereof may direct, a Number of Electors, equal to the whole Number of Senators and Representatives to which the State may be entitled in the Congress; but no Senator or Representative, or Person holding an Office of Trust or Profit under the United States, shall be appointed an Elector.

The Electors shall meet in their respective States, and vote by Ballot for two Persons, of whom one at least shall not be an Inhabitant of the same State with themselves. And they shall make a List of all the Persons voted for, and, of the Number of Votes for each; which List they shall sign and certify, and transmit sealed to the Seat of the Government of the United States, directed to the President of the Senate. The President of the Senate shall, in the Presence of the Senate and House of Representatives, open all the Certificates, and the Votes shall then be counted. The Person having the greatest Number of Votes shall be the President, if such Number be a Majority of the whole Number of Electors appointed; and if there be more than one who have such Majority, and have an equal Number of Votes, then the House of Representatives shall immediately chuse by Ballot one of them for President; and if no Person have a Majority, then from the five highest on the List the said House shall in like Manner chuse the President. But in chusing the President, the Votes shall be taken by States, the Representation from each State having one Vote; A quorum for this Purpose shall consist of a Member or Members from two thirds of the States, and a Majority of all the States shall be necessary to a Choice. In every Case, after the Choice of the President, the Person having the greatest Number of Votes of the Electors shall be the Vice President. But if there should remain two or more who have equal Votes, the Senate shall chuse from them by Ballot the Vice President.

The Congress may determine the Time of chusing the Electors, and the Day on which they shall give their Votes; which Day shall be the same throughout the United States.

No Person except a natural born Citizen, or a Citizen of the United States, at the time of the Adoption of this Constitution, shall be eligible to the Office of President; neither shall any Person be eligible to that Office who shall not have attained to the Age of thirty five Years, and been fourteen Years a Resident within the United States.

In Case of the Removal of the President from Office, or of his Death, Resignation, or Inability to discharge the Powers and Duties of the said Office, the Same shall devolve on the Vice President, and the Congress may by Law provide for the Case of Removal, Death, Resignation or Inability, both of the President and Vice President, declaring what Officer shall then act as President, and such Officer shall act accordingly, until the Disability be removed, or a President shall be elected.

The President shall, at stated Times, receive for his Services, a Compensation, which shall neither be encreased nor diminished during the Period for which he shall have been elected, and he shall not receive within that Period any other Emolument from the United States, or any of them.

Before he enter on the Execution of his Office, he shall take the following Oath or Affirmation—"I do solemnly swear (or affirm) that I will faithfully execute the Office of President of the United States, and will to the best of my Ability, preserve, protect and defend the Constitution of the United States."

Section 2

The President shall be Commander in Chief of the Army, and Navy of the United States, and of the Militia of the several States, when called into the actual Service of the United States; he may require the Opinion, in writing, of the principal Officer in each of the executive Departments, upon any Subject relating to the Duties of their respective Offices, and he shall have Power to grant Reprieves and Pardons for Offences against the United States, except in Cases of Impeachment.

He shall have Power, by and with the Advice and Consent of the Senate, to make Treaties, provided two thirds of the Senators present concur; and he shall nominate, and by and with the Advice and Consent of the Senate, shall appoint Ambassadors, other public Ministers and Consuls, Judges of the supreme Court, and all other Officers of the United States, whose Appointments are not herein otherwise provided for, and which shall be established by Law: but the Congress may by Law vest the Appointment of such inferior Officers, as they think proper, in the President alone, in the Courts of Law, or in the Heads of Departments.

The President shall have Power to fill up all Vacancies that may happen during the Recess of the Senate, by granting Commissions which shall expire at the end of their next Session.

Section 3

He shall from time to time give to the Congress Information of the State of the Union, and recommend to their Consideration such Measures as he shall judge necessary and expedient; he may, on extraordinary Occasions, convene both Houses, or either of them, and in Case of Disagreement between them, with Respect to the Time of Adjournment, he may adjourn them to such Time as he shall think proper; he shall receive Ambassadors and other public Ministers; he shall take Care that the Laws be faithfully executed, and shall Commission all the Officers of the United States.

Section 4

The President, Vice President and all civil Officers of the United States, shall be removed from Office on Impeachment for, and Conviction of, Treason, Bribery, or other high Crimes and Misdemeanors.

ARTICLE III
Section 1

The judicial Power of the United States, shall be vested in one supreme Court, and in such inferior Courts as the Congress may from time to time ordain and establish. The Judges, both of the supreme and inferior Courts, shall hold their Offices during good Behaviour, and shall, at stated Times, receive for their Services, a Compensation, which shall not be diminished during their Continuance in Office.

Section 2

The judicial Power shall extend to all Cases, in Law and Equity, arising under this Constitution, the Laws of the United States, and Treaties made, or which shall be made, under their Authority;—to all Cases affecting Ambassadors, other public Ministers and Consuls;—to all Cases of admiralty and maritime Jurisdiction;—to Controversies to which the United States shall be a Party;—to Controversies between two or more States;—between a State and Citizens of another State;—between Citizens of different States,—between Citizens of the same State claiming Lands under Grants of different States,—and between a State, or the Citizens thereof, and foreign States, Citizens of Subjects.

In all Cases affecting Ambassadors, other public Ministers and Consuls, and those in which a State shall be Party, the supreme Court shall have original Jurisdiction. In all the other Cases before mentioned, the supreme Court shall have appellate Jurisdiction, both as to Law and Fact, with such Exceptions, and under such Regulations as the Congress shall make.

The Trial of all Crimes, except in Cases of Impeachment, shall be by Jury; and such Trial shall be held in the State where the said Crimes shall have been committed; but when not committed within any State, the Trial shall be at such Place or Places as the Congress may by Law have directed.

Section 3

Treason against the United States, shall consist only in levying War against them, or in adhering to their Enemies, giving them Aid and Comfort. No Person shall be convicted of Treason unless on the Testimony of two Witnesses to the same overt Act, or on Confession in open Court.

The Congress shall have Power to declare the Punishment of Treason, but no Attainder of Treason shall work Corruption of Blood, or Forfeiture except during the Life of the Person attainted.

ARTICLE IV
Section 1

Full Faith and Credit shall be given in each State to the public Acts, Records, and judicial Proceedings of every other State. And the Congress may by general Laws prescribe the Manner in which such Acts, Records and Proceedings shall be proved, and the Effect thereof.

Section 2

The Citizens of each State shall be entitled to all Privileges and Immunities of Citizens in the several States.

A Person charged in any State with Treason, Felony, or other Crime, who shall flee from Justice, and be found in another State, shall on Demand of the executive Authority of the State from which he fled, be delivered up, to be removed to the State having Jurisdiction of the Crime.

No Person held to Service or Labour in one State under the Laws thereof, escaping into another, shall, in Consequence of any Law or Regulation therein, be discharged from such Service or Labour, but shall be delivered up on Claim of the Party to whom such Service or Labour may be due.

Section 3

New States may be admitted by the Congress into this Union; but no new State shall be formed or erected within the Jurisdiction of any other State; nor any State be formed by the Junction of two or more States, or Parts of States, without the Consent of the Legislatures of the States concerned as well as of the Congress.

The Congress shall have Power to dispose of and make all needful Rules and Regulations respecting the Territory or other Property belonging to the United States; and nothing in this Constitution shall be so construed as to Prejudice any Claims of the United States, or of any particular State.

Section 4

The United States shall guarantee to every State in this Union a Republican Form of Government, and shall protect each of them against Invasion, and on Application of the Legislature, or of the Executive (when the Legislature cannot be convened) against domestic Violence.

ARTICLE V

The Congress, whenever two thirds of both Houses shall deem it necessary, shall propose Amendments to this Constitution, or, on the Application of the Legislatures of two thirds of the several States, shall call a Convention for proposing Amendments, which, in either Case, shall be valid to all Intents and Purposes, as Part of this Constitution, when ratified by the Legislatures of three fourths of the several States, or by Conventions in three fourths thereof, as the one or the other Mode of Ratification may be proposed by the Congress; Provided that no Amendment which may be made prior to the Year One thousand eight hundred and eight shall in any Manner affect the first and fourth Clauses in the Ninth Section of the first Article; and that no State, without its Consent, shall be deprived of its equal Suffrage in the Senate.

ARTICLE VI

All Debts contracted and Engagements entered into, before the Adoption of this Constitution, shall be as valid against the United States under this Constitution, as under the Confederation.

This Constitution, and the laws of the United States which shall be made in Pursuance thereof; and all Treaties made, or which shall be made, under the Authority of the United States, shall be the supreme Law of the Land; and the Judges in every State shall be bound thereby, any Thing in the Constitution or Laws of any State to the Contrary notwithstanding.

The Senators and Representatives before mentioned, and the Members of the several State Legislatures, and all executive and judicial Officers, both of the United States and of the several States, shall be bound by Oath or Affirmation, to support this Constitution; but no religious Test shall ever be required as a Qualification to any Office or public Trust under the United States.

ARTICLE VII

The Ratification of the Conventions of nine States, shall be sufficient for the Establishment of this Constitution between the States so ratifying the Same.

Done in Convention by the Unanimous Consent of the States present the Seventeenth Day of September in the Year of our Lord one thousand seven hundred and Eighty seven and of the Independence of the United States of America the Twelfth. In witness whereof we have hereunto subscribed our Names,

Go. WASHINGTON
Presid't. and deputy from Virginia

Attest
WILLIAM JACKSON
Secretary

Articles in addition to, and amendment of the Constitution of the United States of America, proposed by Congress and ratified by the Legislatures of the several states, pursuant to the Fifth Article of the original Constitution.

(The first ten amendments were passed by Congress on September 25, 1789, and were ratified on December 15, 1791.)

AMENDMENT I

Congress shall make no law respecting an establishment of religion, or prohibiting the free exercise thereof; or abridging the freedom of speech, or of the press; or the right of the people peaceably to assemble, and to petition the Government for a redress of grievances.

AMENDMENT II

A well regulated Militia, being necessary to the security of a free State, the right of the people to keep and bear Arms, shall not be infringed.

AMENDMENT III

No Soldier shall, in time of peace be quartered in any house, without the consent of the Owner, nor in time of war, but in a manner to be prescribed by law.

AMENDMENT IV

The right of the people to be secure in their persons, houses, papers, and effects, against unreasonable searches and seizures, shall not be violated, and no warrants shall issue, but upon probable cause, supported by Oath or affirmation, and particularly describing the place to be searched, and the persons or things to be seized.

AMENDMENT V

No person shall be held to answer for a capital, or otherwise infamous crime, unless on a presentment or indictment of a Grand Jury, except in cases arising in the land or naval forces, or in the Militia, when in actual service in time of War or public danger; nor shall any person be subject for the same offence to be twice put in jeopardy of life or limb; nor shall be compelled in any criminal case to be a witness against himself, nor be deprived of life, liberty, or property, without due process of law; nor shall private property be taken for public use, without just compensation.

AMENDMENT VI

In all criminal prosecutions, the accused shall enjoy the right to a speedy and public trial, by an impartial jury of the State and district wherein the crime shall have been committed, which district shall have been previously ascertained by law, and to be informed of the nature and cause of the accusation; to be confronted with the witnesses against him; to have compulsory process for obtaining witnesses in his favor, and to have the assistance of counsel for his defence.

AMENDMENT VII

In Suits at common law, where the value in controversy shall exceed twenty dollars, the right of trial by jury shall be preserved, and no fact tried by a jury, shall be otherwise re-examined in any Court of the United States, than according to the rules of the common law.

AMENDMENT VIII

Excessive bail shall not be required, nor excessive fines imposed, nor cruel and unusual punishments inflicted.

AMENDMENT IX

The enumeration in the Constitution, of certain rights, shall not be construed to deny or disparage others retained by the people.

AMENDMENT X

The powers not delegated to the United States by the Constitution, nor prohibited by it to the States, are reserved to the States respectively, or to the people.

AMENDMENT XI
[RATIFIED ON FEBRUARY 7, 1795]

The Judicial power of the United States shall not be construed to extend to any suit in law or equity, commenced or prosecuted against one of the United States by Citizens of another State, or by Citizens or Subjects of any Foreign State.

AMENDMENT XII
[RATIFIED ON JUNE 15, 1804]

The Electors shall meet in their respective states, and vote by ballot for President and Vice-President, one of whom, at least, shall not be an inhabitant of the same state with themselves; they shall name in their ballots the person voted for as President, and in distinct ballots the person voted for as Vice-President, and they shall make distinct lists of all persons voted for as President, and of all persons voted for as Vice-President, and of the number of votes for each, which lists they shall sign and certify, and transmit sealed to the seat of the government of the United States, directed to the President of the Senate;—The President of the Senate shall, in the presence of the Senate and House of Representatives, open all the certificates and the votes shall then be counted;—The person having the greatest number of votes for President, shall be the President, if such number be a majority of the whole number of Electors appointed; and if no person have such majority; then from the persons having the highest numbers not exceeding three on the list of those voted for as President, the House of Representatives shall choose immediately, by ballot, the President. But in choosing the President, the votes shall be taken by states, the representation from each state having one vote; a quorum for this purpose shall consist of a member or members from two-thirds of the states, and a majority of all the states shall be necessary to a choice. And if the House of Representatives shall not choose a President whenever the right of choice shall devolve upon them, before the four th day of March next following, then the Vice-President shall act as President, as in the case of the death or other constitutional disability of the President.—The person having the greatest number of votes as Vice-President, shall be the Vice-President, if such number be a majority of the whole number of Electors appointed, and if no person have a majority, then from the two highest numbers on the list, the Senate shall choose the Vice-President; a quorum for the purpose shall consist of two-thirds of the whole number of Senators, and a majority of the whole number shall be necessary to a choice. But no person constitutionally ineligible to the office of President shall be eligible to that of Vice-President of the United States.

AMENDMENT XIII
[RATIFIED ON DECEMBER 6, 1865]
Section 1

Neither slavery nor involuntary servitude, except as a punishment for crime whereof the party shall have been duly convicted, shall exist within the United States, or any place subject to their jurisdiction.

Section 2

Congress shall have power to enforce this article by appropriate legislation.

AMENDMENT XIV
[RATIFIED ON JULY 9, 1868]
Section 1

All persons born or naturalized in the United States, and subject to the jurisdiction thereof, are citizens of the United States and of the State wherein they reside. No State shall make or enforce any law which shall abridge the privileges or immunities of citizens of the United States; nor shall any State deprive any person of life, liberty, or property, without due process of law; nor deny to any person within its jurisdiction the equal protection of the laws.

Section 2

Representatives shall be apportioned among the several States according to their respective numbers, counting the whole number of persons in each State, excluding Indians not taxed. But when the right to vote at any election for the choice of electors for President and Vice President of the United States, Representatives in Congress, the Executive and Judicial officers of a State, or the members of the Legislature thereof, is denied to any of the male inhabitants of such State, being twenty-one years of age, and citizens of the United States, or in any way abridged, except for participation in rebellion, or other crime, the basis of representation therein shall be reduced in the proportion which the number of such male citizens shall bear to the whole number of male citizens twenty-one years of age in such State.

Section 3

No person shall be a Senator or Representative in Congress, or elector of President and Vice President, or hold any office, civil or military, under the United States, or under any State, who, having previously taken an oath, as a member of Congress, or as an officer of the United States, or as a member of any State legislature, or as an executive or judicial officer of any State, to support the Constitution of the United States, shall have engaged in insurrection or rebellion against the same, or given aid or comfort to the enemies thereof. But Congress may by a vote of two-thirds of each House, remove such disability.

Section 4

The validity of the public debt of the United States, authorized by law, including debts incurred for payment of pensions and bounties for services in suppressing insurrection or rebellion, shall not be questioned. But neither the United States nor any State shall assume or pay any debt or obligation incurred in aid of insurrection or rebellion against the United States, or any claim for the loss or emancipation of any slave, but all such debts, obligations and claims shall be held illegal and void.

Section 5

The Congress shall have power to enforce, by appropriate legislation, the provisions of this article.

AMENDMENT XV
[RATIFIED ON FEBRUARY 3, 1870]

Section 1

The right of citizens of the United States to vote shall not be denied or abridged by the United States or by any State on account of race, color, or previous condition of servitude.

Section 2

The Congress shall have power to enforce this article by appropriate legislation.

AMENDMENT XVI
[RATIFIED ON FEBRUARY 3, 1913]

The Congress shall have power to lay and collect taxes on incomes, from whatever source derived, without apportionment among the several States, and without regard to any census or enumeration.

AMENDMENT XVII
[RATIFIED ON APRIL 8, 1913]

The Senate of the United States shall be composed of two Senators from each State, elected by the people thereof, for six years; and each Senator shall have one vote. The electors in each State shall have the qualifications requisite for electors of the most numerous branch of the State legislatures.

When vacancies happen in the representation of any State in the Senate, the executive authority of such State shall issue writs of election to fill such vacancies: Provided, That the legislature of any State may empower the executive thereof to make temporary appointments until the people fill the vacancies by election as the legislature may direct.

This amendment shall not be so construed as to affect the election or term of any Senator chosen before it becomes valid as part of the Constitution.

AMENDMENT VXIII
[RATIFIED ON JANUARY 16, 1919]

Section 1

After one year from the ratification of this article the manufacture, sale, or transportation of intoxicating liquors within, the importation thereof into, or the exportation thereof from the United States and all territory subject to the jurisdiction thereof for beverage purposes is hereby prohibited.

Section 2

The Congress and the several States shall have concurrent power to enforce this article by appropriate legislation.

Section 3

This article shall be inoperative unless it shall have been ratified as an amendment to the Constitution by the legislatures of the several States, as provided in the Constitution, within seven years from the date of the submission hereof to the States by the Congress.

AMENDMENT XIX
[RATIFIED ON AUGUST 18, 1920]

The right of citizens of the United States to vote shall not be denied or abridged by the United States or by any State on account of sex.

Congress shall have power to enforce this article by appropriate legislation.

AMENDMENT XX
[RATIFIED ON FEBRUARY 6, 1933]

Section 1

The terms of the President and Vice President shall end at noon on the 20th day of January, and the terms of Senators and Representatives at noon on the 3d day of January, of the years in which such terms would have ended if this article had not been ratified; and the terms of their successors shall then begin.

Section 2

The Congress shall assemble at least once in every year, and such meeting shall begin at noon on the 3d day of January, unless they shall by law appoint a different day.

Section 3

If, at the time fixed for the beginning of the term of the President, the President elect shall have died, the Vice President elect shall become President. If a President shall not have been chosen before the time fixed for the beginning of his term, or if the President elect shall have failed to qualify, then the Vice President elect shall act as President until a President shall have qualified; and the Congress may by law provide for the case wherein neither a President elect nor a Vice President elect shall have qualified, declaring who shall then act as President, or the manner in which one who is to act shall be selected, and such person shall act accordingly until a President or Vice President shall have qualified.

Section 4

The Congress may by law provide for the case of the death of any of the persons from whom the House of Representatives may choose a President whenever the rights of choice shall have devolved upon them, and for the case of the death of any of the persons from whom the Senate may choose a Vice President whenever the right of choice shall have devolved upon them.

Section 5

Sections 1 and 2 shall take effect on the 15th day of October following the ratification of this article.

Section 6

This article shall be inoperative unless it shall have been ratified as an amendment to the Constitution by the legislatures of three-fourths of the several States within seven years from the date of its submission.

AMENDMENT XXI
[RATIFIED ON DECEMBER 5, 1933]
Section 1

The eighteenth article of amendment to the Constitution of the United States is hereby repealed.

Section 2

The transportation or importation into any State, Territory, or possession of the United States for delivery or use therein of intoxicating liquors, in violation of the laws thereof, is hereby prohibited.

Section 3

This article shall be inoperative unless it shall have been ratified as an amendment to the Constitution by conventions in the several States, as provided in the Constitution, within seven years from the date of the submission hereof to the States by the Congress.

AMENDMENT XXII
[RATIFIED ON FEBRUARY 27, 1951]

No person shall be elected to the office of the President more than twice, and no person who has held the office of President, or acted as President, for more than two years of a term to which some other person was elected President shall be elected to the office of the President more than once. But this Article shall not apply to any person holding the office of President when this Article was proposed by the Congress, and shall not prevent any person who may be holding the office of President, or acting as President, during the term within which this Article becomes operative from holding the office of President or acting as President during the remainder of such term.

AMENDMENT XXIII
[RATIFIED ON MARCH 29, 1961]

Section 1

The District constituting the seat of Government of the United States shall appoint in such manner as the Congress may direct:

A number of electors of President and Vice President equal to the whole number of Senators and Representatives in Congress to which the District would be entitled if it were a State, but in no event more than the least populous State; they shall be in addition to those appointed by the States, but they shall be considered, for the purposes of the election of President and Vice President, to be electors appointed by a State; and they shall meet in the District and perform such duties as provided by the twelfth article of amendment.

Section 2

The Congress shall have power to enforce this article by appropriate legislation.

AMENDMENT XXIV
[RATIFIED ON JANUARY 23, 1964]

Section 1

The right of citizens of the United States to vote in any primary or other election for President or Vice President, for electors for President or Vice President, or for Senator or Representative in Congress, shall not be denied or abridged by the United States or any State by reason of failure to pay any poll tax or other tax.

Section 2

The Congress shall have power to enforce this article by appropriate legislation.

AMENDMENT XXV
[RATIFIED ON FEBRUARY 10, 1967]

Section 1

In case of the removal of the President from office or of his death or resignation, the Vice President shall become President.

Section 2

Whenever there is a vacancy in the office of the Vice President, the President shall nominate a Vice President who shall take office upon confirmation by a majority vote of both Houses of Congress.

Section 3

Whenever the President transmits to the President pro tempore of the Senate and the Speaker of the House of Representatives his written declaration that he is unable to discharge the powers and duties of his office, and until he transmits to them a written declaration to the contrary, such powers and duties shall be discharged by the Vice President as Acting President.

Section 4

Whenever the Vice President and a majority of either the principal officers of the executive departments or of such other body as Congress may by law provide, transmit to the President pro tempore of the Senate and the Speaker of the House of Representatives their written declaration that the President is unable to discharge the powers and duties of his office, the Vice President shall immediately assume the powers and duties of the office as Acting President.

Thereafter, when the President transmits to the President pro tempore of the Senate and the Speaker of the House of Representatives his written declaration that no inability exists, he shall resume the powers and duties of his office unless the Vice President and a majority of either the principal officers of the executive department or of such other body as Congress may by law provide, transmit within four days to the President pro tempore of the Senate and the Speaker of the House of Representatives their written declaration that the President is unable to discharge the powers and duties of his office. Thereupon Congress shall decide the issue, assembling within forty-eight hours for that purpose if not in session. If the Congress, within twenty-one days after receipt of the latter written declaration, or, if Congress is not in session, within twenty-one days after Congress is required to assemble, determines by two-thirds vote of both Houses that the President is unable to discharge the powers and duties of his office, the Vice President shall continue to discharge the same as Acting President; otherwise, the President shall resume the powers and duties of his office.

AMENDMENT XXVI
[RATIFIED ON JULY 1, 1971]

Section 1

The right of citizens of the United States, who are eighteen years of age or older, to vote shall not be denied or abridged by the United States or by any State on account of age.

Section 2

The Congress shall have power to enforce this article by appropriate legislation.

Amendment XXVII
[Ratified on May 7, 1992]

No law varying the compensation for the services of Senators and Representatives shall take effect until an election of Representatives shall have intervened.

The Federalist No. 10
November 22, 1787
James Madison

TO THE PEOPLE OF THE STATE OF NEW YORK.

Among the numerous advantages promised by a well constructed Union, none deserves to be more accurately developed than its tendency to break and control the violence of faction. The friend of popular governments, never finds himself so much alarmed for their character and fate, as when he contemplates their propensity to this dangerous vice. He will not fail therefore to set a due value on any plan which, without violating the principles to which he is attached, provides a proper cure for it. The instability, injustice and confusion introduced into the public councils, have in truth been the mortal diseases under which popular governments have every where perished; as they continue to be the favorite and fruitful topics from which the adversaries to liberty derive their most specious declamations. The valuable improvements made by the American Constitutions on the popular models, both ancient and modern, cannot certainly be too much admired; but it would be an unwarrantable partiality, to contend that they have as effectually obviated the danger on this side as was wished and expected. Complaints are every where heard from our most considerate and virtuous citizens, equally the friends of public and private faith, and of public and personal liberty; that our governments are too unstable; that the public good is disregarded in the conflicts of rival parties; and that measures are too often decided, not according to the rules of justice, and the rights of the minor party; but by the superior force of an interested and over-bearing majority. However anxiously we may wish that these complaints had no foundation, the evidence of known facts will not permit us to deny that they are in some degree true. It will be found indeed, on a candid review of our situation, that some of the distresses under which we labor, have been erroneously charged on the operation of our governments; but it will be found, at the same time, that other causes will not alone account for many of our heaviest misfortunes; and particularly, for that prevailing and increasing distrust of public engagements, and alarm for private rights, which are echoed from one end of the continent to the other. These must be chiefly, if not wholly, effects of the unsteadiness and injustice, with which a factious spirit has tainted our public administrations.

By a faction I understand a number of citizens, whether amounting to a majority or minority of the whole, who are united and actuated by some common impulse of passion, or of interest, adverse to the rights of other citizens, or to the permanent and aggregate interests of the community.

There are two methods of curing the mischiefs of faction: the one, by removing its causes; the other, by controlling its effects.

There are again two methods of removing the causes of faction: the one by destroying the liberty which is essential to its existence; the other, by giving to every citizen the same opinions, the same passions, and the same interests.

It could never be more truly said than of the first remedy, that it is worse than the disease. Liberty is to faction, what air is to fire, an aliment without which it instantly expires. But it could not be a less folly to abolish liberty, which is essential to political life, because it nourishes faction, than it would be to wish the annihilation of air, which is essential to animal life, because it imparts to fire its destructive agency.

The second expedient is as impracticable, as the first would be unwise. As long as the reason of man continues fallible, and he is at liberty to exercise it, different opinions will be formed. As long as the connection subsists between his reason and his self-love, his opinions and his passions will have a reciprocal influence on each other; and the former will be objects to which the latter will attach themselves. The diversity in the faculties of men from which the rights of property originate, is not less an insuperable obstacle to a uniformity of interests. The protection of these faculties is the first object of Government. From the protection of different and unequal faculties of acquiring property, the possession of different degrees and kinds of property immediately results: and from the influence of these on the sentiments and views of the respective proprietors, ensues a division of the society into different interests and parties.

The latent causes of faction are thus sown in the nature of man; and we see them every where brought into different degrees of activity, according to the different circumstances of civil society. A zeal for different opinions concerning religion, concerning Government and many other points, as well of speculation as of practice; an attachment to different leaders ambitiously contending for pre-eminence and power; or to persons of other descriptions whose fortunes have been interesting to the human passions, have in turn divided mankind into parties, inflamed them with mutual animosity, and rendered them much more disposed to vex and oppress each other, than to cooperate for their common good. So strong is this propensity of mankind to fall into mutual animosities, that where no substantial occasion presents itself, the most frivolous and fanciful distinctions have been sufficient to kindle their unfriendly passions, and excite their most violent conflicts. But the most common and durable source of factions, has been the various and unequal distribution of property. Those who hold, and those who are without property, have ever formed distinct interests in society. Those who are creditors, and those who are debtors, fall under a like discrimination. A landed interest, a manufacturing interest, a mercantile interest, a monied interest, with many lesser interests, grow up of necessity in civilized nations, and divide them into different classes, actuated by different sentiments and views. The regulation of these various and interfering interests forms the principal task of modern Legislation, and involves the spirit of party and faction in the necessary and ordinary operations of Government.

No man is allowed to be a judge in his own cause; because his interest would certainly bias his judgment, and, not improbably, corrupt his integrity. With equal, nay with greater reason, a body of men, are unfit to be both judges and parties, at the same time; yet, what are many of the most important acts of legislation, but so many judicial determinations, not indeed concerning the rights of single persons, but concerning the rights of large bodies of citizens, and what are the different classes of legislators, but advocates and parties to the causes which they determine? Is a law proposed concerning private debts? It is a question to which the creditors are parties on one side, and the debtors on the other. Justice ought to hold the balance between them. Yet the parties are and must be themselves the judges; and the most numerous party, or, in other words, the most powerful faction must be expected to prevail. Shall domestic manufactures be encouraged, and in what degree, by restrictions on foreign manufactures? are questions which would be differently decided by the landed and the manufacturing classes; and probably by neither, with a sole regard to justice and the public good. The apportionment of taxes on the various descriptions of property, is an act which seems to require the most exact impartiality; yet, there is perhaps no legislative act in which greater opportunity and temptation are given to a predominant party, to trample on the rules of justice. Every shilling with which they over-burden the inferior number, is a shilling saved to their own pockets.

It is in vain to say, that enlightened statesmen will be able to adjust these clashing interests, and render them all subservient to the public good. Enlightened statesmen will not always be at the helm: Nor, in many cases, can such an adjustment be made at all, without taking into view indirect and remote considerations, which will rarely prevail over the immediate interest which one party may find in disregarding the rights of another, or the good of the whole.

The inference to which we are brought, is, that the causes of faction cannot be removed; and that relief is only to be sought in the means of controlling its effects.

If a faction consists of less than a majority, relief is supplied by the republican principle, which enables the majority to defeat its sinister views by regular vote: It may clog the administration, it may convulse the society; but it will be unable to execute and mask its violence under the forms of the Constitution. When a majority is included in a faction, the form of popular government on the other hand enables it to sacrifice to its ruling passion or interest, both the public good and the rights of other citizens. To secure the public good, and private rights, against the danger of such a faction, and at the same time to preserve the spirit and the form of popular government, is then the great object to which our enquiries are directed: Let me add that it is the great desideratum, by which alone this form of government can be rescued from the opprobrium under which it has so long labored, and be recommended to the esteem and adoption of mankind.

By what means is this object attainable? Evidently by one of two only. Either the existence of the same passion or interest in a majority at the same time, must be prevented; or the majority, having such co-existent passion or interest, must be rendered, by their number and local situation, unable to concert and carry into effect schemes of oppression. If the impulse and the opportunity be suffered to coincide, we well know that neither moral nor religious motives can be relied on as an adequate control. They are not found to be such on the injustice and violence of individuals, and lose their efficacy in proportion to the number combined together; that is, in proportion as their efficacy becomes needful.

From this view of the subject, it may be concluded, that a pure Democracy, by which I mean, a Society, consisting of a small number of citizens, who assemble and administer the Government in person, can admit of no cure for the mischiefs of faction. A common passion or interest will, in almost every case, be felt by a majority of the whole; a communication and concert results from the form of Government itself; and there is nothing to check the inducements to sacrifice the weaker party, or an obnoxious individual. Hence it is, that such Democracies have ever been spectacles of turbulence and contention; have ever been found incompatible with personal security, or the rights of property; and have in general been as short in their lives, as they have been violent in their deaths. Theoretic politicians, who have patronized this species of Government, have erroneously supposed, that by reducing mankind to a perfect equality in their political rights, they would, at the same time, be perfectly equalized and assimilated in their possessions, their opinions, and their passions.

A republic, by which I mean a government in which the scheme of representation takes place, opens a different prospect, and promises the cure for which we are seeking. Let us examine the points in which it varies from pure democracy, and we shall comprehend both the nature of the cure and the efficacy which it must derive from the union.

The two great points of difference, between a democracy and a republic, are, first, the delegation of the government, in the latter, to a small number of citizens, elected by the rest; secondly, the greater number of citizens, and greater sphere of country, over which the latter may be extended.

The effect of the first difference is, on the one hand, to refine and enlarge the public views, by passing them through the medium of a chosen body of citizens, whose wisdom may best discern the true interest of their country, and whose patriotism and love of justice, will be least likely to sacrifice it to temporary or partial considerations. Under such a regulation, it may well happen, that the public voice, pronounced by the representatives of the people, will be more consonant to the public good, than if pronounced by the people themselves, convened for the purpose. On the other hand the effect may be inverted. Men of factious tempers, of local prejudices, or of sinister designs, may by intrigue, by corruption, or by other means, first obtain the suffrages, and then betray the interest of the people. The question resulting is, whether small or extensive republics are most favorable to the election of proper guardians of the public weal, and it is clearly decided in favor of the latter by two obvious considerations.

In the first place, it is to be remarked that, however small the republic may be, the representatives must be raised to a certain number, in order to guard against the cabals of a few; and that however large it may be, they must be limited to a certain number, in order to guard against the confusion of a multitude. Hence, the number of representatives in the two cases not being in proportion to that of the constituents, and being proportionally greatest in the small republic, it follows, that if the proportion of fit characters be not less in the large than in the small republic, the former will present a greater option, and consequently a greater probability of a fit choice.

In the next place, as each Representative will be chosen by a greater number of citizens in the large than in the small Republic, it will be more difficult for unworthy candidates to practise with success the vicious arts, by which elections are too often carried; and the suffrages of the people being more free, will be more likely to center on men who possess the most attractive merit, and the most diffusive and established characters.

It must be confessed, that in this, as in most other cases, there is a mean, on both sides of which inconveniences will be found to lie. By enlarging too much the number of electors, you render the representatives too little acquainted with all their local circumstances and lesser interests; as by reducing it too much, you render him unduly attached to these, and too little fit to comprehend and pursue great and national objects. The Federal Constitution forms a happy combination in this respect; the great and aggregate interests being referred to the national, the local and particular, to the state legislatures.

The other point of difference is, the greater number of citizens and extent of territory which may be brought within the compass of Republican, than of Democratic Government; and it is this circumstance principally which renders factious combinations less to be dreaded in the former, than in the latter. The smaller the society, the fewer probably will be the distinct parties and interests composing it; the fewer the distinct parties and interests, the more frequently will a majority be found of the same party; and the smaller the number of individuals composing a majority, and the smaller the compass within which they are placed, the more easily will they concert and execute their plans of oppression. Extend the sphere, and you take in a greater variety of parties and interests; you make it less probable that a majority of the whole will have a common motive to invade the rights of other citizens; or if such a common motive exists, it will be more difficult for all who feel it to discover their own strength, and to act in unison with each other. Besides other impediments, it may be remarked, that where there is a consciousness of unjust or dishonorable purposes, communication is always checked by distrust, in proportion to the number whose concurrence is necessary.

Hence it clearly appears, that the same advantage, which a Republic has over a Democracy, in controlling the effects of faction, is enjoyed by a large over a small Republic—is enjoyed by the Union over the States composing it. Does this advantage consist in the substitution of Representatives, whose enlightened views and virtuous sentiments render them superior to local prejudices, and to schemes of injustice? It will not be denied, that the Representation of the Union will be most likely to possess these requisite endowments. Does it consist in the greater security afforded by a greater variety of parties, against the event of any one party being able to outnumber and oppress the rest? In an equal degree does the increased variety of parties, comprised within the Union, increase this security? Does it, in fine, consist in the greater obstacles opposed to the concert and accomplishment of the secret wishes of an unjust and interested majority? Here, again, the extent of the Union gives it the most palpable advantage.

The influence of factious leaders may kindle a flame within their particular States, but will be unable to spread a general conflagration through the other States: a religious sect, may degenerate into a political faction in a part of the Confederacy but the variety of sects dispersed over the entire face of it, must secure the national Councils against any danger from that source: a rage for paper money, for an abolition of debts, for an equal division of property, or for any other improper or wicked project, will be less apt to pervade the whole body of the Union, than a particular member of it; in the same proportion as such a malady is more likely to taint a particular county or district, than an entire State.

In the extent and proper structure of the Union, therefore, we behold a Republican remedy for the diseases most incident to Republican Government. And according to the degree of pleasure and pride, we feel in being Republicans, ought to be our zeal in cherishing the spirit, and supporting the character of Federalists.

PUBLIUS

The Federalist No. 51
February 6, 1788
James Madison

TO THE PEOPLE OF THE STATE OF NEW YORK.

To what expedient then shall we finally resort for maintaining in practice the necessary partition of power among the several departments, as laid down in the constitution? The only answer that can be given is, that as all these exterior provisions are found to be inadequate, the defect must be supplied, by so contriving the interior structure of the government, as that its several constituent parts may, by their mutual relations, be the means of keeping each other in their proper places. Without presuming to undertake a full development of this important idea, I will hazard a few general observations, which may perhaps place it in a clearer light, and enable us to form a more correct judgment of the principles and structure of the government planned by the convention.

In order to lay a due foundation for that separate and distinct exercise of the different powers of government, which to a certain extent, is admitted on all hands to be essential to the preservation of liberty, it is evident that each department should have a will of its own; and consequently should be so constituted, that the members of each should have as little agency as possible in the appointment of the members of the others. Were this principle rigorously adhered to, it would require that all the appointments for the supreme executive, legislative, and judiciary magistracies, should be drawn from the same fountain of authority, the people, through channels, having no communication whatever with one another. Perhaps such a plan of constructing the several departments would be less difficult in practice than it may in contemplation appear. Some difficulties however, and some additional expense, would attend the execution of it. Some deviations therefore from the principle must be admitted. In the constitution of the judiciary department in particular, it might be inexpedient to insist rigorously on the principle; first, because peculiar qualifications being essential in the members, the primary consideration ought to be to select that mode of choice, which best secures these qualifications; secondly, because the permanent tenure by which the appointments are held in that department, must soon destroy all sense of dependence on the authority conferring them.

It is equally evident that the members of each department should be as little dependent as possible on those of the others, for the emoluments annexed to their offices. Were the executive magistrate, or the judges, not independent of the legislature in this particular, their independence in every other would be merely nominal.

But the great security against a gradual concentration of the several powers in the same department, consists in giving to those who administer each department, the necessary constitutional means, and personal motives, to resist encroachments of the others. The provision for defense must in this, as in all other cases, be made commensurate to the danger of attack. Ambition must be made to counteract ambition. The interest of the man must be connected with the constitutional right of the place. It may be a reflection on human nature, that such devices should be necessary to control the abuses of government. But what is government itself but the greatest of all reflections on human nature? If men were angels, no government would be necessary. If angels were to govern men, neither external nor internal controls on government would be necessary. In framing a government which is to be administered by men over men, the great difficulty lies in this: You must first enable the government to control the governed; and in the next place, oblige it to control itself. A dependence on the people is no doubt the primary control on the government; but experience has taught mankind the necessity of auxiliary precautions.

This policy of supplying by opposite and rival interests, the defect of better motives, might be traced through the whole system of human affairs, private as well as public. We see it particularly displayed in all the subordinate distributions of power; where the constant aim is to divide and arrange the several offices in such a manner as that each may be a check on the other; that the private interest of every individual, may be a sentinel over the public rights. These inventions of prudence cannot be less requisite in the distribution of the supreme powers of the state.

But it is not possible to give to each department an equal power of self defense. In republican government the legislative authority, necessarily, predominates. The remedy for this inconveniency is, to divide the legislature into different branches; and to render them by different modes of election, and different principles of action, as little connected with each other, as the nature of their common functions, and their common dependence on the society, will admit. It may even be necessary to guard against dangerous encroachments by still further precautions. As the weight of the legislative authority requires that it should be thus divided, the weakness of the executive may require, on the other hand, that it should be fortified. An absolute negative, on the legislature, appears at first view to be the natural defense with which the executive magistrate should be armed. But perhaps it would be neither altogether safe, nor alone sufficient. On ordinary occasions, it might not be exerted with the requisite firmness; and on extraordinary occasions, it might be perfidiously abused. May not this defect of an absolute negative be supplied, by some qualified connection between this weaker department, and the weaker branch of the stronger department, by which the latter may be led to support the constitutional rights of the former, without being too much detached from the rights of its own department?

If the principles on which these observations are founded be just, as I persuade myself they are, and they be applied as a criterion, to the several state constitutions, and to the federal constitution, it will be found, that if the latter does not perfectly correspond with them, the former are infinitely less able to bear such a test.

There are moreover two considerations particularly applicable to the federal system of America, which place that system in a very interesting point of view.

First. In a single republic, all the power surrendered by the people, is submitted to the administration of a single government; and usurpations are guarded against by a division of the government into distinct and separate departments. In the compound republic of America, the power surrendered by the people, is first divided between two distinct governments, and then the portion allotted to each, subdivided among distinct and separate departments. Hence a double security arises to the rights of the people. The different governments will control each other; at the same time that each will be controlled by itself.

Second. It is of great importance in a republic, not only to guard the society against the oppression of its rulers; but to guard one part of the society against the injustice of the other part. Different interests necessarily exist in different classes of citizens. If a majority be united by a common interest, the rights of the minority will be insecure. There are but two methods of providing against this evil: The one by creating a will in the community independent of the majority, that is, of the society itself, the other by comprehending in the society so many separate descriptions of citizens, as will render an unjust combination of a majority of the whole, very improbable, if not impracticable. The first method prevails in all governments possessing an hereditary or self appointed authority. This at best is but a precarious security; because a power independent of the society may as well espouse the unjust views of the major, as the rightful interests, of the minor party, and may possibly be turned against both parties. The second method will be exemplified in the federal republic of the United States. While all authority in it will be derived from and dependent on the society, the society itself will be broken into so many parts, interests and classes of citizens, that the rights of individuals or of the minority, will be in little danger from interested combinations of the majority. In a free government, the security for civil rights must be the same as for religious rights. It consists in the one case in the multiplicity of interests, and in the other, in the multiplicity of sects. The degree of security in both cases will depend on the number of interests and sects; and this may be presumed to depend on the extent of country and number of people comprehended under the same government. This view of the subject must particularly recommend a proper federal system to all the sincere and considerate friends of republican government: Since it shows that in exact proportion as the territory of the union may be formed into more circumscribed confederacies or states, oppressive combinations of a majority will be facilitated, the best security under the republican form, for the rights of every class of citizens, will be diminished; and consequently, the stability and independence of some member of the government, the only other security, must be proportionally increased. Justice is the end of government. It is the end of civil society. It ever has been, and ever will be pursued, until it be obtained, or until liberty be lost in the pursuit. In a society under the forms of which the stronger faction can readily unite and oppress the weaker, anarchy may as truly be said to reign, as in a state of nature where the weaker individual is not secured against the violence of the stronger: And as in the latter state even the stronger individuals are prompted by the uncertainty of their condition, to submit to a government which may protect the weak as well as themselves: So in the former state, will the more powerful factions or parties be gradually induced by a like motive, to wish for a government which will protect all parties, the weaker as well as the more powerful. It can be little doubted, that if the state of Rhode Island was separated from the confederacy, and left to itself, the insecurity of rights under the popular form of government within such narrow limits, would be displayed by such reiterated oppressions of factious majorities, that some power altogether independent of the people would soon be called for by the voice of the very factions whose misrule had proved the necessity of it. In the extended republic of the United States, and among the great variety of interests, parties and sects which it embraces, a coalition of a majority of the whole society could seldom take place on any other principles than those of justice and the general good; and there being thus less danger to a minor from the will of the major party, there must be less pretext also, to provide for the security of the former, by introducing into the government a will not dependent on the latter; or in other words, a will independent of the society itself. It is no less certain than it is important, notwithstanding the contrary opinions which have been entertained, that the larger the society, provided it lie within a practicable sphere, the more duly capable it will be of self government. And happily for the republican cause, the practicable sphere may be carried to a very great extent, by a judicious modification and mixture of the federal principle.

PUBLIUS

Presidents of the United States

PRESIDENT	YEAR	PARTY	MOST NOTEWORTHY EVENT
George Washington	1789–1797	Federalist	Establishment of Federal Judiciary
John Adams	1797–1801	Federalist	Alien-Sedition Acts
Thomas Jefferson	1801–1809	Dem.-Republican	First President to Defeat Incumbent/Louisiana Purchase
James Madison	1809–1817	Dem.-Republican	War of 1812
James Monroe	1817–1825	Dem.-Republican	Monroe Doctrine/ Missouri Compromise
John Quincy Adams	1825–1829	Dem.-Republican	Elected by "King Caucus"
Andrew Jackson	1829–1837	Democratic	Set up Spoils System
Martin Van Buren	1837–1841	Democratic	Competitive Parties Established
William H. Harrison	1841	Whig	Universal White Male Suffrage
John Tyler	1841–1845	Whig	Texas Annexed
James K. Polk	1845–1849	Democratic	Mexican-American War
Zachary Taylor	1849–1850	Whig	California Gold Rush
Millard Fillmore	1850–1853	Whig	Compromise of 1850
Franklin Pierce	1853–1857	Democratic	Republican Party Formed
James Buchanan	1857–1861	Democratic	Dred Scott Decision
Abraham Lincoln	1861–1865	Republican	Civil War
Andrew Johnson	1865–1869	Dem. (Unionist)	First Impeachment of President
Ulysses S. Grant	1869–1877	Republican	Reconstruction of South
Rutherford B. Hayes	1877–1881	Republican	End of Reconstruction
James A. Garfield	1881	Republican	Assassinated by Job-seeker
Chester A. Arthur	1881–1885	Republican	Civil Service Reform
Grover Cleveland	1885–1889	Democratic	Casts 102 Vetoes in One Year
Benjamin Harrison	1889–1893	Republican	McKinley Law Raises Tarrifs
Grover Cleveland	1893–1897	Democratic	Depression/Pullman Strike

(continued)

Presidents of the United States
(continued)

PRESIDENT	YEAR	PARTY	MOST NOTEWORTHY EVENT
William McKinley	1897–1901	Republican	Spanish-American War
Theodore Roosevelt	1901–1909	Republican	Conservation/Panama Canal
William H. Taft	1909–1913	Republican	Judicial Reform
Woodrow Wilson	1913–1921	Democratic	Progressive Reforms/World War I
Warren G. Harding	1921–1923	Republican	Return to Normalcy
Calvin Coolidge	1923–1929	Republican	Cuts Taxes/Promotes Business
Herbert C. Hoover	1929–1933	Republican	Great Depression
Franklin D. Roosevelt	1933–1945	Democratic	New Deal/World War II
Harry S. Truman	1945–1953	Democratic	Beginning of Cold War
Dwight D. Eisenhower	1953–1961	Republican	End of Korean War
John F. Kennedy	1961–1963	Democratic	Cuban Missile Crisis
Lyndon B. Johnson	1963–1969	Democratic	Great Society/Vietnam War
Richard M. Nixon	1969–1974	Republican	Watergate Scandal
Gerald R. Ford	1974–1977	Republican	War Powers Resolution
James Earl Carter	1977–1981	Democratic	Iranian Hostage Crisis
Ronald Reagan	1981–1989	Republican	Tax Cut/ Expenditure Cuts
George Bush	1989–1993	Republican	End of Cold War/Persian Gulf War
William J. Clinton	1993–2001	Democratic	Deficit Reduction

NOTE: Refer to www.ablongman.com/fiorina

GLOSSARY

A

affirmative action   Programs designed to enhance opportunities for groups that have suffered discrimination in the past. (Chapter 14)

agenda setting   Occurs when the media affect the issues and problems people think about. (Chapter 5)

Aid to Families with Dependent Children (AFDC)   Public assistance program established in 1935 as part of the Social Security Act and replaced in 1996. (Chapter 15)

ambassador   The head of a diplomatic delegation to a major foreign country. (Chapter 11)

Anti-Federalists   Those who opposed ratification of the Constitution. (Chapter 2)

appropriations process   Process of providing funding for governmental activities and programs that have been authorized. (Chapter 9)

Articles of Confederation   The "league of friendship" under which the American colonies operated during and immediately after the Revolutionary War, until ratification of the U.S. Constitution in 1789. (Chapter 2)

authorization process   Term given to the process of providing statutory authority for a government program activity; does not provide funding for the project. (Chapter 9)

B

balancing doctrine   The principle enunciated by the courts that freedom of speech must be balanced against other competing public interests. (Chapter 13)

Bay of Pigs   Location of CIA-supported effort by Cuban exiles in 1961 to invade Cuba and overthrow Fidel Castro. (Chapter 11)

beltway insider   Person living in the Washington metropolitan area who is engaged in, or well informed about, national politics and government. (Chapter 10)

bicameral   A legislature that contains two chambers. (Chapter 9)

Bill of Rights   The first ten amendments to the U.S. Constitution. Promised by the framers to overcome resistance to the new Constitution, and compiled by James Madison, they list some of the most important civil liberties protected in the United States. (Chapter 2)

block grant   Federal grant to a state and/or local government that imposes minimal restrictions on the use of funds. (Chapter 3)

brief   Written arguments presented to a court by lawyers on behalf of clients. (Chapters 11, 12)

Brown v. Board of Education of Topeka, Kansas   Supreme Court decision (1954) declaring racial segregation in schools unconstitutional. (Chapter 14)

bully pulpit   A description of the presidency emphasizing opportunities to preach to voters on behalf of good policy. (Chapter 10)

bureaucracy   Hierarchical organization designed to perform a particular set of tasks. (Chapter 11)

Bush Doctrine   The aggressive foreign policy stance outlined by President George W. Bush after terrorists struck the United States in 2001, which declared as enemies countries who harbor terrorists or promote terrorism. (Chapter 15)

business cycle   The alternation of periods of economic growth with periods of economic slowdown. (Chapter 15)

C

Cabinet   Top administration officials; mostly heads of executive branch departments. (Chapter 10)

categorical grant   Federal grant to a state and/or local government that imposes programmatic restrictions on the use of funds. (Chapter 3)

caucus   Either a meeting to choose delegates to a state or national convention or a collection of like-minded legislators. (Chapters 7, 9)

checks and balances   Limits that one branch of government places on another because they have different interests, preventing an abuse of power. (Chapter 1)

chief of staff   Head of White House staff usually in continuous contact with the president. (Chapter 10)

circuit court of appeals   Court to which decisions by federal district courts are appealed. (Chapters 11, 12)

civic republicanism   A political philosophy that emphasizes the obligation of citizens to act virtuously in pursuit of the common good. (Chapter 4)

civil code   Laws regulating relations among individuals. Alleged violators are sued by presumed victims, who ask courts to award damages and otherwise offer relief. (Chapters 11, 12)

civil disobedience   A peaceful violation of law designed to dramatize injustice. (Chapter 14)

civil liberties   Fundamental freedoms that protect a people from their government. (Chapter 13)

civil rights   Guarantees to equal treatment under the law. (Chapter 14)

civil rights amendments   The Thirteenth, Fourteenth, and Fifteenth Amendments to the U.S. Constitution, designed to abolish slavery and secure rights for freemen. (Chapter 13)

civil service   A system that protects government employees from losing their jobs when elected offices change hands. (Chapter 11)

class action suit   Suit brought on behalf of all individuals in a particular category, whether or not they are actually participating in the suit. (Chapters 11, 12)

classical liberalism   A belief in freedom, individualism, equality, and small government that characterized many, if not most, of the nation's founders. It grew from the social, political, and religious changes of the Enlightenment period. (Chapter 4)

clear and present danger doctrine   The principle that people should have freedom of speech unless their language poses a direct threat that lawmakers have the authority to prevent. (Chapter 13)

closed primaries   Primaries in which only party members can vote—and vote only in the party in which they are registered. (Chapter 7)

cloture   Motion to end debate; requires 60 votes to pass. (Chapter 9)

coattails   Positive electoral effect of a popular presidential candidate on congressional candidates of the party. (Chapter 7)

coercion test   Alternative to the Lemon test preferred by conservative judges defining a religious establishment as an instance when government coerces citizens into following religious practices or punishes those who do not. (Chapter 13)

Cold War   The 43-year period (1946–1989) during which the United States and the Soviet Union threatened one another with mutual destruction. (Chapter 11)

commerce clause   Constitutional provision that gives Congress power to regulate commerce "among the states." (Chapter 3)

communitarianism   A modern revival of the civic republican tradition that characterized some of the nation's founders. It defines freedom not as individual rights and liberties, but as the rights of a community's members to seek the good life using political institutions. (Chapter 4)

compositional effect   A change in the behavior of a group that arises from a change in membership rather than a change in the behavior of individuals in the group. (Chapter 6)

concurring opinion   A written opinion prepared by judges who vote with the majority but who wish to disagree with or elaborate on some aspect of the majority opinion. (Chapters 11, 12)

conference committee   Group of representatives from both the House and the Senate who iron out the differences between the two chambers' versions of a bill or resolution. (Chapter 9)

Connecticut Compromise   The Constitutional Convention's plan to resolve conflicts over the scheme of representation that should appear in the U.S. Constitution. Gave each state equal representation in the Senate and representation in the House of Representative based on a state's population size. (Chapter 2)

constituency   Those legally entitled to vote for a public official. (Chapter 1)

constituency service   The work a member of Congress performs to win federal funds for the state or district and to help constituents deal with federal agencies. (Chapter 9)

containment   U.S. policy that attempted to stop the spread of communism in the expectation that this system of government would eventually collapse on its own. (Chapter 11)

conservatism   A word that differs in meaning depending on the time and place, but in modern America it generally refers to those who prefer to (1) limit government activity in economic affairs, (2) use government to promote morality, (3) allow states wide latitude in shaping social policies, and (4) use foreign policy aggressively to promote national-security interests. (Chapter 4)

constituents   The voters that an elected official represents before the government, who as a group are often called the representative's "constituency." May refer to everyone who constitutes an elected official's jurisdiction rather than only those who actually voted. (Chapter 5)

cooperative federalism   *See marble-cake federalism.*

criminal code   Laws regulating relations between individuals and society. Alleged violators are prosecuted by government. (Chapters 11, 12)

critical election   Election that marks the emergence of a new, lasting alignment of partisan support within the electorate. (Chapter 8)

D

Declaration of Independence   Document signed in 1776 declaring the United States to be a country independent of Great Britain. (Chapter 2)

de facto **segregation**   Segregation that occurs as the result of private decisions. (Chapter 14)

defendant   One accused of violating the civil or criminal code. (Chapters 11, 12)

de jure **segregation**   Segregation that is legally sanctioned. (Chapter 14)

democracy   System in which governmental power is widely shared. (Chapter 1)

department   Organizational unit into which many federal agencies are grouped. (Chapter 11)

devolution   Return of governmental responsibilities to states and localities. (Chapter 3)

direct democracy   System in which ordinary people make all the laws themselves. (Chapter 1)

direct mail   Computer-generated letters, faxes, and other communications to people who might be sympathetic to an appeal for money or support. (Chapter 8)

dissenting opinion   Written opinion presenting the reasoning of judges who vote against the majority. (Chapter 12)

distributive theory   Theory predicting that a legislature's members will serve on the committees most important for delivering benefits to their constituents. (Chapter 9)

district attorney   Person responsible for prosecuting criminal cases. (Chapter 12)

divided government   Said to exist when no single party controls the presidency and both houses of Congress. (Chapter 8)

divine right   Doctrine that says God selects the sovereign for the people. (Chapter 2)

double jeopardy   Fifth Amendment provision that prohibits prosecution for the same offense twice. (Chapters 12, 13)

dual sovereignty   A theory of federalism by which both the national and state governments have final authority over their own policy domains. (Chapter 3)

due process clause   Clause found in the Fifth and Fourteenth Amendments to the Constitution that forbids deprivation of life, liberty, or property without due process of law. (Chapter 13)

E

Earned Income Tax Credit (EITC)   Provision that returns tax payments to those who have little income. (Chapter 15)

elastic clause   An alternate name for the U.S. Constitution's "necessary and proper clause" that stresses how flexibly courts have interpreted the language to reconcile it with congressional activities. (Chapter 3)

Electoral College   The formal name for the electors selected by each U.S. state during presidential elections to cast the state's official "electoral votes." Presidential candidates must win a majority in the Electoral College or the election goes to the U.S. House of Representatives. (Chapter 2)

electoral incentive   Desire to obtain or retain elected office. (Chapter 1)

electoral vote   Votes cast for a presidential candidate, with each state receiving one vote for each of its members of the House of Representatives and one vote for each of its senators. (Chapter 7)

embassy   The structure that houses ambassadors and their diplomatic aides in the capital cities of many foreign countries. (Chapter 11)

equal protection clause   Fourteenth Amendment clause specifying that no state can deny any of its people equal protection under the law. (Chapter 14)

Equal Rights Amendment (ERA)   Failed constitutional amendment to ban gender discrimination. (Chapter 14)

equal-time rule   Promulgated by the FCC, rule that required any station selling time to a candidate to sell time to other candidates at comparable rates. (Chapter 11)

establishment clause   Clause that denies government the power to favor religion or to establish any single religious practice as superior. (Chapter 13)

exclusionary rule   The rule that evidence obtained improperly may not be introduced in a trial. (Chapter 13)

executive agreement   Agreement with foreign countries that requires only a presidential signature. (Chapter 10)

Executive Office of the President (EOP)   Agency that houses both top coordinating offices closely connected to the president; contains the White House office. (Chapter 10)

executive order   A presidential directive that has the force of law. (Chapter 10)

executive privilege   The right of members of the executive branch to have private communications among themselves that need not be shared with Congress. (Chapter 10)

F

fairness doctrine   Promulgated by the FCC, policy that required stations to carry some public affairs programming and to balance the points of view expressed. (Chapter 11)

federal district courts   The lowest level of the federal court system and the courts in which most federal trials are held. (Chapter 12)

Federal Reserve System   The country's central bank, which executes monetary policy by manipulating the supply of funds that lower banks can lend. (Chapter 11)

federalism   Division of sovereignty between at least two different levels of government. (Chapter 3)

Federalist Papers   Essays that were written in support of the Constitution's ratification and have become a classic argument for the American constitutional system. (Chapter 2)

Federalists   Those who campaigned on behalf of the Constitution. (Chapter 2)

filibuster   Delaying tactic by which senators refuse to allow legislation to be considered, usually by speaking indefinitely. (Chapter 9)

filing deadline   The latest date on which a candidate for office may file official papers or pay required fees to state election officials. (Chapter 7)

fiscal policy   The sum total of government taxing and spending decisions. (Chapter 15)

floor   Term for an entire congressional chamber; usually used when bills have left committee and moved to a vote of the full membership. (Chapter 9)

food stamps   Public assistance program providing recipients with stamps that can be used to purchase food. (Chapter 15)

foreign service   Diplomats who staff U.S. embassies and consulates. (Chapter 11)

framing   Stating of an argument in such a way as to emphasize one set of considerations and deemphasize others. (Chapters 5, 12)

franchise   The right to vote. (Chapter 6)

frank   Free mailing privileges enjoyed by members of Congress when communicating with constituents. (Chapter 9)

free exercise clause   Clause that protects the right of individuals to practice their religion. (Chapter 13)

free-rider problem   Barrier to collective action that arises when people can enjoy the benefits of group activity without contributing their limited share of the costs. (Chapter 8)

fundamental freedoms doctrine (preferred freedoms doctrine)   Court doctrine stating that some liberties are fundamental to the preservation of democratic practice—the freedoms of speech, press, assembly, and religion—are to be scrutinized by the courts more closely than other legislation. (Chapter 13)

G

general election   Final election that selects the office holder. (Chapter 1)

gerrymandering   Drawing of boundary lines of congressional districts in order to confer an advantage on some partisan or political interest. (Chapter 7)

government corporation   Independent organization created by Congress to fulfill functions related to business. (Chapter 11)

grandfather clause   Racially restrictive provision of certain southern laws after Reconstruction permitting a man to vote if his grandfather could have voted. (Chapter 14)

H

Hatch Act   Law enacted in 1939 prohibiting federal employees from engaging in political campaigning and solicitation. (Chapter 11)

honeymoon   The first several months of a presidency, when reporters are more forgiving than usual, Congress more inclined to be cooperative, and the public receptive to new approaches. (Chapter 10)

horse-race coverage   The tendency of news organizations to emphasize who is winning and losing when they cover elections, rather than covering the issues prominent in the elections. (Chapter 5)

I

ideology   System of beliefs in which one or more organizing principles connect the individual's views on a wide range of issues. (Chapters 4, 5)

impeachment   Recommendation by a majority of the House of Representatives that a president, other executive-branch official, or judge of the federal courts be removed from office; removal depends on a two-thirds vote of the Senate. (Chapter 10)

incumbency advantage   The electoral advantage a candidate enjoys by virtue of being an incumbent, over and above his or her other personal and political characteristics. (Chapter 7)

incumbent   The politician who currently holds an elective office and therefore may enjoy an "incumbency advantage" over challengers when running for reelection. (Chapter 7)

independent agencies   Agencies that have quasi-judicial responsibilities. (Chapter 11)

independent counsel   Originally called special prosecutor, legal officer appointed by a court to investigate allegations of criminal activity against high-ranking members of the executive branch. Law expired in 1999. (Chapter 10)

inflation   A sustained rise in the price level such that people need more money to purchase the same amount of goods and services. (Chapter 15)

information cost   The time and mental effort required to absorb and store information, whether from conversations, personal experiences, or the media. (Chapter 5)

informational theory   Theory that sees committees as means of providing reliable information about the actual consequences of the legislation that members could adopt. (Chapter 9)

interest group   Private associations or organizations, made up of people with common interests, that participate in politics on behalf of their members. (Chapter 8)

initiative   Proposed laws or state constitutional amendments placed on the ballot via citizen petition. (Chapter 1)

Iran–Contra affair   An allegedly illegal diversion of funds from the sale of arms to Iran to a guerrilla group in Nicaragua. (Chapter 11)

iron curtain   Armed barrier during the Cold War that prevented movement across national borders between communist Eastern Europe and democratic Western Europe. (Chapters 11, 15)

iron triangle   A congressional committee, bureaucratic agency, and allied interest groups who combine to dominate policy making in some specified policy area. (Chapter 8)

isolationism   A foreign policy that keeps the United States separate from the conflicts taking place among other nations. (Chapter 15)

issue network   A loose constellation of larger numbers of committees, agencies, and interest groups active in a particular policy area. (Chapter 8)

issue public   Group of people particularly affected by or concerned with a specific issue. (Chapter 5)

J

Jim Crow laws   Segregation laws passed after Reconstruction. (Chapter 14)

Joint Chiefs of Staff   The heads of all the military services, together with a chair and vice-chair nominated by the president and confirmed by the Senate. (Chapter 11)

judicial activism   Doctrine that indicates the principles of *stare decisis* and legislative deference should sometimes be sacrificed in order to adapt the Constitution to changing conditions. (Chapter 12)

judicial restraint   Doctrine that indicates courts should, if at all possible, avoid overturning a prior court decision or legislative act. (Chapter 12)

judicial review   Court authority to declare null and void laws of Congress and of state legislatures on the grounds that they violate the Constitution. (Chapters 2, 3, 12)

justices   The nine judges who make up the U.S. Supreme Court. (Chapter 12)

K

Keynesianism   Economic policy based on the belief that governments can control the economy by running deficits to expand it and surpluses to contract it. (Chapter 15)

L

law clerk   Young, influential aide to a Supreme Court justice. (Chapter 12)

Lemon test   Three-part test developed in the early 1960s and formalized in 1971; determines whether a law violates the Constitution's establishment clause. (Chapter 13)

libel   False statement damaging to someone's reputation. (Chapter 13)

liberalism   A philosophy that elevates and empowers the individual as opposed to religious, hereditary, governmental, or other forms of authority. (Chapter 4)

libertarianism   A modern revival of the classical liberal tradition that characterized many, if not most, of the nation's founders. It favors small government in all areas of public policy, not just in some public-policy areas. (Chapter 4)

line item veto   Power of most governors to reject specific components of legislation rather than reject entire bills. (Chapter 3)

lobbying   Attempts by interest group representatives to influence the decisions of government officials directly. (Chapter 8)

logrolling   Colloquial term given to politicians' trading of favors, votes, or generalized support for each other's proposals. (Chapter 9)

M

machine   A highly organized party under the control of a boss, based on patronage and control of government activities. (Chapter 8)

majority leader   The Speaker's chief lieutenant in the House and the most important officer in the Senate. He or she is responsible for managing the floor. (Chapter 9)

marble-cake federalism (cooperative federalism)   The theory that all levels of government can work together to solve common problems. (Chapter 3)

Marbury **v.** *Madison*   Supreme Court decision (1803) in which the court first exercised the power of judicial review. (Chapter 12)

markup   Process in which a committee or subcommittee considers and revises a bill that has been introduced. (Chapter 9)

mass media   Means of communication that are technologically capable of reaching most people and economically affordable to most. (Chapters 5, 12)

mass public   Ordinary people for whom politics is a peripheral concern. (Chapter 5)

matching funds   Public moneys (from $3 checkoffs on income tax returns) that the FEC distributes to primary candidates. (Chapter 7)

McCulloch **v.** *Maryland*   Decision of 1819 in which the Supreme Court declared unconstitutional the state's power to tax a federal government entity. (Chapter 3)

measurement error   Polling error that arises from questioning rather than sampling. (Chapter 5)

Medicaid   Program that provides medical care to those of low income. (Chapter 15)

Medicare   Program that provides medical benefits to Social Security recipients. (Chapter 15)

midterm loss   When the president's party loses seats in Congress during the off-year election, which failed to happen only twice in the twentieth century: 1934 and 1998. (Chapter 7)

minority leader   Leader of the minority party in the House or Senate. (Chapter 9)

Miranda warning   The specific words used by police officers to inform accused persons of their constitutional rights; necessary before questioning suspects. (Chapter 13)

mobilization   The efforts of parties, groups, and activists to encourage their supporters to participate in politics. (Chapter 6)

monetarism   An economic school of thought that rejects Keynesianism, arguing that the money supply is the most important influence on the economy. (Chapter 15)

monetary policy   The actions taken by government to affect the level of interest rates by varying the supply of money. (Chapter 15)

Monroe Doctrine   Policy (1819) that declared the Western Hemisphere to be free of European colonial influence. (Chapter 15)

mugwumps   A group of civil service reformers organized in the 1880s who maintained that government officials should be chosen on a merit basis. (Chapter 11)

multiple referrals   Practice of party leaders who give more than one committee responsibility for considering a bill. (Chapter 9)

N

natural rights   Fundamental rights such as life, liberty, and property to which classical liberals considered all people entitled and therefore upon which legitimate governments could not infringe. (Chapter 2)

necessary and proper clause   Constitutional clause that gives Congress the power to take all actions that are "necessary and proper" to the carrying out of its delegated powers. Also known as the *elastic clause*. (Chapters 2, 3)

neutrality test   Test allowing restrictions on the exercise of religion when they are part of a neutral criminal law generally applied to the population. Replaced the Sherbert test. (Chapter 13)

New Deal   Programs created by Franklin Roosevelt's administration that expanded the power of the federal government over economic affairs. (Chapter 3)

new media   Cable and satellite TV, the fax, e-mail, and the Internet—the consequences of the technological advances of the past few decades. (Chapters 5, 12)

NIMBY problem   The problem that results when everyone wants the problem solved, but "Not In My Back Yard." (Chapter 3)

nullification   A doctrine that gives states the authority to declare acts of Congress unconstitutional. (Chapter 3)

O

obscenity   Publicly offensive language or portrayals with no redeeming social value. (Chapter 13)

Office of Management and Budget (OMB)   Agency responsible for coordinating the work of departments and agencies of the executive branch. (Chapter 10)

open primaries   Primaries in which any registered voter can vote in any party's primary. (Chapter 7)

open seat   A House or Senate race with no incumbent (because of death or retirement). (Chapter 7)

opinion of the court   A court's written explanation for its decision. (Chapter 12)

override   Congressional passage of a bill by a two-thirds vote over the president's veto. (Chapter 10)

P

party identification   A person's subjective feeling of affiliation with a party. (Chapter 7)

patronage   Jobs, contracts, or favors in exchange for their political support. Widely practiced in the eighteenth and nineteenth centuries and continues to present day. (Chapters 2, 8, 11)

Pendleton Act   Legislation in 1881 creating the Civil Service Commission. (Chapter 11)

permanent campaign   Term describing the tendency for election campaigns to begin as soon as the last election has ended and for the line between electioneering and governing to disappear. (Chapter 1)

plaintiff   One who brings legal charges against another. (Chapter 12)

plea bargain   Agreement between prosecution and defense that the accused will admit having committed a crime, provided that other charges are dropped or the recommended sentence shortened. (Chapter 13)

plenary session   Activities of a court in which all judges participate. (Chapter 12)

pluralism   A school of thought holding that politics is the clash of groups that represent all important interests in society and check and balance each other. (Chapter 8)

pocket veto   Presidential veto after congressional adjournment, executed merely by not signing a bill into law. (Chapter 10)

political action committee (PAC)   Specialized organization for raising and contributing campaign funds. (Chapter 8)

political culture   Collection of beliefs and values about government. (Chapter 4)

political efficacy   The belief that one can make a difference in politics. (Chapter 5)

political elite   Activists and officeholders who are deeply interested in and knowledgeable about politics. (Chapter 5)

political entrepreneurs   People willing to assume the costs of forming and maintaining an organization even when others may free ride on them. (Chapter 8)

political parties   Groups of like-minded people who band together in an attempt to take control of government. (Chapter 8)

popular vote   The total vote cast for a presidential candidate nationwide. (Chapter 7)

precedent   Previous court decision or ruling applicable to a particular case. (Chapter 11)

president pro tempore   Leader of the Senate, who presides in the absence of the vice president. (Chapter 9)

primary election   Preliminary election that narrows the number of candidates by determining who will be the party nominees in the general election. (Chapters 1, 7)

priming   What occurs when the media affect the standards people use to evaluate political figures or the severity of a problem. (Chapters 5, 12)

prior restraint doctrine   Legal doctrine that gives individuals the right to publish without prior restraint—that is, without first submitting material to a government censor. (Chapter 13)

proportional representation (PR)   An electoral system that assigns legislative seats in a manner roughly proportional to the number of votes each party received. (Chapters 7, 8)

public defender   Attorney whose full-time responsibilities are to provide for the legal defense of indigent criminal suspects. (Chapter 13)

public goods   Goods that you can enjoy without contributing. (Chapter 8)

Q

quorum   Number of members of a council or legislative body who must be present for official business to take place. (Chapter 2)

quota   Specific number of positions set aside for a specific group; said by the Supreme Court to be unconstitutional. (Chapter 14)

R

"rally 'round the flag" effect   The tendency for the public to back presidents in moments of crisis. (Chapters 10, 15)

random sample   A representative subset of a larger group, chosen in such a way that each member of the group had roughly the same chance of being selected. (Chapter 5)

realignment   Arrangement that ccurs when the pattern of group support for political parties shifts in a significant and lasting way, such as in the latter half of the twentieth century, when the white South shifted from Democratic to Republican. (Chapter 8)

reapportionment   The allocation of House seats to the states after each decennial census. (Chapter 7)

recall election   Attempt to remove an official from office before the completion of the term. (Chapter 1)

recession   A slowdown in economic activity, officially defined as a decline that persists for two quarters (six months). (Chapter 15)

Reconstruction   Period after the Civil War when southern states were subject to a federal military presence. (Chapter 14)

redistricting   Drawing of new boundaries of congressional districts. (Chapter 7)

referenda   Laws or state constitutional amendments that are proposed by a legislative body but do not go into effect unless the required number of voters approve it. (Chapter 1)

registered voters   Those legally eligible to vote who have registered in accordance with the requirements prevailing in their states and localites. (Chapter 6)

remand   To send a case to a lower court to determine the best way of implementing the higher court's decision. (Chapter 12)

remedy   Court-ordered action designed to compensate plaintiffs for wrongs they have suffered. (Chapter 12)

republic   *See direct democracy.* (Chapter 1)

restrictive housing covenant   Legal promise by home buyers that they would not resell to black households; enforcement declared unconstitutional by Supreme Court. (Chapter 14)

retrospective voting   Voting on the basis of the past performance. (Chapter 7)

right to privacy   Right to keep free of government interference those aspects of one's personal life that do not affect others. (Chapter 13)

roll-call vote   A congressional vote in which the specific choice of each member is recorded, allowing constituents to learn how their representative voted. (Chapter 9)

rule   Specification of the terms and conditions under which a bill or resolution will be considered on the floor of the House—in particular, how long debate will last, how time will be allocated, and the number and type of amendments that will be in order. (Chapter 9)

S

safe seat   A congressional district almost guaranteed to elect either a Democrat or a Republican because the distribution of partisans is so lopsided. (Chapter 7)

sampling error   The error that arises in public opinion surveys as a result of relying on a representative but small sample of the larger population. (Chapter 5)

Second Continental Congress   Political authority that directed the struggle for independence beginning in 1775. (Chapter 2)

select committee   Temporary Congressional committee appointed to deal with a specific issue or problem. (Chapter 9)

selection bias The error that occurs when a sample systematically includes or excludes people with certain attitudes. (Chapter 5)

selective benefits Side benefits of belonging to an organization that are limited to contributing members of the organization. (Chapter 8)

selective incorporation The case-by-case incorporation, by the courts, of the Bill of Rights into the due process clause of the Fourteenth Amendment. (Chapter 13)

selective perception The tendency of listeners, such as a media audience, to distort a message so that they hear what they already believe or hear what they want to hear. (Chapter 5)

senatorial courtesy An informal rule that the Senate will not confirm nominees within or from a state unless they have the approval of the senior senator of the state from the president's party. (Chapters 11, 12)

seniority Congressional practice by which the majority party member with the longest continuous service on a committee becomes the chair. (Chapter 9)

separate but equal doctrine Obsolete rule stating that racial segregation did not violate the equal protection clause as long as the facilities were equivalent. (Chapter 14)

separation of powers A system of government in which different institutions exercise different components of governmental power. (Chapter 2)

Shays's Rebellion Uprising in western Massachusetts in 1786 led by Revolutionary War captain Daniel Shays. (Chapter 2)

Sherbert test Three-part test formalized in the early 1960s but overruled in 1990 that determined whether a law violates the Constitution's free exercise clause. (Chapter 13)

sin tax Tax intended to discourage unwanted behavior. (Chapter 15)

single-issue voter Voter for whom one issue is so important that it determines which political candidates attract his or her votes or campaign activism. (Chapter 5)

single-member, simple plurality (SMSP) system Electoral system in which the country is divided into geographic districts, and the candidates who win the most votes within their districts are elected. (Chapters 7, 8)

social connectedness The degree to which individuals are integrated into society—families, churches, neighborhoods, groups, and so forth. (Chapter 6)

social-contract theory An approach to political philosophy starting from the hypothetical assumption that there was a time before society or before government, and that people accepted such innovations as part of a contract in which they gained some sort of guarantee as the terms of cooperating. (Chapter 2)

social issues Issues such as obscenity, feminism, gay rights, capital punishment, and prayer in schools that reflect personal values more than economic interests. (Chapter 6)

social movement Broad-based demand for government action on some problem or issue, such as civil rights for blacks and women or environmental protection. (Chapter 8)

socializing agent A person or institution that teaches social values and political attitudes. (Chapter 5)

soft money Campaign funds that are spent on a candidate's behalf by an interest group or political party but that the candidate does not receive or coordinate directly. (Chapters 7, 8)

solicitor general   Government official responsible for presenting before the courts the position of the presidential administration. (Chapter 12)

sovereign immunity   The legal doctrine protecting states from lawsuits filed under national legislation. (Chapter 3)

Speaker   The presiding officer of the House of Representatives; normally, the Speaker is the leader of the majority party. (Chapter 9)

spending clause   Constitutional provision that gives Congress the power to collect taxes to provide for the general welfare. (Chapter 3)

spoils system   A system of government employment in which workers are hired on the basis of party loyalty. (Chapter 11)

sponsor   Representative or senator who introduces a bill or resolution. (Chapter 9)

standing committee   Committee with fixed membership and jurisdiction, continuing from Congress to Congress. (Chapter 9)

stare decisis   In court rulings, remaining consistent with precedents. (Chapter 12)

state action doctrine   Rule stating that only the actions of state and local governments, not those of private individuals, must conform to the equal protection clause. (Chapter 14)

State of the Union address   Annual speech delivered by the president in fulfillment of the constitutional obligation of reporting to Congress on the state of the Union. (Chapter 10)

statutory interpretation   The judicial act of applying laws to particular cases. (Chapter 12)

suffrage   Another term for the right to vote. (Chapter 6)

supremacy clause   Part of the Constitution that says the Constitution is the "supreme Law of the Land," to which all judges are bound. (Chapters 2, 3)

suspect classification   Categorization of a particular group that will be strictly scrutinized by the courts to see whether its use is unconstitutional. (Chapter 14)

suspension of the rules   Fast-track procedure for considering bills and resolutions in the House; debate is limited to 40 minutes, no amendments are in order, and a two-thirds majority is required for passage. (Chapter 9)

T

tariffs   Taxes on imported goods. (Chapter 2)

tax preferences   Special tax treatment received by certain activities, property, or investments. (Chapter 15)

Temporary Assistance for Needy Families (TANF)   Reformed welfare program established by Congress in 1996. (Chapter 15)

three-fifths compromise   Constitutional provision that counted each slave as three-fifths of a person when calculating representation in the House of Representatives; repealed by the Fourteenth Amendment. (Chapter 2)

ticket splitting   Occurs when a voter chooses candidates from multiple parties. (Chapter 8)

transition   The period after a presidential candidate has won the November election but before the candidate assumes office as president on January 20. (Chapter 10)

treaties   Official agreements with foreign countries ratified by the Senate. (Chapter 10)

two-thirds rule   Rule governing Democratic national conventions from 1832 to 1936. It required that the presidential and vice presidential nominees receive at least two-thirds of the delegates' votes. (Chapter 8)

two-presidency theory   Idea that a president has so much more power in foreign affairs than in domestic policy that there are two presidencies. (Chapter 10)

U

U.S. attorney   Person responsible for prosecuting violations of the federal criminal code. (Chapter 12)

unanimous-consent agreement   Agreement that sets forth the terms according to which the Senate will consider a bill; these are individually negotiated by the leadership for each bill. (Chapter 9)

unemployment   When people who are willing to work at the prevailing wage cannot get jobs. (Chapter 15)

unfunded mandates   Federal regulations that impose burdens on state and local governments without appropriating enough money to cover costs. (Chapter 3)

V

veto   Executive rejection of legislation, which usually may be overridden by a supermajority in the legislature. (Chapter 10)

Virginia Plan   James Madison's rough draft of the U.S. Constitution, especially his proposal that states would receive representation in the national legislature proportional to their population sizes. (Chapter 2)

voting-age population   All people in the United States over the age of 18. (Chapter 6)

W

War on Poverty   One of the most controversial of the Great Society programs, it was designed to enhance the economic opportunity of low-income citizens. (Chapter 3)

War Powers Resolution   Congressional resolution in 1973 requiring the president to notify Congress formally upon ordering U.S. troops into military action. (Chapter 10)

Whigs   Political opposition to royal power in eighteenth-century England. (Chapter 2)

whips   Members of Congress who serve as informational channels between the leadership and the rank and file. (Chapter 9)

White House Office   Political appointees who work directly for the president, many of whom occupy offices in the White House. (Chapter 10)

winner-take-all voting   Any voting procedure in which the side with the most votes gets all of the seats or delegates at stake. (Chapter 7)

writ of *certiorari* (cert)   A document issued by the Supreme Court indicating that the Court will review a decision made by a lower court. (Chapter 12)

Y

yeoman   Independent farmers who made up approximately four-fifths of the U.S. population at the time of the founding and who tended to embrace a radical version of revolutionary ideals such as "liberty" and "equality. (Chapter 2)

ENDNOTES

PREFACE

1. On the limited importance of elections, see for example the string of works by Benjamin Ginsberg, including an influential book with Martin Shefter, *Politics By Other Means: The Declining Importance of Elections in America* (New York: Basic, 1990). On the dominance of elites, see the running textbook series by Thomas R. Dye, including listed in their first editions *Who's Running America?* (Englewood Cliffs, NJ: Prentice-Hall, 1976) and, with L. Harmon Ziegler, *The Irony of Democracy* (Belmont, CA: Wadsworth, 1970).

2. Morris P. Fiorina and Paul E. Peterson, *The New American Democracy,* 2nd ed. (New York: Longman, 2001).

CHAPTER 1

1. David Bauder (Associated Press), "TV Networks Lambasted for Election Coverage," *Lexington Herald–Leader* (February 3, 2001): A7.

2. On Republican reliance on the South, see Earl Black and Merle Black, *The Vital South* (Cambridge, MA: Harvard University Press, 1992).

3. Election-night quotations come from ABC-NEWS television coverage presented the night of the election through the following morning.

4. Henry E. Brady, Michael C. Herron, Walter R. Mebane, Jr., Jasjeet Singh Sekhon, Kenneth W. Shotts, and Jonathan Wand, "Law and Data: The Butterfly Ballot Episode," *PS: Political Science and Politics* 34 (2001): 59–69.

5. Manny Garcia and Tom Dubocq, "Unregistered Voters Cast Ballots in Dade," *Miami Herald* (December 24, 2000); and David Kidwell, Phil Long, and Geoff Dougherty, "Hundreds of Felons Cast Votes Illegally," *Miami Herald* (December 1, 2000).

6. Joseph S. Nye, Jr., Philip D. Zelikow, and David C. King, eds., *Why People Don't Trust Government* (Cambridge, MA: Harvard University Press, 1997).

7. H. H. Gerth and C. W. Mills, trans., *From Max Weber* (New York: Oxford University Press, 1946), p. 78.

8. Chuck Henning, *The Wit and Wisdom of Politics: Expanded Edition* (Golden, CO: Fulcrum, 1992), p. 91.

9. Thomas Hobbes, *Leviathan* (New York: Dutton, 1973), p. 65.

10. "Federalist No. 51." See the Appendix to this book.

11. Henning, *Wit and Wisdom,* p. 89.

12. "Federalist No. 51."

13. Good surveys of democratic theory include J. Roland Pennock, *Democratic Political Theory* (Princeton, NJ: Princeton University Press, 1979); Giovanni Sartori, *The Theory of Democracy*

Revisited (Chatham, NJ: Chatham House, 1987); and Carole Pateman, *Participation and Democratic Theory* (New York: Cambridge University Press, 1970). A critical summary appears in James Marone, *The Democratic Wish: Popular Participation and the Limits of American Government* (New York: Basic Books, 1990), p. 5.

14. Angus Campbell, Philip E. Converse, Warren E. Miller, and Donald E. Stokes, *The American Voter* (New York: Wiley, 1960); Deborah R. Hensler and Carl P. Hensler, *Evaluating Nuclear Power: Voter Choice on the California Nuclear Energy Initiative* (Santa Monica, CA: Rand Corporation, 1979), p. 106; David Magleby, *Direct Legislation: Voting on Ballot Propositions in the United States* (Baltimore: Johns Hopkins University Press, 1984), p. 144; Barbara S. Gamble, "Putting Civil Rights to a Popular Vote," *American Journal of Political Science* 41 (1997): 245–269; and D. Stephen Voss and Penny Miller, "The Phantom Segregationist: An Aggregate-Data Analysis of Kentucky's 1996 Constitutional Amendment Vote," paper presented at the annual meeting of the Kentucky Political Science Association, Lexington, Kentucky, March 5–6, 1999.

15. John Adams, *The Political Writings of John Adams,* George Peek, Jr., ed. (New York: Macmillan, 1985), p. 89.

16. Alexis de Tocqueville, *Democracy in America,* 2nd ed., Henry Reeve, trans., 2 vols. (Cambridge, MA: Sever & Francis, 1863), I, pp. 318–319, as quoted in Marone, *The Democratic Wish*, p. 86.

17. "Half a Million Voters' Choices," *Governing* (April 1995): 15.

18. Herbert Jacob and Kenneth Vines, "Courts," in Virginia Gray, Herbert Jacob, and Kenneth Vines, eds., *Politics in the American States: A Comparative Analysis*, 4th ed. (Boston: Little, Brown, 1983), p. 238.

19. Professor Richard Murray, as reported by Professor Jay Greene, personal communication, April 10, 1997.

20. Thomas Cronin, *Direct Democracy* (Cambridge, MA: Harvard University Press, 1989); and Magleby, *Direct Legislation*.

21. For an analysis of the 1995 Canadian referendum, see David Lublin and D. Stephen Voss, "Context and Francophone Support for Sovereignty: An Ecological Analysis," *Canadian Journal of Political Science* 35 (2002): 75–101.

22. Anthony King, *Running Scared: Why America's Politicians Campaign Too Much and Govern Too Little* (New York: Free Press, 1996), pp. 2–3.

23. Susan A. Macmanus, *Young v. Old: Generational Combat in the 21st Century* (Boulder, CO: Westview Press, 1996), Ch. 2.

24. Sidney Blumenthal, *The Permanent Campaign* (New York: Simon & Schuster, 1982).

25. Hugh Heclo, "The Permanent Campaign: A Conspectus," in *Campaigning to Govern or Governing to Campaign?* ed. Thomas Mann and Norman Ornstein (Washington, DC: Brookings, 2000).

26. Woodrow Wilson, *Congressional Government* (Cleveland, OH: Meridian Books, 1956), p. 39.

27. Richard Boyd, "Decline of U.S. Voter Turnout: Structural Explanations," *American Politics Quarterly* 9 (1981): 133–159.

28. Frank Sorauf, *Political Parties in the American System* (Boston: Little, Brown, 1964); and Martin Wattenberg, *The Decline of American Political Parties, 1952–1984* (Cambridge, MA: Harvard University Press, 1986).

29. Gary Jacobson finds that national swings in House elections are much more heterogeneous than at mid-century. See "The Marginals Never Vanished: Incumbency and Competition in Elections to the U.S. House of Representatives, 1952–1982," *American Journal of Political Science* 31 (1987): 126–141.

30. Norman Ornstein, Thomas Mann, and Michael Malbin, *Vital Statistics on Congress, 1997–1998* (Washington, DC: Congressional Quarterly, 1998), Table 3.1.

31. U.S. Senate Republican Policy Committee, 107th Congress 2nd Session, Senate Record Vote Analysis No. 54 (March 20, 2002): S-2160.

32. Council of State Governments, *The Book of the States 2002* (Lexington, KY: 2002): 140, Table C.

33. Benjamin Ginsberg and Martin Shefter, *Politics By Other Means: The Declining Importance of Elections in America* (New York: Basic, 1990); and Terry Moe, "The Politics of Bureaucratic Structure," in John Chubb and Paul Peterson, eds., *Can the Government Govern?* (Washington, DC: Brookings, 1989), pp. 267–329.

34. John Dewey, as quoted in Marone, *The Democratic Wish,* p. 322.

35. R. Douglas Arnold, *The Logic of Congressional Action* (New Haven, CT: Yale University Press, 1990).

36. Marone, *The Democratic Wish*.

37. Henning, *Wit and Wisdom*, p. 58.

38. "A League of Evil," *The Economist* (September 11, 1999): 7.

39. Craig Smith, "Chinese Fight Crime with Torture and Executions," *New York Times* (September 9, 2001): 8.

40. Henning, *Wit and Wisdom*, p. 94.

41. Details of the 9/11 story come from the following sources: David Maraniss, "A Day Like No Other," *Washington Post Weekly Edition* (September 24–30, 2001): 8–13; John Dorschner, "It Began As Such an Ordinary Day," Knight-Ridder News Service (September 16, 2001); and the December 31, 2001/January 7, 2002, special edition of *Newsweek*.

CHAPTER 2

1. Details for the Shays's Rebellion story come primarily from David P. Szatmary, *Shays' Rebellion: The Making of an Agricultural Insurrection* (Amherst: University of Massachusetts Press, 1980); and Merrill Jensen, *The New Nation: A History of the United States During the Confederation, 1781–1789* (New York: Vintage, 1965).

2. Szatmary, *Shays' Rebellion,* p. 36.

3. Szatmary, *Shays' Rebellion,* p. 82.

4. James W. Loewen, *Lies My Teacher Taught Me* (New York: New Press, 1995), Ch. 3.

5. Thomas A. Bailey, *The American Pageant: A History of the Republic* (Boston: D. C. Heath, 1956).

6. Gordon S. Wood, *The Radicalism of the American Revolution* (New York: Knopf, 1992), p. 55.

7. Merrill D. Peterson, *Thomas Jefferson and the New Nation* (New York: Oxford University Press, 1970), pp. 22–23.

8. John Locke, *Two Treatises on Civil Government* (London: Dent, 1924). Originally published in 1690.

9. J. H. Plumb, *The Origins of Political Stability* (Boston: Houghton Mifflin, 1967).

10. Samuel H. Beer, *To Make a Nation: The Rediscovery of American Federalism* (Cambridge, MA: Harvard University Press, 1993).

11. Thomas Paine, *Common Sense* (New York: Penguin, 1986). Originally published in 1776.

12. Edmund S. Morgan and Helen M. Morgan, *The Stamp Act Crisis: Prologue to Revolution* (Chapel Hill: University of North Carolina Press, 1953), p. 106.

13. Greg Smith, *Beer: A History of Suds and Civilization from Mesopotamia to Microbreweries* (New York, Avon, 1995), p. 52.

14. Morgan and Morgan, *Stamp Act Crisis,* p. 106.

15. Interesting discussions of both Locke's influence on Jefferson and Jefferson's introduction of the phrase *pursuit of happiness* appear in David Freeman Hawke, *A Transaction of Free Men:The Birth and Course of the Declaration of Independence* (New York: Da Capo, 1989), pp. 50, 148–151. Originally published in 1964.

16. Robert J. Dinkin, *Voting in Revolutionary America:A Study of Elections in the Original Thirteen States, 1776–1789* (Westport, CT: Greenwood Press, 1982); and Robert J. Dinkin, *Voting in Provincial America:A Study of Elections in the Thirteen Colonies, 1689–1776* (Westport, CT: Greenwood Press, 1977).

17. Willi Paul Adams, *The First American Constitutions: Republican Ideology and the Making of the State Constitutions in the Revolutionary Era* (Chapel Hill, NC: University of North Carolina Press, 1980), pp. 245, 308–311.

18. Gordon S. Wood, *The Creation of the American Republic, 1776–1787* (Chapel Hill: University of North Carolina Press, 1969), pp. 396–403; Szatmary, *Shays' Rebellion,* p. 77; Hawke, *Transaction of Free Men,* p. 112.

19. Wood, *Creation of the American Republic,* Ch. 8.

20. Bailey, *American Pageant,* p. 136.

21. Stanley M. Elkins and Eric McKitrick, *The Age of Federalism* (New York: Oxford University Press, 1993), Ch. 1.

22. Warren E. Burger, *It Is So Ordered:A Constitution Unfolds* (New York:William Morrow, 1995), p. 7.

23. Herbert J. Storing, ed., *The Complete Anti-Federalist: Maryland and Virginia and the South,* Vol. 5 (Chicago: University of Chicago Press, 1981), p. 210.

24. Merrill Jensen, *The New Nation,* p. 33.

25. Charles A. Beard, *An Economic Interpretation of the Constitution of the United States* (New York: Free Press, 1913).

26. Robert E. Brown, *Charles Beard and the Constitution* (Princeton, NJ: Princeton University Press, 1956); and Forrest McDonald, *We the People* (Chicago: University of Chicago Press, 1958).

27. John P. Roche, "The Founding Fathers:A Reform Caucus in Action," *American Political Science Review* 55 (December 1961): 799–816.

28. Max Farrand, *The Framing of the Constitution of the United States* (New Haven, CT:Yale University Press, 1913), p. 113.

29. Thornton Anderson, *Creating the Constitution:The Convention of 1787 and the First Congress* (University Park: Pennsylvania State University Press, 1993).

30. C. M. Kenyon, "Men of Little Faith:The Anti-Federalists on the Nature of Representative Government," in Jack P. Greene, *The Reinterpretation of the American Revolution, 1763–1789* (New York: Harper & Row, 1968), pp. 526–567; and Herbert J. Storing, ed., *The Anti-Federalist* (Chicago: University of Chicago Press, 1986).

31. Arthur M. Schlesinger, *Prelude to Independence* (New York: Knopf, 1958), p. 229.

32. Jane Mansbridge, *Why We Lost the ERA* (Chicago: University of Chicago Press, 1986).

33. Henry Steele Commager, ed., *Documents of American History* (New York:Appleton, 1958), p. 104; and Adams, *First American Constitutions.*

34. Charles A. Beard, *An Economic Interpretation of the Constitution of the United States.*

35. Bernard Bailyn, *The Ideological Origins of the American Revolution* (Cambridge, MA: Harvard University Press, 1967); and Wood, *Creation of the American Republic.*

CHAPTER 3

1. Candy Lightner's story comes from Jay Mathews, "One California Mother's MADD Drive to Bar Highways to Drunken Killers," *Washington Post* (June 16, 1984): A2; and John J. O'Connor, "'MADD' Drama Fights Drunken Driving," *New York Times* (March 14, 1983): C14.

2. Jane Perlez, "Teen-Age Drinking Vote: Crusader Is 'Delighted,'" *New York Times* (June 9, 1984): 5.

3. The story of the National Minimum Drinking Age Act of 1984 comes primarily from two sources: Perlez, "Teen-Age Drinking Vote," and Douglas B. Feaver, "Reagan Now Wants 21 as Drinking Age," *Washington Post* (June 14, 1984): A1.

4. Martin Tolchin, "Senate Votes Bill Aimed at Forcing Drinking Age of 21," *New York Times* (June 27, 1984): 1.

5. Al Kamen, "High Court Upholds Law Linking U.S. Highway Funds, State Drinking Age," *Washington Post* (June 24, 1987): A8.

6. Lu Ann Snider, "The Politics and Consequences of the New Drinking Age Law," *Florida State University Law Review* 13 (Fall 1985): 847–861.

7. Stuart Taylor, Jr., "Justices Back Use of Aid to Get States to Raise Drinking Age," *New York Times* (June 24, 1987): 20.

8. David G. Savage, "Justices Support Move for Drinking Age of 21," *Los Angeles Times* (June 24, 1987): 15.

9. South Louisiana differs from the rest of the U.S. South in other ways as well, including political preferences and approaches to race. See D. Stephen Voss, "Beyond Racial Threat: Failure of an Old Hypothesis in the New South," *Journal of Politics* 58 (1996): 1156–1170; James G. Dauphine, *A Question of Inheritance: Religion, Education, and Louisiana's Cultural Boundary, 1880–1940* (Lafayette, LA: Center for Louisiana Studies, 1993); and John H. Fenton and Kenneth N. Vines, "Negro Registration in Louisiana," *American Political Science Review* 51 (1957): 704–713.

10. James Gill, "Court Tampers with Drinking Age," *New Orleans Times-Picayune* (March 13, 1996): B7.

11. Details on Louisiana's battle to keep its lower drinking age come from the following sources: Bill Voelker and Susan Finch, "21-Year Limit Discriminates, High Court Says," *New Orleans Times-Picayune* (March 9, 1996): A1; Bruce Alpert, "Drinking Age Ruling May Slash Road Aid," *New Orleans Times-Picayune* (March 15, 1996): A1; Susan Finch and Ed Anderson, "Court Reverses on Age to Drink; It's 21 to Imbibe or to Buy Liquor," *New Orleans Times-Picayune* (July 3, 1996): A1; and Joe Gyan, Jr., "Drinking Age Revived," *Baton Rouge Advocate* (July 3, 1996): 1A.

12. Doug Myers, "Poll Shows Voters Want Drinking Age Set at 21," *New Orleans Times-Picayune* (March 17, 1996): 1A. Despite the mixed feelings of Louisiana men and the strong feelings of the state's young adults, the statewide results supported a higher drinking age because women overwhelmingly endorsed the higher limit. It is unclear how much of the position reflected sincere policy preferences and how much represented desire for the "blackmail portion" of the funds.

13. Ed Anderson, "Gamblers, Drinkers Still Must Be 21," *New Orleans Times-Picayune* (June 5, 1999): A2. At least some members of the House said they opposed the bill not because it would lower the drinking age but because it would also lower the gambling age and might prevent companies from giving senior citizens special discounts.

14. Manuel Roig-Franzia and Ed Anderson, "Lower Alcohol Limit Clears Hurdle, But Drinking Age Measure Blocked," *New Orleans Times-Picayune* (April 3, 1998): A1; and Sherry Sapp, "Try Fails to Close Drinking Age Law Loophole," *Baton Rouge Advocate* (April 4, 1998): 8A.

15. Associated Press, "Law Doesn't Stop Teen Drinkers," *Dubuque Telegraph Herald* (August 12, 1996): B10.

16. John Bartlett, *Familiar Quotations: Revised and Enlarged,* 15th ed. (Boston: Little, Brown, 1980), p. 452.

17. Alexis de Tocqueville, *Democracy in America,* Vol. I, ed. Philips Bradley (New York: Knopf, 1945), p. 169.

18. Jean E. Smith, *John Marshall: Definer of a Nation* (New York: Henry Holt, 1996), pp. 440–446.

19. *Board of Trustees of the University of Alabama v. Garrett,* 99-1240 (2001).

20. Stephen Henderson, "Family Leave Covers State Employees, Justices Rule," *Lexington Herald-Leader* (May 28, 2003): A1.

21. *McCulloch* v. *Maryland* (1819), 4 Wheaton 316, as reprinted in Henry Steele Commager, ed., *Documents of American History,* 6th ed. (New York: Appleton, 1949), p. 217.

22. *McCulloch* v. *Maryland* (1819), as reprinted in Commager, *Documents of American History,* p. 217.

23. *United States* v. *E. C. Knight Co.,* 156 U.S. 1 (1895).

24. *NLRB* v. *Jones & Laughlin Co.,* 317 U.S. 111 (1937).

25. *Wickard* v. *Filburn,* (1942).

26. *Helvering* v. *Davis,* 301 U.S. 548, 599 (1937).

27. *South Dakota* v. *Dole,* 483 U.S. 203 (1987).

28. Barry Friedman, "The Law and Economics of Federalism: Valuing Federalism," *Minnesota Law Review* 82 (December 1997): 317.

29. Lynn A. Baker, "Conditional Federal Spending and States' Rights," *Annals of the American Academy of Political and Social Science* 574 (March 2001): 105.

30. Morton Grodzins, *The American System: A New View of Government in the United States,* ed. Daniel J. Elazar (Chicago: Rand McNally, 1966).

31. Ibid.

32. Calculated from data in Ester Fuchs, *Mayors and Money* (Chicago: University of Chicago Press, 1992), p. 210.

33. Jeffrey L. Pressman and Aaron Wildavsky, *Implementation,* 3rd ed. (Berkeley: University of California Press, 1984); Martha Derthick, *New Towns in Town: Why a Federal Program Failed* (Washington, DC: Urban Institute, 1972); and Eugene Bardach, *The Implementation Game,* 4th ed. (Cambridge, MA: MIT Press, 1982).

34. Derthick, *New Towns in Town.*

35. Pressman and Wildavsky, *Implementation,* p. 118.

36. Dirk Johnson, "In Fight Against the River, A Victory in North Dakota," *New York Times* (April 12, 1997): 7.

37. Timothy Conlan, *New Federalism: Intergovernmental Reform from Nixon to Reagan* (Washington, DC: Brookings, 1988).

38. Executive Office of the President, Office of Management and Budget, *Budget for Fiscal Year 2000, Historical Tables,* Table 12.3.

39. David McKay, *Domestic Policy and Ideology: Presidents and the American State, 1964–1987* (New York: Cambridge University Press, 1989), Ch. 4.

40. Lynda McDonnell, "Will Our State Be a Magnet for Poor from Across Nation?" *Pioneer Press* (December 31, 1995): 1A, 10A.

41. John Holahan et al., "Explaining the Recent Growth in Medicaid Spending," *Health Affairs* 12 (Fall 1993): 177–193.

42. Murray Evans, "Cities' Leaders Describe Budget Woes," Associated Press, June 7, 2003. Also see Gregory S. Lashutka, "Local Rebellion: How Cities Are Rising Up Against Unfunded Mandates," *Commonsense* 1 (Summer 1994): 66.

43. Donald Kettl, "10th Amendment Turf War," *Governing Magazine* (October 1998): 13.

44. Dan M. Berkovitz, "Waste Wars: Did Congress 'Nuke' State Sovereignty in the Low-Level Radioactive Waste Policy Amendments Act of 1985?" *Harvard Environmental Law Review* 11 (1987): 437–440; *New York Times* (January 18, 1991).

45. *New York* v. *U.S., 112 Supreme Court Reporter,* 2414–47 301 U.S. 1 (1991).

46. Robert R. Alford and Eugene C. Lee, "Voting Turnout in American Cities," *American Political Science Review* 62 (1968): 796–813.

47. Village politics are well described in A. J. Vidich and J. Bensman, *Small Town in Mass Society* (New York: Harper & Row, 1972). For descriptions of courthouse gangs in the county politics of the South, see V. O. Key, *Southern Politics* (New York: Random House, 1949).

48. Paul E. Peterson, *City Limits* (Chicago: University of Chicago Press, 1981).

49. *Statistical Abstract of the United States, 1992,* Table 22.

50. "Money to Burn," *The Economist* (August 14, 1993): 23.

51. Steve Rushin, "The Heart of a City," *Sports Illustrated* (December 4, 1995).

52. Amy Pyle, "Bond Backers Weigh Second Try," *Los Angeles Times* (March 24, 2000): A3; Randal C. Archibold, "School Budgets: Many Reasons Why Voters May Say No," *New York Times* (May 21, 2001): B1; Iver Peterson, "As Taxes Rise, Suburbs Work to Keep Elderly," *New York Times* (February 27, 2001): A1; Martha Groves and Duke Helfand, "Schools Prepare Fresh Set of Bond Issues," *Los Angeles Times* (November 9, 2000): A3; Martha Groves, "Voters Ready to Give Vouchers a Drubbing," *Los Angeles Times* (October 26, 2000): A3; and Lisa Frazier, "In Bowie, 'White Angst' Bubbles Beneath Secession Movement,'"*Washington Post* (October 26, 2000): M2.

53. "Land Ordinance of 1785," in Henry S. Commager, ed., *Documents of American History,* 6th ed. (New York: Appleton, 1958), p. 124.

54. The Gallup Organization, Roper Center for Public Opinion Research Database, Question ID Numbers USGALLUP. 870.Q005A; USGALLUP. 99JNE25R11E.

55. Eric A Hanushek, "School Resources and Student Performance," in *Does Money Matter? The Effect of School Resources on Student Achievement and Adult Success,* ed. Gary Burtless (Washington, DC: Brookings, 1996), pp. 43–73.

56. Helen F. Ladd, "Introduction," in Helen F. Ladd, ed., *Holding Schools Accountable: Performance-Based Reform in Education* (Washington, DC: Brookings, 1996), pp. 1–22.

57. U.S. Department of Education, National Center for Education Statistics, *Digest of Education Statistics,* 1999, May 2000 (NCES 2000-031), Table 419, p. 471.

58. National Education Association Research Division, *Salaries Paid Classroom Teachers, Principals, and Certain Others,* 1960–61, *Urban Districts 100,000 and Over in Population;* ibid., 1970–71; Educational Research Service, *Salaries Paid Professional Personnel in Public Schools,* 1974–75; ibid., 1979–80; ibid., 1984–85; ibid., 1989–90; National Education Association, *Estimates of School Statistics,* 1960–61, p. 13; ibid., 1989–90, p. 19; and National Center for Education Statistics, *Digest of Education Statistics,* 1988, Table 57, p. 72.

59. David Osborne, *Laboratories of Democracy* (Boston: Harvard Business School Press, 1991).

60. Morris Fiorina, *Divided Government* (New York: Macmillan, 1992).

61. Calculated from U.S. Bureau of the Census, *State and Local Finance Estimates by State: 1995–1996,* www.census.gov/govs/www/esti96.html accessed November 11, 1999. Data on

state expenditures combine expenditures by state and local governments. Because the balance between these levels varies greatly, any interstate comparison that looks at one level alone can be misleading.

62. Paul E. Peterson, *The Price of Federalism* (Washington, D.C.: Brookings, 1995), p. 105.

63. The Council of State Governments, *The Book of the States: 1996–97 Edition,* Lexington, KY: Council of State Governments.

64. Thad Beyle, "Being Governor," in Carl E. Van Horn, ed., *The State of the States,* 2nd ed. (Washington, DC: Brookings, 1993).

65. Douglas Turner, "Governors Issue Call for States to Get Share of Anti-Terror Funding," *Buffalo News,* December 6, 2001: A10.

66. George Skelton, "Lessons from an Earlier Foreign Journey," *Los Angeles Times,* October 25, 1999.

67. This Aftershock draws on two sources in addition to those cited specifically below. Those are David S. Broder, "Talk vs. Action," *Washington Post Weekly Edition* (August 20–26, 2001): 4; and David S. Broder, "A Matter of Money," *Washington Post Weekly Edition* (May 6–12, 2002): 4.

68. Margie Wylie, "Cash-Strapped States Press to Tax Internet Sales," Newhouse News Service (November 16, 2001); Jon Swartz and Theresa Howard, "More Holiday Shoppers Take Their Lists Online," *USA Today* (November 23, 2001): 1B; David S. Broder, "States in Fiscal Crisis," *Washington Post Weekly Edition* (May 27–June 2, 2002): 4.

69. Broder, "States in Fiscal Crisis"; David S. Broder, "What About the States?" *Washington Post Weekly Edition* (March 4–10, 2002): 4.

70. Robert E. Pierre, "The Budget Squeeze," *Washington Post Weekly Edition* (March 25–31, 2002): 6.

CHAPTER 4

1. Joseph B. Mitchell, *Military Leaders of the American Revolution* (McLean, VA: EPM Publications, 1967), pp. 138–149.

2. Louis des Cognets, Jr., *Black Sheep and Heroes of the American Revolution* (Princeton, NJ: Cognets, 1965), Ch. 15.

3. Jan Stanislaw Kopczewski, *Kosciuszko and Pulaski* (Warsaw, Poland: Impress Publishers, 1976).

4. See Alvin Rabushka and Kenneth Shepsle, *Politics in Plural Societies* (Columbus, OH: Merrill, 1972).

5. Carl J. Friedrich, *Problems of the American Public Service* (New York: McGraw-Hill, 1935), p. 12.

6. John A. Garrity and Peter Gay, eds., *The Columbia History of the World* (New York: Harper & Row, 1972), p. 673.

7. Garrity and Gay, eds., *Columbia History of the World,* pp. 669–670.

8. Israel Zangwill, *The Melting Pot* (New York: Macmillan, 1912, ©1909).

9. Quoted in Marc Shell, "Babel in America; or, The Politics of Language Diversity in the United States," *Critical Inquiry* 20 (1993): 109.

10. Richard McCormick, "Ethno-Cultural Interpretations of Nineteenth-Century American Voting Behavior," *Political Science Quarterly* 89 (1974): 351–377.

11. Richard Wayman, "Wisconsin Ethnic Groups and the Election of 1890," *Wisconsin Magazine of History* 51 (1968): 273. More generally, see Paul Kleppner, *The Third Electoral System, 1853–1892: Parties, Voters, and Political Cultures* (Chapel Hill: University of North Carolina Press, 1979).

12. See Oscar Handlin, *Race and Nationality in American Life* (Boston: Little, Brown, 1957), p. 95.

13. Madison Grant, *The Passing of the Great Race* (New York: Scribner's, 1916), pp. 80–81.

14. *Abstracts of Reports of the Immigration Commission* (Washington, DC: Government Printing Office, Vol. 1, 1911). See pp. 229, 244–265.

15. John Miller, "Chinese Exclusion Act," *Congressional Record–Senate 1882*, 13, Pt. 2: 1484–1485.

16. J. Morgan Kousser, *The Shaping of Southern Politics* (New Haven, CT: Yale University Press, 1974).

17. Seymour Martin Lipset and Earl Raab, *The Politics of Unreason* (New York: Harper & Row, 1970), p. 111.

18. Henry Cabot Lodge, "Immigration Restriction," *Congressional Record—Senate 1896*, 28, Pt. 3: 2817.

19. "Emergency" immigration restrictions passed in 1921 were fine-tuned and formalized in the National Origins Act of 1924 and the National Origins Quota Act of 1929.

20. Spencer Rich, "A 20-Year High Tide of Immigration," *Washington Post National Weekly Edition* (September 4–10, 1995): 30.

21. Caroline J. Tolbert and Rodney E. Hero, "Race/Ethnicity and Direct Democracy: An Analysis of California's Illegal Immigration Initiative," *Journal of Politics* 58 (1996): 806–818.

22. George Borhas, "The New Economics of Immigration," *The Atlantic Monthly* (November 1996): 72–80.

23. National Research Council, *The New Americans: Economic, Demographic, and Fiscal Effects of Immigration* (Washington, DC: National Academy Press, 1977), Chs. 4–6.

24. Brad Knickerbocker, "Environment vs. Immigrants," *Christian Science Monitor* (April 27, 1998): 3; and William Branigin, "Sierra Club Votes for Neutrality on Immigration; Population Issue 'Intensely Debated,'" *Washington Post* (April 26, 1998): A16.

25. David Kennedy, "Can We Still Afford to Be a Nation of Immigrants?" *The Atlantic Monthly* (November 1996): 67.

26. Arthur Schlesinger, Jr., *The Disuniting of America* (Knoxville, TN: Whittle, 1991).

27. Louis Hartz, *The Liberal Tradition in America* (New York: Harcourt, 1955).

28. On Madison's pessimistic view of human nature, see Richard Matthews, *If Men Were Angels* (Lawrence, KS: University of Kansas Press, 1995), especially Ch. 3.

29. Ayn Rand, *The Virtue of Selfishness: A New Concept of Egoism*, New American Library (New York: Signet, 1964), pp. 80–91.

30. Bernard Bailyn, *The Ideological Origins of the American Revolution* (Cambridge, MA: Harvard University Press, 1967).

31. Gordon Wood. *The Creation of the American Republic* (New York: Norton, 1972); and J. G. A. Pocock, *The Machiavellian Moment* (Princeton, NJ: Princeton University Press, 1975).

32. Michael J. Sandel, *Democracy's Discontent: American in Search of a Public Philosophy* (Cambridge, MA: Belknap Press of Harvard University Press, 1996).

33. Rogers Smith, "Beyond Tocqueville, Myrdal and Hartz: The Multiple Traditions in America," *American Political Science Review* 87 (1993): 549–566. These inconsistencies were not lost on earlier thinkers, to be sure. Recall Jefferson's pessimistic predictions in his *Notes on the State of Virginia 1781–1785*. Also see Alexis de Tocqueville, *Democracy in America,* ed. J. P. Mayer (New York: Harper, 1969), pp. 340–363.

34. Samuel Huntington, *American Politics: The Promise of Disharmony* (Cambridge, MA: Harvard University Press, 1981).

35. Everett Carl Ladd, *The American Ideology* (Storrs, CT: The Roper Center, 1994), p. 79.

36. I. A. Lewis and William Schneider, "Hard Times: The Public on Poverty," *Public Opinion* (June/July 1985): 2–8, 59–60.

37. "Income Tax Irritation," *Public Perspective* (July/August, 1990): 86.

38. Stanley Feldman, "Structure and Consistency in Public Opinion: The Role of Core Beliefs and Values," *American Journal of Political Science* 32 (1988): 416–440.

39. Alexis de Tocqueville, *Democracy in America*, ed. J. P. Mayer (New York: HarperPerennial, 1969), p. 506.

40. Madison, "Federalist No. 10." See the Appendix to this book.

41. Krissah Williams, "Rich, Poor and Making Ends Meet," *Washington Post Weekly Edition*, July 9–15, 2001: 34.

42. Geoffrey Colvin, "The Great CEO Pay Heist," *Fortune*, June 25, 2001; Mark Gimien, "You Bought. They Sold," *Fortune*, September 2, 2002.

43. Jane Weaver, "Deadbeat CEOs: Will They Pay Up?" MSNBC News, August 9, 2002; CBS News, "GE: SEC Probing Welch Compensation," September 16, 2002.

44. Paul Krugman, *Peddling Prosperity* (New York: Norton, 1994), Ch. 5.

45. Karl Mannheim, *Ideology and Utopia* (New York: Harcourt, 1936), pp. 55–79.

46. Hartz, *The Liberal Tradition,* p. 89.

47. Frederick Jackson Turner, *The Frontier in American History* (New York: Holt, 1920).

48. For a discussion, see Seymour Martin Lipset, "Why No Socialism in the United States?" in Seweryn Bialer and Sophia Sluzar, eds., *Sources of Contemporary Radicalism* (New York: Westview Press, 1977).

49. Sven Steinmo, "American Exceptionalism Reconsidered," in Larry C. Dodd and Calvin Jillson, eds., *The Dynamics of American Politics* (Boulder, CO: Westview, 1994), pp. 106–131.

50. For a sympathetic description of the trials and ordeals of the immigrants, see Oscar Handlin, *The Uprooted,* 2nd ed. (Boston: Little, Brown, 1973).

51. *Abstracts of Reports of the Immigration Commission*, p. 170.

52. William Bennett and Jack Kemp, "The Fortress Party?" *Wall Street Journal* (October 21, 1994): A14.

53. David Firestone, "Mayor Seeks Immigration Coalition," *New York Times* (October 11, 1996): B-3.

54. Dana Milbank, "On Amnesty, Shifting into Low Gear," *Washington Post Weekly Edition*, August 27–September 2, 2001: 11; and Dana Milbank, "The White House Lightning Rod," *Washington Post Weekly Edition* (July 23–29, 2001): 13.

55. Rodolfo de la Garza, "The Effects of Ethnicity on Political Culture," in Paul Peterson, ed., *Classifying by Race* (Princeton, NJ: Princeton University Press, 1995), pp. 351–352. See also Rodolfo de la Garza, Angelo Falcon, and F. Chris Garcia, "Will the Real Americans Please Stand Up: Anglo and Mexican American Support of Core American Political Values," *American Journal of Political Science* 40 (1996): 335–351; and Lydia Saad, "Immigrants See United States as Land of Opportunity," *The Gallup Poll Monthly* (July 1995): 19–33.

56. Gregory Rodriguez, quoted in Patrick McDonnell, "Immigrants Quickly Becoming Assimilated, Report Concludes," *San Francisco Chronicle* (July 7, 1999): A4.

57. Philip Martin and Elizabeth Midgley, "Immigration to the United States" (Washington, DC: Population Reference Bureau, June 1999): 37.

58. Anne Hull, "A New Anxiety," *Washington Post Weekly Edition* (December 3–9, 2001): 9.

59. Mary Jordan, "It's Harder to Cross the Mexican Border," *Washington Post Weekly Edition* (June 3–9, 2002): 17.

60. Hanna Rosin, "The Faded American Dream," *Washington Post Weekly Edition* (April 1–7, 2002): 29.

61. T. Alexander Aleinikoff and David A. Martin, "Ashcroft's Immigration Threat," *Washington Post Weekly Edition* (March 4–10, 2002): 26.

62. David J. Jefferson, "Stopped at the Border," *Newsweek* (October 14, 2002): 59; and Hull, "A New Anxiety."

63. Robert Pear, "Bush Wants Food Stamps for Legal Immigrants," New York Times News Service (January 10, 2002).

64. Michelle Malkin, "Congress Piling Up Measures to Aid, Abet Illegal Immigration," Creators Syndicate (July 5, 2002).

CHAPTER 5

1. For background on the Gulf War, see "Gulf Crisis Grows into War with Iraq," in *1990 Congressional Quarterly Almanac* (Washington, DC: Congressional Quarterly, 1991), pp. 717–756; and "1991 Begins with War in the Mideast," in *1991 Congressional Quarterly Almanac* (Washington, DC: Congressional Quarterly, 1992), pp. 437–450.

2. Jon Krosnick and Laura Brannon, "The Impact of the Gulf War on the Ingredients of Presidential Evaluations," *American Political Science Review* 87 (1993): 963–975.

3. V. O. Key, *Public Opinion and American Democracy* (New York: Knopf, 1961).

4. Carl Friedrich, *Man and His Government* (New York: McGraw-Hill, 1963), pp. 199–215.

5. Robert Hess and Judith Horney, *The Development of Political Attitudes in Children* (Garden City, NY: Doubleday, 1967).

6. Elizabeth Cook, Ted Jelen, and Clyde Wilcox, *Between Two Absolutes: Public Opinion and the Politics of Abortion* (Boulder, CO: Westview Press, 1992).

7. For a survey of positive and negative findings, see Jack Citrin and Donald Green, "The Self-Interest Motive in American Public Opinion," *Research in Micropolitics,* Vol. 3 (Greenwich, CT: JAI Press, 1993), pp. 1–28.

8. Douglas Hibbs, *The American Political Economy* (Cambridge, MA: Harvard University Press, 1987), Ch. 5.

9. David Sears and Jack Citrin, *Tax Revolt* (Cambridge, MA: Harvard University Press, 1985), Chs. 6–7.

10. Jennifer A. Lindholm, Alexander W. Astin, Linda J. Sax, and William S. Korn, *The American College Teacher: National Norms for the 2001–2002 HERI Faculty Survey* (Los Angeles, CA: Higher Education Research Institute). Also, Karl Zinsmeister, "The Shame of America's One-Party Campuses," *American Enterprise Online* (September 2002), but see Martin Plissner, "Flunking Statistics," *American Prospect Online* 13 (December 30, 2002).

11. Norman Nie, Jane Junn, and Kenneth Stehlik-Barry, *Education and Democratic Citizenship in America* (Chicago: University of Chicago Press, 1996).

12. John G. Geer, *From Tea Leaves to Opinion Polls: A Theory of Democratic Leadership* (New York: Columbia University Press, 1996).

13. Details on how these polls are conducted appear in D. Stephen Voss, Andrew Gelman, and Gary King, "Preelection Survey Methodology: Details from Eight Polling Organizations, 1988 and 1992," *Public Opinion Quarterly* 59 (Spring 1995): 98–132.

14. Don Van Natta, Jr., "Polling's 'Dirty Little Secret': No Response," *New York Times* (November 21, 1999, Sect. 4): pp. 1, 16.

15. John Brehm, *The Phantom Respondents* (Ann Arbor, MI: University of Michigan Press, 1993), Ch. 2.

16. Everett Ladd, "The Pollsters' Waterloo," *Wall Street Journal* (November 19, 1996).

17. "Poll Leaves Democrats with Red Faces," (Reuters, January 5, 2000).

18. Jon Krosnick and Matthew Barent, "Comparisons of Party Identification and Policy Preferences: The Impact of Survey Question Format," *American Journal of Political Science* 37 (1993): 941–964.

19. For a full discussion, see David Moore and Frank Newport, "Misreading the Public: The Case of the Holocaust Poll," *Public Perspective* (March/April 1994): 28–30; and Tom Smith, "Review: The Holocaust Denial Controversy," *Public Opinion Quarterly* 59 (1995): 269–295. D. Stephen Voss and Penny Miller present two other instances in which a double negative apparently caused many people to misreport their policy preferences in "Following a False Trail: The Hunt for White Backlash in Kentucky's 1996 Desegregation Vote," *State Politics and Policy Quarterly* 1 (2001): 63–82.

20. Tom Smith, "Public Support for Public Spending, 1973–1994," *The Public Perspective* 6 (April/May 1995): 2.

21. "Abortion: Overview of a Complex Opinion," *The Public Perspective* (November/December, 1989): 19, 20.

22. Ibid., p. 20.

23. "Abortion," *The American Enterprise* (July/August 1995): 107.

24. Cook, Jelen, and Wilcox, *Between Two Absolutes,* Ch. 2.

25. Tamar Lewin, "Study Points to Increase in Tolerance of Ethnicity," *New York Times* (January 8, 1992): A12.

26. For a comprehensive breakdown of federal spending, see "Where the Money Goes," *Congressional Quarterly* (December 11, 1993).

27. Anthony Downs, *An Economic Theory of Democracy* (New York: Harper & Row, 1957), Chs. 11–13.

28. Morris P. Fiorina, "Information and Rationality in Elections," in John Ferejohn and James Kuklinski, eds., *Information and Democratic Processes* (Urbana: University of Illinois Press, 1990), pp. 329–342.

29. John Krosnick, "Government Policy and Citizen Passion: A Study of Issue Publics in Contemporary America," *Political Behavior* 12 (1990): 59–92; and Peter Natchez and Irvin Bupp, "Candidates, Issues, and Voters," *Public Policy* 1 (1968): 409–437.

30. Anthony Downs, "Up and Down with Ecology—The Issue Attention Cycle," *The Public Interest* 28 (1972): 38–50.

31. Fiorina, "Information and Rationality."

32. Anthony King, "Names and Places Lost in the Mists of Time," *Daily Telegraph* (August 26, 1997): 4.

33. Philip Converse, "The Nature of Belief Systems in Mass Publics," in David Apter, ed., *Ideology and Discontent* (New York: Free Press, 1964), pp. 206–261.

34. Warren Miller and Santa Traugott, *American National Election Studies Data Sourcebook, 1952–1986,* (Cambridge, MA: Harvard University Press, 1990), p. 94.

35. James A. Davis, "Changeable Weather in a Cooling Climate Atop the Liberal Plateau," *Public Opinion Quarterly* 56 (1992): 261–306; and Morris P. Fiorina, "The Reagan Years: Turning to the Right or Groping Toward the Middle?" in Barry Cooper, Allan Kornberg, and William Mishler, eds., *The Resurgence of Conservatism in Anglo-American Democracies* (Durham, NC: Duke University Press, 1988), pp. 430–459.

36. "Public Expects GOP Miracles," *Times-Mirror News Release* (December 8, 1994).

37. Samuel Stouffer, *Communism, Conformity, and Civil Liberties* (New York: Doubleday, 1955); and James Prothro and Charles Grigg, "Fundamental Principles of Democracy: Bases of Agreement and Disagreement," *Journal of Politics* 22 (1960): 176–194.

38. For evidence that people's opinions reflect a smaller number of "core beliefs" that may conflict with each other or situational characteristics, see Stanley Feldman, "Structure and Consistency in Public Opinion: The Role of Core Beliefs and Values," *American Journal of Public Opinion* 32 (1988): 416–440; and Stanley Feldman and John Zaller, "A Simple Theory of the Survey Response: Answering Questions versus Revealing Preferences," *American Journal of Political Science* 36 (1992): 579–616.

39. On the effects of posing political conflicts as matters of conflicting rights, see Mary Anne Glendon, *Rights Talk: The Impoverishment of Political Discourse* (New York: Free Press, 1991).

40. All quotations are from John F. Harris, "Campaign Promises Aside, It's Politics as Usual: Policy Shifts, Internal Debates—The Bush White House Looks a Lot Like the Clinton One," *Washington Post Weekly Edition* (July 2–8, 2001): 11.

41. Dan Carney, "House GOP Embrace of Gun Curbs Not Yet Lock, Stock and Barrel, *CQ Weekly* (May 29, 1999): 1267.

42. Dan Carney, "Beyond Guns and Violence: A Battle for House Control," *CQ Weekly* (June 1999): 1426–1432.

43. Kathy Keily, "After Failed Gun Legislation, Political Finger Pointing Begins," *USA Today* (June 21, 1999): 14A.

44. ABC News/*Washington Post* poll of August 30–September 2, 1999.

45. Benjamin Page and Robert Shapiro, *The Rational Public* (Chicago: University of Chicago Press, 1992).

46. James Stimson, "A Macro Theory of Information Flow," in John Ferejohn and James Kuklinski, eds., *Information and Democratic Processes* (Urbana: University of Illinois Press, 1990), pp. 345–368.

47. Arthur Lupia, "Shortcuts versus Encyclopedias: Information and Voting Behavior in California Insurance Reform Elections," *American Political Science Review* 88 (1994): 63–76.

48. James Stimson, *Public Opinion in America: Moods, Cycles, and Swings* (Boulder, CO: Westview Press, 1991).

49. Page and Shapiro, *The Rational Public*; and Christopher Wlezien, "The Public as Thermostat: Dynamics of Preferences for Spending," *American Journal of Political Science* 39 (1995): 981–1000.

50. William Mayer, "Trends in Media Usage," *Public Opinion Quarterly* 57 (1993): 597, 610.

51. For example, Doris Graber, *Mass Media and American Politics* (Washington, DC: CQ Press, 1993), Ch. 7.

52. Russell Neuman, Marion Just, and Ann Crigler, *Common Knowledge: News and the Construction of Political Meaning* (Chicago: University of Chicago Press, 1992); and Jeffrey Mondak, "Newspapers and Political Awareness," *American Journal of Political Science* 39 (1995): 513–527.

53. S. Robert Lichter and Stanley Rothman, "Media and Business Elites," *Public Opinion* (October/November 1981): 43; and Freedom Forum survey cited in Jill Zuckman, "Dole Says Media Overplay GOP View on Abortion," *Boston Globe* (June 25, 1996): 10.

54. William Schneider and I. A. Lewis, "Views on the News," *Public Opinion* (August/September 1985): 6–11; and "Ordinary Americans More Cynical Than Journalists: News Media Differs with Public and Leaders on Watchdog Issues" (Washington, DC: Times-Mirror Center on People and the Press, May 22, 1995).

55. Maura Clancy and Michael Robinson, "The Media in Campaign '84: General Election Coverage, Part I," *Public Opinion* (December/January 1985): 49–54, 59.

56. Daniel Amundson and S. Robert Lichter, "Heeeeeeree's Politics," *Public Opinion* (July/August 1988): 46.

57. Martha Moore, "Candidates Try to Reach Voters by Joking with Jay, Dueling with Dave," *USA Today* (March 1, 2000): 14A.

58. S. Robert Lichter, Stanley Rothman, and Linda S. Lichter, *The Media Elite: America's New Powerbrokers* (New York: Hastings House, 1990).

59. G. C. Stone and E. Grusin, "Network TV as Bad News Bearer," *Journalism Quarterly* 61 (1984), 517–523; R. H. Bohle, "Negativism as News Selection Predictor," *Journalism Quarterly* 63 (1986): 789–796; and D. E. Harrington, "Economic News on Television: The Determinants of Coverage," *Public Opinion Quarterly* 53 (1989): 17–40.

60. Larry Sabato, *Feeding Frenzy* (New York: Simon and Schuster, 1991).

61. A widely cited study of what constitutes news is provided by Herbert Gans, *Deciding What's News: A Case Study of CBS Evening News, NBC Nightly News, Newsweek and Time* (New York: Vintage, 1979).

62. The following account is based on Thomas Romer and Barry Weingast, "Political Foundations of the Thrift Debacle," in Alberto Alesina and Geoffrey Carliner, eds., *Politics and Economics in the 1980s* (Chicago: University of Chicago Press, 1981), pp. 175–214.

63. Ellen Hume, "Why the Press Blew the S&L Scandal," *New York Times* (May 24, 1990): A25.

64. Mark Rom, *Public Spirit in the Thrift Tragedy* (Pittsburgh, PA: University of Pittsburgh Press, 1996).

65. John David Rausch, Jr., "The Pathology of Politics: Government, Press, and Scandal," *Extensions: A Publication of the Carl Albert Congressional Research and Studies Center* (Norman, OK: Carl Albert Congressional Research and Studies Center, Fall 1990), pp. 11–12.

66. A Gallup survey of former Nieman Journalism Fellows found that more than three-quarters believe that traditional journalism is being replaced by tabloid journalism. See "The State of the Public Media Today" (Cambridge, MA: Nieman Foundation, April 1995).

67. Sabato, *Feeding Frenzy.*

68. Michael Robinson and Margaret Sheehan, *Over the Wire and on TV* (New York: Russell Sage, 1983).

69. S. Robert Lichter and Daniel Amundson, "Less News Is Worse News: Television News Coverage of Congress, 1972–92," in Thomas Mann and Norman Ornstein, eds., *Congress, the Press, and the Public* (Washington, DC: American Enterprise Institute, 1994), pp. 131–140.

70. Shanto Iyengar, *Is Anyone Responsible?* (Chicago: University of Chicago Press, 1991).

71. Lichter and Amundson, "Less News Is Worse News."

72. Thomas Patterson, *Out of Order* (New York: Knopf, 1993), Ch. 2.

73. Kiku Adatto, *Picture Perfect* (New York: Basic Books, 1993), Ch. 25.

74. Elihu Katz and Jacob Feldman, "The Debates in the Light of Research: A Survey of Surveys," in Sidney Kraus, ed., *The Great Debates* (Bloomington: University of Indiana Press, 1962), pp. 173–223.

75. Thomas Holbrook, "Campaigns, National Conditions, and U.S. Presidential Elections," *American Journal of Political Science* 38 (1994): 973–998.

76. David von Drehle and Ceci Connolly, "The Truth About Gore's Credibility: Republicans Are Trying to Use the Tall Tales He Tells on the Stump to Trip Him Up," *Washington Post Weekly Edition* (October 16, 2000): 11; Jim Hoagland, "The 'BS' Factor," *Washington Post Weekly Edition* (October

2, 2000): 5; Jonathan Alter, "Al Gore and the Fib Factor," *Newsweek* (October 16, 2000): 43; and "Face to Face Combat," *Newsweek* (November 20, 2000): 102–103.

77. Dan Balz, "Still Neck-and-Neck: With No Major Errors, the First Debate Nonetheless Exposed Weaknesses in Both Candidates,"*Washington Post Weekly Edition* (October 9, 2000): 14; Dan Balz, "Tests Passed, But Questions Remain: Bush Showed a Mastery of Foreign Policy, and Gore Appeared Tentative in the Second Debate,"*Washington Post Weekly Edition* (October 16, 2000): 14; David von Drehle, "The Candidates, Great and Small: Gore Looms Large in the 3rd Debate, But Is That Good?"*Washington Post Weekly Edition* (October 23, 2000): 11; Richard Morin, "For Better and for Worse: Post-Debate Polls Show No Clear-Cut Winner, with Good and Bad News for Both Candidates,"*Washington Post Weekly Edition* (October 23, 2000): 34; and "Face to Face Combat," *Newsweek* (November 20, 2000): 102.

78. Alison Carper, "Paint-by-Numbers Journalism: How Reader Surveys and Focus Groups Subvert a Democratic Press," discussion paper D–19, Barone Center on the Press, Politics and Public Policy, Harvard University Kennedy School of Government, April 1995.

79. Dave Barry, "Scandal Sheep," *Boston Globe Magazine* (March 15, 1998): 12–13.

80. Peter Canellos, "Perot Ad Announcement Is Also-Ran Against Reruns," *Boston Globe* (September 13, 1996): A24.

81. William Kornhauser, *The Politics of Mass Society* (New York: Free Press, 1959).

82. An example is the study of the 1940 presidential campaign reported in Paul Lazarsfeld, Bernard Berelson, and Hazel Gaudet, *The People's Choice* (New York: Columbia University Press, 1948).

83. Joseph Klapper, *The Effects of Mass Communication* (New York: Free Press, 1960).

84. Presentation by Steven Livingston at the John F. Kennedy School of Government, Harvard University, March 1996.

85. Robert Rotberg and Thomas Weiss, eds., *From Massacres to Genocide* (Washington, DC: Brookings, 1996).

86. Bernard Cohen, *The Press and Foreign Policy* (Princeton, NJ: Princeton University Press, 1963), p. 13.

87. M. McCombs and D. Shaw, "The Evolution of Agenda-Setting: Twenty-Five Years in the Marketplace of Ideas," *Journal of Communications* 43 (1993): 58–67.

88. Steven Livingston and Todd Eachus, "Humanitarian Crises and U.S. Foreign Policy: Somalia and the CNN Effect Reconsidered," *Political Communication* 12 (1995): 413–429.

89. Shanto Iyengar and Donald Kinder, *News That Matters: Television and American Opinion* (Chicago: University of Chicago Press, 1987).

90. Jon Krosnick and Laura Brannon, "The Impact of the Gulf War on the Ingredients of Presidential Evaluations," *American Political Science Review* 87 (1993): 963–975.

91. Everett C. Ladd, "As Much About Continuity as Change: As Much About Restoration as Rejection," *The American Enterprise* (January/February 1993): 49–50; and Marc Hetherington, "The Media's Role in Forming Voters' National Economic Evaluations in 1992," *American Journal of Political Science* 40 (1996): 372–395.

92. The most extensive study of framing is Iyengar, *Is Anyone Responsible?*

93. Iyengar and Kinder, *News That Matters*, Chs. 6, 10.

94. Bernard Cohen, *The Press and Foreign Policy*. See also Lutz Erbring, Edie Goldenberg, and Arthur Miller, "Front-Page News and Real-World Clues: A New Look at Agenda-Setting by the Media," *American Journal of Political Science* 24 (1980): 16–49.

95. Frank Luther Mott, *American Journalism* (New York: Macmillan, 1950).

96. Samuel Kernell, *Going Public: New Strategies of Presidential Leadership* (Washington, DC: CQ Press, 1986). Compare Mel Laracey, "The Presidential Newspaper: The Forgotten Way of Going Public," manuscript, Harvard University, 1993.

97. Mott, *American Journalism,* p. 216.

98. Personal communication of Premier Radio, which manages and distributes the Limbaugh show, with research assistant Sam Abrams, March 28, 2000.

99. The 1999 annual radio station survey by M Street Corporation of Nashville, http://www.mstreet.net

100. Mary Ann Watson, *The Expanding Vista: American Television in the Kennedy Years* (New York: Oxford University Press, 1990), p. 76.

101. Austin Ranney, "Broadcasting, Narrowcasting, and Politics," in Anthony Kind, ed., *The New American Political System,* second version (Washington, DC: AEI Press, 1990), pp. 175–201.

102. Pew Research Center for the People and the Press (http://www.peoplepress.org/med98rpt.htm); and Mediamark Research Inc., "Multimedia Audiences," 1999.

103. William Mayer, "The Rise of the New Media," *Public Opinion Quarterly* 58 (1994): 124–146.

104. www.nua.ie/surveys/how_many_online/index.html

105. Mark Gillespie, "'Cyber-Politics' May be More Hype Than Reality . . . So Far," Gallup Poll Release (February 25, 2000).

106. Jim Puzzanghera, "Candidates Rake in Funds on Internet, *San Jose Mercury News* (January 5, 2000).

107. Jeff Glasser, "Virtual Campaign Pays Off," *U.S. News and World Report* (March 6, 2000).

108. Eve Gerber, "Six Arguments for Online Fund Raising," *Slate* (January 18, 2000); and Lindsey Arent, "Candidates Eye Check Republic," *Wired News* (January 13, 2000).

109. Larry Bartels, "Messages Received: The Political Impact of Media Exposure," *American Political Science Review* 87 (1993): 267–285.

CHAPTER 6

1. Tom Fiedler, "Introduction: The Encore of *Key Largo*," in *Overtime*, ed. Larry Sabato (New York: Longman, 2002), pp. 12–13.

2. Dan Keating and Dan Balz, "Election 2000: Closer Than Close," *Washington Post* (November 12, 2001).

3. Benjamin Barber, *Strong Democracy: Participatory Politics for a New Age* (Berkeley: University of California Press, 1984), p. xiii.

4. Jeff Jacoby, "Making It Too Easy to Vote," *Boston Globe* (July 18, 1996): A15.

5. John Aldrich, *Why Parties?* (Chicago: University of Chicago Press, 1995), pp. 106–107.

6. "18-Year-Old Vote: Constitutional Amendment Cleared," *Congressional Quarterly Almanac* (Washington, DC: Congressional Quarterly, 1972), pp. 475–477.

7. For a comparative study of the American and Swiss suffrage movements, see Lee Ann Banaszak, *Why Movements Succeed or Fail* (Princeton, NJ: Princeton University Press, 1996).

8. Howard Rosenthal and Subrata Sen, "Electoral Participation in the French Fifth Republic," *American Political Science Review* 67 (1973): 29–54.

9. Raymond E. Wolfinger and Steven J. Rosenstone, *Who Votes?* (New Haven, CT: Yale University Press, 1980), p. 116.

10. Ruy Teixeira, *The Disappearing American Voter* (Washington, DC: Brookings, 1992), p. 10.

11. "Can the Black Vote Hold Up? *The Economist* (April 3, 1999): 24.

12. Martha Angle, "Low Voter Turnout Prompts Concern on Hill," *Congressional Quarterly Weekly Report* (April 2, 1988): 864; and Stephen Bennett, "The Uses and Abuses of Registration and Turnout Data," *PS: Political Science and Politics* 23 (1990): 166–171.

13. Stephen Knack, "Drivers Wanted: Motor Voter and the Election of 1996," *PS: Political Science and Politics* 32 (1999): 237–243; and Michael Martinez and David Hill, "Did Motor Voter Work? *American Politics Quarterly* 27 (1999): 296–315.

14. Wolfinger and Rosenstone, *Who Votes?,* p. 88.

15. Richard Hasen, "Voting Without Law," *University of Pennsylvania Law Review* 144 (1996): 2135–2179.

16. Mark Franklin, "Electoral Engineering and Cross-National Turnout Differences: What Role for Compulsory Voting? *British Journal of Political Science* 29 (1999): 205.

17. Richard Boyd, "Decline of U.S. Voter Turnout: Structural Explanations," *American Politics Quarterly* 9 (1981): 133–159.

18. Stephen Knack, "The Voter Participation Effects of Selecting Jurors from Registration Lists," Working Paper No. 91–10, University of Maryland, Department of Economics; and J. Eric Oliver and Raymond Wolfinger, "Jury Aversion and Voter Registration," paper presented at the 1997 Annual Meeting of the American Political Science Association, Washington, DC.

19. G. Bingham Powell, "American Voter Turnout in Comparative Perspective," *American Political Science Review* 80 (1986): 17–43; and Robert Jackman, "Political Institutions and Voter Turnout in the Industrial Democracies," *American Political Science Review* 81 (1987): 405–423.

20. Steven J. Rosenstone and John Mark Hansen, *Mobilization, Participation, and Democracy* (New York: Macmillan, 1993), pp. 63–70. There is some conflict between their figures and those reported by Sidney Verba, Kay Lehman Schlozman, and Henry E. Brady in *Voice and Equality: Civic Volunteerism in American Politics* (Cambridge, MA: Harvard University Press, 1995), pp. 69–74. Part of the explanation may be that the survey items relied on by Rosenstone and Hansen generally have more specific referents (such as this year's elections), whereas the items relied on by Verba, Schlozman, and Brady ask more generally about activity in the last year or two years. Thus the Verba, Schlozman, and Brady figures may reflect the increasing number of opportunities.

21. Jack Citrin, "Comment: The Political Relevance of Trust in Government," *American Political Science Review* 68 (1974): 973–988.

22. Teixeira, *The Disappearing American Voter,* p. 49.

23. "Politics Brief: Is There a Crisis?" *The Economist* (July 17, 1999): 50.

24. Rosenstone and Hansen, *Mobilization, Participation, and Democracy,* Ch. 2.

25. Jeffrey Jones, "Does Bringing Out the Candidate Bring Out the Votes?" *American Politics Quarterly* 26 (1998): 406.

26. John Milholland, "The Danger Point in American Politics," *North American Review* 164 (1897).

27. Wolfinger and Rosenstone, *Who Votes?,* p. 101.

28. John Ferejohn and Morris Fiorina, "The Paradox of Not Voting: A Decision Theoretic Analysis," *American Political Science Review* 68 (1974): 525–535.

29. Anthony Downs, *An Economic Theory of Democracy* (New York: Harper & Row, 1957), Ch. 14.

30. Richard Brody, "The Puzzle of Political Participation in America," in Anthony King, ed., *The New American Political System* (Washington, DC: American Enterprise Institute, 1978), pp. 287–324; and Paul Abramson and John Aldrich, "The Decline of Electoral Participation in America," *American Political Science Review* 76 (1982): 502–521.

31. Rosenstone and Hansen, *Mobilization, Participation, and Democracy,* p. 183.

32. Marshall Ganz, "Motor Voter or Motivated Voter," *The American Prospect* (September–October, 1996): 46–48; Marshall Ganz, "Voters in the Crosshairs," *The American Prospect* (Winter 1994): 100–109; and Michael Scherer, "Campaign Finance Reform School," *Columbia Journalism Review* (September/October 2002): 54.

33. Stephen Knack, "Civic Norms, Social Sanctions, and Voter Turnout," *Rationality and Society* 4 (1992): 133–156.

34. Warren Miller, "The Puzzle Transformed: Explaining Declining Turnout," *Political Behavior* 14 (1992): 1–43.

35. Rosenstone and Hansen, *Mobilization, Participation, and Democracy*, Ch. 7; and Teixeira, *The Disappearing American Voter*, Ch. 2.

36. Laura Stoker and M. Kent Jennings, "Life-Cycle Transitions and Political Participation: The Case of Marriage," *American Political Science Review* 89 (1995): 421–433.

37. For detailed analyses of the relationship between demographic characteristics and voting, see Wolfinger and Rosenstone, *Who Votes?*, and Rosenstone and Hansen, *Mobilization, Participation, and Democracy*, Ch. 5.

38. Sidney Verba and Norman Nie, *Participation in America: Political Democracy and Social Equality* (New York: Harper & Row, 1972), pp. 170–171; and Wolfinger and Rosenstone, *Who Votes?* p. 90.

39. Rosenstone and Hansen, *Mobilization, Participation, and Democracy in America*, Ch. 5.

40. Katherine Tate, "Black Political Participation in the 1984 and 1988 Presidential Elections," *American Political Science Review* 85 (1991): 1159–1176.

41. On language and political participation, see Verba, Schlozman, and Brady, *Voice and Equality*.

42. Russell Dalton, *Citizen Politics in Western Democracies* (Chatham, NJ: Chatham House, 1988), pp. 51–52.

43. Herbert Tingsten, *Political Behavior: Studies in Election Statistics* (London: King & Son, 1937), pp. 225–226.

44. "The Democratic Distemper," *The Public Interest* 41 (1975), pp. 36–37.

45. Quoted in Seymour Martin Lipset, *Political Man* (New York: Anchor, 1963), p. 228, note 90.

46. George Will, "In Defense of Nonvoting," in George Will, ed., *The Morning After* (New York: Free Press, 1986), p. 229.

47. Political theorist Benjamin Barber refers to the former as an example of "strong democracy" and to the latter as an example of "thin democracy." See Barber, *Strong Democracy*, note 2.

48. Stephen Bennett and David Resnick, "The Implications of Nonvoting for Democracy in the United States," *American Journal of Political Science* 34 (1990): 771–802.

49. U.S. Bureau of the Census, *Current Population Reports*, P20–485, Table B. For a general discussion, see Peverill Squire, Raymond Wolfinger, and David Glass, "Residential Mobility and Voter Turnout," *American Political Science Review* 81 (1987): 45–65.

50. Teixeira, *The Disappearing American Voter*, p. 92.

51. Rosenstone and Hansen, *Mobilization, Participation, and Democracy*, p. 51.

52. David Nexon, "Asymmetry in the Political System: Occasional Activists in the Democratic and Republican Parties, 1956–1964," *American Political Science Review* 65 (1971): 716–730; and Warren Miller and M. Kent Jennings, *Parties in Transition* (New York: Russell Sage, 1986), Ch. 2.

CHAPTER 7

1. For a full discussion, see Barbara Sinclair, "Trying to Govern Positively in a Negative Era: Clinton and the 103rd Congress," in Colin Campbell and Bert Rockman, eds., *The Clinton Presidency: First Appraisals* (Chatham, NJ: Chatham House, 1996), pp. 101–109.

2. Dana Milbank, "Staring History in the Face," *Washington Post Weekly Edition* (October 30, 2000): 21–22; David Stout, "Experts, Once Certain, Now Say Gore Is a Maybe," *New York Times* (November 7, 2000); Richard Morin, "It's Not Easy to Pick a Winner," *Washington Post Weekly Edition* (September 11, 2000): 34; and Karl Eisenhower and Pete Nelson, "The Phony Science of Predicting Elections," Slate Archives, http://slate.msn.com/Features/forecast/forecast.asp (accessed August 15, 2001).

3. Hanna Rosin, "Personal Faith and Public Policy," *Washington Post Weekly Edition* (September 11, 2000): 10–11.

4. Nina J. Easton, "For Now, Silence Is Golden," *Washington Post Weekly Edition* (October 9, 2000): 21; Richard L. Berke, "A Race in Which Candidates Clung to the Center," *New York Times* (November 7, 2000); and George Stephanopoulos, "Clinton's Long Shadow," *Newsweek* (August 21, 2000): 35.

5. David Brooks, "The Revenge of the Liberals," *Newsweek* (October 30, 2000): 39; David S. Broder, "Still the Economy, Stupid," *Washington Post Weekly Edition* (September 18, 2000): 4; Sebastian Mallaby, "The Paradox of Prosperity," *Washington Post Weekly Edition* (September 18, 2000): 29; George Packer, "Gore Says He'll Protect the Middle Class, But His Rhetoric Is 100 Years Out of Date," *Washington Post Weekly Edition* (November 6, 2000): 21–22; and Richard Morin and Claudia Deane, "The Nader Factor," *Washington Post Weekly Edition* (November 6, 2000): 34.

6. Dan Balz, "Still Neck-and-Neck," *Washington Post Weekly Edition* (October 9, 2000): 14; Dan Balz, "Tests Passed, But Questions Remain," *Washington Post Weekly Edition* (October 16, 2000): 14; David von Drehle, "The Candidates, Great and Small," *Washington Post Weekly Edition* (October 23, 2000): 11; Richard Morin, "For Better and For Worse," *Washington Post Weekly Edition* (October 23, 2000): 34; and "Face to Face Combat," *Newsweek* (November 20, 2000): 102.

7. David von Drehle and Ceci Connolly, "The Truth About Gore's Credibility," *Washington Post Weekly Edition* (October 16, 2000): 11; Jim Hoagland, "The 'BS' Factor," *Washington Post Weekly Edition* (October 2, 2000): 5; Jonathan Alter, "Al Gore and the Fib Factor," *Newsweek* (October 16, 2000): 43; and "Face to Face Combat," *Newsweek*, pp. 102–103.

8. Andrew Gelman and Gary King, "Why Are American Presidential Election Campaign Polls So Variable When Votes Are So Predictable?" *British Journal of Political Science* 23 (1993): 409–451; Dan B. Thomas and Larry R. Baas, "The Postelection Campaign: Competing Constructions of the Clinton Victory in 1992," *Journal of Politics* 58 (1996): 309–331; and Richard Morin, "The True Political Puppeteers," *Washington Post Weekly Edition* (February 20–26, 1989): 37.

9. Although the general notion of "partisanship" has been around for centuries, the social–psychological concept of party ID was advanced in the pioneering work of Angus Campbell, Philip Converse, Warren Miller, and Donald Stokes, *The American Voter* (New York: Wiley, 1960), Chs. 6–7.

10. Donald Philip Green and Bradley Palmquist, "How Stable Is Party Identification?" *Political Behavior* 16 (1994): 437–466.

11. Morris Fiorina, *Retrospective Voting in American National Elections* (New Haven, CT: Yale University Press, 1981); and Michael MacKuen, Robert Erikson, and James Stimson, "Macropartisanship," *American Political Science Review* 83 (1989): 1125–1142. On the latter piece, though, see Donald Green, Bradley Palmquist, and Eric Schickler, "Macropartisanship: A Replication and Critique," *American Political Science Review* 92 (1998): 883–899.

12. Bruce E. Keith et al., *The Myth of the Independent Voter* (Berkeley, CA: University of California Press, 1992).

13. Jane Mansbridge, "Myth and Reality: The ERA and the Gender Gap in the 1980 Election," *Public Opinion Quarterly*, 49 (1985): 164–178.

14. Emily Stoper, "The Gender Gap Concealed and Revealed," *Journal of Political Science* 17 (1989): 50–62; and Tom Smith, "Gender and Attitudes Toward Violence," *Public Opinion Quarterly* 48 (1984): 384–396.

15. For discussions, see Pamela Conover, "Feminists and the Gender Gap," *Journal of Politics* 50 (1988): 985–1010; and Elizabeth Cook and Clyde Wilcox, "Feminism and the Gender Gap—A Second Look," *Journal of Politics* 53 (1991): 1111–1122.

16. This was first noted by Herbert Weisberg, "The Demographics of a New Voting Gap: Marital Differences in American Voting Behavior," *Public Opinion Quarterly* 51 (1987): 335–343.

17. "Where the Parties Are," *The Public Perspective* (March/April 1994): 78–79; and "Which Party Is Better on Which Issues?" *The Public Perspective* (June/July 1996): 65.

18. Fiorina, *Retrospective Voting.*

19. Scott Teeter, "Public Opinion in 1984," and Gerald Pomper, "The Presidential Election," both in Gerald Pomper et al., *The Election of 1984* (Chatham, NJ: Chatham House, 1985).

20. Samuel Popkin, *The Reasoning Voter* (Chicago: University of Chicago Press, 1991), pp. 60–67.

21. Michael Kinsley, as quoted by Howard Kurtz, "The Premature Post-Mortems Are Starting," *Washington Post* (online extras, October 31, 2000).

22. The classic demonstration in Chapter 8 of Campbell et al.'s *The American Voter* almost certainly overstates the case. Balanced treatments of policy issues in recent campaigns appear in the series of *Change and Continuity* volumes by Paul Abramson, John Aldrich, and David Rohde, published by CQ Press.

23. Benjamin Page and Richard Brody, "Policy Voting and the Electoral Process: The Vietnam War Issue," *American Political Science Review* 66 (1972): 979–995.

24. Edward Carmines and James Stimson, "The Two Faces of Issue Voting," *American Political Science Review* 74 (1980): 78–91.

25. Donald Stokes, "Some Dynamic Elements of Contests for the Presidency," *American Political Science Review* 60 (1966): 19–28.

26. Fiorina, *Retrospective Voting,* pp. 150–153; and Andrew Kohut, "The Vox Pop on Malaprops," *Washington Post Weekly Edition* (October 2, 2000): 22.

27. Stokes, "Some Dynamic Elements," p. 222.

28. Indeed, by some calculations, Kennedy's results were worse than those of a "generic" Democrat for that time. See Angus Campbell et al., "Stability and Change in 1960; and A Reinstating Election," in *Elections and the Political Order* (New York: Wiley, 1966), pp. 78–95.

29. On the failure of incumbency to provide a complete explanation of Democratic dominance during this era, see Morris Fiorina, *Divided Government,* 2nd ed. (Boston: Allyn & Bacon, 1996),

pp. 18–23. D. Stephen Voss and David Lublin offer evidence of a candidate overstating her own incumbency advantage in "Black Incumbents, White Districts: An Appraisal of the 1996 Congressional Elections," *American Politics Research* 29 (2001):141–182. Ironically, that candidate lost her party primary in 2002.

30. Norman Ornstein, Thomas Mann, and Michael Malbin, *Vital Statistics on Congress, 1998–2000* (Washington, DC: American Enterprise Institute, 2000).

31. Robert Erikson, "Malapportionment, Gerrymandering and Party Fortunes in Congressional Elections," *American Political Science Review* 66 (1972): 1234–1245. Gary King and Andrew Gelman, "Systemic Consequences of Incumbency Advantage in U.S. House Elections," *American Journal of Political Science* 35 (1991): 110–138.

32. Gary W. Cox and Jonathan N. Katz, *Elbridge Gerry's Salamander: The Electoral Consequences of the Reapportionment Revolution* (New York: Cambridge University Press, 2002).

33. David Brady and Morris Fiorina, "Ruptured Legacy: Presidential Congressional Relations in Historical Perspective," in Larry Berman, ed., *Looking Back on the Reagan Presidency* (Baltimore, MD: Johns Hopkins University Press, 1989), pp. 268–287.

34. John Ferejohn and Randall Calvert, "Presidential Coattails in Historical Perspective," *American Journal of Political Science* 28 (1984): 127–146.

35. Fiorina, *Divided Government*, p. 14.

36. Ibid., pp. 135–139.

37. Ronald Keith Gaddie and Charles S. Bullock, III, *Elections to Open Seats in the U.S. House: Where the Action Is* (Lanham, MD: Rowman and Littlefield, 2000), pp. 4–5, 24–35; and David Lublin and D. Stephen Voss, "Boll-Weevil Blues," *American Review of Politics* 22 (2000): 427–450.

38. Jon Healey, "Projects Are His Project," *Congressional Quarterly Weekly Report* (September 21, 1996): 2672. Also see Jonathan Salant, "Some Republicans Turned Away from Leadership," *Congressional Quarterly Weekly Report* (December 7, 1996): 3352–3354; and Andrew Taylor, "GOP Pet Projects Give Boost to Shaky Incumbents," *Congressional Quarterly Weekly Report* (August 3, 1996): 2169–2173.

39. Karen Foerstel, "Slouching Toward Election Day, Democrats Are Anxious and Angry," *Congressional Quarterly Weekly Report* (September 12, 1998): 2383-2385.

40. www.commoncause.org

41. David Rohde, *Parties and Leaders in the Postreform House* (Chicago: University of Chicago Press, 1991).

42. Donna Cassate, "'Independent Groups' Ads Increasingly Steer Campaigns," *Congressional Quarterly Weekly Report* (May 2, 1998): 1114.

43. Max Farrand, ed., *The Records of the Federal Convention of 1787* (New Haven, CT: Yale University Press, 1966), Vol. 1, p. 151.

44. Joe Foote and David Weber, "Network Evening News Visibility of Congressmen and Senators," paper presented to the Association for Education in Journalism and Mass Communication (August 1984).

45. James Campbell, "When Have Presidential Campaigns Decided Election Outcomes?" paper presented at the 1999 Annual Meeting of the American Political Science Association, Atlanta.

46. See Thomas Holbrook, *Do Campaigns Matter?* (Thousand Oaks, CA: Sage, 1996).

47. For a discussion, see Marjorie Hershey, "The Campaign and the Media," in Gerald Pomper et al., *The Election of 1988* (Chatham, NJ: Chatham House, 1989), Ch. 3.

48. See, for example, Adam Nagourney and Elizabeth Kolbert, "Missteps Doomed Dole from the Start," *New York Times* (November 8, 1996): A1.

49. Jim Drinkard, "Let the Fundraising Begin—Again," *USA Today* (March 10, 2000): 14A.

50. Thomas B. Edsall and Juliet Eilperin, "PAC Attack II," *Washington Post* (August 18, 2002): B02.

51. During the last two months of the presidential campaigns of 1976 to 1988, about 40 percent of the lead stories on the CBS evening news were about the election, as were 20 percent of all the stories reported. See Steven J. Rosenstone and John Mark Hansen, *Mobilization, Participation, and Democracy in America* (New York: Macmillan, 1993), p. 178, n. 26.

52. Anthony Corrado, "Financing the 1996 Presidential General Election," in John Green, *Financing the 1996 Election* (Armonk, NY: Sharpe, 1999), pp. 84–85.

53. Thomas Patterson and Robert McClure, *The Unseeing Eye: The Myth of Television Power in National Elections* (New York: Putnam, 1976); and Darrel West, *Air Wars: Television Advertising in Election Campaigns, 1952–1992* (Washington, DC: Congressional Quarterly, 1993).

54. Edwin Diamond and Stephen Bates, *The Spot,* 3rd ed. (Cambridge, MA: MIT Press, 1992); and Craig Brians and Martin Wattenberg, "Campaign Issue Knowledge and Salience: Comparing Reception from TV Commercials, TV News, and Newspapers," *American Journal of Political Science* 40 (1996): 172–193.

55. Federal Election Commission (www.fec.gov).

56. Gary Jacobson, "Practical Consequences of Campaign Finance Reform: An Incumbent Protection Act?" *Public Policy* 42 (1976): 1–32.

57. Gary Jacobson, *Money in Congressional Elections* (New Haven, CT: Yale University Press, 1980).

58. Jacobson, *Politics of Congressional Elections*, p. 40; Kenneth Bickers and Robert Stein, "The Electoral Dynamics of the Federal Pork Barrel," *American Journal of Political Science* 40 (1996): 1300–1326.

59. Dave Barry, "Direct Deposit," *Boston Globe Magazine* (November 30, 1997): 12–13.

60. Charles Lane, "Kohl Train," *The New Republic* (February 14, 2000): 17.

61. Richard Katz, "Party Organizations and Finance," in Lawrence LeDuc, Richard Niemi, and Pippa Norris, eds., *Comparing Democracies* (Thousand Oaks, CA: Sage, 1996), pp. 129–132.

62. Howard Margolis, "The Banzhaf Fallacy," *American Journal of Political Science* 27 (1983): 321–326; George Rabinowitz and Stuart Elaine MacDonald, "The Power of the States in U.S. Presidential Elections," *American Political Science Review* 80 (1986): 65–87; and James C. Garand and T. Wayne Parent, "Representation, Swing, and Bias in U.S. Presidential Elections, 1872–1988," *American Journal of Political Science* 35 (1991): 1011–1031.

63. For a discussion, see Nelson Polsby and Aaron Wildavsky, *Presidential Elections*, 10th ed. (Chatham, NJ: Chatham House, 2000), pp. 245–253.

64. Frederick D. Weil, "The Sources and Structure of Legitimation in Western Democracies," *American Sociological Review* 54 (1989): 682–706; and Frederick D. Weil, "Political Culture, Political Structure and Democracy: The Case of Legitimation and Opposition Structure," in Frederick D. Weil, ed., *Research on Democracy and Society, Vol. 2, Political Culture and Political Structure: Theoretical and Empirical Studies* (Greenwich, CT: JAI Press, 1994).

65. "Fresh Light on Primary Colors," *The Economist* (February 24, 1996): 23.

66. A good current description of the caucus system can be found in William Mayer, "Caucuses: How They Work, What Difference They Make," in William Mayer, ed., *In Pursuit of the White House* (Chatham, NJ: Chatham House, 1996).

67. Marianne Means, "Downfall of the Reform Party," Hearst Newspapers (August 3, 2001).

68. On the history of the presidential primary, see James Davis, *Springboard to the White House* (New York: Crowell, 1967).

69. John Kessel, *The Goldwater Coalition* (Indianapolis, IN: Bobbs-Merrill, 1968), Ch. 3.

70. Nelson Polsby, *Consequences of Party Reform* (New York: Oxford University Press, 1983), Ch. 1.

71. For a participant observer's account of the post-1968 reforms, see Austin Ranney, *Curing the Mischiefs of Faction* (Berkeley, CA: University of California Press, 1975).

72. On primary dynamics, see John Aldrich, *Before the Convention* (Chicago: University of Chicago Press, 1980); and Larry Bartels, *Presidential Primaries and the Dynamics of Public Choice* (Princeton, NJ: Princeton University Press, 1988).

73. John Haskell, *Fundamentally Flawed* (Lanham, MD: Rowman and Littlefield, 1996).

74. Pew Research Center for the People and the Press, "It's Still Too Early for the Voters," http://www. people-press.org/june99rpt.htm

75. Kathy Kiely, "Wealth of Debates Keeps the Hopefuls Talking," *USA Today* (January 26, 2000): 8A.

76. Pew Research Center for the People and the Press, "It's Still Too Early for the Voters," http://www.people-press.org/june99rpt.htm

77. Larry Sabato, "Presidential Nominations: The Front-Loaded Frenzy of '96," in Larry Sabato, ed., *Toward the Millennium: The Elections of 1996* (Boston: Allyn & Bacon, 1997), pp. 37–91.

78. "A Good Fight Draws a Crowd," *New York Times* (March 12, 2000): 5.

79. See John G. Geer, *Nominating Presidents* (New York: Greenwood Press, 1989), Ch. 2; and Barbara Norander, "Nomination Choices: Caucus and Primary Outcomes, 1976–1988," *American Journal of Political Science* 37 (1993): 343–364.

80. See, for example, the ABC News/*Washington Post* poll of August 30–September 2, 1999.

81. Thomas Patterson, *Out of Order* (New York: Vintage, 1994), p. 74.

82. "Once Again, 2 Small States Warp Political Process, *USA Today* (January 24, 2000): 18A.

83. Patterson, *Out of Order*, p. 82.

84. Most research finds only small electoral impacts for the vice-presidential nominees. See Steven Rosenstone, *Forecasting Presidential Elections* (New Haven, CT: Yale University Press, 1983), pp. 64–66, 87–88.

85. "Congressional Primary Schedule," *Congressional Quarterly Weekly Report* (January 1, 2000): 16–17.

CHAPTER 8

1. Derek Bok, *The State of the Nation* (Cambridge, MA: Harvard University Press), pp. 235–255.

2. Bok, *State of the Nation*, p. 252.

3. Haynes Johnson and David Broder, *The System: The American Way of Politics at the Breaking Point* (Boston: Little, Brown, 1996), p. 81.

4. Ibid., p. 205.

5. Ibid., p. 94.

6. Helen Dewar and Amy Goldstein, "Partisan Bickering Is a Side Effect," *Washington Post Weekly Edition* (July 22–28, 2002): 14.

7. This short account is based on James MacGregor Burns, *The Deadlock of Democracy* (Englewood Cliffs, NJ: Prentice-Hall, 1964), Ch. 2.

8. Jackson Turner Main, *Political Parties Before the Constitution* (New York: Norton, 1973).

9. Steven Rosenstone, Roy Behr, and Edward Lazarus, *Third Parties in America* (Princeton, NJ: Princeton University Press, 1981).

10. Maurice Duverger, *Political Parties: Their Organization and Activity in the Modern State* (New York: Wiley, 1963), Book II, Ch. 1.

11. Ibid. For elaboration, see Thomas Palfrey, "A Mathematical Proof of Duverger's Law," in Peter Ordeshook, ed., *Models of Strategic Choice in Politics* (Ann Arbor: University of Michigan Press, 1989), pp. 69–91.

12. Douglas Rae, *The Political Consequences of Electoral Laws,* rev. ed. (New Haven, CT: Yale University Press, 1971), p. 98. Compare Arend Lijphart, who argues that Rae's figures exaggerate the difference; see Lijphart, "The Political Consequences of Electoral Laws, 1945–1985," *American Political Science Review* 84 (1990): 481–496.

13. The seminal contribution was V. O. Key, Jr., "A Theory of Critical Elections," *Journal of Politics* 17 (1955): 3–18. The most influential elaborations and extensions of the idea are Walter Dean Burnham, *Critical Elections and the Mainsprings of American Politics* (New York: Norton, 1970) and James Sundquist, *Dynamics of the Party System,* rev. ed. (Washington, DC: Brookings, 1983).

14. Robert Remini, *Martin Van Buren and the Making of the Democratic Party* (New York: Columbia, 1959); and Donald Cole, *Martin Van Buren and the American Political System* (Princeton, NJ: Princeton University Press, 1984).

15. For a recent history of the period, see Paul Kleppner, *The Third Electoral System, 1853–1892: Parties, Voters, and Political Cultures* (Chapel Hill: University of North Carolina Press, 1979).

16. Charles Stewart and Barry Weingast, "Stacking the Senate, Changing the Nation: Republican Rotten Boroughs, Statehood Politics, and American Political Development," *Studies in American Political Development* 6 (1992): 223–271.

17. Michael McGerr, *The Decline of Popular Politics* (New York: Oxford University Press, 1986).

18. Harold Gosnell provides a classic study of a machine. See his *Machine Politics: Chicago Model* (Chicago: University of Chicago Press, 1937). For a more recent study, see M. C. Brown and C. N. Halaby, "Machine Politics in America, 1870–1945," *Journal of Interdisciplinary History* 17 (1987): 587–612.

19. John D. Hicks, *The Populist Revolt* (Minneapolis, MN: University of Minnesota Press, 1931).

20. E. E. Schattschneider, "United States: The Functional Approach to Party Government," in Sigmund Neumann, ed., *Modern Political Parties* (Chicago: University of Chicago Press, 1956), pp. 194–215.

21. George Brown Tindall, *America: A Narrative History* (New York: Norton, 1984), p. 1025.

22. Alan Lichtman, *Prejudice and the Old Politics* (Chapel Hill: University of North Carolina Press, 1979).

23. Stanley Lebergott, *The Americans: An Economic Record* (New York: Norton, 1984), Ch. 34.

24. Joel Silbey, "Beyond Realignment and Realignment Theory," in Byron Shafer, ed., *The End of Realignment?* (Madison: University of Wisconsin Press, 1991), pp. 3–23.

25. Martin Wattenberg, *The Decline of American Political Parties, 1952–1992* (Cambridge, MA: Harvard University Press, 1994).

26. E. E. Schattschneider, *Party Government* (New York: Farrar and Rinehart, 1942), p. 1.

27. American Political Science Association, "Toward a More Responsible Two-Party System: A Report of the Committee on Political Parties," *Supplement to the American Political Science Review* 44 (1950).

28. John Aldrich, *Why Parties?* (Chicago: University of Chicago Press, 1995), Ch. 2.

29. See, for example, James Campbell, *The Presidential Pulse of Congressional Elections* (Lexington: University Press of Kentucky, 1993).

30. Richard Fenno, *Home Style* (Boston: Little, Brown, 1978), Ch. 3.

31. V. O. Key, Jr., *Southern Politics* (New York: Knopf, 1949).

32. Anthony Downs, *An Economic Theory of Democracy* (New York: Harper & Row, 1957).

33. R. Michael Alvarez and Jonathan Nagler, "Economics, Issues, and the Perot Candidacy: Voter Choice in the 1992 Presidential Election," *American Journal of Political Science* 39 (1995): 714–744.

34. Morris Fiorina, *Divided Government,* 2nd ed. (Boston: Allyn & Bacon, 1996), pp. 107–110.

35. Julius Turner, *Party and Constituency: Pressures on Congress* (Baltimore, MD: Johns Hopkins University Press, 1951).

36. Burns, *Deadlock of Democracy.*

37. Writing in the 1970s, Hugh Heclo put the number at 3000. See his *A Government of Strangers* (Washington, DC: Brookings, 1977). By 1992, Thomas Weko put the number at about 3700. See *The Politicizing Presidency* (Lawrence: University of Kansas Press, 1995), p. 161.

38. Stephen Skowronek, *Building a New American State* (New York: Cambridge University Press, 1992), p. 69.

39. Stephen Frantzich, *Political Parties in the Technological Age* (New York: Longman, 1989).

40. Gordon Baker, *The Reapportionment Revolution* (New York: Random House, 1966).

41. Cornelius Cotter, James Gibson, John Bibby, and Robert Huckshorn, *Party Organizations in American Politics* (New York: Praeger, 1984).

42. Ibid.

43. Robert Dahl, *Dilemmas of Pluralist Democracy* (New Haven, CT: Yale University Press, 1982).

44. There is some controversy about how to measure group membership—and consequently about the exact figures. For differing viewpoints, see Frank Baumgartner and Jack Walker, "Survey Research and Membership in Voluntary Associations," *American Journal of Political Science* 32 (1988): 908–928; Tom Smith, "Trends in Voluntary Group Membership: Comments on Baumgartner and Walker," *American Journal of Political Science* 34 (1990): 646–661; and Baumgartner and Walker, "Response to Smith's 'Trends in Voluntary Group Membership,'" *American Journal of Political Science* 34 (1990): 662–670.

45. Alexis de Tocqueville, *Democracy in America,* ed. J. P. Mayer (New York: HarperPerennial, 1969), p. 513.

46. Kay Schlozman and John Tierney, *Organized Interests and American Democracy* (New York: Harper & Row, 1981), p. 75.

47. Robert Wiebe, *The Search for Order, 1877–1920* (New York: Hill and Wang, 1967).

48. Jack Walker, *Mobilizing Interest Groups in America* (Ann Arbor: University of Michigan Press, 1991), p. 10.

49. Jeffrey Berry, *Lobbying for the People* (Princeton, NJ: Princeton University Press, 1977).

50. An excellent source of basic information about groups and associations in the United States is the *Encyclopedia of Associations,* Carol Schwartz and Rebecca Turner, eds. (Detroit, MI: Gale Research, Inc., annual editions).

51. James Q. Wilson, *Political Organizations* (New York: Basic Books, 1973), Ch. 3.

52. Mancur Olson, *The Logic of Collective Action* (Cambridge, MA: Harvard University Press, 1965).

53. The term is from Richard Wagner, "Pressure Groups and Political Entrepreneurs," *Papers in Nonmarket Decision Making* 1 (1966): 161–170. For extended discussions, see Norman Frolich, Joe Oppenheimer, and Oran Young, *Political Leadership and Collective Goods* (Princeton, NJ: Princeton University Press, 1971); and Terry Moe, *The Organization of Interests* (Chicago: University of Chicago Press, 1980), Chs. 3–4.

54. Walker, *Mobilizing Interest Groups,* pp. 98–99.

55. Expenditures were $1.4 billion in 1998, the latest year for which we have figures. "Spending on Lobbying Rises," *USA Today* (November 16, 1999): 11A.

56. Carl Weiser, "Enforcement of Law Almost Non-existent," *USA Today* (November 16, 1999): 11A.

57. *American Lobbyists Directory,* Robert Wilson, ed. (Detroit, MI: Gale Research Inc., 1995). The estimate of Washington lobbyists is that of James Thurber, cited in Burdett Loomis, *The Contemporary Congress* (New York: St. Martin's Press, 1996), p. 35.

58. Lobbyist Michael Bromberg, quoted in Eleanor Clift and Tom Brazaitis, *War Without Bloodshed: The Art of Politics* (New York: Scribner, 1996), p. 100.

59. Peter Odegard, *Pressure Politics: The Story of the Anti-Saloon League* (New York: Columbia University Press, 1928), p. 76.

60. Frank Sorauf, *Inside Campaign Finance* (New Haven, CT: Yale University Press, 1992), Ch. 4. A basic reference on PACs is *The PAC Directory* (Cambridge, MA: Ballinger, various editions).

61. Ross Baker, *The New Fat Cats: Members of Congress as Political Benefactors* (New York: Priority Press, 1989); and Eliza Carney, "PAC Men," *National Journal* (October 1, 1994): 2268–2273.

62. See Edward Epstein, "Business and Labor Under the Federal Election Campaign Act of 1971," in Michael Malbin, ed., *Parties, Interest Groups, and Campaign Finance Laws* (Washington, DC: American Enterprise Institute, 1980), pp. 107–151.

63. Thomas Ferguson and Joel Rogers, *Right Turn: The Decline of the Democrats and the Future of American Politics* (New York: Hill and Wang, 1986).

64. For a discussion, see Richard Hall and Frank Wayman, "Buying Time: Moneyed Interests and the Mobilization of Bias in Congressional Committees," *American Political Science Review* 84 (1990): 797–820.

65. Jim Drinkard, "Issue Ads Crowd Airwaves Before 2000 Election," *USA Today* (November 29, 1999): 11A.

66. R. Kenneth Godwin, *One Billion Dollars of Influence* (Chatham, NJ: Chatham House, 1988).

67. Andrew McFarland, *Common Cause: Lobbying for the People* (Chatham, NJ: Chatham House, 1984), pp. 74–81.

68. For an analysis of the expansion by the judiciary of federal programs for the handicapped and the poor, see R. Shep Melnick, *Between the Lines* (Washington, DC: Brookings, 1994).

69. For elaboration, see Hugh Graham and Ted Gurr, *The History of Violence in America* (New York: Bantam, 1969).

70. Jonathan Rauch, *Demosclerosis* (New York: Random House, 1994).

71. Philip Stern, *The Best Congress Money Can Buy* (New York: Pantheon, 1988).

72. John Heinz, Edward Laumann, Robert Nelson, and Robert Salisbury, *Representing Interests: Structure and Uncertainty in National Policy Making* (in press).

73. J. Leiper Freeman, *The Political Process*, rev. ed. (New York: Random House, 1965); Grant McConnell, *Private Power and American Democracy* (New York: Knopf, 1966); and Theodore Lowi, *The End of Liberalism* (New York: Norton, 1969).

74. David Hosansky, "House and Senate Assemble Conflicting Farm Bills," *Congressional Quarterly Weekly Report* (February 3, 1996): 298.

75. Hugh Heclo, "Issue Networks and the Executive Establishment," in Anthony King, ed., *The New American Political System* (Washington, DC: Brookings, 1978), pp. 87–124.

76. Robert Salisbury, John Heinz, Robert Nelson, and Edward Laumann, "Triangles, Networks, and Hollow Cores: The Complex Geometry of Washington Interest Representation," in Mark Petracca, ed., *The Politics of Interests* (Boulder, CO: Westview Press, 1992), pp. 130–149.

77. Schlozman and Tierney, *Organized Interests and American Democracy*, pp. 314–317.

78. Henry Brady, Sidney Verba, and Kay Schlozman, "Beyond SES: A Resource Model of Political Participation," *American Political Science Review* 89 (1995): 271–294.

79. John Hibbing and Elizabeth Theiss-Morse, *Congress as Public Enemy* (New York: Cambridge University Press, 1995), pp. 63–65, 147.

80. Earl Latham, *The Group Basis of Politics* (New York: Cornell University Press, 1952); and David Truman, *The Governmental Process* (New York: Knopf, 1958).

81. E. E. Schattschneider, *The Semisovereign People* (New York: Holt, 1960), pp. 34–35.

82. Peter Aranson and Peter Ordeshook, "A Prolegomenon to a Theory of the Failure of Representative Democracy," in Peter Aranson and Peter Ordeshook, eds., *American Re-evolution* (Tucson, AR: University of Arizona, 1977), pp. 23–46.

83. Jane Mansbridge, *Why We Lost the ERA* (Chicago: University of Chicago Press, 1986), p. 73.

CHAPTER 9

1. "Pushing the Limit," *New York Times* (May 19, 2002): 14; "While Farmers Milk Public for Billions More," *USA Today* (May 15, 2002): 12A; and "Bush the Anti-Globaliser," *The Economist* (May 11, 2002): 14.

2. Data found at www.cbo.gov

3. Gebe Martinez, "Playing the Blame Game on Farm-Friendly Politics," *CQ Weekly* (April 20, 2002): 1008–1014.

4. Dan Morgan, "For Bush's Ranch Neighbors, Money Grows from Grain," *Washington Post Weekly Edition* (September 10–16, 2001): 12.

5. Dave Barry, "The Mohair of the Dog that Bites You," *Miami Herald* (June 23, 2002).

6. Quoted in David Sanger, "Bush OKs Farm Subsidies," *San Francisco Chronicle* (May 14, 2002).

7. For colorful accounts of these congressional leaders, see Neil McNeil, *Forge of Democracy* (New York: McKay, 1963).

8. Speaker Thomas Reed, as quoted in McNeil, *Forge of Democracy.*

9. Richard Fenno, *The United States Senate: A Bicameral Perspective* (Washington, DC: American Enterprise Institute, 1982).

10. Nelson Polsby, Miriam Gallagher, and Barry Rundquist, "The Growth of the Seniority System in the U.S. House of Representatives," *American Political Science Review* 63 (1969): 787–807.

11. George H. Mayer, *The Republican Party, 1854–1966,* 2nd ed. (New York: Oxford University Press, 1967).

12. Charles Jones, "Joseph G. Cannon and Howard W. Smith: An Essay on the Limits of Leadership in the House of Representatives," *Journal of Politics* 30 (1968): 617–646.

13. Barbara Sinclair, *Majority Leadership in the U.S. House* (Baltimore, MD: Johns Hopkins University Press, 1983).

14. For a full discussion, see Steven S. Smith and Marcus Flathman, "Managing the Senate Floor: Complex Unanimous Consent Agreements Since the 1950s," *Legislative Studies Quarterly* 14 (1989): 349–374.

15. Lawrence Dodd and Richard Schott, *Congress and the Administrative State* (New York: Wiley, 1979), Ch. 3. For further discussion, see Kenneth Shepsle, "The Changing Textbook Congress," in John Chubb and Paul Peterston, eds., *Can the Government Govern?* (Washington, DC: Brookings, 1989).

16. "Democrats Oust Hebert, Poage; Adopt Reforms," *Congressional Quarterly Weekly Report* (January 18, 1975): 114.

17. Barbara Sinclair, *Legislators, Leaders, and Lawmaking: The U.S. House of Representatives in the Postreform Era* (Baltimore, MD: Johns Hopkins University Press, 1995).

18. David Brady, *Congressional Voting in a Partisan Era* (Lawrence: University of Kansas Press, 1973).

19. Gary Cox and Mathew McCubbins, *Legislative Leviathan* (Berkeley: University of California Press, 1993).

20. David Rohde, *Parties and Leaders in the Postreform House* (Chicago: University of Chicago Press, 1991).

21. Jim Drinkard, "Confident Candidates Share Campaign Wealth," *USA Today* (April 19, 2000): 10A.

22. Gerald Gamm and Kenneth Shepsle, "Emergence of Legislative Institutions: Standing Committees in the House and Senate, 1810–1825," *Legislative Studies Quarterly* 14 (1989): 39–66; and Joseph Cooper, *The Origins of the Standing Committees and the Development of the Modern House* (Houston, TX: Rice University Studies, 1970).

23. Richard Fenno, *Congressmen in Committees* (Boston: Little, Brown, 1973), p. 172.

24. Karen Foerstel, "Gingrich Flexes His Power in Picking Panel Chiefs," *Congressional Quarterly Weekly Report* (November 19, 1994): 3326.

25. Mark Ferber, "The Formation of the Democratic Study Group," in Nelson Polsby, ed., *Congressional Behavior* (New York: Random House, 1971), pp. 249–267.

26. Norman Ornstein, "Causes and Consequences of Congressional Change: Subcommittee Reforms in the House of Representatives, 1970–1973," in Norman Ornstein, ed., *Congress in Change* (New York: Praeger, 1975), pp. 88–114; and Roger Davidson and Walter Oleszek, *Congress Against Itself* (Bloomington: Indiana University Press, 1977).

27. Barry Weingast and William Marshall, "The Industrial Organization of Congress," *Journal of Political Economy* 91 (1988): 132–163.

28. John Ferejohn, *Pork Barrel Politics* (Stanford, CA: Stanford University Press, 1974); and R. Douglas Arnold, *Congress and the Bureaucracy* (New Haven, CT: Yale University Press, 1979).

29. Keith Krehbiel, *Information and Legislative Organization* (Ann Arbor: University of Michigan Press, 1991).

30. Morris Fiorina, *Representatives, Roll Calls, and Constituencies* (Lexington, MA: D.C. Heath, 1974), Chs. 2–3; and R. Douglas Arnold, *The Logic of Congressional Action* (New Haven, CT: Yale University Press, 1990), Chs. 2–4.

31. Jeffrey Talbert, Bryan Jones, and Frank Baumgartner, "Nonlegislative Hearings and Policy Change in Congress," *American Journal of Political Science* 39 (1995): 391–392.

32. For a detailed study of how and why individual members participate at these various stages of the legislative process, see Richard Hall, *Participation in Congress* (New Haven, CT: Yale University Press, 1996).

33. On the conference committee in recent years, see Stephen Van Beek, *Post-Passage Politics: Bicameral Relations in Congress* (Pittsburgh, PA: University of Pittsburgh Press, 1995).

34. Richard Munson, *The Cardinals of Capitol Hill* (New York: Grove Press, 1993).

35. James Young, *The Washington Community, 1800–1828* (New York: Harcourt, 1966), Ch. 2.

36. The South was primarily agricultural and had fewer high-status career opportunities outside of politics. From the very beginning, southern members of Congress stayed longer than northerners. Morris Fiorina, David Rohde, and Peter Wissel, "Historical Change in House Turnover," in Norman Ornstein, ed., *Congress in Change* (New York: Praeger, 1975), pp. 34–38.

37. Robert Struble, Jr., "House Turnover and the Principle of Rotation," *Political Science Quarterly* 94 (1979–1980): 660.

38. Douglas Price, "The Congressional Career—Then and Now," in Nelson Polsby, ed., *Congressional Behavior* (New York: Random House, 1971), pp. 14–27.

39. Douglas Arnold, *The Logic of Congressional Action* (New Haven, CT: Yale University Press, 1990), Ch. 2.

40. Glenn Parker, *Homeward Bound* (Pittsburgh, PA: University of Pittsburgh Press, 1986).

41. John G. Geer, *From Tea Leaves to Opinion Polls: A Theory of Democratic Leadership* (New York: Columbia University Press, 1996).

42. Ornstein, Mann, and Malbin, *Vital Statistics*, pp. 67–68.

43. John Ferejohn, "On the Decline of Competition in Congressional Elections," *American Political Science Review* 71 (1977): 172–174.

44. Gary Jacobson, *The Politics of Congressional Elections*, 4th ed. (New York: Longman, 1997).

45. Heinz Eulau, "Changing Views of Representation," in Heinz Eulau and John Wahlke, eds., *The Politics of Representation* (Beverly Hills, CA: Sage, 1978), pp. 31–53.

46. Morris Fiorina, *Congress—Keystone of the Washington Establishment*, 2nd ed. (New Haven, CT: Yale University Press, 1989).

47. Ibid., Ch. 10. See also Bruce Cain, John Ferejohn, and Morris Fiorina, *The Personal Vote* (Cambridge, MA: Harvard University Press, 1987), Ch. 2.

48. Burdett Loomis, "The Congressional Office As a Small Business: New Members Set Up Shop," *Publius* 9 (1979): 35–55.

49. Ornstein, Mann, and Malbin, *Vital Statistics*, pp. 126, 130.

50. Walter Gellhorn, *Ombudsmen and Others: Citizens' Protectors in Nine Countries* (Cambridge, MA: Harvard University Press, 1966).

51. Morris Fiorina, "Congressmen and Their Constituents: 1958 and 1978," in Dennis Hale, ed., *The United States Congress: Proceedings of the Thomas P. O'Neill, Jr., Symposium* (Leominster, MA: Eusey Press, 1982), pp. 33–64.

52. Richard H. Shapiro, *Frontline Management* (Washington, DC: Congressional Management Foundation, 1989), p. 94.

53. Quoted in Stephen Skowronek, *The Politics Presidents Make* (Cambridge, MA: Harvard University Press, 1993), p. 389.

54. Harrison Donnelly, "Reagan Opposition Threatens EDA Development Program," *Congressional Quarterly Weekly Report* 40 (1982): 2295–2296.

55. Chuck Henning, *The Wit and Wisdom of Politics* (Golden, CO: Fulcrum, 1992), p. 39.

56. For institutional comparisons, see John Hibbing and Elizabeth Theiss-Morse, *Congress as Public Enemy* (New York: Cambridge University Press, 1995), Ch. 2.

...son and David Magleby, "Trends: Public Support for Congress," *Public Opinion* (1992): 539–551.

...ard Fenno, "If, As Ralph Nader Says, Congress Is the 'Broken Branch,' How Come We ...Our Congressmen So Much?" in Norman Ornstein, ed., *Congress in Change* (New York: ...aeger, 1975), pp. 277–287.

59. Richard Fenno, *Home Style: House Members in Their Districts* (Boston: Little, Brown, 1978), p. 168.

60. Glenn Parker and Roger Davidson, "Why Do Americans Love Their Congressman So Much More Than Their Congress? *Legislative Studies Quarterly* 4 (1979): 52–61.

CHAPTER 10

1. *New York Times* (September 8, 1993): B10.

2. Bill Clinton and Al Gore, *Putting People First: How We Can All Change America* (New York: Times Books, 1992).

3. Sources for the "reinventing government" story include Lisa Getter, "GAO Report Disputes Gore Claims on Red-Tape Cuts," *Los Angeles Times* (August 14, 1999): A6; Stephen Barr, "Some Pessimism on 'Reinvention,'" *Washington Post* (March 31, 2000): A27; Tome Brune and William Douglas, "Reinvention Reality: Gore Boasts REGO Success, But Critics See New Problems," *Newsday* (July 17, 2000): A5; Stephen Barr, "Reinventing Government Is an Idea Whose Time Has Come—Again," *Washington Post* (October 22, 2000): C2; Jonathan Weisman, "Gore Misstates Job-Cutting Role: 'Reinventing' Results Do Not Match Claims, Many Analysts Say," *Baltimore Sun* (October 27, 2000): 1A; and Stephen Barr, "Members of Campaign to Reinvent Government Packing Up, Not Giving Up," *Washington Post* (January 14, 2001): C2.

4. *New York Times* (September 9, 1993): D20.

5. *New York Times* (September 8, 1993): B10.

6. *Washington Post* (August 12, 1993): A6.

7. *New York Times* (September 5, 1993, Sec. I): 39.

8. *New York Times* (September 5, 1993, Sec. I): 39.

9. Brune and Douglas, "Reinvention Reality."

10. Terry Moe, "The Politicized Presidency," in John Chubb and Paul E. Peterson, eds., *The New Direction in American Politics* (Washington, DC: Brookings, 1985).

11. Mark Peterson, *Legislating Together: The White House and Capitol Hill from Eisenhower to Reagan* (Cambridge, MA: Harvard), p. 157.

12. Richard E. Neustadt, *Presidential Power and the Modern Presidents* (New York: Free Press, 1990), p. 29.

13. James S. Young, *The Washington Community 1800–1828* (New York: Columbia University Press, 1966).

14. Benjamin Ginsberg and Martin Shefter, *Politics by Other Means: The Declining Importance of Elections in America* (New York: Basic Books, 1990).

15. Thomas Bailey, *The American Pageant* (Boston: D. C. Heath, 1956), p. 669.

16. Samuel Kernell, *Going Public* (Washington, DC: CQ Press, 1986).

17. Daniel Stid, *The Statesmanship of Woodrow Wilson: Responsible Government Under the Constitution* (Lawrence: University Press of Kansas, 1998), Ch. 6.

18. Neustadt, *Presidential Power,* p. 274.

19. Denis G. Sullivan and Roger D. Masters, "Happy Warriors: Leaders' Facial Displays, Viewers' Emotions and Political Support," *American Journal of Political Science* 32 (1988): 345–368.

20. Chuck Henning, *The Wit and Wisdom of Politics* (Golden, CO: Fulcrum, 1992), p. 240.

21. Jeffrey Tulis, *The Rhetorical Presidency* (Princeton, NJ: Princeton University Press, 1987), Ch. 3.

22. Ibid.

23. John W. Kingdon, *Agendas, Alternatives and Public Policies* (Boston: Little, Brown, 1981).

24. Harry McPherson, *A Political Education* (Boston: Little, Brown, 1972), p. 268, as quoted in Paul C. Light, *The President's Agenda: Domestic Policy Choice from Kennedy to Reagan* (Baltimore, MD: Johns Hopkins University Press, 1991), p. 13.

25. Stephen Hess, *Organizing the Presidency* (Washington, DC: Brookings, 1988), pp. 11–18.

26. Herbert Kaufman, *The Administrative Behavior of Federal Bureau Chiefs* (Washington, DC: Brookings, 1981), p. 183, n. 8.

27. Hugh Heclo, "OMB and the Presidency—the Problem of 'Neutral Competence,'" *Public Interest* 38 (Winter 1975): 80–98; and Karen Hult, "Advising the President," in George C. Edwards, John H. Kessel, and Bert A. Rockman, *Researching the Presidency: Vital Questions, New Approaches* (Pittsburgh, PA: University of Pittsburgh Press, 1992), p. 126.

28. David Stockman, *The Triumph of Politics* (New York: Harper & Row, 1986).

29. Haynes Johnson and David Broder, *The System: The American Way of Politics at the Breaking Point* (Boston: Little, Brown, 1996), p. 116.

30. Norman C. Thomas, Joseph A. Pika, and Richard A. Watson, *The Politics of the Presidency,* 3rd ed. (Washington, DC: CQ Press, 1993), p. 204.

31. John F. Harris, "Both Sides Frustrated as Budget Wars End," *Washington Post* (November 15, 1999): A1.

32. As quoted in James P. Pfiffner, *The Modern Presidency* (New York: St. Martin's, 1994), p. 114.

33. James L. Sundquist, *The Decline and Resurgence of Congress* (Washington, DC: Brookings, 1981), p. 93.

34. *United States* v. *Belmont* 301 US 324 (1937).

35. Ann Devroy, "Pact Reached to Dismantle Ukraine's Nuclear Force; Detailed Plan to Be Signed Friday, Clinton Announces," *Washington Post* (January 11, 1994): A1.

36. *U.S.* v. *Curtiss Wright Export Corporation* 299 US 304 (1936).

37. *Youngstown Sheet & Tube Co.* v. *Sawyer* 343 US 579 (1952).

38. Joint Resolution of Congress, H.J. RES 1145 August 7, 1964.

39. Louis Fisher and David Gray Adler, "The War Powers Resolution: Time to Say Goodbye," *Political Science Quarterly* 113/3: 1–20.

40. *United States* v. *Belmont* 301 US 324 (1936); Harold Bruff and Peter Shane, *The Law of Presidential Powers: Cases and Materials* (Durham, NC: Carolina Academic Press, 1988), p. 88; and Joseph Paige, *The Law Nobody Knows: Enlargement of the Constitution—Treaties and Executive Orders* (New York: Vantage Press, 1977), p. 63.

41. Louis Fisher, *Constitutional Conflicts Between Congress and the President,* 3rd ed. rev. (Lawrence: University of Kansas, 1991), p. 154.

42. Bob Woodward and Scott Armstrong, *The Brethren: Inside the Supreme Court* (New York: Simon and Schuster, 1979), Ch. 5 (1973 Term), especially p. 365.

43. *United States* v. *Nixon,* 418 US 683, 709 (1974).

44. Walter Bagehot, *The English Constitution* (London: Fantana, 1993).

and Eric McKitrick, *Age of Federalism* (New York: Oxford University Press,

...earns Goodwin, *No Ordinary Time: Franklin and Eleanor Roosevelt: The Home Front in World
...New York: Simon & Schuster, 1994).

...ert Rockman, "Leadership Style and the Clinton Presidency," in Colin Campbell and Bert
...ockman, eds., *The Clinton Presidency: First Appraisals* (Chatham, NJ: Chatham House, 1996),
pp. 334–336.

48. David Johnston, "With Counsel Law Expiring, Attorney General Takes Reins," *New York Times*
(June 30, 1999).

49. John Hart, *The Presidential Branch: From Washington to Clinton,* 2nd ed. (Chatham, NJ: Chatham
House, 1995), pp. 26–30.

50. See Matthew Dickinson, *Bitter Harvest: FDR, Presidential Power, and the Growth of the Presidential
Branch* (New York: Cambridge University Press, 1997).

51. Paul Quirk, "Presidential Competence," in Michael Nelson, ed., *The Presidency and the
Political System,* 4th ed. (Washington, DC: CQ Press, 1994), pp. 171–221; and John P. Burke,
The Institutional Presidency (Baltimore, MD: Johns Hopkins University Press, 1992),
pp. 40–42.

52. Colin Campbell, "Management in a Sandbox," in Campbell and Rockman, *The Clinton
Presidency,* p. 60.

53. Charles O. Jones, "Campaigning to Govern: The Clinton Style," in Campbell and Rockman,
The Clinton Presidency, p. 16.

54. Terry Moe, "The Politicized Presidency," in Chubb and Peterson, *New Direction in American
Politics;* and Andrew Rudalevige, "The President's Program and the Politicized Presidency," paper
presented at the Annual Meeting of the American Political Science Association, Atlanta, GA,
September 2–5, 1999.

55. Bruce E. Altshuler, *LBJ and the Polls* (Gainesville, FL: University of Florida Press, 1990);
and Lawrence R. Jacobs, "The Recoil Effect: Public Opinion in the U.S. and Britain,"
Comparative Politics 24 (1992): 199–217. On the importance of political consultant Karl
Rove to George W. Bush's White House, see Dana Milbank, "The White House Lightning Rod:
If Sparks are Flying, Karl Rove Is Probably at the Center," *Washington Post Weekly Edition*
(July 23–29, 2001): 13–14; and Thomas B. Edsall, "Bush's Big Gamble: An Amnesty Proposal
for Illegal Immigrants Angers GOP Conservatives," *Washington Post Weekly Edition* (July 23–29,
2001): 14.

56. *Wall Street Journal* (December 22, 1993): A4.

57. Jack Mitchell, *Executive Privilege: Two Centuries of White House Scandals* (New York: Hippocrene
Books, 1992), pp. 89–90.

58. John Farrell, "Embattled Security Official Quits, Calls Getting FBI Files a 'Mistake,'" *Boston
Globe* (June 27, 1996): 12.

59. Aaron Wildavsky, "The Two Presidencies [1965]," in Steven A. Shull, *The Two Presidencies: A
Quarter Century Assessment* (Chicago: Nelson Hall, 1991), pp. 11–25.

60. Wildavsky, "The Two Presidencies," p. 17.

61. Barry M. Blechman, *The Politics of National Security: Congress and U.S. Defense Policy* (New York:
Oxford University Press, 1990); Duane M. Oldfield and Aaron Wildavsky, "Reconsidering the
Two Presidencies," in Steve A. Shull, ed., *The Two Presidencies: A Quarter Century Assessment* (Chicago:
Nelson Hall, 1991), pp. 181–90; Thomas Franck and Edward Weisband, *Foreign Policy by Congress*

(New York: Oxford University Press, 1979); Thomas E. Mann, ed., *A Question of Balance: The President, the Congress and Foreign Policy* (Washington, DC: Brookings, 1990); and Stephen R. Weissman, *A Culture of Deference: Congress's Failure of Leadership in Foreign Policy* (New York: Basic Books, 1955).

62. James Baker, III, with Thomas M. DeFrank, *The Politics of Diplomacy: Revolution, War, and Peace, 1989–1992* (New York: Putnam, 1995), p. 116.

63. *Statistical Abstract,* 1996, p. 3.

64. Wildavsky, "The Two Presidencies," p. 16.

65. Wildavsky, "The Two Presidencies," p. 15.

66. John E. Mueller, *War, Presidents and Public Opinion* (New York: Wiley, 1973); and Gary King and Lyn Ragsdale, *The Elusive Executive: Discovering Statistical Patterns in the Presidency* (Washington, DC: CQ Press, 1988).

67. Mueller, War, *Presidents and Public Opinion.*

68. George F. Kennan, "Somalia, Through a Glass Darkly," *New York Times* (September 30, 1993): A25.

69. Jessica Mathews, "Policy vs. TV," *Washington Post* (March 8, 1994): A19.

70. Neustadt, *Presidential Power,* Ch. 4.

71. As quoted in Henning, *Wit and Wisdom,* p. 222

72. The effect of time on presidential support is stressed by Paul Brace and Barbara Hinckley, "The Structure of Presidential Approval: Constraints Within and Across Presidencies," *Journal of Politics* 53 (1991): 993–1017; and John Mueller, "Presidential Popularity from Truman to Johnson," *American Political Science Review* 64 (1970): 18–34. For contrasting views, which stress events rather than time, see Richard A. Brody, *Assessing the President: The Media, Elite Opinion, and Public Support* (Stanford, CA: Stanford University Press, 1991); and Samuel Kernell, "Explaining Presidential Popularity," *American Political Science Review* 72 (1978): 506–522. Also see Michael MacKuen, "Political Drama, Economic Conditions, and the Dynamic of Public Popularity," *American Journal of Political Science* 27 (1983): 165–192; Charles Ostrom and Dennis Simon, "Promise and Performance: A Dynamic Model of Presidential Popularity," *American Political Science Review* 79 (1985): 334–358; and James Stimson, "Public Support for American Presidents," *Public Opinion Quarterly* 40 (1976): 401–421.

73. James Barber, *The Presidential Character: Predicting Performance in the White House* (Englewood Cliffs, NJ: Prentice-Hall, 1972).

74. Richard Morin and Claudia Deane, "Americans Approve of Bush's Handling of Crisis," *Washington Post* (September 13, 2001); Richard Benedetto and Patrick O'Driscoll, "Poll Finds a United Nation," *USA Today* (September 18, 2001).

75. Charles O. Jones, "Separating to Govern: The American Way," in Byron E. Shafer, ed., *Present Discontents: American Politics in the Very Late 20th Century* (Chatham, NJ: Chatham House, 1997), pp. 56–59.

CHAPTER 11

1. Clinton Rossiter, ed., *The Federalist Papers* (New York: Mentor, 1961), No. 4.

2. Rossiter, *Federalist Papers,* No. 3.

3. Barton Gellman, "A Missed Opportunity?" *Washington Post Weekly Edition* (October 8–14, 2001): 18.

4. Bob Woodward, "The CIA's Eye on Bin Laden," *Washington Post Weekly Edition* (January 7–13, 2002): 9; and Bob Woodward and Thomas E. Ricks, "The Foiled Plot to Nab Bin Laden," *Washington Post Weekly Edition* (October 8–14, 2001): 6.

5. Barton Gellman, "Clinton's Covert War," *Washington Post Weekly Edition* (January 7–13, 2002): 6.

6. Mary Pat Flaherty, David B. Ottaway, and James V. Grimaldi, "Ignored at Our Own Peril," *Washington Post Weekly Edition* (November 12–18, 2001): 10.

7. Gellman, "Clinton's Covert War."

8. Flaherty et al., "Ignored at Our Own Peril."

9. James V. Grimaldi, Steve Fainaru, and Gilbert M. Gaul, "So Easy to Hide," *Washington Post Weekly Edition* (October 15–21, 2001): 9.

10. Dan Eggen and Cheryl W. Thompson, "The Tip of the INS Iceberg," *Washington Post Weekly Edition* (March 25–31, 2002): 29.

11. Bill Miller, "Minding the Gaps," *Washington Post Weekly Edition* (April 15–21, 2002): 8.

12. Grimaldi et al., "So Easy to Hide."

13. Miller, "Minding the Gaps."

14. Eric Pianin, Bradley Graham, and Ceci Connolly, "Defending the Homeland," *Washington Post Weekly Edition* (October 1–7, 2001): 9.

15. Grimaldi et al., "So Easy to Hide."

16. Neely Tucker and Petula Dvorak, "Lessons from Oklahoma City Still Unlearned," *Washington Post Weekly Edition* (October 8–14, 2001): 32.

17. James Bamford, "Missing in Action: The NSA . . .," *Washington Post Weekly Edition* (June 10–16, 2002): 21.

18. Joby Warrick et al., "Despite Improvements, the FBI's Efforts Still Fall Short," *Washington Post Weekly Edition* (October 1–7, 2001): 31.

19. Gwen Kinkead, "One Measure of the FBI?" *Washington Post Weekly Edition* (April 22–28, 2002): 23; and Warrick et al., "Despite Improvements."

20. Steve Fainaru and Dan Eggen, "Chief Among the Changes," *Washington Post Weekly Edition* (June 10–16, 2002): 30; and Warrick et al., "Despite Improvements."

21. "The Informant Who Lived with the Hijackers," *Newsweek* (September 16, 2002): 6.

22. Fainaru and Eggen, "Chief Among the Changes."

23. John Donnelly, "U.S. Security Aspects Familiar to Some," *Boston Globe* (September 12, 2001): A9.

24. Richard Morin and Claudia Deane, "Trust It to Do the Right Thing," *Washington Post Weekly Edition* (October 8–14, 2001): 35.

25. John F. Harris and Dana Milbank, "A New Conservative Agenda," *Washington Post Weekly Edition* (October 1–7, 2001): 14.

26. Charles E. Schumer, "Big Government Looks Better Now," *Washington Post Weekly Edition* (December 17–23, 2001): 26.

27. Committee on Government Reform and Oversight, U.S. House of Representatives, *U.S. Government Policy and Supporting Positions ("Plum Book")* (Washington, DC: U.S. Government Printing Office, 1996).

28. General Accounting Office, *Government Corporations: Profiles of Existing Government Corporations*, (GAO/GGD-96-14) (Washington, DC: General Accounting Office, 1995).

29. Lyn Ragsdale, "Studying the Presidency: Why Presidents Need Political Scientists," in Michael Nelson, ed., *The Presidency and the Political System,* 5th ed. (Washington, DC: CQ Press, 1998), p. 50.

30. Max Weber, *Essays in Sociology* (New York: Oxford University Press, 1958); and Max Weber, *Economy and Society* (Berkeley, CA: University of California Press, 1978).

31. Henning, *Wit and Wisdom,* p. 92.

32. James Q. Wilson, "The Bureaucracy Problem," *The Public Interest* (Winter 1967): 3–9.

33. Graham Allison, *Essence of Decision: Explaining the Cuban Missile Crisis* (Boston: Little, Brown, 1971), Ch. 3.

34. Herbert Kaufman, *Red Tape: Its Origins, Uses and Abuses* (Washington, DC: Brookings, 1977), as reprinted in Francis E. Rourke, *Bureaucratic Power in National Policy Making,* 4th ed. (Boston: Little, Brown, 1986), p. 442.

35. Laurence J. Peter, as quoted in Chuck Henning, *The Wit and Wisdom of Politics: Expanded Edition* (Golden, CO: Fulcrum Publishing, 1992), p. 16.

36. William A. Niskanen, *Bureaucracy and Representative Government* (Chicago: Aldine-Atherton, 1971), Chs. 2–4.

37. Aaron Wildavsky, *The New Politics of the Budgetary Process* (Boston: Little, Brown, 1988), pp. 84–85.

38. Michael Lipsky, *Street-Level Bureaucracy: Dilemmas of the Individual in Public Services* (New York: Russell Sage, 1980).

39. Ibid.

40. Kaufman, *Red Tape,* p. 434.

41. James Young, *The Washington Community 1800–1828* (New York: Harcourt, 1966), p. 49. Ellipses deleted.

42. John Bartlett, *Familiar Quotations: Revised and Enlarged,* 15th ed. (Boston: Little, Brown, 1980), p. 455.

43. Seymour J. Mandelbaum, *Boss Tweed's New York* (New York: Wiley, 1965).

44. As quoted in Henning, *Wit and Wisdom,* p. 11.

45. A. James Reichley, *The Life of the Parties* (New York: Free Press, 1992), pp. 157–158.

46. Robert Dahl, *Who Governs?* (New Haven, CT: Yale University Press, 1961); Raymond E. Wolfinger, *The Politics of Progress* (Englewood Cliffs, NJ: Prentice-Hall, 1974), Ch. 4; Edward Banfield and James Q. Wilson, *City Politics* (New York: Random House, 1963); and Robert K. Merton, *Social Theory and Social Structure* (Glencoe, IL: Free Press, 1957), pp. 71–81.

47. Quoted in Reichley, *Life of the Parties,* p. 212.

48. Paul E. Peterson, *The Politics of School Reform, 1870–1940* (Chicago: University of Chicago Press, 1985), pp. 86–87.

49. Rufus P. Browning, Dale Rogers Marshall, and David H. Tabb, *Protest Is Not Enough: The Struggle of Blacks and Hispanics for Equality in Urban Politics* (Berkeley, CA: University of California Press, 1984), Ch. 5.

50. Alben W. Barkley, vice president of the United States, 1949–1953, as quoted in Henning, *Wit and Wisdom,* p. 17.

51. Paul Light, *Thickening Government: Federal Hierarchy and the Diffusion of Accountability* (Washington, DC: Brookings, 1995), Ch. 1.

52. G. Calvin MacKenzie, "The Presidential Appointment Process: Historical Development, Contemporary Operations, Current Issues," background paper for the Twentieth Century Fund Panel on Presidential Appointments, March 1, 1994, p. 1.

53. Leonard White, *Introduction to the Study of Public Administration,* 4th ed. (New York: Macmillan, 1955), p. 80.

54. *Wall Street Journal* (February 9, 1994): 1.

55. President George W. Bush's nominations began running into trouble soon after the Senate switched to Democratic control.

56. David King, "The Nature of Congressional Committee Jurisdictions," *American Political Science Review* 88 (March 1995): 48–62.

57. Beryl A. Radin and Willis D. Hawley, *The Politics of Federal Reorganization: Creating the U.S. Department of Education* (New York: Pergamon Press, 1988).

58. R. Shep Melnick, *Regulation and the Courts: The Case of the Clean Air Act* (Washington, DC: Brookings, 1983).

59. Dick Kirschten, "Slicing the Turf," *Government Executive* (April 1999); and Graeme Browning, "Fiscal Fission," *National Journal* (June 8, 1996): 1259.

60. Bill McAllister, "Byrd's Big Prize: Bringing Home the FBI," *Washington Post* (March 13, 1991): A1.

61. Joel Aberbach, *Keeping a Watchful Eye* (Washington, DC: Brookings, 1990), p. 38.

62. R. Shep Melnick, *Between the Lines* (Washington, DC: Brookings).

63. Martha Derthick, *Agency Under Stress: The Social Security Administration in American Government* (Washington, DC: Brookings, 1990).

64. Paul E. Peterson, Barry G. Rabe, and Kenneth K. Wong, *When Federalism Works* (Washington, DC: Brookings, 1986), Ch. 8; John J. Harrigan, *Political Change in the Metropolis,* 2nd ed. (Boston: Little, Brown, 1981), pp. 267–268, 350–351; Rochelle L. Stanfield, "Communities Reborn," *National Journal* (June 22, 1966): 1371; and "Bush Admits Intelligence-Sharing Lapses," *Pittsburgh Post-Gazette* (June 5, 2002): A8.

65. Patrick Wolf, "What History Advises About Reinventing Government," Ph.D. dissertation, Department of Government, Harvard University, 1996.

66. John Dilulio, *No Escape: The Future of American Corrections* (New York: Basic Books, 1991), pp. 19–26.

67. James A. Morone, *The Democratic Wish: Popular Participation and the Limits of American Government* (New York: Basic Books, 1990).

68. Francis Rourke, "Executive Secrecy: Change and Continuity," in Rourke, *Bureaucratic Power in National Policy Making,* pp. 536–537.

69. Jeffrey Birnbaum, Eileen Gunn, et al., "Unbelievable! The Mess at the IRS *Is* Worse Than You Think" *Fortune* (April 13, 1998).

70. Ibid.

71. Ibid.

72. Albert B. Crenshaw, "IRS Overhaul Set for Passage; Measure Gives Taxpayers New Rights, Includes Capital Gains Break," *Washington Post* (June 25, 1998): A1.

73. Martha Derthick, *Agency Under Stress,* p. 87.

74. Former Bureau of the Budget Director Kermit Gordon, as quoted in Kaufman, *Administrative Behavior,* p. 443.

75. Paul J. Quirk, "Food and Drug Administration," in James Q. Wilson, *The Politics of Regulation* (New York: Basic Books, 1980), p. 199.

76. Terry Moe, "The Politics of Bureaucratic Structure," in John E. Chubb and Paul E. Peterson, *Can the Government Govern?* (Washington, DC: Brookings, 1988).

77. Robert Manor, "Firms Linked in Plane Crash Ignored Rules, Oxygen Generators Improperly Loaded," *St. Louis Post-Dispatch* (June 2, 1996): 11A.

78. *Heart of Atlanta Motel* v. *United States* 322 US 533 (1964); and *United States* v. *South-Eastern Underwriters Association* 322 US 533 (1944).

79. Paul Attewell and Dean R. Gerstein, "Government Policy and Local Practice," *American Sociological Review* 44 (1979): 311–327. For a banking example, see John T. Woolley, "Conflict Among Regulators and the Hypothesis of Congressional Dominance," *Journal of Politics* 55 (1993): 102–103.

80. Marc K. Landy, Marc J. Roberts, and Stephen R. Thomas, *The Environmental Protection Agency: Asking the Wrong Questions from Nixon to Clinton,* expanded edition (New York: Oxford University Press, 1994).

81. Kenneth Meier, *Regulation: Politics, Bureaucracy, and Economics* (New York: St. Martin's Press, 1985).

82. Martha Derthick and Paul Quirk, *The Politics of Deregulation* (Washington, DC: Brookings, 1985); and Mark C. Rom, *Public Spirit in the Thrift Tragedy* (Pittsburgh, PA: University of Pittsburgh Press, 1996).

83. H. Craig Petersen, *Business and Government,* 2nd ed. (New York: Harper & Row, 1985), p. 198.

84. Marver H. Bernstein, *Regulating Business by Independent Commission* (Princeton, NJ: Princeton University Press, 1955); Harold Seidman, *Politics, Position and Power: The Dynamics of Federal Organization*, 2nd ed. (New York: Oxford University Press, 1975); George J. Stigler, "The Theory of Economic Regulation," *Bell Journal of Economics and Management Science* 2 (Spring 1971): 3–21; Terry Moe, "Regulatory Performance and Presidential Administration," *American Journal of Political Science* 16 (1982), 197–224; and B. R. Weingast and M. J. Moran, "Bureaucratic Discretion or Congressional Control? Regulatory Policymaking by the Federal Trade Commission," *Journal of Political Economy* 91 (1983): 765–800; and B. R. Weingast, "The Congressional-Bureaucratic System: A Principal–Agent Perspective (with Application to the SEC)," *Public Choice* 44, 1 (1984): 147–191.

85. Robyn Meredith, "Credit Unions Help Finance a Bid for Reinstatement by a Dismissed Federal Regulator," *New York Times* (July 20, 1996): 7; and United States Court of Appeals for the District of Columbia Circuit, November 22, 1996, No. 96–5193.

86. Address at Westminster College, Fulton, Missouri, March 5, 1946, as reprinted in John Bartlett, *Familiar Quotations* (Boston: Little, Brown, 1980), p. 746.

87. George Marshall, secretary of state under Harry Truman, as quoted in Alexander De Conde, "George C. Marshall," in Norman A. Graebner, ed., *An Uncertain Tradition: American Secretaries of State in the Twentieth Century* (New York: McGraw Hill, 1961), p. 252.

88. Henning, *Wit and Wisdom,* p. 69.

89. Barry Rubin, *Secrets of State: The State Department and the Struggle Over U.S. Foreign Policy* (New York: Oxford University Press, 1985), p. 64.

90. Stephen Holmes, "What Russia Teaches Us Now; How Weak States Threaten Freedom," *The American Prospect* (July–August 1997): 30.

91. Andrew Krepinevich, quoted in Justin Brown, "How Many Weapons Is Too Many?" *Christian Science Monitor* (November 4, 1999): 1.

92. Bradley Graham, "Senators Scold Military Chiefs, Top Officers Accused of Failing to Warn Soon Enough of Readiness Decline," *Washington Post* (September 30, 1998): A2.

93. Loch K. Johnson, *America's Secret Power* (New York: Oxford University Press, 1989), Ch. 2.

94. Johnson, *America's Secret Power;* and Rhodri Jeffreys-Johnes, *The CIA and American Democracy* (New Haven, CT: Yale University Press, 1989).

95. *Director of Central Intelligence Annual Report for the United States Intelligence Community* (Washington, DC: Central Intelligence Agency, 2000).

96. Rubin, *Secrets of State,* p. 50.

97. As quoted in Robert Pastor, "Disagreeing on Latin America," in Paul E. Peterson, ed., *The President, the Congress, and the Making of Foreign Policy* (Norman: Oklahoma University Press, 1994), p. 217.

98. Donald Kettl, *Leadership at the Fed* (New Haven, CT: Yale University Press, 1986).

99. John M. Berry, "Where's the Rebound? The Fed, Increasingly Concerned That Its Rate Cuts Haven't Worked, Is Poised to Act Again," *Washington Post Weekly Edition* (June 25–July 1, 2001): 18.

100. Susan Milligan, "Greenspan Nominated to Fourth Term as Fed Chairman," *Boston Globe* (January 5, 2000): C1.

101. *Annual Report: Budget Review* (Washington, DC: Board of Governors of the Federal Reserve System, 1999).

102. James Livingston, *Origins of the Federal Reserve System* (Ithaca, NY: Cornell University Press, 1986).

103. John Woolley, *Monetary Politics: The Federal Reserve and the Politics of Monetary Policy* (New York: Cambridge University Press, 1984).

104. Douglas Hibbs, "The Partisan Model of Macroeconomic Cycles: More Theory and Evidence for the United States," *Economics and Politics* 6 (1994): 1–23.

105. Edward Tufte, *Political Control of the Economy* (Princeton, NJ: Princeton University Press, 1978), Ch. 2.

106. William Greider, *Secrets of the Temple: How the Federal Reserve Runs the Country* (New York: Simon & Schuster, 1987).

107. Michael Schrage, "It's Time to Put a Transaction Tax on Credit Card Purchases," *Washington Post* (October 17, 1990): F3.

108. "Steady Greenspan; Clinton Plays It Safe on Choice of Fed Chief," *San Diego Union-Tribune* (February 26, 1996): B4.

109. "The Race Is On—For 2004," *Slate* (August 14, 2000).

110. "Fresh Light on Primary Colors," *The Economist* (February 24, 1996): 23.

111. A good current description of the caucus system appears in William Mayer, "Caucuses: How They Work, What Difference They Make," in *In Pursuit of the White House*, ed. William Mayer (Chatham, NJ: Chatham House, 1996).

112. On the history of the presidential primary, see James Davis, *Springboard to the White House* (New York: Crowell, 1967).

113. Harry Truman, *Memoirs*, Vol. 2: *Years of Trial and Hope* (Garden City, NY: Doubleday, 1956), p. 51.

114. David Von Drehle and Mike Allen, "Bush Plan's Underground Architects," *Washington Post* (June 9, 2002): A1.

115. Adriel Bettelheim, "Lawmakers with a List of Concerns Are Sure to Add Strings to Bush Proposal," *CQ Weekly* (June 15, 2002): 1577.

116. Nick Anderson and Richard Simon, "Democrats Attack Item in Bush's Security Plan," *Los Angeles Times* (June 21, 2002): A26.

117. "Daschle Says Bush Attack Politicizes Debate," *Seattle Post-Intelligencer* (September 26, 2002): A1; and Jim VandeHei, "Daschle Angered by Bush Statement," *Washington Post* (September 26, 2002): A1.

118. Tod Lindberg, "The Homeland Security Two-fer," *Weekly Standard* (June 24, 2002): 13.

119. See, for example, Theodore Lowi, *The End of Liberalism* (New York: Norton, 1969); and than Rauch, *Demosclerosis* (New York: Times Books, 1994).

CHAPTER 12

1. As quoted in Chuck Henning, *The Wit and Wisdom of Politics* (Golden, CO: Fulcrum Publishing, 1992), p. 250.

2. Ruth Marcus, "Plain-Spoken Marshall Spars with Reporters," *Washington Post* (June 29, 1991): A1.

3. David Brock, *The Real Anita Hill: The Untold Story* (New York: Free Press, 1993), p. 66. On the understanding that Bush would appoint an African American, see, for example, David G. Savage, "Court Nominee Warfare Opens," *Los Angeles Times* (July 6, 2001): A18.

4. Paul Simon, *Advice and Consent* (Washington, DC: National Press Books, 1992), p. 89.

5. Ibid., p. 93.

6. Bob Dart, "Abortion Key to Hearing Today," *Atlanta Journal and Constitution* (September 11, 1991): A1.

7. Simon, *Advice and Consent*, Chs. 5–6.

8. Ibid., p. 122.

9. Ibid., p. 122.

10. Brock, *The Real Anita Hill*, p. 17.

11. Gerald Pomper, "The Presidential Election," in Gerald M. Pomper et al., *The Election of 1992: Reports and Interpretations* (Chatham, NJ: Chatham House, 1993), p. 138.

12. Henning, *Wit and Wisdom*, p. 108.

13. Richard N. Smith, *Thomas E. Dewey and His Times* (New York: Simon & Schuster, 1982), Chs. 5–9.

14. Linda Greenhouse, "Legacy of a Term," *New York Times* (July 3, 1996): A1.

15. H. W. Perry, Jr., *Deciding to Decide: Agenda Setting in the United States Supreme Court* (Cambridge, MA: Harvard University Press, 1991), p. 27.

16. Ibid., pp. 218–219.

17. Ibid., p. 99.

18. Joan Biskupic and Howard Kurtz, "Police Can Be Sued for Letting Media See Raids," *Washington Post* (May 25, 1999): A8.

19. Simon, *Advice and Consent*, p. 128.

20. As quoted in Henning, *Wit and Wisdom*, p. 106.

21. Rodney R. Jones and Gerald F. Uelmen, *Supreme Folly* (New York: Norton, 1990), p. 151.

22. John C. Jeffries, Jr., *Justice Lewis F. Powell, Jr: A Biography* (New York: Scribner, 1994), pp. 245–247.

23. Bob Woodward and Scott Armstrong, *The Brethren: Inside the Supreme Court* (New York: Simon and Schuster, 1979), pp. 126, 286–287, 297–298, 311.

24. *Parts and Electric Motors v. Sterling Electric* 866 F 2d 288 (1988).

25. Jones and Uelmen, *Supreme Folly*, p. 114.

26. Henning, *Wit and Wisdom*, p. 213.

27. Hart Pomerantz, as quoted in Henning, *Wit and Wisdom*, p. 250.

28. *Harris v. Forklift* 508 US 938 (1993).

29. Jeffries, *Justice Lewis F. Powell, Jr.*, p. 323.

30. Jones and Uelmen, *Supreme Folly*, p. 146.

31. Woodward and Armstrong, *The Brethren*, pp. 71, 199.

32. This was true for the period 1958–1967; with the reduction in the number of certs accepted, this percentage has undoubtedly declined. Robert Scigliano, *The Supreme Court and the Presidency* (New York: Free Press, 1971), as quoted in Rebecca M. Salokar, *The Solicitor General: The Politics of Law* (Philadelphia, PA: Temple University Press, 1992), p. 3.

33. Jeffrey A. Segal, "*Amicus Curiae* Briefs by the Solicitor General During the Warren and Burger Courts: A Research Note," *Western Political Quarterly* 41 (March 1988): 135–144.

34. Perry, *Deciding to Decide,* p. 71.

35. Perry, *Deciding to Decide*; and Bernard Schwartz, *A History of the Supreme Court* (New York: Oxford University Press, 1993), Ch. 16.

36. Abram Chayes, "The Role of the Judge in Public Law Litigation," *Harvard Law Review* 89 (May 1976): 1281–1316.

37. Alexis de Toqueville, *Democracy in America*, J. P. Mayer, ed. (New York: Harper, 1988), p. 270.

38. Myron Levin and Henry Weinstein, "Big Tobacco Must Pay Damages in Florida Case," *Los Angeles Times* (April 8, 2000): A1.

39. Robert J. Samuelson, "Delegating Democracy: Government by Litigation Has Become Increasingly Popular," *Newsweek* (June 12, 2000): 59; and "Perspectives," *Newsweek* (May 29, 2000): 19.

40. As quoted in Henning, *Wit and Wisdom,* p. 107.

41. David O'Brien, "Background Paper," in Twentieth Century Fund, *Judicial Roulette* (New York: Priority Press, 1988), p. 37.

42. C. K. Rowland, Donald Songer, and Robert Carp, "Presidential Effects on Criminal Justice Policy in the Lower Federal Courts: The Reagan Judges," *Law and Society Review* 22/1 (1988): 191–200.

43. Carl B. Swisher, *American Constitutional Development,* 2nd ed. (Boston: Houghton Mifflin, 1954), pp. 1075–1079.

44. Simon, *Advice and Consent,* p. 275.

45. Henry J. Abraham, *Justices and Presidents: A Political History of Appointments to the Supreme Court,* 3rd ed. (New York: Oxford University Press, 1992).

46. Warren Richey, "After GOP Senate Sweep, Judiciary Is Set to Shift Right," *Christian Science Monitor,* November 8, 2002: 4.

47. Stephen L. Carter, "Looking for Law in All the Wrong Places," *Manhattan Lawyer* (September 1990): 20.

48. Ethan Bronner, *Battle for Justice: How the Bork Nomination Shook America* (New York: Norton, 1989), pp. 158–159.

49. Robert G. McCloskey, *The American Supreme Court* (Chicago: University of Chicago Press, 1960), p. 14.

50. Marbury's story is drawn primarily from Jean Edward Smith, *John Marshall: Definer of a Nation* (New York: Holt, 1996), Ch. 13, as well as the case itself, *Marbury v. Madison* 5 U.S. 137 (1803).

51. *Lochner v. New York* 195 US 45 (1905).

52. University of Wisconsin Law School, "Supreme Court Justice Scalia Speaks at Law School," *Law School News* (March 2001, accessed at http://www.law.wisc.edu/news/main.asp on July 30, '01).

53. Jeffrey A. Segal and Albert D. Cover, "Ideological Values and the Votes of U.S. Supreme Court Justices," *American Political Science Review 83* (June 1989): 557–565.

54. Woodward and Armstrong, *The Brethren,* p. 193.

55. Institute for Justice, *State of the Supreme Court 2000: The Justices' Record on Individual Liberties* (Washington, DC: Institute for Justice, 2000, accessed at http://www.ij.org/PDF_folder/supreme_court_report.pdf on August 13, 2001).

56. Joan Biskupic, "The Rehnquist Court," *Washington Post* (May 25, 1999): B3.

57. *Lynch* v. *Donnelly* 465 US 668 (1984); and *County of Allegheny* v. *ACLU* 492 US 573 (1989).

58. *City of Erie* v. *Pap's A. M.,* "Kandyland" 98–1161 (2000).

59. *Schechter Poultry Corp.* v. *United States* 295 US 495 (1935).

60. Congressional Research Service, Library of Congress, *The Constitution of the United States of America: Analysis and Interpretation, 1998 Supplement* (Washington, DC: Government Printing Office, 1999).

61. James A. Stimson, Michael B. Mackuen, and Robert S. Erikson, "Dynamic Representation," *American Political Science Review* 89 (1995): 555. Also see William Mishler and Reginald S. Sheehan, "The Supreme Court as a Counter-Majoritarian Institution? The Impact of Public Opinion on Supreme Court Decisions," *American Political Science Review* 87 (1993): 87–101; and Helmut Norpoth and Jeffery Segal, "Popular Influence on Supreme Court Decisions," *American Political Science Review* 88 (1994): 711–724.

62. As quoted by Austin Ranney, "Peltason Created a New Way to Look at What Judges Do," Public Affairs Report, Institute of Governmental Studies, Vol. 36, No. 6 (November 1995), p. 7.

63. R. Shep Melnick, *Between the Lines* (Washington, DC: Brookings, 1994), Ch. 1.

64. C. Herman Pritchett, *The American Constitution* (New York: McGraw-Hill, 1959), p. 99.

65. Lee Epstein and Thomas G. Walker, *Constitutional Law for a Changing America: Rights, Liberties, and Justice,* 3rd ed. (Washington, DC: Congressional Quarterly, 1998), pp. 200–201.

66. John Paul Ryan, Allen A. Ashman, Bruce D. Sales, and Sandra Shane-Dubow, *American Trial Judges* (New York: Free Press, 1980), p. 125.

67. "Investigate, Then Prosecute; Bungled Lewis Trial: Atlanta Prosecutors, Police Rushed to Indict Before They Had All the Evidence," *Baltimore Sun* (June 14, 2000): 22A.

68. Cynthia Tucker, "My Opinion; Murder Acquittals: Running for Glory, Fulton DA Fumbles." *Atlanta Constitution* (June 14, 2000): 14A.

69. Herbert Jacob and Kenneth Vines, "Courts," in Virginia Gray, Herbert Jacob, and Kenneth Vines, eds., *Politics in the American States: A Comparative Analysis*, 4th ed. (Boston: Little, Brown, 1983), p. 238.

70. Jacob and Vines, "Courts," p. 239.

71. Excerpted with ellipses deleted. Milton Rakove, *Don't Make No Waves; Don't Back No Losers* (Bloomington: Indiana University Press, 1975), pp. 223–225.

72. Mark Hansen, "A Run for the Bench," *ABA Journal* (October 1998): 68.

73. As quoted in Pritchett, *The American Constitution*, pp. 65, 215.

74. Congressional Research Service, Library of Congress, *The Constitution of the United States of America: Analysis and Interpretation, 1998 Supplement* (Washington, DC: Government Printing Office, 1999).

75. *In re Chapman* 16 US 661 (1897).

CHAPTER 13

1. Details for the McVeigh story came from the following sources: Lou Michel and Dan Herbeck, "Live from Death Row," *Newsweek* (April 9, 2001): 24–28; Michael Isikoff and Evan Thomas, "Waiting for Justice," *Newsweek* (May 21, 2001): 23–27; and Andrew Murr and Flynn McRoberts, "'It Just Goes On and On': For the Families and Survivors, the FBI Prolongs the Pain," *Newsweek* (May 21, 2001): 28.

2. Isikoff and Thomas, "Waiting for Justice," p. 27.

3. ABC News broadcast, June 11, 2001.

4. Michel and Herbeck, "Live from Death Row."

5. Peter Annin, "Inside the New Alcatraz: The ADX 'Supermax' Prison Redefines Hard Time," *Newsweek* (July 13, 1998): 35.

6. Michel and Herbeck, "Live from Death Row."

7. Jonathan Alter, "Why the Mess Really Matters," *Newsweek* (May 21, 2001): 29; Mike Tharp, Chitra Ragavan, and Angie Cannon, "A Notch in the Paranoia Belt," *U.S. News and World Report* (May 21, 2001): 20; and Jonah Goldberg, "Just Kill Him," *National Review Online* (May 14, 2001).

8. "The Executions Continue," *New York Times* (June 19, 2001): A22; and James Gill, "Europeans' Outrage Rings False," *New Orleans Times–Picayune* (June 20, 2001): 7.

9. Arthur M. Schlesinger, *Prelude to Independence: The Newspaper War on Britain, 1764–1776* (New York: Knopf, 1958), p. 299.

10. *Barron v. Baltimore*, 1833, as quoted in C. Herman Pritchett, *Constitutional Civil Liberties* (Englewood Cliffs, NJ: Prentice-Hall, 1984), p. 6.

11. *Stromberg v. California* 283 US 359 (1931).

12. *United States v. Carolene Products Co.* 304 US 144 (1938).

13. George Anastaplo, as quoted in Goldstein, *Political Repression,* p. 532.

14. *Papish v. the Board of Curators of the University of Missouri* 410 US 667 (1973).

15. *New York Times v. United States* 403 US 713 (1971).

16. Robert Goldstein, *Saving "Old Glory": The History of the Desecration Controversy* (Boulder, CO: Westview Press, 1995).

17. *Texas v. Johnson* 491 US 397 (1989).

18. *United States v. Eichman* 496 US 310, (1990).

19. *Jenkins v. Georgia* 418 US 153 (1974).

20. Linda Greenhouse, "Court, 9 0, Upholds State Laws Prohibiting Assisted Suicide, Protects Speech on Internet," *New York Times* (June 27, 1997): A1; Stephen V. Treglia, "After 'Ashcroft', Is Virtual Child Pornography a Crime?" *New York Law Journal* 228 (September 17, 2002): 5.

21. Michael W. McConnell, "Stuck with a Lemon: A New Test for Establishment Clause Cases Would Help Ease Current Confusion," *ABA Journal* (February 1997): 46–47.

22. Scalia concurrence, *City of Erie v. Pap's A. M.,* "Kandyland" 98-1161 (2000).

23. Kennedy partial concurrence, *County of Allegheny v. ACLU* 492 US 573 (1989).

24. Scalia dissent, *Lee v. Weisman* 505 US 577 (1992).

25. *Sante Fe v. Doe* 99-62 (2000).

26. As quoted in Charles L. Glenn, Jr., *The Myth of the Common School* (Amherst, MA: University of Massachusetts Press, 1987), p. 84.

27. *Fe v. Doe* 99-62 (2000).

28. Benjamin I. Page and Robert Y. Shapiro, *The Rational Public: Fifty Years of Trends in Americans' Policy Preferences* (Chicago: University of Chicago Press, 1992), p. 113.

29. *Board of Education* v. *Mergens* 496 US 226 (1990).

30. *Sherbert* v. *Verner* 374 US 398 (1963).

31. C. Herman Pritchett, *The American Constitution* (New York: McGraw-Hill, 1959), p. 477.

32. James F. Simon, *The Antagonists: Hugo Black, Felix Frankfurter and Civil Liberties in Modern America* (New York: Simon and Schuster, 1989), pp. 106–114.

33. Pritchett, *The American Constitution*, p. 478.

34. Samuel Warren and Louis Brandeis, "The Right to Privacy," *Harvard Law Review* 4 (1890): 193–220.

35. *Griswold* v. *Connecticut* 381 US 479 (1965).

36. Ibid.

37. Michael J. Sandel, *Democracy's Discontent: American in Search of a Public Philosophy* (Cambridge, MA: Belknap Press of Harvard University Press, 1996), pp. 93–94.

38. Bob Woodward and Scott Armstrong, *The Brethren: Inside the Supreme Court* (New York: Simon and Schuster, 1979), pp. 198–206.

39. *Harris* v. *McRae* 448 US 297 (1980).

40. *Webster* v. *Reproductive Health Services* 492 US 490 (1989).

41. *Planned Parenthood* v. *Casey* 112 SCt 291 (1992).

42. *Stenberg* v. *Carhart* 99-830 (3000).

43. Pamela Coyle, "Second State Court Overturns Sodomy Law," *New Orleans Times–Picayune* (March 18, 1999): A1; and Amy Argetsinger, "Maryland Judge's Ruling Protects Private, Consensual Sex Acts," *Washington Post* (January 20, 1999): B8.

44. "The Gallup Poll: Social and Economic Indicators—Homosexual Relations," accessed at www.gallup.com/poll/ indicators/indhomsexual.asp on March 22, 2000.

45. *Mapp* v. *Ohio* 167 US 643 (1961).

46. *Washington* v. *Chrisman* 455 US 1 (1982), p. 182.

47. John C. Domino, *Civil Rights and Liberties in the 21st Century* (New York: Longman), pp. 176–177.

48. *Kyllo* v. *United States* 99-8508 (2001).

49. Pritchett, *Constitutional Civil Liberties*, p. 78.

50. *Sheppard* v. *Maxwell* 384 US 333 (1966).

51. *Nebraska Press Association* v. *Stuart* 427 US 539 (1976).

52. Lisa J. McIntyre, *The Public Defender: The Practice of Law in the Shadows of Repute* (Chicago: University of Chicago Press, 1987), p. 162.

53. Jonathan D. Casper, *American Criminal Justice: The Defendant's Perspective* (Englewood Cliffs, NJ: Prentice-Hall, 1972), p. 101.

54. Toni Locy, "Okla. Trial for Nichols Rethought: New Prosecutor Reviewing Options," *USA Today* (June 19, 2001): 6A.

55. Domino, *Civil Rights and Liberties*, p. 218.

56. Casper, *American Criminal Justice;* and Jerome Skolnick, *Justice Without Trial* (New York: Wiley, 1966).

57. Sharon Begley, "What Price Security?" *Newsweek* (October 1, 2001): 58–62.

58. Jim Burns, "Libertarians Frown on New FBI Surveillance Powers," CNSNews.com (October 3, 2001).

59. George Lardner, Jr., "Are Civil Liberties in Jeopardy?" *Washington PostWeekly Edition* (November 26–December 2, 2001): 29.

60. Richard Morin, "What Are We Willing to Sacrifice?" *Washington PostWeekly Edition* (October 1–7, 2001): 35; Brian Whitson, "49% of Americans Would Trade Privacy for Protection, Poll Says," *Lexington Herald-Leader* (July 2, 2002): A3; and Evan Thomas and Michael Isikoff, "Justice Kept in the Dark," *Newsweek* (December 10, 2001): 37.

61. Bob Egelko, "FBI Begins Secretly Observing Library Patrons," *San Francisco Chronicle* (June 25, 2002); and Adam Piore, "Librarians Keep Quiet," *Newsweek* (October 28, 2002): 12.

62. Dan Eggen, "Justice for All?" *Washington PostWeekly Edition* (December 3–9, 2001): 7.

63. Lardner, "Are Civil Liberties in Jeopardy?"; Thomas and Isikoff, "Justice Kept in the Dark"; Adam Roberts, "Apply Existing Laws to the Prisoners," *Washington PostWeekly Edition* (February 11–17, 2002): 21.

64. Eggen, "Justice for All?"

CHAPTER 14

1. John Meacham, "A Man Out of Time," *Newsweek* (December 23, 2002); and Howard Fineman, "Ghosts of the Past," *Newsweek* (December 23, 2002).

2. Ibid.

3. David Brooks, "We Don't Talk This Way," *Newsweek* (December 23, 2002).

4. Ellis Cose, "Lessons of the Trent Lott Mess," *Newsweek* (December 23, 2002).

5. Wes Carter, "The Newspapers Tell Only Half of the Story," *Newsweek* (January 13, 2003).

6. Meacham, "A Man Out of Time"; and Fineman, "Ghosts of the Past."

7. Ibid.

8. Ibid.

9. Cose, "Lessons of the Trent Lott Mess."

10. Ruth Bader Ginsburg, "Employment of the Constitution to Advance the Equal Status of Men and Women," in Shlomo Slonim, ed., *The Constitutional Bases of Political and Social Change in the United States* (New York: Praeger, 1990), p. 188.

11. Robert F. Nagel, *Constitutional Cultures: The Mentality and Consequences of Judicial Review* (Berkeley, CA: University of California Press, 1989), Chs. 5–6.

12. Philip Converse, "The Nature of Belief Systems in Mass Publics," in David E. Apter, *Ideology and Discontent* (New York: Free Press, 1964), pp. 206–261.

13. John D. Hicks, *The American Nation* (Cambridge, MA: Riverside Press, 1949), p. 21.

14. Eric Foner, *A Short History of Reconstruction* (New York: Harper & Row, 1990).

15. Richard M. Valelly, "National Parties and Racial Disfranchisement," in Paul E. Peterson, ed., *Classifying by Race* (Princeton, NJ: Princeton University Press, 1995), pp. 188–216.

16. U.S. Commission on Civil Rights, *Report of the Commission on Civil Rights* (Washington, DC: Government Printing Office, 1959), p. 32. Ellipses deleted.

17. V. O. Key, Jr., *Southern Politics* (New York: Random House, 1949).

18. J. Morgan Kousser, *The Shaping of Southern Politics: Suffrage Restriction and the Establishment of the One-Party South, 1880–1910* (New Haven, CT: Yale University Press, 1974), p. 61.

19. *Civil Rights Cases* 109 US 3 (1883).

Plessy v. *Ferguson* 163 US 537 (1896).

ward Banfield and James Q. Wilson, *City Politics* (New York: Vintage Books, 1963); and Wilson, *Negro Politics* (New York: Free Press, 1960). For caveats, see Steven P. Erie,

Rainbow's End: Irish-Americans and the Dilemmas of Urban Machine Politics, 1840–1985 (Berkeley, CA: University of California Press, 1990).

22. Gerald N. Rosenberg, *The Hollow Hope: Can Courts Bring About Social Change?* (Chicago: University of Chicago Press, 1991), p. 61.

23. *Smith* v. *Allwright* 321 US 649 (1944).

24. *Shelley* v. *Kraemer* 334 US 1 (1948).

25. Howard Ball and Phillip J. Cooper, *Of Power and Right: Hugo Black, William O. Douglas, and America's Constitutional Revolution* (New York: Oxford University Press, 1992), p. 172.

26. James F. Simon, *The Antagonists: Hugo Black, Felix Frankfurter, and Civil Liberties in Modern America* (New York: Simon and Schuster, 1989), pp. 219–223; and Ball and Cooper, *Of Power and Right*, pp. 171–175.

27. Bob Woodward and Scott Armstrong, *The Brethren: Inside the Supreme Court* (New York: Simon and Schuster, 1979), Prologue.

28. *Brown* v. *Board of Education* 347 US 483 (1954), note 11. The citation of six psychological and sociological studies in this note led Herbert Garfinkel to charge that the Court was making decisions on the basis of sociology, not law. "Social Science Evidence and the School Segregation Cases," *Journal of Politics* 21 (February 1959): 37–59. Kenneth B. Clark, "Effect of Prejudice and Discrimination on Personality Development" (Midcentury White House Conference on Children and Youth 1950, as cited in note 11 to *Brown*).

29. A. D. Morris, *Origins of the Civil Rights Movement: Black Communities Organizing for Change* (New York: Free Press, 1984).

30. Ibid., pp. 51–63.

31. Michael Lipsky, "Protest as a Political Resource," *American Political Science Review* LXII (December 1968): 1144–1158.

32. University of Georgia, Carl Vinson Institute of Government, "Historical Documents Related to Georgia," accessed at http://www.cviog.uga.edu/Projects/gainfo/gahisdoc.htm on April 6, 2000.

33. Rosenberg, *The Hollow Hope,* p. 50.

34. Gerald D. Jaynes and Robin M. Williams, Jr., eds., *A Common Destiny: Blacks and American Society* (Washington, DC: National Academy Press, 1989), p. 224.

35. Patricia Gurin, Shirley Hatchett, and James S. Jackson, *Hope and Independence: Blacks' Response to Electoral and Party Politics* (New York: Russell Sage, 1989), pp. 42–49.

36. Jaynes and Williams, *A Common Destiny,* p. 233.

37. Joint Center for Political and Economic Studies, *Focus* (Washington, DC: Joint Center for Political and Economic Studies 1993); and "Joint Center Releases 1998 National Count of Black Elected Officials," press release (Washington, DC: Joint Center for Political and Economic Studies, November 9, 1999).

38. William J. Grimshaw, *Bitter Fruit: Black Politics and the Chicago Machine, 1931–1991* (Chicago: University of Chicago Press, 1992).

39. Gary Orfield, *The Reconstruction of Southern Education: The Schools and the 1964 Civil Rights Act* (New York: Wiley, 1969); and Jennifer Hochschild, *The New American Dilemma* (New Haven, CT: Yale University Press, 1984).

40. Katherine Tate, *From Protest to Politics* (Cambridge, MA: Harvard University Press, 1993), Ch. 8.

41. *Milliken* v. *Bradley* I 418 US 717 (1974); 433 US 267 (1977).

42. *Regents of the University of California* v. *Bakke* 438 US 265 (1978).

43. U.S. Bureau of the Census, *Statistical Abstract of the United States, 1999*, Table 760.

44. U.S. Bureau of the Census, *Statistical Abstract of the United States, 1999*, Table 680; and Amitabh Chandra, "Is the Convergence in the Racial Wage Gap Illusory?" *American Economic Review* 90 (2000).

45. U.S. Bureau of the Census, *Statistical Abstract of the United States, 1999*, Tables 99 and 133.

46. Jaynes and Williams, *A Common Destiny*, p. 313.

47. U.S. Bureau of the Census, *Statistical Abstract of the United States, 1999*, Tables 298 and 302.

48. Lisa Handley and Bernard Grofman, "The Impact of the Voting Rights Act on Minority Representation: Black Officeholding in Southern State Legislatures," in Chandler Davidson and Bernard Grofman, eds., *Quiet Revolution in the South: The Impact of the Voting Rights Act, 1965–1990* (Princeton, NJ: Princeton University Press, 1994), pp. 335–350; Margaret Edds, *Claiming the Dream: The Victorious Campaign of Douglas Wilder of Virginia* (Chapel Hill, NC: Algonquin Books, 1990); and D. Stephen Voss and David Lublin, "Black Incumbents, White Districts: An Appraisal of the 1996 Congressional Elections," *American Politics Research* 29 (2001): 141–182.

49. Frederic Cople Jaher, *A Scapegoat in the Wilderness: The Origins and Rise of Anti-Semitism in America* (Cambridge, MA: Harvard University Press, 1994); Leonard Dinnerstein, *Anti-Semitism in America* (New York: Oxford, 1994); and Jack Nelson, *Terror in the Night: The Klan's Campaign Against the Jews* (New York: Simon & Schuster, 1993).

50. U.S. Bureau of the Census, *Profiles of General Demographic Characteristics* (Washington, DC: U.S. Department of Commerce, 2001).

51. Michael Jones-Correa, *Between Two Nations: The Political Predicament of Latinos in New York City* (Ithaca, NY: Cornell University Press, 1998).

52. National Election Studies; and *Newsweek* poll conducted by Princeton Survey Research Associates, June 25–30, 1999.

53. Geoffrey Fox, *Hispanic Nation: Culture, Politics, and the Constructing of Identity* (Secaucus, NJ: Birch Lane, 1996).

54. *Lau* v. *Nichols* 414 US 563 (1974).

55. Bernard Grofman, Lisa Handley, and Richard G. Niemi, *Minority Representation and the Quest for Voting Equality* (New York: Cambridge University Press, 1992), pp. 16–25. Also see Thomas Weyr, *Hispanic U.S.A.: Breaking the Melting Pot* (New York: Harper, 1959); and Peter Skerry, *Mexican Americans: The Ambivalent Minority* (New York: Free Press, 1993).

56. U.S. Bureau of the Census, *Statistical Abstract of the United States, 1999*, Tables 18 and 57.

57. Stanley Karnow and Nancy Yoshihara, *Asian Americans in Transition* (New York: Asia Society, 1992).

58. William Schneider, "Asian Americans Will Matter More," *National Journal* (August 14, 1999): 2398.

59. Asian Pacific American Institute for Congressional Studies, "Statement from APA Community Organizations," accessed at http://www.apaics.org/statement.html on April 10, 2000.

60. Vine Deloria, Jr., "The Distinctive Status of Indian Rights," in Peter Iverson, ed., *The Plains Indians of the Twentieth Century* (Norman, OK: University of Oklahoma Press, 1985), p. 241.

1. Deloria, ibid., pp. 237–248.

Deloria, ibid., p. 237.

Agresto, *The Supreme Court and Constitutional Democracy* (Ithaca, NY: Cornell University), pp. 148–149.

64. Theda Skocpol, *Protecting Soldiers and Mothers: The Political Origins of Social Policy in the United States* (Cambridge, MA: Harvard University Press, 1992); and Sara Evans, *Personal Politics: The Roots of Women's Liberation in the Civil Rights Movement and the New Left* (New York: Knopf, 1979).

65. Nancy McGlen and Karen O'Conner, *Women's Rights: The Struggle for Equality in the Nineteenth and Twentieth Centuries* (New York: Praeger, 1983), Ch. 9.

66. Jane J. Mansbridge, *Why We Lost the ERA* (Chicago: University of Chicago Press, 1986).

67. *Craig* v. *Boren* 429 US 190 (1976).

68. Ginsburg, *Employment of the Constitution,* p. 191.

69. *Rostker* v. *Goldberg* 453 US 65 (1981).

70. Mansbridge, *Why We Lost the ERA,* Ch. 7.

71. *Watson* v. *Fort Worth Bank & Trust* 487 US 997–999; *New York City Transit Authority* v. *Beazer* 440 US at 587, no 31; and *Griggs* v. *Duke Power,* 401 US at 432.

72. *Wards Cove* v. *Antonio* 490 US 642 (1989).

73. *Meritor Savings Bank* v. *Vinson* 477 US 57 (1986).

74. *Harris* v. *Forklift Systems* 510 US 77 (1993).

75. "Hillary's Class," *Frontline* (PBS television broadcast, No. 15, 1994), as cited in Karla Cooper-Boggs, "The Link Between Private and Public Single-Sex Colleges: Will Wellesley Stand or Fall with the Citadel?" *Indiana Law Review* 29 (1995), p. 137.

76. Cooper-Boggs, "The Link Between Private and Public Single-Sex Colleges," p. 135.

77. *United States* v. *Virginia* 116 SCt 2264 (1996).

78. Shawn Zeller, "Gay Rites: Giving to Democrats," *National Journal* (May 8, 1999): 1241.

79. Matthew Brelis, "From the Closet to the Campaign Trail; Being Gay Once Defined a Candidate. Now the Issues Do," *Boston Globe* (August 30, 1998): E1.

80. Deb Price, "Gays Need Democrats to Win 2000 Elections," *Detroit News* (November 1, 1999): A7; and Human Rights Campaign, accessed at http://www.hrc.org on April 11, 2000.

81. Stephen L. Percy, *Disability, Civil Rights, and Public Policy: The Politics of Implementation* (Tuscaloosa, AL: University of Alabama Press, 1989), p. 3.

82. Authors' 1995 estimate based on 1989 estimate provided by Percy, ibid., Ch. 5.

83. Robert A. Katzman, *Institutional Disability: The Saga of Transportation Policy for the Disabled* (Washington, DC: Brookings, 1986).

84. Frederick J. Weintraub, ed., *Public Policy and the Education of Exceptional Children* (Washington, DC: Council for Exceptional Children, 1976).

85. Paul E. Peterson, "Background Paper," in Twentieth Century Fund, *Making the Grade: Report of the Twentieth Century Fund Task Force on Federal Elementary and Secondary Education Policy* (New York: Twentieth Century Fund, 1983), Ch. 5.

86. Lynn Sweet, "1 in 5 Arab Americans Say They've Experienced Bias," *Chicago Sun-Times* (October 12, 2001): 9.

87. *Los Angeles Times,* "Rights and the New Reality" (September 21, 2002): Part 2, p. 22.

88. Eric Lichtblau and James Gerstenzang, "Anti-Muslim Violence Up, Officials Say," *Los Angeles Times* (September 18, 2001): 3.

89. Saeed Ahmed, "Overcoming the Stereotypes," *Atlanta Journal and Constitution* (October 4, 2001): 12A.

90. Sam Howe Verhovek, "Americans Give In to Racial Profiling," *New York Times* (September 23, 2001): 1A; and Sandra Tan, "Change of Heart," *The Buffalo News* (October 22, 2001): A1.

91. Sweet, "1 in 5 Arab Americans."

92. Rufus Browning, Dale Rogers Marshall, and David H. Tabb, *Protest Is Not Enough: The Struggle of Blacks and Hispanics for Equality in Urban Politics* (Berkeley, CA: University of California Press, 1984).

CHAPTER 15

1. Clarke Canfield, "Prescription Drugs Take Center Stage for Fall Elections in States with Many Elderly People," Associated Press, August 2, 2002.

2. Arthur Maass, *Congress and the Common Good* (New York: Basic Books, 1983).

3. Eugene Bardach, *The Implementation Game,* 4th ed. (Cambridge, MA: M.I.T. Press, 1982); and Jeffrey L. Pressman and Aaron Wildavsky, *Implementation,* 3rd ed. (Berkeley, CA: University of California Press, 1984).

4. Thomas R. Dye, *Politics, Economics and the Public: Policy Outcomes in the American States* (Chicago: Rand McNally, 1966).

5. Amy Goldstein, "Forgotten Issues; Welfare Reform's Progress Is Stalled," *Washington Post* (June 1, 2000): A1.

6. Timothy Smeeding, Michael O'Higgins, and Lee Rainwater, eds., *Poverty, Inequality and Income Distribution in Comparative Perspective* (New York: Harvester Wheatsheaf, 1990); and Lee Rainwater and Timothy M. Smeeding, "Doing Poorly: The Real Income of American Children in a Comparative Perspective," working paper no. 127, Maxwell School of Citizenship and Public Affairs, Syracuse University, Syracuse, NY, August 1995.

7. Neil Howe and Richard Jackson, *Entitlements and the Aging of America* (Washington, DC: National Taxpayers Union Foundation, 1994).

8. Martha Derthick, *Policymaking for Social Security* (Washington, DC: Brookings, 1979); and Theda Skocpol, *Protecting Soldiers and Mothers: The Politics of Social Provision in the United States* (Cambridge, MA: Harvard University Press, 1993).

9. R. Kent Weaver, *Automatic Government: The Politics of Indexation* (Washington, DC: Brookings, 1988).

10. Neil Howe and Richard Jackson, *1998 Chartbook: Entitlements and the Aging of America* (Washington, DC: National Taxpayers Union Foundation, 1998), Chart 4-26.

11. Because these figures are in constant dollars, one should not compare social security benefits directly to other possible forms of investment.

12. *Boston Globe* (December 27, 1994): 70.

13. John F. Harris and Glenn Kessler, "Who Shrank the Surplus? Both Sides Place Blame as the Effects of a Slow Economy and a Tax Cut Set In," *Washington Post Weekly Edition* (July 16–22, 2001): 6.

14. *Budget of the United States Government, Fiscal Year 2001, Historical Tables* (Washington, DC: Office of Management and Budget, 2000), Table 16.1, p. 279.

15. Ibid.

16. Elizabeth Drew, *Showdown: The Struggle Between the Gingrich Congress and the Clinton White House* (New York: Simon & Schuster, 1996), pp. 238–242, 318–321.

 U.S. Bureau of the Census, *Current Population Reports* (July 1998), pp. 20–504; and U.S.
 of the Census, *Current Populations Reports* (May 2000), pp. 20–523.
 A. MacManus, with Patricia A. Turner, *Young v. Old: Generational Combat in the 21st Century* Westview Press, 1996), pp. 60, 141.

19. Employment information: Susan Levine, "AARP Hopes Boom Times Are Ahead," *Washington Post* (June 2, 1998): A1; membership and volunteer numbers, "What Is AARP?" accessed at http://www.aarp. org/what_is.html on May 28, 2000; and budget figures, *AARP: 1999 Financial Statements* (Washington, DC: AARP, 2000).

20. Survey by the Luntz Research Companies/Mark A. Siegal and Associates, September 8–10, 1994; and *The Public Perspective: People, Opinions, & Polls* (February/March 1995).

21. *Publication 596: Earned Income Tax Credit* (Washington, DC: Internal Revenue Service, 1999); and John F. Harris and Dan Balz, "A Delicate Balance: The Steady Courtship of Senate Moderates Was Key to the Passage of the Tax Bill," *Washington Post Weekly Edition* (June 4–10, 2001): 8–10.

22. Percentage of monies going for services to the elderly in fiscal year 1993. Marilyn Werber Serafini, "Pinching Pennies," *National Journal* 27/37 (September 16, 1995): 2273. Also see Mark Rom, "Health and Welfare in the American States," *Politics in the American States,* 6th ed., Virginia Gray and Herbert Jacob, eds. (Washington, DC: CQ Press, 1995).

23. *Public Perspective* (February/March 1995): p. 39; and *The Gallup Poll*, accessed at www.gallup.com on July 24, 2000.

24. Jeff Shear, "The Credit Card," *National Journal* 27/32 (August 12, 1995): 2056–2058; and Marilyn W. Serafini, "Turning Up the Heat," *National Journal* 27/32 (August 12, 1995): 2051–2055.

25. Paul E. Peterson, "An Immodest Proposal," *Daedalus* 121 (Fall 1992): 151–174.

26. Calculated from the Green Book, Table 1, 1579. Until 1995, the Green Book, issued annually since 1981, was one of the most comprehensive sources of information on U.S. social policy. U.S. House of Representatives, Committee on Ways and Means, *Overview of Entitlement Programs: Background Material and Data on Programs Within the Jurisdiction of the Committee on Ways and Means* (otherwise known as the 1992 Green Book) (Washington, DC: U.S. Government Printing Office, 1992), Table 1, p. 1579. All subsequent references to this document in this chapter will be simply to the Green Book. They refer to the 1992 edition.

27. Green Book, Table 2, p. 1582.

28. U.S. Department of Health and Human Services, Administration for Children and Families, Office of Family Assistance, *TANF Selected Provisions of State Plans*, accessed at http://www.acf.dhhs.gov/ programs/ofa/provis.htm on July 24, 2000.

29. Paul E. Peterson and Mark Rom, *Welfare Magnets: A New Case for a National Standard* (Washington, DC: Brookings, 1990).

30. Green Book, Table 12, pp. 643–645.

31. Green Book, Table 12, p. 1212.

32. "Social Security Penalty on Earnings Is Repealed," *Los Angeles Times* (April 8, 2000): A14.

33. David K. Kirkpatrick, *Choice in Schooling: A Case for Tuition Vouchers* (Chicago: Loyola University Press, 1990); and Terry Moe, ed., *Private Vouchers* (Stanford, CA: Hoover Institution Press, 1995).

34. A. W. Phillips, "The Relationship Between Unemployment and the Rate of Change of Money Wage Rates in the United Kingdom 1862–1957," *Economica* 25 (1958): 283–299.

35. Morris Fiorina, "Elections and Economics in the 1980s," in Alberto Alesina and Geoffrey Carliner, eds., *Politics and Economics in the 1980s* (Chicago: University of Chicago Press, 1991), pp. 17–38.

36. For a summary of the relevant literature, see Fiorina, "Elections and Economics in the 1980s." Also see John Chubb, "Institutions, the Economy, and the Dynamics of State Elections," *American Political Science Review* 82 (1988): 133–154; and Dennis Simon, Charles Ostrom, and Robin Marra, "The President, Referendum Voting, and Subnational Elections in the United States," *American Political Science Review* 85 (1991): 1177–1192.

37. Paul Peretz, *The Political Economy of Inflation in the United States* (Chicago: University of Chicago, Press, 1983).

38. The following summary account is drawn from Allen Schick, *The Federal Budget* (Washington, DC: Brookings, 1995); and Steven Smith, *The American Congress* (Boston, MA: Houghton Mifflin, 1995), Ch. 11.

39. Tim Weiner, "Criticism Appears to Doom Republican Budget Tactic," *New York Times* (October 1, 1999): A20.

40. Bruce Oppenheimer, "The Importance of Elections in a Strong Congressional Party Era: The Effect of Unified v. Divided Government," manuscript, 1995.

41. *Budget and Economic Outlook, Fiscal Years 2000–2009* (Washington, DC: Congressional Budget Office, January 1999).

42. David Bradford, *Untangling the Income Tax* (Cambridge, MA: Harvard University Press, 1986); and surveys by the National Opinion Research Center.

43. Ballard C. Campbell, *The Growth of American Government: Governance from the Cleveland Era to the Present* (Bloomington: Indiana University Press, 1995), p. 181.

44. Calculated by authors from U.S. Bureau of the Census, *Statistical Abstract of the United States, 1999*, Tables 1434 and 1443.

45. Howard Schuman, *Politics and the Budget,* 3rd ed. (Englewood Cliffs, NJ: Prentice-Hall, 1992), p. 121.

46. For a critical survey, see Paul Krugman, *Peddling Prosperity* (New York: Norton, 1994), Ch. 5.

47. Speech at the Constitutional Convention, as quoted in Hans J. Morgenthau, *Politics Among Nations,* 4th ed. (New York: Knopf, 1966), p. 12.

48. Speech in Philadelphia, February 22, 1861, as quoted in Morgenthau, *Politics Among Nations,* p. 35.

49. Annual Message to Congress, December 2, 1823, as quoted in Bartlett, *Familiar Quotations,* p. 408.

50. Address to Congress, asking for a declaration of war, April 2, 1917, as reprinted in Bartlett, *Familiar Quotations*, p. 682.

51. Carl B. Swisher, *American Constitutional Development,* 2nd ed. (Boston: Houghton Mifflin, 1958), pp. 992–993.

52. George Washington, *Farewell Address*, September 17, 1796, as quoted in Bartlett, *Familiar Quotations,* p. 379.

53. Message to the Senate, August 19, 1914, as quoted in Bartlett, *Familiar Quotations,* p. 682.

54. Campaign speech in Boston, October 30, 1940, as reprinted in Bartlett, *Familiar Quotations,* p. 780.

55. "Fireside Chat to the Nation," December 29, 1940, as quoted in Bartlett, *Familiar Quotations,* p. 0.

ge Brown Tindall, *America: A Narrative History* (New York: Norton, 1984), p. 380.

on Cooper, Jr., *The Warrior and the Priest* (Cambridge, MA: Harvard University Press,

PHOTO CREDITS

CHAPTER 1

4 (left): Gary I. Rothstein/AP/Wide World Photos; **4 (right):** Reuters NewMedia Inc./CORBIS; **8:** Faleh Kheiber/Reuters; **13:** Charles Ommanney/Corbis Saba Press; **23:** Chris Collins/CORBIS.

CHAPTER 2

59: Tiffany K. Goodell/AP/Wide World Photos.

CHAPTER 3

66: Dan Lamont/CORBIS; **93:** Bettmann/CORBIS.

CHAPTER 4

95: Thomas Nast/Harper's Weekley, March 17, 1867; **116:** Ethel Wolvovitz/The Image Works.

CHAPTER 5

129: Brad Markell/Getty Images; **139:** Forest McMullin/STOCKPHOTO/Black Star; **149:** Calvin and Hobbs ©Watterson, distributed by Universal Press Syndicate. Reprinted with permission. All rights reserved; **152:** Doug Mills/AP/Wide World Photos.

CHAPTER 6

182: Dilbert reprinted by permission of United Feature Syndicate, Inc.; **187:** Gary Markstein/Milwaukee Journal Sentinel/Copley News Service; **190:** Richard Ellis/Corbis Sygma.

CHAPTER 7

197: Jim Bourg/Reuters/Getty Images; **205:** Mark Peterson/Corbis Saba Press; **214:** Joe Marquette/AP/Wide World Photos; **223:** Thompson/The Detroit Free Press; **232:** ROB ROGERS reprinted by permission of United Feature Syndicate, Inc.

CHAPTER 8

249: Reuters NewMedia, Inc./CORBIS; **251:** PETT © 2001 Lexington Herald-Leader. Distributed by UNIVERSAL PRESS SYNDICATE. Reprinted with permission. All rights reserved; **253:** Steve Breen/Asbury Park Press/Copley News Service; **265:** Joe Marquette/AP/Wide World Photos; **271:** Andrew Lichtenstein/Corbis Sygma.

CHAPTER 9

281: Nick Anderson/© 2002 The Washington Post Writers Group. Reprinted with permission; **284 (left):** Hulton|Archive Photos/ Getty Images; **284 (right):** Dennis Brack/STOCKPHOTO/Black Star; **301:** ©Tribune Media Services. All rights reserved. Reprinted with permission.

CHAPTER 10

329: J.B. Russell/Corbis Sygma; **331 (top):** National Archives and Records Administration; **331 (bottom):** Eric Draper/ White House/Getty Images; **332:** Win McNamee/Reuters NewMedia, Inc./CORBIS.

CHAPTER 11

353: Walt Handlesman/Copyright, Tribune Media Services, Inc. All rights reserved. Reprinted with permission; **368:** Richard Falco/STOCKPHOTO /Black Star; **377:** © 2001 by John Trever/The Albuquerque Journal; **379:** Saurabh Das/AP/Wide World Photos; **383:** Robert Trippet/SIPA Press; **385:** Doug Mills/AP/Wide World Photos.

CHAPTER 12

407: Craig Buck; **410:** CORBIS; **412:** Mark Reinstein/The Image Works; **414:** PF Bently/PFPIX.COM; **420 and 421:** Bettmann/CORBIS.

CHAPTER 13

432: HO/AP/Wide World Photos; **438:** Robert Phillips/STOCKPHOTO/ Black Star; **440:** Nick Anderson/© 2002, The Washington Post Writers Group. Reprinted with permission; **449:** AP/Wide World Photos; **455:** AP/Wide World Photos; **461:** Getty Images.

CHAPTER 14

472: Hulton/Archive Photos/ Getty Images; **477:** Hulton | Archive Photos/ Getty Images; **478:** Hulton | Archive Photos/ Getty Images; **481:** Reuters NewMedia, Inc./CORBIS; **487:** Tina Fineberg/AP/Wide World Photos; **492:** Les Stone/Corbis Sygma; **495:** PETT © 2001 Lexington Herald-Leader. Distributed by Universal Press Syndicate. Reprinted with permission. All rights reserved.

CHAPTER 15

503: Beth A. Keiser/Reuters; **508:** A. Ramey/PhotoEdit, Inc.; **518:** CARLSON © 2001 Milwaukee Sentinel. Reprinted with permission of UNIVERSAL PRESS SYNDICATE. All rights reserved; **521:** Mike Thompson/The Detroit Free Press/ Copley News Service; **526:** Dilbert reprinted by permission of United Feature Syndicate, Inc.

NAME INDEX

SUBJECT INDEX

Boldface pages locate figures; *Italicized* pages locate tables.

ADDITIONAL TITLES
OF INTEREST

Note to Instructors: Any of these Penguin-Putnam, Inc., titles can be packaged with this book at a special discount. Contact your local Longman sales representative for details on how to create a Penguin-Putnam, Inc. Value Package.

Stephen E. Ambrose, *Rise to Globalism*

Alexis De Tocqueville (edited by Richard D. Heffner), *Democracy in America*

The Federalist Papers
(edited by Clinton Rossiter and new introduction by Charles R. Kesler)

Al Gore, *Earth in the Balance*

Peter Irons, *The Courage of Their Convictions*

Martin Luther King, Jr., *Why We Can't Wait*

Philip B. Kunhardt and Peter W. Kunhardt, *The American President*

Joe McGinniss, *Selling of the President*

David Osborne and Ted Gaebler, *Reinventing Government*

Thomas Paine, *Common Sense*

William L. Riordan, *Plunkitt of Tammany Hall*

Upton Sinclair, *The Jungle*

Harriet Beecher Stowe, *Uncle Tom's Cabin*

Stephen Waldman, *The Bill*

Juan Williams (introduction by Julian Bond), *Eyes on the Prize*